The Clipper® Interface Handbook

John Mueller

Windcrest®/McGraw-Hill

FIRST EDITION
SECOND PRINTING

Library of Congress Cataloging-in-Publication Data

Mueller, John, 1958–
The Clipper interface handbook / by John Mueller.
p. cm.
Includes index.
ISBN 0-8306-3532-7 (pbk.)
1. Compilers (Computer programs) 2. Clipper (Computer program)
I. Title.
QA76.76.C65M83 1991
005.75′65—dc20 91-34294
CIP

TAB Books offers software for sale. For information and a catalog, please contact TAB Software Department, Blue Ridge Summit, PA 17294-0850.

Acquisitions Editor: Brad Schepp
Book Editor: Kellie Hagan
Director of Production: Katherine G. Brown
Series Design: Jaclyn J. Boone
Cover: Sandra Blair Design and Brent Blair Photography, Harrisburg, PA WP1

There are always those people who affect the lives of others in such a way as to leave them permanently changed. I met my best friend that way and couldn't think of spending time away from her, so I married her. My wife has been my tower of strength, my counselor, and my joy for many years, and her efforts helped produce this book.

Contents

APPENDICES

Acknowledgments

My friend Wallace Wang helped get me started writing and encourages me to do so with a fervor unmatched by anyone. His gift to me has always been laughter in the face of overwhelming odds. Everyone should have someone like this to cheer them on.

A good technical editor is hard to find, at least that is what I've heard. Dian Schaffhauser has been an example to me of what an editor should be. Never harsh, and always willing to talk, Dian led me on the chase for perfection. She encouraged me to find that elusive thing called truth.

I want to thank David Frier for technically reviewing this book. I can't help but feel his contribution has made this book better than I could have alone.

I also want to acknowledge the contributions of those people who made parts of this book possible. Tanya VanDam of Microsoft Corporation graciously helped me obtain the best information possible about Macro Assembler and the C compiler. Frances Jackson and Craig Ogg of Nantucket Corporation assisted me in every way possible to obtain and understand the Clipper compiler. Artist Graphics provided the Artist TI12, which I used to document the TMS34010 processor. And finally, I want to thank all those technicians, developers, and consultants who cheered me on, provided criticism and ideas, and generally helped me shape this book.

Introduction

This book conveys four main ideas that anyone using Clipper needs to consider. First, "What does Clipper provide in the way of programming tools?" The Introduction looks at what you should expect from Clipper as a compiler. Second, "How does Clipper interface with Assembler and C?" This is the basis for building your own tools to enhance the Clipper programming environment. Third, "How can you enhance Clipper-provided programming tools?" Once you understand the application program interface (API), you can begin to modify your working environment. Doing so will increase your productivity while decreasing the amount of work required to create a program. Fourth, "How can I create entirely new programming tools?" Enhancements are often not enough to give a developer an edge over the competition. Programming tools are the means by which you cannot only reduce programming time, but differentiate your product from someone else's. This book assumes that you are an intermediate to advanced programmer, so actual implementation of an idea takes precedence over the theory behind the idea.

What is in this book?

The *Clipper Interface Handbook* begins with a brief discussion of all the Clipper commands and functions already available. This is important because some readers might not know that a particular capability already exists or that there are problems with a particular capability. The main reason for this lack of user knowledge is the relatively poor documentation supplied by Nantucket with Clipper. The newest release does not even supply hardcopy documentation. As a result, there are new features that many people are not familiar with.

Part 1: Clipper introduction This introductory section contains the first four chapters. Chapters 1 and 2 discuss Clipper commands and functions, and each description highlights any anomalies you should expect to see when using the command or function. It also tells you when the command or function first appeared in Clipper. This will help you determine when to use an advanced feature and when to maintain compatibility with older versions of Clipper. Chapter 3 discusses the preprocessor and how to use code blocks. Both of these features are new to version 5.0 of Clipper. Understanding what they can do for you is paramount to tool building. Chapter 4 is a detailed discussion of the object-oriented features in Clipper. In many cases, these new object-oriented features allow you to redefine your programming environment without resorting to C or assembler add-on functions.

Part 2: Interfacing Clipper The second section of the book discusses the Clipper interface to other programming languages. It is divided into two chapters, one for Assembly Language and another for C. Each chapter discusses Nantucket-supplied interface aids, user additions to these interfaces, and new interface aids that you can create. Many of the differences between C and assembler add-ons are discussed as well, for example, using assembler or C to create an add-on.

Part 3: Clipper add-ons The third section of the book discusses Clipper add-ons, in other words, using the supplied functions as a base and adding to them. This section is also split into two chapters. The first chapter covers standard functions and the second covers network-related functions. Enhancing existing commands and functions is often easier than programming them from the beginning. This section will help you determine when you can use this relatively simple technique in place of a full-blown C or assembler add-on.

Part 4: New functions The fourth and final section looks at creating entirely new functions. Once you determine that Clipper does not supply a required function and that an existing function cannot be modified, you can use this book to create entirely new functions. This section contains four chapters, and is therefore a major portion of the book. Chapter 9 discusses Clipper interfaces to other programs. This is intended to illustrate how to create a data (versus programming language) interface. For example, you could write a program where the client wants a program to call a cash register, download information, convert it to dBASE III format, and then analyze the receipt and employee information. Without the proper interface to the cash register, this program couldn't work. Chapter 10 discusses how to create libraries of routines. This is important in a group programming environment. Using a library of routines is far more convenient than using individual object modules. Chapters 11 and 12 discuss low-level access to DOS routines not exploited by Clipper, specifically mouse routines and graphic displays.

Appendices The seven appendices contain reference material that you might need to create a program. This includes information about Clipper responses to the keyboard, a summary of commands for both Assembly Language and C, and two appendices describing how to directly access the computer's peripheral chips.

Why is this book unique?

Most Clipper programming books leave you stranded with untested code fragments that may or may not work when used. This book provides complete programs as examples. Therefore, you not only see how to include a feature as part of a program, but you know that the code works as well. Also, no other book attempts to cover low-level programming techniques in the detail that this book does. Even though some books tell you that you can access hardware, they fail to show you how. The *Clipper Interface Handbook* provides you with complete coverage of how to use Clipper to your best advantage.

Programming conventions

There are several programming conventions used throughout this book. An understanding of these conventions will help you receive more information from the examples in this book and from the Nantucket manuals in general. In addition, these same concepts are equally applicable to Clipper, C, and assembly code. Many of these conventions have been discussed by developers at conferences and on bulletin board systems (BBSs).

The first stage of development for this system was started by Charles Simonyi of Microsoft Corporation. He called his system *Hungarian notation*. There are many places that you can obtain a copy of his work, including many BBSs. His work was further enhanced by developers in close association with the Nantucket Corporation. A final copy of the enhancement to the original Hungarian notation was published by Robert A. Difalco of Fresh Technologies. You can find his work on many BBSs as well, including the Nantucket-supported forum on CompuServe.

Much of the information in this section can be found in one of the two previously mentioned documents in one form or another. The purpose in presenting them here is to make you aware of the exact nature of the conventions and show you how to use them to your best advantage. There are four reasons why you should use these naming conventions in your programs:

Mnemonic value This allows the programmer to remember the name of a variable more easily, an important consideration for team projects.

Suggestive value You might not be the only person modifying your code. If you're working on a team project, others in the team will most likely look at the code you've written. Using these conventions will help others understand your work.

Consistency A programmer's ability is often evaluated on the basis of not only how efficiently he programs or how well the programs he creates function, but also how easily another programmer can read his code. Using these conventions will help you maintain uniform code from one project to another. Other programmers will be able to anticipate the value or function of a section of code simply by the conventions you use.

Speed of decision In the business world, the speed at which you can create and modify code will often determine how successful a particular venture will be. Using consistent code will reduce the time you spend trying to decide what someone meant when creating a variable or function. This reduction in decision time will increase the amount of time you have available for productive work.

Procedure and function naming conventions

This book uses the same conventions for naming both functions and procedures. To make the text easier to understand, I will refer to both procedures and functions as functions. The following rules will help you understand the conventions used to name functions throughout the book.

- Some languages allow you to type a function by the value it returns. This is not the case with Clipper, however, because it is not a strongly typed language. Because you can't rely on a specific return value from a function, you can't use an indicator to show its return type. For example, a variable returning a numeric value would begin with a lowercase *n* to show its type. Therefore, all Clipper functions begin with an uppercase character for an external third-party function, a lowercase letter for a native external function, or an underscore for an internal function.
- You can further differentiate between native and third-party functions because native functions use all lowercase letters. A third-party function might use a combination of upper- and lowercase, providing the first character is always uppercase.
- In many cases, a function converts one value to another value. To differentiate these functions from functions that perform a more generalized task, you type the input value, a 2, and then the output value. For example, if you wanted to create a function for converting a value from the frequency domain to the time domain, you could name the function Freq2Time.
- Even though you can't type a function to return a specific value, there are instances where the purpose of a function is clearly outlined and you know that it returns a specific value. In those cases you can use a standard qualifier to help define the function. A list-

ing of these standard qualifiers appears in the section on variable naming conventions.

- Always define a function using only one or two standard qualifiers. Some programmers use so many qualifiers to define a function name that they actually make their code less rather than more descriptive. The purpose of a function can become difficult to determine if you use too many qualifiers.
- It is always convenient to be able to quickly find where a function is defined within the source code. To help in this, always capitalize the keywords PROCEDURE, FUNCTION, and RETURN. This will make the task of finding function definitions easier.
- To help differentiate native standard functions from those using the object-oriented programming (OOP) exported method, use a combination of upper- and lowercase letters for the OOP function, and always make the first letter of the function lowercase. For example, oBrowse:goBottom( ) is an exported instance variable of the TBrowse class.

Using these seven rules will make it much easier to determine the purpose and origin of the functions you use within a program. The following examples illustrate the seven rules.

```
SomeFunc( )               // third-party function
cls                       // native external function
__retni( )                // native internal function
Num2Char( )               // third-party conversion function
Bin2W( )                  // native conversion function
SetColor( )               // qualified function
FUNCTION SetColor( )      // keyword capitalization
oGet:KillFocus            // OOP function
```

DBF and field-related naming conventions

One of the things that differentiates database programming from other types of programming is the use of databases and indexes. These file structures rely on the contents of fields within the structure. Because these are of such importance in a Clipper program, you need to differentiate between a database, field, index, and standard variable. Often, a database is assigned an alias when the user opens it. For the purpose of this discussion, aliases will have the same naming conventions as database files.

One way to make a piece of code stand out from the code around it is by using capitalization. To differentiate the three parts of a database from the rest of the code, the database filenames, index filenames, and field names will always be expressed in capital letters.

Just like other variables, it makes sense to give database variables logical names. Whenever possible, use the same standard qualifiers for database filenames, index filenames, and field names as you use for standard variables.

Even with the precaution of using all capital letters to reference a database filename and field name, it might still be possible for someone to confuse the two variables within your code. Because of this and also the possibility of confusing the compiler, always reference a field name with an alias. This will ensure that anyone reading your code will instantly recognize a field. In addition, you'll ensure that the compiler knows that you're referring to a field name rather than a variable. An example of this approach is SOMEDATA→FIELD NAME, where SOMEDATA is an alias for a database file, and FIELD NAME is the name of a field.

It's always best to show an association where one exists. For this reason, when a variable is used to store the contents of a field, it's best to give it the same name as the field, with the addition of a standard prefix. For example, if you have a field named FIELDNAME, and that field stores character values, then the variable name would be cFieldName. A list of variable prefixes is provided in the variable naming convention section.

There is also the question of exactly how to name a database file. One strategy is to build a database filename out of various parts. For example, if you had a database that was used for accounting, you might start each file specifically for that purpose with the prefix ACT. That way, you could easily separate the accounting files from other files in the directory. Another typical database is one that contains customer addresses and other information. You could give these files a prefix of CUST.

Just as a variable can be associated with a specific field in a database, index files are always associated with a specific database file. Because you want to be able to see a relationship where it occurs, you should always use the same name for an index file as you do for the database file. However, then you have to handle databases with multiple indexes. In these cases, it's better to give the database file a seven-character name and sequentially number the index files. For example, the first index file of a database used to store customer address information might be CUSTADR1.NTX. This approach is much better than trying to indicate the indexing scheme as part of the index filename.

Variable naming conventions

Variables are one of the hardest parts of a program to understand. Unlike functions and procedures, variables are not defined in the manual anywhere and few programs have published data dictionaries. As a result, there is often a lot of confusion about the exact meaning of a variable. There are several ways to understand the variables you use within a program.

Always prefix a variable with a single lowercase letter, indicating its type. In most cases this is the first letter of the variable type, so it's easy to remember what letter to use. The following examples show the most common prefixes. Note that these prefixes are also the values returned by the ValType( ) function described in chapter 2.

Prefix	**Variable type**
a	Array
b	Code block
c	Character
d	Date
h	Handle
l	Logical
n	Numeric
o	Object
x	Variable type (macro or changing value)

Some variables represent the state of a database, or store the state of another variable. You can identify these variables using a three-character state qualifier. The following examples represent the most common state qualifiers.

Qualifier	**State**
New	a new state
Sav	a saved state
Tem	a temporary state

A standard qualifier can help someone see the purpose of a variable almost instantly. For example, using the Clr qualifier tells you that this variable is used in some way with color. You can even combine the qualifiers to amplify their effect and describe how the variable is used. For example, cClrCrs is a character variable that determines the color of the cursor. Using from one to three of these qualifiers is usually sufficient to describe the purpose of a variable. The following standard qualifiers are examples of the more common types.

Qualifier	**Type**	**Qualifier**	**Type**
Ar	Array	Msg	Message
Attr	Attribute	Name	Name
B	Bottom	Ntx	Index File
Clr	Color	R	Right
Col	Column	Rec	Record number
Crs	Cursor	Ret	Return value
Dbf	Database file	Scr	Screen
F	First	Str	String
File	File	T	Top
Fld	Field	X	Row
L	Last/left	Y	Column

Use the following specifications to refer to optional pointer references:

Qualifier	**Reference**
1,2,3	State pointer references, as in cSavClr1, cSavClr2, etc.
Max	Strict upper limit, as in nFldMax, maximum number of fields
Min	Strict lower limit, as in nRecMin, minimum number of records

Other conventions

Besides programming conventions, there are some book conventions I use to illustrate examples more clearly. These conventions are not part of the programs, but are used to illustrate the use of a command, function, or procedure. These book conventions are as follows:

<**EXP**> A standard expression of no particular type. This usually refers to a command or function that accepts multiple types as input.

<**aEXP**> An array is required as input. The command or function description will tell you if it is a single or multidimensional array. It will also tell you the variable type required as input.

<**bEXP**> A code block is required as input. The command or function description will provide the parameters that the code block must meet. The example section of the description will show how to format the code block.

<**cEXP**> A character expression is required as input.

<**dEXP**> A date expression is required as input.

<**hEXP**> A file handle is required as input. The description will tell you how the handle is obtained and for what purpose it is used.

<**lEXP**> A logical expression is required as input. This is always the Boolean operators .T. or .F., or some expression that equates to a Boolean.

<**nEXP**> A numeric expression is required as input.

<**oEXP**> An object is required as input.

<**xEXP**> Some type of variable expression is required as input. The command or procedure description will tell you what types of input you can provide.

[<EXP>] The requested expression is optional. This usually means that the command or function will perform the specified task correctly without this input. The optional expression merely enhances program operation in some way.

EXP LIST A list of expressions separated by commas or combined with math operators is required. A single expression constitutes a subset of the list in most cases.

KeyWord Type this word exactly as written in the heading of the description, using the proper capitalization (as described in the previous section) within your program.

<**SCOPE**> This usually appears in conjunction with a database or array command or function. It indicates that you can specify the range of records on which the command or function operates.

<**FIELD**> You must supply a field expression as input. This usually means that the command or function works directly with the database instead of variables.

<**CONDITION**> An expression that equates to a Boolean output. It is used in conjunction with the scope clause of a command or function to further define the range of records on which the command or function operates.

The book uses other conventions in special cases. In these instances, the exact meaning of the convention is stated in the description of the command or function.

1
Clipper commands

This chapter contains an alphabetical listing of all Clipper commands. In many cases, the use and execution of these commands vary widely from other *x*base (generic database) dialects. The preprocessor found in versions 5.0 and above of Clipper will allow you to modify this behavior. To find out how to enhance the capabilities provided by these versions, read chapter 3.

Each command description in this chapter also provides you with the version in which the command first appeared. If the command appeared in more than one version (Summer 87, 5.0, or 5.01), then the version information will tell you how the command changed. In many cases it will become apparent that version 5.0 enhanced the language, while 5.01 increased compatibility. Some of the version-specific information provides warnings about using certain commands under specific conditions. These warnings include unimplemented features between versions, enhancements, anomalies, and fixes that change the behavior of the command.

This chapter uses the conventions explained in the introduction to the book. Reading the introduction will increase your understanding of the examples provided as part of each description.

Each command entry contains the command line interface for the command and a description of how to use it. Notice how each version changes the behavior of some commands. These differences determine how you should use the command while programming. In this chapter, I assume that you're using the default Clipper configuration, libraries, and other support files.

?/?? <EXP LIST>

Summer 87, 5.0, 5.01

A change in versions 5.0 and 5.01 is that the preprocessor actually substitutes the QOut( ) function for the ? command, and the QQOut( ) function for the ?? command. This command is provided for compatibility reasons only.

This command displays the results of the expression list. It does not provide any method of formatting the output. The output appears at the current cursor position unless the expression list contains the control codes necessary to change the cursor position. In most cases, use the @ Say/Get command in place of this command for standard output. Use the QOut( ) or QQOut( ) function within code blocks. Version 5.01 provides the Alert( ) function for error messages.

The ? command displays a single line of text or numbers. It always ends the text with a carriage return and line feed combination. The ?? places the text or numbers on the current line. EXAMPLE:

```
? "Some Text"
```

@ <nEXP1>, <nEXP2>, <nEXP3>, <nEXP4> Box <cEXP1> [Color <cEXP2>]

Summer 87, 5.0, 5.01

5.01 provides a new function, DispBox( ), in place of this command. The DispBox( ) function provides greater flexibility and is easier to use than the @...Box command. In addition, both 5.0 and 5.01 allow you to use a numeric argument in place of cEXP1. A value of 1 draws a single box, while 2 draws a double box. 5.01 also adds cEXP2, which allows you to change the color of the box.

Use this command to draw a box around a display area. nEXP1 contains the top row offset. nEXP2 contains the left column offset, nEXP3 contains the bottom row offset, and nEXP4 contains the right column offset. cEXP1 contains a string of nine characters. The first eight characters are the line-drawing characters used for corners and sides of the box. Clipper begins a box at the upper left corner of the defined area. The ninth character is the box fill character. cEXP2 sets the border color of the box. It uses the same colors described for the SetColor( ) function. The optional Color argument provides the means to set the colors for that specific say or get. It uses the same color setup described in chapter 2 for the SetColor( ) function. EXAMPLE:

```
cFILL = chr(218) + chr(196) + chr(191) + chr(179) + chr(217) + ;
      chr(196) + chr(192) + chr(179) + chr(176)

@ 01, 01, 23, 79 box cFILL
```

@ 01, 01, 23, 79 box cFILL

@ <nEXP1>, <nEXP2> Clear [To <nEXP3>, <nEXP4>]

Summer 87, 5.0, 5.01

5.01 uses a combination of the Scroll( ) and SetPos( ) functions to accomplish this command. Depending on the effect you want to create, it might be more efficient to use a combination of these two commands rather than using @...Clear.

Use this command to clear a rectangular area of a display. nEXP1 contains the starting row and nEXP2 contains the starting column. If you don't specify the optional To argument, Clipper clears a single line starting at nEXP2 and going to column 79. nEXP3 specifies the ending row and nEXP4 specifies the ending column. This command removes windows of information from the display. EXAMPLE:

```
* Clear the upper left corner of the display.

@ 01, 01 clear to 15, 24
```

@ 01, 01 clear to 15, 24

@ <nEXP1>, <nEXP2> Prompt <cEXP1> [Message <cEXP2>]

Summer 87, 5.0, 5.01

Starting with version 5.0, the number of prompts has been increased from 32 to 4,096.

Create menus using this command in conjunction with the MENU TO command. nEXP1 contains the prompt row, nEXP2 contains the prompt column, and cEXP1 contains the menu prompt. Specify an optional help message using the Message argument. If you specify this argument, Clipper displays the cEXP2 associated with the currently highlighted prompt. Set the message location using the Set Message To command. EXAMPLE:

```
@ 01, 20 prompt "Display Database"
@ 02, 20 prompt "Print Database"
@ 03, 20 prompt "Exit Program"
menu to SELECTION
```

@ <nEXP1>, <nEXP2> [Say <EXP> [Picture <cEXP1>]] [Color <cEXP2>] [Get <VARIABLE> [Picture <cEXP3>] [Color <cEXP4>] [When <lEXP>] [Range <nEXP3>, <nEXP4>] [Valid <lEXP>]]

Summer 87, 5.0, 5.01

The When clause was added in version 5.0 and the Color clause in 5.01. The Valid and Range clauses are mutually exclusive in versions 5.0 and above. 5.0 and 5.01 handle incorrect date entry differently than Sum-

mer 87. They don't restore the original date as did Summer 87. Instead, the newer versions home the cursor in the get field and allow the user to edit the incorrect date. Pressing Escape in a get field restores the original value to the field and redisplays the value on-screen. Summer 87 doesn't redisplay the value. The 5.0 and 5.01 versions also clip any gets or says that extend past the end of line rather than continuing them on the next line of the screen. Most of these changes are due to the fact that both versions 5.0 and 5.01 provide enhanced get handling through internal routines. Using the get object provides additional flexibility over the get command at the expense of increased complexity. Chapter 4 describes get objects in detail. In addition, both versions use two new functions, DevOut( ) and DevPos( ), to handle says. These functions are not documented in the 5.0 manual, but you can use DevOut( ) to perform any full-screen display task.

This command performs three separate and independent functions. The first function positions the cursor. nEXP1 is the cursor row and nEXP2 is the cursor column. Using the optional Say argument displays EXP at the specified location. Using the optional Get argument obtains keyboard input up to the length of VARIABLE at the specified location. In both cases, the optional Picture argument formats the input or output. TABLE 1-1 provides a listing of the legal picture functions and templates. A function is a shorthand method of formatting the picture string. Precede each picture function with the @ symbol. A template specifies the format of each character separately. The optional Color argument provides the means to set the colors for that specific say or get. It uses the same color setup described in chapter 2 for the SetColor( ) function. The optional When argument allows you to display the say and get portions of the command, but does not allow the user to enter information unless lEXP is satisfied. The optional Range argument determines the range of numbers Clipper accepts for numeric input. nEXP3 determines the lower limit and nEXP4 determines the upper limit. The optional Valid argument determines legal input criteria. Clipper accepts input that results in a true condition. This allows you to create UDFs for processing data input by the user. However, at this level of complexity it's easier to use a get object in place of the @...Get command when using version 5.0 or above. EXAMPLE:

```
@ 15, 15 say "Enter your age: " get AGE picture '999' range 5, 100
```

@ <nEXP1>, <nEXP2>
To <nEXP3>, <nEXP4> [Double] [Color <cEXP>]

Summer 87, 5.0, 5.01

5.01 provides a new function, DispBox( ), in place of this command. The DispBox( ) function provides greater flexibility and is easier to use than the @...Box command. The Color clause was added in version 5.01.

Table 1-1 **Clipper picture functions and templates**

Symbol	Variable type	Description
Picture functions		
A	C	Alphabetic character input only.
B	N	Numbers displayed left justified instead of right justified.
C	N	Displays CR (representing credit) after positive numbers.
D	D, N	Displays dates in the SET DATE format and numbers in American format (9,999,999.99).
E	D, N	Displays dates in British format and numbers in European format (9.999.999,99).
K	All	Clears the pending GET if the first key is not a cursor key.
R	C	Inserts nontemplate characters in the character stream. You do this by using the @R function followed by the entire template. For example, typing @R RJ21-9999 creates a special nine-digit number. The inserted characters do not appear in the output stream.
S<N>	C	Permits scrolling within a GET. N is the number of characters the user sees at any given time.
X	N	Displays DB (representing debit) after a negative number.
Z	N	Displays a variable containing a zero as blank.
(	N	Displays negative numbers enclosed in parentheses with leading spaces.
)	N	Displays negative numbers enclosed in parentheses without leading spaces.
!	C	Display alphabetic characters in uppercase. Converts input alphabetic characters to uppercase.

Table 1-1 Continued.

Symbol	Variable type	Description
Picture templates		
A		Displays or allows the user to input only alphabetic characters.
N		Displays or allows the user to input only numeric or alphabetic characters.
X		Displays or allows the user to input any character.
9		Displays or allows the user to input only numeric characters and signs (+ or -).
#		Displays or allows the user to input only numeric characters, spaces, and signs (+ or -).
L		Displays logicals, such as T or F. Allows the user to input only T, F, Y, or N.
Y		Displays logicals as Y or N. Allows the user to input only Y or N.
!		Displays or allows the user to input any character. Converts alphabetic characters to uppercase.
$		Displays a dollar sign ($) in place of the leading space for numeric variables. Specifies the location of a dollar sign ($) for character variables.
*		Displays an asterisk (*) in place of the leading space. Specifies the location of an asterisk for character variables.
.		Specifies the location of a decimal point for either numeric or character variables.
,		Specifies the location of a comma for either numeric or character variables.

NOTE:
Variable types include: D - Date
C - Character N - Numeric

This command creates standard boxes using either single or double lines. Use the Double argument to create double line boxes. nEXP1 contains the upper row, nEXP2 contains the left column, nEXP3 contains the lower row, and nEXP4 contains the right column. The optional Color argument provides the means to set the colors for that specific say or get. It uses the same color setup described in chapter 2 for the SetColor( ) function. EXAMPLE:

```
@ 01, 01 to 24, 79 double
```

Accept [<cEXP>] To <xEXP>

Summer 87, 5.0, 5.01

Use this command to retrieve characters from the keyboard and place them in a variable (xEXP). The optional cEXP displays a message (prompt). The display appears at the current cursor position unless cEXP contains cursor-positioning control codes, including tabs, spaces, carriage returns, and line feeds. Clipper retrieves the keyboard characters immediately following the prompt (if provided). Nantucket provided this command for compatibility purposes only. Use the @ Say/Get command in place of this command for general purposes and a get object for more complex programming environments. EXAMPLE:

```
accept 'Enter something: ' to SOMEVAR
```

Append Blank

Summer 87, 5.0, 5.01

5.01 adds a new function, DBAppend( ), that can take the place of this command. 5.0 translates the Append Blank command to _DBAppend( ). Currently, there is no advantage to using the new functions over the command.

This command adds a new record to the end of the selected database. When using this command in a network environment, Clipper attempts to lock the newly created record. If another user locked the database previous to using this command, the append fails. EXAMPLE:

```
append blank
```

Append [<SCOPE>] [Fields <FIELD LIST>] From <FILE>/(<cEXP1>) [For <CONDITION>] [While <CONDITION>] [SDF]/[Delimited [With Blank/<DELIMITER>/(<cEXP2>)]]

Summer 87, 5.0, 5.01

Versions 5.0 and 5.01 will no longer accept a delimited character string as input for the Delimited With clause. You must supply a character expression. When using 5.0, make certain that any delimited file uses commas as delimiters. The use of other delimiters with this version might produce undesired results. 5.01 corrects this problem. In addition, text files should end with a carriage return/line feed combination or an end-of-file character (^Z).

This command adds records to the selected database using the contents of another database or ASCII text file. Don't lock the file before using this command in a network. Clipper automatically arbitrates between application programs during the append process.

The SCOPE argument determines how many of the source records appear in the selected database. You can use three keywords with SCOPE. All adds every source record to the selected database. Next <*n*> adds the number of records specified by *n*. Clipper starts adding records from the record pointed to by the record pointer. Record <*n*> adds a single record; *n* specifies the record number.

The Fields argument specifies which fields to transfer from the source database to the target. The From argument specifies which file to append from, and the For argument specifies which source records to append to the selected database. You must use a scope of all or next.

The While argument also specifies which source records to append to the selected database, but, unlike the For argument, the While argument stops appending records when the source record no longer meets the specified criteria.

The SDF and Delimited arguments import records from files that use an alternate format. An SDF file contains fixed-length records separated by a carriage return and line feed. A delimited file contains variable-length records separated by a carriage return and line feed. A comma separates each field in the record, and double quotations mark the boundaries of character fields. Use the Delimited argument with the With Blank modifier when a space marks the boundary between fields. Use the Delimited argument with the DELIMITER modifier to use a different delimiter as a field boundary. EXAMPLE:

```
append ALL from SOMEFILE
```

Average [<SCOPE>] <nEXP LIST> To <MEMVAR LIST> [For <CONDITION>] [While <CONDITION>]

Summer 87, 5.0, 5.01

Both versions 5.0 and 5.01 translate this command into a set of three commands that uses the DBEval( ) function to compute the average. Depending on your program's needs, you might be able to increase program execution speed and decrease program size by using the DBEval( ) function directly.

This command averages a range of records in the selected database and places the result in a memory variable list. Use one variable for every separately averaged field. The SCOPE argument determines how many records Clipper averages. You can use two different keywords with SCOPE. All averages every source record to the selected database. Next <*n*> averages the number of records specified by *n*. Clipper starts averaging records from the record pointed to by the record pointer. The For argument specifies which records to average. The While argument specifies which records to average, but, unlike the For argument, the While argument stops averaging records when the current record no longer meets the specified criteria. EXAMPLE:

```
Average SOMEFIELD to SOMEVAR for FIELD = CONDITION
```

Begin Sequence

```
Begin Sequence
    <STATEMENTS> ...
    [BREAK [<ERROR>] ]
    <STATEMENTS> ...
    [RECOVER [<EXP>] ]
    <STATEMENTS> ...
    [RETRY]
end [SEQUENCE]
```

The BREAK ERROR, RECOVER, RETRY, and End SEQUENCE clauses were added in Clipper 5.0. Avoid using the LOOP, EXIT, and RETURN clauses within a Begin Sequence structure when using 5.0 and 5.01. Of the two, 5.0 is more sensitive to this condition. 5.01 always generates an error message when using these clauses would prevent the program from operating correctly. The Summer 87 version doesn't have any restrictions on use of the LOOP, EXIT, and RETURN clauses within the Begin Sequence control structure.

The Begin Sequence control structure separates an area of critical code. The BREAK argument provides a method of leaving the control structure or reacting to error conditions. Execution continues at the nearest RECOVER clause. If you don't provide a RECOVER clause, then Clipper resumes program execution at the first statement after the control structure ends. When you specify the optional ERROR number, Clipper sends this number to the RECOVER clause or first statement at the end of the control structure. The RECOVER clause specifies the point in the control structure dedicated to error recovery. The optional EXP receives the error number value sent by the BREAK clause. The RETRY clause restarts program execution at the nearest Begin Sequence clause. When the control structure completes or encounters a BREAK clause, Clipper continues execution at the statement following the control structure. EXAMPLE:

```
<PROGRAM STATEMENTS>
do CRIT_CODE
<PROGRAM STATEMENTS>

* Perform a critical code section.
```

```
procedure CRIT_CODE
begin sequence
        <PROGRAM STATEMENTS>
        if CONDITION
                break
        endif
        return
end
<ERROR HANDLING STATEMENTS>
return
```

Call <cEXP> [With <EXP LIST>]

Summer 87, 5.0, 5.01

The 5.0 version has a problem where the parameters in the expression list are passed in reverse order to the separately assembled routine. For example, Call SOMEPROC With cA, cB, nC would send the parameters as nC, cB, cA. This problem has been corrected in 5.01.

The CALL command temporarily suspends execution of a Clipper program, then passes control to a separately compiled or assembled routine or program. The parameters present in EXP LIST are passed on the stack employing the same method used by the Extend System. The program must observe all the conventions observed by routines created for the Extend System. Nantucket provided this command for compatibility purposes only. Use the procedures described in later chapters of this book to include separately compiled or assembled routines. Use the Run command to execute external programs.

Cancel/Quit

Summer 87, 5.0, 5.01

This command closes all files, terminates the current program, and returns control to the operating system. The Cancel command is provided for compatibility purposes only in versions 5.0 and 5.01. Use the Quit command instead. EXAMPLE:

```
<PROGRAM STATEMENTS>
quit
```

Clear [Screen]/CLS

Summer 87, 5.0, 5.01

5.0 added the CLS command as a substitute for the Clear Screen command. There is no advantage to using either command, and there is no substitute for the Clear command.

Use this command to clear the display and all pending gets, then place the cursor in the upper left corner. The optional Screen argument suppresses the automatic clearing of gets. The Summer 87 version of Clipper clears an actual get parameter when you use the Clear command. Versions 5.0 and 5.01 write an empty array to the GetList array to clear the gets. EXAMPLE:

```
clear screen
<DISPLAY STATEMENTS>
```

Clear All

Summer 87, 5.0, 5.01

The Clear All command closes all open database and associated files, releases all memory variables, and selects work area 1. Use this command in place of the Close/Clear Memory command combination when using Summer 87. This is a compatibility command for 5.0 and 5.01. When using these versions, you should close databases and release variables using separate commands as required. This command does not release local or static variables. In addition, it might have unexpected consequences due to the lexical scoping used in 5.0 and 5.01. EXAMPLE:

```
procedure DOIT
use DATA
SOMEVAR = 'String'
<PROGRAM STATEMENTS>
* Terminate the procedure and return to main.
clear all
return
```

Clear Gets

Summer 87, 5.0, 5.01

This command writes a blank array to the current GetList array (there could be a different variable name when using the ReadModal( ) function) when using versions 5.0 and above. It does not clear previous levels in a multilevel get imposed by a Valid clause.

This command clears all pending gets. Use it when a read statement cannot clear the pending gets automatically. You can also clear all pending gets using the Read or Clear command. EXAMPLE:

```
<PROGRAM STATEMENTS>
do while .not. updated()
      <DISPLAY STATEMENTS>
      read save
enddo
clear gets
```

Clear Memory

Summer 87, 5.0, 5.01

Use this command to release all private and public variables. It has the same effect as using the Release All command in Summer 87. When using 5.0 or 5.01, you should release variables using separate commands as required. However, this is the only command that can actually remove public and private variables from memory. (The Release command assigns a value of NIL to variables when using 5.0 and 5.01.) This command does not remove local or static variables. In addition, it might have unexpected consequences due to the lexical scoping used in 5.0 and 5.01. EXAMPLE:

```
procedure NEWPROC
<VARIABLE DECLARATIONS>
<PROGRAM STATEMENTS>
clear memory
return
```

Clear Typeahead

Summer 87, 5.0, 5.01

Removes all characters from the keyboard buffer. Two other commands, Set Typeahead and Keyboard, perform the same task as one of their duties. EXAMPLE:

```
if nextkey() <> 0
     clear typeahead
endif
```

Close [<cEXP>/All/Alternate/Databases/Format/Index]

Summer 87, 5.0, 5.01

The Close<cExp> form of this command was added in Clipper 5.0, and there is added documented function translation in Clipper 5.01.

The command closes all databases and associated files when used by itself. The cEXP argument allows you to specify a work area other than the current work area where all files are closed. Both forms of the Close command translate to the DBCloseArea( ) function in Clipper 5.01. The All argument closes all databases and associated files. It also releases all active filters, formats, and relations.

This command equates to using the DBCloseAll( ) function, followed by a DBSelectArea( ) function and the Set Format command when using Clipper 5.01. The Alternate argument closes the alternate database and associated files only. The Databases argument closes all databases and associated files. It also releases all active filters. This is the same as issuing a DBCloseAll( ) function by itself in Clipper 5.01. The Format argument closes all active formats without affecting the databases. The Index argument closes all active index files without affecting the databases. This equates to the DBClearIndex( ) function in Clipper 5.01. EXAMPLE:

```
* Close all formats and indexes.
close format
close index
```

Commit

Summer 87, 5.0, 5.01

Commit flushes all DOS buffers to disk when using DOS versions greater than 3.2. It ensures that all file updates appear on disk prior to program termination. When using DOS versions 3.2 and below, this command merely flushes the Clipper buffers to DOS. It will not supersede the buffering provided by disk caches. The Commit command equates to the DBCommitAll( ) function when using 5.01. If you want to flush the Clipper buffers for the current work area, use the DBCommit( ) function (5.01 only). You must use the Commit command when you want to update a database in a network environment. This also makes any changes visible to any other processes running on the network. EXAMPLE:

```
<PROGRAM STATEMENTS>
clear all
commit
quit
```

Continue

Summer 87, 5.0, 5.01

This command finds the next record matching the conditions set using the LOCATE command. If no record matches the search conditions, FOUND( ) returns .F. EXAMPLE:

```
locate for FIELD = CONDITION
@ 01, 01 say FIELD
do while found()
      continue
      @ 01, 01 say FIELD
      skip
enddo
```

Copy File <FILE1>.<EXT1>/(<cEXP1>) To <FILE2>.<EXT2>/(<cEXP2>)

Summer 87, 5.0, 5.01

This command creates a copy of a file of any type. You must specify both the filename and extension. If the filename is in the form of a character expression, you must enclose the variable in parentheses. Copy File will overwrite existing files without error or warning, so you should always check for the existence of the target file before using it. EXAMPLE:

```
copy FILEA.DBF to FILEB.DBF
```

Copy Structure [Fields <FIELD LIST>] To <FILE>/(<cEXP>)

Summer 87, 5.0, 5.01

This command copies the structure of the selected database to a new file, creating an empty database. When used by itself, this command performs the same task as Copy Structure Extended for versions 5.0 and above. The optional Fields argument specifies which fields to copy from the selected database. EXAMPLE:

```
copy structure to NEWFILE
```

Copy Structure Extended to <FILE>/(<cEXP>)

Summer 87, 5.0, 5.01

This command creates a database containing four fields: FIELD_NAME, FIELD_TYPE, FIELD_LEN, and FIELD_DEC. Each record in the database describes one field of the selected database. EXAMPLE:

```
copy structure extended to NEWFILE
```

Copy To <FILE>/(<cEXP1>) [<SCOPE>] [Fields <FIELD LIST>] [For <CONDITION>] [While <CONDITION>] [SDF/Delimited/Delimited With <DELIMITER>/(<cEXP2>)]

Summer 87, 5.0, 5.01

When using 5.0, make certain that any delimited file uses commas as delimiters. The use of other delimiters with this version could produce undesired results. 5.01 corrects this problem. In addition, you must use a character expression when using the Delimited With clause in 5.0. It no longer accepts literal characters as Summer 87 did.

This command adds records to the specified file using the contents of the currently selected database. Don't lock the file before using this command in a network. Clipper automatically opens the file in the EXCLUSIVE mode. If another user opens the file before the program issues this command, the copy fails.

The To argument specifies a filename to send the output to. The SCOPE argument determines how many of the source records appear in the specified file. There are three different scopes. All adds every source record to the specified file. Next <*n*> adds the number of records specified by *n*. Clipper starts adding records from the record pointed to by the record pointer. Record <*n*> adds a single record; *n* specifies the record number. The default scope is all.

The Fields argument specifies which fields to transfer from the source database to the specified file. The For argument specifies which source records to send to the specified file. You must use a scope of all or next with this argument. The While argument also specifies which source records to send to the specified file, but, unlike the For argument, the While argument stops outputting records when the source record no longer meets the specified criteria.

The SDF and Delimited arguments export records to files that use an alternate format. An SDF file contains fixed-length records separated by a carriage return and line feed. A delimited file contains variable length records separated by a carriage return and line feed. A comma separates each field in the record, and double quotations mark the boundaries of character fields. Use the Delimited With argument to specify a different character to mark the boundary between fields. EXAMPLE:

```
copy to SOMEFILE SDF
```

Count [<SCOPE>] [For <CONDITION>] [While <CONDITION>] to <nEXP>

Summer 87, 5.0, 5.01

Both 5.0 and 5.01 translate this command into a set of three commands that uses the DBEval( ) function to compute the average. Depending on your program's needs, you might be able to increase program execution speed and decrease program size by using the DBEval( ) function directly.

This command totals the number of records matching a specific criteria to a numeric variable. The SCOPE argument determines how many of the source records appear in the specified file. There are two different scopes. All counts every record. Next <*n*> counts the number of records specified by *n*. Clipper starts counting records from the record pointed to by the record pointer.

The For argument specifies which records to count. The While argument also specifies which records to count, but, unlike the For argument, the While argument stops counting records when the current record no longer meets the specified criteria. Use the LastRec( ) function in place of this command when you need to know the total number of records in the database. EXAMPLE:

```
count next 15 for FIELD = SOMEVAR to COUNTVAR
```

Create <FILE>/(<cEXP>)

Summer 87, 5.0, 5.01

This command creates a database containing four fields: FIELD_NAME, FIELD_TYPE, FIELD_LEN, and FIELD_DEC. Each record in the database describes one field of the selected database. Unlike the Copy Structure Extended command, this command does not require you have a database in use. EXAMPLE:

```
create NEWFILE
```

Create <FILE1>/(<cEXP1>) From <FILE2>/(<cEXP2>)

Summer 87, 5.0, 5.01

This command creates a database from a structure extended file. A structure extended file contains four fields: FIELD_NAME, FIELD_TYPE, FIELD_LEN, and FIELD_DEC. Each record in the database describes one field of the new database. FILE1 is the new database and FILE2 is the structure extended database. EXAMPLE:

```
create NEWDATA from STRUCT
```

Declare <ARRAY1/MEMVAR1> [<nEXP1>] [:= <EXP1>] [<ARRAY2/MEMVAR2> [<nEXP2>]] [:= <EXP2>] ...

Summer 87, 5.0, 5.01

The Assignment Operator and EXP were added in Clipper 5.0. This command is provided for compatibility purposes only. It performs the same function as the Private command in versions 5.0 and above.

This command creates an array (or other variable when using Clipper 5.0) with nEXP elements. The square brackets must appear as part of the nEXP argument. nEXP is not an optional part of the command when using the Summer 87 version of Clipper 5.0. When using Clipper 5.0, you can use Declare to create private variables by excluding the brackets and nEXP. The assignment operator (:=) and EXP allow you to place a value in private variables created using Declare. Excluding EXP creates a private variable with a value of NIL. All array elements automatically receive a value of NIL. You cannot assign a value to arrays. Use this command before using any array function described in the next chapter when using Summer 87. EXAMPLE:

```
declare SOMEARRAY[2]
SOMEARRAY[1] = 1
SOMEARRAY[2] = 2
```

Delete [<SCOPE>] [For <CONDITION>] [While <CONDITION>]

Summer 87, 5.0, 5.01

Both 5.0 and 5.01 translate this command into a DBEval( ) function to delete multiple records. Only 5.01 uses DBEval( ) for single-record deletions (5.0 uses an internal function). Depending on your program's needs, you might be able to increase program execution speed and decrease program size by using the DBEval( ) function directly. 5.01 also includes a new function, DBDelete( ), which performs the same task as the Delete command with a scope of the current record.

Use this command to remove records from the selected database. The SCOPE argument determines how many of the source records Clipper removes from the specified file. There are three different scopes. All removes every record in the specified file. Next <*n*> removes the number of records specified by *n*. Clipper starts removing records from the record pointed to by the record pointer. Record <*n*> removes a single record; *n* specifies the record number. The default scope is Record <*n*> where *n* equals the current record.

The For argument specifies which records to delete from the specified file. You must use a scope of all or next with this argument. The While argument specifies which records to delete from the specified file. However, unlike the For argument, the While argument stops deleting records when the current record no longer meets the specified criteria. EXAMPLE:

```
* Remove the records meeting a specific condition.
delete all for FIELD = CONDITION
```

Delete File <cExp>

Summer 87, 5.0, 5.01

See the Erase command description.

Dir [<DRIVE>:] [<PATH> \] [<SKELETON>]/(<cEXP>)

Summer 87, 5.0, 5.01

This is a compatibility command in versions 5.0 and above. It is recommended that you use the Directory( ) function instead.

Dir retrieves the files appearing the specified directory and places the list on the display. DRIVE specifies the disk drive. PATH specifies the directory. SKELETON specifies the file types to retrieve. Clipper allows you to use the asterisk (*) and question mark (?). Nantucket supplies this command for compatibility purposes only. The ADir( ) function replaces this command when using Summer 87. Use the Directory( ) function appearing in the next chapter for most directory searches when using 5.0 and above. The Directory( ) function allows you to manipulate and store the retrieved directory, providing more flexibility. EXAMPLE:

```
* Display all the files on drive A.
dir A:*.*
```

Display [Off] [<SCOPE>] <EXP LIST> [For <CONDITION>] [While <CONDITION>] [To Print] [To File <FILE>/(<cEXP>)]

Summer 87, 5.0, 5.01

When using 5.0, the To Printer clause must be specified as To Print. This has been fixed in 5.01.

This command outputs a listing of the current database to the display, printer, file, or any combination of the three. The Off arguments sets the output of record numbers off.

The SCOPE argument determines how many of the source records Clipper displays from the selected database. There are three different scopes. All displays every record in the selected database. Next <*n*> displays the number of records specified by *n*. Clipper starts displaying records from the record pointed to by the record pointer. Record <*n*> displays a single record; *n* specifies the record number. The default scope is Record <*n*> where *n* equals the current record.

EXP LIST defines what information Clipper displays from the database and in what format. The For argument specifies which records to display from the selected database. You must use a scope of all or next with this argument. The While argument also specifies which records to display from the selected database, but, unlike the For argument, the While argument stops displaying records when the current record no longer meets the specified criteria. The To Print argument sets the printer on. The To File argument sends the output to the specified file. EXAMPLE:

```
* Display every field of every record to all three outputs.
display all to print to file
```

Do <PROCEDURE> [With <PARAMETER LIST>]

Summer 87, 5.0, 5.01

The Do command is listed as a compatibility feature in 5.0 and above. The new procedure execution method is to place the procedure name on a line by itself. You can place any passed parameters in parentheses following the procedure name.

Do executes PROCEDURE and returns to the following command. This is a temporary branch to a subroutine. The optional With argument passes PARAMETER LIST to the called procedure. Clipper passes fields and expressions to the procedure by value. In other words, the called procedure obtains a copy of the variable. Clipper passes single memory variables by reference as a default. In other words, the called procedure directly manipulates the original copy of the variable. To pass a single memory variable by value, enclose it in parentheses. EXAMPLE:

```
<PROGRAM STATEMENTS>
do SOMEPROC                    && Execute SOMEPROC.
<PROGRAM STATEMENTS>           && Return here when finished.

procedure SOMEPROC
<PROGRAM STATEMENTS>
return
```

Do Case
    Case <CONDITION>
        <COMMANDS>
    [Case <CONDITION>
        <COMMANDS>] ...
    [Otherwise
        <COMMANDS>]
Endcase

Summer 87, 5.0, 5.01

This control structure executes one of several options and then exits to the command following the control structure. The Case argument specifies an instance of CONDITION. Clipper compares each condition with the actual conditions until it finds a comparison or the end of the control structure. The Otherwise argument always matches the current conditions. Clipper executes the commands appearing between two sets of conditions or a condition and Endcase.

Use the IF control structure whenever possible in place of this control structure. The IF control structure uses an average of four bytes less per condition and incurs no penalty in execution speed. However, the Do Case control structure does produce more readable code. EXAMPLE:

```
do case
      case CONDITION = X
            <PROGRAM STATEMENTS>
      case CONDITION = Y
            <PROGRAM STATEMENTS>
      otherwise
            <PROGRAM STATEMENTS>
endcase
```

Do While <CONDITION>
    <PROGRAM STATEMENTS>
    [Exit]
    <PROGRAM STATEMENTS>
    [Loop]
    <PROGRAM STATEMENTS>
Enddo

Summer 87, 5.0, 5.01

This control structure executes a set of instructions until the specified condition becomes false. The Exit argument terminates the while loop prematurely and transfers control to the first instruction after the control structure. The Loop argument terminates the current loop and transfers control to the first argument in the control structure. EXAMPLE:

```
do while CONDITION = .T.
      <PROGRAM STATEMENTS>
      if CONDITION = .T.
            exit
      elseif CONDITION = .T.
            loop
      endif
      <PROGRAM STATEMENTS>
enddo
```

Eject

Summer 87, 5.0, 5.01

This command advances the print head to the top of the next page. EXAMPLE:

```
set print on
@ row(), col() say 'Some String'
eject
```

Erase/Delete File <FILENAME>.<EXT>/(<cEXP>)

Summer 87, 5.0, 5.01

This command has been replaced by the FErase( ) function in 5.0 and above.

It removes the specified file, if present, from the disk. You can specify a drive and path when using this command. EXAMPLE:

```
if file(NOFILE.TXT)
      erase NOFILE.TXT
endif
```

External <PROCEDURE LIST>

Summer 87, 5.0, 5.01

Use this command to declare one or more procedures, format files, or user-defined functions external to the current file. This is especially important if you access the procedures using macro substitution, because Clipper and the linker don't know to look for the procedure on disk. EXAMPLE:

```
external SOMEPROC
```

Field <cEXP1> [In <cEXP2>]

5.0, 5.01

The Field command declares a field within a database to the compiler. This allows you to reference a field without using an alias before the field name (for example, B– >FIELD). cEXP1 contains a list of one or more field names. Separate each field name with a comma. cEXP2 contains the name of the database. If you don't use the optional In cEXP2 clause, then Clipper assigns the special FIELD alias to the field. This means that the field name is referenced as a field in the current database rather than a variable. The Field command must appear before any executable statements in a procedure or function. You can override the Field command definitions by providing an alias before the field or variable name. EXAMPLE:

```
field F_NAME, L_NAME in DB1
```

Find <CHARACTER STRING>/(<cEXP>)

Summer 87, 5.0, 5.01

Find is a compatibility command in 5.0 and above. Use the Seek command whenever possible. In addition, 5.01 adds a new function, DBSeek( ), which is more flexible than either the Find or Seek commands.

This command looks for the desired search string in the selected database. It uses the index associated with the database to find the string and then updates the database record pointer. In most cases, use the SEEK command instead of this command. The SEEK command provides greater flexibility and requires the same amount of memory as this command. EXAMPLE:

```
find "SOME STRING"
```

For <MEMVAR> = <nEXP1> To <nEXP2> [Step <nEXP3>]

<PROGRAM STATEMENTS>
[Exit]
<PROGRAM STATEMENTS>
[Loop]
<PROGRAM STATEMENTS>
Next

Summer 87, 5.0, 5.01

This control structure creates a program loop. Unlike the Do While command, this control structure executes a fixed number of times and exits. MEMVAR contains the current count. nEXP1 contains the starting count. nEXP2 contains the ending count. The optional Step argument controls how Clipper increments the counter. Normally, Clipper increments the counter by one after each loop. nEXP3 contains the step value. The Exit argument terminates the while loop prematurely and transfers control to the first instruction after the control structure. The Loop argument terminates the current loop and transfers control to the first argument in the control structure. EXAMPLE:

```
for COUNTVAR = 1 to 100
      <PROGRAM STATEMENTS>
      if CONDITION = X
            exit
      elseif CONDITION = Y
            loop
      endif
      <PROGRAM STATEMENTS>
next
```

[Static] Function <FUNCTION NAME>
[(<PARAMETER LIST>)]
    [Local <ARRAY1> [<nEXP1>] [:= <EXP1>]]
    [Static <ARRAY1> [<nEXP1>] [:= <EXP1>]]
    [Field <cEXP1> [In <cEXP2>]]
    [MemVar <cEXP>]
    <PROGRAM STATEMENTS> ...
Return <EXP>

Summer 87, 5.0, 5.01

This command was completely revamped for Clipper 5.0. All clauses except FUNCTION and RETURN are new. The Function control structure separates a section of code from the main body of code. This allows the program to use the code repeatedly without writing it more than once. The main difference between this control structure and the Procedure control structure is that this control structure returns a value to the calling program.

When using Clipper 5.0, you can return a NIL value. When the program doesn't require a return value from the code segment, use the Procedure control structure. The Procedure control structure requires an average of four bytes less per occurrence and incurs no performance penalty. The Static clause in front of the Function clause allows you to specify functions used within the current PRG file only. Using the Static clause reduces the size of your object file by 15 bytes per occurrence. It does not affect the EXE file size. Using the Static clause does not affect program execution speed. The variables declared in PARAMETER LIST are local to the function. See the appropriate commands in this chapter for a discussion of the Local, Static, Field, and MemVar clauses. EXAMPLE:

```
<PROGRAM STATEMENTS>
SOMEVAR = sample()
```

```
function SAMPLE
      <PROGRAM STATEMENTS>
      OUTVALUE = RESULT
return OUTVALUE
```

Go/Goto <nEXP>/Bottom/Top

Summer 87, 5.0, 5.01

Version 5.01 of Clipper replaces this command with three new functions: DBGoTop( ), DBGoBottom( ), and DBGoTo( ). There is no advantage to using these functions over the Go/Goto command, however, because the preprocessor translates the command to the function. 5.0 had the same functions as undocumented internal functions: _DBGoTop( ), _DBGoBottom( ), and _DBGoTo( ).

This command places the record pointer at the specified position in the database. The nEXP argument places the record pointer at a specific record number. The Bottom argument places the record pointer at the last record in the database. The Top argument places the record pointer at the first record in the database. When using either the Top or Bottom arguments, the first or last record is affected by any indexes or filter conditions attached to the database. EXAMPLE:

```
goto top
```

If <CONDITION>
<PROGRAM STATEMENTS> ...
[Elseif <CONDITION>
<PROGRAM STATEMENTS> ...]
[Else
<PROGRAM STATEMENTS> ...]
Endif

Summer 87, 5.0, 5.01

This control structure performs conditional execution of a group of program statements that exits to the program statement following the control structure. EXAMPLE:

```
if CONDITION = X
      <PROGRAM STATEMENTS>
elseif CONDITION = Y
      <PROGRAM STATEMENTS>
else
      <PROGRAM STATEMENTS>
endif
```

Index On <KEY EXP> To <FILE>/(<cEXP>) [UNIQUE]

Summer 87, 5.0, 5.01

5.0 adds the UNIQUE clause to the Index command, making the Set Unique command obsolete. 5.01 uses a new function, DBCreateIndex( ), in place of the Index command. The command form gets translated to the function form. The DBCreateIndex( ) function is more flexible than the Index command because you can include a code block as one of the parameters.

This command creates an index to a database using KEY EXP as the basis for the index contents. Clipper places the key expressions in sorted order and includes all deleted and filtered records. FILE specifies the file to use. Clipper uses a default file extension of NTX. You can create dBASE III compatible indexes by specifying the NDX extension when using Summer 87. Version 5.0 and above require a special driver to create dBASE III compatible index files. EXAMPLE:

```
index on FIELD to INDXFILE
```

Input [<PROMPT>] To <MEMVAR>

Summer 87, 5.0, 5.01

5.0 sets the value of MEMVAR to NIL if the user fails to input a value. 5.01 maintains Summer 87 compatibility by preserving the value of MEMVAR if the user doesn't input a value.

Use this command to retrieve characters from the keyboard. Clipper places the input in MEMVAR. The optional PROMPT displays a message. The display appears at the current cursor position unless PROMPT contains cursor positioning control codes. Clipper retrieves the keyboard characters immediately following the prompt (if provided). Nantucket provided this command for compatibility purposes only. In most cases, use the @ Say/Get command in place of this command. The @ Say/Get command requires an average of only nine bytes more per command occurrence to use. EXAMPLE:

```
input 'Enter something: ' to SOMEVAR
```

Join With <ALIAS>/(<cEXP1>) To <FILE>/(<cEXP2>) For <CONDITION> [Fields <FIELD LIST>]

Summer 87, 5.0, 5.01

Versions 5.0 and above require that you specify secondary fields to include in the resultant database.

This command creates a new database using the records and fields from two other databases. ALIAS specifies one database to use as a source of records. Clipper uses the selected database as the second source of records. FILE specifies the file to copy the records to. The For argument specifies which records to output from the specified and selected databases. Both databases must contain any fields used as a condition. The optional Fields argument specifies which fields to transfer from the source databases to the specified file. Only one source database needs to contain the specified fields. EXAMPLE:

```
join with DATA2 to NEWDATA for FIELD = CONDITION
```

Keyboard <cEXP>

Summer 87, 5.0, 5.01

The Keyboard command places cEXP in the keyboard buffer, simulating user input. EXAMPLE:

```
keyboard "Some String"
```

Label Form <FILE1>/(<cEXP1>) [<SCOPE>] [For <CONDITION>] [While <CONDITION>] [Sample] [To Print] [To File <FILE>/(<cEXP>)] [No Console]

Summer 87, 5.0, 5.01

The NoConsole clause, undocumented in 5.0, is available to versions 5.0 and above. Specifying this clause removes output from the display while the report is printing.

This command outputs a listing of the current database to the display, printer, file, or any combination of the three using the criteria in a LBL file. FILE specifies which label form definition file to use. The SCOPE argument determines how many of the source records Clipper displays from the selected database. There are three different scopes. All displays every record in the selected database. Next <*n*> displays the number of records specified by *n*. Clipper starts displaying records from the record pointed to by the record pointer. Record <*n*> displays a single record; *n* specifies the record number. The default scope is all.

The For argument specifies which records to display from the selected database. You must use a scope of all or next with this argument. The While argument specifies which records to display from the selected database. However, unlike the For argument, the While argument stops displaying records when the current record no longer meets the specified criteria. The Sample argument sends a group of Xs to the printer showing the maximum character positions for the label. The To Print argument sets the printer on. The To File argument sends the output to the specified file. EXAMPLE:

```
* Send all the labels in the database to the printer only.
set console off
label form SOMEFILE to print
set console on
```

List [Off] [<SCOPE>] <EXP LIST> [For <CONDITION>] [While <CONDITION>] [To Print] [To File <FILE>/(<cEXP>)]

Summer 87, 5.0, 5.01

When using 5.0, the To Printer clause must be specified as To Print. This has been fixed in 5.01.

This command outputs a listing of the current database to the display, printer, file, or any combination of the three. The Off arguments sets output of record numbers off. The SCOPE argument determines how many of the source records Clipper displays from the selected database. There are three different scopes. All displays every record in the selected database. Next <*n*> displays the number of records specified by *n*. Clipper starts displaying records from the record pointed to by the record pointer. Record <*n*> displays a single record; *n* specifies the record number. The default scope is all.

EXP LIST defines what information Clipper displays from the database and in what format. The For argument specifies which records to display from the selected database. You must use a scope of all or next with this argument. The While argument specifies which records to display from the selected database. However, unlike the For argument, the While argument stops displaying records when the current record no longer meets the specified criteria. The To Print argument sets the printer on. The To File argument sends the output to the specified file.

Use the Display command in place of this command when code size is more important than execution speed. The Display command uses 12 bytes per occurrence less than the List command. However, the List command executes 289% faster than the Display command. EXAMPLE:

```
* Send all the records to the printer and display.
list SOMEFIELD to print
```

Local <aARRAY1> [<nEXP1>] [:= <EXP1>] [<aARRAY2> [<nEXP2>]] [:= <EXP2>] ...

5.0, 5.01

There are two known anomalies with this command in 5.0 and 5.01. First, declaring more than one variable will result in one local variable and at least one private variable. For example, the statement local nA := nB := 0 *produces one local variable, nA, and one private variable, nB. In addition, you can't create dependent declarations. For example, the statement* local nA := 0, nB := nA + 1 *will result in an argument error during runtime.*

This command creates an array with nEXP elements or a local variable. The square brackets must appear as part of the nEXP argument when declaring an array. Exclude the nEXP argument to create a local variable. The assignment operator (:=) and EXP allow you to place a value in local variables created using Local. Excluding EXP creates a local variable with a value of NIL. All array elements automatically receive a value of NIL. You cannot assign a value to arrays. Use this command before using any array function described in the next chapter.

Local variables take precedence over any private, public, or field variables with the same name. Clipper resolves the value of a local variable at compile time. This means that local variables offer you significant performance gains over other variable types. Local variables exist for the duration of the current and any called procedures or functions.

Clipper creates a new instance of the variable each time you call the procedure or function in which it resides. This includes recursive calls. You must use the Local command before any executable statements in a procedure or function. This includes the Private, Public, and Parameters commands. You cannot use macro substitution with a Local command because the value of a local variable is resolved at compile time. Clipper will not save local variable to a MEM file. In addition, you cannot determine the type of a local variable using the Type( ) function. Use the ValType( ) function instead. EXAMPLE:

```
* Declare a local variable with a value of 5.
local SOMEVAR := 5
```

Locate [<SCOPE>] For <CONDITION> [While <CONDITION>]

Summer 87, 5.0, 5.01

This command finds the first occurrence of the specified condition in the selected database. The SCOPE argument determines how in how many records of the selected database Clipper searches for CONDITION. There are two different scopes. All searches every record in the selected database. Next <*n*> searches the number of records specified by *n*. Clipper starts searching records from the record pointed to by the record pointer. The default scope is all.

The For argument specifies which records to display from the selected database. The While argument specifies which records to display from the selected database. However, unlike the For argument, the While argument stops displaying records when the current record no longer meets the specified criteria. The SCOPE and While arguments do not affect the outcome of any Continue commands following the Locate command. EXAMPLE:

```
* Find a specific record in a database.
locate for FIELD = CONDITION
```

MemVar <cEXP>

5.0, 5.01

Tells the compiler to resolve all unaliased variables in the variable list (cEXP) as memory variables. This means that these variables automatically assume an alias of M - >. You can override the effects of this command by using an alias in front of the variable or field. MemVar does not create variables, it only provides a reference to them. This command does not affect the contents of macro variables. EXAMPLE:

```
memvar SOMEVAR, SOMEVAR2
```

Menu To <MEMVAR>

Summer 87, 5.0, 5.01

5.0 encountered some problems returning the correct procedure, line, and variable parameters to a procedure called with the SetKey( ) function from a Menu To command. 5.01 corrects this problem.

Use this command with the @ Prompt command to create light-bar menus. Clipper places the user selection as a number in MEMVAR. The number represents the prompt hierarchy on the display. The first prompt equals 1, the second 2, and so forth. EXAMPLE:

```
@ 01, 20 prompt "Display Database"
@ 02, 20 prompt "Print Database"
@ 03, 20 prompt "Exit Program"
menu to SELECTION
```

Note/*/&&

Summer 87, 5.0, 5.01

Use this command to place comments in the source code file. Clipper ignores any text appearing after the Note command. EXAMPLE:

```
* This is a note on a single line.
@ 01, 01 say 'Something' && This is an in-line note.
```

Pack

Summer 87, 5.0, 5.01

Some multi-index packs fail when using 5.0. Always close the indexes, pack the database, then reindex the index files. 5.01 corrects this problem.

This command physically removes records marked for deletion from a database. It automatically reindexes any open index files attached to the packed database. EXAMPLE:

```
use SOMEDATA                          && Open database
delete for FIELD = CONDITION          && Mark records
pack                                  && Remove marked records
```

Parameters <MEMVAR LIST>

Summer 87, 5.0, 5.01

Versions 5.0 and above assign a value of NIL to parameters that don't receive input from the calling routine. Summer 87 allowed the parameters to retain their previous value.

Use this command to specify the parameters required by a function or procedure. Clipper ignores extra parameters passed to the function or procedure. If the calling program does not pass enough parameters, the extra memory variables specified by MEMVAR remain undefined. EXAMPLE:

```
procedure NEW
parameters SOMEVAR, MOREVAR
      <PROGRAM STATEMENTS>
return
```

Private <ARRAY1/MEMVAR1> [<nEXP1>] [:= <EXP1>] [<ARRAY2/MEMVAR2> [<nEXP2>]] [:= <EXP2>] ...

Summer 87, 5.0, 5.01

This command was redefined for Clipper 5.0. It was previously used to declare variables private, not create them. When used with the Summer 87 version of Clipper, this command defines the variables in MEMVAR LIST as private. Procedures at the same level or above the current procedure cannot use the variable. Use this command before actually assigning a value to the variable. Clipper automatically releases private variables when the procedure terminates.

When used with the 5.0 version of Clipper, it creates an array with nEXP elements or a private variable. The square brackets must appear as part of the nEXP argument. You can use Private to create private variables by excluding the brackets and nEXP. The assignment operator (:=) and EXP allow you place a value in private variables created using Private. Excluding EXP creates a private variable with a value of NIL. All array elements automatically receive a value of NIL. You cannot assign a value to arrays. Use this command before using any array function described in the next chapter. Summer 87 EXAMPLE:

```
Declare an existing variable private.
private SOMEVAR
SOMEVAR = 0
```

5.0 EXAMPLE:

```
* Create a variable.
private SOMEVAR := 1
```

[Static] Procedure <PROCEDURE NAME> [(<PARAMETER LIST>)]
[Local <ARRAY1> [<nEXP1>] [:= <EXP1>]]
[Static <ARRAY1> [<nEXP1>] [:= <EXP1>]]
[Field <cEXP1> [In <cEXP2>] CB
[MemVar <cEXP>]
<PROGRAM STATEMENTS> ...
[RETURN]

Summer 87, 5.0, 5.01

This command was completely revamped for Clipper 5.0. All clauses except PROCEDURE and RETURN are new.

The Procedure control structure appears in two places. First, the main body of program code is considered a procedure. Second, a procedure separates a section of code from the main body of code. This allows the program to use the code repeatedly without writing the code more than once. Unlike the Function control structure, this structure does not return a value to the calling program.

The Procedure control structure requires an average of four bytes less per occurrence than the Function control structure, and incurs no performance penalty. The Static clause in front of the Procedure clause allows you to specify procedures used within the current PRG file only. Using the Static clause reduces the size of your object file by 15 bytes per occurrence. It does not affect the EXE file size. Using the Static clause does not affect program execution speed. The variables declared in PARAMETER LIST are local to the procedure. See the appropriate commands in this chapter for a discussion of the Local, Static, Field, and MemVar clauses. EXAMPLE:

```
<PROGRAM STATEMENTS>
do SAMPLE

procedure SAMPLE
      <PROGRAM STATEMENTS>
return
```

Public <ARRAY1/MEMVAR1> [<nEXP1>] [:= <EXP1>] [<ARRAY2/MEMVAR2> [<nEXP2>]] [:= <EXP2>] ...

Summer 87, 5.0, 5.01

This command was redefined for Clipper 5.0; it was previously used to declare variables public, not create them.

When used with the Summer 87 version of Clipper, this command declares a variable public. All procedures within a program have access to all public variables. Clipper does not allow you to declare variables public after declaring them private. However, you can declare a variable private after declaring it public. Clipper assigns all public variables an initial value of false.

When used with the 5.0 version of Clipper, it creates an array with nEXP elements or a public variable. The square brackets must appear as part of the nEXP argument. You may use Public to create public variables by excluding the brackets and nEXP. The assignment operator (:=) and EXP allows you to place a value in public variables created using Public. Excluding EXP creates a Public variable with a value of NIL. All array elements automatically receive a value of NIL. You cannot assign a value to arrays. Use this command before using any array function described in the next chapter. Summer 87 EXAMPLE:

```
public SOMEVAR, MOREVAR
SOMEVAR = 0
MOVEVAR = 'String'
```

5.0 EXAMPLE:

```
* Create a multidimensional array.
private SOMEARRAY [1024, 109, 52]
```

Quit/Cancel

Summer 87, 5.0, 5.01

The Cancel command is provided for compatibility purposes in versions 5.0 and above.

Using this command closes all open files, terminates program execution, and returns control to the operating system. EXAMPLE:

```
<PROGRAM STATEMENTS>
quit
```

Read [Save]

Summer 87, 5.0, 5.01

Starting with version 5.0, this command uses the ReadModal( ) function and get objects to perform its work. If the command excludes the Save clause, then the new command clears all pending gets by assigning an empty list to the GetList variable.

This command appears after one or more @ GET commands. It places Clipper in the full-screen editing mode, allowing the user to enter information in the blanks provided by the @ GET commands. Normally, Clipper clears all pending gets after a READ command. Using the optional Save argument preserves the status of the pending gets. The full-screen editing mode uses a special set of control keys to navigate, edit, change the editing mode, and escape during a READ. TABLE 1-2 contains a listing of these control keys. EXAMPLE:

```
@ 01, 01 say 'Enter a string: ' get STRING
read
```

Table 1-2 Full-screen edit-mode control keys

Key	Edit type	Description
Backspace	Edit	Removes the character to the left of the cursor.
Ctrl-A	Navigation	Moves the cursor one word left.
Ctrl-C	Escape	Terminate the READ. Save any changes to the current GET.
Ctrl-D	Navigation	Moves the cursor one character right. Does not move past the end of the current GET.
Ctrl-E	Navigation	Moves the cursor to the previous GET.
Ctrl-End	Navigation	Moves the cursor to the beginning of the last GET displayed.
Ctrl-F	Navigation	Moves the cursor one word right.
Ctrl-G	Edit	Removes the character at the cursor position.
Ctrl-H	Edit	Removes the character to the left of the cursor.
Ctrl-Home	Navigation	Moves the cursor to the beginning of the first GET.
Ctrl-left arrow	Navigation	Moves the cursor one word left.

Key	Edit type	Description
Ctrl-M	Escape	Terminates the READ from the last GET.
Ctrl-M	Navigation	Moves the cursor to the next GET.
Ctrl-right arrow	Navigation	Moves the cursor one word right.
Ctrl-S	Navigation	Moves the cursor one character left. Does not move past the end of the current GET.
Ctrl-T	Edit	Removes the word to the right of the cursor.
Ctrl-U	Edit	Restores the GET to its original value.
Ctrl-V	Mode	Toggles the insert mode between insert and overwrite.
Ctrl-W	Escape	Terminates the READ. Saves any changes to the current GET.
Ctrl-X	Navigation	Moves the cursor to the next GET.
Ctrl-Y	Edit	Removes any input appearing to the right of the cursor position to the end of the GET.
Del	Edit	Removes the word at the cursor position.
Down arrow	Escape	Terminates the READ from the last GET. Valid only if READEXIT() = .T.
Down arrow	Navigation	Moves the cursor to the next GET.
End	Navigation	Moves the cursor to the end of the current GET. Does not move past the end of the current GET.
Enter	Escape	Terminates the READ from the last GET.
Enter	Navigation	Moves the cursor to the next GET.

Table 1-2 Continued.

Key	Edit type	Description
Esc	Escape	Terminates the READ. Does not save any changes to the current GET.
Home	Navigation	Moves the cursor to the beginning of the current GET.
Ins	Mode	Toggles the insert mode between insert and overwrite.
Left arrow	Navigation	Moves the cursor one character left. Does not move past the end of the current GET.
PgDn	Escape	Terminates the READ. Saves any changes to the current GET.
PgUp	Escape	Terminates the READ. Saves any changes to the current GET.
Right arrow	Navigation	Moves the cursor one character right. Does not move past the end of the current GET.
Up arrow	Escape	Terminates the READ from the first GET. Valid only if READEXIT = .T.
Up arrow	Navigation	Moves the cursor to the previous GET.

Recall [<SCOPE>] [For <CONDITION>] [While <CONDITION>]

Summer 87, 5.0, 5.01

Both 5.0 and 5.01 translate this command into the DBEval( ) function. Within the DBEval( ) function is a code block using the DBRecall( ) function for 5.01. This function is documented for the 5.01 version in the Norton Guides. The 5.0 version uses the undocumented _DBRecall( ) function. Depending on your program's needs, you might be able to increase program execution speed and decrease program size by using the DBEval( ) function directly.

This command reinstates records previously marked for deletion. It doesn't recover packed records, only marked records. The SCOPE argument determines how many of the source records Clipper reinstates in the selected database. There are three different scopes. All reinstates every record in the selected database. Next <*n*> reinstates the number of records specified by *n*. Clipper starts reinstating records from the record pointed to by the record pointer. Record <*n*> reinstates a single record; *n* specifies the record number. The default scope is record <*n*>, where *n* equals the current record.

The For argument specifies which records to reinstate in the selected database. You must use a scope of all or next with this argument. The While argument also specifies which records to reinstate in the selected database, but, unlike the For argument, the While argument stops reinstating records when the current record no longer meets the specified criteria. EXAMPLE:

```
* See if user wants to reverse deletes before packing.
@ 01, 01 say 'Reinstate records before packing? ' get ANSWER picture '!'
read
iif (ANSWER = 'Y', recall all, pack)
```

Reindex

Summer 87, 5.0, 5.01

The 5.0 version uses the existing index file header to create the updated index. If this header is corrupted, then Reindex will not properly update the index file. 5.01 fixes this problem. In addition, 5.01 adds the DBReindex( ) function, which is a direct replacement for this command. There is no advantage to using the command version over the function version of Reindex.

Use this command to rebuild any indexes associated with a database. When used in a network environment, you must obtain exclusive use the database before using this command. EXAMPLE:

```
use DATABASE index DATAIND
reindex
```

Release <MEMVAR LIST>/[All [Like/Except <SKELETON>]]

Summer 87, 5.0, 5.01

This command deallocates the memory used by one or more memory variables. MEMVAR LIST is a list of memory variables to release. The All argument releases all memory variables. The Like and Except arguments modify the All argument. SKELETON specifies a wildcard match for variables to release or retain. EXAMPLE:

```
* Release all variables beginning with R.
release all like R*
```

Rename <FILE1>.<EXT1>/(<cEXP1>) To <FILE2>.<EXT2>/(<cEXP2>)

Summer 87, 5.0, 5.01

Versions 5.0 and above use the FRename( ) function to replace this command. There is no advantage to using the command version over the function version.

This command changes the name of a disk file. The specification includes the drive, path, filename, and file extension. FILE1 is the original filename. FILE2 is the new filename. EXAMPLE:

```
rename OLDFILE.TXT to NEWFILE.TXT
```

Replace [<SCOPE>] [<ALIAS> – >] <FIELD1> With <EXP1> [, [<ALIAS> – >] <FIELD2> with <EXP2> ...] [For <CONDITION>] [While <CONDITION>]

Summer 87, 5.0, 5.01

Both 5.0 and 5.01 translate this command into the DBEval( ) function. Depending on your program's needs, you might be able to increase program execution speed and decrease program size by using the DBEval( ) function directly.

The REPLACE command changes the contents of one or more fields to match the specified expression. The SCOPE argument determines how many of the source records Clipper replaces in the selected database. There are three different scopes. All replaces every record in the selected database. Next <*n*> replaces the number of records specified by *n*. Clipper starts replacing records from the record pointed to by the record pointer. Record <*n*> replaces a single record, and *n* specifies the record number. The default scope is all.

ALIAS is the name used to specify a particular database. Clipper assumes a default of the selected database. FIELD is the database field you want to replace. EXP is the replacement contents for the specified field. The For argument specifies which records to replace in the selected database. You must use a scope of all or next with this argument. The While argument specifies which records to replace in the selected database. However, unlike the For argument, the While argument stops replacing records when the current record no longer meets the specified criteria. EXAMPLE:

```
* Replace the contents of a field meeting a specified condition.
use SOMEDATA
replace FIELD_NAME with "New Contents" for FIELD_NAME = CONDITION
```

Report Form <FILE1>/(<cEXP1>) [<SCOPE>] [For <CONDITION>] [While <CONDITION>] [To Print] [To File <FILE2>/(<cEXP2>)] [Summary] [Plain] [Heading <cEXP3>] [NoEject] [NoConsole]

Summer 87, 5.0, 5.01

The NoConsole clause, undocumented in 5.0, is available to versions 5.0 and above. Specifying this clause removes output from the display while the report is printing.

This command outputs a listing of the current database to the display, printer, file, or any combination of the three using the criteria in a FRM file. FILE specifies which report form definition file to use.

The SCOPE argument determines how many of the source records Clipper displays from the selected database. There are three different scopes. All displays every record in the selected database. Next <*n*> displays the number of records specified by *n*. Clipper starts displaying records from the record pointed to by the record pointer. Record <*n*> displays a single record; *n* specifies the record number. The default scope is all.

The For argument specifies which records to display from the selected database. You must use a scope of all or next with this argument. The While argument specifies which records to display from the selected database. However, unlike the For argument, the While argument stops displaying records when the current record no longer meets the specified criteria.

The To Print argument sets the printer on. The To File argument sends the output to the specified file. The Summary argument prints a report containing the group, subgroup, and grand-total lines. Clipper does not print the detail lines. The Heading argument places a heading on the first line of each page. EXP3 contains the heading to print. The NoEject argument suppresses the initial form feed sent to the printer at the beginning of a printout. EXAMPLE:

```
* Send all the records in the database to the printer and display.
report form SOMEFILE to print
```

Restore From <FILE>/(<cEXP>) [Additive]

Summer 87, 5.0, 5.01

5.0 experienced some reliability problems with the additive clause of this command. The exact reason for these problems is unknown. However, the effect seems most prominent with public and private variables. All the reliability problems are fixed in version 5.01.

Use this command to retrieve variables stored in a MEM file. Normally, Clipper overwrites any variables already existing in memory. Using the Additive argument retains the current variables and adds the stored variables to them. Clipper always overwrites any variables with the same name as the stored variables. EXAMPLE:

```
restore from OLDVAR additive
```

Restore Screen [From <MEMVAR>]

Summer 87, 5.0, 5.01

Restore Screen is classified as a compatibility command for versions 5.0 and above. Use the RestScreen( ) function in its place.

This command restores previously saved screens. The optional From argument restores a screen from a specific memory variable. Otherwise, Clipper uses the standard buffer (contains a single screen). EXAMPLE:

```
* Save the display, perform some display oriented
* tasks, then restore the original display.
save screen to SOMEVAR
<PROGRAM STATEMENTS>
restore screen from SOMEVAR
```

Return [<EXP>]

Summer 87, 5.0, 5.01

This command terminates the current procedure or function and returns control to the calling procedure or function. Clipper deallocates any memory used by private variables in the terminated procedure or function. Functions use the optional EXP to return a value to the calling procedure or function. EXAMPLE:

```
procedure NEW
        <PROGRAM STATEMENTS>
return
```

Run/! <DOS COMMAND>/(<cEXP>)

Summer 87, 5.0, 5.01

The ! form is provided for compatibility purposes with versions 5.0 and above. You should always use the Run form of the command whenever possible.

This command temporarily suspends the current application, invokes a new copy of the command processor, and executes the desired command.

WARNING: Never run a memory-resident program from within Clipper because you could lose memory available to the Clipper application. In addition, the memory-resident program could interact with Clipper in ways that could cause memory corruption. EXAMPLE:

```
* Allow the user to exit to DOS to perform a task.
<PROGRAM STATEMENTS>
run COMMAND
<PROGRAM STATEMENTS>
```

Save To <FILE>/(<cEXP>) [All [Like/Except <SKELETON>]]

Summer 87, 5.0, 5.01

Use the SAVE TO command to place a copy of all or part of the currently active variables in a MEM file. The All argument saves all nonhidden private and public variables. This is the default condition. The Like and Except arguments limit the number of variables saved. Clipper allows use of the asterisk (*) and question mark (?) as wildcards. The asterisk represents multiple character positions. The question mark represents a single character position. Clipper does not allow you to save arrays. EXAMPLE:

```
TEMP1 = 'Some String'
VAR1 = 2
VAR2 = 3
* Save only VAR1 and VAR2.
save to TEMP1 all like VAR*
* Save all the variables.
save to TEMP2
```

Save Screen [To <MEMVAR>]

Summer 87, 5.0, 5.01

This command is classified as a compatibility command for versions 5.0 and above. Use the SaveScreen( ) function in its place.

Save Screen places a copy of the current screen display in a buffer or variable. Using the command by itself places the screen in a buffer. You can save a single screen in the buffer. The optional To argument places the screen in a variable. Clipper allows you to place screens in an array, making screen management easier. EXAMPLE:

```
* Save the display, perform some display oriented
* tasks, then restore the original display.
save screen to SOMEVAR
<PROGRAM STATEMENTS>
restore screen from SOMEVAR
```

Seek <EXP>

Summer 87, 5.0, 5.01

Version 5.01 added a new function, DBSeek( ), which replaces this command. The DBSeek( ) function is more flexible than the command it replaces. For example, the DBSeek( ) function allows you to locally set softseek on or off without changing the global softseek setting.

The SEEK command searches an index for an expression, then updates the database record pointer to point to the appropriate record. EXP contains the search expression. EXAMPLE:

```
use SOMEDATA index SOMEINDX
seek "Some String"
```

Select <WORK AREA>/<ALIAS>/(<nEXP>)

Summer 87, 5.0, 5.01

Version 5.01 added the DBSelectArea( ) function to replace the Select command. There is no advantage to using the function form of the command over the command form.

Use this command to change the selected work area. Each work area contains one or no database. WORK AREA contain a work area number 0 through 254. ALIAS is a database or work area alias. You can refer to the first 10 work areas using letters A through J. nEXP is a numeric expression evaluating to a number between 0 and 254. EXAMPLE:

```
* Open a database in the first and second work areas.
select 0
use SOMEDATA index SOMEINDX
select 1
use OTHDATA index OTHINDX
```

Set Alternate To [<FILE>/(<cEXP>) [ADDITIVE]]
Set Alternate On/Off/(<lEXP>)

Summer 87, 5.0, 5.01

Version 5.01 adds the ADDITIVE clause to this command. Clipper always truncates the file before writing information to it. Adding the ADDITIVE clause allows you to add information without truncating the file first.

Use Set Alternate To to echo the screen display to an ASCII text file. FILE is the file that Clipper uses for output. The Set Alternate On command enables screen echo. The Set Alternate Off command disables screen echo, but does not close the text file. EXAMPLE:

```
use SOME DATA
set alternate to AFILE
set alternate on
do while .not. eof()
      ? FIELD1, FIELD2
      skip
enddo
set alternate off
close all
```

Set Bell On/Off/(<lEXP>)

Summer 87, 5.0, 5.01

Use this command to enable or disable the bell during full-screen operations. The bell sounds whenever the user commits an error. EXAMPLE:

```
set bell off
```

Set Century On/Off/(<lEXP>)

Summer 87, 5.0, 5.01

When in the on condition, this command causes Clipper to display the century digits in a date. Clipper normally displays the year digits only. For example, 05/19/89 when set off, or 05/19/1989 when set on. EXAMPLE:

```
set century off
```

Set Color/Colour To [<STANDARD> [, <ENHANCED>] [, <BORDER>] [, <BACKGROUND>] [, <UNSELECTED>]]/[(<cEXP>)]

Summer 87, 5.0, 5.01

This command was classified as a compatibility command for versions 5.0 and above. Use the SetColor( ) function in its place.

Use this command to define the colors used by Clipper to present various display elements. STANDARD contains the color used for all normal text, for example, the output of every @ SAY command. ENHANCED contains the color used for all inverted text, for example, the output of the currently selected @ GET command.

BORDER contains the color used for the area around the edge of the display. Clipper never places text in this area. No display adapter currently supports the BACKGROUND argument. UNSELECTED contains the color of all unselected inverted text elements. For example, the output of all currently unselected @ GET commands.

Clipper allows the use of numbers or letters to designate which colors appear on screen. TABLE 1-3 provides a listing of the color numbers and letters. To obtain an intensified color, add 8 to the foreground color. To obtain a blinking color, add 8 to the background color. When using numbers in place of letters, make sure you use character numbers, not actual numbers. EXAMPLE:

```
* This program demonstrates the 256 color combinations
* available using numbers.
COUNT1 = 0
COUNT2 = 0
clear screen
for COUNT1 = 0 to 15                    && Foreground Count
      for COUNT2 = 0 to 15              && Background Count
            * Change numbers to a string.
```

```
        COLORSTR = ltrim(str(COUNT1, 2, 0)) + '/' +  ltrim(str(COUNT2, 2, 0))
        set color to &COLORSTR
        clear screen
        @ 12, 29 say 'This is color ' + COLORSTR
        inkey(1)                && Display 5 Seconds
    next
next
set color to 7/0
clear screen
```

Table 1-3 Color combinations

Name	Number	Letter
Black	0	N
Blue	1	B
Green	2	G
Cyan	3	BG
Red	4	R
Magenta	5	RB
Brown	6	GR
Light gray	7	W
Dark gray	8	N+
Light blue	9	B+
Light green	10	G+
Light cyan	11	BG+
Light red	12	R+
Light magenta	13	RB+
Yellow	14	GR+
White	15	W+
Blank		X

Name	Number	Letter
Underline		U
Inverse video		I
Blink	8 + Color 1 - 7	*

NOTES:
1. Colors 8 through 15 available with foreground color only.
2. Blink used with background color only.

Set Confirm On/Off/(<lEXP>)

Summer 87, 5.0, 5.01

Set this command on to demand a keypress before leaving a get. Clipper normally sets this command off. EXAMPLE:

```
set confirm on
```

Set Console On/Off/(<lEXP>)

Summer 87, 5.0, 5.01

There are some occasions where the Set Console condition is ignored by the Report Form and Label Form commands in 5.0. Always use the NoConsole clause to remove output from the display with these two commands. This problem does not appear in version 5.01 and above.

Use this command to set the console on or off. If a program sets this command off, Clipper does not echo commands or other display information to the console. EXAMPLE:

```
<PROGRAM STATEMENTS>
* Get ready to print.
set console off
<PRINT STATEMENTS>
* Stop printing.
set console on
<PROGRAM STATEMENTS>
```

Set Cursor On/Off/(<lEXP>)

Summer 87, 5.0, 5.01

Versions 5.0 and above add a new function, SetCursor( ), which allows you to control the shape and size of the cursor. This function is a much more versatile replacement for the Set Cursor command.

Clipper normally displays a cursor. Setting this command off disables cursor display. EXAMPLE:

```
set cursor off
```

Set Date American/ANSI/British/French/German/Italian/Japan/USA

Summer 87, 5.0, 5.01

Versions 5.0 and above add Japan and USA as new standard date formats. In addition, you can now create user-defined date formats using the Set Date Format To command described next.

Use this command to control the way Clipper displays and returns the date. The default Clipper setting is AMERICAN. TABLE 1-4 contains a listing of date formats provided by Clipper. EXAMPLE:

```
* Set the date for ANSI format.
set date ANSI
```

Table 1-4 Date formats

Format	Description
American	MM/DD/YY
ANSI	YY.MM.DD
British	DD/MM/YY
French	DD/MM/YY
German	DD.MM.YY
Italian	DD.MM.YY
USA*	MM-DD-YY
Japan*	YY/MM/DD

NOTE:
By using the appropriate operating system call, you can return date formats other than those described above. However, these formats are limited to user-written commands and functions only. Clipper-provided functions return only the date formats shown above.

* The USA and Japan formats are available only when you're using Clipper versions 5.0 and above.

Set Date Format To <cEXP>

5.0, 5.01

Sets the date format used by Clipper. You can choose from several nonstandard display formats, as well. This command overrides the value set by the Set Date command. Clipper allows you to specify up to 12 characters in the format string. It interprets *m* as month, *d* as day, and *y* as year. Clipper copies all other characters verbatim onto the output device. EXAMPLE:

```
* Set the date format for a previous time.
set date format to "mm/dd/yyyyBC"
```

Set Decimals To <nEXP>

Summer 87, 5.0, 5.01

Use this command to change the number of decimal places Clipper displays as the result of numeric calculations and functions. This command does not change the representation of the number in memory. EXAMPLE:

```
set decimals to 4
```

Set Default To <DRIVE>[:<PATH>]/(<cEXP>)

Summer 87, 5.0, 5.01

The Set Default To command changes the drive and optionally the directory path used by Clipper for file searches. Using Set Default To with no arguments sets the drive and path to the currently selected drive and path. EXAMPLE:

```
set default to C:\DATA
```

Set Deleted On/Off/(<lEXP>)

Summer 87, 5.0, 5.01

Specific ordering and filtering conditions occasionally allowed 5.0 programs to display deleted records even with Set Deleted On. Adding a clause ".and. !Deleted( )" to display routines seems to solve the problem. This condition does not occur in version 5.01.

Clipper does not display records marked for deletion when the program sets this command on. The command defaults to off, which displays all records marked for deletion. EXAMPLE:

```
set deleted on
```

Set Delimiters On/Off/(<lEXP>) Set Delimiters To [<cEXP>/Default]

Summer 87, 5.0, 5.01

Use the Set Delimiters On command to display delimiters on either side of a data entry blank. Setting delimiters off inhibits the display of delimiters. The Set Delimiters To command changes the characters Clipper uses for the delimiters. Specifying the Default or no argument sets the delimiters to colons (:) on either side of the data entry blank. EXAMPLE:

```
* Display asterisks as delimiters.
set delimiters to "**"
set delimiters on
```

Set Device To Screen/Print

Summer 87, 5.0, 5.01

The Set Device To command determines in Clipper outputs the results of an @ Say command to the printer or display. The Screen argument ignores the settings of the Set Console and Set Print commands. It outputs all @ Say command information to the display. The Print argument uses the destination defined by the Set Printer To command as the output for all @ Say command information. Clipper ignores all @ Get commands when the program specifies the Print argument. EXAMPLE:

```
<PROGRAM STATEMENTS>
* Set the display off and print.
set device to print
<PRINT STATEMENTS>
* Set the display back on.
set device to screen
<PROGRAM STATEMENTS>
```

Set Epoch <nEXP>

5.0, 5.01

Sets the 100-year period used for all dates. nEXP contains a number between 0100 and 2999. The Clipper year range extends from 0100 to 2999. The default epoch is 1900. When Clipper sees a two-digit year, it assumes a value for the century set by the Epoch command. EXAMPLE:

```
* Set the century to 18 then display a date.
* Displays 01/02/1890.
set epoch 1800
set date format to "mm/dd/yyyy"
@ 01, 01 say ctod("01/02/90")
```

Set Escape On/Off/(<lEXP>)

Summer 87, 5.0, 5.01

Clipper normally allows the user to terminate a read using Escape. When the program sets Escape off, the user must press Enter to terminate a read. EXAMPLE:

```
* Make sure the user enters a value.
set escape off
do while .not. updated()
      <DISPLAY STATEMENTS>
      read
enddo
set escape on
```

Set Exact On/Off/(<lEXP>)

Summer 87, 5.0, 5.01

This command is provided for compatibility purposes only in versions 5.0 and above.

Use this command when the program requires an exact match between two strings. For example, with Set Exact Off, "some string" equals "some string." However, with Set Exact On, Clipper regards the two strings as different. The Seek command ignores this setting and conducts all searches with Set Exact Off. EXAMPLE:

```
* See if two strings match exactly.
set exact on
if STRINGA = STRINGB
      @ 01, 01 say "The Strings Match"
endif
```

Set Exclusive On/Off/(<lEXP>)

Summer 87, 5.0, 5.01

This command is provided for compatibility purposes only in versions 5.0 and above. Use the Shared or Exclusive clauses provided as part of the Use command instead. Some networks return a DOS error 5 (access denied) on a second Use Exclusive attempt on the same file with version 5.0. You can get around this problem by writing your own network error handler for this condition. This problem has been corrected with 5.01.

Use this command in a network environment to ensure that the USE command opens all files for shared or single use. When set on, the Set Exclusive command opens all files for single use. When set off, the Set Exclusive command opens all files for shared use. Clipper uses a default condition of On. EXAMPLE:

```
* Open a file for shared use.
set exclusive on
use SOMEDATA
```

Set Filter To [<CONDITION>]

Summer 87, 5.0, 5.01

5.01 replaces this command with two functions, DBClearFilter( ) and DBSetFilter( ). The DBClearFilter( ) function performs the same task as using Set Filter To with no arguments. The DBSetFilter( ) function provides greater functionality than the Set Filter To command. 5.0 provides these features as the undocumented functions _DBClearFilter( ) and _DBSetFilter( ).

The Set Filter To command defines the records Clipper displays. CONDITION contains a logical argument consisting of one or more field names and a value for each field. Using this command with no condition displays all records. This command does not affect the status of the Set Deleted command. EXAMPLE:

```
* Display a subset of the available records.
set filter to (AGE > 21) .and. (AGE < 100)
<DISPLAY STATEMENTS>
```

Set Fixed On/Off/(<lEXP>)

Summer 87, 5.0, 5.01

Use this command to toggle the Set Decimals command on and off. Using the On argument displays all numbers with the number of decimal places specified by the Set Decimals command. The Off arguments tells Clipper to ignore the Set Decimals status. EXAMPLE:

```
* Display all numbers with 2 decimal places.
set decimals to 2
set fixed on
<DISPLAY STATEMENTS>
```

Set Format To <PROCEDURE>

Summer 87, 5.0, 5.01

The Set Format To command is classified as a compatibility command for versions 5.0 and above. The recommended way to call a procedure is to include the procedure name on a line by itself.

The Set Format To command selects a procedure Clipper uses for displaying database information. Each time Clipper encounters a read statement, it executes the contents of the format file. EXAMPLE:

```
* Display a database record.
set format to SOMEFORM
do while .not. eof()
      read
      skip
enddo
```

```
procedure SOMEFORM
<DISPLAY STATEMENTS>
return
```

Set Function <nEXP> To <cEXP>

Summer 87, 5.0, 5.01

The Set Function command translates to a Set Key command in versions above 5.0. This makes the command incompatible with previous versions that maintained separate Set Function and Set Key lists.

Use this command to assign a string to a function key. Each time a user presses the function key, Clipper executes the assigned string. nEXP contains the function key number. F1 through F10 use numbers 1 through 10. Shift–F1 through Shift–F10 use numbers 11 through 20. Ctrl–F1 through Ctrl–F10 use numbers 21 through 30. Alt–F1 through Alt–F10 use numbers 31 through 40. cEXP contains the string to execute each time the user presses the function key. In most cases this string contains a procedure name. EXAMPLE:

```
* Assign a procedure to a function key.
set function 10 to "SOMEPROC" + chr(13)  && Return
```

Set Index To [<FILE LIST>/(<cEXP>) ...]

Summer 87, 5.0, 5.01

5.01 replaces this command with two functions, DBClearIndex( ) and DBSetIndex( ). The DBClearIndex( ) function performs the same task as using Set Index To with no arguments. The DBSetIndex( ) function provides greater functionality than the Set Index To command. 5.0 provides these features as the undocumented functions _DBClearIndex( ) and _DBSetIndex( ).

The Set Index To command opens one or more index files and attaches them to the database in the current work area. FILE LIST contains the name of the index file to use. Clipper assumes a file extension of NTX or NDX when using this command. Using the Set Index To command without the optional FILE LIST closes all index files in the current work area. Open index files in other work areas remain unaffected. EXAMPLE:

```
use SOMEDATA index SOMEINDX
<PROGRAM STATEMENTS>
* Change the index.
set index to OTHINDEX
```

Set Intensity On/Off/(<lEXP>)

Summer 87, 5.0, 5.01

When set to Off, this command tells Clipper to display all gets using the standard instead of the enhanced color. Clipper defaults to using the enhanced color. EXAMPLE:

```
set intensity off
```

Set Key <nEXP> To [<PROCEDURE>]

Summer 87, 5.0, 5.01

5.0 replaces this command with the SetKey( ) function. The function form of the command is more versatile.

The Set Key command sets a key equal to the desired procedure. Whenever the user presses the key, Clipper executes the procedure. This command takes precedence over the settings of the Set Function and Set Escape commands, and the SetCancel( ) function. nEXP contains the keyboard key value to assign. Appendix A contains a listing of keyboard key values. PROCEDURE contains the name of the procedure clipper executes when the user presses the specified key. EXAMPLE:

```
set key -1 to SOMEPROC  && F2
```

Set Margin To <nEXP>

Summer 87, 5.0, 5.01

This command affects the starting column position of all printed output. nEXP contains the left margin setting. Clipper uses a default setting of zero. EXAMPLE:

```
* Create a 1/2-inch margin for pica type.
set margin to 5
<PRINT STATEMENTS>
```

Set Message To [<nEXP> [Center/Centre]]

Summer 87, 5.0, 5.01

Use this command to define where Clipper displays messages specified by the @ Prompt command. nEXP specifies the display row. If the program omits the optional nEXP argument, Clipper does not display the messages. The Center argument displays the messages in the center of the display. Clipper uses a default column of 0. EXAMPLE:

```
* Create a menu with messages centered at the bottom of
* the display.
set message to 22 center
@ 01, 20 prompt "Display Database"
```

```
@ 02, 20 prompt "Print Database"
@ 03, 20 prompt "Exit Program"
menu to SELECTION
```

Set Order To [<nEXP>]

Summer 87, 5.0, 5.01

5.01 replaces this command with the DBSetOrder( ) function. There is no advantage to using either the command or function format.

Use this command to change the controlling index in the selected work area. Clipper uses a default of 1. In other words, the first index opened control database order. nEXP contains the new index number. If the program uses this command without nEXP, Clipper resets the controlling index to 1. EXAMPLE:

```
use SOMEDATA index AGE, NAME
* Change the controlling index to name.
set order to 2
```

Set Path To [<PATH LIST>/(<cEXP>)]

Summer 87, 5.0, 5.01

The Set Path To command specifies the path Clipper uses when searching for files. EXAMPLE:

```
set path to C:\CLIPPER\DATA
```

Set Print On/Off/(<lEXP>)

Summer 87, 5.0, 5.01

When set to On, this command outputs all console information to the printer. Clipper uses a default condition of Off. EXAMPLE:

```
<PROGRAM STATEMENTS>
set print on
<PRINT STATEMENTS>
set print off
<PROGRAM STATEMENTS>
```

Set Printer To [<DEVICE>/<FILE>/(<cEXP>) [Additive]]

Summer 87, 5.0, 5.01

Version 5.01 adds the Additive clause to this command. Clipper always truncates the file before writing information to it. Adding the additive clause allows you to add information without truncating the file first.

Use this command to change the destination for all printed output. DEVICE contains a device name. Clipper recognizes PRN, LPT1, LPT2, LPT3, COM1, and COM2 as legal devices. FILE contains a filename. You cannot use a filename and device at the same time. Specifying a nonexistent port creates a file with the port name as a destination. Using this command with no device or file argument empties the print buffer and closes the file or device. Clipper uses a default destination of PRN. EXAMPLE:

```
* Ask the user where to send the printed output.
PRINT = string(8)
@ 01, 01 say 'Enter a Print Destination: ' get PRINT
read
if PRINT <> string(8)
      set printer to &PRINT
endif
```

Set Procedure To [<FILE>]

Summer 87, 5.0, 5.01

Versions 5.0 and above provide this command for compatibility purposes only.

Use this command to include procedures and functions from other files in the current object module. FILE contains the name of the procedure file to include. Clipper assumes an extension of PRG. EXAMPLE:

```
* Include the procedure SOMEPROC in the current file
* then, set F2 to point to it.
set procedure to SOMEPROC
set key -1 to SOMEPROC  && F2
```

Set Relation [Additive] to [<KEY EXP1>/<nEXP1> Into <ALIAS1>/(<EPXC1>)] [, <KEY EXP2>/<nEXP2> Into <ALIAS2>/(<EPXC2>) ...]

Summer 87, 5.0, 5.01

Version 5.0 allows you to exclude the To clause for multiple relations. 5.01 replaces this command with two functions, DBClearRelation( ) and DBSetRelation( ). The DBClearRelation( ) function performs the same task as using Set Relation To with no arguments. The DBSetRelation( ) function provides greater functionality than the Set Relation To command. 5.0 provides these features as the undocumented functions _DBClearRelation( ) and _DBSetRelation( ).

The Set Relation command associates two different work areas using a key expression, record number, or numeric expression. A relation consists of a parent and a child work area. The current work area is the parent. The Additive argument retains all previously defined relations. Clipper normally clears all old relations when the program defines a new relation. KEY EXP contains the fields to relate. Each time the record in the parent work area changes, Clipper performs a seek for the appropriate record in the child work area using the expression as a criteria. To use this relation type, the child work area must use an index. nEXP is an alternate relation containing a record number expression. Each time the record changes in the parent work area, Clipper performs a goto using the record evaluation as a criteria. To use this relation type, the child work area must not use an index. ALIAS contains the name of the child work area. EXAMPLE:

```
select 1
use MAINDATA index SOMEINDX
select 2
use OTHDATA index OTHINDX
select 1
set relation to FIELDNAME into OTHDATA
```

Set Scoreboard On/Off/(<lEXP>)

Summer 87, 5.0, 5.01

The scoreboard contains mode information and appears on line 0 of the display. This information includes the range clause error message, MemoEdit( ) abort query message, and the insert mode indicator during MemoEdit( ) and Read. Setting the scoreboard off inhibits the mode message display. EXAMPLE:

```
set scoreboard off
```

Set Softseek On/Off/(<lEXP>)

Summer 87, 5.0, 5.01

This command affects how Clipper performs the Seek command. If the program sets softseek On, Clipper places the record pointer to the record closest to the requested information if no exact match exists. If the program sets softseek Off and no exact match to a Seek command exists, Clipper places the record pointer at LastRec( ) + 1. EXAMPLE:

```
set softseek off
```

Set Typeahead To <nEXP>

Summer 87, 5.0, 5.01

Version 5.0 limits the typeahead buffer to 15 characters. Use the undocumented Set(_SET_TYPEAHEAD, <nKey>) function to relieve this condition. The Set Typeahead To command works properly in version 5.01. Version 5.0 translates this command to the SetTypeahead( ) function, whereas 5.01 uses the Set( ) function.

Use the Set Typeahead command to control the size of the keyboard buffer. nEXP contains the number of characters that the keyboard buffer accepts. Clipper allows a maximum buffer size of 32,767 characters/bytes. EXAMPLE:

```
* Create a 512 character buffer.
set typeahead to 512
```

Set Unique On/Off/(<lEXP>)

Summer 87, 5.0, 5.01

Versions 5.0 and above provide this command for compatibility purposes only.

Use the Unique clause of the Index command in its place. Use the Set Unique command to control the method Clipper uses to create an index. If the program sets unique On, Clipper creates index with a single occurrence of each key. Normally, Clipper includes all keys. EXAMPLE:

```
* Set unique to its default condition.
set unique off
```

Set Wrap On/Off/(<lEXP>)

Summer 87, 5.0, 5.01

The Set Wrap controls wrapping in menus. If the program sets wrap to On, and the user presses the down arrow at the last menu item, Clipper places the highlight on the first menu item. Clipper performs the opposite procedure when the highlight appears on the first menu item and the user presses the up arrow. Clipper normally sets this command to Off. EXAMPLE:

```
set wrap on
```

Skip [<nEXP1>] [Alias <ALIAS>/(<nEXP2>)]

Summer 87, 5.0, 5.01

Version 5.01 replaces this command with the DBSkip( ) function. There is no advantage to using either the function or command version of the command. The Alias clause of this command does not work correctly in some releases of version 5.0. You can replace this command with cALIAS – > (_dbskip(nEXP1)) to force proper operation of the Alias clause. This problem has been fixed in version 5.01.

The Skip command moves the record pointer one or more positions. nEXP1 contains the number of records to move. If the program does not specify nEXP1, Clipper moves the record pointer one record. The Alias argument specifies a work area. If the program does not specify an ALIAS, Clipper moves the record pointer in the current work area. EXAMPLE:

```
* Display a database record.
do while .not. eof()
     <DISPLAY STATEMENTS>
     read
     skip
enddo
```

Sort [<SCOPE>] On <FIELD1> [/A] [/C] [/D] [, <FIELD2> [/A] [/C] [/D] ...] To <FILE>/(<cEXP>) [For <CONDITION>] [While <CONDITION>]

Summer 87, 5.0, 5.01

Use this command to create a sorted version of all or part of the selected database. The SCOPE argument determines how many of the source records Clipper sorts in the selected database. There are two different scopes. All sorts every record in the selected database. Next <*n*> sorts the number of records specified by *n*. Clipper starts sorting records from the record pointed to by the record pointer. The default scope is All.

FIELD is the field Clipper uses as a sort key. When the program uses more than one field, the first field always takes precedence. The /A argument sorts the database in ascending order. This is the default condition. The /C argument tells Clipper to ignore case when sorting the database. The /D argument tells Clipper to sort the database in descending order.

The For argument specifies which records to sort from the selected database. The While argument specifies which records to sort from the selected database. However, unlike the For argument, the While argument stops sorting records when the current record no longer meets the specified criteria. EXAMPLE:

```
* Create a sorted database.
use SOMEDATA
sort on FIELDNAME to NEWDATA
```

Static <ARRAY1> [<nEXP1>] [:= <EXP1>] [<ARRAY2> [<nEXP2>]] [:= <EXP2>] ...

5.0, 5.01

Creates an array with nEXP elements or a static variable. The square brackets must appear as part of the nEXP argument when declaring an array. Exclude the nEXP argument to create a static variable. The assignment operator (:=) and EXP allows you to place a value in static variables created using Static. Excluding EXP creates a static variable with a value of NIL. All array elements automatically receive a value of NIL. You cannot assign a value to arrays. Use this command before using any array function described in the next chapter.

Static variables take precedence over any private, public, or field variables with the same name. Clipper resolves the value of a static variable at compile time. This means that static variables offer you significant performance gains over other variable types. Static variables exist for the duration of the current and any called procedures or functions. Clipper retains the value of a static variable for the duration of the program. This means that even though a parent procedure cannot see the variable, the variable retains its value each time the procedure or function gets called.

You must use the Static command before any executable statements in a procedure or function. This includes the Private, Public, and Parameters commands. You cannot use macro substitution with a Static command since the value of a static variable is resolved at compile time. Clipper will not save static variable to a MEM file. In addition, you cannot determine the type of a static variable using the Type( ) function. Use the ValType( ) function instead. EXAMPLE:

```
* Declare two three-dimensional static arrays.
static SOMEARRAY [42, 102, 88]
static SECOND [1024] [4096] [18]
```

Store <EXP> to <MEMVAR LIST> <MEMVAR> = <EXP> <MEMVAR1> := [<MEMVAR2> := ...] <EXP>

Summer 87, 5.0, 5.01

The Store command was rendered obsolete by the in-line assignment operator (:=) presented as the third option in versions 5.0 and above.

The Store command places EXP in the variables contained in MEMVAR LIST. The assignment operator (=) performs the same task on a single variable. Use the in-line assignment operator (:=) to assign the same value to multiple variables. While the Store command is provided for compatibility purposes (Clipper provides the easier to use in-line assignment operators :=, ++, --, +=, -= *=, and /=), it does not incur any program size or speed penalties when you use it. EXAMPLE:

```
* Initialize program variables.
store space(8) to SOMESTRING, OTHSTRING
NUMVAR = 0
SOMESTRING := OTHSTRING := space(8)
```

Sum [<SCOPE>] <nEXP LIST> To <MEMVAR LIST> [For <CONDITION>] [While <CONDITION>]

Summer 87, 5.0, 5.01

Both 5.0 and 5.01 translate this command into a code block that uses the DBEval( ) function to sum matching database fields. Depending on your program's needs, you might be able to increase program execution speed and decrease program size by using the DBEval( ) function directly.

The Sum command calculates the numeric total for one or more fields in an expression for a range of records. The SCOPE argument determines how many of the source records Clipper sums in the selected database. There are two different scopes. All sums every record in the selected database. Next <*n*> sums the number of records specified by *n*. Clipper starts summing records from the record pointed to by the record pointer. The default scope is All.

nEXP LIST contains the expression to use while summing the database fields. MEMVAR LIST contains the names of the memory variables Clipper stores the result in. The program must specify one memory variable for each expression. The For argument specifies which records to sum from the selected database. The While argument also specifies which records to sum from the selected database, but, unlike the For argument, the While argument stops summing records when the current record no longer meets the specified criteria. EXAMPLE:

```
use SOMEDATA
sum SOMEFIELD+10, OTHFIELD/2 to FIRSTSUM, SECONDSUM
```

Text [To Print] [To File <FILE>/(<cEXP>)] <TEXT> ... EndText

Summer 87, 5.0, 5.01

Versions 5.0 and above provide this command for compatibility purposes only. In addition, you cannot send output to both the printer and a file simultaneously. You must specify either a printer or a file. This problem has not been fixed in version 5.01.

This command sends TEXT to the display and optionally the printer and/or a file. Clipper automatically expands any macro definitions found within TEXT. The To Print argument sends the text output to the printer. The To File argument sends the text output to a file. FILE specifies the name of a file to use. If the program does not provide an extension, Clipper automatically uses the TXT extension. EXAMPLE:

```
text to print to file SOMETEXT
      This is some example text.
endtext
```

Total On <KEY EXP> [<SCOPE>] [Fields <FIELD LIST>] To <FILE>/(<cEXP>) [For <CONDITION>] [While <CONDITION>]

Summer 87, 5.0, 5.01

The Total On command summarizes a database using KEY EXP as the basis for grouping. Always sort or index the database using KEY EXP before using this command. The SCOPE argument determines how many of the records Clipper summarizes in the selected database. There are two different scopes. All summarizes every record in the selected database. Next <*n*> summarizes the number of records specified by *n*. Clipper starts summarizing records from the record pointed to by the record pointer. The default scope is All.

FIELD LIST contains a list of fields to total. If the program does not use the Fields argument, Clipper does not total any of the numeric fields. It places the value of the first numeric field in the target database instead.

FILE contains the name of the target database. Clipper automatically assumes an extension of DBF. The For argument specifies which records to summarize from the selected database. The While argument also specifies which records to summarize from the selected database. However, unlike the For argument, the While argument stops summarizing records when the current record no longer meets the specified criteria. EXAMPLE:

```
use SOMEDATA index SOMEINDX
total on SOMEFIELD fields NUMFIELD to NEWDATA
```

Type <FILE1>.<EXT1>/(<cEXP1>) [To Print] [To File <FILE2>.<EXT2>/(<cEXP2>)]

Summer 87, 5.0, 5.01

Version 5.0 does not allow you to send output to both the printer and a file simultaneously. You must specify either a printer or a file. This problem has been fixed in version 5.01.

Use this command to send the contents of a text file to the display. FILE1.EXT1 contains the name of the file to use. The To Print argument sends the output to the printer. The To File argument sends the output to a file. FILE2.EXT2 contains the name of the output file. If the program does not specify EXT2, Clipper automatically uses an extension of TXT. EXAMPLE:

```
type SOMETEXT.TXT to print
```

Unlock [All]

Summer 87, 5.0, 5.01

5.01 replaces this command with the DBUnlock( ) function. There is no advantage to using either the command or function form of the command.

The Unlock command frees a previously locked file in the current work area for use by other people on a network. The optional All argument frees the locked files in all work areas. EXAMPLE:

```
unlock all
```

Update On <KEY EXP> From <ALIAS>/(<cEXP>) Replace <FIELD1> With <EXP1> [, <FIELD2> With <EXP2>] [Random]

Summer 87, 5.0, 5.01

This command updates the contents of the database in the current work area with the contents of another database. KEY EXP contains the field expressions that match in both databases. Clipper uses this expression to determine which records to replace. ALIAS is the name of another work area containing the source database. FIELD is the name of the field to replace in the current work area. EXP is an expression defining how Clipper replaces the contents of the specified field.

The Random argument allows the source database to appear in any order. Clipper searches the current work area for all occurrences of the key expression of the source database. The program must index the target database using KEY EXP to use the Random argument. EXAMPLE:

```
update on SOMEFIELD from OTHDATA replace CHARFIELD with CHARFIELD
```

Use [<FILE>/(<cEXP1>)] [Index <FILE LIST>/(<cEXP2>) [, (<cEXP3>)] ...] [Exclusive/Shared] [Alias <ALIAS>] [New] [ReadOnly] [Via <cEXP4>]

Summer 87, 5.0, 5.01

Version 5.0 added the New, ReadOnly, and Shared clauses. The Shared clause allows you to open the database in shared mode on a network. The New clause opens the database in the next available work area. If you do not specify this clause, Clipper opens the database in the current work area. The ReadOnly clause opens the database in read-only mode. If you do not specify this clause, Clipper opens the database in read-write mode. This feature does not work properly in version 5.0. Version 5.01 implements it fully. 5.01 adds the Via clause. This allows you to use replaceable database drivers. If you do not specify this clause, Clipper uses the standard DBFNTX driver.

The USE command opens and closes the database and, optionally, any associated index files. FILE contains the name of the database to open. If the program specifies USE without a database name, Clipper closes the database in the current work area. FILE LIST contains the names of the index files to open and associate with the database. The program must separate each index using a comma. The Exclusive argument opens the database in the single-user mode. Other users can't open the database when using this argument with a database on a network. ALIAS contains the name Clipper uses to reference the work area. If the program does not specify an alias, Clipper uses the database name as an alias. EXAMPLE:

```
use SOMEDATA index SOMEINDX
```

Wait [<PROMPT>] [To <MEMVARC>]

Summer 87, 5.0, 5.01

Versions 5.0 and above supply this command for compatibility purposes only. Use the Inkey( ) function or the @...Get command whenever possible.

Use this command to pause program execution until the user presses a key. PROMPT contains a string Clipper displays. If the program does not specify a prompt, Clipper uses the default prompt *Press any key to continue....* MEMVARC contains the name a variable Clipper uses to store the key pressed by the user. If the program does not specify MEMVARC, Clipper discards the character. EXAMPLE:

```
wait "Press a key" to SOMEVAR
```

Zap

Summer 87, 5.0, 5.01

The ZAP command removes all records from the database in the current work area. It also removes the contents from any open index files associated with the selected database. EXAMPLE:

```
zap
```

2
Clipper functions

This chapter contains an alphabetical listing of all Clipper functions. In many cases the use and execution of these functions vary widely from other *x*base dialects. The preprocessor found in versions 5.0 and above will allow you to modify this behavior. To find out how to enhance the capabilities provided by these versions, read chapter 3.

Each function description also provides you with the version in which the function first appeared. If the function appeared in more than one version (Summer 87, 5.0, or 5.01), then the version information tells you how the function changed. In many cases it will become apparent that version 5.0 enhanced the language, while 5.01 increases compatibility. Some of the version-specific information provides warnings about using certain functions under specific conditions. These warnings include unimplemented features between versions, enhancements, anomalies, and fixes that change the behavior of the function.

This chapter uses the conventions specified in the introduction to the book. Reading the introduction will increase your understanding of the examples that are provided as part of each description.

Each function entry contains the command-line interface for the function and a description of how to use it. In many cases, the description tells which function provides better functionality for little or no increase in program size. This will help you determine which functions Nantucket provided for compatibility reasons only. It also helps you to avoid using archaic functions. In addition to these descriptions and hints, each function tells which version of Clipper you can use it with. If a function contains updated features in one of the newer versions, you will be provided with this information as well. You will be told how each version enhances the function.

AAdd(<aEXP>, <xEXP>)

5.0, 5.01

This function adds a new element to an array. Unlike AIns( ), this function actually changes the length of the array by one. Use the ASize( ) function to add more than one element to an array. aEXP contains the name of the array you want to change. xEXP contains the value of the new array element. EXAMPLE:

```
* Add a new element at the end of SOMEARRAY with a value of 5.
aadd(SOMEARRAY, 5)
```

ABS(<nEXP>)

Summer 87, 5.0, 5.01

This function returns the absolute value of nEXP. EXAMPLE:

```
SOMEVAR = abs(-22)  && SOMEVAR = 22
```

AChoice(<nEXP1>, <nEXP2>, <nEXP3>, <nEXP4>, <aEXP1> [, <aEXP2> [, <cEXP> [, <nEXP5 [, <nEXP6>]]]])

Summer 87, 5.0, 5.01

5.0 added a header file called ACHOICE.CH to reduce the effort required for the programmer and increase source code readability.

The AChoice function displays a pop-up menu based on the contents of one or more arrays. nEXP1 contains the top row offset. nEXP2 contains the left column offset. nEXP3 contains the bottom row offset. nEXP4 contains the right column offset. aEXP1 contains the character strings AChoice displays. aEXP2 is a logical array containing one element for each element in aEXP1. If an element in aEXP2 contains .F., the corresponding element in aEXP1 is not available. cEXP is the name of a user-defined function that Clipper executes when the user presses an undefined key. Clipper uses two default states for keypresses. The table shows the result if the keypress occurs with and without a user-defined function available.

TABLE 2-1 contains a listing of defined keys. TABLE 2-2 contains the status messages sent from AChoice to the user-defined function. TABLE 2-3 contains the request messages sent from the user-defined function to AChoice. nEXP5 contains the starting position for the menu highlight. For example, if nEXP5 equals 5, then Clipper highlights the fifth menu item. If the program uses AChoice without specifying nEXP5, Clipper highlights the first menu item. nEXP6 contains the relative window row. For example, if nEXP6 equals 2, then Clipper starts the menu display with the second menu item. If the program uses AChoice without specifying nEXP6,

Clipper uses the currently highlighted menu item as the relative window row. EXAMPLE:

```
* Create the menu choices and available choices arrays.

declare MENU1[5], MENU2[5]

* Menu Choices

MENU1[1] = 'Edit'
MENU1[2] = 'View'
MENU1[3] = 'Sort'
MENU1[4] = 'Utility'
MENU1[5] = 'Quit'

* Available Choices

MENU2[1] = .T.
MENU2[2] = .T.
MENU2[3] = .T.
MENU2[4] = .T.
MENU2[5] = .T.

* User Selection
SELECT = 1

* Display Menu

save screen
clear screen
@ 10, 36 to 16, 44 double
do while SELECT <> 5
      SELECT = achoice(11, 37, 15, 43, MENU1, MENU2, "CHOICE")
enddo
restore screen
quit

* User Defined Function for Menu Control

function CHOICE
parameters STATUS, ELEMENT, REL_POS

* Assign Variables

RET_TYPE = 0  && UDF Request Message

if STATUS = 0
      RET_TYPE = 2
else
      do case
            case lastkey() = 13
                  RET_TYPE = 1
            case (lastkey() > 65) .and. (lastkey() < 122)
```

```
                RET_TYPE = 3
          otherwise
                RET_TYPE = 2
      endcase
endif
return RET_TYPE
```

Table 2-1 Standard menu keys

Key	With UDF	Without UDF (normal)
Up arrow	Same as normal	Moves highlight up one menu item.
Down arrow	Same as normal	Moves highlight down one menu item.
Home	Defined as part of UDF	Selects the first item in the menu.
End	Defined as part of UDF	Selects the last item in the menu.
PgUp	Same as normal	Moves the cursor up the number of menu items defined by the current window. If the menu does not contain a sufficient number of items, it displays the first item in the menu at the top of the window. The highlight appears in the same relative position after the keypress.
PgDn	Same as normal	Moves the cursor down the number of menu items defined by the current window. If the menu does not contain a sufficient number of items, it displays the last item in the menu at the bottom of the window. The highlight appears in the same relative position after the keypress.

Key	With UDF	Without UDF (normal)
Ctrl-PgUp	Same as normal	Selects the first item in the menu.
Ctrl-PgDn	Same as normal	Selects the last item in the menu.
Return	Defined as part of UDF	Selects the highlighted menu item. Returns the menu item number to the calling procedure or function.
Esc	Defined as part of UDF	Exits the menu. Returns a zero to the calling procedure or function.
Left arrow	Defined as part of UDF	Exits the menu. Returns a zero to the calling procedure or function.
Right arrow	Defined as part of UDF	Exits the menu. Returns a zero to the calling procedure or function.
First letter	Defined as part of UDF	Selects the next item in the menu containing the first letter. If Clipper reaches the bottom of the menu without finding an appropriate menu choice, it searches from the top of the menu to the current highlight position. If no menu item contains the letter pressed as its first letter, Clipper does not move the highlight.

ıle 2-2 UDF status messages

Mode	Description
0	No user action since the last call.
1	User pressed a key that placed the cursor past the beginning of the menu.
2	User pressed a key that placed the cursor past the end of the menu.
3	User pressed an undefined key.
4	Menu does not contain any selectable items.

Table 2-3 UDF request messages

Return value	Description
0	Exit the menu. Return zero to the calling procedure or function.
1	Exit the menu. Return the number of the currently highlighted menu item.
2	Do not exit the menu. Continue the selection process.
3	Do not exit the menu. Highlight the next item with a first letter matching the key pressed by the user.

AClone(<aEXP>)

5.0, 5.01

This function makes an exact duplicate of either a one-dimensional or multidimensional array. You can also use this function with arrays containing subarrays. ACopy( ) will not reproduce nested arrays. aEXP contains the name of the array to clone. EXAMPLE:

```
aEXPCOPY = aclone(SOMEARRAY)
```

ACopy(<aEXP1>, <aEXP2> [, <nEXP1> [, <nEXP2> [, <nEXP3>]]])

Summer 87, 5.0, 5.01

This function copies the elements in aEXP1 to aEXP2. nEXP1 contains the starting element in aEXP1. If the program omits nEXP1, Clipper uses element 1 as the starting location. nEXP2 contains the number of elements to copy. If the program omits nEXP2, Clipper copies all the elements in aEXP1 to aEXP2, starting at nEXP1. If nEXP2 contains a larger number than aEXP1 contains elements after nEXP1, Clipper copies to the end of aEXP1. nEXP3 contains the starting position in aEXP2. If the program omits nEXP3, Clipper starts copying to element 1 of aEXP2. EXAMPLE:

```
acopy(SOURCE_ARRAY, TARGET_ARRAY)
```

ADel(<aEXP>, <nEXP>)

Summer 87, 5.0, 5.01

Use this function to remove an unwanted element from an array. nEXP contains the element number that Clipper removes. All elements greater than nEXP move one position toward the beginning of the array. The last array element becomes undefined. EXAMPLE:

```
* Remove element 3 from SOME_ARRAY.
adel(SOME_ARRAY, 3)
```

ADir(<DIRECTORY SKELETON> [, <aEXP1> [, <aEXP2> [, <aEXP3> [, <aEXP4> [, <aEXP5>]]]]])

Summer 87, 5.0, 5.01

ADir( ) is supplied for compatibility purposes only in versions 5.0 and above. Use the Directory( ) function, which provides enhanced functionality, whenever possible.

The ADir function retrieves one or more types of information about the specified directory. DIRECTORY SKELETON contains the drive, path, and file specification. Clipper allows the program to use the asterisk and question mark as wildcards. aEXP1 contains the name of an array used to store the filenames matching the file specification. The filenames include extensions.

aEXP2 contains the name of an array used to store the file size of the corresponding element (filename) in aEXP1. aEXP3 contains the name of an array used to store the file date of the corresponding element in aEXP1. aEXP4 contains the name of an array used to store the file time of the corresponding element in aEXP1. aEXP5 contains the name of an array used to store the file attributes of the corresponding element in aEXP1. These attributes include R for read-only, H for hidden, S for system, D for directory, and A for archive.

Clipper requires that the program declare a dummy variable to retrieve the information contained in a later variable without retrieving the information in the previous variables. For example, if the program needs the information in aEXP5 but not the information in aEXP4, use a dummy variable in place of aEXP4. A dummy variable consists of a null string.

Use the ADir( ) function in place of the Dir command for most directory searches. The ADir( ) function allows you to manipulate and store the retrieved directory, providing more flexibility. EXAMPLE:

```
* Create an array capable of storing 128 filenames.
declare NAME_ARRAY[128]
* Get the filenames in the current directory.
adir(*.*, NAME_ARRAY)
* Display the filenames.
clear screen
for COUNT = 1 to 128
     if len(trim(NAME[COUNT])) > 0
          @ row()+1, 0 say NAME[COUNT]
     endif
next
```

AEval(<aEXP>, <bEXP> [, <nEXP1>] [, <nEXP2>])

5.0, 5.01

The documentation does not specify that AEval( ) sends values to the code bloc (bEXP). The first parameter is the value of the array element being evaluated. The second is the element number within the array. Therefore, you could have a code block that uses both parameters. For example, {|nValue, nElement| aArray [nElement] := nValue / 100} divides the array element by 100.

This function evaluates each element of an array and performs some action based on its contents. aEXP contains the name of the array you want to evaluate. bEXP is a section of code that you pass to the function. The function uses this code to evaluate the contents of the array. Because AEval( ) can return only one value, you must use the code block to create any multivalue returns required by an application. nEXP1 contains the starting element. If you don't specify a starting element, Clipper assumes you want to begin with the element 1 of the array. nEXP2 contains the number of elements you want to evaluate. If you don't supply a value, Clipper assumes you want to evaluate all array elements. EXAMPLE:

```
* Display the number of employees in each age group, then
* calculate their average age.

COUNT := COUNT2 := COUNT3 := 0
```

```
use EMP_DATA
EMP_AGE := array(70)
afill (EMP_AGE, 0)

* This code block fills an array with the number of employees in
* each age group.

dbeval({ || iif(AGE > 0, EMP_AGE[AGE]++, qout("End")) })

* Display the array.

cls
@ 00, 00 say "Age | Number"
@ 01, 00 say "----┼──────────"
for COUNT = 18 to 65
   if row() < 23
      @ row()+1, 01 say str(COUNT,2)+' | '+str(EMP_AGE[COUNT],6)
   else
      @ 24, 01 say "Press any key when ready..."
      inkey(0)
      cls
      @ 00, 00 say "Age | Number"
      @ 01, 00 say "----┼──────────"
      @ 02, 01 say str(COUNT,2)+' | '+str(EMP_AGE[COUNT],6)
   endif
next

* This code block creates a total age for all employees using the
* equation TOTAL = TOTAL + (AGE * NUMBER).

aeval(EMP_AGE, {|COUNT|COUNT, COUNT3++, COUNT2+=(COUNT3*COUNT)})

* Find the average by dividing by the number of employees.

COUNT2 = COUNT2/lastrec()

* Display the average and end the program.

@ row()+2, 01 say "Average age is: " + str (COUNT2, 6, 3)
@ 24, 01 say "Press any key when ready..."
inkey(0)
close all
return
```

AFields([<aEXP1> [, <aEXP2> [, <aEXP3> [, <aEXP4>]]]])

Summer 87, 5.0, 5.01

AFields( ) is supplied for compatibility purposes only in versions 5.0 and above. Use the DBStruct( ) function, which provides enhanced functionality, whenever possible.

This function returns one or more types of information about the database in the current work area. If the program uses AFIELDS with no arguments, it returns the number of fields in the current work area.

AFIELDS returns 0 if the current work area has no database in use. aEXP1 contains the name of an array used to store the field names. aEXP2 contains the name of an array used to store the field types for the corresponding element (field name) in aEXP1. aEXP3 contains the name of an array used to store the field widths for the corresponding element in aEXP1. aEXP4 contains the name of an array used to store the number of decimals for the corresponding element in aEXP1.

Clipper requires that the program declare a dummy variable to retrieve the information contained in a later variable without retrieving the information in the previous variables. For example, if the program needs the information in aEXP3, but not the information in aEXP2, use a dummy variable in place of aEXP2. A dummy variable consists of a null string. EXAMPLE:

```
* Initialize Variables

SUCCESS = 0                 && AFIELDS Successful?
COUNT = 0                   && Display Count
NUMPARM = 0                 && Number of Parameters

* Get the parameter count, then the parameters.

parameters DATAFILE         && DBF File to Read
NUMPARM = pcount()
if NUMPARM = 0
     ? chr(7) + "Specify a database name."
     quit
endif

* Obtain the database structure.

use &DATAFILE
declare FLD[fcount()], TYP[fcount()], WDTH[fcount()], DEC[fcount()]
SUCCESS = afields(FLD, TYP, WDTH, DEC)

* Display the database structure.

if SUCCESS > 0
     clear screen
     for COUNT = 1 to SUCCESS
          @ row()+1, 0 say FLD[COUNT]
          @ row(), 12 say TYP[COUNT]
          @ row(), 15 say str(WDTH[COUNT], 4, 0)
          @ row(), 22 say str(DEC[COUNT], 4, 0)
     next
endif
quit
```

AFill(<aEXP>, <xEXP> [, <nEXP1> [, <nEXP2>]])

Summer 87, 5.0, 5.01

The AFill function fills aEXP with EXP. nEXP1 contains the number of the first element to fill. Clipper uses a default condition of element one. nEXP2 contains the number of elements to fill starting at nEXP1. If nEXP2 is greater than the total number of elements from nEXP1 to the end of the array, Clipper fills to the end of the array only. Clipper normally fills all array elements. EXAMPLE:

```
afill(SOME_ARRAY, 0)
```

AIns(<aEXP>, <nEXP>)

Summer 87, 5.0, 5.01

Use this function to insert an undefined element at nEXP in aEXP. Clipper discards the last element of the array. EXAMPLE:

```
* Place an undefined element in position 3 of an array.
ains(SOME_ARRAY, 3)
```

Alert(<cEXP1> [, <aEXP> [, <cEXP2>]])

5.01

This function allows you to display a message centered in a box in the center of the display. cEXP1 contains the message you want displayed. If you add semicolons to the expression, then Clipper breaks the line at that point to allow for multiline messages. You can optionally define a set of actions that the user can perform. aEXP contains a list of these actions.

Normally, Clipper displays the message and waits for the user to press a key. If you include aEXP, then the user is allowed to use the cursor to select the desired action before pressing Enter. Alert returns the number of the action selected by the user. For example, selecting the first choice and pressing Enter returns a value of 1. If the user presses Escape, then Alert returns a value of 0. cEXP2 contains a color string used to modify the colors used to display the message box. EXAMPLE:

```
// Define the variables required to display a complete
// Alert() message box.

aSomeArray := {"Abort", "Retry", "Fail"}
cMessage := "An error has occured!;Select an alternative"
cColorStr := "W+/R+,R/W"
nRetValue := 0

// Keep displaying the alert message until the user
// selects a valid action.
```

```
do while nRetValue == 0
     nRetValue := alert(cMessage, aSomeArray, cColorStr)
enddo

// Display the selected action.

cls
@ 01, 01 say nRetValue

return
```

Alias([<nEXP>])

Summer 87, 5.0, 5.01

This function retrieves the alias for the specified work area. nEXP contains the work area number. If the program uses Alias without specifying a work area, Clipper obtains the alias for the current work area. Alias returns a null string if the specified work area does not have a database in use. EXAMPLE:

```
* Retrieve the alias of work area two.
SOMEVAR = alias(2)
```

AllTrim(<cEXP>)

Summer 87, 5.0, 5.01

The 5.0 version would not allow you to use AllTrim within macro expression or in indexes. The only way to correct this situation was to create an AllTrim( ) function, compile it with the /N parameter, and link it with your program. This problem has been fixed in version 5.01.

Use the AllTrim function to remove the leading and trailing spaces from a string. cEXP contains the character string to trim. EXAMPLE:

```
@ 01, 01 say alltrim(SOMESTR)
```

AltD([<nEXP>])

Summer 87, 5.0, 5.01

Version 5.0 updated AltD( ) to return a value of NIL. It also uses the enhanced debugger provided with versions 5.0 and above.

The AltD function activates the debugging features of Clipper. To use the debug features, link DEBUG.OBJ with the other object files of the program. nEXP contains the status of debug. If the program omits nEXP, Clipper invokes the debugger. A value of 0 disables the debugger. A value of 1 enables the debugger. A value of 2 invokes the debugger with View Privates selected. EXAMPLE:

```
<PROGRAM STATEMENTS>
* Invoke the debugger to find a bug.
altd()
<PROGRAM STATEMENTS>
```

Array(<nEXP1> [, <nEXP2>...])

5.0, 5.01

Creates an array containing nEXP elements. nEXP1 contains the number of elements for the first dimension, and nEXP2 contains the number of elements for the second dimension. Clipper allows you to specify an array size of 4,096 elements. An array can have an unlimited number of dimensions. Use this function within expressions or code blocks to create arrays dynamically. EXAMPLE:

```
* Create a four-dimensional array with 20 elements in
* each dimension.
SOMEARRAY := array(20, 20, 20, 20)
```

ASC(<cEXP>)

Summer 87, 5.0, 5.01

This function returns the ASCII value of the leftmost character in a string. cEXP contains the string to evaluate. EXAMPLE:

```
SOMESTR = 'A'
<PROGRAM STATEMENTS>
asc(SOMESTR)
```

AScan(<aEXP>, <xEXP> [, <nEXP1> [, <nEXP2>]])

Summer 87, 5.0, 5.01

Version 5.01 adds the ability to supply a code block in place of a simple search expression. When your program uses a code block in place of a standard search expression, AScan( ) sends the value of the array element to the code block and then executes an Eval( ) on the code block. The search ends when the code block either returns true or AScan( ) reaches the last element in the array.

The ASCAN function searches for EXP in aEXP and returns the element number containing EXP. If Clipper does not find EXP within aEXP, it returns a 0. nEXP1 contains the array element to start the search. Clipper uses a default value of one. nEXP2 contains the number of elements to search. Clipper uses a default value of all array elements. EXAMPLE:

```
declare SOMEARRAY[15]
<PROGRAM STATEMENTS>
ascan(SOMEARRAY, SOMESTR)
<PROGRAM STATEMENTS>
```

ASize (<aEXP>, <nEXP>)

5.0, 5.01

This function changes the size of an array. If you shorten the array, Clipper removes elements from the end of the array and you can no longer access these elements. If you lengthen an array, Clipper adds elements with a value of NIL to the end of the array. aEXP contains the name of an array. nEXP contains the new array length. EXAMPLE:

```
asize(SOMEARRAY, 25)
```

ASort(<aEXP> [, <nEXP1> [, <nEXP2>] [, <bEXP>]]])

Summer 87, 5.0, 5.01

Version 5.0 adds the ability to supply a code block in place of a simple sort expression. When your program uses a code block in place of a standard sort expression, ASort( ) sends the value of two array elements to the code block then executes an Eval( ) on the code block. The code block must return true if the two elements are in sorted order.

Use this function to sort the elements in aEXP. nEXP1 contains the array element to start the sort. Clipper uses a default value of one. nEXP2 contains the number of elements to sort. Clipper uses a default value of all array elements. When using Clipper 5.0, you can provide an alternate sorting routine using the bEXP entry. You normally use code blocks with multidimensional arrays, but you can also use code blocks to support nonstandard array sorts. (You must supply a code block to sort multidimensional arrays; the ASort( ) function does not support them.) This function does not return a value. EXAMPLE:

```
declare SOMEARRAY[15]
<PROGRAM STATEMENTS>
asort(SOMEARRAY, SOMESTR)
<PROGRAM STATEMENTS>
```

AT(<cEXP1>, <cEXP2>)

Summer 87, 5.0, 5.01

The AT function searches for the first occurrence of cEXP1 in cEXP2. If Clipper finds the search string in cEXP2, it returns the starting character position. Otherwise, Clipper returns a zero. EXAMPLE:

```
TARGET = "ABCDEFGHIJKLMNOPQRSTUVWXYZ"
SEARCH = "X"
SOMEVAR = at(SEARCH, TARGET)
```

ATail(<aEXP>)

5.01

The ATail( ) function provides a shorthand method of returning the contents of the last element of an array. It is equivalent to the expression xSomeVar := aSomeArray [len(aSomeArray)]. The ATail( ) function does not alter the contents of the array. EXAMPLE:

```
aSomeArray := { 1, 2, 3, 4 }
nSomeValue := atail(aSomeArray)      // Returns 4.
```

Bin2I(<cEXP>)

Summer 87, 5.0, 5.01

This function converts a character string formatted as a 16-bit signed integer to Clipper integer format. cEXP contains the two-byte integer Clipper converts. Clipper automatically ignores any extra characters in the character string. The maximum range of this conversion is –32,768 to 32,767. EXAMPLE:

```
* Declare the variables.

SOMESTR = space(2)
HANDLE = fopen("TEMP.TXT")

* Get the string from the file.

fread(HANDLE, @SOMESTR, 2)

* Display the converted value.

clear screen
@ 01, 01 say bin2i(SOMESTR)
fclose(HANDLE)
quit
```

Bin2L(<cEXP>)

Summer 87, 5.0, 5.01

This function converts a character string formatted as a 32-bit signed integer to Clipper integer format. cEXP contains the four-byte integer Clipper converts. Clipper automatically ignores any extra characters in the character string. The maximum range of this conversion is –2,147,483,648 to 2,147,483,647. EXAMPLE:

```
SOMEVAR = bin2l(SOMESTR)
```

Bin2W(<cEXP>)

Summer 87, 5.0, 5.01

This function converts a character string formatted as a 16-bit unsigned integer to Clipper integer format. cEXP contains the two-byte integer Clipper converts. Clipper automatically ignores any extra characters in the character string. The maximum range of this conversion is 0 to 65535. EXAMPLE:

```
SOMEVAR = bin2w(SOMESTR)
```

BOF( )

Summer 87, 5.0, 5.01

This function occasionally returns false indications in versions 5.0 and above. For example, if you execute goto lastrec( ) + 1, the BOF( ) function will return a value of true. Version 5.0 also returns true if you perform a database operation before testing its value. In most cases you can get around this problem by evaluating BOF( ) before you perform any other database operation.

The BOF function returns true when the database record pointer points to the beginning of the file. Clipper sets this switch after a Skip command. EXAMPLE:

```
* Open a database and try to skip past the beginning of
* the file. Display a message if bof() is true.
use SOMEDATA
goto top
skip -1
if bof()
     @ 01, 01 say 'Beginning of file'
endif
```

Browse([<nEXP1> [, <nEXP2> [, <nEXP3> [, <nEXP4>]]]])

5.0, 5.01

The Browse( ) function provides a general-purpose editor and browser for a single database file. TABLE 2-4 describes the keys you can use while editing the database (they are exactly the same as the keys provided by the DBEdit( ) function). This function supports a status line in the upper right corner of the display.

The five keywords displayed on the status line include <new>, <bof>, <eof>, <Delete>, and Record. New appears whenever the user enters append mode. Bof appears whenever the user attempts to go past the first record of the database using the PgUp, Ctrl–PgUp, or up arrow keys. Eof appears whenever the user attempts to go past the last record of the database using the PgDn or Ctrl–PgDn keys. Delete appears whenever the user places the cursor on a record marked for deletion. The Record keyword is followed by the current record number. This function is much easier to use than the DBEdit( ) function, but the DBEdit( ) function provides greater flexibility.

This function supports four parameters. nEXP1 defines the top line of the browse area. If you don't provide this parameter, Clipper uses a default value of 1. nEXP2 defines the left-most column of the browse area. If you don't provide this parameter, Clipper uses a default value of 0. nEXP3 defines the bottom line of the browse area. If you don't provide this parameter, Clipper uses a default value of MaxRow( ). nEXP4 defines the right-most column of the browse area. If you don't provide this parameter, Clipper uses a default value of MaxCol( ). You can provide any or all of the parameters. EXAMPLE:

```
use SOMEDATA
browse(5, 10, maxrow(), 70)
```

Table 2-4 Standard database edit keys

Key	With UDF	Without UDF (normal)
Up arrow	Same as normal	Moves highlight up one row.
Down arrow	Same as normal	Moves highlight down one row.
Left arrow	Same as normal	Moves highlight left one column.
Right arrow	Same as normal	Moves highlight right one column.
Ctrl-left arrow	Same as normal	Pans the display left one column.
Ctrl-right arrow	Same as normal	Pans the display right one column.
Home	Same as normal	Selects the first displayed column in the current row.
End	Same as normal	Selects the last displayed column in the current row.
Ctrl-Home	Same as normal	Selects the first actual column in the current row.

Table 2-4 Continued.

Key	With UDF	Without UDF (normal)
Ctrl-End	Same as normal	Selects the last actual column in the current row.
PgUp	Same as normal	Moves the cursor up the number of records defined by the number of rows in the current window. If the database does not contain a sufficient number of records, it displays the first item in the database at the top of the window. The highlight appears in the same relative position after the keypress.
PgDn	Same as normal	Moves the cursor down the number of records defined by the number of rows in the current window. If the database does not contain a sufficient number of records, it displays the last item in the database at the bottom of the window. The highlight appears in the same relative position after the keypress.
Ctrl-PgUp	Same as normal	Selects the first record in the database.
Ctrl-PgDn	Same as normal	Selects the last record in the database.
Return	Defined as part of UDF	Terminates the database edit.
Esc	Defined as part of UDF	Terminates the database edit.

CDow(<dEXP>)

Summer 87, 5.0, 5.01

The CDow function converts a date to a string containing the day of the week. dEXP contains the date to convert. A null date value returns a null string. EXAMPLE:

```
SOMESTR = cdow(date())
```

CHR(<nEXP>)

Summer 87, 5.0, 5.01

Use the CHR function to convert a number to its ASCII equivalent. Clipper accepts a range of numbers from 0 to 255. EXAMPLE:

```
* Display a string then move the cursor to the next line.
* ASCII 10 is line feed and 13 is carriage return.
? 'Some Statement' + chr(10) + chr(13)
```

CMonth(<dEXP>)

Summer 87, 5.0, 5.01

The CMonth function converts a date to a string containing the month. dEXP contains the date to convert. A null date value returns a null string. EXAMPLE:

```
SOMESTR = cmonth(date())
```

COL( )

Summer 87, 5.0, 5.01

The COL function returns the column position of the cursor position. EXAMPLE:

```
* Create a generic display routine.
@ row()+1, 00 say VAL1              && Appears at next row, column 0.
@ row(), col()+5 say VAL2           && Appears 5 characters after entry.
```

CToD(<cEXP>)

Summer 87, 5.0, 5.01

Use this function to convert a character string to a date. cEXP contains the character string to convert. The character string must appear in the format specified by the Set Date command. The default format is American, or MM/DD/YY. If the program uses an empty date form (" / / "), then Clipper returns a null date. EXAMPLE:

```
DATESTR = "01/01/89"
SOMEDATE = ctod(DATESTR)
```

CurDir([<cEXP>])

Summer 87, 5.0, 5.01

This function retrieves the current directory and places the path in a string. The optional cEXP specifies a drive letter to retrieve. If the program omits cEXP, Clipper uses a default of the current drive. EXAMPLE:

```
SOMESTR = curdir("A")
```

Date( )

Summer 87, 5.0, 5.01

The Date function returns the system date. Clipper uses the date format set with the Set Date command. If Set Century is on, then Clipper returns a four-digit year value. EXAMPLE:

```
@ 01, 01 say date()
```

Day(<dEXP>)

Summer 87, 5.0, 5.01

The Day function converts a date to a number containing the day of the month. dEXP contains the date to convert. A null date value returns 0. Clipper automatically accounts for leap years when returning the day. EXAMPLE:

```
SOMESTR = day(date())
```

DBAppend( )

5.01

Use this function to add a blank record to the end of the database file, the same way you would use the Append Blank command. It follows the same rules as the Append Blank command for both single-user and network applications. You can, however, alias the function. This means that you can record to a database in an unselected work area. EXAMPLE:

```
// Add a record to the database using the CUSTOMER alias.
CUSTOMER -> dbappend()
```

DBClearFilter( )

5.01

This function performs the same task as the Set Filter command without any arguments. It resets the filter in the current work area. You cannot alias this function. EXAMPLE:

```
// Clear the filter in the current work area.
dbclearfilter()
```

DBClearIndex( )

5.01

This function performs the same task as the Set Index command without any arguments. It resets the index in the current work area. You cannot alias this function. EXAMPLE:

```
// Clear the index in the current work area.
dbclearindex()
```

DBClearRelation( )

5.01

This function performs the same task as the Set Relation To command without any arguments. It resets the relation in the current work area. You cannot alias this function. EXAMPLE:

```
// Clear the relation in the current work area.
dbclearrelation()
```

DBCloseAll( )

5.01

Use this function to release all work areas from use. It has the same effect as issuing the DBCloseArea( ) function for each work area. You cannot alias this function. EXAMPLE:

```
// Close all work areas in use.
dbcloseall()
```

DBCloseArea( )

5.01

The DBCloseArea command closes all databases, indexes, and other files in the current work area. In addition, it releases any resources used by the work area. This function is equivalent to issuing a standard Close command or the Use command without arguments. You can alias this function so that you do not need to actually be in the desired work area to close it. EXAMPLE:

```
// Close the CUSTOMER work area.
CUSTOMER -> dbclosearea()
```

DBCommit( )

5.01

Use this function to flush all Clipper buffers for the current work area to the operating system. In a single-user application using DOS, the information gets written to the disk. In a multiuser application, the information is written to the network buffers where it becomes visible to other processes. The information does not get written to disk until the network operating system issues a command to do so. You cannot alias this command. It is functionally equivalent to the Commit command. EXAMPLE:

```
// Flush the Clipper buffers.
dbcommit()
```

DBCommitAll

5.01

Use this function to flush all Clipper buffers for all work areas to the operating system. In a single-user application using DOS, the information gets written to the disk. In a multiuser application, the information is written to the network buffers where it becomes visible to other processes. The information does not get written to disk until the network operating system issues a command to do so. You cannot alias this command. It is functionally equivalent to using the Commit command in every work area. EXAMPLE:

```
// Flush the Clipper buffers in all work areas.
dbcommitall()
```

DBCreate(<cEXP>, <aEXP>)

5.0, 5.01

This function creates a database with the name contained in cEXP using the parameters contained in aEXP. If you don't supply a file extension, Clipper assumes a default of DBF. You can create the array by hand or use an array created by the DBStruct( ) function. Each array element corresponds to one field in the database. For example, if your database has five fields, then the array must contain five elements. Each element contains a subarray with four elements. Each element in the subarray corresponds to a different database parameter in the following order: name, type, length, and decimals. You access these subarrays by referencing the field element and then the subarray element. The four subarray names are: DBS_NAME, DBS_TYPE, DBS_LEN, and DBS_DEC. EXAMPLE:

```
use SOMEDATA
SOMEARRAY = dbstruct()
dbcreate("NEWDATA", SOMEARRAY)
```

DBCreateIndex(<cEXP1>, <cEXP2>, <bEXP>, [<lEXP>])

5.01

The manual states that the code block is an optional parameter for this function. You must include a basic code block with the key field names as a minimum.

Use this function to create new indexes to a database. cEXP1 contains the name of the file. If you don't specify a file extension, Clipper automatically appends an extension of NTX. cEXP2 contains the key expression used to index the file. This contains a string with any legal Clipper expression. The string appears at the beginning of the index file. It allows other programs to determine the key you used to create the index. bEXP contains a code block that creates the actual index. In most cases, this code block contains the field names used to create the index as a minimum. You can add other commands as required to obtain a desired level of functionality from the index routine, but the field names must appear as the last item in the code block. Otherwise you'll create a corrupted index file.

lEXP determines whether or not you create a unique index. Setting this value to .T. creates a unique index. Clipper automatically assumes a value of .F. if you don't specify a value. The following example shows how you would create an index routine with the added functionality of displaying record numbers. This function provides the features of the Index command while providing increased functionality. EXAMPLE:

```
// This example opens a sample database, clears the screen,
// displays an indexing message, then indexes the database.
// Notice that it automatically updates the number of records
// indexed.

static nCount := 0
use SAMPLE3 alias NUMBER
cls
@ 01, 01 say "Indexing record:          of " + ltrim(str(lastrec()))
NUMBER -> (dbcreateindex("SAMPLE3",;
                         "FIELD1+FIELD2+FIELD3",;
                         {| | devpos(01, 18),;
                              devout(nCount),;
                              ++nCount,;
                              FIELD1+FIELD2+FIELD3}))

return
```

DBDelete( )

5.01

DBDelete marks the current record as deleted. It does not remove the record from the database. You must use the Pack command to physically remove the deleted record from the database. This command requires that you have the record locked in a multiuser environment. This function performs the same task as the Delete command with a scope of the current record. EXAMPLE:

```
// Mark the current database record for deletion.
dbdelete()
```

DBEdit([nEXP1>] [, <nEXP2>] [, <nEXP3>] [, <nEXP4>] [, <aEXP1>] [, <cEXP1>] [, <aEXP2>/<cEXP2>] [, <aEXP3>/<cEXP3>] [, <aEXP4>/<cEXP4>] [, <aEXP5>/<cEXP5>] [, <aEXP6>/<cEXP6>] [, <aEXP7>/<cEXP7>])

Summer 87, 5.0, 5.01

The DBEdit( ) function is supplied for compatibility purposes in versions 5.0 and above. Use a TBrowse object instead whenever possible. Version 5.0 also modified DBEdit( ) to return a value of NIL instead of nothing. DBEdit( ) also refreshes the screen each time the user moves the cursor. Summer 87 refreshed the screen only when the user moved the record pointer to a record that didn't appear on the display.

DBEDIT provides the means for creating a full-screen editing facility within a program. Unlike the AChoice function, Clipper can execute this function without specifying any parameters. However, the program must open a database before using this function. nEXP1 contains the top row offset. nEXP2 contains the left column offset. nEXP3 contains the bottom row offset. nEXP4 contains the right column offset. If the program does not specify the screen coordinates, Clipper uses a default of the entire screen. aEXP1 contains a list of database fields to display. cEXP is the name of a user-defined function that Clipper executes when the user presses an undefined key.

TABLE 2-4 contains a listing of the active keys for DBEdit. TABLE 2-5 contains a listing of the status messages passed from DBEDIT to the user-defined function (UDF). TABLE 2-6 contains a listing of the request messages passed from the UDF to DBEdit. aEXP2 contains the name of an array containing picture strings. Most picture strings work as stated in TABLE 1-2. However, the @S (scroll) function does not perform any function. If the argument contains a string (cEXP2) in place of an array, Clipper uses the same formatting for all columns. aEXP3 contains the name of an array containing column headings. If the argument contains a string (cEXP3) in place of an array, Clipper uses the same heading for all columns. aEXP4 contains an array of line-drawing characters used to separate the heading from the fields. If the argument contains a string (cEXP4) in place of an array, Clipper uses the same string for all columns. aEXP5 contains an array of line-drawing characters used to separate the individual columns. If the argument contains a string (cEXP5) in place of an array, Clipper uses the same string between all columns. aEXP6 contains an array of line-drawing characters used to separate the footer from the fields. If the argument contains a string (cEXP6) in place of an array, Clipper uses the same string for all columns. aEXP7 contains the name of an array containing column footers. If the argument contains a string (cEXP8) in place of an array, Clipper uses the same heading for all columns. For general-purpose browsing and editing of the contents of a database, use the Browse( ) function provided with Clipper 5.0. EXAMPLE:

```
* Setup Environment

set deleted on

* Initialize Variables

DUMMY = ""

declare FORMAT[9]
FORMAT[1] = ""
FORMAT[2] = "@!"
FORMAT[3] = ""
FORMAT[4] = ""
FORMAT[5] = ""
FORMAT[6] = "99999-9999"
FORMAT[7] = "(999)999-9999"
FORMAT[8] = "(999)999-9999"
FORMAT[9] = ""

declare HEADING[9]
HEADING[1] = "First Name"
HEADING[2] = "MI"
HEADING[3] = "Last Name"
HEADING[4] = "Address Line 1"
HEADING[5] = "Address Line 2"
HEADING[6] = "Zip Code"
HEADING[7] = "Telephone 1"
HEADING[8] = "Telephone 2"
HEADING[9] = "Company Name"

* Open the database.

use SAMPLE1

* Display the database.

clear screen
@ 01, 00 to 24, 79 double
dbedit(02, 01, 23, 78, DUMMY, "CHOICE", FORMAT, HEADING)
```

```
pack
clear screen
quit

* User Defined Function for Database Edit Control

function CHOICE
parameters STATUS, FLD

* Assign Variables
RET_TYPE = 0                            && UDF Request Message

if STATUS = 0
      RET_TYPE = 1
elseif STATUS = 4
      do case
            case lastkey() = 13
                  do EDITREC with FLD
                  RET_TYPE = 2
            case (lastkey() > 65) .and. (lastkey() < 122)
                  keyboard chr(lastkey())
                  do EDITREC with FLD
                  RET_TYPE = 2
            case lastkey() = 27
                  RET_TYPE = 0
            case lastkey() = 7
                  delete
                  RET_TYPE = 2
            otherwise
                  RET_TYPE = 2
      endcase
elseif STATUS = 2
      append blank                      && Add a record.
      @ row()+1, col()                  && Move the cursor.
      do EDITREC with FLD
      RET_TYPE = 2
elseif STATUS = 1
      ? chr(7)
      RET_TYPE = 1
endif
return RET_TYPE

* Edit the selected record.

procedure EDITREC
parameters FLDNUM

* Assign Variables

FIELD_NAME = field(FLDNUM)

* Edit the field.
```

```
set cursor on
 @ row(), col() get &FIELD_NAME
read
set cursor off
@ 01, 00 to 24, 79 double          && Refresh the border.

return
```

Table 2-5 UDF status messages for database edit

Mode	Description
0	No undefined user action since the last call.
1	User pressed a key that placed the record pointer past the beginning of the file.
2	User pressed a key that placed the record pointer past the end of the file.
3	Database does not contain any records.
4	User pressed an undefined key.

Table 2-6 UDF request messages for database edit

Return value	Description
0	Terminates the database edit.
1	Continues the database edit.
2	Repaints the database edit screen. Continues the database edit.
3	Append mode.

DBEval(<bEXP1> [, <bEXP2> [, <bEXP3> [, <nEXP1> [, <nEXP2> [, <lEXP>]]]]])

5.0, 5.01

Use this function to evaluate the contents of a database. bEXP1 contains the code you want to execute for each selected record. bEXP2 contains a For condition that limits the number of records selected. Clipper processes all records that meet the required condition. This code block is used for the same purpose as the For clause in any record-processing command. bEXP3 contains a While condition that limits the number of records selected. Unlike the For condition, record processing stops at the first record that fails to meet the required condition. This code block is used for the same purpose as the While clause in any record-processing command.

nEXP1 contains the number of records to process, beginning at the current record. This number represents the next clause in any record processing command. nEXP2 contains the number of a specific record to process. This number represents the record clause in any record processing command. lEXP contains a logical statement. If the statement is true, Clipper processes the records beginning at the current record and going to the end of the database. If the statement is false, Clipper processes all records in the database. EXAMPLE:

```
* Display the number of employees in each age group, then
* calculate their average age.

COUNT := COUNT2 := COUNT3 := 0
use EMP_DATA
EMP_AGE := array(70)
afill (EMP_AGE, 0)

* This code block fills an array with the number of employees in
* each age group.

dbeval({ || iif(AGE > 0, EMP_AGE[AGE]++, qout("End")) })

* Display the array.

cls
@ 00, 00 say "Age | Number"
@ 01, 00 say "───┼──────"
for COUNT = 18 to 65
    if row() < 23
        @ row()+1, 01 say str(COUNT,2)+' | '+str(EMP_AGE[COUNT],6)
    else
        @ 24, 01 say "Press any key when ready..."
        inkey(0)
        cls
        @ 00, 00 say "Age | Number"
        @ 01, 00 say "───┼──────"
        @ 02, 01 say str(COUNT,2)+' | '+str(EMP_AGE[COUNT],6)
    endif
next

* This code block creates a total age for all employees using the
* equation TOTAL = TOTAL + (AGE * NUMBER).

aeval(EMP_AGE, {|COUNT|COUNT, COUNT3++, COUNT2+=(COUNT3*COUNT)})
```

```
* Find the average by dividing by the number of employees.

COUNT2 = COUNT2/lastrec()

* Display the average and end the program.

@ row()+2, 01 say "Average age is: " + str (COUNT2, 6, 3)
@ 24, 01 say "Press any key when ready..."
inkey(0)
close all
return
```

DBF( )

5.0, 5.01

Use this function to determine the alias of the current database. Nantucket furnished this function to provide compatibility with dBASE III Plus. The Alias( ) function performs the same task as the DBF( ) function. Use the Alias( ) function whenever possible. EXAMPLE:

```
SOMEVAR = dbf()
```

DBFilter( )

Summer 87, 5.0, 5.01

This function returns the value of the filter for the current work area. If the program has not set a filter in the current work area, DBFilter returns a null string. EXAMPLE:

```
SOMESTR = dbfilter()
```

DBGoBottom( )

5.01

This function places the record pointer at the last logical record in the database. EXAMPLE:

```
dbgobottom()
```

DBGoto(nEXP)

5.01

This function places the record pointer at the record number specified by nEXP. EXAMPLE:

```
// Go to the second record of the database.
dbgoto(2)
```

DBGoTop( )

5.01

This function places the record pointer at the first logical record in the database. EXAMPLE:

```
dbgotop()
```

DBRecall( )

5.01

DBRecall marks the current record as undeleted (not deleted). You cannot recall a record that has been physically removed from the database using the Pack command. This function performs the same task as the Recall command with a scope of the current record. EXAMPLE:

```
// Mark the current database record for undeletion.
dbrecall()
```

DBReindex( )

5.01

Use this function to reindex all the indexes in the current work area. It provides the samc functionality as the Reindex command. The DBReindex function does not provide the same capabilities as the DBCreateIndex function previously described. EXAMPLE:

```
// Open then reindex a database.
use SAMPLE3 index SAMPLE3 alias NUMBER
NUMBER -> (dbreindex())
```

DBRelation(<nEXP>)

Summer 87, 5.0, 5.01

This function returns the value of the specified relation set for the current work area. nEXP contains the number of the relation to return. If the program has not created any links to other databases for the current work area, DBRelation returns a null string. EXAMPLE:

```
SOMESTR = dbrelation()
```

DBSelect(<nEXP>)

Summer 87, 5.0, 5.01

This function returns the target work area of the specified relation set for the current work area. nEXP contains the number of the relation to return. If the program has not created any links to other databases for the current work area, DBSelect returns zero. EXAMPLE:

```
SOMENUM = dbrelation()
```

DBSeek(<xEXP> [, <lEXP>])

5.01

The DBSeek function searches for the key expression specified by xEXP. If found, DBSeek returns true; otherwise, it returns false. lEXP turns softseek on or off. Supplying a value of true turns softseek on. DBSeek always returns true when softseek is turned on. This function performs the same task as the Seek command. EXAMPLE:

```
// Find the first occurrence of the requested name.
local cSeek := space(30)
use SAMPLE1 index SAMPLE1
cls
 @ 01, 01 say "Enter a name: " get cSeek picture '@!'
read
@ 02, 01 say "Name " + iif(dbseek(cSeek),;
                          "record " + ltrim(str(recno())),;
                          "not found")
return
```

DBSelectArea(<nEXP>/<cEXP>)

5.01

This function performs the same task as the Select command. You can provide either a work area number or an alias as input. nEXP contains the number of a work area in the range 0 through 250. Specifying work area 0 selects the lowest numbered active work area. cEXP contains an alias. DBSelectArea always returns NIL. It is usually more efficient to use work area aliasing in place of this command. For example, NUMBER -> (go-top( )) selects the work area aliased by NUMBER and goes to the top of that database. EXAMPLE:

```
// Select the database aliased as NUMBER.
dbselectarea(NUMBER)
```

DBSetFilter(<bEXP> [, <cEXP>])

5.01

This function displays the first record in a database when used with a TBrowse object, whether or not the first record fits the filter criteria. Therefore, you must use a positioning command after setting the filter to get the filter to work properly with a TBrowse object. See the following example for further details.

Use this function to set a filter condition for the current or aliased database. You must specify the filter as a code block (bEXP). The optional string (cEXP) allows you to identify the filter in textual form. Both bEXP and cEXP must express the same condition. If you don't include cEXP, then Clipper displays a blank when asked for the filter expression. The DBSetFilter function performs the same task as the Set Filter command. EXAMPLE:

```
// Open the database and set a filter.
use SAMPLE3 index SAMPLE3
dbsetfilter({||FIELD1 > 4 .and. FIELD1 < 8},;
            "FIELD1 > 4 .and. FIELD1 < 8")

// Added to set filter without changing the record pointer.

goto top
```

DBSetIndex(<cEXP>)

5.01

This function sets the index in the current or aliased work area to the filename specified by cEXP. If you don't specify a file extension, Clipper automatically appends NTX as an extension. This function performs the same task as the Set Index To command. There is no benefit to using the command form over the function form of the function. DBSetIndex( ) always returns a value of NIL. EXAMPLE:

```
use SAMPLE3
dbsetindex("SAMPLE3")
```

DBSetOrder(<nEXP>)

5.01

Use this function to determine which of the active index files is the controlling index. nEXP contains the number of the controlling index. DBSetOrder( ) performs the same function as the Set Order To command. There is no benefit to using the command form over the function form of the function. DBSetOrder( ) always returns a value of NIL. EXAMPLE:

```
use SAMPLE3 index SAMPLE3, NUMBER
// Select NUMBER as the controlling index.
dbsetorder(2)
```

DBSetRelation(<nEXP>/<cEXP1>, <bEXP> [, <cEXP2>])

5.01

Use this function to set a relation between a parent and child database. It performs the same task as the Set Relation To command using the Additive clause. The function variant offers greater flexibility than the command variant. You must specify either nEXP or cEXP1 as the child work area. nEXP contains the work area number. cEXP1 contains the work area alias. bEXP is a code block describing the relation. The optional string (cEXP2) allows you to identify the filter in textual form. Both bEXP and cEXP2 must express the same condition. If you do not include cEXP2, then Clipper displays a blank when asked for the relation expression. EXAMPLE:

```
// Create a relation between a names and a contribution
// database.
use SAMPLE6 index SAMPLE6 alias CONT
use SAMPLE5 index SAMPLE5 alias NAME new
select CONT
dbsetrelation("NAME", {|| str(CONT->REFERENCE)}, ;
       "str(CONT->REFERENCE)")
```

DBSkip([<nEXP>])

5.01

The DBSkip( ) function performs the same task as the Skip command. There is no benefit to using the command form over the function form of the function. nEXP contains the number of records, plus or minus, to skip. When using an index, DBSkip( ) always uses the logical record order set by the index. If you don't specify nEXP, then Clipper assumes a value of 1 record. EXAMPLE:

```
use SAMPLE3 index SAMPLE3
// Skip one record.
skip()
// Skip five records.
skip(5)
```

DBStruct( )

5.0, 5.01

While version 5.0 returns NIL if no fields are active in the current or aliased work area, version 5.01 returns an empty array.

Use this function to create an array containing the structure of a database. Each element corresponds to one field in the database. For example, if your database has five fields, then DBStruct( ) creates an array with five elements. Each element contains a subarray with four elements. Each element in the subarray corresponds to a different database parameter in the following order: name, type, length, and decimals. You access these subarrays by referencing the field element and then the subarray element. The four subarray names are: DBS_NAME, DBS_TYPE, DBS_LEN, and DBS _DEC. EXAMPLE:

```
* Get the structure of the current database, then
* display the field names.
#include "DBSTRUCT.H"
use SOMEDATA
SOMEARRAY := dbstruct()
COUNT = len(SOMEARRAY)
cls
for COUNT = 1 to COUNT
     @ row()+1 say SOMEARRAY[COUNT].DBS_NAME
next
```

DBUnlock( )

5.01

Use this function to remove any locks in the current or aliased database file. It performs the same task as the Unlock command. There is no benefit to using the command form over the function form. EXAMPLE:

```
// Unlock the database aliased as NUMBER.
NUMBER -> (dbunlock())
```

DBUnlockAll( )

5.01

Use this function to remove all locks in all currently active work areas. It performs the same task as the Unlock All command. There is no benefit to using the command form over the function form. It achieves the same result as using the DBUnlock( ) function on all active work areas. EXAMPLE:

```
// Unlock all currently active work areas.
dbunlockall()
```

DBUseArea([<lEXP1>], [<cEXP1>], <cEXP2>, [<cEXP3>], [<lEXP2>], [<lEXP3>])

5.01

This function equates to the Use command. There is no benefit to using the command form over the function form. lEXP1 is an optional parameter. Setting this value to true selects the lowest number unoccupied work area before opening the database. The default is .F., which uses the current work area. If a database is open in the current work area, Clipper closes the file before opening the new one.

cEXP1 is an optional parameter that contains the name of the database driver used to service the database. If left blank, Clipper uses the default DBFNTX driver. cEXP2 contains the name of the database file you want opened. You must specify a value for this parameter. cEXP3 contains the alias of the database file. You don't have to specify an alias. lEXP2 determines whether or not the database is opened in exclusive mode. Specifying a value of true opens the database in shared mode. lEXP3 contains a value that determines if the user can write to the database. Specifying a value of true opens the database in read-only mode, which prohibits the user from writing to the file. EXAMPLE:

```
// Open SAMPLE3 using an alias of NUMBER. Service it
// with the default DBFNTX driver. Open it in exclusive
// mode and allow updates.
dbUseArea( .F., , "SAMPLE3", "NUMBER", .F., .F. )
```

Deleted( )

Summer 87, 5.0, 5.01

The Deleted function returns the status of the current record. If the program marks the current record for deletion, Deleted returns true. EXAMPLE:

```
if deleted()
      @ 01, 01 say 'Record is deleted.'
endif
```

Descend(<xEXP>)

Summer 87, 5.0, 5.01

The Descend function creates and searches descending order indexes. Clipper normally creates and searches indexes in ascending order only. EXP is an expression of any type. EXAMPLE:

```
use SOMEDATE
index on descend(FLDNAME)
seek descend(FLDNAME=VALUE)
```

DevOut(<xEXP> [, <cEXP>])

5.0, 5.01

This function was undocumented in the version 5.0 manual. Version 5.01 adds the capability of specifying color through the cEXP parameter. If you don't specify a color string, then Clipper uses the colors set by the SetColor( ) function.

The DevOut( ) function sends the specified expression to the current output device at the current cursor position. xEXP contains the expression that you want to display. EXAMPLE:

```
// Output a string to the display at position 01,01.
devpos(01, 01)
devout("Hello World")
```

DevPos(<nEXP1>, <nEXP2>)

5.0, 5.01

The DevPos( ) function positions the cursor on the current output device. nEXP1 contains the row and nEXP2 contains the column position. If the output device selected is the printer, then DevPos( ) also updates the PRow( ) and PCol( ) information. EXAMPLE:

```
// Output a string to the display at position 01,01.
devpos(01, 01)
devout("Hello World")
```

Directory(<cEXP1> [, <cEXP2>])

5.0, 5.01

While version 5.0 returns NIL if no files match the requested directory skeleton, version 5.01 returns an empty array.

Use this function to create an array containing the contents of the specified directory. Each element corresponds to one directory entry. Two factors control which entries Directory( ) places in the array. cEXP1 contains the directory skeleton. You can include a legal DOS path, drive, or wildcard (* or ?) characters. cEXP2 contains the file attributes to look for. The H attribute includes hidden files. The S attribute includes system files. The D attribute includes directory entries. The V attribute includes the DOS volume label for the drive. cEXP2 is an optional parameter. If you don't include it, Directory( ) places files with the normal attribute set into the array. In fact, the only time that Directory( ) excludes normal files is when you specify the V attribute.

Each array element contains a subarray with five elements. Each subarray element corresponds to a different file parameter in the following order: name, size, date, time, and attributes. You access these subarrays by referencing the field element and then the subarray element. The four subarray names are: F_NAME, F_SIZE, F_DATE, F_TIME, and F_ATT. EXAMPLE:

```
* Get a listing of all the files and subdirectories in
* the current directory, then list their names and
* sizes.
#include "DIRECTORY.CH"
```

```
SOMEARRAY := directory("*.*", "HSD")
COUNT = len(SOMEARRAY)
cls
for COUNT = 1 to COUNT
       @ row()+1 say SOMEARRAY[COUNT].F_NAME + ' ' + ;
       str(SOMEARRAY[COUNT].F_SIZE, 7)
```

DiskSpace([<nEXP>])

Summer 87, 5.0, 5.01

Use the DiskSpace function to determine the amount of memory left on the current or other drive. Clipper uses a default of the current drive. nEXP contains the number of the drive to query. One is drive A, two is drive B, and three is drive C. EXAMPLE:

```
* Get the amount of space left on drive A.
SOMENUM = diskspace(1)
```

DispBegin( )

5.01

Use this function to tell Clipper when your program is about to begin a series of display operations. Every display operation appearing between the DispBegin( ) and the DispEnd( ) function is buffered. The result is that your screen updates appear to happen more quickly. This function is especially useful on complex displays where screen performance is lacking. Your program must avoid any peripheral device communication between the time you issue DispBegin( ) and DispEnd( ). Peripheral device communication (for example with the keyboard) can cause loss of display data. EXAMPLE:

```
// Clear the display and display preliminary box and
// identifying text in preparation for using the program.

dispbegin()
setcolor("w+/b, w+/g,, w+/bg, w+/rb")
cls
dispbox(01, 00, 24, 79, B_SINGLE_DOUBLE)
@00, 00 say padc(" Donator Contribution Status ", 80, chr(176))
dispend()
```

DispBox(<nEXP1>, <nEXP2>, <nEXP3>, <nEXP4> [, <cEXP1>] [, <cEXP2>])

5.01

The DispBox( ) function displays a box at the coordinates specified by nEXP1 through nEXP4. It is equivalent to using the @...Box command. There is no benefit to using the command form over the function form.

nEXP1 defines the upper line position, nEXP2 defines the left line position, nEXP3 defines the bottom line position, and nEXP4 defines the right line position. The optional cEXP1 parameter contains a character string that defines the characters used to draw the box. A set of predefined characters are contained in BOX.CH. cEXP2 contains an optional string that describes the colors used to draw the box. If you don't supply this parameter, then DispBox( ) uses the default colors specified by the SetColor( ) function. EXAMPLE:

```
// Clear the display and display preliminary box and
// identifying text in preparation for using the program.

dispbegin()
setcolor("w+/b, w+/g,, w+/bg, w+/rb")
cls
dispbox(01, 00, 24, 79, B_SINGLE_DOUBLE)
@00, 00 say padc(" Donator Contribution Status ", 80, chr(176))
dispend()
```

DispEnd( )

5.01

Use this function to tell Clipper when your program is ending a series of display operations. Every display operation appearing between the DispBegin( ) and the DispEnd( ) function is buffered. The result is that your screen updates appear to happen more quickly. This function is especially useful on complex displays where screen performance is lacking. Your program must avoid any peripheral device communication between the time you issue DispBegin( ) and DispEnd( ). Peripheral device communication (for example with the keyboard) can cause loss of display data. EXAMPLE:

```
// Clear the display and display preliminary box and
// identifying text in preparation for using the program.

dispbegin()
setcolor("w+/b, w+/g,, w+/bg, w+/rb")
cls
dispbox(01, 00, 24, 79, B_SINGLE_DOUBLE)
@00, 00 say padc(" Donator Contribution Status ", 80, chr(176))
dispend()
```

DispOut(<xEXP> [, <cEXP>])

5.01

Use this function to send output to the display at the current cursor position. It does not follow any of the Set command settings other than color. Output always goes to the display. xEXP contains the value you want sent to the display. The optional cEXP string contains a color value. If you don't supply this parameter, then DispOut( ) uses the default colors specified by the SetColor( ) function. EXAMPLE:

```
dispout("Hello World", "W+/R")
```

DOSError([<nEXP>])

Summer 87, 5.0, 5.01

Version 5.01 adds the ability to set the DOS errorlevel by providing a value for the optional nEXP parameter.

This function returns the value of the last DOS error. TABLE 2-7 contains a listing of the applicable DOS error numbers. EXAMPLE:

```
ERRORNUM = doserror()
if ERRORNUM <> 0
     do SOMEPROC with ERRORNUM
endif
```

DOW(<dEXP>)

Summer 87, 5.0, 5.01

Use the DOW function to convert a date value into a number identifying the day of the week. The days of the week begin with Sunday as one and end with Saturday as seven. EXAMPLE:

```
DAYNUM = dow(date())
```

DToC(<dEXP>)

Summer 87, 5.0, 5.01

Use the DToC function to convert a date value into a string. The string appears in the format specified by the Set Date command. The default setting is American. The Set Century command affects whether Clipper adds the century to the year entry of the date. If the program sets century on, Clipper adds the two-digit century number to the date string. EXAMPLE:

```
SOMESTR = dtoc(date())
```

DToS(<dEXP>)

Summer 87, 5.0, 5.01

Use the DToS function to convert a date value into a string suitable for indexes. The string appears in the format YYYYMMDD. EXAMPLE:

```
SOMESTR = dtos(date())
```

Empty(<xEXP>)

Summer 87, 5.0, 5.01

Empty( ) was updated in version 5.0 to check the contents of NIL and array data types. The Empty function returns true if the result of an expression is empty. A null string, null date, false logical, or zero numeric value are all empty. EXAMPLE:

```
if empty(SOMEVAR = 0)
        do SOMEPROC
endif
```

EOF( )

Summer 87, 5.0, 5.01

This function returns true if the record pointer for the database in the current work area is at the end of file. EOF equals LASTREC + 1. EXAMPLE:

```
do while .not. eof()
        <PROGRAM STATEMENTS>
enddo
```

ErrorLevel([<nEXP>])

Summer 87, 5.0, 5.01

The ErrorLevel function returns the current DOS errorlevel. nEXP optionally sets the errorlevel to a new value. If the program omits nEXP, then Clipper does not change the errorlevel. EXAMPLE:

```
if SOMEVAR = 0
        errorlevel(1)
else
        errorlevel(0)
endif
```

Eval(<bEXP> [, <PARAMETER LIST>])

5.0, 5.01

Use this function to evaluate bEXP. A code block contains executable code. You pass parameters to the code block through PARAMETER LIST. EXAMPLE:

```
* Display a column of numbers.
CBLOCK := &("{ |NUM| NUM + 1}" )
cls
do while row() < maxrow() - 1
      @ row()+1, 01 say eval(CBLOCK, row())
enddo
```

EXP(<nEXP>)

Summer 87, 5.0, 5.01

Use this function to calculate e^x, where e is the natural logarithm and x is the exponent. nEXP contains the exponent. EXP performs the inverse task of the LOG function. EXAMPLE:

```
* Compute continuous compound interest.
END_AMT = PRINCIPLE * exp(INT_RATE * TIME)
```

FClose(<nEXP>)

Summer 87, 5.0, 5.01

This function closes a file. nEXP contains the file handle obtained during opening. FClose returns true if the file closed successfully. EXAMPLE:

```
* Initialize Variables
 HANDLE = 0    && DOS File Handle

* Open the file

if .not. file("TEMP.TXT")
      HANDLE = fcreate("TEMP.TXT", 0)
else
      HANDLE = fopen("TEMP.TXT", 0)
endif

<PROGRAM STATEMENTS>

* Close the file and exit.

fclose(HANDLE)
quit
```

FCount( )

Summer 87, 5.0, 5.01

The FCount function returns the number of fields in the database in the current work area. If the current work area does not contain an open database, Clipper returns zero. EXAMPLE:

```
* Return the number of fields in the current database.
SOMENUM = fcount()
```

FCreate(<cEXP> [, <nEXP>])

Summer 87, 5.0, 5.01

This function creates a file. cEXP contains the name of a file to open. nEXP contains the attribute DOS uses to create the file. Clipper uses a default attribute of 0 (normal). TABLE 2-8 contains a listing of DOS file attributes. This function returns a file handle that DOS uses for all subsequent access if successful. If unsuccessful, this function returns −1. Clipper opens the new file in the read/write access mode. EXAMPLE:

```
* Initialize Variables
HANDLE = 0     && DOS File Handle

* Open the file

if .not. file("TEMP.TXT")
     HANDLE = fcreate("TEMP.TXT", 0)
else
     HANDLE = fopen("TEMP.TXT", 0)
endif

<PROGRAM STATEMENTS>

* Close the file and exit.

fclose(HANDLE)
quit
```

Table 2-7 DOS extended error information

Code	Description
0	No error
1	Function number invalid
2	File not found
3	Path not found
4	Too many open files
5	Access denied
6	Handle invalid
7	Memory control block destroyed
8	Insufficient memory
9	Memory block address invalid
10	Environment invalid
11	Format invalid
12	Access code invalid
13	Data invalid
14	Unknown unit
15	Disk drive invalid

Code	Description
16	Attempted to remove current directory
17	Not same device
18	No more files
19	Disk write-protected
20	Unknown unit
21	Drive not ready
22	Unknown command
23	Data error (CRC)
24	Bad request structure length
25	Seek error
26	Unknown media type
27	Sector not found
28	Printer out of paper
29	Write fault
30	Read fault
31	General failure
32	Sharing violation
33	Lock violation
34	Disk change invalid
35	FCB unavailable
36	Sharing buffer exceeded
37 - 49	Reserved
50	Unsupported network request
51	Remote machine not listening
52	Duplicate name on network
53	Network name not found
54	Network busy
55	Device no longer exists on network
56	NetBIOS command limit exceeded
57	Error in network adapter hardware
58	Incorrect response from network
59	Unexpected network error
60	Remote adapter incompatible
61	Print queue full
62	Not enough space for print file
63	Print file canceled
64	Network name deleted
65	Network access denied
66	Incorrect network device type
67	Network name not found
68	Network name limit exceeded
69	NetBIOS session limit exceeded

Table 2-7 Continued.

Code	Description
70	File sharing temporarily paused
71	Network request not accepted
72	Print or disk redirection paused
73 - 79	Reserved
80	File already exists
81	Reserved
82	Cannot make directory
83	Fail on Int 24h
84	Too many redirections
85	Duplicate redirection
86	Invalid password
87	Invalid parameter
88	Network device fault
89	Function not supported by network
90	Required system component not installed

FError( )

Summer 87, 5.0, 5.01

This function returns a DOS error number if an error occurs during a file function. TABLE 2-7 contains a listing of DOS errors. If no file error occurs, this function returns zero. EXAMPLE:

```
* Initialize Variables
HANDLE = 0     && DOS File Handle

* Open the file

if .not. file("TEMP.TXT")
      HANDLE = fcreate("TEMP.TXT", 0)
else
      HANDLE = fopen("TEMP.TXT", 0)
endif
if ferror() > 0
      <ERROR RECOVERY STATEMENTS>
endif
```

Table 2-8 DOS file attributes

Attribute	Value	Description
Normal	0	This is the standard file attribute. Allows read/write access.
Read only	1	This is a protected file attribute. Allows read access only.
Hidden	2	This is a protected file attribute. Allows read/write access. The file does not appear in most directory searches using DOS.
System	4	This is a protected file attribute. Allows read/write access. The file does not appear in most directory searches using DOS. Normally used by DOS system files only.

Field(<nEXP>)/Fieldname(<nEXP>)

Summer 87, 5.0, 5.01

The Field/Fieldname function returns the name of the specified field in the database in the current work area. nEXP contains the field number to retrieve. If the database doesn't contain the number of fields specified by nEXP or the current work area doesn't contain an open database, this function returns a null string. EXAMPLE:

```
use SOMEDATE
SOMESTR = field(1)
```

FieldBlock(<cEXP>)

5.0, 5.01

Version 5.01 adds the capability of using this function even if the specified field does not exist. The field must exist, however, prior to executing the code block.

The FieldBlock( ) function creates a code block for the field specified by cEXP. When your program evaluates the code block, you can either get or set the value of the field. Evaluating the code block without a value gets the current field value. Evaluating the code block with a value sets the current field value. If the field does not exist, then FieldBlock returns NIL. EXAMPLE:

```
bFCodeBlock := fieldblock(SOMEFIELD)
```

FieldGet(<nEXP>)

5.0, 5.01

The FieldGet( ) function retrieves the value for a field based on its ordinal position within the database structure. nEXP contains the ordinal position of the field. EXAMPLE:

```
// Get the value of the 4th field in a database.
xSomeVar := fieldget(4)
```

FieldPOS(<cEXP>)

5.01

Use this function to determine the position of the field name contained in cEXP within the current or aliased work area. FieldPos( ) returns the field number of the specified field. If the field doesn't appear within the specified work area, then FieldPos( ) returns a value of zero. EXAMPLE:

```
// Check for the existence of a field.  If it doesn't
// exist, then display a database error message.
nFieldNum := NUMBER -> (fieldpos(SOMEFIELD))
if nFieldNum == 0
     alert("Database Error")
     return
endif
```

FieldPut(<nEXP>, <xEXP>)

5.0, 5.01

The FieldPut( ) function assigns the value of a field based on its ordinal position within the database structure. nEXP contains the ordinal position of the field. xEXP contains an expression for assigning the value to the field. EXAMPLE:

```
// Put a value of 14 in the 4th field the of a database.
fieldput(4, 14)
```

FieldWBlock(<cEXP>, <nEXP>)

5.0, 5.01

Version 5.01 adds the capability of using this function even if the specified field doesn't exist. The field must exist, however, prior to executing the code block.

The FieldWBlock( ) function creates a code block for the field specified by cEXP for the work area specified by nEXP. When your program evaluates the code block, you can either get or set the value of the field. Evaluating the code block without a value gets the current field value. Evaluating the code block with a value sets the current field value. If the field does not exist, then FieldWBlock returns NIL. EXAMPLE:

```
bFCodeBlock := fieldwblock(SOMEFIELD, 2)
```

File(<cEXP>)

Summer 87, 5.0, 5.01

This function checks the status of a file. cEXP contains the name of the file to check. cEXP can contain a drive and directory path. If the file exists in the specified path, this function returns true. EXAMPLE:

```
* Initialize Variables
HANDLE = 0    && DOS File Handle

* Open the file

if .not. file("TEMP.TXT")
      HANDLE = fcreate("TEMP.TXT", 0)
else
      HANDLE = fopen("TEMP.TXT", 0)
endif

<PROGRAM STATEMENTS>

* Close the file and exit.

fclose(HANDLE)
quit
```

FKLabel(<nEXP>)

5.0, 5.01

This function provides compatibility with dBASE III's FKLabel( ) function. It returns a string containing the name of the function key associated with a specific number. You don't need to use it with Clipper-specific programs because the function keys are numbered from 1 through 40. EXAMPLE:

```
SOMEVAR = fklabel(1)    && Returns "F1"
```

FKMax( )

5.0, 5.01

This function provides compatibility with dBASE III's FKMax( ) function. It returns a number corresponding to the maximum number of function keys. You don't need to use it with Clipper-specific programs because Clipper returns a constant value of 40. EXAMPLE:

```
SOMEVAR = fkmax() && Returns 40
```

Flock( )

Summer 87, 5.0, 5.01

Use this function to lock the entire database. This allows a program to perform tasks that require exclusive use of the database. Flock returns true when the database lock becomes successful. EXAMPLE:

```
do while .not. flock()
      @ 01, 01 say "Locking file. Press any key to exit."
      SOMEVAR = inkey(2)
      if SOMEVAR <> 0
            exit
      endif
enddo
```

FOpen(<cEXP> [, <nEXP>])

Summer 87, 5.0, 5.01

This function opens a file. cEXP contains the name of a file to open, and can contain a drive and directory path. nEXP contains the mode DOS uses to open the file. Clipper uses a default attribute of 0 (read only). TABLE 2-9 contains a listing of DOS file open modes. This function returns a file handle that DOS uses for all subsequent access if successful. If unsuccessful, this function returns –1. EXAMPLE:

```
* Initialize Variables
HANDLE = 0  && DOS File Handle

* Open the file

if .not. file("TEMP.TXT")
      HANDLE = fcreate("TEMP.TXT", 0)
else
      HANDLE = fopen("TEMP.TXT", 0)
endif

<PROGRAM STATEMENTS>

* Close the file and exit.

fclose(HANDLE)
quit
```

Table 2-9 DOS file open modes

Mode	Description
0	Read only -- DOS outputs an error if the program attempts to write to the file.
1	Write only -- DOS outputs an error if the program tries to read the file.
2	Read/Write -- DOS allows both reading and writing of the file.

Found( )

Summer 87, 5.0, 5.01

The Found function returns true if the previous search succeeded. EXAMPLE:

```
if .not. found()
      @ 01, 01 say "Search String Not Found"
endif
```

FRead(<nEXP1>, @<MEMVARC>, <nEXP2>)

Summer 87, 5.0, 5.01

Use this function to read the contents of a file. nEXP1 contains the file handle obtained when Clipper opened or created the file. @MEMVARC contains the name of a string variable initialized to a length equal to or greater than nEXP2. If the string isn't longer than the value of nEXP2, Clipper uses the length of MEMVARC in place of nEXP2. nEXP2 contains the number of bytes to read. This function returns the number of bytes actually read from the file. If the number of bytes read doesn't match the number of bytes requested, it means that DOS found the end of file or a file-read error occurred. EXAMPLE:

```
* Initialize Variables
HANDLE = 0                  && DOS File Handle
SUCCESS = 0                 && Number of Bytes Read
SOMESTR = space(10)         && String Holding Data

* Open the file.

HANDLE = fopen("TEMP.TXT", 0)

* Read the file.

SUCCESS = fread(HANDLE, SOMESTR, 10)
```

FReadStr(<nEXP1>, <nEXP2>)

Summer 87, 5.0, 5.01

Use this function to read the contents of a file. nEXP1 contains the file handle obtained when Clipper opened or created the file. nEXP2 contains the number of bytes to read. Clipper allows the program to read up to 65,535 bytes. This function returns the data read from the file as a string. EXAMPLE:

```
* Initialize Variables
HANDLE = 0                  && DOS File Handle
SOMESTR = space(10)         && String Holding Data

* Open the file.

 HANDLE = fopen("TEMP.TXT", 0)

* Read the file.

SOMESTR = freadstr(HANDLE, 10)
```

FSeek(<nEXP1>, <nEXP2> [, <nEXP3]])

Summer 87, 5.0, 5.01

Use thc FSeek function to move the file pointer of the specified file. nEXP1 contains the file handle obtained when Clipper opened or created the file. nEXP2 contains the number of bytes to move the file pointer. nEXP3 contains the method used to move the file. Clipper uses a default position of the beginning of the file (method 0). Method 1 moves the file pointer from the current cursor position. Method 2 moves the file pointer from the end of the file. This function returns the new file pointer position relative to the beginning of the file. EXAMPLE:

```
* Initialize Variables
HANDLE = 0  && DOS File Handle

* Open the file.

fopen("TEMP.TXT", 0)

* Move the file pointer 12 bytes from the beginning of
* the file.

fseek(HANDLE, 12)
```

FWrite(<nEXP1>, <cEXP> [, <nEXP2>])

Summer 87, 5.0, 5.01

Use this function to write the contents of a string to a file. nEXP1 contains the file handle obtained when Clipper opened or created the file. cEXP contains the name of a variable containing the string to write. nEXP2 contains the number of bytes to write. If the program doesn't include nEXP2, Clipper writes the entire contents of cEXP. This function returns the number of bytes actually written to the file. If the number of bytes written doesn't match the number of bytes requested, it means a file-write error occurred. EXAMPLE:

```
* Initialize Variables
HANDLE = 0                  && DOS File Handle
SUCCESS = 0                 && Number of Bytes Written
SOMESTR = space(1)          && String Holding Data

* Open the file.

HANDLE = fopen("TEMP.TXT", 2)

<PROGRAM STATEMENTS>

* Write the file.

SUCCESS = fwrite(HANDLE, SOMESTR)
```

GetE(<cEXP>)/GetEnv(<cEXP>)

Summer 87, 5.0, 5.01

Version 5.0 changed the syntax of GetE to GetEnv, but you can still use the shortened version.

The GetE( )/GetEnv( ) function retrieves the contents of a DOS environment variable. cEXP contains the name of the environment variable to retrieve. If the variable doesn't exist, Clipper returns a null string. Otherwise, Clipper returns the value of the environment variable. GetEnv( ) is the Clipper version 5.0 form of the command. You can still use the abbreviated form, GetE( ), with this new version. EXAMPLE:

```
SOMESTR = gete("ENV_VAR")
```

HardCr(<cEXP>)

Summer 87, 5.0, 5.01

Use this function to convert the soft carriage returns (ASCII 141) in cEXP with hard carriage returns (ASCII 13). HardCr returns the converted string to a variable without changing cEXP. EXAMPLE:

```
* Remove the soft carriage returns from a memo field.
SOMESTR = hardcr(SOMEMEMO)
```

Header( )

Summer 87, 5.0, 5.01

This function returns the number of bytes in the header of the database in the current work area. If Header returns zero, the current work area does not contain an open database. EXAMPLE:

```
HDR_LENGTH = header()
```

I2Bin(<nEXP>)

Summer 87, 5.0, 5.01

I2Bin converts a Clipper integer to standard binary 16-bit integer format. This function places the results in a string for use with one of the file functions. EXAMPLE:

```
* Initialize Variables
HANDLE = 0                  && DOS File Handle
SUCCESS = 0                 && Number of Bytes Written
SOMESTR = space(2)          && String Holding Data

* Open the file.

HANDLE = fopen("TEMP.TXT", 2)

<PROGRAM STATEMENTS>

* Write the file.

SOMESTR = i2bin(12)
SUCCESS = fwrite(HANDLE, SOMESTR)
```

If/IIf(<lEXP>, <xEXP1>, <xEXP2>)

Summer 87, 5.0, 5.01

The If/IIf function conditionally performs one of two options. lEXP contains a conditional statement. If the statement is true, Clipper performs EXP1. Otherwise, Clipper performs EXP2. Both EXP1 and EXP2 usually contain a legal Clipper command or function. EXP1 and EXP2 can optionally contain a string or other Clipper command or function subsection.

Use the If control structure whenever possible in place of Do Case control structure. The If control structure uses an average of four bytes less per condition and incurs no penalty in execution speed. However, use the IIf( ) function whenever possible in place of an If control structure using a condition, a single If result, and a single Else result. The IIf( ) function uses 11 less bytes per occurrence. EXAMPLE:

```
@ 01, 01 say iif(file("TEMP.TXT"), "File Found", "File Not Found")
```

IndexExt( )

Summer 87, 5.0, 5.01

This function returns the file extension of the indexes used with the current application. If the file extension is NTX, the application uses Clipper-specific indexes. Otherwise, the application uses dBASE III compatible index files. EXAMPLE:

```
IND_NAME = "INDX" + iif(indexext() = "NTX", "NTX", "NDX")
```

IndexKey(<nEXP>)

Summer 87, 5.0, 5.01

The IndexKey function returns a string containing the key expression used for an index file. nEXP contains the number of the index file key to retrieve in the current work area. Clipper numbers the indexes from 1 to *n* in the order the program opened them. EXAMPLE:

```
SOMESTR = indexkey(1)
```

IndexOrd( )

Summer 87, 5.0, 5.01

This function returns the ordinal number of the controlling index in the current work area. Clipper uses a default of 1 when the program opens the index files. EXAMPLE:

```
SOMENUM = indexord()
```

InKey(<nEXP>])

Summer 87, 5.0, 5.01

InKey creates a wait state until the user presses a key. It then returns the value of the keystroke as an integer. nEXP contains the number of seconds that InKey waits for a keypress. If the time expires before the user presses a key, InKey returns 0. If the program omits nEXP, Clipper waits indefinitely for the keypress. Clipper returns the ASCII value of any characters input by the user. Clipper uses special number values for function keys and control characters. These numbers range from −39 to 386. Appendix A contains a complete listing of the numbers returned for function keys. Appendix B contains a complete ASCII chart. EXAMPLE:

```
@ 01, 01 say "Press any key to continue..."
inkey(5)
```

Int(<nEXP>)

Summer 87, 5.0, 5.01

Use the INT function to convert a real number to an integer. A real number always contains a fractional part, even if it represents a whole number. INT truncates the fractional portion. EXAMPLE:

```
SOMENUM = int(100.00)
```

IsAlpha(<cEXP>)

Summer 87, 5.0, 5.01

Use the IsAlpha function to determine the status of the beginning letter of a character string. If the first character position contains a letter, IsAlpha returns true. cEXP contains the character string to examine. EXAMPLE:

```
@ 01, 01 say "Enter a string: " get SOMESTR
read
if isalpha(SOMESTR)
        <PROGRAM STATEMENTS>
endif
```

IsColor/IsColour( )

Summer 87, 5.0, 5.01

The IsColor function returns true if the computer contains a color graphics card. EXAMPLE:

```
if iscolor()
        set color to B+/G
else
        set color to W/N
endif
```

IsDigit(<cEXP>)

5.0, 5.01

Use the IsDigit( ) function to determine the status of the beginning letter of a character string. If the first character position contains a digit, IsDigit( ) returns true. cEXP contains the character string to examine. EXAMPLE:

```
if isdigit(SOMEVAR)
        ? "Please type a letter."
endif
```

IsLower(<cEXP>)

Summer 87, 5.0, 5.01

Use the IsLower function to determine the status of the beginning letter of a character string. If the first character position contains a lowercase letter, IsLower returns true. cEXP contains the character string to examine. EXAMPLE:

```
@ 01, 01 say "Enter a string: " get SOMESTR
read
if islower(SOMESTR)
     <PROGRAM STATEMENTS>
endif
```

IsPrinter( )

Summer 87, 5.0, 5.01

Use this function to determine the status of LPT1. IsPrinter returns true if LPT1 is ready for printing. EXAMPLE:

```
<PRINT STATEMENTS>
do while .not. isprinter()
     @ 01, 01 say "Printer Not Ready!"
enddo
<PRINT STATEMENTS>
```

IsUpper(<cEXP>)

Summer 87, 5.0, 5.01

Use the IsUpper function to determine the status of the beginning letter of a character string. If the first character position contains an uppercase letter, IsUpper returns true. cEXP contains the character string to examine. EXAMPLE:

```
@ 01, 01 say "Enter a string: " get SOMESTR
read
if isupper(SOMESTR)
     <PROGRAM STATEMENTS>
endif
```

L2Bin(<nEXP>)

Summer 87, 5.0, 5.01

L2Bin converts a Clipper integer to standard binary 32-bit integer format. This function places the results in a string for use with one of the file functions. EXAMPLE:

```
* Initialize Variables
HANDLE = 0               && DOS File Handle
SUCCESS = 0              && Number of Bytes Written
SOMESTR = space(4)       && String Holding Data
```

```
* Open the file.

HANDLE = fopen("TEMP.TXT", 2)

<PROGRAM STATEMENTS>

* Write the file.

SOMESTR = l2bin(12)
SUCCESS = fwrite(HANDLE, SOMESTR)
```

LastKey( )

Summer 87, 5.0, 5.01

Use this function to retrieve the last character fetched from the keyboard buffer. Clipper returns the ASCII value of any characters input by the user. Clipper uses special number values for function keys and control characters that range from −39 to 386. Appendix A contains a complete listing of the numbers returned for function keys, and appendix B contains a complete ASCII chart. EXAMPLE:

```
if lastkey() = 27 && Escape
      quit
endif
```

LastRec/Reccount( )

Summer 87, 5.0, 5.01

This function obtains the total number of records in the database in the current work area. If the current work area does not contain an open database, this function returns zero.

Use the LastRec( ) function in place of the Count command when you need to know the total number of records in the database. The LastRec( ) function provides almost instantaneous results and uses 35 less bytes per occurrence. EXAMPLE:

```
for COUNT = 1 to lastrec()
      <PROGRAM STATEMENTS>
next
```

Left(<cEXP>, <nEXP>)

Summer 87, 5.0, 5.01

This function returns the number of characters in cEXP specified by nEXP. It begins at the left side of the character string and works right. EXAMPLE:

```
* Display the filename part of a file string.
FILESTR = "SOMENAME.EXT"
DOTPOS = rat(".", FILESTR)
@ 01, 01 say left(FILESTR, DOTPOS - 1)
```

Len(<cEXP>/<aEXP>)

Summer 87, 5.0, 5.01

This function returns the number of characters in cEXP or aEXP. EXAMPLE:

```
* Display the filename part of a file string.
FILESTR = "SOMENAME.EXT"
EXTSTART = len(FILESTR) - rat(".", FILESTR)
@ 01, 01 say right(FILESTR, EXTSTART)
```

Log(<nEXP>)

Summer 87, 5.0, 5.01

The Log function calculates the natural logarithm of nEXP. Use this function to calculate $e^x = y$, where e is the natural logarithm, x is the exponent, and y is the numeric equivalent. nEXP contains y. Log performs the inverse task of the EXP function. EXAMPLE:

```
* Compute the time required to accrue an amount
* given a specific investment at a continuously
* compounded interest rate.
TIME = log(END_AMT / PRINCIPLE) / INT_RATE
```

Lower(<cEXP>)

Summer 87, 5.0, 5.01

This function converts the characters in cEXP to lowercase. EXAMPLE:

```
@ 01, 01 get SOMESTR
read
SOMESTR = lower(SOMESTR)
```

LTrim(<cEXP>)

Summer 87, 5.0, 5.01

This function removes the leading spaces from cEXP. EXAMPLE:

```
@ 01, 01 say ltrim(SOMESTR)
```

LUpdate( )

Summer 87, 5.0, 5.01

LUpdate returns the date that a program modified and closed the database in the current work area. If the current work area doesn't contain an open database, LUpdate returns a blank date. EXAMPLE:

```
if lupdate() < date()
      @ 01, 01 say "Database not modified today."
endif
```

Max(<nEXP1>/<dEXP1>, <nEXP2>/<dEXP2>)

Summer 87, 5.0, 5.01

Use this function to determine the larger of two numeric or date expressions. Both expressions must contain the same type information. This expression returns the larger value instead of a logical expression. EXAMPLE:

```
@ 01, 01 say max(SOMENUM, OTHNUM)
```

MaxCol( )

5.0, 5.01

This function returns the maximum screen column for the current display adapter mode. Clipper begins all screen numbers with zero. EXAMPLE:

```
SOMEVAR = maxcol()
```

MaxRow( )

5.0, 5.01

This function returns the maximum screen row for the current display adapter mode. Clipper begins all screen numbers with zero. EXAMPLE:

```
SOMEVAR = maxrow()
```

MemoEdit([<cEXP1>] [, <nEXP1>] [, <nEXP2>] [, <nEXP3>] [, <nEXP4>] [, <lEXP1>] [, <cEXP2>] [, <nEXP5>] [, <nEXP6>] [, <nEXP7>] [, <nEXP8>] [, <nEXP9>] [, <nEXP10>])

Summer 87, 5.0, 5.01

Version 5.0 added a new header file, MEMOEDIT.CH, to make MemoEdit( ) more readable. In addition, it changed the manner in which soft carriage returns were added to text. Instead of replacing spaces in the text with the soft carriage returns, 5.0 adds them without modifying the text. The same principle applies when a program changes the width of the display area. The old soft carriage returns are no longer replaced with spaces. This has the effect of implanting the soft carriage returns without modifying the text.

MemoEdit provides the means for creating a full-screen editing facility for memo fields and strings within a program. Unlike the AChoice function, the program can execute this function without specifying any parameters. However, the program must open a database containing a memo field before using this function. cEXP1 contains the name of the memo field or string to edit or display. nEXP1 contains the top row offset. nEXP2 contains the left column offset. nEXP3 contains the bottom row offset. nEXP4 contains the right column offset. If the program doesn't specify the screen coordinates, Clipper uses a default of the entire screen.

lEXP1 determines if Clipper displays the memo field or opens it for editing. Clipper uses a default state of true (edit mode). cEXP2 contains the name of a user-defined function (UDF). Clipper executes the UDF whenever an undefined condition exists. TABLE 2-10 contains a listing of memo field configurable and nonconfigurable keys, and TABLE 2-11 contains a listing of UDF status messages. TABLE 2-12 contains a listing of UDF request messages.

Table 2-10 Standard memo field and string edit keys

Key	With UDF	Without UDF (normal)
Up arrow	Same as normal	Moves cursor up one line.
Down arrow or Ctrl-X	Same as normal	Moves cursor down one line.
Left arrow or Ctrl-S	Same as normal	Moves cursor left one character.
Right arrow or Ctrl-D	Same as normal	Moves cursor right one character.
Ctrl-left arrow or Ctrl-A	Same as normal	Moves cursor left one word.
Ctrl-right arrow or Ctrl-F	Same as normal	Moves cursor right one word.
Home	Same as normal	Moves cursor to the beginning of the current line.

Table 2-10 Continued.

Key	With UDF	Without UDF (normal)
End	Same as normal	Moves cursor to the end of the current line.
Ctrl-Home	Same as normal	Moves the cursor to the first character in the current window.
Ctrl-End	Same as normal	Moves the cursor to the last character in the current window.
PgUp	Same as normal	Moves the cursor up one edit screen.
PgDn	Same as normal	Moves the cursor down one edit screen
Ctrl-PgUp	Same as normal	Moves the cursor to the beginning of the memo field or string.
Ctrl-PgDn	Same as normal	Moves the cursor to the end of the memo field or string.
Return	Same as normal	Moves the cursor to the beginning of the next line.
Delete	Same as normal	Removes the character under the cursor.
Backspace	Same as normal	Removes the character to the left of the cursor.
Tab	Same as normal	Inserts a tab is EXPN6 defined. Otherwise, insert four spaces.
Any printable character	Same as normal	Inserts the requested character.

Key	With UDF	Without UDF (normal)
Ctrl-Y	Definable as part of UDF	Deletes the current line.
Ctrl-T	Definable as part of UDF	Delete the word to the right of the current cursor position.
Ctrl-B	Definable as part of UDF	Reformats the paragraph to conform to formatting parameters.
Ctrl-V or Ins	Definable as part of UDF	Toggles insert/overwrite mode.
Ctrl-W	Definable as part of UDF	Ends the current editing session. Save all changes.
Esc	Definable as part of UDF	Terminates the memo field or string edit. Removes any edits made to the memo field or string.

Table 2-11 UDF status messages for memo field and string edit

Mode	Description
0	No undefined user action since the last call.
1	User pressed a reconfigurable or undefined key. Memo field or string unaltered.
2	User pressed a reconfigurable or undefined key. Memo field or string altered.
3	Startup

Table 2-12 UDF request messages for memo field and string edit

Return value	Description
0	Perform default edit action.
1 - 31	Perform the default action for the requested ASCII key value. For example, 13 equals Return and 27 equals Escape.
32	Ignore the keypress.
33	Process the control key (ASCII values 1 to 31) as data entry.
34	Toggle word wrap
35	Toggle scroll state
100	Resolve a key value collision. If the control key was 2, reformat the document. Otherwise, move the cursor to the next word.
101	Resolve a key value collision. If the control key was 23, save the document and exit. Otherwise, move the cursor to the last character in the window (bottom right of display).

nEXP5 contains the line length. If nEXP5 is greater than nEXP4 – nEXP2, then Clipper scrolls the screen horizontally. nEXP6 contains the tab width. If a program specifies a tab width, Clipper uses real tabs within the string or memo field. Otherwise, Clipper uses spaces to simulate tabs. nEXP7 contains initial cursor line. Clipper uses a default of one. nEXP8 contains the initial cursor column. Clipper uses a default of one. nEXP9 contains the initial cursor row relative to the top of the window. The default is zero. nEXP10 contains the initial cursor column relative to the left side of the window. The default is zero. EXAMPLE:

```
* Get the display ready.

clear screen

* Get the parameter count, then the parameters.

parameters DATAFILE                        && DBF File to Read
NUMPARM = pcount()
```

```
if NUMPARM = 0
      ? chr(7) + "Specify a database name."
      quit
endif

* Check if the database exists, then open it.

DATAFILE = DATAFILE + ".DBF"
if file(DATAFILE)
      use &DATAFILE
endif

* Initialize Variables

COUNT1 = 0                                      && Loop Count Holder
COUNT2 = 1                                      && Loop Count Holder
COUNT3 = 0                                      && Number of Fields
SELECT = 0                                      && User Memo Field Selection
MEMONAME = space(10)                            && Edited Memo Field
CHNGSTR = space(10)                             && Changed Memo Field

* Create an array to hold all the memo field names.

declare FIELDN[fcount()]
declare FIELDT[fcount()]

* Initialize the arrays and remove non-memo fields.

afields(FIELDN, FIELDT)
COUNT3 = fcount()
for COUNT1 = 1 to COUNT3
      if FIELDT[COUNT2] <> "M"
            adel(FIELDN, COUNT2)
            adel(FIELDT, COUNT2)
      else
            COUNT2 = COUNT2 + 1
      endif
next

* Check the number of memo fields.

if (COUNT2 = 1)

      ? chr(7) + "No memo fields in database."
      quit
endif

* Display the memo fields and ask the user to select one.

@ 01, 00 to 24, 79 double
@ 08, 33 to 18, 47 double
@ 20, 18 say 'Please select one of the memo fields to edit.'
SELECT = achoice(09, 35, 15, 45, FIELDN)

* Edit the Memo Field.
```

```
@ 23, 22 say "Press F10 to Save Document and Exit."
MEMONAME = "A->" + FIELDN[SELECT]
CHNGSTR = memoedit(&MEMONAME, 02, 01, 21, 78, .T., "MEMOKEY")
replace &MEMONAME with CHNGSTR

* Exit to DOS.

clear screen
quit

* User Defined Function for Database Edit Control

function MEMOKEY
parameters STATUS, LINE, COLUMN

* Initialize Variables.

RET_CODE = 0                          && UDF Action Request Message

* Check status and take appropriate action.
* RET_CODE contains correct value for start-up and idle.

if (STATUS = 1) .or. (STATUS = 2)
     do case
          case lastkey() = 12        && Form Feed
               RET_CODE = 33
          case lastkey() = 14        && Shift Out, Expanded Print
               RET_CODE = 33
          case lastkey() = 15        && Shift In, Compressed Print
               RET_CODE = 33
          case lastkey() = 18        && DC2, Compressed Print Off
               RET_CODE = 33
          case lastkey() = 20        && DC4, Expanded Print Off
               RET_CODE = 33
          case lastkey() = -9        && F10
               RET_CODE = 23         && Ctrl-W, Save and Exit
          otherwise
               RET_CODE = 0
     endcase
endif

return RET_CODE
```

MemoLine(<cEXP> [, <nEXP1>] [, <nEXP2>] [, <nEXP3>] [, <lEXP>])

Summer 87, 5.0, 5.01

The MemoLine function returns a formatted line of text from a memo field or character string. cEXP is the memo field or character string to extract the string from. nEXP1 is the number of characters per line to use in the output string. Clipper uses a default of 79 characters and allows a maximum of 254 characters per line. nEXP2 contains the line number to extract. Clipper assumes a default of one if the program omits this argument. nEXP3 contains the tab size. Clipper uses a default of four. If the tab size is equal to or greater than nEXP1, Clipper uses a value of nEXP1 – 1. lEXP toggles word wrap on when true, and off when false. Clipper uses a default of true. EXAMPLE:

```
SOMESTR = memoline(MEMOFLD, 102)
```

MemoRead(<cEXP>)

Summer 87, 5.0, 5.01

Use this command to import text files stored on disk. cEXP contains the name of the text file to import. Clipper allows a maximum file import size of 65,353 characters (64Kb). EXAMPLE:

```
* Get a text file from disk and store it in a memo field.
SOMESTR = memoread("TEST.TXT")
replace MEMOFLD with SOMESTR
```

Memory(<nEXP>)

Summer 87, 5.0, 5.01

The 1 and 2 arguments were added with Clipper 5.0. When using the Summer 87 version of Clipper, this function determines the amount of free character memory in kilobytes. Because DOS fragments memory as a program allocates and deallocates it, this memory estimate does not represent contiguous memory space. As a result, some memory allocations might fail even if DOS reports that enough memory exists to make the allocation. You must pass a zero as a parameter.

Clipper 5.0 adds two new arguments. The 1 argument returns the largest available block of memory for character values. This represents the maximum amount of memory you can allocate for any given function. The 2 argument returns the largest block of memory available for Run commands. If a program requires more than the available memory, then you cannot run it from within Clipper. EXAMPLE:

```
SOMENUM = memory(0)
```

MemoTran(<cEXP1> [, <cEXP2> [, <cEXP3>]])

Summer 87, 5.0, 5.01

Use the MemoTran function to replace the hard and soft carriage returns in a character string or memo field with other characters. cEXP1 contains the name of the character string or memo field to perform the replacement on. cEXP2 contains the character you want Clipper to replace the hard carriage returns with. Clipper automatically uses semicolons. cEXP3 contains the character you want Clipper to replace the soft carriage returns with. Clipper automatically uses spaces. In all cases Clipper automatically removes all linefeeds. EXAMPLE:

```
SOMESTR = memoline(MEMOFLD, 102)
UNFORMAT = memotran(SOMESTR, " ", " ")
```

MemoWrit(<cEXP1>, <cEXP2>)

Summer 87, 5.0, 5.01

Use the MemoWrit function to export a memo field or character string to an ASCII text file. cEXP1 contains the name of the disk file. cEXP2 contains the name of the memo field or character string. EXAMPLE:

```
memowrit("TEST.TXT", SOMESTR)
```

Min(<nEXP1>/<dEXP1>, <nEXP2>/<dEXP2>)

Summer 87, 5.0, 5.01

Use this function to determine the smaller of two numeric or date expressions. Both expressions must contain the same type information. This expression returns the smaller value instead of a logical expression. EXAMPLE:

```
@ 01, 01 say min(SOMENUM, OTHNUM)
```

MLCount(<cEXP> [, <nEXP1>] [, <nEXP2>] [, <lEXP>])

Summer 87, 5.0, 5.01

Use MLCount to obtain the number of word-wrapped lines in a character string or a memo field. cEXP contains the name of the memo field or character string to analyze. nEXP1 contains the number of characters per line. Clipper uses a default of 79 characters per line. nEXP2 is the tab size. Clipper uses a default of four. lEXP toggles word wrap on and off. Clipper uses a default of true (word wrap on). EXAMPLE:

```
COUNT = mlcount(SOMEMEMO, 102)
for LOOPVAR = 1 to COUNT
      @ row() + 1, 01 say memoline(SOMEMEMO, 102, LOOPVAR)
next
```

MLCToPos(<cEXP>, <nEXP1>, <nEXP2>, <nEXP3>, [, <nEXP4>] [, <lEXP>])

5.01

This function returns the byte position of a line and column within a memo field or other formatted text. It is used mainly within memo field search functions. cEXP contains the text string you want to check. This can be a string or memo field. nEXP1 contains the formatted width of the field. nEXP2 contains the line you want to check. The first line in the field begins at one. nEXP3 contains the column position you want to check. The first column begins at zero. nEXP4 is an optional parameter that specifies the tab width. If you don't supply a tab width, Clipper uses a default of four. lEXP is an optional parameter that turns word wrap on or off. Clipper uses a default of on (true). EXAMPLE:

```
cString := "Hello World."
// Returns a value of 10.
? mlctopos(cString, 6, 2, 3)
```

MLPos(<cEXP>, <nEXP1>, <nEXP2> [, <nEXP3>] [, <lEXP>])

Summer 87, 5.0, 5.01

Use this function to determine the character position of a numbered line in a memo field or character string. cEXP contains the name of the memo field or character string to analyze. nEXP1 contains the number of characters per line. Clipper normally uses a default of 79 characters per line. Unlike other memo commands, this command requires a characters-per-line argument. nEXP2 contains the line number to search for. If the memo field or character string doesn't contain the required number of lines, Clipper returns the memo field length. nEXP3 is the tab size. Clipper uses a default of four. lEXP toggles word wrap on and off. Clipper uses a default of true (word wrap on). EXAMPLE:

```
SOMENUM = mlpos(SOMEMEMO, 102, 14)
```

MLPosToLC(<cEXP>, <nEXP1>, <nEXP2>, [, <nEXP3>] [, <lEXP>])

5.01

This function returns the line and column value of a byte position within a memo field or other formatted text. It is used mainly within memo field search functions. The value is returned as a two-element array. The line value appears first and the column value second. cEXP contains the text string you want to check. This can be a string or memo field. nEXP1 contains the formatted width of the field. nEXP2 contains the byte position you want to check. The byte positions begin with one. nEXP3 is an optional parameter that specifies the tab width. If you don't supply a tab width, Clipper uses a default of four. lEXP is an optional parameter that turns word wrap on or off. Clipper uses a default of on (true). EXAMPLE:

```
cString := "Hello World."
// Returns a value of {2, 3}.
aPosit := mpostolc(cString, 6, 10)
```

Mod(<nEXP1>, <nEXP2>)

5.0, 5.01

Use this function to determine the modulo (remainder) of two numbers. nEXP1 contains the dividend. nEXP2 contains the divisor. This is a compatibility function for dBASE III. Use the Clipper modulus function (%) whenever possible. EXAMPLE:

```
* The following example returns 1.
SOMEVAR = mod(4, 3)
```

Month(<dEXP>)

Summer 87, 5.0, 5.01

The Month function converts a date to a number containing the month. dEXP contains the date to convert. A null date value returns 0. EXAMPLE:

```
SOMESTR = month(date())
```

NetErr([<nEXP>])

Summer 87, 5.0, 5.01

Version 5.01 adds the ability to set the network errorlevel by providing a value for the optional nEXP parameter.

NetErr returns true if one or more network specific commands fail. Network commands include Use, Use...Exclusive, and Append Blank. The Use and Use...Exclusive commands fail if another user opens the database for exclusive use. The Append Blank command fails if another user has a file lock on the current file or a record lock on last record + 1 (end of file). EXAMPLE:

```
* Add a new record.
append blank
do while neterr()
       @ 01, 01 say "Record Add Failed. Try Again? " get SOMESTR
       read
       if SOMESTR = "Y"
              append blank
       else
              exit
       endif
enddo
```

NetName( )

Summer 87, 5.0, 5.01

This function returns the name of the current workstation. If the workstation is not operating under the IBM-PC Network, this function returns a null string. EXAMPLE:

```
* Obtain the network name for the current workstation.
SOMESTR = netname()
```

NextKey( )

Summer 87, 5.0, 5.01

The NextKey function reads the first character in the keyboard buffer without removing it. NextKey returns the ASCII value of the character. Clipper uses special number values for function keys and control characters. These numbers range from –39 to 386. Appendix A contains a complete listing of the numbers returned for function keys. Appendix B contains a complete ASCII chart. EXAMPLE:

```
SOMESTR = nextkey()
```

OS( )

5.0, 5.01

OS( ) was changed in version 5.01 to return the real value of the operating system version number rather than a constant.

This function returns the name of the current operating system as a string. The string includes the operating system version number. OS allows you to determine the availability of certain operating-specific features. EXAMPLE:

```
SOMESTR = os()
```

PadC(<xEXP>, <nEXP> [, <cEXP>]) PadL(<xEXP>, <nEXP> [, <cEXP>]) PadR(<xEXP>, <nEXP> [, <cEXP>])

5.0, 5.01

All three of these functions add to the length of a character, date, or numeric expression. PadC centers the expression within a given length. PadR adds to the right side of the expression. PadL adds to the left side of the expression. EXP contains the expression you want to pad. nEXP contains the new length of the expression. The optional cEXP contains a specific pad character. You can use this with character expressions only. In all cases this function outputs a string. EXAMPLE:

```
* Center a string on the display.
? padc("This is a string", 80)
```

PCol( )

Summer 87, 5.0, 5.01

This function returns the current printer column. The Eject command resets PCol to 0. EXAMPLE:

```
@ prow(), pcol() say SOMESTR
```

PCount( )

Summer 87, 5.0, 5.01

The PCount function returns the number of parameters sent by a calling function or procedure. This includes any parameters sent to the main procedure from the DOS command line on program startup. EXAMPLE:

```
if pcount() < 2
      @ 01, 01 say "Not Enough Parameters Specified!"
      @ 02, 01 say "Use SOMECOM PARAM1 PARAM2"
      quit
endif
```

ProcLine([<nEXP>])

Summer 87, 5.0, 5.01

Starting with version 5.0, ProcLine( ) accepts a modifier, nEXP, that determines which activation it returns the procedure line number from. It defaults to a value of zero, or the current activation.

This function returns the current procedure line number. Clipper counts line numbers starting from the beginning of the file, not the beginning of the procedure. EXAMPLE:

```
@ 01, 01 say procline() + " " + procname()
```

ProcName([<nEXP>])

Summer 87, 5.0, 5.01

Starting with version 5.0, ProcName( ) accepts a modifier, nEXP, that determines which activation it returns the procedure line number from. It defaults to a value of zero, or the current activation.

This function returns the current procedure name. If the current procedure is the main procedure for a file, Clipper returns the filename. EXAMPLE:

```
@ 01, 01 say procline() + " " + procname()
```

PRow( )

Summer 87, 5.0, 5.01

This function returns the current printer row. The Eject command resets PRow to 0. EXAMPLE:

```
@ prow(), pcol() say SOMESTR
```

QOut([<xEXP>]) QQOut([<xEXP>])

5.0, 5.01

These functions act similar to the ? and ?? commands. QOut sends EXP to the display then places the cursor at the beginning of the next row. QQOut sends EXP to the display without updating either row or column position. The cursor remains at the space following the final character in the output. The difference between these functions and the ? and ?? commands is that you can use QOut and QQOut within code blocks and other expressions. EXAMPLE:

```
eval({iif(SOMENUM>0, QOut("Greater than zero."),;
QOut("Less than or equal to zero."))})
```

Rat(<cEXP1>,<cEXP2>)

Summer 87, 5.0, 5.01

This function returns the last instance of cEXP1 in cEXP2. It begins at the right side of the character string and works left. EXAMPLE:

```
* Display the filename part of a file string.
FILESTR = "SOMENAME.EXT"
DOTPOS = rat(".", FILESTR)
@ 01, 01 say left(FILESTR, DOTPOS - 1)
```

ReadExit([<lEXP>])

Summer 87, 5.0, 5.01

This function toggles use of the up and down arrows as read-exit keys. The optional lEXP contains true (.T.) to activate the up and down arrow keys, or false (.F.) to deactivate them. Clipper uses a default of false. ReadExit returns the current read-exit state. EXAMPLE:

```
* Force the user into entering some data.
readexit(.F.)
@ 01, 01 say "Enter your name: " get SOMESTR
read
```

ReadKey( )

5.0, 5.01

Use the ReadKey( ) function to determine which key the user pressed to exit a read. TABLE 2-13 shows the code returned for various keypresses. Nantucket provided this function for compatibility with dBASE III Plus. Use the LastKey( ) function whenever possible. EXAMPLE:

```
SOMEVAR = readkey()
```

Table 2-13 ReadKey( ) return values

Key	Return value
Ctrl-End	14
Ctrl-PgDn	30
Ctrl-PgUp	31
Ctrl-W	14
Down arrow	2
Esc	12
PgDn	7
PgUp	6
Return	15
Type past end	15
Up arrow	5

ReadInsert([<lEXP>])

Summer 87, 5.0, 5.01

This function toggles the insert state for the Read and MemoEdit( ) commands. The optional lEXP contains true to activate insert or false to deactivate insert. Clipper uses a default state of false. READINSERT returns the current insert state. EXAMPLE:

```
ISINSERT = readinsert()
```

ReadVar( )

Summer 87, 5.0, 5.01

This function returns the current variable name. This function works with the Get and Menu commands only. Clipper returns a null string for an Accept, Input, or Wait command, or a DBEdit, AChoice, MemoEdit, or ReadVar function. EXAMPLE:

```
if readvar() = "SOMESTR"
     @ 01, 01 say "Enter a string."
endif
```

RecNo( )

Summer 87, 5.0, 5.01

Use this function to obtain the current record number. EXAMPLE:

```
@ 01, 01 say recno()
```

RecSize( )

Summer 87, 5.0, 5.01

Use this function to obtain the current record length. EXAMPLE:

```
@ 01, 01 say recsize()
```

Replicate(<cEXP>, <nEXP>)

Summer 87, 5.0, 5.01

The Replicate function returns a character string, cEXP, repeated nEXP times. Always use the Space function in place of the Replicate function to create sequences of blanks. The Space function provides less flexibility, but requires four bytes less per occurrence and executes 3% faster. EXAMPLE:

```
* Create a rectangle of asterisks
? replicate("*", 20)
? replicate("*"+replicate(" ", 18)+"*"+chr(13)+chr(10), 17)
? "*"+replicate(" ", 18)+"*"
? replicate("*", 20)
```

RestScreen(<nEXP1>, <nEXP2>, <nEXP3>, <nEXP4>, <cEXP>)

Summer 87, 5.0, 5.01

Starting with version 5.0, RestScreen( ) returns a value of NIL instead of nothing.

RestScreen restores a previously saved display to the screen. nEXP1 contains the top row offset. nEXP2 contains the left column offset. nEXP3 contains the bottom row offset. nEXP4 contains the right column offset. cEXP contains the name of the screen variable to restore.

Always use the Restore Screen command in place of the RestScreen( ) function. The RestScreen( ) function requires 51 bytes more memory per occurrence. In addition the RestScreen( ) function requires EXTEND library, which consumes another 82Kb. Finally, the RestScreen( ) function executes 19% more slowly than this command. However, the RestScreen( ) function does provide more flexibility than the Restore Screen command. EXAMPLE:

```
SOMEVAR = savescreen(00, 00, 23, 79)
do SOMEPROC
restscreen (00, 00, 23, 79, SOMEVAR)
```

Right(<cEXP>, <nEXP>)

Summer 87, 5.0, 5.01

Version 5.0 of Clipper would not allow you to use Right( ) within macro expression or in indexes. The only way to correct this situation was to create a Right( ) function, compile it with the /N parameter, and link it with your program. This problem has been fixed in version 5.01.

This function returns the number of characters in cEXP specified by nEXP. It begins at the right side of the character string and works left. EXAMPLE:

```
* Display the filename part of a file string.
FILESTR = "SOMENAME.EXT"
EXTSTART = len(FILESTR) - rat(".", FILESTR)
@ 01, 01 say right(FILESTR, EXTSTART)
```

RLock/Lock( )

Summer 87, 5.0, 5.01

Use this function to lock a single record in a database. This allows a program to perform tasks that require use of only one record in the database. RLock returns true when the database record lock becomes successful. EXAMPLE:

```
do while .not. rlock()
     @ 01, 01 say "Locking Record. Press any key to exit."
     SOMEVAR = inkey(2)
     if SOMEVAR <> 0
          exit
     endif
enddo
```

Round(<nEXP1>, <nEXP2>)

Summer 87, 5.0, 5.01

This function rounds variable nEXP1 to the number of decimal places specified by nEXP2. If nEXP2 is greater than zero, Clipper rounds the specified number of places before the decimal point. If nEXP2 is less than zero, Clipper rounds the specified number of places after the decimal point. If the rounded portion of the input value is greater than five, then Clipper adds one to the result. EXAMPLE:

```
* Round to the nearest whole number.
NEWNUM = round(SOMENUM, 0)
```

Row( )

Summer 87, 5.0, 5.01

The Row function returns the row position of the cursor. EXAMPLE:

```
* Create a generic display routine.
@ row()+1, 00 say VAL1        && Appears at next row, column 0.
@ row(), col()+5 say VAL2     && Appears 5 characters after entry.
```

SaveScreen(<nEXP1>, <nEXP2>, <nEXP3>, <nEXP4>)

Summer 87, 5.0, 5.01

SaveScreen saves the specified screen portion to a variable. nEXP1 contains the top row offset. nEXP2 contains the left column offset. nEXP3 contains the bottom row offset. nEXP4 contains the right column offset.

Always use the Save Screen command in place of the SaveScreen( ) function. The SaveScreen( ) function requires 50 bytes more memory per occurrence. In addition the SaveScreen( ) function requires EXTEND library, which consumes another 82 kilobytes. Finally, the SaveScreen( ) function executes 16% more slowly than this command. However, the SaveScreen( ) function does provide more flexibility than the Save Screen command. EXAMPLE:

```
SOMEVAR = savescreen(00, 00, 23, 79)
do SOMEPROC
restscreen (00, 00, 23, 79, SOMEVAR)
```

Scroll(<nEXP1>, <nEXP2>, <nEXP3>, <nEXP4>, <nEXP5>)

Summer 87, 5.0, 5.01

Starting with version 5.0, Scroll( ) returns a value of NIL instead of nothing. Version 5.01 added the capability of using Scroll( ) without any parameters. The entire display is the default area and 0 is the default number of rows (the entire display).

Scroll moves a portion of the display up or down. nEXP1 contains the top row offset. nEXP2 contains the left column offset. nEXP3 contains the bottom row offset. nEXP4 contains the right column offset. nEXP5 contains the number of rows to scroll the display portion. If nEXP5 contains a positive number, Clipper scrolls up the specified number of rows. If nEXP5 contains a negative number the display scrolls down. Specifying 0 blanks the specified scroll area. This function does not return a value. EXAMPLE:

```
scroll(01, 01, 20, 15, 5)
```

Seconds( )

Summer 87, 5.0, 5.01

Use this function to obtain the number of seconds elapsed since midnight (12:00 A.M.). EXAMPLE:

```
* Time the user response time.
START = seconds()
@ 01, 01 say "Press any key when ready." get SOMESTR
```

```
read
FINISH = seconds()
TOTAL = FINISH - START
```

Select([<cEXP>])

Summer 87, 5.0, 5.01

This function returns the number of the specified work area. cEXP contains the work area alias. If the program uses Select without specifying cEXP, Clipper returns the number of the current work area. Never confuse this function with the Select command. It does not change the selected work area. EXAMPLE:

```
select 1
? select()
```

Set(<nEXP> [, <xEXP>] [, <lEXP>])

5.0, 5.01

Version 5.01 adds a third parameter to the Set( ) function that performs the tasks described in the following paragraph.

Use this function to inspect or change the value of any of the Set command values listed in TABLE 2-14. Always use the manifest constant located in SET.CH in place of a number for nEXP. Because Nantucket will automatically make the required changes to the header file for each version of the compiler, this eliminates problems of interversion numbering differences. You can optionally place a value in EXP to change the current value of the Set command. TABLE 2-14 lists the types of values expected by each manifest constant.

Version 5.01 adds lEXP, which is used to control how a file is opened for the following three values: _SET_ALTFILE, _SET_PRINTFILE, and _SET_EXTRAFILE. Setting the value to true opens the file in append mode. Setting the value to false opens the file in truncate mode. The Set( ) function assumes a value of false when no value is supplied. In either case, the file is created if it doesn't already exist.

5.01 also adds the _SET_SCROLLBREAK manifest constant. When set to true, this setting interprets the scroll break as a request to pause the display the next time Clipper outputs. When set to false, the setting interprets the keypress as a cursor control key. EXAMPLE:

```
* Get the current margin width.
STATUS = set(_SET_MARGIN)
```

Table 2-14 Set( ) manifest constant values

Constant association	Type	Command/Function
_SET_ALTERNATE	Logical	Set Alternate
_SET_ALTFILE	Character	Set Alternate To
_SET_BELL	Logical	Set Bell
_SET_CANCEL	Logical	SetCancel()
_SET_COLOR	Character	SetColor()
_SET_CONFIRM	Logical	Set Confirm
_SET_CONSOLE	Logical	Set Console
_SET_CURSOR	Numeric	SetCursor()
_SET_DATEFORMAT	Character	Set Date
_SET_DEBUG	Logical	AltD()
_SET_DECIMALS	Numeric	Set Decimals
_SET_DEFAULT	Character	Set Default
_SET_DELETED	Logical	Set Deleted
_SET_DELIMCHARS	Character	Set Delimiters To
_SET_DELIMITERS	Logical	Set Delimiters
_SET_DEVICE	Character	Set Device
_SET_EPOCH	Numeric	Set Epoch
_SET_ESCAPE	Logical	Set Escape
_SET_EXACT	Logical	Set Exact
_SET_EXCLUSIVE	Logical	Set Exclusive
_SET_EXIT	Logical	ReadExit()
_SET_FIXED	Logical	Set Fixed
_SET_INSERT	Logical	Set Insert
_SET_INTENSITY	Logical	Set Intensity
_SET_MARGIN	Numeric	Set Margin
_SET_MCENTER	Logical	Set Message
_SET_MESSAGE	Numeric	Set Message
_SET_PATH	Character	Set Path
_SET_PRINTER	Logical	Set Printer
_SET_PRINTFILE	Character	Set Printer To
_SET_SCOREBOARD	Logical	Set Scoreboard
_SET_SOFTSEEK	Logical	Set Softseek
_SET_SCROLLBREAK*	Logical	N/A
_SET_UNIQUE	Logical	Set Unique
_SET_WRAP	Logical	Set Wrap

* Available with version 5.01 and above.

SetCancel([<lEXP>])

Summer 87, 5.0, 5.01

Version 5.0 added the Ctrl-Break key to the list of keys allowed to terminate program execution. SetCancel( ) controls this ability the same way it controls the Alt-C key.

The SetCancel function changes the status of the Alt-C key. Normally, Alt-C terminates program execution. lEXP contains the status. If the program specifies true, Clipper enables Alt-C. Otherwise, it disables Alt-C. The Set Key command takes precedence over the settings of the Set Function and Set Escape commands, and the SetCancel( ) function. EXAMPLE:

```
* Do not allow the user to exit the program.
setcancel(.F.)
```

SetColor([<cEXP>])

Summer 87, 5.0, 5.01

Use this function to change the colors used by Clipper to present various display elements. cEXP contains a string with the following elements: STANDARD, ENHANCED, BORDER, BACKGROUND, and UNSELECTED. STANDARD contains the color used for all normal text. For example, the output of every @ Say command. ENHANCED contains the color used for all inverted text. For example, the output of the currently selected @ Get command. BORDER contains the color used for the area around the edge of the display. Clipper never places text in this area. No display adapter currently supports the BACKGROUND argument. UNSELECTED contains the color of all unselected inverted text elements, for example, the output of all currently unselected @ Get commands. This function returns the current color selections. If the program doesn't specify cEXP, Clipper won't change the current color selections.

Clipper allows the use of numbers or letters to designate which colors appear on screen. TABLE 1-4 provides a listing of the color numbers and letters. To obtain an intensified color, add 8 to the foreground color. To obtain a blinking color, add 8 to the background color. When using numbers in place of letters, make sure you use character numbers, not actual numbers. EXAMPLE:

```
* Save the current display colors, change the colors to
* display an error message, then change the colors back
* to their original state.
SOMESTR = setcolor("R/W, W/R")
<ERROR STATEMENTS>
setcolor(SOMESTR)
```

SetPRC(<nEXP1>, <nEXP2>)

Summer 87, 5.0, 5.01

Starting with version 5.0, SetPRC( ) returns a value of NIL instead of nothing.

SetPRC changes the current printer row and column returned by the Clipper functions PRow and PCol. It doesn't physically change the print head position. nEXP1 contains the printer row. nEXP2 contains the printer column. This function does not return a value. EXAMPLE:

```
* Set the printer row to 40 and the column to 20.
setprc(40, 20)
```

SetKey(<nEXP> [, <bEXP>])

5.0, 5.01

This function allows you to assign a code block to a particular key. nEXP contains the InKey( ) value of the key. Appendix A contains a complete listing of the numbers for function keys, and appendix B contains a complete ASCII chart. bEXP contains the code you want executed each time the user presses the key. EXAMPLE:

```
* This example shows you how to automatically insert
* the current date in a date field.
#include "INKEY.CH"                          && Key definition file.
setkey(K_F2, {|| outdate() })          && Set F2 to our function.
DATEVAR = ctod("  /  /  ")             && Display a date field.
cls
@ 01, 01 say "Type the date" get DATEVAR picture '@D'
read
return

* This function performs the actual task of placing the
* date in the date field.
function OUTDATE()

CMON = substr(dtoc(date()),1,2)        && Declare the date
CDAY = substr(dtoc(date()),4,2)        && variables.
CYR = substr(dtoc(date()),7,2)

keyboard CMON + CDAY + CYR             && Stuff the keyboard.

return NIL
```

Soundex(<cEXP>)

Summer 87, 5.0, 5.01

This function converts cEXP to its soundex equivalent. *Soundex* is a phonetic method of spelling words so that words with phonetically similar sounds use the same spelling. This allows a database to find all occurrences of a word even if the user inputs an incorrect or incomplete spelling. This function returns a string in the form A9999, where A is the first letter of the word and 9999 is a numeric evaluation of the rest of the word. EXAMPLE:

```
* Search for a specific name in a database using
* soundex format.
use SOMEDATA
index on soundex(SOMEFIELD) to SOMEINDX
@ 01, 01 say "Enter a name: " get SOMESTR
seek soundex(SOMESTR)
```

Space(<nEXP>)

Summer 87, 5.0, 5.01

The Space function returns a sequence of spaces. nEXP determines the number of spaces created. Always use the SPACE function in place of the Replicate function to create sequences of blanks. The Space function provides less flexibility, but requires four bytes less per occurrence and executes 3% faster. EXAMPLE:

```
SOMESTR = space(8)
```

SQRT(<nEXP>)

Summer 87, 5.0, 5.01

The SQRT function returns the square root of nEXP. This function accepts only positive numbers as arguments. EXAMPLE:

```
SOMENUM = sqrt(4)
```

STR(<nEXP1> [, <nEXP2> [, <nEXP3>]])

Summer 87, 5.0, 5.01

The STR function converts a number to a string. nEXP1 contains the number to convert. If the program specifies nEXP1 without nEXP2 or nEXP3, Clipper outputs a standard string. TABLE 2-15 contains the standard character lengths returned. nEXP2 contains the number of places to return. This includes the decimal point. If the program uses STR and specifies nEXP2 without specifying nEXP3, Clipper rounds the number to an integer. nEXP3 contains the number of decimal places. EXAMPLE:

```
@ 01, 01 say "Using Work Area: " ltrim(str(select()))
```

Table 2-15 Standard STR( ) character-return lengths

Expression type	Returned string length
Field	Field length plus decimals
Expressions or constants	10 digits in integer plus decimals
VAL()	3 digits minimum
MONTH()/DAY()	3 digits
YEAR()	5 digits

STRTran(<cEXP1>, <cEXP2> [, <cEXP3>] [, <nEXP1>] [, <nEXP2>])

Summer 87, 5.0, 5.01

The STRTRAN function performs a search and replace within a character string. cEXP1 contains the name of the string to search. cEXP2 contains the characters to search for. cEXP3 contains the search string replacement value. If the program doesn't specify cEXP3, Clipper replaces all occurrences of the search string with a null string. nEXP1 contains the number of the first occurrence to replace. Clipper uses a default of the first occurrence. nEXP2 contains the number of occurrences to replace. Clipper uses a default of all occurrences. STRTran returns a character string with appropriate changes. It doesn't modify the original string. EXAMPLE:

```
* Remove all the asterisks from a character string.
SOMESTR = strtran(OTHSTR, "*")
```

Stuff(<cEXP1>, <nEXP1>, <nEXP2>, <cEXP2>)

Summer 87, 5.0, 5.01

This function performs six different functions on a character string. These functions include: insert, replace, delete, replace and insert, replace and delete, and replace and delete rest. cEXP1 contains the name of the string Clipper uses to perform the desired function. nEXP1 contains the replacement starting position. nEXP2 contains the number of characters to replace. cEXP2 contains the replacement string.

To perform an insert, place the insert starting position in nEXP1. Set nEXP2 to zero. Place the insert string in cEXP2. To perform a replace, set nEXP1 equal to the replace starting position. Set nEXP2 equal to the length of cEXP2. Place the replacement string in cEXP2. To perform a delete, set nEXP1 equal to the delete starting position. Set nEXP2 equal to the number of characters you want deleted. Set cEXP2 equal to "" (null string).

To perform a replace and insert, set nEXP1 equal to the replace starting position. Set nEXP2 equal to the length of the characters you want removed in cEXP1. Place a replacement string longer than nEXP2 in cEXP2. To perform a replace and delete, set nEXP1 equal to the replace starting position. Set nEXP2 equal to the length of the characters you want removed in cEXP1. Place a replacement string shorter than nEXP2 in cEXP2. To perform a replace and delete rest, set nEXP1 equal to the replace starting position. Set nEXP2 equal to one greater than the length of cEXP1. Place a replacement string in cEXP2. EXAMPLE:

```
NEWSTR = stuff(SOMESTR, 5, len(SOMESTR) + 1, "*")
```

SubSTR(<cEXP>, <nEXP1> [, <nEXP2>])

Summer 87, 5.0, 5.01

This function returns a portion of cEXP. nEXP1 contains the starting position. Normally Clipper starts from the left side of the string. However, if the program uses a negative value for nEXP1, Clipper starts returning characters from the right side of the string. nEXP2 contains the number of characters to return. If the program doesn't provide an argument for nEXP2, Clipper returns the rest of the string. EXAMPLE:

```
* Reduces the size of string to 12 characters.
NEWSTR = substr(SOMESTR, 1, 12)
@ 01, 01 say NEWSTR
```

Time( )

Summer 87, 5.0, 5.01

The Time function returns the current system time in the form HH:MM:SS. EXAMPLE:

```
@ 01, 01 say time()
```

Tone(<nEXP1>, <nEXP2>)

Summer 87, 5.0, 5 01

Starting with version 5.0, Tone( ) returns a value of NIL instead of nothing.

This function produces a tone for a specified duration. nEXP1 contains the frequency of the tone. nEXP2 contains the duration of the tone in increments of 1/18 second. To produce a tone one second long, specify a value of 18. To calculate the value of specific notes, use the following equation: 61.73541 × (1.059463^NOTEVALUE), where NOTEVALUE = 25 for middle C and 26 for C sharp. EXAMPLE:

```
* Play notes until the user presses Q.
NOTE = 25
do while .not. NOTE = 39
```

```
        NOTE = inkey(1) - 42
        tone (61.73541 * (1.059463 ^ NOTE), 9)
enddo
quit
```

Transform(<xEXP>, <cEXP>)

Summer 87, 5.0, 5.01

Use this function to format the results of any expression of any data type. EXP contains the expression to format. cEXP contains a string for formatting EXP. TABLE 1-2 contains a complete description of the format functions and templates. This function returns a formatted character string. EXAMPLE:

```
* Convert the string to uppercase.
SOMESTR = transform(SOMEVAR, "@!")
```

Trim/RTrim(<cEXP>)

Summer 87, 5.0, 5.01

This function removes the trailing spaces from cEXP. EXAMPLE:

```
@ 01, 01 say rtrim(SOMESTR)
```

Type(<cEXP>)

Summer 87, 5.0, 5.01

5.0 expanded the number of types returned by Type( ) to handle the new data types. You must use the ValType( ) function to determine the type of static and local variable.

This function returns the type of an expression. cEXP contains the name of the expression to evaluate. TABLE 2-16 contains a listing of all the data types supported by Clipper. This function returns a letter representing the data type. You cannot use Type( ) on static and local variables. EXAMPLE:

```
if type(SOMEVAR) = "U"
      @ 01, 01 say "Error, Incorrect Input"
endif
```

Updated( )

Summer 87, 5.0, 5.01

This function returns true if the user made any changes in any of the pending gets during the last read. EXAMPLE:

```
if updated()
      do DATA_UPDATE
endif
```

Upper(<cEXP>)

Summer 87, 5.0, 5.01

This function converts the characters in cEXP to uppercase. EXAMPLE:

```
@ 01, 01 get SOMESTR
read
SOMESTR = upper(SOMESTR)
```

Used( )

Summer 87, 5.0, 5.01

Use this function to determine if the current work area contains an open database. EXAMPLE:

```
if used()
      SOMESTR = alias()
endif
```

Val(<cEXP>)

Summer 87, 5.0, 5.01

Use the Val function to convert the numbers in a character string to a number. cEXP contains the character string to convert. Val continues to convert the character string until it reaches a nonnumeric character or it converts the entire string. EXAMPLE:

```
SOMENUM = val(SOMESTR)
```

ValType(<cEXP>)

5.0, 5.01

This function returns the type of an expression. cEXP contains the name of the expression to evaluate. TABLE 2-16 contains a listing of all the data types supported by Clipper. This function returns a letter representing the data type. The ValType( ) function differs from the Type( ) function by the method used to evaluate an expression. ValType( ) evaluates the actual expression, while Type( ) uses the macro (&) operator to evaluate its expression. You can use ValType( ) on static and local variables. EXAMPLE:

```
static SOMEVAR = "Character"
VARTYPE = valtype(SOMEVAR)    && Returns C.
```

Version( )

5.0, 5.01

This function returns the version number of the Clipper EXTEND.LIB as a character string. This allows you to determine if specific features are available with the user's version of the Clipper compiler. EXAMPLE:

```
SOMENUM = version()
```

Table 2-16 Clipper data types

Data type letter	Represents
A	Array
B*	Code block
C	Character
D	Date
L	Logical
M	Memo field
N	Numeric
O*	Object
U	Undefined, local/static variables*, NIL*
UE	Error in syntax
UI	Error indeterminate

* Available in versions 5.0 and above only.

Word(<nEXP>)

Summer 87, 5.0, 5.01

Starting with version 5.0, Word( ) returns a value of NIL instead of nothing. This function is supplied for compatibility purposes only.

The Word function converts a number from Double format to Int. The number cannot exceed the range of −32,767 to 32,767. Using this function reduces Clipper overhead in calling external routines. EXAMPLE:

```
call SOMEROUT with word(500)
```

Year(<dEXP>)

Summer 87, 5.0, 5.01

The Year function converts a date to a number containing the year. dEXP contains the date to convert. A null date value returns 0. EXAMPLE:

```
SOMESTR = year(date())
```

3

Preprocessor directives and code blocks

The first section in this chapter describes the preprocessor and compiler directives provided by Clipper. These directives help you communicate your wishes to the preprocessor and therefore the compiler. For example, if you want to include a specific program or header filer, then you would use the #Include directive. This control extends to the definition or redefinition of commands and the creation of manifest variables. A thorough understanding of these directives is required to fully implement the new and enhanced features of Clipper versions 5.0 and 5.01. While you can use the extend system without understanding the preprocessor, you can greatly enhance the functionality of the program by using it to reference external code.

Another feature that is new to Clipper 5.0 and 5.01 is code blocks. The second section of this chapter describes the uses for code blocks and shows you how to create them. Many of the remaining chapters in this book contain detailed examples of how to use code blocks as well. A basic definition for a *code block* is an unnamed assignable function. You assign a code block to a variable and pass it to a function as you would any other variable.

By implementing code blocks correctly, you can create self-modifying code. In essence, the code block that you pass to a function modifies its behavior. You can therefore create functions that are generic in nature, and pass a code block that makes the function specific to the task at hand. This is, in fact, how many of the native functions supplied with Clipper are implemented. The function library supplies a generic function that you modify with a code block. This, in turn, creates a function that's specific to your programming needs. Nantucket also supplies code block-specific functions like Eval( ). In this case, the code block becomes essential to the operation of the program. You cannot safely pass any other variable type to the function and expect it to operate correctly. The second section of this chapter will cover UDFs of this type as well.

Preprocessor directives

The preprocessor looks at your code and translates it into library calls that the compiler can understand. This allows you to use terminology that is fairly easy to understand, while reducing the number of object modules that the library contains. You could look at each Clipper command as a macro that the preprocessor expands. The following sections describe each directive in detail.

There are, however, a few rules that every directive follows. For example, you must precede all preprocessor and compiler directives with the pound sign (#). In addition, some directives use special characters that you must translate directly into your program. For example, the #Command directive uses square brackets ([ ]) to define some clauses. Each description tells you when, where, and how to use the directive. The best place to look for practical examples of these directives is the Clipper header files. However, each of the following descriptions shows a typical example of how to use the directive.

#Command <MATCH PATTERN> = > <RESULT PATTERN>

5.0, 5.1

The #Command directive tells the preprocessor to translate a statement it finds in your source files when that statement matches a predefined pattern. The pattern must form a complete statement. Therefore, use the #Command to translate source code in your program to library calls and compiler commands. A #Command directive takes the following form: MATCH_PATTERN = > RESULT_PATTERN. The = > symbol is a literal part of the entire directive. You must include it for the directive to work properly. #Command directive essentially takes the information in the match pattern and makes it look like the result pattern. This translation process is helpful when you want to make a function easier to use, or if you want to make your commands compatible with a foreign command. (For example, some dBASE III commands don't directly translate into Clipper commands.)

A match pattern describes what the preprocessor should look for when it parses your program. There are different types of match pattern types that perform different tasks. You can use one or more of each type within a single directive. In fact, most commands are a composite of more than one match pattern. TABLE 3-1 lists and describes each type and subtype of match pattern.

Table 3-1 #Command/#Translate directive match pattern types

Type/Subtype	Description
Literal tokens	Characters that appear in the directive. The pre-processor interprets these characters exactly. Literal tokens are case sensitive. If you want to use the angle bracket (<) as a literal token, you must precede it with a backward slash (\). For example, in the directive: #command TEXT TO PRINTER ; => __TextSave("PRINTER") ; ; text QOut, __TextRestore the word PRINTER is a literal value.
Words	Keywords or identifiers that appear in the directive. The pre-processor uses the dBASE convention for comparison purposes (case insensitive, first four letters mandatory, etc.) This is how Clipper differentiates one command or function from another. For example, in the directive: #command TEXT TO PRINTER ; => __TextSave("PRINTER") ; ; text QOut, __TextRestore the words TEXT TO are word match patterns.
Match markers	Names assigned to the text appearing in the match pattern. The form that this name takes depends on the match marker you choose. Clipper uses them to create variable entries. Match markers always follow the Clipper naming convention. You must place all match markers within angle brackets, as shown below.
Regular match marker <ID MARKER>	Matches the next legal expression. This marker does not place any other restriction on the input text. For example, in the directive: #command TEXT TO FILE <(file)> ; => __TextSave(<(file)>) ; ; text QOut, __TextRestore Clipper substitutes the filename in the input text for the variable in the output string.
List match marker <ID MARKER, ...>	Matches a list of legal expressions. Each expression is separated by a comma. This marker does not place

Table 3-1 Continued.

Type/Subtype	Description
	any other restriction on the input text. For example, in the directive: #command @ <row>, <col> SAY <sayxpr> ; [<sayClauses,...>] ; GET <var> ; [<getClauses,...>] ; ; => @ <row>, <col> SAY <sayxpr> [<sayClauses>] ; ; @ Row(), Col()+1 GET <var> [<getClauses>] both the sayClauses and getClauses variables are looking for a list of expressions.
Restricted Match marker <ID MARKER: WORD LIST>	Matches the input text to one of the words in a list of words. The match fails if the input text does not match one of the words. Each marker matches a single word in the input text. For example, in the directive: #command SET EXCLUSIVE <x:ON,OFF,&> ; => Set(_SET_EXCLUSIVE, <(x)>) the variable x can accept one of three values as input: ON, OFF, or & (macro). If the input text does not contain one of these three values, then the match fails and the variable doesn't contain anything.
Wildcard match marker <*ID MARKER*>	Matches all the input text from the current position to the end of the line. The pre-processor does not determine the legality of the statement. For example, in the directive: #command FIND <*text*> ; => dbSeek(<(text)>) text can be anything. It could contain numbers or characters.
Optional clauses	This is a superset of all the other match patterns. An optional clause always appears within brackets and can include any of the previously described match pattern types. The statement does not depend on the outcome of this match pattern. If the input text does not contain the appropriate text, then the pre-

Type/Subtype	Description
	processor excludes any result patterns that reference this match. You can next optional clauses within other optional clauses. For example, in the directive: #command REPLACE <f1> WITH <v1> [, <fN> WITH <vN>] ; => _FIELD-><f1> := <v1> [; _FIELD-><fN> := <vN>] the programmer must supply one set of parameters (f1 and v1), while the other parameters (fN and vN) are optional.

A result pattern describes how the preprocessor should translate the command you specify. It contains a description of the actual commands required by the compiler to implement your command. TABLE 3-2 lists and describes each type and subtype of result pattern.

Table 3-2 #Command/#Translate directive request pattern types

Type/Subtype	Description
Literal tokens	Outputs the characters to the result text. The pre-processor interprets the characters exactly. If you want to use the angle bracket (<) as a literal token, you must precede it with a backward slash (\). This result pattern performs the same function on output text as the match pattern performs on the input string.
Words	Outputs the specified keywords or identifiers to the result text. This result pattern performs the same function on output text as the match pattern performs on the input string.
Result markers	There are six types of result markers. Each type outputs the input text referenced by a match marker to the result text. The result marker must use the same name as the match marker. You must place result markers within angle brackets, as shown below.

Table 3-2 **Continued.**

Type/Subtype	**Description**
Regular result marker <ID MARKER>	Outputs the matched input text to the result text. If no match exits, the pre-processor writes nothing. For example, in the directive: #command TEXT TO FILE <(file)> ; => __TextSave(<(file)>) ; ; text QOut, __TextRestore the variable (file) contains the name of the output text file. Clipper substitutes the filename in the input text for the variable in the output text.
Dumb stringify result marker #<ID MARKER>	The matched input text is placed within quotes (") and output to the result text. The pre-processor writes a null string ("") if no match exists. If the matched text is a list, then each element of the list is placed in quotes and written to the result text. The list items remain separated by commas. For example, in the directive: #command SET COLOR TO [<*spec*>] ; => SetColor(#<spec>) the wild match marker is converted to a string. Therefore, if the input text contained N/W, then the output text would be "N/W". Likewise, markers produce a single quoted string. For example, A, B, C produces "A, B, C" in the output text.
Normal stringify result marker <"ID MARKER">	The matched input text is placed within quotes (") and output to the result text. The pre-processor writes the NIL keyword if no match exists. If the matched text is a list, then each element of the list is placed in quotes and written to the result text. The list items remain separated by commas. For example, A, B, C produces "A", "B", "C" in the output text.
Smart stringify result marker <(ID MARKER)>	The pre-processor stringifies the input text only if the result text does not already contain a complex expression. For example, (A, B, C) produces "A", "B", "C" in the output text. If the result text does contain a complex expression, it writes the input text to the result text unchanged. For example, the expression (A + B) remains unchanged. The pre-processor writes the NIL keyword if no match exists.

Type/Subtype	Description

Blockify result marker <{ID MARKER}>	Outputs the input text to the result text as a code block. The pre-processor writes the NIL keyword if no match exists. For example, in the directive:
	`#command INDEX ON <key> TO <(file)>`
	`[<u: UNIQUE>] ;`
	`=> dbCreateIndex( ;`
	`<(file)>, <"key">, <{key}>, ;`
	`if( <.u.>, .t., NIL ) ;`
	`)`
	the field name is passed as a string and a code block. The string provides the field name to the function. The code block evaluates the data at the record pointed to by that field. List elements are evaluated one at a time and converted to individual code blocks.

Logify result marker <.ID MARKER.>	Does not output the input text to the result text. Writes .T. if a match exits and .F. if a match does not exist. For example, in the directive:
	`#command INDEX ON <key> TO <(file)>`
	`[<u: UNIQUE>] ;`
	`=> dbCreateIndex( ;`
	`<(file)>, <"key">, <{key}>, ;`
	`if( <.u.>, .t., NIL ) ;`
	`)`
	if the command line contains the word UNIQUE as the final entry on the line, then the variable u is matched. This results in the logify result marker .u. writing .T. to the output text. Otherwise, the logify result marker writes .F. to the output text.

Repeating clauses	Always place repeating clauses within square brackets ([]). The pre-processor outputs the repeating text zero or more times, once for each element in the input text.

The combination of a match pattern and a result pattern produces a unique output. You must take both halves of the directive into account when you create a new directive. By using the /P parameter when you compile your program, you can compare the input in your program file (PRG) with the output in the preprocessed output file (PPO). The following example illustrates the interaction between the match pattern and the result pattern (I placed the #Command directive in JOHN.CH). EXAMPLE:

```
* Convert a standard output statement to an @ say
* command equivalent.  In addition, change the output
* to upper case.
#command ? <*EXP*> => @ row()+1, 01 say <EXP> picture '@!'

* Given the following program.
#include "JOHN.CH"
? "Hello World"

* We get the following output in the PPO file.
#line 1 "C:\clipper5\include\JOHN.CH"
#line 2 "TEMP.PRG"
DevPos( row()+1, 01 ) ; DevOutPict( "Hello World", "@!" )
* Notice the ? command now uses the @ Say calling
* convention rather than using the QOut() function as
* it did before.
```

#Define <ID CONSTANT> [<RESULT TEXT>]
#Define <ID FUNCTION> ([<ARGUMENT LIST>]) [<EXP>]

5.0, 5.1

There are three types of #Define directives. Each type declares a different type of information to the preprocessor. You can tell the preprocessor that an identifier exists, identify a manifest constant, or define a pseudo-function. Use the first command-line syntax of the #Define directive for identifiers and manifest constants. The second command line syntax defines pseudo-functions. Note: The #Define directive is case-sensitive. You must use the exact name and letter styles of identifiers and literal text or the preprocessor will display an error message.

The identifier/manifest constant version of #Define directive consists of two parts. The ID CONSTANT contains the name of the identifier or manifest constant. The RESULT TEXT contains the replacement value of the manifest constant. If you add this optional text, the preprocessor will replace every occurrence of the identifier with the text you define. For example, if you add the directive #Define ENTER 13 to your program, then the preprocessor will replace every occurrence of ENTER with the number 13.

For the purposes of this book, an *identifier* is a manifest constant without an assigned value. For example, #Define NETWORK is an example of an identifier. Identifiers are used to modify the behavior of the program and/or preprocessor depending on existing conditions. You can use identifiers in conjunction with other directives in this chapter in order to include or exclude optional code. Manifest constants, on the other hand, reduce the amount of work required to assign a value to specific operations. You can use manifest constants to reduce memory requirements and improve execution speed when the value of a variable won't change during program execution. In addition, both identifiers and manifest constants improve program readability if the programmer uses descriptive names.

The pseudo-function version of #Define consists of three parts. ID FUNCTION contains the name of the pseudo-function. ARGUMENT LIST contains a list of arguments the function requires to work correctly. If the function doesn't require any arguments, you must still add a set of parentheses after the function name. EXP contains a definition of the function. As with the previous version of #Define, the preprocessor replaces every occurrence of the function name with the function definition if you specify this parameter. The function might consist of no more than a single line of code. Psuedo-functions are most useful for quick conversions, for example, converting temperature in degrees Celsius to degrees Fahrenheit. EXAMPLE:

```
#define LARGE                             ;Define an identifier.
#define ENTER 13                          ;Define a manifest constant.
#define SQUARE(SOMENUM) SOMENUM*SOMENUM ;Define a pseudo-function.
```

#Error [<MESSAGE>]

5.1

This new directive is the only one specifically designed to enhance the preprocessor file itself. It displays an error message whenever that section of preprocessor code is run. For example, if you want to make certain that the network version of some command or function gets implemented, you could display an error message each time the code to perform this task is bypassed. This directive always displays error number 2074. The optional message allows you to further define the error condition. The message is a literal string and does not require quotes unless you want the quotes displayed in the message. EXAMPLE:

```
* Display an error message if your preprocessor code
* isn't added correctly.
#ifdef ADDFUNC
     #translate ADDFUNC(X, Y) => X + Y
#else
     #error You didn't define ADDFUNC.
#endif
```

#IfDef <IDENTIFIER>
<STATEMENTS>
[#Else]
<STATEMENTS>
[#EndIf]

5.0, 5.01

The #IfDef directive allows you to perform conditional compilation of a section of code based on the existence of a variable or other identifier. If the identifier exists, then the preprocessor compiles the code. The optional #Else clause allows you to specify an alternate code section. Define an identifier using the #Define directive, or undefine it using the #UnDef directive. EXAMPLE:

```
#define DOUBLE
.
.
.
#ifdef DOUBLE                      && Compile if DOUBLE exists.
      @02, 02 say "Double"
#else
      @01, 01 say "Single"
#endif
#IfNDef <IDENTIFIER>
      <STATEMENTS>
[#Else]
      <STATEMENTS>
```

[#IfNDef] <IDENTIFIER>
<STATEMENTS>
[#Else]
<STATEMENTS>
[#EndIf]

5.0, 5.01

The #IfNDef directive allows you to perform conditional compilation of a section of code based on the lack of a variable or other identifier. If the identifier does not exist, then the preprocessor compiles the code. The optional #Else clause allows you to specify an alternate code section if the variable does exist. You can define an identifier using the #Define directive or undefine it using the #UnDef directive. EXAMPLE:

```
#undef DOUBLE
.
.
.
#ifndef DOUBLE                     && Compile if DOUBLE does not exist.
      @02, 02 say "Double"
#else
      @01, 01 say "Single"
#endif
```

#Include "<HEADER FILE NAME>"

5.0, 5.1

The #Include directive allows you to add header code contained in another file to the current file. The preprocessor treats both files as a single file. The contents of the include file are placed at the same point as the #Include directive in the source file. You must place the include filename in quotes, as shown above. Most Clipper include files use the CH file extension. Clipper allows you to include files up to 16 levels deep. If you don't specify a path as part of the include filename, and the file doesn't reside in the current directory, then the preprocessor searches any paths specified with the /I option or the Include environment variable. EXAMPLE:

```
#Include "SOMEFILE"
```

#Translate <MATCH PATTERN> => <RESULT PATTERN>

5.0, 5.1

The #Translate directive tells the preprocessor to translate a statement it finds in your source files when that statement matches a predefined pattern. Unlike the #Command directive, the match pattern need not form a complete statement. Therefore, you can use the #Translate directive to translate pseudo-functions and clauses into working code.

A #Translate directive takes the following form: MATCH_PATTERN => RESULT_PATTERN. The => symbol is a literal part of the entire directive. You must include it for the directive to work properly. The #Translate directive essentially takes the information in the match pattern and makes it look like the result pattern. This translation process is helpful when you want to make a function easier to use, or if you want to make your commands compatible with a foreign command. (For example, some dBASE III commands don't directly translate into Clipper commands.)

A match pattern describes what the preprocessor should look for when it parses your program. There are different types of match pattern types to perform different tasks. You can use one or more of each type within a single directive. In fact, most commands are a composite of more than one match pattern. TABLE 3-1 lists and describes each type and subtype of match pattern.

A result pattern describes how the preprocessor should translate the command you specify. It contains a description of the actual commands required by the compiler to implement your command. TABLE 3-2 lists and describes each type and subtype of match pattern.

As with the #Command directive, the match pattern and result pattern used with the #Translate directive work together to produce the desired output. You may use the /P parameter of the compiler to create a PPO file showing how the #Translate directive changed your input. The following example shows how you can use a #Translate directive to produce a psuedo-function. Notice that unlike the #Command directive, we use the

#Translate directive to create a new function which may or may not be a complete statement. EXAMPLE:

```
;Define a math pseudo-function.
cls
IN1 = 0.000
IN2 = 0.000
#translate Hyp(<LEG1>, <LEG2>) => sqrt((<LEG1>*<LEG1>)+(<LEG2>*<LEG2>))
@ 01, 01 say 'Type the first number:  ' get IN1
@ 02, 01 say 'Type the second number: ' get IN2
read
OUT = Hyp(IN1, IN2)
@ 03, 01 say 'The third side is:       '+str(OUT,15,3)
```

#UnDef <IDENTIFIER>

5.0, 5.1

The #UnDef directive allows you to revoke the definition of a manifest constant or pseudo-function. One of the most common reasons to use this directive is to remove the definition of a manifest constant or pseudo-function before redefining it with the #Define directive. Failure to do so can result in a noncritical compiler error message. You can perform the same task using the /U option of the compiler. EXAMPLE:

```
#undef SOMEDEF
```

#XCommand <MATCH PATTERN> = > <RESULT PATTERN>
#XTranslate <MATCH PATTERN> = > <RESULT PATTERN>

5.1

Both of these commands operate the same way as their predecessors, #Command and #Translate. However, the user must specify the exact spelling and capitalization to use the command translated by these directives. This means that a program using a #XCommand or #XTranslate directive cannot use the four-character dBASE III calling convention. This is extremely useful when you want to create a function that uses part of a current command's syntax. EXAMPLE:

```
* Standard output command.
#command ? [ <list,...> ]      => QOut( <list> )
* Extended output command (double space).
#xcommand ?ext [ <list,...> ]   => QOut( <list> );
                                   QOut()
```

Code blocks

Code blocks are new to Clipper versions 5.0 and above. You can view them in one of two ways: the way they work and the result they produce. Many programmers refer to code blocks as *unnamed assignable functions*. In essence, code blocks have many of the attributes of functions. They perform their work in much the same way as a function would. A code block accepts variable input, performs some operation on it, and returns a result. At the same time, you can perform some tasks with code blocks that you can't do with a function.

For example, you can assign a code block to a variable and pass that variable to a procedure or function. A code block is compiled code, so you are passing a new piece of code to the function or procedure. Because this new code affects the behavior of the function or procedure, you could look at code blocks as the means to creating self-modifying code. This view looks at the result of a code block.

There are others who look at code blocks as enhanced macros. In fact, code blocks do replace most of the functions performed by macros in earlier versions of Clipper. As with public and private variables, you should avoid using macros whenever possible.

There are two major differences between code blocks and macros. First, a code block is compiled at compile time, while a macro gets compiled on the fly during runtime. This means that a code block will execute quicker than a macro will. It also means that the compiler can check the code block for errors before you try to run it. Second, because a code block does get compiled at compile time, you can use both dynamically and lexically scoped variables.

Both static and local variables are invisible to the macro operator, while you can freely access them within a code block. This is due to the fact that the compiler does not include the names of static and local variables in the executable code. Because a macro is compiled at runtime, the variable names no longer exist and therefore can't be accessed. The only time it's acceptable to use a macro in place of a code block is when a value cannot be ascertained at compile time. For example, if you want to create a generic procedure for opening a database and its associated indexes, you might have to use a macro to store the filenames.

No matter what your viewpoints on code blocks are, they are a powerful feature used throughout the Clipper programming environment. Even the preprocessor makes extensive use of code blocks to perform its work. One look at STD.CH shows how important they are. It's the combination of code blocks and the preprocessor that gives Clipper 5.0 and above its flexibility.

This section looks at three general aspects of code blocks: how you create them, what their limitations are, and how you use them. Other areas of this book contain specific examples of using code blocks to enhance the programming environment. Combining the general ideas here with the specific examples found in later sections is essential to a complete understanding of how code blocks operate in the Clipper environment. This section will provide you with sufficient information to determine how code blocks work.

Creating code blocks

A code block is very simple to construct. It takes the form of { | <PARAMETER LIST> | <EXPRESSION LIST> }. The parameter list contains variables or constants that you want the code block to operate on. Just like functions, you don't have to pass parameters to a code block. However, not passing parameters restricts the type of output you can expect from a code block. The expression list contains the executable statements that you want the code block to perform.

The following code block displays *Hello World* on the screen. This is one of the simplest variations of code block that you'll see. Notice that you assign the code block to a variable and then evaluate the variable using a function. As with the game *Othello*, code blocks take a minute to learn and a lifetime to master. EXAMPLE:

```
bSomeBlock := "{ | | qout('Hello World') }"
eval(bSomeBlock)
```

Code block limitations

There are a few limitations to using code blocks. For instance, you can use only valid Clipper expressions in a code block. That means that you can't use commands or control structures. This is where a function is more flexible than a code block. Functions allow you to use commands and control structures. Some people get around this limitation in code blocks by declaring a function with the command as the only statement, and then using the function within the code block. For example, you can't use the Index command within a code block. The following example shows how to get around this limitation. EXAMPLE:

```
// Create the code block.
bIEval := {| cIKey, cIName | findex (cIKey, cIName)}
// Declare the index name and key value.
LOCAL cThisKey := "L_NAME + F_NAME",;
      cThisName := "SOMEINDX"
// Evaluate the code block.
eval(bIEval, cThisKey, cThisName)
// Create a function containing the Index command.
function FINDEX (cKey, cName)
      index on cKey to cName
return NIL
```

This is only one way of getting around the command limitation with code blocks. Most, if not all, commands are implemented with functions. Clipper simply uses a #Command or #Translate directive to change the command into its function form. STD.CH contains a complete listing of

Clipper commands. By observing the conversion technique outlined in STD.CH, you can convert many commands into their functional form for use in code blocks. For example, the ? command is translated to the QOut( ) function. Another reference for command-to-function conversion can be found in chapter 1 of this book. Many of the command descriptions also contain a reference to the function counterpart in chapter 2.

This same principle does not hold true for control structures. The only control structure you can use within a code block is the IIf( ) function. If you need more control over a particular situation, then you need to use a function. There are, fortunately, many ways in which you can create structures using the IIf( ) function. One way to do this is to nest functions. This allows you to conditionally evaluate the next parameter in a string of parameters based on the previous results. In many respects, this particular structure looks and acts like an If Then Else construct. It provides you many of the same features as using the full-blown command version. The following example shows how to do this. EXAMPLE:

```
// Create a code block to evaluate multiple conditions.
lCheck1 := .T.
lCheck2 := .T.
bCheckLog := { |lX, lY| iif(lX,;
                         iif(lY, "True  * True", "True  * False"),;
                         iif(lY, "False * True", "False * False"))}
? eval(bCheckLog, lCheck1, lCheck2)  // Outputs True  * True
lCheck2 := !lCheck2
? eval(bCheckLog, lCheck1, lCheck2)  // Outputs True  * False
lCheck1 := !lCheck1
lCheck2 := !lCheck2
? eval(bCheckLog, lCheck1, lCheck2)  // Outputs False * True
lCheck2 := !lCheck2
? eval(bCheckLog, lCheck1, lCheck2)  // Outputs False * False
```

Another commonly required construct is the case statement. You can implement this construct by cascading IIf( ) functions together, as shown in the following example. Notice that you could add further flexibility as required by using both the true and false outputs of the IIf( ) function or by using the true output in place of the false output to create the cascade effect. Also, this method of using the IIf( ) function preserves one of the characteristics of a case construct; the control structure is evaluated only as far as required to find a true result. EXAMPLE:

```
// Create a code block to simulate a Case Statement.
nCount := 1
bCase := { | nVal | iif(nVal == 1, "One",;
                        iif(nVal == 2, "Two",;
                        iif(nVal == 3, "Three",;
                        iif(nVal == 4, "Four", "Other"))))}
```

```
do while nCount < 6
     ? eval(bCase, nCount)  // Output One, Two, Three, Four & Other.
     ++ncount
enddo
```

These examples show just two of the ways in which you can use the IIf( ) function to create a control structure within a code block. Through judicious use of the IIf( ) function, you can create any nonrepetitive control structure used in ordinary programming. Repetitive structures like Do While and For Next control structure represent a special problem. Forcing the code block to imitate one of these control structures completely is somewhat difficult. However, you can use recursion to at least partially solve this problem.

The following example acts much like a For Next loop. It accepts the number of iterations you want to perform as input and allows you to directly manipulate output variables, once for each loop. You could implement the step clause of the For Next loop by simply passing another variable to control the amount by which the control variable gets updated each iteration. EXAMPLE:

```
// Create a code block to simulate a For Next control
// structure.
static nCount := 1,;     // n! Result.
       nTimes := 0       // n! Input (number of loops).
cls
@ 01, 01 say "Enter a number: " get nTimes picture '@9'
read

// This particular code block uses recursion to compute
// n! (factorial).  However, the principles would allow
// you to create any looping structure required.

bCase := { | nVal | iif(nVal == 0,;
                        NIL,;
                        eval(bCase, nVal - 1)),;
                        iif(nVal == 0,;
                            NIL,;
                            nCount := nCount * nVal)}

// Check the output of the code block against the value
// returned by the control variable nCount.

? eval(bCase, nTimes)
? nCount
```

The previous examples show you how to create code block constructs that simulate common control structures. Like any simulation, code blocks have their limitations as well. For example, it would be very difficult (if not impossible) to simulate the Break clause of a Do While control structure. These limitations aside, a properly constructed code block can do just about anything that a full-fledged function can do. The overriding limitation, of course, is the length of string that the Clipper compiler will accept as input. Even the most carefully constructed code block cannot overcome this limitation.

Using code blocks

There are three main functions and a host of auxiliary functions that accept code blocks as input. The three main functions are Eval( ), AEval( ), and DBEval( ). Chapter 2 describes each one of these functions in detail. The following section will show you how to use these functions to accomplish various tasks.

The Eval( ) function is the easiest to understand and use of the code block evaluation functions. The input to a code block evaluated with the Eval( ) function comes from variables found in the function or procedure in which the code block appears. The Eval( ) function accepts a list of parameters to pass to the code block. The following example illustrates a code block that accepts variables as input, indirectly modifies some variables, directly modifies others, and creates an output in the process. EXAMPLE:

```
// Create a code block that determines if a number is
// in range and converts it to a string automatically.

static cOutStr := "     "
local nConvNum := 0

// To use a code block as part of an @...Get command it
// must be either a public or private variable.  This
// code block converts the input number to a string
// then checks its value against a predefined range.
// If the number is in range, the code block returns
// true.

bCheckSize := {| nIn | cOutStr := ltrim(str(nIn)),;
                       iif(nIn >= 0 .and. nIn < 10000,;
                           .T.,;
                           .F.)}

// Clear the display, prompt for input, and use a valid
// clause to verify it using the code block.

cls
@01, 01 say "Enter a number: ";
        get nConvNum valid eval(bCheckSize, nConvNum) picture '@9'
read

// Display the input and output values.

? cOutStr
? nConvNum
return
```

The AEval( ) function is used on arrays. In many respects it works the same way as the Eval( ) function. You still create a code block and supply it with values to manipulate. However, the AEval( ) function performs these manipulations on more than one value without resorting to recursion or other methods. It causes the code block to evaluate one or more values in an array automatically. Each array element is looked at in turn and a value returned. The AEval( ) function begins to look very much like the Eval( ) function when you keep this difference in mind.

While chapter 2 provides a complete description of the AEval( ) function and its arguments, I'll take another look at those arguments from a usage point of view in this chapter. The four input parameters are aArray, bCodeBlock, nStartElement, and nEndElement. Of the four parameters, nStartElement and nEndElement are optional. The aArray parameter provides the input values to bCodeBlock. As with the Eval( ) function example, an AEval( ) function can manipulate values both inside and outside of the code block. nStartElement defines the beginning array element, while nEndElement defines the ending array element used as arguments to the code block. AEval( ) defaults to using the entire array if you don't supply these values.

The following example provides an illustration of how you would use AEval( ) within a program. It begins by creating a two-dimensional array and filling it with data. The first dimension contains a color code. The first half of the code determines the foreground color and the second half determines the background color of the display. These codes are in the form of number strings separated by a slash (*nn/nn*). The second dimension contains a number from 1 to 256 that identifies the color combination being displayed. The code block receives a one-dimensional array from AEval( ) consisting of two items, the color code, and the color string. It takes these two inputs, changes the on-screen color, and outputs the string. EXAMPLE:

```
// The following program illustrates one method of
// handling multi-dimensional arrays using AEval().  It
// displays the various color combinations available
// when using Clipper by filling an array with the
// appropriate values then evaluating it with a code
// block.
// Create and initialize the program variables.

static aColorArray[256, 2],;  // Array containing color codes/strings.
       nCount1 := 0,;         // First color code counter.
       nCount2 := 0,;         // Second color code counter.
       nCount3 := 1           // Color string counter.

// Create the code block used to display the colors and associated
// color number strings.

bColorBlock := { | aIn | setcolor(aIn[2]), qqout(aIn[1])}
```

```
// Initialize the color array.

for nCount1 := 0 to 15
   for nCount2 := 0 to 15
       aColorArray[nCount3, 1] := str(nCount3, 4) + " "
       aColorArray[nCount3, 2] := str(nCount1) + "/" + str(nCount2)
       ++nCount3
   next
next

// Clear the display and print a header.

cls
? padc(" The Colors of Clipper ", 80, chr(219))
?

// Evaluate the code block to display the colors and associated
// color number strings.

 aeval(aColorArray, bColorBlock)

// Exit the program.

return
```

The DBEval( ) function is actually the most useful of the three functions described so far. It is also the most complex of the three. Using DBEval( ) with the appropriate code blocks, you can create unique methods of viewing the contents of a database. As with the AEval( ) function, you supply a code block. The function automatically feeds one or more data values, and the code block directly or indirectly changes the environment or variable contents based on that input.

There are a number of optional parameters you can supply to the DBEval( ) function. Chapter 2 provides a complete description of all these optional parameters. The only parameter that you must supply is the code block itself. DBEval( ) assumes that you want to use the database in the current or aliased database for input.

The following example shows one method of using DBEval( ) within a program. It begins by creating and initializing the appropriate variables. As you can see, the code block itself is fairly simple. Notice that you must directly reference the field names within the code block. There are other techniques you can use to access the fields if you don't know their names. For example, you could use the FieldName( ) function to retrieve the field names one at a time. The other parts of the program are similar to those found in the Eval( ) and AEval( ) examples. EXAMPLE:

```
// This code fragment demonstrates one of the basic uses for the
// DBEval() function.  It begins by reading a value from the database
// record, adding the value to a total variable, and then averaging
// it.
```

```
// Create and initialize program variables.

static nTotal := 0,;     // The total of all records averaged.
       nCount := 0,;     // The number of records averaged.
       nAve   := 0       // The record running average.

// This code block input, totals, then averages the value from
// FIELD3 of the database record.  Once it performs this math
// operations, it displays the results on-screen.

bAveBlock := {| | nIn := FIELD3,;
                  nTotal := nIn + nTotal,;
                  ++nCount,;
                  nAve := nTotal / nCount,;
                  qout(str(nCount, 5) + "   "),;
                  qqout(str(nIn, 5, 2) + "   "),;
                  qqout(str(nTotal, 10, 2) + "   "),;
                  qqout(str(nAve, 7, 3))}

// Open the database.

use SAMPLE3 index SAMPLE3 alias NUMBER

// Clear the screen and display a header.

cls
? "Count  Field   Cumulative   Average"
? "        Value     Total        Value"

// Evaluate the code block for every record in the database.

dbeval(bAveBlock)

return
```

Summary

This chapter concentrates on the basics of both the preprocessor and code blocks as they are applied in this book. The rest of this book is dedicated to showing how to create interfaces between Clipper and the outside world. A complete understanding of the preprocessor is required in order to add external functions in such a way as to make them easy to use. The preprocessor can make new commands appear as an extension to an old one or simply as a new command.

Code blocks can greatly enhance the functionality of new interfaces that are added to your Clipper environment. Using code blocks to good effect requires a complete and thorough understanding of how they react differently than macros and functions. Learning how code blocks react under various conditions is essential to understanding many of the more complex issues discussed in the following chapters.

4
Object-oriented programming techniques

There are four object classes provided with Clipper 5.0 and 5.01. Each class performs a different task using object-oriented programming (OOP) methods. These tasks can be performed using conventional procedural methods, but the OOP techniques provide greater flexibility. You can use this additional programming power to create dramatic screen effects or reduce the chances of user input errors.

The procedural methods of previous versions of Clipper didn't allow you to control your programming environment to the same degree as these new OOP techniques do. Of course, you must exercise greater care when using this additional flexibility. In addition, the OOP methods are more complex than the procedural techniques, requiring greater programming skill as well. This chapter will provide a description of the various object classes and examples of some of the ways you can use them. While the examples use all the capabilities of version 5.01, the techniques they illustrate are equally applicable to version 5.0. In many cases the example will run in 5.0 unaltered.

Using the Get System

The Get System is an object class that performs the same tasks as the @...Get command, except that it uses OOP techniques to accomplish them. In fact, the preprocessor translates every @...Get command into a get object. To perform this task, the preprocessor uses the following code from STD.CH:

```
#command @ <row>, <col> GET <var>                        ;
                        [PICTURE <pic>]                  ;
                        [VALID <valid>]                  ;
```

```
                        [WHEN <when>]                              ;
                        [SEND <msg>]                               ;
=> SetPos( <row>, <col> )                                          ;
 ; AAdd(                                                           ;
        GetList,                                                   ;
        _GET_( <var>, <(var)>, <pic>, <{valid}>, <{when}> ) ;
      )                                                            ;
[; ATail(GetList):<msg>]
```

Notice that the @...Get command makes use of a special array called GetList to hold the get objects. This array is automatically defined when you start your Clipper program. If you were to examine this array after filling it with one or more variables, you would see one unnamed object for each get in the get list. For example, the following code produces an array containing two elements. The first element contains cSomeVar and the second contains nSomeVar:

```
local cSomeVar := space(40),;
      nSomeVar := 0
@01,01 get cSomeVar
@02,01 get nSomeVar picture '9999.99'
read
```

The code begins by creating two variables of a specific type and initializing them. It then creates two get objects, one for each variable, and uses the Read command to read them. Given this code fragment, the preprocessor produces the following code:

```
local cSomeVar := space(40), nSomeVar := 0
SetPos( 01, 01 ) ; AAdd( GetList, _GET_( cSomeVar, "cSomeVar",,, ) )
SetPos( 02, 01 ) ; AAdd( GetList, _GET_( nSomeVar, "nSomeVar", "9999.99",, ) )
ReadModal(GetList) ; GetList := {}
```

One difference between a standard get object and the preprocessor output is that the preprocessor uses a special internal function, _get_, to create the get objects. The preprocessor uses the AAdd( ) function to add the new get object to the GetList array. Also notice that the code clears the get list after reading by assigning an empty array to GetList. If you use the Read command with the Save clause, the preprocessor omits the assignment.

The Get System offers additional flexibility by allowing you to define many of the elements used to manipulate data on screen. For example, instead of using the default code blocks to determine how the cursor keys react, you can add your own code block. In addition, you can control the on-screen colors and other screen characteristics by using a get object in place of the @...Get command. The following section describes how the

Get System works and provides examples of how you can use it in your programs.

Get System description

The Get System consists of three parts: the class function, exported instance variables, and exported methods. Each part plays a role in creating, monitoring, and manipulating a get object.

The only class function associated with the Get System is GetNew([<nEXP1>], [<nEXP2>], [<bEXP>], [<cEXP1>], [<cEXP2>], [<cEXP3>]). The first argument, nEXP1, accepts a number describing the screen row at which the entry appears. If you don't specify a screen row, the get object uses a default of row 0. nEXP2 accepts a number describing the screen column at which the entry appears. As with the row argument, this argument defaults to column 0 if you don't supply a value. The third variable, bEXP, accepts a code block. ReadModal( ) uses this code block to determine how to interpret information input by the user. If you don't supply a code block, the Get System defaults to a NIL code block. You must, as a minimum, supply a code block in order for the get object to perform useful work. However, you don't need to declare the code block when you create the object. cEXP1 contains a string containing the name of the variable that the get object will modify.

The Get System uses a default of " " if you don't supply this value. cEXP2 contains a character string describing the picture function and/or template used for data entry. The user is allowed to input anything if you don't supply this argument (it defaults to NIL). cEXP3 contains a color string that determines the colors used to display the entry blank. If you don't supply this argument, the Get System defaults to the current Set Color defaults. The standard color setup is "N/W, N/W". The following example shows the minimum GetNew( ) configuration that performs useful work without modification. EXAMPLE:

```
local cSomeVar := space(40),;
     oGetVar := getnew(,,{| | cSomeVar})
aadd(GetList, oGetVar)
readmodal(GetList)
```

The exported instance variables allow you to monitor the condition of the get object. In some cases they also allow you to reconfigure the get object. For example, you can change the row at which a get object appears by modifying the Row variable. TABLE 4-1 contains a complete listing of the Get System exported instance variables and their functions.

The exported methods provided by the Get System allow you to modify the operation of the get object, display it on screen, determine its current condition, and change the way specific keys react when the user presses them. Use these methods to interact with the get object. In many cases you'll want to use a method to manipulate the contents of a variable, rather than changing the variable itself. This is especially true when one variable affects the contents of another. You always need to use a method to move the cursor within a get object. TABLE 4-2 provides a complete listing and description of the exported methods.

Table 4-1 Get-class exported-instance variables

Variable	Description
badDate	This variable returns true when the date entered by the user is invalid. It returns false for a good date entry. Use the badDate variable as follows: `lDateChk := oGetOBJ:badDate`

block	Use this variable to specify which variable you want the get object to operate on. The block variable can contain any valid code block that returns a legal value for the variable. Use the block variable as follows:
	`bGetVar := {| cInVal | if(pcount() > 0,;`
	`cVar := cInVal,;`
	`cVar) }`
	`oGetOBJ:block := bGetVar`
	`ReadModal ({oGetVar})`

buffer	The buffer variable contains the name of a buffer used while editing a get object. Normally, this variable contains a value of NIL. Attempts to assign a name to the buffer are futile until the get object has input focus.
cargo	This variable contains the value of any data type not used by the get system. You can use this variable to keep track of data that does not have a standard slot in the get object. For example, some programmers use this variable to track the edit status of the get object. Use the cargo variable as follows: `oGetOBJ:cargo := "Some Value"`
changed	Use this variable to determine if the user changed the contents of a get object during a read (when the get object had the input focus). If the buffer changed, then the changed variable contains true; otherwise, it contains false. Use the changed variable as follows: `lDChanged := oGetOBJ:changed`

Variable	Description
col	The col variable determines the column where the get object appears on the display. Use the col variable as follows: oGetOBJ:col := 4
colorSpec	This variable contains a character string that defines the colors used to display the get object. The string contains two sets of color specifications. The first set is the unselected color for the get. The second color is the selected color for the get. A get is selected when it has the input focus. Clipper automatically uses the colors defined with Setcolor() for the get object. Use the colorSpec variable as follows: oGetOBJ:colorSpec := "N/W, W/N"
decPos	The decPos variable contains the position of the decimal point within a get object. For example, if the decimal point is on the eighth position of a ten-digit number, then this variable returns 8. The contents of this variable are meaningful only when the get object has input focus. Otherwise, the variable contains NIL. Use the decPos variable as follows: nSomeVar := oGetOBJ:decPos
exitState	The Readmodal() function updates the exitState variable to show how a get object was exited when last read. There are nine potential exit states: GE_NOEXIT 0 No exit attempted GE_UP 1 Up arrow pressed GE_DOWN 2 Down arrow pressed GE_TOP 3 User went past first get GE_BOTTOM 4 User went past last get GE_ENTER 5 Enter pressed GE_WRITE 6 Get written GE_ESCAPE 7 Escape pressed GE_WHEN 8 When condition not satisfied The variable returns a number that you can match to a text expression if you include GETEXIT.CH in your program. This method is available in Clipper versions 5.01 and above. Use the exitState variable as follows: nSomeVar := oGetOBJ:exitState

Table 4-1 Continued.

Variable	Description
hasFocus	The hasFocus variable returns true if the get object has the input focus (is selected for editing); otherwise, it returns false. Use the hasFocus variable as follows: lGFocus := oGetOBJ:hasFocus
name	The Readmodal() and Readvar() functions use this variable to determine the name of the get variable. You don't need to define this variable. The get object ignores the value contained in this variable. It was added for Summer 87 compatibility purposes. Use the name variable as follows: oGetOBJ:name := "Some Value"
original	The get object stores the original value of the get variable in the original variable when the object receives input focus. This allows the get system to undo user input using the undo() method. Never modify this variable.
picture	Use this variable to define a picture string for the get variable. The @ Get module of this manual contains a complete description of the pictures available for the get object. Use the picture variable as follows: oGetOBJ:picture := "999.99"
pos	The pos variable contains the position of the cursor within a get object. For example, if the cursor is on the last position of a ten-character string, then this variable returns 10. The contents of this variable are meaningful only when the get object has input focus. Otherwise, the variable contains NIL. Use the decPos variable as follows: nSomeVar := oGetOBJ:pos
postBlock	This variable contains a code block used to validate the contents of a get object after editing. If the get object contains a legal value, then the code block should return true. The get object ignores the code block contained in this variable. It is used by the standard Read command, replacing the Valid clause. This allows the Valid clause to verify the get variable without directly looking at it.
preBlock	This variable contains a code block that determines when the user can edit the get variable. If the code block returns true,

Variable	Description
	then the user can edit the get variable. The get object ignores the code block. It is used by the standard Read command, replacing the When clause. This allows the When clause to verify that the get is open for editing without looking directly at the get variable.
reader	Use this variable to create special effects using a standard Get command. You supply a code block as input to the variable, which modifies the behavior of the specified get object. The code block can include calls to specialized procedures and functions. If the reader variable does not contain a code block, Readmodal() automatically uses the standard get routine. This method is available in Clipper versions 5.01 and above.
rejected	Use the rejected variable to determine if the last character specified by a insert() or overstrike() method was rejected. If the get object rejected the input, then the rejected variable returns true. Any subsequent entry resets this variable. Use the rejected variable as follows: lWasRej := oGetOBJ:rejected
row	The row variable determines the row where the get object appears on the display. Use the row variable as follows: oGetOBJ:row := 4
subscript	Use this variable to determine the array element subscripts contained in a get object. The variable returns an array of numeric values relating to the subscripts used in the @ Get statement. There is one array element for each dimension of the get variable. If the get variable contains three dimensions, the subscript variable returns a one-dimensional array with three elements. If the get object contains a regular variable, the subscript variable returns NIL. This method is available in Clipper versions 5.01 and above. Use the subscript variable as follows: local a := "John " local b := "Mary " local c := "David " local aVar := {{a, b, c}, {c, b, a}} @ 01, 01 get aVar[1, 3]

Table 4-1 Continued.

Variable	Description
	oGetVar := GetList [Len(GetList)] // aSub[1] = 1, aSub[2] = 3 aSub := oGetVar:subscript
type	This variable returns the type of the get variable. These are the same types described in the ValType() module of this book. Use the type variable as follows: cSomeVar := oGetOBJ:type
typeOut	Use the typeOut variable to determine if the most recent method attempted to move the cursor outside the get or if the get does not contain any editable positions. If the user can no longer move the cursor in a specific direction, or if there aren't any editable positions, this variable returns true. Use the typeOut variable as follows: lSomeVar := oGetOBJ:typeOut

Table 4-2 Get-class methods

Method	Description
State change methods	
assign()	This method assigns the value in the editing buffer to the get object by evaluating the get code block. You can use this method only when the get object has the input focus.
colorDisp()	Use this method to reassign the colors used by a get object and then redraw the screen. It is equivalent to setting the color using the colorSpec instance variable and issuing a display() method. This method is available in Clipper versions 5.01 and above.
display()	The display() method redraws the get object on screen. If the get object has the input focus, it places the cursor in the position indicated by the pos variable and uses the selected color. Otherwise, it redraws the get object using the unselected color.

Method	Description
killFocus()	Use this method to remove the input focus from a get object. Once the input focus is removed, the get object redisplays itself and discards any internal state information.
reset()	The reset() method resets a get object's internal state information. It also places the current value of the get variable into the editing buffer. Finally, it places the cursor in column one of the buffer. You can use this method only when the get object has the input focus.
setFocus()	Use this method to give a get object the input focus. Once the get object receives the input focus, it creates and initializes the internal state information. This includes the exported instance variables: buffer, pos, decPos, and original. Finally, the get object displays the editing buffer in the selected color.
undo()	This method copies the contents of the original instance variable to the editing buffer, returning the buffer to its unedited state. You can use this method only when the get object has the input focus.
updateBuffer()	Use the updateBuffer() method to update the editing buffer with the current value of the get variable. This method automatically redisplays the get. You can use this method only when the get object has the input focus.
Cursor movement methods	
end()	This method moves the cursor to the rightmost column in the object and redraws the screen.
home()	This method moves the cursor to the leftmost column in the object and redraws the screen.
left()	This method moves the cursor one column left in the object. If the cursor is on the last column, the cursor position remains unchanged.

Table 4-2 Continued.

Method	Description
right()	This method moves the cursor one column right in the object. If the cursor is on the last column, the cursor position remains unchanged.
toDecPos()	Use this method to move the cursor to the first column position to the right of the decimal point. This method is valid only when editing numeric values.
wordLeft()	This method moves the cursor one word left in the object. If the cursor is on the last editable column, the cursor position remains unchanged.
wordRight()	This method moves the cursor one word right in the object. If the cursor is on the first column, the cursor position remains unchanged.
Editing methods	
backspace()	The backspace() method moves the cursor one column to the left in the object. It removes the character to the left of the original cursor position. If the cursor is on the first column, the cursor position remains unchanged.
delLeft()	Use this method to remove a character to the left of the cursor.
delRight()	Use this method to remove a character to the right of the cursor.
delWordLeft()	Use this method to remove a word to the left of the cursor.
delWordRight()	Use this method to remove a word to the right of the cursor.
Text entry methods	
insert (<cChar>)	The insert() method inserts cChar at the current cursor position in the object. It moves the contents of the buffer to the right of the cursor enough space to

Method	Description
	accommodate the entry. cChar can contain a single character or a string. Once the get object inserts the string, it moves the cursor to the first position to the right of the last insertion column.
overStrike (<cChar>)	The overStrike() method places cChar at the current cursor position in the object. It overwrites the contents of the buffer to the right of the cursor. cChar can contain a single character or a string. Once the get object overwrites the string, it moves the cursor to the first position to the right of the last overwritten column.

Get System functions

Version 5.01 of Clipper provides five Get System functions in addition to the class function. These functions change the behavior of a specific get object rather than interact with the class itself. The following sections describe each Get System function in detail and provide an example of how you would use them within a program.

GETAPPLYKEY(<oEXP>, <nEXP>)

The GetApplyKey( ) function sends an InKey( ) value to the specified get object. The get object reacts as if the user had pressed a key when it receives the InKey( ) value. For example, if you were to send the letter A and if the picture function of the get object permitted you to enter characters, then an A would appear on the screen and the cursor would advance to the next position. Likewise, if you sent a down-arrow keystroke to the get object, the cursor would go down to the next position on the display. oEXP contains the name of the get object that you want to send keystrokes to. nEXP contains the InKey( ) value you want to send to the get object.

There are several restrictions you must observe while using this function. First, the get object must have the input focus or it will ignore all the keystrokes that you send to it. Second, if you send a keystroke that executes a Set Key command and if that procedure contains a Clear Gets command, then the get object will terminate when you return from the Set Key procedure.

This function is most useful in creating demonstration versions of your program or in implementing pick lists. In the first instance, you could create entire routines that would manipulate the get objects on screen automatically. Using the GetApplyKey( ) function would allow you to create macro functions for your get object. In the second instance, you could use a Set Key procedure to display a pick list on screen, allow the user to select an item, and then paste that item into the get object. The following example shows how you would use the GetApplyKey( ) function to paste a zero into a numeric entry after the user responds favorably to a question. EXAMPLE:

```
// Clear the screen, display a header and any display questions.
// Ask the user if they want to zero the displayed values.  Zero them
// using the GetApplyKey() function if required. An Inkey() value of
// 48 equals the character zero.

set scoreboard off
setcolor("W/B,W+/G")
cls
@00, 00 say padc(" Get Object Demonstration Number 2 ", 80, chr(176))

// Use the Get2Reader() function in place of ReadModal().  Notice that
// the object does not appear within an array and that Get2Reader()
// operates on a single variable at a time.  This function is bypassed
// if the get object Reader exported instance variable contains a code
// block.  Using ReadModal() allows you to implement the special
// behavior when necessary, but using Get2Reader() allows you to
// implement a standard behavior as well.

@ 02, 01 say "Zero the database variables prior to displaying them? "
Get2Reader(oZero)

@ 02, 01 clear

if lZero

   // Zero the First Field

   oGetFld1:setfocus()
   getapplykey(oGetFld1, 48)
   oGetFld1:assign()
   oGetFld1:killfocus()

   // Zero the Second Field

   oGetFld2:setfocus()
   getapplykey(oGetFld2, 48)
   oGetFld2:assign()
   oGetFld2:killfocus()

   // Zero the Third Field

   oGetFld3:setfocus()
   getapplykey(oGetFld3, 48)
   oGetFld3:assign()
   oGetFld3:killfocus()
```

```
    // Zero the Fourth Field

    oGetFld4:setfocus()
    getapplykey(oGetFld4, 48)

    oGetFld4:assign()
    oGetFld4:killfocus()

endif
```

GETDOSETKEY(<bEXP>, <oEXP>)

The GetDOSetKey function executes a Set Key code block after preserving the state of the current get. bEXP contains the code block you want to execute. oEXP contains the get object whose state you want to preserve. You can use any standard code block as input to this function. If the code block contains a Clear Gets command, then the get object will terminate when you return. The code block called by GetDOSetKey( ) receives the line number and procedure name that called the ReadModal( ) function as input.

You would normally use this function as part of an extension to the standard Get System. For example, you could check the status of the get object and perform a procedure based on that status without affecting the get object. However, you can also use it whenever it is important to save and restore the current get object before you satisfy the requirements of a Set Key code block. EXAMPLE:

```
local bDispMsg := {|cProc, nLine| devpos(0,0),;
                                  devout(cProc),;
                                  devout("   "),;
                                  devout(nLine)}

// activate the GET for reading

get:SetFocus()

// Display the procedure name and line number which called
// Get2Reader() in the upper left corner of the display.

getdosetkey(bDispMsg, get)
```

GETPOSTVALIDATE(<oEXP>)

The GetPostValidate( ) function allows you to check the status of a get object after the user edits it. This is the function that Clipper calls as part of the Valid clause of an @...Get command. oEXP contains the get object you want to validate. The exported instance variable, get:postBlock, contains a code block used to validate the get object. If the exported instance variable contains NIL or if the validation succeeds (the code block returns true), then GetPostValidate( ) returns true. It returns false if the code block does not succeed. If the code block contains a Clear Gets command or its equivalent, the ReadModal( ) function normally terminates upon return from the validation code block.

This function is normally found within the Get System. However, you could use it to perform conditional validations of a get object based on the needs of the program, for example, if there were specific rules governing the value of a price input to an accounting program based on the area of the country where a specific product was sold. EXAMPLE:

```
// This section of code adds validation code to the four field get
// objects.  The code ensures that the user does not enter a number
// greater than or equal to 1,000.

oGetFld1:postblock := {| oIn | iif(val(oIn:buffer) >= -999 .and.;
                                   val(oIn:buffer) <= 999,;
                                   .T.,;
                                   .F.)}
oGetFld2:postblock := {| oIn | iif(val(oIn:buffer) >= -999.9 .and.;
                                   val(oIn:buffer) <= 999.9,;
                                   .T.,;
                                   .F.)}
oGetFld3:postblock := {| oIn | iif(val(oIn:buffer) >= -999.99 .and.;
                                   val(oIn:buffer) <= 999.99,;
                                   .T.,;
                                   .F.)}
oGetFld4:postblock := {| oIn | iif(val(oIn:buffer) >= -999.999 .and.;
                                   val(oIn:buffer) <= 999.999,;
                                   .T.,;
                                   .F.)}

// The following cargo entries work with the modified Get2Reader()
// function below.  They allow the program to display appropriate
// error messages when the validation range is exceeded.

oGetFld1:cargo := "Enter a value between -999 and 999."
oGetFld2:cargo := "Enter a value between -999.9 and 999.9."
oGetFld3:cargo := "Enter a value between -999.99 and 999.99."
oGetFld4:cargo := "Enter a value between -999.999 and 999.999."

// disallow exit if the VALID condition is not satisfied

if ( !GetPostValidate(get) )
   get:exitState := GE_NOEXIT
   alert(get:cargo)
end
```

GETPREVALIDATE(<oEXP>)

The GetPreValidate( ) function allows you to check the condition of a variable before the user edits it. oEXP contains the get object you intend to validate. The exported instance variable, get:preBlock, contains a code block used to validate the get object. If the exported instance variable contains NIL or if the validation succeeds (the code block returns true), then GetPreValidate( ) returns true. It returns false if the code block does not succeed. If the code block contains a Clear Gets command or its equivalent, the ReadModal( ) function normally terminates upon return from the validation code block.

This function is normally found within the Get System. However, you could use it to ensure database integrity and other maintenance tasks within a program. EXAMPLE:

```
// This section of code adds pre-validation routines which check for the
// existence of errors in the database.  For example, if the database
// were to get corrupted and the value of field contained characters or
// a value greater than 1,000.  The routine works by using the val
// function to determine the numeric value of the buffer.  If that value
// is zero, and the first character in the buffer is not a zero, then
// the buffer must contain non-numeric characters.  Once it checks for
// this error, the routine checks for out of range numeric values.  If
// everything checks out, then the code block returns true.

oGetFld1:preblock := {| oIn | iif(!valtype(FIELD1) == "N",;
                                .F.,;
                                iif(FIELD1 > -1000 .and.;
                                    FIELD1 <  1000,;
                                    .T.,;
                                    .F.))}
oGetFld2:preblock := {| oIn | iif(!valtype(FIELD2) == "N",;
                                .F.,;
                                iif(FIELD2 > -1000 .and.;
                                    FIELD2 <  1000,;
                                    .T.,;
                                    .F.))}
oGetFld3:preblock := {| oIn | iif(!valtype(FIELD3) == "N",;
                                .F.,;
                                iif(FIELD3 > -1000 .and.;
                                    FIELD3 <  1000,;
                                    .T.,;
                                    .F.))}
oGetFld4:preblock := {| oIn | iif(!valtype(FIELD4) == "N",;
                                .F.,;
                                iif(FIELD4 > -1000 .and.;
                                    FIELD4 <  1000,;
                                    .T.,;
                                    .F.))}

// Check the database for errors.

if !(getprevalidate(oGetFld1))
   alert("Database Error!;Call your supervisor!")
   return
endif
if !(getprevalidate(oGetFld2))
```

```
   alert("Database Error!;Call your supervisor!")
   return
endif
if !(getprevalidate(oGetFld3))
   alert("Database Error!;Call your supervisor!")
   return
endif
if !(getprevalidate(oGetFld4))
   alert("Database Error!;Call your supervisor!")
   return
endif
```

GETREADER(<oEXP>)

The GetReader( ) function is normally called by ReadModal( ) as part of an @...Get/Read sequence. oEXP contains the get object you want to edit. In standard mode, ReadModal( ) removes the get objects from the array supplied as input one at a time and sends them to GetReader( ). To perform its work, GetReader( ) calls other functions like GetPreValidate( ) and GetPostValidate( ).

When the get object you construct contains a code block entry in the get:reader exported instance variable, ReadModal( ) does not send the get object to GetReader( ). It evaluates the code block instead. This essentially allows you to create two behaviors for a single get object. You can implement the standard behavior by calling GetReader( ) directly, and a special behavior by calling ReadModal( ). EXAMPLE:

```
// Clear the screen, display a header and any display questions.
// Ask the user if they want to zero the displayed values.  Zero them
// using the GetApplyKey() function if required. An Inkey() value of
// 48 equals the character zero.

set scoreboard off
setcolor("W/B,W+/G")
cls
@00, 00 say padc(" Get Object Demonstration Number 2 ", 80, chr(176))

// Use the Get2Reader() function in place of ReadModal().  Notice that
// the object does not appear within an array and that Get2Reader()
// operates on a single variable at a time.  This function is bypassed
// if the get object Reader exported instance variable contains a code
// block.  Using ReadModal() allows you to implement the special
// behavior when necessary, but using Get2Reader() allows you to
// implement a standard behavior as well.

@ 02, 01 say "Zero the database variables prior to displaying them? "
Get2Reader(oZero)
```

Get System programming examples

The Get System is an extremely powerful tool for manipulating the presentation, editing, and validating of data. The example program presented in FIG. 4-1 provides a complete example of how to use most of the Get System capabilities within a program. Notice that this example uses the modified GETSYS.PRG provided as part of the sample program disk. While this example does not show every Get System environment variable or programming construct, it does show many of the more common ones. The program is split into four main sections.

4-1 Get system programming example

```
// This example shows you how to use the various Get System functions by
// adding to the original Get System example in GET01.PRG.  You can
// compile it as you would any other Clipper program.  To use this
// example, compile the example GETSYS.PRG and add it to the RTLINK
// command line (ie RTLINK FI GET02, GETSYS).  This will add the extra
// functionality included with the example Get System program (some of
// which was originally contained in GET01.PRG).
// Written by: John Mueller
// Copyright 1991 John Mueller - Tab Books

// Create some holding variables.

local nField1 := 0,;
      nField2 := 0,;
      nField3 := 0,;
      nField4 := 0

static lZero := .T.              // Zero the variables before display?

public aGetArray[4]              // Contains an array of Get Objects.

// Create the get objects.

// Database Specific.

oGetFld1 := getnew(02, 10, {| nIn | if(pcount()>0,;
                                       nField1 := nIn,;
                                       nField1) },;
                                    "Field 1",;
                                    "9999999999",;
                                    "W+/B,W+/R")
oGetFld2 := getnew(03, 11, {| nIn | if(pcount()>0,;
                                       nField2 := nIn,;
                                       nField2) },;
                                    "Field 2",;
                                    "9999999.9",;
                                    "W+/B,W+/R")
oGetFld3 := getnew(04, 12, {| nIn | if(pcount()>0,;
                                       nField3 := nIn,;
```

4-1 Continued.

```
                                               nField3) },;
                                            "Field 3",;
                                            "99999.99",;
                                            "W+/B,W+/R")
oGetFld4 := getnew(05, 13, {| nIn | if(pcount()>0,;
                                               nField4 := nIn,;
                                               nField4) },;
                                            "Field 4",;
                                            "999.999",;
                                            "W+/B,W+/R")

// Variable Specific Get Object.

oZero := getnew(02, 55, {| lIn | if(pcount()>0,;
                                         lZero := lIn,;
                                         lZero) },;
                                         "Zero Database Variable",;
                                         "Y",;
                                         "W+/B,W+/R")

// Open the database.

use SAMPLE3 index SAMPLE3 alias NUMBER

// Place the values contained in the first record in the first holding
// variable.

nField1 := NUMBER->FIELD1
nField2 := NUMBER->FIELD2
nField3 := NUMBER->FIELD3
nField4 := NUMBER->FIELD4

// Clear the screen, display a header and any display questions.
// Ask the user if they want to zero the displayed values.  Zero them
// using the GetApplyKey() function if required. An Inkey() value of
// 48 equals the character zero.

set scoreboard off
setcolor("W/B,W+/G")
cls
@00, 00 say padc(" Get Object Demonstration Number 2 ", 80, chr(176))

// Use the Get2Reader() function in place of ReadModal().  Notice that
// the object does not appear within an array and that Get2Reader()
// operates on a single variable at a time.  This function is bypassed
// if the get object Reader exported instance variable contains a code
// block.  Using ReadModal() allows you to implement the special
// behavior when necessary, but using Get2Reader() allows you to
// implement a standard behavior as well.

@ 02, 01 say "Zero the database variables prior to displaying them? "
Get2Reader(oZero)
```

```
@ 02, 01 clear

if lZero

   // Zero the First Field

   oGetFld1:setfocus()
   getapplykey(oGetFld1, 48)
   oGetFld1:assign()
   oGetFld1:killfocus()

   // Zero the Second Field

   oGetFld2:setfocus()
   getapplykey(oGetFld2, 48)
   oGetFld2:assign()
   oGetFld2:killfocus()

   // Zero the Third Field

   oGetFld3:setfocus()
   getapplykey(oGetFld3, 48)
   oGetFld3:assign()
   oGetFld3:killfocus()

   // Zero the Fourth Field

   oGetFld4:setfocus()
   getapplykey(oGetFld4, 48)
   oGetFld4:assign()
   oGetFld4:killfocus()

endif

// This section of code adds validation code to the four field get
// objects.  The code ensures that the user does not enter a number
// greater than or equal to 1,000.

oGetFld1:postblock := {| oIn | iif(val(oIn:buffer) >= -999 .and.;
                                   val(oIn:buffer) <= 999,;
                                   .T.,;
                                   .F.)}
oGetFld2:postblock := {| oIn | iif(val(oIn:buffer) >= -999.9 .and.;
                                   val(oIn:buffer) <= 999.9,;
                                   .T.,;
                                   .F.)}
oGetFld3:postblock := {| oIn | iif(val(oIn:buffer) >= -999.99 .and.;
                                   val(oIn:buffer) <= 999.99,;
                                   .T.,;
                                   .F.)}
oGetFld4:postblock := {| oIn | iif(val(oIn:buffer) >= -999.999 .and.;
                                   val(oIn:buffer) <= 999.999,;
                                   .T.,;
                                   .F.)}
```

4-1 Continued.

```
// This section of code adds pre-validation routines which check for the
// existance of errors in the database.  For example, if the database
// were to get corrupted and the value of field contained characters or
// a value greater than 1,000.  The routine works by using the val
// function to determine the numeric value of the buffer.  If that value
// is zero, and the first character in the buffer is not a zero, then
// the buffer must contain non-numeric characters.  Once it checks for
// this error, the routine checks for out of range numeric values.  If
// everything checks out, then the code block returns true.

oGetFld1:preblock := {| oIn | iif(!valtype(FIELD1) == "N",;
                                  .F.,;
                                  iif(FIELD1 > -1000 .and.;
                                      FIELD1 <  1000,;
                                      .T.,;
                                      .F.))}
oGetFld2:preblock := {| oIn | iif(!valtype(FIELD2) == "N",;
                                  .F.,;
                                  iif(FIELD2 > -1000 .and.;
                                      FIELD2 <  1000,;
                                      .T.,;
                                      .F.))}
oGetFld3:preblock := {| oIn | iif(!valtype(FIELD3) == "N",;
                                  .F.,;
                                  iif(FIELD3 > -1000 .and.;
                                      FIELD3 <  1000,;
                                      .T.,;
                                      .F.))}
oGetFld4:preblock := {| oIn | iif(!valtype(FIELD4) == "N",;
                                  .F.,;
                                  iif(FIELD4 > -1000 .and.;
                                      FIELD4 <  1000,;
                                      .T.,;
                                      .F.))}

// The following cargo entries work with the modified Get2Reader()
// function below.  They allow the program to display appropriate
// error messages when the validation range is exceeded.

oGetFld1:cargo := "Enter a value between -999 and 999."
oGetFld2:cargo := "Enter a value between -999.9 and 999.9."
oGetFld3:cargo := "Enter a value between -999.99 and 999.99."
oGetFld4:cargo := "Enter a value between -999.999 and 999.999."

// Create the get array.  Each element consists of one get object.

aGetArray[1] := oGetFld1
aGetArray[2] := oGetFld2
aGetArray[3] := oGetFld3
aGetArray[4] := oGetFld4

// Check the database for errors.
```

```
if !(getprevalidate(oGetFld1))
   alert("Database Error!;Call your supervisor!")
   return
endif
if !(getprevalidate(oGetFld2))
   alert("Database Error!;Call your supervisor!")
   return
endif
if !(getprevalidate(oGetFld3))
   alert("Database Error!;Call your supervisor!")
   return
endif
if !(getprevalidate(oGetFld4))
   alert("Database Error!;Call your supervisor!")
   return
endif

// Display some field descriptors and get user input using the get
// array.

@02, 01 say "Field 1:"
@03, 01 say "Field 2:"
@04, 01 say "Field 3:"
@05, 01 say "Field 4:"
readmodal(aGetArray)

// Replace the current database record contents with the new values
// input by the user.

NUMBER->FIELD1 := nField1
NUMBER->FIELD2 := nField2
NUMBER->FIELD3 := nField3
NUMBER->FIELD4 := nField4

// Clear the screen, close the database, and return to the DOS prompt.

setcolor("W/N")
cls
close all
return
```

The first section declares variables and objects used to manipulate the data found in a database. When you create a program using the Get System, it is often important to declare not only the variables and objects, but all the exported instance variables at the beginning of the program. This will ensure that you can find the variables easier later and reduce the number of errors resulting from undefined code blocks required to manipulate the data.

The second section of the program opens the database and places data from the first logical record into the get objects. By adding a loop and a menu, this program could be used to manipulate any record in the database. A single-record example was used to simplify the code. Notice especially the ability to zero the database using an automated macro. You could use similar techniques to create demo programs or other automated processes that rely on pasting characters into a field as if the user typed them.

The third section contains the code used to actually manipulate the data. Much of the data manipulation occurs in the GETSYS.PRG file, which is included as part of the sample program disk.

The fourth section replaces the data in the database with the edited and verified data contained in the get objects. This section also closes the database and exits the program.

Using the TBrowse System

The TBrowse System is an OOP replacement for the DBEdit( ) function. It provides greater flexibility and improves the handling characteristics of the browse display. In addition, you can add specialized character-handling features that were unavailable for DBEdit( ). However, TBrowse is also much more complex than the DBEdit( ) function. There are many instances where you need to display data in a generic fashion and don't require the added flexibility provided by the TBrowse System. In these cases, it is more efficient to use the Browse( ) function described in chapter 2.

TBrowse System description

The TBrowse System is composed of three elements: the class functions required to create an object, the TBColumn objects that define the contents of each column within the TBrowse object, and the object itself. A complete description of a TBColumn object appears in the following section. The components that make up a TBrowse object appear in the following section. A complete description of the two TBrowse class functions appears in TABLE 4-3.

As you can see, there are two different TBrowse class functions. This might seem confusing at first because both functions are designed to create TBrowse objects. In essence, you use the TBrowseNew( ) function to create an object capable of handling any type of tabular data. This data does not necessarily come from a database file. You could display the information contained in an array using an object created with this function. In most instances, TBrowseNew( ) provides the greatest flexibility, but requires a considerable amount of additional programming. For example, you must define all the code blocks required to move around within the object.

Table 4-3 TBrowse-class functions

Function	Description
TBrowseNew (<nTop>, <nLeft>, <nBottom>, <nRight>)	This function creates a new, uninitialized TBrowse object that uses the specified screen coordinates. You must create the columns required to contain data and the data positioning code blocks. Use this function when you need to create an object that allows maximum flexibility. The command line format for creating an object that uses the entire display is, as follows: `oBrowseDB := TBrowseNew (0, 0, 24, 79)`
TBrowseDB (<nTop>, <nLeft>, <nBottom>, <nRight>)	This function creates a new, initialized TBrowse object that uses the specified screen coordinates. You must create the columns required to contain data. However, this function automatically creates data positioning code blocks which use default values. These positioning blocks include: Go Top, Go Bottom, and Skip. Use this function when you need to create an object that requires a minimum of programming effort. The command line format for creating an object that uses the entire display is, as follows: `oBrowseDB := TBrowseDB (0, 0, 24, 79)`

The TBrowseDB( ) function, on the other hand, is specifically designed to create an object for displaying database file information. It automatically creates many of the code blocks required to manipulate data within the object. As a result, this function is less flexible, but requires a minimum of code to use. Both functions create TBrowse objects. The one you choose to use within your code is determined by the requirements of the program you want to create.

A major part of the programming associated with a TBrowse object revolves around the object itself. Each TBrowse object consists of two parts: exported instance variables and methods. You determine the behavior and status of a TBrowse object by monitoring and manipulating these components. TABLE 4-4 contains a listing and description of every TBrowse exported instance variable and TABLE 4-5 contains descriptions of the various TBrowse methods.

Table 4-4 TBrowse-class exported-instance variables

Variable	Description
Cargo	This variable contains the value of any data type as a user definable slot. Think of cargo as a place to store information that doesn't belong anywhere else. It usually contains information specific to the instance of a TBrowse object. Use the cargo variable as follows: oTObject:Cargo := "Some Value"
colCount	This variable contains a number representing the total number of columns in the browse. There is one TBColumn object for each column in the browse. Use the colCount variable as follows: nCol := oTObject:colCount
colorSpec	The colorSpec variable contains the colors used by the TBrowse object to display data on screen. It contains the colors defined by Setcolor() when you initialize the TBrowse object. Use the colorSpec variable as follows to save the current color: cColors := oTObject:colorSpec and use the colorSpec variable as follows to change the current color: oTObject:colorSpec := cColors
colPos	Use this variable to determine the current position of the browse cursor. The columns are numbered starting at 1 from the leftmost column. Use the colPos variable as follows: nCol := oTObject:colPos
colSep	This variable determines what TBrowse uses as a separator between columns that don't have a separator defined. Use colSep variable as follows: oTObject:colSep := chr(186)
freeze	Use this variable to define the number of columns that are visible on the display at all time. The number of columns always begin at the left side of the display starting with column 1. Use the freeze variable as follows to freeze the first column in place: oTObject:freeze := 1

Variable	Description
goBottomBlock	This variable contains the code block executed whenever the program issues a goBottom() message.
goTopBlock	This variable contains the code block executed whenever the program issues a goTop() message.
headSep	This variable determines what TBrowse uses as a separator between headers and detail that don't have a separator defined. Use the colSep variable as follows: oTObject:headSep := chr(196)
hitBottom	This variable returns true whenever the user makes an attempt to navigate past the bottom of the file. Many programs use this as a signal to append a new record.
hitTop	This variable returns true whenever the user makes an attempt to navigate past the top of the file. Many programs use the tone() function to signal the user that he is at the beginning of the file.
LeftVisible()	Use this variable to determine the leftmost unfrozen column visible on the browse display. This variable is available in Clipper versions 5.01 and above. Use the LeftVisible() variable as follows: nCol := oTObject:LeftVisible()
nBottom	Use this variable to define the bottom of the display area. TBrowse automatically sets it as part of defining the original object. Use the nBottom variable as follows: oTObject:nBottom := 24
nLeft	Use this variable to define the left side of the display area. TBrowse automatically sets it as part of defining the original object. Use the nLeft variable as follows: oTObject:nLeft := 0
nRight	Use this variable to define the right side of the display area. TBrowse automatically sets it as part of defining

Table 4-4 Continued.

Variable	Description
	the original object. Use the nRight variable as follows: oTObject:nRight := 78
nTop	Use this variable to define the top of the display area. TBrowse automatically sets it as part of defining the original object. Use the nTop variable as follows: oTObject:nTop := 0
RightVisible()	Use this variable to determine the rightmost unfrozen column visible on the browse display. This variable is available in Clipper versions 5.01 and above. Use the RightVisible() variable as follows: nCol := oTObject:RightVisible()
rowCount	This variable contains the number of detail rows visible on the screen. It does not include rows occupied by headers, footers, or separators. Use the rowCount variable as follows: nRow := oTObject:rowCount
rowPos	This variable contains a number that indicates the current browse cursor position in the detail rows. It does not include rows occupied by headers, footers, or separators. Do not confuse this number with the record number or any other database positioning information. It indicates only screen rows. Use the rowPos variable as follows: nRow := oTObject:rowPos
skipBlock	This variable contains a code block that defines the method used to skip records. TBrowse provides a default skipBlock entry that is sufficient for most purposes when you initialize the object.
stable	Use this variable to determine if the TBrowse object is in a stable state. It returns true if the object is stable and false when it isn't. Most screen repositioning and data editing commands place the TBrowse object in an unstable state. Therefore, your program must monitor this variable and use the stabilize() method as appropriate to restabilize the object.

Table 4-5 TBrowse-class methods

Method	Description
Cursor movement methods	
delColumn(nPos)	Use this method to remove a column object from the middle of a browse. It returns a reference to the column. This method is available in Clipper versions 5.01 and above.
down()	This method moves the browse cursor down one row. If the cursor is already at the bottom of the display, the method scrolls the screen up one row and places the browse cursor on the new value displayed at the bottom of the display. When a user tries to move the cursor past the last record in the database, the method retains the current cursor position and sets the hitBottom variable true.
end()	This method moves the browse cursor to the rightmost column in the browse object and redraws the screen.
goBottom()	This method moves the browse cursor to the last record in the database and redraws the screen.
goTop()	This method moves the browse cursor to the first record in the database and redraws the screen.
home()	This method moves the browse cursor to the leftmost column in the browse object and redraws the screen.
insColumn(nPos, oColumn)	Use this method to insert a column object into the middle of a browse. It returns a reference to the column. This method is available in Clipper versions 5.01 and above.
invalidate()	Use this method to invalidate the entire browse display. TBrowse redraws the entire screen, including headers, footers, and separators during the next stabilize. The invalidate() method will not refresh the data displayed on the screen. In other words, it uses the current data values. Use the refresh() method if

Table 4-5 Continued.

Method	Description
	you need to refresh the data values in a column. This method is available in Clipper versions 5.01 and above.
left()	This method moves the browse cursor one column left in the browse object. If the cursor is already at the leftmost position on the display, the method pans the display one column to the left. If the cursor is on the last column, the browse cursor position remains unchanged.
pageDown()	Use this method to skip down the number of records appearing in one display. The method automatically places the browse cursor on the first record in the new display. If the cursor is already on the last display page of records, the method simply places the browse cursor on the last record in the database. When a user tries to move the cursor past the last record in the database, the method retains the current cursor position and sets the hitBottom variable true.
pageUp()	Use this method to skip up the number of records appearing in one display. The method automatically places the browse cursor on the first record in the new display. If the cursor is already on the first display page of records, the method simply places the browse cursor on the first record in the database. When a user tries to move the cursor past the first record in the database, the method retains the current cursor position and sets the hitTop variable true.
panEnd()	This method moves the browse cursor to the rightmost data column. This pans the display completely to the right.
panHome()	This method moves the browse cursor to the leftmost data column. This pans the display completely to the left.

Method	Description
panLeft()	Use this method to pan the display one screen to the left without changing the position of the browse cursor. If the leftmost column is already in view, the position of the browse cursor remains unchanged.
panRight()	Use this method to pan the display one screen to the right without changing the position of the browse cursor. If the rightmost column is already in view, the position of the browse cursor remains unchanged.
right()	This method moves the browse cursor one column right in the browse object. If the cursor is already at the rightmost position on the display, the method pans the display one column to the right. If the cursor is on the last column, the browse cursor position remains unchanged.
up()	This method moves the browse cursor up one row. If the cursor is already at the top of the display, the method scrolls the screen down one row and places the browse cursor on the new value displayed at the top of the display. When a user tries to move the cursor past the first record in the database, the method retains the current cursor position and sets the hitTop variable true.
Miscellaneous methods	
addColumn (<oColumn>)	Use this method to add a new column to the TBrowse object. This method automatically increments the colCount variable.
configure()	This method forces TBrowse to reexamine all instance variables and TBColumn objects. The object then reconfigures its internal settings as required. Use this method after you modify the TBrowse instance variables manually.
getColumn (<nColumn>)	The getColumn method returns the TBColumn object specified by nColumn.

Table 4-5 Continued.

Method	Description
refreshAll()	This method marks all data rows invalid. The next stabilize() method call refreshes all the values displayed on screen from the database.
refreshCurrent()	This method marks the current data row invalid. The next stabilize() method call refreshes the current data row values displayed on screen from the database.
setColumn (<nColumn>, <oColumn>)	Use this method to replace the column object used by the column pointed to by nColumn with the object contained in oColumn.
stabilize()	This method stabilizes the current TBrowse object and displays the results on screen. You must call the stabilize() method until the stabilize variable returns true because this method is incremental. An incremental stabilize allows asynchronous events such as keystrokes to occur. The method returns false until the TBrowse object is stable.

The exported instance variables described in TABLE 4-4 allow you to monitor the condition of the TBrowse object. For example, the ColCount variable allows you to determine the number of columns the TBrowse object contains. Because each column is composed of and controlled by a TBColumn object, you cannot change this statistic directly, but you can use it to determine how to manage the TBrowse object. In other words, the ColCount variable is provided for informational purposes only.

You can also use exported instance variables to manipulate specific aspects of the TBrowse object. For example, the nTop variable allows you to change the top screen row used by Clipper to display the object. By saving and then changing nTop, you can modify the appearance of the table on screen. Saving the value of nTop allows you to return the table to its original appearance. There are other variables that allow you to control the appearance of the table. Notice that none of the exported instance variables directly modify data. They are always used to change the appearance of the table, not the data.

Unlike the exported instance variables, the TBrowse exported methods are used to directly and indirectly manipulate the data. They do not change the value of the data, they simply manipulate it. All cursor movement methods are examples of indirect manipulation. These methods provide the interface between the data and the table. For example, the Up( ) method monitors the cursor position within the table. If the cursor is at the top of the table, then Up( ) retrieves the previous record from the database. As you can see, the method provides access to the data without actually changing it.

An example of direct manipulation can be seen in the GetColumn( ) method. In this instance, the method retrieves a TBColumn object from the TBrowse object and places it in a variable. By changing the contents of the variable you can change the value of the data. As with the other methods provided with the TBrowse class, this method does not modify the data, it only makes it available for modification. Once modified, you can use the SetColumn( ) method to replace the contents of the TBColumn( ) object with the contents of the variable.

It's essential that you understand the relationship between a TBrowse object and the TBColumn objects it contains before you attempt to use the TBrowse System. The TBrowse object is responsible for the appearance of the table and manipulation of the data. The TBColumn object is responsible for the actual changing and handling of the data. Another way of looking at this relationship is that the TBrowse object handles the higher-level functions, while the TBColumn objects perform the lower-level work. Once you grasp this concept, you'll find it easier to determine which object you need to work with in your program, TBrowse or TBColumn.

TBColumn System description

The TBColumn System is the means by which you can add new column to a TBrowse object or manipulate the data contained in the column. It consists of two elements, a class function for creating a new column and exported instance variables used to change the data. The following section describes the class function, TBColumnNew( ). TABLE 4-6 contains a listing and description of all the TBColumn exported instance variables.

TABLE 4-6 clearly illustrates the biggest differences between a TBrowse object and a TBColumn object. All of the TBColumn exported instance variables are directly involved in modifying and displaying the data contained in a single column of the table. One of the most important variables is the data retrieval code block, Block. The code block contained in this variable determines how the object reacts when asked to retrieve or replace data in a database, array, or other variable. The syntax for TBColumnNew is as follows:

```
TBCOLUMNNEW(<cEXP>, <bEXP>)
```

Table 4-6 TBColumn-class exported-instance variables

Variable	Description

block	You use this variable to define the code block that retrieves data for the column. This code block can contain any code required to perform the task. The TBColumn object does not supply any input. The block must supply data of the appropriate type for the column as output. You can create a noneditable code block as follows:
	`bNewBlock := {|| MAILLIST->FIRST_NAME}`
	`oTBObj := oNewBrowse:getColumn(1)`
	`oTBObj:block := bNewBlock`
	`oNewBrowse:setColumn(1, oTBObj)`

Cargo	This variable contains the value of any data type as a userdefinable slot. Think of cargo as a place to store information that doesn't belong anywhere else. It usually contains information specific to the instance of a TBrowse object. Use the cargo variable as follows:
	`oTBObj := oNewBrowse:getColumn(1)`
	`oTBObj:Cargo := "Some Value"`
	`oNewBrowse:setColumn(1, oTBObj)`

colorBlock	Use this variable if you want to create a code block that determines the color of a row in a column by the value of the data. The code block must return a two-element array. The array contains numbers that are an index into the color table for the TBrowse object. This is very useful if, for example, you wanted to display positive numbers in black and negative numbers in red. Use the colorBlock variable as shown below:
	`local aClr1 := {1, 2}`
	`local aClr2 := {2, 3}`
	`local bColBlock := {| cFld |;`
	`iif(len(alltrim(cFld)) == 0, aClr2, aClr1)}`
	`oTBObj := oNewBrowse:getColumn(5)`
	`oTBObj:colorBlock := bColBlock`
	`oNewBrowse:setColumn(5, oTBObj)`

colSep	This variable determines what TBrowse uses as a separator between columns that don't have a separator defined. Use colSep variable as follows:
	`oTBObj := oNewBrowse:getColumn(1)`
	`oTBObj:colSep := chr(186)`
	`oNewBrowse:setColumn(1, oTBObj)`

Variable	Description

defColor	The defColor variable lets you redefine the color of a column. As with the colorBlock variable, the defColor variable uses a two-element array. The array contains numbers that are an index into the color table for the TBrowse object. Use the defColor variable as shown below:
	local aColor := {2, 3}
	  oTBObj := oNewBrowse:getColumn(5)
	  oTBObj:defColor := aColor
	  oNewBrowse:setColumn(5, oTBObj)

footing	This variable contains text that the TBColumn object displays at the bottom of the display area. Use the footing variable as follows:
	  oTBObj := oNewBrowse:getColumn(1)
	  oTBObj:footing := "Some Text"
	  oNewBrowse:setColumn(1, oTBObj)

footSep	This variable determines what TBrowse uses as a separator between footers and detail. Use the footSep variable as follows:
	  oTBObj := oNewBrowse:getColumn(1)
	  oTBObj:footSep := chr(196)
	  oNewBrowse:setColumn(1, oTBObj)

heading	This variable contains text that the TBColumn object displays at the top of the display area. Use the heading variable as follows:
	  oTBObj := oNewBrowse:getColumn(1)
	  oTBObj:heading := "Some Text"
	  oNewBrowse:setColumn(1, oTBObj)

headSep	This variable determines what TBrowse uses as a separator between headers and detail. Use the headSep variable as follows:
	  oTBObj := oNewBrowse:getColumn(1)
	  oTBObj:headSep := chr(196)
	  oNewBrowse:setColumn(1, oTBObj)

width	Use this variable to define the width of a column. If this variable is left blank, the TBColumn object uses the width of the input returned by TBColumn:block. Use the width

Table 4-6 Continued.

Variable	Description
	variable as follows: oTBObj := oNewBrowse:getColumn(1) oTBObj:width := 20 oNewBrowse:setColumn(1, oTBObj)

The TBColumnNew( ) function creates a new column object. This object contains the header defined by cEXP and the data retrieval code block defined by bEXP. Simply creating the TBColumn object does not add it to the TBrowse object. You must create the object and then add it to the TBrowse object using the AddColumn method. You must supply both parameters to create a new object. However, you can display a blank heading by providing a null string (" ") to cEXP. EXAMPLE:

```
// Create a rudimentary TBrowse object and add the appropriate
// column objects.

oBrowse := tbrowsedb(02, 01, 23, 78)
oBrowse:addcolumn(tbcolumnnew("Reference;Number", {|| NAME->REFERENCE}))
oBrowse:addcolumn(tbcolumnnew("Name", {|| NAME->FIRST}))
oBrowse:addcolumn(tbcolumnnew(" ", {|| NAME->MIDDLE}))
oBrowse:addcolumn(tbcolumnnew(" ", {|| NAME->LAST}))
oBrowse:addcolumn(tbcolumnnew("Date", {|| CONT->DATE}))
oBrowse:addcolumn(tbcolumnnew("Purpose", {|| CONT->CONTRIBUTE}))
oBrowse:addcolumn(tbcolumnnew("Amount", {|| CONT->AMOUNT}))
```

TBrowse and TBColumn programming examples

The preceding text described how and when to use the TBrowse and TBColumn Systems in detail. This section introduces you to some of the practical considerations for using them. Figure 4-2 contains a programming example that illustrates some of the features of both TBrowse and TBColumn. Notice that it specifically covers some of the additional programming required when more than one database is used to store data. This example shows a one-to-many relationship between the parent and child database.

While the remarks sprinkled throughout the source code example should help you understand the mechanics of how the code works, an explanation of the overall theory is in order. This example demonstrates three reasons why TBrowse is superior to its predecessor DBEdit( ). First, you can display data from more than one database at a time. Second, you can use color and other visual aids to help the user see the relationship between the various data elements. Third, you can exercise greater control over the cursor and data-editing environment.

```
// This example program shows an expanded TBrowse object.  It includes
// all the features of TBROW02.PRG.  Enhanced features include more
// precise cursor control and the ability to edit field contents.  You
// can compile this program as you would any other Clipper program.
// Written by: John Mueller
// Copywrite 1991 John Mueller - Tab Books
// Works with Version 5.01 and above only.

// Include some pre-defined InKey() manifest constants
// and box drawing characters.

#include "INKEY.CH"
#include "BOX.CH"

// Create program variables.

local nChar := 0,;       // InKey() value.
      nDispRow := 0,;    // Display row during stabilize.
      oEditCol           // Column we wish to edit.
static aCVar1[2],;       // First foreground color array.
       aCVar2[2],;       // Second foreground color array.
       aCVar3[2],;       // Background color array.
       aNVar[50],;       // New value tracking array.
       nRef := 0,;       // Previous reference value.
       nRow := 0,;       // Current cursor row within a browse.
       cName := " ",;    // Name of the field we want to edit.
       lEqRef := .F.     // Are the two reference numbers equal?

// Assign the array colors.

aCVar1[1] := 4
aCVar1[2] := 2
aCVar2[1] := 5
aCVar2[2] := 2
aCVar3[1] := 1
aCVar3[2] := 2

// Clear the display and display preliminary box and identifying text in
// preparation for using the program.

set scoreboard off
dispbegin()
setcolor("w+/b, w+/g,, w+/bg, w+/rb")
cls
dispbox(01, 00, 24, 79, B_SINGLE_DOUBLE)
@00, 00 say padc(" Donator Contribution Status ", 80, chr(176))
dispend()

// Open the database and set a relation.

use SAMPLE6 index SAMPLE6 alias CONT
use SAMPLE5 index SAMPLE5 alias NAME new
```

4-2 Continued.

```
select CONT
dbsetrelation("NAME", {|| str(CONT->REFERENCE)}, "str(CONT->REFERENCE)")

// Create a rudimentary TBrowse object and add the appropriate
// column objects.

oBrowse := tbrowsedb(02, 01, 23, 78)
oBrowse:addcolumn(tbcolumnnew("Reference;Number", {|| NAME->REFERENCE}))
oBrowse:addcolumn(tbcolumnnew("Name", {|| NAME->FIRST}))
oBrowse:addcolumn(tbcolumnnew(" ", {|| NAME->MIDDLE}))
oBrowse:addcolumn(tbcolumnnew(" ", {|| NAME->LAST}))
oBrowse:addcolumn(tbcolumnnew("Date", {|| CONT->DATE}))
oBrowse:addcolumn(tbcolumnnew("Purpose", {|| CONT->CONTRIBUTE}))
oBrowse:addcolumn(tbcolumnnew("Amount", {|| CONT->AMOUNT}))

// Define the header and column separators.

oBrowse:colSep := chr(186)
oBrowse:headSep := chr(196)

// Remove the column separator for the name columns.

// Assign the columns to objects.

oColumn1 := oBrowse:getcolumn(1)
oColumn2 := oBrowse:getcolumn(2)
oColumn3 := oBrowse:getcolumn(3)
oColumn4 := oBrowse:getcolumn(4)
oColumn5 := oBrowse:getcolumn(5)
oColumn6 := oBrowse:getcolumn(6)
oColumn7 := oBrowse:getcolumn(7)

// Store the field name for every column in the cargo variable.  This
// will allow us to quickly identify the column later for editing.

oColumn1:cargo := "NAME->REFERENCE"
oColumn2:cargo := "NAME->FIRST"
oColumn3:cargo := "NAME->MIDDLE"
oColumn4:cargo := "NAME->LAST"
oColumn5:cargo := "CONT->DATE"
oColumn6:cargo := "CONT->CONTRIBUTE"
oColumn7:cargo := "CONT->AMOUNT"

// Assign new column separators.  Since we want the entire name to
// appear as a single entity, the line separators are inappropriate.

oColumn3:colSep := " "
oColumn4:colSep := " "

// Assign new colors.  The first four columns check to see if there
// is data to display, if not, they use the background color.
// Otherwise, they use the appropriate foreground color.
```

```
oColumn1:colorBlock := {| cIn | iif(len(trim(cIn))>0, aCVar1, aCVar3)}
oColumn2:colorBlock := {| cIn | iif(len(trim(cIn))>0, aCVar2, aCVar3)}
oColumn3:colorBlock := {| cIn | iif(len(trim(cIn))>0, aCVar2, aCVar3)}
oColumn4:colorBlock := {| cIn | iif(len(trim(cIn))>0, aCVar2, aCVar3)}
oColumn5:colorBlock := {| | aCVar1}
oColumn6:colorBlock := {| | aCVar2}
oColumn7:colorBlock := {| | aCVar1}

// Change the data display blocks for the first four columns.
// The first column code block performs three tasks.  First, it
// compares the current value of Reference with the previous value
// stored in nRef.  If the value is the same, it sets the value of
// lEqRef to True.  The value nDispRow verifies that this is not
// the first data row.  If it is, then the header already set nRef
// to equal Reference and the data row won't display otherwise. The
// second task is to store the current value of Reference to nRef.
// Finally, if the lEqRef is true, then we've already displayed the
// value.  Therefore, we output a blank in place of the value in
// Reference.  The value of lEqRef is checked for the other three
// rows as well and appropriate action taken.

oColumn1:block := {|| iif(nRef == NAME->REFERENCE .and.;
                          ! nDispRow == 0,;
                          lEqRef := .T.,;
                          lEqRef:= .F.),;
                      nRef := NAME->REFERENCE,;
                      iif(lEqRef,;
                          " ",;
                          str(NAME->REFERENCE))}
oColumn2:block := {|| iif(lEqRef, space(20), NAME->FIRST)}
oColumn3:block := {|| iif(lEqRef, " ", NAME->MIDDLE)}
oColumn4:block := {|| iif(lEqRef, space(30), NAME->LAST)}

// Send the changes to the TBrowse object.

oBrowse:setColumn(1, oColumn1)
oBrowse:setColumn(2, oColumn2)
oBrowse:setColumn(3, oColumn3)
oBrowse:setColumn(4, oColumn4)
oBrowse:setColumn(5, oColumn5)
oBrowse:setColumn(6, oColumn6)
oBrowse:setColumn(7, oColumn7)

// Continue this loop until the user presses ESC.

do while ! nChar == K_ESC
   nChar := inkey()

// Display the TBrowse object.

   nDispRow := 0
   do while (! oBrowse:stabilize)
      ++nDispRow
      if oBrowse:colPos == 1
```

4-2 Continued.

```
         aNVar[row()] := lEqRef
      endif
   enddo

// Interpret the InKey() value.  Manipulate the browse cursor position
// using the appropriate TBrowse method.

   do case

// If the user presses the up arrow, check the current column position.
// If the position is less than 5, then there is data displayed on every
// row.  Move the cursor up one row unless we are at the top of the
// file.  If the column position is between 1 and 4, then some rows are
// blank.  Move the cursor up one row and place the current row position
// in a row counting variable.  aNVar contains true if the row is blank,
// false if the row contains data, and NIL if the row does not contain
// data.  If the current row is NIL (does not contain data), then move
// down one row to the first row (always contains data) and exit.
// Otherwise, check to see if the row is blank.  Continue to move up one
// row at a time until we find a row that isn't blank.

      case nChar == K_UP
         if oBrowse:colPos < 5
            oBrowse:up()
            nRow := row() - 1
            if aNVar[nRow] == NIL
               oBrowse:down()
            else
               while aNVar[nRow]
                  oBrowse:up()
                  nRow--
               enddo
            endif
         else
            oBrowse:up()
         endif

// If the user presses the down arrow and the column position is less
// than 5, move the cursor down one row, and place the current row value
// in a row counting variable.  aNVar contains true if the row is blank,
// false if the row contains data, and NIL if the row does not contain
// data.  If the row is blank, continue to move down until we find
// either a row that contains data or does not contain data.  If the row
// does not contain data, move up until we find one that does and exit.
// If the column position is 5 or greater, then there is data on every
// row.  Move down one row if we are not at the bottom of the file.

      case nChar == K_DOWN
         if oBrowse:colPos < 5
            oBrowse:down()
            nRow := row() + 1
            while aNVar[nRow]
```

```
            oBrowse:down()
            nRow++
            if aNVar[nRow] == NIL
               nRow--
               while aNVar[nRow]
                  oBrowse:up()
                  nRow--
               enddo
               oBrowse:up()
               exit
            endif
         enddo
      else
         oBrowse:down()
      endif

// If the user presses the right arrow, move right one column unless we
// are already at the rightmost column.

      case nChar == K_RIGHT
         oBrowse:right()

// If the user presses the left arrow, more left one column unless we
// are already at the leftmost column.  Since we could run into a blank
// row when moving left, check the column number.  If the column number
// is less than 5 and aNVar is true (row is blank), then move down one
// row.  Place the current row in a row counting variable.  If the row
// is blank move down one row.  Check to see if the row contains data
// (false) or does not contain data (NIL).  If the row does not contain
// data, then move up until we find a non-blank row that does.
// Otherwise, continue to move down until we find a non-blank row.

      case nChar == K_LEFT
         nRow := row() + 1
         oBrowse:left()
         if oBrowse:colPos < 5 .and. aNVar[row()]
            oBrowse:down()
            while aNVar[nRow]
               oBrowse:down()
               nRow++
               if aNVar[nRow] == NIL
                  nRow--
                  while aNVar[nRow]
                     oBrowse:up()
                     nRow--
                  enddo
                  oBrowse:up()
                  exit
               endif
            enddo
         endif

// If the user presses enter, then allow them to modify any field except
// the key field.  We determine the current field name by obtaining the
```

4-2 Continued.

```
// current TBColumn object and examining the cargo value which contains
// the field name.  If the user chooses the key field, display an error
// message.  Otherwise, place the name of the field in a variable and
// perform a standard get on the field.  Mark the field invalid so that
// TBrowse will display the new value the next time it refreshes the
// display.

      case nChar == K_ENTER
         oEditCol := oBrowse:getcolumn(oBrowse:colPos)
         cName := oEditCol:cargo
         if !(cName == "NAME->REFERENCE")
            @ row(), col() get &cName color "W+/R"
            read
            oBrowse:refreshCurrent()
         else
            alert("You cannot edit this field!")
         endif
   endcase


enddo

// Clear the display and exit the program.

setcolor("w/n, n/w")
cls
return
```

You can attain the first goal by using two techniques. First, set up a relationship between the parent and child database. This relationship is based on a numeric key field where each key is unique. Obtaining uniqueness with the parent database, NAME, is simply a matter of indexing the REFERENCE field. Because the child database, CONT, contains multiple instances of a single REFERENCE, add DATE to the indexing scheme to create a unique key. You can also make use of various code blocks to determine when and where to display the data. Only one instance of data in the NAME database is displayed for all instances of that reference number in the CONT database. Because each TBColumn Block exported instance variable references a separate, aliased field, you can mix data from the two databases.

The use of color is one of the most apparent features for the user. Your second goal is to use color to make the data easier to see and work with. In this case, make alternating sections the same color. This helps differentiate one column of data from another. Notice that if you use the same highlight color for every column, the get highlight color is the same for every column as well. This allows the user to know the exact position of the cursor and the edit state at all times. In addition, blank spaces use the same color as the screen background. This emphasizes the fact that a specific coordinate does not contain any data to edit.

The programmer's third goal in this example might not be apparent to users the first few times they browse through the database. The cursor positions itself only on row/column coordinates that contain data. If the coordinate is blank, then the cursor skips to the first nonblank coordinate it finds. This means that users cannot accidentally try to modify a blank area on the screen, reducing chances of errors in the database. To prevent users from corrupting the index key, you can prevent them from editing the key field. If an attempt is made to edit the key field, the program displays an error message telling the user that this action is not permitted. Implementing safeguards of this type are essential to maintaining referential integrity in the database. Both the cursor-control and edit-control features of TBrowse allow the programmer to maintain the database with a higher level of integrity.

Using the Error System

The Error System is one of the most important sections of code in a Clipper program. This is the section of code designed to protect users from themselves. The main purpose for the Error System is to track the condition of the program and report any errors it finds. It's also responsible for helping users recover from any errors they might encounter. However, this is also the least used and therefore least tested section of code in any program. Because of the job it's designed to perform, the programmer hopes never to use the Error System code. There are also inherent dangers associated with this section of code. For example, it's almost impossible to determine every source of errors during program design. The computer or user will always cause errors in some way that was not originally envisioned by the programmer.

Because the Clipper Error System uses OOP techniques, it's possible to build error-control code that is less susceptible to mistakes and more likely to catch errors. In addition, it's easier to add new controls as the need arises because of the modularity enforced by OOP techniques.

Error System description

Considering the importance of the job it performs, the Error System is quite simple. It consists of one class function, described below, and several exported instance variables described in TABLE 4-7. You don't need exported methods to perform the functions required by an error object. The main purpose of the error object itself is to retrieve the data that's required to classify the error and recover from it. A separate program performs the actual classification and recovery tasks. The error object also maintains status information. For example, it tracks the number of times that the Error System has tried to correct the error and provides a status indicator showing whether or not the program can recover from the error.

Table 4-7 Error-class exported-instance variables

Variable	Description
args	This variable contains a list of the arguments supplied to an operator or function when an argument error occurs. Monitoring this variable allows you to check the type and value of the parameters sent from one area to another area of your code. The args variable contains NIL for other types of errors.
canDefault	Use this variable to determine if the error can use the default error handler to recover. A return value of false means that it can't. The result is that the user will receive an error message and the program will end. By adding your own error-handling routines, you can help the user recover from many errors. If the variable returns true, you can safely ignore the error because the default recovery routines will handle it. This variable never returns true if the canSubstitute variable is true.
canRetry	Use this variable to determine if the subsystem can retry the operation that failed. If the variable returns true, then the default error handler will allow the user to fix the problem and retry the operation. This variable never returns true if the canSubstitute variable is true.
canSubstitute	Monitor the canSubstitute variable to determine when the error handler can safely substitute a new value for a failed operation. This normally occurs when a function or operator receives invalid arguments. You must perform the substitution by returning a new result value from the code block invoked to handle the error. The canSubstitute variable is never true when the canDefault or canRetry variables are true.
cargo	This variable contains the value of any data type not used by the get system. You can use this variable to keep track of data that doesn't have a standard slot in the error object. For example, you could use it to store additional error information for a custom error handler to aid in recovery.

Variable	Description
description	The description variable contains a string describing the failure condition. A zero-length string indicates the system doesn't recognize the specific error that occurred. In most cases it is not safe to try to recover from unrecognized error conditions. If the genCode variable does not contain zero, a printable error description is always available.
filename	The filename variable contains the name of the file associated with the error condition. If this string is empty, then the error did not occur as the result of a particular file. Other conditions that output a null string include failure to provide a filename and loss of the filename by the subsystem.
genCode	Use the genCode variable to determine if the error is one of the generic errors described in ERROR.CH or if it is subsystem specific. A subsystem-specific error requires special handling. In most cases it results in a unrecoverable error unless your code contains special error-handling code.
operation	This variable contains the name of the operation being performed when the error occurred. When the error occurs in an operator or function, the operation variable contains the name of the operator or function. If the error occurs due to an undefined variable or function, operator contains the name of the variable or function. In most cases you can use this variable to determine the exact nature of an error. If the operator variable is blank, the subsystem doesn't recognize the particular operation in effect during the error.
osCode	Use this variable to determine if the error is operating system specific. If the variable contains a zero, then the error is Clipper specific. Otherwise, the error occurred as the result of a DOS operation. The osCode variable returns the same value as the DOSError() function.

Table 4-7 Continued.

Variable	Description
subCode	The subCode variable contains the subsystem error number. If this variable contains a zero, then the subsystem does not recognize a specific error code.
subSystem	This variable contains the name of the subsystem experiencing the error. For Clipper-specific errors, the subSystem variable returns BASE. Database specific errors return the name of the database driver.
tries	The tries variable contains the number of times that the retry operation has failed. If this number is zero, then the subsystem does not allow retries for this particular error.

The ErrorNew( ) function creates a new error object. It doesn't require arguments as input. In most cases, in fact, the default error object provides sufficient functionality. EXAMPLE:

```
oErrorObj := errornew()
```

Error System programming examples

In most cases, you'll want to add to the capability of the Error System rather than create a new one. One of the ways to test these additions is to create a program that generates specific errors and observe how the Error System traps them. Figure 4-3 is an example of a program designed to generate errors. The error number expected is listed next to the piece of code generating the error.

Nantucket provides a copy of the Error System code with the Clipper distribution disks. The Error System program consists of procedures for creating an error object, determining what error has occurred, and generating error messages. Figure 4-4 shows a modified version of the Error System program, ERRORSYS.PRG. The modifications include enhanced message support, an option to ignore the error, and a means of determining where the error occurred simply by observing the error message. As you can see, while it's time-consuming to add these enhancements, the actual procedure for doing so is not complicated.

4-3 An example program designed to generate errors

```
// This is an error generation program.  It is not designed to work, or
// do anything spectacular.  Use it to test the ERRORSYS.PRG file
// contained on this disk.  Do not use it with the standard error system
// included within Clipper.
// Written by: John Mueller
// Copyright 1991 John Mueller - Tab Books

local xSomeVar := " "
static nTest1 := 100,;
       cTest2 := "This is a string"
       dTest3 := ctod("01/01/91")
       nTest4 := 100.1
       cTest5 := "SOMEPROC"

do &cTest5                              // Generate error 1001.
eval(nTest1, cTest2)                    // Generate error 1004.
? !nTest4                               // Generate error 1077.
? nTest1 + cTest2                       // Generate error 1081.
xSomeVar := nTest1 - dTest3             // Generate error 1082.
? xSomeVar                              // Generate error 1083.
? cTest2 * dTest3
? abs(dTest3)                           // Generate error 1089.
```

4-4 Error-system programming example

```
// Sections of this code come from the ERRORSYS.PRG provided by
// Nantucket on the distribution disks for Clipper 5.01.
// Enhancements to the original program include more detailed error
// messages.  The messages now provide a more meaningful explanation of
// the error.  In addition, you may now choose to ignore the error.
// This is useful during troubleshooting.  Unfortunately, this also
// could mean that your machine will freeze after you tell Clipper to
// ignore the error.  The on screen error messages also display the
// procedure and line number at which the error occurred.
// Portions Written by: John Mueller
// Copyright 1991 John Mueller - Tab Books

/***
*   Errorsys.prg
*   Standard Clipper 5.0 error handler
*   Copyright (c) 1990 Nantucket Corp.  All rights reserved.
*
*   Compile:  /m/n/w
*/

#include "error.ch"
```

4-4 Continued.

```
// put messages to STDERR
#command ? <list,...>   =>  ?? Chr(13) + Chr(10) ; ?? <list>
#command ?? <list,...>  =>  OutErr(<list>)


// used below
#define NTRIM(n)       ( LTrim(Str(n)) )



/***
*   ErrorSys()
*
*   Note:  automatically executes at startup
*/

proc ErrorSys()
   ErrorBlock( {|e| DefError(e)} )
return



/***
*   DefError()
*/
static func DefError(e)
local i, cMessage, aOptions, nChoice


   // by default, division by zero yields zero
   if ( e:genCode == EG_ZERODIV )
   return (0)
end


// for network open error, set NETERR() and subsystem default
if ( e:genCode == EG_OPEN .and. e:osCode == 32 .and. e:canDefault )

   NetErr(.t.)
   return (.f.)                                    // NOTE

end


// for lock error during APPEND BLANK, set NETERR() and subsystem default
if ( e:genCode == EG_APPENDLOCK .and. e:canDefault )

   NetErr(.t.)
   return (.f.)                                    // NOTE

end
```

```
// build error message
cMessage := ErrorMessage(e)


// build options array
// aOptions := {"Break", "Quit"}
aOptions := {"Quit"}

if (e:canRetry)
   AAdd(aOptions, "Retry")
end

if (e:canDefault)
   AAdd(aOptions, "Default")
end

 AAdd(aOptions, "Ignore")     // This new option allows you to
                              // continue program execution after an
                              // error occurs.  This is especially
                              // during debugging.


// put up alert box
nChoice := 0
while ( nChoice == 0 )

   if ( Empty(e:osCode) )
      nChoice := Alert( cMessage, aOptions )

   else
      nChoice := Alert( cMessage + ;
                  ";(DOS Error " + NTRIM(e:osCode) + ")", ;
                  aOptions )
   end


   if ( nChoice == NIL )
      exit
   end

end


if ( !Empty(nChoice) )

   // do as instructed
   if ( aOptions[nChoice] == "Break" )
      Break(e)

   elseif ( aOptions[nChoice] == "Retry" )
      return (.t.)

   elseif ( aOptions[nChoice] == "Default" )
      return (.f.)
```

4-4 Continued.

```
    elseif ( aOptions[nChoice] == "Ignore" )  // Implement the new
        return (.f.)                          // option.

    end

end


// display message and traceback
if ( !Empty(e:osCode) )
    cMessage += " (DOS Error " + NTRIM(e:osCode) + ") "
end

? cMessage
i := 2
while ( !Empty(ProcName(i)) )
    ? "Called from", Trim(ProcName(i)) + ;
        "(" + NTRIM(ProcLine(i)) + ")  "

    i++
end


// give up
ErrorLevel(1)
    QUIT

return (.f.)



/***
*   ErrorMessage()
*/
static func ErrorMessage(e)
local cMessage, nCount


    // start error message
    cMessage := if( e:severity > ES_WARNING, "Error ", "Warning " )


    // add subsystem name if available
    if ( ValType(e:subsystem) == "C" )
        cMessage += e:subsystem()
    else
        cMessage += "???"
    end
```

```
    // add subsystem's error code if available
    if ( ValType(e:subCode) == "N" )
       cMessage += ("/" + NTRIM(e:subCode))

// Provide extended message support.  The program currently supports a
// subset of the total number of messages.  The remainder are left as an
// exercise for the reader.

       do case

          case e:subCode == 1001
             cMessage += (";The specified function or " + ;
                ";procedure was not linked with the " + ;
                ";application or was never directly " + ;
                ";referred to by the application.;")

          case e:subCode == 1002
             cMessage += (";The specified alias is not " + ;
                ";currently associated with any work area.;")

          case e:subCode == 1003
             cMessage += (";The specified MEMVAR or FIELD " + ;
                ";variable does not exist or is not visible.;")

          case e:subCode == 1004
             cMessage += (";A message was sent using the" + ;
                ";send operator (:), but the left operand" + ;
                ";is not an object or the object has no" + ;
                ";method with the specified name.  This" + ;
                ";error may also occur if the first" + ;
                ";parameter to the EVAL() function is not" + ;
                ";a code block or if a value other than a" + ;
                ";code block is supplied in a context" + ;
                ";where a code block is required.;")

          case e:subCode == 1005
             cMessage += (";An attempt was made to assign" + ;
                ";an exported instance variable using the" + ;
                ";send operator (:), but the left operand" + ;
                ";is not an object or the object has no" + ;
                ";exported variable with the specified name.;")

          case e:subCode == 1065
             cMessage += (";The argument to the macro (&)" + ;
                ";operator was not a character value.;")

          case e:subCode == 1066
             cMessage += (";The result of the expression in" + ;
                ";a conditional statement such as IF or" + ;
                ";DO WHILE, or the value of the first" + ;
                ";parameter to the IF() function, was not" + ;
                ";a logical value.;")
```

4-4 Continued.

```
case e:subCode == 1067
   cMessage += (";The value specifying the length" + ;
      ";of a new array was missing or non-numeric.;")

case e:subCode == 1068
   cMessage += (";When attempting to retrieve the" + ;
      ";value of an array element, the subscript" + ;
      ";value was non-numeric or the variable" + ;
      ";being subscripted was not an array.;")

case e:subCode == 1069
   cMessage += (";When attempting to assign a new" + ;
      ";value to an array element, the subscript" + ;
      ";value was non-numeric or the variable" + ;
      ";being subscripted was not an array.;")

case e:subCode > 1069 .and. e:subCode < 1077
   cMessage += (";The arguments to the " + ;
      e:operation + ;
      " operator;were of incompatible types.;")

case e:subCode > 1076 .and. e:subcode < 1081
   cMessage += (";The argument to the " + ;
      e:operation + ;
      ";operator was not a logical value.;")

case e:subCode > 1080 .and. e:subCode < 1089
   cMessage += (";The arguments to the " + ;
      e:operation + ;
      " operator;were of incompatible types.;")

case e:subCode > 1088 .and. e:subCode < 1092
   cMessage += (";The argument to " + ;
      e:operation + ;
      " was non-numeric.;")

   endcase

else
   cMessage += "/???"
end


// add error description if available
if ( ValType(e:description) == "C" )
   cMessage += ("  " + e:description)
end


// add either filename or operation
if ( !Empty(e:filename) )
   cMessage += (": " + e:filename)
```

```
    elseif ( !Empty(e:operation) )
        cMessage += (": " + e:operation)

    end

// Add the procedure name and line number to the error message.  This
// allow you to use the ignore option and still know where the error
// actually occurred in the code.

    nCount := 2
    while ( !Empty(ProcName(nCount)) )
        cMessage += ";Called from " + Trim(ProcName(nCount)) + ;
            "(" + NTRIM(ProcLine(nCount)) + ")  "
        nCount++
    end

return (cMessage)
```

5
Interfacing Clipper to assembly language

Assembler was once the language that everyone used to create complete applications. It was one of the easiest ways to guarantee absolute access to the hardware. However, as the time allocated to create an application decreased and the needs of users increased, programmers found other, more efficient, ways of creating programs. While assembler supplied all the flexibility anyone would ever want, there was simply not enough time to use it for every project.

High-level languages are a real time saver for programmers. Unfortunately, there are many cases where a high-level language like Clipper cannot provide every feature that every person needs. Nantucket left some features out because not everyone will need to use them. They left others out because the need for the feature did not exist at the time they created the compiler. Therefore, Clipper, like any other high-level language, cannot guarantee total access to the hardware or provide every low-level routine needed for every application. When you need to provide a specific feature in a program, there are two ways to add it. You can either build the feature out of native compiler commands or create it using an external language.

Nantucket provides a documented application program interface (API), which you can use to manipulate the variables contained in your program directly. You can also use it to obtain program status information and call Clipper internal functions (although Nantucket doesn't recommend using them unless they document the function). The Clipper documentation calls this API the Extend System. The Extend System is a set of protocols that allows you to create external routines that react with Clipper programs. These routines typically provide some functionality not found in Clipper. For example, you might need to create a direct interface to some esoteric piece of hardware. Some types of hardware could include point-of-sale systems or RS-422 ports. You might even want to access some special feature of a display adapter used on the machines you build or buy.

Nantucket wrote Clipper in Microsoft C 5.1. This presents some interesting challenges to users of assembler. You can use the C parameter of the .MODEL directive, or hand code every call to a Clipper function to ensure your routine uses the correct calling conventions. However, Clipper uses the Pascal calling convention for all its functions, so using the C parameter of the .MODEL directive presents certain disadvantages. Of course, hand coding all the calls in your routine means that you need to take these calling convention needs into consideration as you create your routine.

The examples in this book assume that you're using the Microsoft MASM 5.1 compiler. They also use the simplified segment and other directives provided by that assembler. This will help simplify the examples so you can concentrate on what the code does rather than exactly how it does it. You might need to modify the sample code slightly to meet the requirements of assemblers created by other vendors.

Using the Clipper-supplied header file

As high-level languages proliferate, assembly-language programmers have gotten used to using some of the tools used by these languages as well. For example, most C compilers provide access to libraries through the use of header files. These files normally define what the library contains so *you* don't have to each time you start to write a program. They also define constants and other general-purpose variables. The file that Nantucket supplies to document its library routines (API) for assembler is EXTASM.INC. Unlike a high-level language header, Nantucket specially designed this include file for use with assembly-language programs.

EXTASM.INC is split into two sections. The first section defines the Clipper Extend System function calls. This is the mechanism your external program uses to interface with your Clipper program. TABLE 5-1 provides a listing of these Extend System function calls and their purpose. Notice that both C and assembler use essentially the same calls, the only difference being the method used to call the API. The second section defines the data type return values using equates. These values tell you what type of data you're receiving from Clipper. For a complete description of the Clipper data types, refer to the ValType( ) function in chapter 2.

As you can see, the Extend System function call table groups the API calls by function. There are two major groups and eight minor groups. The first major group contains all parameter calls. These calls both send and retrieve values from your application program. The second major group allocates and deallocates memory for your add-on routine. The following sections describe the six minor groups in further detail.

Table 5-1 **Extend-system function calls**

Function	Description
NOTE: The descriptions in this table use the C calling conventions for the purpose of clarity. Assembler routines use the same function names and pass parameters using the stack, as noted in the text. All function descriptions assume you are using Microsoft C 5.1 or Microsoft MASM 5.1.	
Parameter count/type	
_ParInfa(int, unsigned int)	Use this function to determine the type or length of an array element. The first parameter contains the number of the parameter within the parameter list. Use _ParInfo() if you need to determine the number of parameters passed by the calling procedure. Do not pass a value of zero. The second parameter contains the array index number. If you pass a value of zero, Clipper returns the number of elements in the array. Passing any other value returns the type of that array element.
_ParInfo(int)	The _ParInfo() function returns information about the specified or last parameter passed by Clipper. If you pass a zero to the function, it returns the number of the last parameter. This allows you to quickly determine how many parameters the calling procedure passed. Passing a specific number retrieves the type for that parameter. Both EXTEND.INC and EXTEND.H define default values (equates) for each type of parameter passed by Clipper. These values are further defined in Table 5-2.
Parameter values	
CAUTION: Never directly modify the value of a parameter passed by reference. Always read the value into a variable local to your program and pass the modified value back to Clipper using one of the return or store functions. This is especially true of character values because direct manipulation of the variable can produce unpredictable results.	
_ParC(int [, unsigned int])	This function returns a pointer to a character parameter. The pointer takes the form of a segement/offset pair (FAR pointer) within the Clipper DGROUP. The first parameter specifies the position of

Table 5-1 Continued.

Function	Description
	the string within the parameter list. The second, optional parameter contains the array index for the string.
_ParCLen(int [, unsigned int])	The ParCLen function returns the length of the specified string. The length does not include the null terminator at the end of the string. It does include any embedded null values. Clipper strings can contain embedded nulls, so you should use this function to determine string length rather than searching for the first null value. The first parameter specifies the position of the string within the parameter list. The second, optional parameter contains the array index for the string.
_ParCSiz(int [, unsigned int])	This is a summer '87 Extend System function that allows you to determine the size of a character variable. It won't work with the static and local variables created by 5.0 programs. The first parameter specifies the position of the string within the parameter list. The second, optional parameter contains the array index for the string. This function is provided for compatibility purposes only. Use the ParCLen() function whenever possible.
_ParDS(int [, unsigned int])	The ParDS() function returns a date value formatted as a null terminated string. The date takes the form YYYYMMDD. The first parameter specifies the position of the date string within the parameter list. The second, optional parameter contains the array index for the date string. This function uses a single buffer to hold the date string, so you should store any date value retrieved in a local variable before calling ParDS() again.
_ParL(int [, unsigned int])	This function returns 0 for a false (.F.) variable and 1 for a true (.T.) variable. The first parameter specifies the position of the logical variable within the parameter list. The second, optional parameter contains the array index for the logical variable.
_ParND(int [, unsigned int])	Use this function to retrieve a numeric variable passed from Clipper to your routine. This function

Function	Description
	returns the number as a double precision integer. The first parameter specifies the position of the number within the parameter list. The second, optional parameter contains the array index for the number.
_ParNI(int [, unsigned int])	Use this function to retrieve a numeric variable passed from Clipper to your routine. This function returns the number as an integer. The first parameter specifies the position of the number within the parameter list. The second, optional parameter contains the array index for the number.
_ParNL(int [, unsigned int])	Use this function to retrieve a numeric variable passed from Clipper to your routine. This function returns the number as a long integer. The first parameter specifies the position of the number within the parameter list. The second, optional parameter contains the array index for the number.
Return a value	
_RetC(far pointer)	The RetC() function returns a string from your routine to the calling Clipper procedure or function. Your procedure supplies a far pointer to the string's location as the only input. Clipper determines string length by scanning for a null terminator. If your string contains embedded nulls, then you need to use the RetCLen() function instead.
_RetCLen(far pointer, unsigned int)	This function works the same way as the RetC() function does. The first parameter contains a far pointer to the string you want to return to the calling Clipper procedure or function. Unlike the RetC() function, you also supply a integer value, which specifies the length of the string. This allows you to return binary values to a calling procedure or function. You don't need to null terminate a string returned with this function. The integer value should not include the null terminator in the character count.
_RetDS(far pointer)	The RetDS() function returns a date value to the calling Clipper procedure or function. The only input to this function is a far pointer to a null-terminated

Table 5-1 Continued.

Function	Description
	date string in the format YYYYMMDD. If the string pointed to does not contain a valid date, Clipper returns a blank date.
_RetL(int)	The RetL() function returns a value of true or false to your program. If you provide a value of zero as the parameter, Clipper returns false. Any other integer value results in a return value of true.
_RetND(double int)	Use this function to return a double precision integer to the calling procedure or function.
_RetNI(int)	Use this function to return an integer to the calling procedure or function.
_RetNL(long);	Use this function to return a long integer to the calling procedure or function.
Return No Value (NIL)	
_Ret()	This is a special function that will always return a NIL (void) value to the calling Clipper procedure or function. Use this function when your routine won't return any other value to Clipper.
Store values	
NOTE: To use these functions you must pass the variable by reference. A successful attempt at storing the variable results in a return value of one. Unsuccessful attempts return zero. Variables are numbered in the order in which you pass them to the called routine, starting with one. Clipper places stored strings on the heap. This means that you don't need to retain the original string once you call the store function successfully.	
_StorC(far pointer, int [, int])	The StorC() function stores a null-terminated string on the heap. When your routine returns control to the calling Clipper procedure or function, Clipper replaces the contents of the appropriate variable with the value you stored. The first parameter contains a far pointer to the string you want to store. The second parameter specifies the position of the string within the parameter list. The third, optional parameter

Function	Description
	contains the array index for the string. You cannot store a string containing embedded nulls with this function. Use the StorCLen() function instead.
_StorCLen(far pointer, unsigned int, int [, int])	Use the StorCLen() function to store a string. When your routine returns control to the calling Clipper procedure or function, Clipper replaces the contents of the appropriate variable with the value you stored. The first parameter contains a far pointer to the string you want to store. Unlike the string stored using the StorC() function, this string can contain embedded nulls and does not require a null terminator. The second parameter contains the length of the string. Do not include the null terminator as part of the length. The third parameter specifies the position of the string within the parameter list. The fourth, optional parameter contains the array index for the string.
_StorL(int, int [, int])	The _StorL() function allows you to store a logical value to a variable. The first parameter contains a zero for a false value or any other number for true. The second parameter specifies the position of the logical variable within the parameter list. The third, optional parameter contains the array index for the logical variable.
_StorDS(far pointer, int [, int])	The _StorDS() function allows you to store a date string in the form of YYYYMMDD to the calling procedure. Clipper automatically converts the date string to a date value. If your routine attempts to pass an invalid date, then Clipper stores a blank date. The second parameter specifies the position of the date string within the parameter list. The third, optional parameter contains the array index for the date string.
_StorNI(int, int [, int])	Use this function to store the value of an integer. The first parameter contains the value of the integer. The second parameter specifies the position of the number within the parameter list. The third, optional parameter contains the array index for the number.

Table 5-1 Continued.

Function	Description
_StorNL(int, int [, int])	Use this function to store the value of an long integer. The first parameter contains the value of the long integer. The second parameter specifies the position of the number within the parameter list. The third, optional parameter contains the array index for the number.
_StorND(int, int [, int])	Use this function to store the value of an double precision integer. The first parameter contains the value of the double precision integer. The second parameter specifies the position of the number within the parameter list. The third, optional parameter contains the array index for the number.
Allocate memory	
_XAlloc(unsigned int)	The _XAlloc() function allocates memory from Clipper's heap for your routine. It returns a far pointer to the memory when Clipper has the memory to allocate. If you request more memory than Clipper can allocate, _XAlloc() returns a null pointer. This function will not "fall back" to the number of bytes available. It will allocate either the entire request or none at all. The only parameter required by this function is an unsigned integer containing the number of bytes you want allocated.
_XFree(far pointer)	Use the _XFree() function to deallocate memory allocated with the _XAlloc() or _XGrab() functions. This function does not provide any return value. The only parameter is a far pointer to the memory block you want deallocated.
_XGrab(unsigned int)	The _XGrab() function allocates memory from Clipper's heap for your routine. It returns a far pointer to the memory when Clipper has the memory to allocate. If you request more memory than Clipper can allocate, _XGrab() generates a runtime error. This function will not "fall back" to the number of bytes available. It will allocate either the entire request or none at all. The only parameter required by this function is an unsigned integer containing the number of bytes you want allocated.

Function	Description
Summer '87 compatible memory allocation	
_EXMGrab(unsigned int)	This function translates to the _XGrab() function. It is provided for compatibility purposes only.
_EXMBack(far pointer)	This function translates to the _XFree() function. It is provided for compatibility purposes only.

Typing and counting parameters

The Parameter Count/Type group contains functions that obtain information about the parameters passed to your routine. Because Clipper is not a strongly typed language, you need to check the values passed to your routine before you attempt to process them. The user could accidently pass some illegal value that would result in an illegal or unusable return value to the calling procedure or function. Using these functions helps to eliminate any possible corruption of your routine's results due to invalid input values.

Retrieving a parameter and parameter characteristics

The Parameter Values group contains functions that determine specific characteristics about the values passed to your routine. For example, the _parclen( ) function returns the length of a character parameter. It is essential to obtain this information because your routine knows nothing about the values you're using within Clipper. This group also contains the functions that actually retrieve data from Clipper. For example, the _parc( ) function returns a pointer to a string in the Clipper data segment. Once you determine that the user's Clipper program has passed your routine the correct type of value and you know the characteristics of that parameter, you can retrieve it and use it in your routine.

Returning a value

The Return a Value group allows you to return a value to your Clipper program. For example, if you had the statement cSomeVar := yourfunc(cOtherVar) embedded in your Clipper code, then your external routine would have to use one of the return functions to place a value in cSomeVar. This differentiates a return value from a function that stores a value in a Clipper variable. Your routine can store values to multiple variables, but it can return only a single value.

The Return No Value group is the specialization of a function to return a value. Because your routine must return some value, it can choose to return something or nothing. NIL essentially returns a value of nothing to the calling Clipper procedure or function. Use it when the routine you create does not return a value to Clipper, but simply performs a task based on existing data. For example, a function to display data on screen would not necessarily return a value to Clipper.

Storing values

The Store Values group places a value into one of the parameters passed to your routine. Using a store function allows you to return multiple values from a single function by directly manipulating the contents of the Clipper variables. To use a store function, you must pass the parameter by reference. For example, if you called an external function with SomeFunc(cSomeStr, @nSomeNum), you could store a value to nSomeNum, but not to cSomeStr. This differentiates a store function from a return function, which allows your routine to return a value using the same methods as a standard function. While your routine can provide only one return value, it can store values to any number of parameters.

Allocating memory

The Allocate Memory group obtains and frees memory for your routine. You cannot use the standard DOS calls to obtain memory from DOS. Clipper automatically allocates all available memory for its own use. The DOS call (interrupt) will execute, but will return a failure code. You must use the Allocate Memory functions to obtain the memory from Clipper instead. This allows Clipper to maintain firm control over the allocation and use of memory.

Definitions not included in EXTASM.INC

The EXTASM.INC file does not contain definitions for two groups found in the EXTEND.H file. The first definition group contains the two special memory-allocation functions that allow you to maintain compatibility with the Summer 87 version of Clipper. In addition, there is the Parameter Check Macros group, which allows you to check the type of the parameters input to your program using more easily remembered functions. I will add these to the MACROS.INC include file discussed later in this chapter.

Using the assembler header file

Understanding these include file entries is only the first step in using them. Combining these entries into useful code is the second step. Figures 5-1 and 5-2 show a program that illustrates some of the simpler techniques for combining the header file with your code. Figure 5-1 contains the Clipper code used to test the assembler function shown in FIG. 5-2.

5-1 Programming example number one, Clipper source

```
// Program Number 1 - Clipper to ASM Interface Example
// This example shows how to link an assembler program with a Clipper
// program.  It was purposely designed to perform a simple task so that
// the illustration would clearly show the linkage requirments.  The
// other half of this program is PROG-01A.ASM.  It contains the
// function, DispString().  This function returns a value of true if
// the calling programs provides a string as input or a value of false
// if it does not.
// Written by John Mueller
// Copyright 1991 John Mueller - Tab Books, Inc.

// Create an array with four different variable types.  Create and
// initialize a counter variable.

local aSomeArray := {"Hello World", 3, .T., ctod("01/01/91")},;
      nCount := 1

// Clear the display.

cls

// Check all array inputs.  If the array element contains a string, then
// display it.  It it doesn't contain a string, display an error message.

for nCount := 1 to len(aSomeArray)
   if !dispstring(aSomeArray[nCount])

      // Error message for non-string input.

      qout(aSomeArray[nCount])
      qqout(" is Not a String")

   endif

next
```

5-2 Programming example number one, assembler source

```
;*********************************************************************
;* Program Number 1 - Clipper to ASM Interface Example              *
;* This program contains a rudimentary example of how to implement a  *
;* function using assebler for use with Clipper.  There are six main  *
;* sections to the program.  First you include any required include   *
;* files.  There is one include file used in this example.  EXTASM.INC *
;* contains the Nantucket provided declarations.  The second section   *
;* contains any variable declarations required to complete the         *
;* specified task.  The third section contains code used to check      *
;* parameter type and number.  In this case there is one parameter and *
;* it must be a string.  The fourth section contains the actual        *
;* working code.  The fifth section contains an error handling routine *
```

5-2 Continued.

```
;* used when the user provides incorrect input to the function.  The     *
;* final section contains storage and return value code.  This allows    *
;* you directly modify Clipper variables if necessary and return a       *
;* value to the calling program.  You must, as a minimum, return a       *
;* value of NIL to the calling program.  Compare this program with       *
;* programs 2 and 3.  Notice how much less readable and longer it is     *
;* than the other two.                                                   *
;* Written by: John Mueller                                              *
;* Copyright 1991 John Mueller - Tab Books                               *
;*************************************************************************

;*************************************************************************
;* SECTION 1 - Make any required declarations.                           *
;*************************************************************************

.MODEL LARGE

INCLUDE EXTASM.INC

PUBLIC DispString

;*************************************************************************
;* SECTION 2 - Declare and required variables.                           *
;*************************************************************************

.DATA

SomeStr         DB      254 DUP (' '), '$'       ; Input String Holder.

;*************************************************************************
;* SECTION 3 - Check the number and types of parameters.                 *
;*************************************************************************

.CODE

DispString      PROC    FAR

                PUSH    SI              ;Save SI.

                MOV     AX,0            ;Check the number of parameters.
                PUSH    AX
                CALL    __parinfo
                ADD     SP,2

                CMP     AX,0            ;If there aren't any, exit.
                JE      NoParms

                MOV     AX,1            ; Check the first parameter to see if
                PUSH    AX              ; it's a character.  If not exit.
                CALL    __parinfo
                ADD     SP,2
                TEST    AX,Character
                JZ      NoParms
```

```
;**********************************************************************
;* SECTION 4 - Do something with the input string.  In this particular *
;*            case we output it to the display.                        *
;**********************************************************************
              MOV    AX,1        ; Get the first character parameter.
              PUSH   AX
              CALL   __parc
              ADD    SP,2
              PUSH   AX          ; Save the string offset.
              PUSH   DX          ; Save the Clipper DATA segment.

              MOV    AX,1        ; Retrieve the string length.
              PUSH   AX
              CALL   __parclen
              ADD    SP,2
              MOV    CX,AX

              POP    DS          ; Point to the Clipper DATA segment.
              POP    SI          ; Point to the string.

              MOV    AX,@DATA    ; Point to our data segment.
              MOV    ES,AX
              LEA    DI,SomeStr ; Load the offset of SomeStr.
              REP    MOVSB       ; Move the string to our data segment.

              PUSH   ES          ; Point DS to our data segment.
              POP    DS
              LEA    DX,SomeStr ; Point to SomeStr.
              MOV    AX,0900h    ;Display the string.
              INT    21h
              JMP    GoodExit

;**********************************************************************
;* SECTION 5 and 6 - Handle any errors by returning a value of false.  *
;*                   Otherwise, return a value of true to the calling  *
;*                   procedure.                                        *
;**********************************************************************
NoParms:      MOV    AX,0        ;Return a value of false to Clipper.
              PUSH   AX
              CALL   __retl
              ADD    SP,2
              JMP    Exit

GoodExit:     MOV    AX,1        ;Return a value of true to Clipper.
              PUSH   AX
              CALL   __retl
              ADD    SP,2

Exit:         POP    SI
              RET

DispString    ENDP

END
```

The example program offers several tips on creating an add-on routine for Clipper in assembler. First, there are six parts to the standard Clipper assembly language program. Notice that FIG. 5-2 clearly indicates where each of the six parts start. Each section performs a different function, as listed in the source code and described in the following text.

Of the six sections, sections 1 and 2 appear only once, at the beginning of the source code file. In fact, you don't necessarily have to include section 2. There are many methods of manipulating Clipper variables that don't require the use of a separate data segment in your code. For example, you could directly modify the variable in the Clipper data segment once you receive a segment and offset pointer. However, using a separate data section will eliminate many problems that some programmers experience with corruption of the Clipper data area. As a result, all programs in this book will include a private data area that the external routine can use to manipulate data.

Every routine that you create contains the information stored in sections 3 through 6 of the example program. Clipper is not a strongly typed language; therefore, a programmer could unknowingly pass an incorrect variable type to your routine. To prevent this, you should always check the data type you receive to make certain it's the correct type. The need for section 4 is obvious. The whole purpose of creating the routine is to manipulate data. Section 5 provides error handling.

It's important to keep the error-handling section of the routine separate from the rest of the routine for two reasons. First, it makes the routine easier to maintain because there is a clearly defined line between functional code and error-handling code. Second, it makes the program easier to debug. As your debugger steps through the routine code, you can instantly detect when an error occurs because the debugger cursor will shift to the error section. In fact, this technique allows you to set a breakpoint within the error section that stops program execution quickly whenever Clipper detects an error.

Section 6 contains the code that returns a value to Clipper and ends the program. The Summer 87 version of Clipper did not mandate that you always return a value from your routine. This had the one disadvantage that you never knew whether an error occurred in the Clipper code or the routine code. By forcing you to return a value, more recent versions of Clipper ensure that you will be able to determine exactly where the error occurred. Even a return of NIL is better than no return at all.

Creating add-on macros

One of the reasons that many developers don't use assembler add-ons in their Clipper code is the expense of doing so. One of the reasons that high-level languages are so prolific is that they are less time-consuming to use. Hiring a programmer to create a C or assembly language routine is expensive. However, you can create add-on macros for assembly language to reduce the work required to interface an assembler program with Clipper.

As FIG. 5-2 illustrates, some code is so redundant that it's more efficient to generate it and place it in an include file. For example, every function you create will need to return some value to Clipper (even if that value is NIL). Placing the code to generate a return value in an include file will also reduce the probability of error in your program. Most programmers agree that many of their errors occur in places where they had redundant or familiar code. Finally, macros will improve the consistency of coding within a team. Because all the members are using the same include file, the only difference in code will be where that difference is important—in the code that performs the work.

Figure 5-3 shows a typical include file designed to reduce the labor required to create a program. Notice that the macros are generic enough in function that you could use them for a variety of purposes. Figure 5-4 shows the reduction in source-code size when you use the include file on the program in FIG. 5-2.

5-3 Sample assembly-language macros for Clipper

```
;*************************************************************************
;* MASM Macro Add-On for Clipper                                         *
;* This file provides most of the macros you will need to use            *
;* Microsoft Macro Assembler with Clipper.  You include in your          *
;* program by adding INCLUDE MACROS.INC at the beginning of your         *
;* program.  Most of the macros are illustrated throughout the book.     *
;* Written by: John Mueller                                              *
;* Copyright 1991 John Mueller - Tab Books                               *
;*************************************************************************

;*************************************************************************
;* This section contains parameter information macros                    *
;*************************************************************************

; This macro is called by the other parameter information macros in this
; file.

ParInfo         MACRO           ParNumber

                MOV             AX,ParNumber
                PUSH            AX
                CALL            __parinfo
                ADD             SP,2

ENDM

; This macro obtains the parameter count.

PCount          MACRO
```

5-3 Continued.

```
                ParInfo         0

ENDM

; This macro determines if the specified parameter is type character.

IsChar          MACRO           ParNum

                ParInfo         ParNum
                TEST            AX,Character

ENDM

; This macro determines if the specified parameter is type numeric.

IsNum           MACRO           ParNum

                ParInfo         ParNum
                TEST            AX,Numeric

ENDM

; This macro determines if the specified parameter is type logical.

IsLog           MACRO           ParNum

                ParInfo         ParNum
                TEST            AX,Logical

ENDM

; This macro determines if the specified parameter is type date.

IsDate          MACRO           ParNum

                ParInfo         ParNum
                TEST            AX,Date

ENDM

; This macro determines if the specified parameter is type memo.

IsMemo          MACRO           ParNum

                ParInfo         ParNum
                TEST            AX,Memo

ENDM

; This macro determines if the specified parameter is type mptr.
```

```
IsByRef        MACRO          ParNum

               ParInfo        ParNum
               TEST           AX,MPtr

ENDM

 ; This macro determines if the specified parameter is type array.

IsArray        MACRO          ParNum

               ParInfo        ParNum
               TEST           AX,Array

ENDM

;**********************************************************************
;* This section contains macros that obtain array information.        *
;**********************************************************************

; This macro is called by the other parameter information macros in this

; file.

ParInfa        MACRO          ParNum, AOffset

               MOV            AX,AOffset      ; Load the array element number.
               PUSH           AX
               MOV            AX,ParNum       ; Load the array's parameter number.
               PUSH           AX
               CALL           __parinfa
               ADD            SP,4

ENDM

; This macro determine the length of an array.

ALength        MACRO          ParNum

               ParInfa        ParNum, 0

ENDM

; This macro determines if the specified parameter is type character.

AIsChar        MACRO          ParNum, AOffset

               ParInfa        ParNum, AOffset
               TEST           AX,Character

ENDM

; This macro determines if the specified parameter is type numeric.
```

5-3 Continued.

```
AIsNum          MACRO           ParNum, AOffset

                ParInfa         ParNum, AOffset
                TEST            AX,Numeric

ENDM

; This macro determines if the specified parameter is type logical.

AIsLog          MACRO           ParNum, AOffset

                ParInfa         ParNum, AOffset
                TEST            AX,Logical

ENDM

; This macro determines if the specified parameter is type date.

AIsDate         MACRO           ParNum, AOffset

                ParInfa         ParNum, AOffset
                TEST            AX,Date

ENDM

; This macro determines if the specified parameter is type memo.

AIsMemo         MACRO           ParNum, AOffset

                ParInfa         ParNum, AOffset
                TEST            AX,Memo

ENDM

; This macro determines if the specified parameter is type mptr.

AIsByRef        MACRO           ParNum, AOffset

                ParInfa         ParNum, AOffset
                TEST            AX,MPtr

ENDM

; This macro determines if the specified parameter is type array.

AIsArray        MACRO           ParNum, AOffset

                ParInfa         ParNum, AOffset
                TEST            AX,Array

 ENDM
```

```
;***********************************************************************
;* This section contains macros that obtain a variable from Clipper.   *
;***********************************************************************

; This macro returns a pointer to a character string.

GetChar         MACRO           ParNum

                MOV             AX,ParNum
                PUSH            AX
                CALL            __parc
                ADD             SP,2

ENDM

; This macro retrieves the length of a character string.

GetCharLen      MACRO           ParNum

                MOV             AX,ParNum
                PUSH            AX
                CALL            __parclen
                ADD             SP,2

ENDM

; This macro retrieves a date string.

GetDate         MACRO           ParNum

                MOV             AX,ParNum
                PUSH            AX
                CALL            __pards
                ADD             SP,2

ENDM

; This macro retrieves a logical value.

GetLog          MACRO           ParNum

                MOV             AX,ParNum
                PUSH            AX
                CALL            __parl
                ADD             SP,2

ENDM

; This macro retrieves a double precision number.

GetDouble       MACRO           ParNum, StoreArea

                MOV             AX,ParNum
                PUSH            AX
```

5-3 Continued.

```
                CALL            __parnd
                ADD             SP,2
                MOV             ES,DX
                MOV             BX,AX
                MOV             WORD PTR StoreArea, ES:[BX]
                MOV             WORD PTR StoreArea, ES:[BX+2]
                MOV             WORD PTR StoreArea, ES:[BX+4]
                MOV             WORD PTR StoreArea, ES:[BX+6]

ENDM

; This macro retrieves an integer.

GetInt          MACRO           ParNum

                MOV             AX,ParNum
                PUSH            AX
                CALL            __parni
                ADD             SP,2

ENDM

; This macro retrieves a long integer.

GetLong         MACRO           ParNum

                MOV             AX,ParNum
                PUSH            AX
                CALL            __parnl
                ADD             SP,2

ENDM

;**********************************************************************
;* This section contains return value macros.                         *
;**********************************************************************

; This macro returns NIL.

RetNIL          MACRO

                CALL            __ret

ENDM

; This macro returns a null terminated string.

RetChar         MACRO           ParName

                MOV             DX,DS
                LEA             AX,ParName
                PUSH            DX
                PUSH            AX
```

```
                CALL            __retc
                ADD             SP,4

ENDM

; This macro returns a non-null terminated string.

RetCharLen      MACRO           ParName, ParLen

                MOV             AX,ParLen
                PUSH            AX
                MOV             DX,DS
                LEA             AX,ParName
                PUSH            DX
                PUSH            AX
                CALL            __retclen
                ADD             SP,6

ENDM

; This macro returns a date string.

RetDate         MACRO           ParName

                MOV             DX,DS
                LEA             AX,ParName
                PUSH            DX
                PUSH            AX
                CALL            __retds
                ADD             SP,4

ENDM

; This macro returns a value of False as a boolean.

RetFalse        MACRO

                MOV             AX,0
                PUSH            AX
                CALL            __retl
                ADD             SP,2

ENDM

; This macro returns a value of True as a boolean.

RetTrue         MACRO

                MOV             AX,1
                PUSH            AX
                CALL            __retl
                ADD             SP,2

ENDM
```

5-3 Continued.

```
; This macro returns a double integer.

RetDouble     MACRO         ParName

              PUSH          WORD PTR (ParNam+6)
              PUSH          WORD PTR (ParNam+4)
              PUSH          WORD PTR (ParNam+2)
              PUSH          WORD PTR ParNam
              CALL          __retnd
              ADD           SP,8

ENDM

; This macro returns an integer.

RetInt        MACRO         ParName

              MOV           AX,ParName
              PUSH          AX
              CALL          __retni
              ADD           SP,2

ENDM

; This macro returns a long integer.

RetLong       MACRO         ParName

              MOV           AX,[ParName+2]
              PUSH          AX
              MOV           AX,ParName
              PUSH          AX
              CALL          __retnl
              ADD           SP,4

ENDM

;**********************************************************************
;* This section contains macros that store values to a variable.      *
;**********************************************************************

; This macro stores a value to a null terminated character.

StorChar      MACRO         ParNum, ParName

              MOV           AX,ParNum
              PUSH          AX
              MOV           DX,DS
              LEA           AX,ParName
              PUSH          DX
              PUSH          AX
              CALL          __storc
              ADD           SP,6
```

```
ENDM

; This macro stores a value to a non-null terminated string.

StorCharLen     MACRO           ParNum, ParName, ParLen

                MOV             AX,ParNum
                PUSH            AX
                MOV             AX,ParLen
                PUSH            AX
                MOV             DX,DS
                LEA             AX,ParName
                PUSH            DX
                PUSH            AX
                CALL            __storclen
                ADD             SP,8

ENDM

; This macro stores a value to a date string.

StorDate        MACRO           ParNum, ParName

                MOV             AX,ParNum
                PUSH            AX
                MOV             DX,DS
                LEA             AX,ParName
                PUSH            DX
                PUSH            AX
                CALL            __stords
                ADD             SP,6

ENDM

; This macro stores a value to a value of False as a boolean.

StorFalse       MACRO           ParNum

                MOV             AX,ParNum
                PUSH            AX
                MOV             AX,0
                PUSH            AX
                CALL            __storl
                ADD             SP,4

ENDM

; This macro stores a value to a value of True as a boolean.

StorTrue        MACRO           ParNum

                MOV             AX,ParNum
                PUSH            AX
                MOV             AX,1
```

5-3 Continued.

```
                PUSH            AX
                CALL            __storl
                ADD             SP,4

ENDM

; This macro stores a value to a double integer.

StorDouble      MACRO           ParNum, ParName

                MOV             AX,ParNum
                PUSH            AX
                PUSH            WORD PTR (ParNam+6)
                PUSH            WORD PTR (ParNam+4)
                PUSH            WORD PTR (ParNam+2)
                PUSH            WORD PTR ParNam
                CALL            __stornd
                ADD             SP,10

ENDM

; This macro stores a value to an integer.

StorInt         MACRO           ParNum, ParName

                MOV             AX,ParNum
                PUSH            AX
                MOV             AX,ParName
                PUSH            AX
                CALL            __storni
                ADD             SP,4

ENDM
; This macro stores a value to a long integer.

StorLong        MACRO           ParNum, ParName

                MOV             AX,ParNum
                PUSH            AX
                MOV             AX,[ParName+2]
                PUSH            AX
                MOV             AX,ParName
                PUSH            AX
                CALL            __stornl
                ADD             SP,6

ENDM

;*************************************************************************
;* This section contains macros that assist in the allocation and       *
;* deallocation of memory.                                               *
;*************************************************************************
```

```
; This macro allocates memory from Clipper's heap.  It returns a
; value of NULL if not successful.

XAlloc          MACRO           MemSize

                MOV             AX,MemSize
                PUSH            AX
                CALL            __xalloc
                ADD             SP,2

ENDM

; This macro frees previously allocated memory.

XFree           MACRO           MemSeg, MemOff

                MOV             AX,MemOff
                MOV             DX,MemSeg
                PUSH            DX
                PUSH            AX
                CALL            __xfree
                ADD             SP,4

ENDM

; This macro allocates memory from Clipper's heap.  If the function it
; calls fails, Clipper will generate a run time error.  The function
; never returns a NULL pointer.

XGrab           MACRO           MemSize

                MOV             AX,MemSize
                PUSH            AX
                CALL            __xgrab
                ADD             SP,2

ENDM
```

As you can see from FIG. 5-3, adding macros to an include file is really very simple. Using them produces a great reduction in the amount of source code that you must create without affecting program performance. Figure 5-4 shows how great this reduction can be, even in a simple program. As you begin to create larger programs, the need for wise management of programming resources increases. Reducing the time spent creating redundant code is of paramount importance, especially in team projects.

```
;*************************************************************************
;* Program Number 2 - Using Macros Example                              *
;* This program contains a rudimentary example of how to implement a    *
;* function using assebler for use with Clipper.  There are six main    *
;* sections to the program.  First you include any required include     *
;* files.  There are two include files used in this example.  The       *
;* first include file, EXTASM.INC contains the Nantucket provided       *
;* declarations.  The second file, MACROS.INC, is used throughout this *
;* book and included as part of the source code disk.  It contains      *
;* macros that make the job of creating a program easier.  The second  *
;* section contains any variable declarations required to complete the *
;* specified task.  The third section contains code used to check       *
;* parameter type and number.  In this case there is one parameter and *
;* it must be a string.  The fourth section contains the actual         *
;* working code.  The fifth section contains an error handling routine *
;* used when the user provides incorrect input to the function.  The   *
;* final section contains storage and return value code.  This allows  *
;* you directly modify Clipper variables if necessary and return a      *
;* value to the calling program.  You must, as a minimum, return a      *
;* value of NIL to the calling program.                                 *
;* Written by: John Mueller                                             *
;* Copyright 1991 John Mueller - Tab Books                              *
;*************************************************************************

;*************************************************************************
;* SECTION 1 - Make any required declarations.                          *
;*************************************************************************

.MODEL LARGE

INCLUDE EXTASM.INC
INCLUDE MACROS.INC

PUBLIC DispString

;*************************************************************************
;* SECTION 2 - Declare and required variables.                          *
;*************************************************************************

.DATA

SomeStr    DB 254 DUP (' '), '$'        ; Input String Holder.

;*************************************************************************
;* SECTION 3 - Check the number and types of parameters.                *
;*************************************************************************

.CODE

DispString     PROC        FAR
```

```
            PUSH        SI          ; Save SI.

            PCount                  ; Check the number of parameters.
            CMP         AX,0        ; If there aren't any, exit.
            JE          NoParms

            IsChar      1           ; Check the first parameter to see if
            JZ          NoParms     ; it's a character.  If not exit.

;*************************************************************************
;* SECTION 4 - Do something with the input string.  In this particular *
;*             case we output it to the display.                       *
;*************************************************************************

            GetChar     1           ; Get the first character parameter.
            PUSH        AX          ; Save the string offset.
            PUSH        DX          ; Save the Clipper DATA segment.

            GetCharLen 1            ; Retrieve the string length.
            MOV         CX,AX

            POP         DS          ; Point to the Clipper DATA segment.
            POP         SI          ; Point to the string.

            MOV         AX,@DATA    ; Point to our data segment.
            MOV         ES,AX
            LEA         DI,SomeStr  ; Load the offset of SomeStr.
            REP         MOVSB       ; Move the string to our data segment.

            PUSH        ES          ; Point DS to our data segment.
            POP         DS
            LEA         DX,SomeStr  ; Point to SomeStr.
            MOV         AX,0900h    ; Display the string.
            INT         21h
            JMP         GoodExit

;*************************************************************************
;* SECTION 5 and 6 - Handle any errors by returning a value of false.  *
;*                   Otherwise, return a value of true to the calling  *
;*                   procedure.                                        *
;*************************************************************************

NoParms:    RetFalse
            JMP         Exit

GoodExit:   RetTrue

Exit:       POP SI
            RET

DispString  ENDP

END
```

Developing an interface without using macros

Some projects require that code be absolutely readable, for example, contract programming, where you're a member of a team and don't expect to be the one maintaining the code that you produce. While macros could reduce the time required for you to complete the project, they would certainly reduce the readability of the code. In these cases, there are still a few things you can do to reduce coding time. Figure 5-5 shows an example of a program that doesn't use macros in the form of an include file, yet reduces the amount of code required to create the program. This is another example of how to implement the code in FIG. 5-2.

The example in FIG. 5-5 illustrates several important concepts. First, you can use functions to reduce the amount of redundant code in your program. While the source code is a little longer, the resulting object file and therefore the executable file are actually smaller. The macro example reduces the size of the source code, but the code is still in an in-line format. The compiler still sees the same amount of code. On the other hand, functions physically reduce the size of the code. By placing these functions in a separate file, you could implement them in a work-group situation and again reduce the code size. Placing this redundant code in a library would reduce the size of the executable file even further.

5-5 Programming example number three, assembler source

```
;*************************************************************************
;* Program Number 3 - Using Functions Example                            *
;* The purpose of this program is to show an alternative to using        *
;* macros or in-line code for your add-on routines.  Notice that the     *
;* main area of this program looks less complex than the other two       *
;* programming examples.  Unlike the other two programs, this program    *
;* contains seven, instead of six, sections.  First you include any      *
;* required include files.  There is one include file used in this       *
;* example.  EXTASM.INC contains the Nantucket provided declarations.    *
;* Notice that this first section also contains public declarations      *
;* for any procedures we want Clipper to access.  This example shows     *
;* that you do not declare any local procedures PUBLIC.  The second      *
;* section contains any variable declarations required to complete the  *
;* specified task.  Notice that besides holding variables for            *
;* parameters we recieve from Clipper, this section also contains any    *
;* variables used by the local procedures.  The third section contains  *
;* code used to check parameter type and number.  In this case there     *
;* is one parameter and it must be a string.  The fourth section         *
;* contains the actual working code.  The fifth section contains an      *
;* error handling routine used when the user provides incorrect input    *
;* to the function.  The sixth section contains storage and return       *
;* value code.  This allows you directly modify Clipper variables if     *
;* necessary and return a value to the calling program.  You must, as    *
;* a minimum, return a value of NIL to the calling program.  The         *
;* seventh section, used only in this example, contains all the local    *
;* procedures used by the program.                                       *
```

```
;* Written by: John Mueller                                             *
;* Copyright 1991 John Mueller - Tab Books                              *
;************************************************************************

;************************************************************************
;* SECTION 1 - Make any required declarations.                          *
;************************************************************************

.MODEL LARGE

INCLUDE EXTASM.INC

PUBLIC DispString       ; Only declare the procedure that Clipper will
                        ; access directly public.  None of the local
                        ; procedures are declared public.

;************************************************************************
;* SECTION 2 - Declare and required variables.                          *
;************************************************************************

.DATA

SomeStr         DB      254 DUP (' '), '$'      ; Input String Holder.

ParNum          DW      0               ; Current Parameter Number.

;************************************************************************
;* SECTION 3 - Check the number and types of parameters.                *
;************************************************************************

.CODE

DispString      PROC    FAR

                PUSH    SI              ; Save SI.

                CALL    CheckParm       ; Check the number of parameters.
                JE      NoParms         ; If there aren't any, exit.

                MOV     ParNum,1        ; Check to see if the parameter was a character.
                CALL    CheckChar
                JZ      NoParms         ; If not, exit.

;************************************************************************
;* SECTION 4 - Do something with the input string.  In this particular *
;*             case we output it to the display.                        *
;************************************************************************

                CALL    GetChar         ; Get the first character parameter.
                PUSH    AX              ; Save the string offset.
                PUSH    DX              ; Save the Clipper DATA segment.

                CALL    GetCharLen      ; Retrieve the string length.
                MOV     CX,AX           ; Place the number of characters in CX.
```

5-5 Continued.

```
              POP     DS            ; Point to the Clipper DATA segment.
              POP     SI            ; Point to the string.

              MOV     AX,@DATA      ; Point to our data segment.
              MOV     ES,AX
              LEA     DI,SomeStr    ; Load the offset of SomeStr.
              REP     MOVSB         ; Move the string to our data segment.

              PUSH    ES            ; Point DS to our data segment.
              POP     DS
              LEA     DX,SomeStr    ; Point to SomeStr.
              MOV     AX,0900h      ; Display the string.
              INT     21h
              JMP     GoodExit

;*************************************************************************
;* SECTION 5 and 6 - Handle any errors by returning a value of false.    *
;*                   Otherwise, return a value of true to the calling    *
;*                   procedure.                                          *
;*************************************************************************

NoParms:      CALL    RetFalse      ; Return a value of false to Clipper.
              JMP     Exit

GoodExit:     CALL    RetTrue       ; Return a value of true to Clipper.

Exit:         POP     SI
              RET

DispString    ENDP

;*************************************************************************
;* SECTION 7 - Begin Local Procedures                                    *
;*************************************************************************

;*************************************************************************
;* This procedure checks to make sure that the calling procedure         *
;* provided the correct number of parameters.  In this case at least     *
;* one.                                                                  *
;*************************************************************************

CheckParm     PROC    NEAR

              MOV     AX,0          ; Load AX with parameter 0.  This tells
              PUSH    AX            ; ParInfo() to return the number of
              CALL    __parinfo     ; parameters.
              ADD     SP,2
              CMP     AX,0          ; Compare the number returned with zero.

              RET

CheckParm     ENDP
```

```
;************************************************************************
;* This procedure validates the specified parameter number again type  *
;* character.                                                           *
;************************************************************************

CheckChar       PROC    NEAR

                MOV     AX,ParNum  ; Load the parameter number, then call
                PUSH    AX         ; ParInfo() to see if its a character.
                CALL    __parinfo
                ADD     SP,2
                TEST    AX,Character    ; Compare the result with the character
                                        ; return value.

                RET

CheckChar       ENDP

;************************************************************************
;* This procedure retrieves the specified character parameter from     *
;* Clipper using the Parc() function.  It returns the segment value in *
;* DX and the offset in AX.                                             *
;************************************************************************

GetChar         PROC    NEAR

                MOV     AX,ParNum  ; Load the parameter number, then call
                PUSH    AX         ; Parc() to retrieve the character value.
                CALL    __parc
                ADD     SP,2

                RET

GetChar         ENDP

;************************************************************************
;* This procedure retrieves the number of characters in the specified  *
;* string.  It returns this value in AX.                                *
;************************************************************************

GetCharLen      PROC    NEAR

                MOV AX,ParNum      ; Load the parameter number, then call
                PUSH    AX         ; ParcLen() to retrieve the character length.
                CALL    __parclen
                ADD SP,2

                RET

GetCharLen      ENDP

;************************************************************************
;* This procedure returns a value of false to the calling Clipper      *
;* procedure or function.                                               *
;************************************************************************
```

5-5 Continued.

```
RetFalse      PROC   NEAR

              MOV    AX,0          ; Load a value of false, then call RetL().
              PUSH   AX
              CALL   __retl
              ADD    SP,2

              RET
RetFalse      ENDP

;************************************************************************
;* This procedure returns a value of true to the calling Clipper        *
;* procedure or function.                                               *
;************************************************************************

RetTrue       PROC   NEAR

              MOV    AX,1          ; Load a value of true, then call RetL().
              PUSH   AX
              CALL   __retl
              ADD    SP,2

              RET
RetTrue       ENDP

END
```

Of course, the risk associated with this is that the program would again become less readable. Therefore, you must always balance the requirements for readability, source code size, and executable size with the need to decrease program costs by increasing programmer productivity. Other factors include program execution speed and the time required to produce and update the centralized files. Because functions add to the program's overhead, your program execution speed decreases slightly when you use functions.

Adding your routines to Clipper using the preprocessor

Once you've created some new routines to enhance the functionality of Clipper, you need to be able to access them from your Clipper program. This requires that you add definitions telling the Clipper compiler when and where to use your routines. There are two ways of doing this. You could add the calls directly to your Clipper source code (as shown in FIG. 5-2), or you can define a Clipper header file and use the preprocessor to add them to your code.

The first method is acceptable if you plan to use the routine only once. Unlike many C routines, programmers often find that they design assembly-language routines to interface with an esoteric piece of equipment. This is one of assembly language's fortes. Because of this, you need to determine if you plan to use this routine again. If so, this method is less acceptable than the second method of defining a header file. When you don't plan to use the routine again, make certain that you document this fact in both the Clipper and assembly source-code files. In this way you document the reason that you didn't build a Clipper header file at the time you created the routine. Always consider the cost of adding the routine directly to your Clipper source versus easier access through a Clipper header file later.

The second method adds the proper definitions to your Clipper program using the preprocessor. Because the definitions appear in a header file, the call is less error-prone. A header file either exists or it doesn't. The worst thing that could happen is that the programmer using your routine will type the wrong header filename as part of the #Include statement in the Clipper program. You can even get around this problem somewhat by adding your routine to STD.CH. (Although you should keep an unaltered version of STD.CH for future reference.) In addition, you can force the preprocessor to perform some formatting work for you. Figure 5-6 shows one technique for adding the function described in FIG. 5-2 to your Clipper program. Notice that this technique assumes your routine is stand-alone. In other words, it does not directly enhance an existing Clipper command.

5-6 Programming example number two, header file

```
// This header file shows how you can create a new command which
// includes an external C or assembler routine.
// Written by: John Mueller
// Copyright 1991 John Mueller - Tab Books

#command SHOWSTRING <list,...> => if ( !dispstring( <list> ) );
            ; qout( <list> );
            ; qqout( " is Not a String" );
            ; end
```

Using a header file containing the information shown allows you to access the function within Clipper, as shown in FIG. 5-1. You no longer need to include the preprocessor directive located at the beginning of the source code because the header file does this for you automatically. However, you *do* need to add an #Include directive to force Clipper to scan the header file. Using a Clipper header file also allows you to make some modifications to the function without changing the user interface. For example, you could create a new command that adds another parameter to the function. If the user executes the function without the parameter, then it performs its original task. Executing the new command allows the same function to perform an enhanced task.

You can also modify an existing Clipper command to use your new function. Figure 5-7 shows an example of how you would accomplish this task. Notice that, in this case, the command calling syntax is changed, but in such a way that the user can employ the original calling syntax without error.

5-7 Programming example number three, header file

```
// This header file shows how you can modify an existing command using
// an external C or assembler routine.
// Written by: John Mueller
// Copyright 1991 John Mueller - Tab Books

#command ? TEXT [ <list,...> ] => if ( !dispstring( <list> ) );
              ; qout( <list> );
              ; qqout( " is Not a String" );
              ; end
```

Using the original command with the new clause you just defined activates your routine and enhances the overall operation of the command. This is one technique for getting around limitations in the Clipper command structure.

Summary

This chapter shows you the basics of creating and using assembler routines with Clipper. It explains the purpose behind various construction techniques and how to use these techniques to their best advantage. In addition to techniques, it explains some of the functions that assembler performs rather than C. This will allow you to make a wise choice in selecting a language for your routine. The chapter finishes by showing you how to incorporate these new routines into your Clipper program. The following chapters (7 and above) will concentrate on building on this base of knowledge by showing you practical applications for external routines.

6
Interfacing Clipper to C

There are many cases where a compiler cannot provide every feature that every person needs. The vendor leaves some features out because not everyone will need to use them. Others fail to appear because the need for the feature didn't exist at the time the vendor created the compiler. For example, not everyone will perform financial analysis using a Clipper program, so Nantucket left out functions specific to that need.

When you need to provide a specific feature in a program, there are two ways you can use to add it. You can either build the feature out of native compiler commands or create them using an external language. This is especially true of many different types of arithmetic functions. Many programmers forgo the use of external routines to maintain the readability of their code. However, in some cases speed becomes more important than using native Clipper code for readability. In these instances you would use a C routine in place of the native Clipper code. Therefore, the choice of whether you build a routine using C and attach it to Clipper or use native commands to build the feature is often a matter of speed versus readability.

Nantucket provides a documented application program interface (API), which you can use to manipulate the variables contained in your program directly. You can also use it to obtain program status information and call Clipper internal functions (although Nantucket does not generally recommend that you do this unless they document the function). The Clipper manual refers to this API as the Extend System. The Extend System is a set of protocols that allows you to create external routines that react with Clipper programs. These routines typically provide some functionality not found in Clipper, for example, a routine to graph the results of a series of calculations.

Because Nantucket wrote Clipper using Microsoft C 5.1, employing that particular compiler and version ensures compatibility with the existing compiler. You can also choose to use any compiler that integrates with the Microsoft C 5.1 compiler code. These compilers might provide enhanced capabilities or a friendlier programming environment than Microsoft C. The examples in this book assume that you're using the Microsoft compiler. This means that, if your compiler performs a task in a different way than the Microsoft C compiler, you might need to modify the routines slightly to meet the requirements of compilers created by other vendors. More importantly, you might have to perform special setups or other modifications to allow your compiler to generate code that is 100% Microsoft C compatible.

Note: Keep in mind that, because there are many similarities in the Clipper/assembler and Clipper/C interfaces, some of this chapter is a repetition of the previous chapter.

Using the Clipper-supplied header file

Most C compilers provide access to libraries through the use of header files. These files normally define what the library contains so *you* don't have to each time you start to write a program. They also define constants and other general-purpose variables. The file that Nantucket supplies to document its library routines (API) is EXTEND.H.

This file is split into three sections. The first section defines some basic Clipper data types like NIL and NULL. This allows you to use the same data-type calls (provided that C supports them, some Clipper data types require translation to their C equivalent) in your external program as you do within Clipper. It also ensures that the data your external program generates is a valid type within Clipper. The second section defines the data-type return values. These values tell you what type of data you're receiving from Clipper. For a complete description of the Clipper data types, refer to the ValType( ) function in chapter 2. The third section defines the Clipper Extend System function calls. This is the mechanism your external program uses to interface with your Clipper program. Table 5-1 provides a listing of these Extend System function calls and their purpose.

As you can see, the Extend System function call table groups the calls by function. There are two major groups and eight minor groups. The first major group contains all parameter calls. These calls both send and retrieve values from your application program. The second major group allocates and deallocates memory for your add-on routine. The following sections explain the eight minor groups in further detail.

Typing and counting parameters

The Parameter Count/Type group contains functions that obtain information about the parameters passed to your routine. Because Clipper is not a strongly typed language, you need to check the values passed to your routine before you attempt to process them. The user could accidently pass some illegal value that would result in an illegal return value. Using these functions helps to eliminate any possible corruption of your routine's results due to invalid input values.

Determining parameter characteristics

The Parameter Values group contains functions that determine specific characteristics about the values passed to your routine. For example, the _parclen( ) function returns the length of a character parameter. It is essential to obtain this information since your routine knows nothing about the values you are using within Clipper. Using these functions could help eliminate memory corruption and other external routine problems.

Returning a value

The Return a Value group allows you to return a value to your Clipper program. This is the value returned by the routine. It reacts like any other Clipper function. For example, if you had the statement cSomeVar := yourfunc(cOtherVar) embedded in your Clipper code, then your external routine would have to use one of the return functions to place a value in cSomeVar. A program views a return value differently than a function that stores a value in a Clipper variable. Your routine can store values to multiple variables. It can return only a single value.

The Return No Value group contains the specialization of a function to return a value. Because your routine must return some value, it can choose to return something or nothing. NIL essentially returns a value of nothing to the calling Clipper procedure or function. Use it when the routine you create does not return a value to Clipper, but simply performs a task based on existing data. For example, a function to display data on screen would not necessarily return a value to Clipper. This differentiates Clipper 5.01 from Summer 87 version functions, which might not return anything to the calling program (i.e., no value at all instead of NIL).

Storing values

The Store Values group places a value into one of the parameters passed to your routine. Using a store function allows you to return multiple values from a single function by directly manipulating the contents of the Clipper variables. The function does not actually return these values; it modifies the contents of the variables before it returns to Clipper.

To use a store function you must pass the parameter by reference. Instead of passing the actual value, Clipper passes a pointer to the variable. You pass a value by reference by preceding it with an @ symbol. For example, in the line of code SomeVar := SomeFunc (Val1, @Val2), Clipper passes Val1 by value and Val2 by reference. The Store Values group differs from a Return a Value group, which allows your routine to return a value using the same methods as a standard function. While your routine can provide only one return value, it can store values to any number of parameters.

Allocating memory

The Allocate Memory group obtains and frees memory for your routine. You cannot use the standard C functions to obtain memory from DOS. Clipper automatically allocates all available memory for its own use. You must use these functions to obtain the memory from Clipper instead. This allows Clipper to maintain firm control over the allocation and use of memory.

Two special memory-allocation functions allow you to maintain compatibility with the Summer 87 version. These functions appear in the S87 Compatibility group. You should use the Clipper 5.01 specific functions, however, unless you need to maintain Summer 87 compatibility.

Checking macro parameters

The final group of functions, Parameter-Check Macros, allow you to check the type of the parameters input to your program using more easily remembered functions. You don't have to use these functions because they equate to the _parinfo( ) function. They do, however, improve the readability of your code and reduce the probability of errors. For example, PCount( ) is easier to read than _parinfo(0), and IsChar(1) is much more concise than (_parinfo(1) & CHARACTER).

Using the C header file

Understanding these header file entries, however, is only the first step in using them. You must then combine them into useful code. Figures 6-1 and 6-2 show a program that illustrates some of the simpler techniques for combining the header file with your code. Figure 6-1 contains the Clipper code used to test the C function shown in FIG. 6-2.

The example program in FIG. 6-2 offers several tips on creating an add-on routine for Clipper in C. First, there are six parts to the standard Clipper C language program. Notice that FIG. 6-2 clearly indicates where each of the six parts start. Each section performs a different function, as listed in the source code and described in the following text.

Of the six sections, sections 1 and 2 appear only once, at the beginning of the source code file. Use section 1 to make any required declarations. This includes adding the include file declaration to use the Clipper Extend System. You don't necessarily have to include section 2. There are many methods of manipulating Clipper variables that don't require the

6-1 Programming example number four, Clipper source

```
// Program Number 4 - Clipper to C Interface Example
// This example shows how to link a C program with a Clipper program.
// It was purposely designed to perform a simple task so that the
// illustration would clearly show the linkage requirments.  The other
// half of this program is PROG-04C.C.  It contains the function,
// GetHyp().  This function returns a 0 if the calling programs provides
// no input or an answer if it does.
// Written by John Mueller
// Copyright 1991 John Mueller - Tab Books, Inc.

// Create the variables required to calculate the sides of a triangle.

static nSide1 := 0,;
       nSide2 := 0,;
       nHyp   := 0

// Clear the display and request input for the two sides from the user.

cls
@ 01, 01 say "Enter the length of the first side:  ";
         get nSide1 picture '999.99'
@ 02, 01 say "Enter the length of the second side: ";
         get nSide2 picture '999.99'
read

// Call the C routine to compute the hypotenuese value.  Display the
// value out to four decimal places.

@ 03, 01 say "The length of the hypotenuese is:      " + ;
             str(GetHyp(nSide1, nSide2), 8, 4)

// Exit the program.

return
```

6-2 Programming example number four, C source code

```
/*
   This program contains a rudimentary example of how to implement a
   function using C for use with Clipper.  There are six main sections
   to the program.  First you include any required header files.  There
   are two include files required.  The first file is EXTEND.H which
   contains the Clipper calls.  The second file is MATH.H which defines
   the square root function.  The second section contains any variable
   declarations required to complete the specified task.  The third
   section consists of an If statement or other means of checking for
   parameter type and number.  In this case there two parameters, both
   of which must be double precision floating point numbers.  The fourth
   section contains the actual working code.  The fifth section contains
   an error handling routine used when the user provides incorrect input
   to the function.  The final section contains storage and return value
```

6-2 Continued.

```
   code.  This allows you directly modify Clipper variables if necessary
   and return a value to the calling program.  You must, as a minimum,
   return a value of NIL to the calling program.
   Written by John Mueller
   Copyright 1991 John Mueller - Tab Books, Inc.
*/

/* SECTION 1 - Header Files */

#include "EXTEND.H"
#include "MATH.H"

CLIPPER GetHyp(void)
{

/* SECTION 2 - Variable Declarations */

   double Side1 = 0;         // Value of the first side
   double Side2 = 0;         // Value of the second side
   double Hyp = 0;           // Value of the hypotenuse
   double ErrorCode = 0;     // Error code value

/* SECTION 3 - Variable Checking */

   if ( PCOUNT == 2 && ISNUM(1) && ISNUM(2) )
   {

/* SECTION 4 - Working Code */

/* Retrieve the individual values, compute the sum of the squares
   of the two sides, then the square root of this value.  Place
   the value of the hypotenuse in the return variable.
*/

                          Side1 = _parnd(1);
                          Side2 = _parnd(2);
                          Hyp = Side1 * Side1 + Side2 * Side2;
                          Hyp = sqrt(Hyp);

/* SECTION 6 - Return Value */

                          _retnd(Hyp);
                          }

/* SECTION 5 - Error Handling Routine */

                          else
                          {
                          _retnd(ErrorCode);
                          }

}
```

use of a separate data segment in your code. For example, you could directly modify the variable in the Clipper data segment once you receive a segment and offset pointer. However, using a separate data section will eliminate many problems that some programmers experience with corruption of the Clipper data area. Clipper doesn't know that you've updated the value of a variable unless you tell it you've done so. The functions included with the Extend System provide the means.

Using a separate data segment also reduces the risk of losing a pointer and corrupting memory. This usually results in the program locking up the host machine. The only drawback to using a separate data segment is that you're drawing directly from the memory available to Clipper. However, even considering this drawback, programs that use a separate data segment are inherently more reliable than those that don't. As a result, all programs in this book will include a private data area that the external routine can use to manipulate data.

Every routine that you create contains the information stored in sections 3 through 6 of the example program. Clipper is not a strongly typed language; therefore, a programmer could unknowingly pass an incorrect variable type to your routine. To prevent this, you should always check the data type you receive to make certain it is the correct type. The need for section 4 is obvious. The whole purpose of creating the routine is to manipulate data. Section 5 provides error handling.

It is important to keep the error-handling section of the routine separate from the rest of the routine for two reasons. First, it makes the routine easier to maintain because there's a clearly defined line between functional code and error-handling code. Second, it makes the program easier to debug. As your debugger steps through the routine code, you can instantly detect when an error occurs because the debugger cursor will shift to the error section. In fact, this technique allows you to set a breakpoint within the error section that stops program execution quickly whenever Clipper detects an error. Section 6 contains the code that returns a value to Clipper and ends the program.

The Summer 87 version of Clipper did not mandate that you always return a value from your routine. This had one disadvantage—you never know whether an error occurred in the Clipper code or the routine code. By forcing you to return a value, Clipper ensures that you'll be able to determine exactly where the error occurred. Even a return of NIL is better than no return at all.

As FIG. 6-1 illustrates, it's relatively easy to call a C routine from within Clipper. In fact, the call looks exactly the same as if the function were a part of Clipper in the first place. This easy integration of C source with Clipper source is one of the reasons that it's often easier to create an add-on than try to implement the same function using native commands and functions.

Unfortunately, as easy as it is to integrate new features into your program, you must weigh the cost of decreased program readability as a result of doing so. Adding a new C function to your source code means that the person who modifies your code after you leave must know both C and Clipper to fully appreciate what task the code performs.

Using external routines affects team projects as well. The team members will have a harder time keeping track of what functions are available and what tasks they perform. Keeping this in mind when you decide to implement a new function will allow you to choose native code versus C code wisely. Of prime importance is the number of times you plan to use the new function. If the function performs a generic task and you could use it for multiple programming assignments, then you can spread the cost of completely documenting the function over several jobs. This makes the function practical to create.

Another good reason to use an add-on function is if no combination of native code will achieve the results you need, for example, if you need to access a cash register port or some other piece of esoteric hardware directly. Imagine trying to solve some complex financial or scientific equations using Clipper. While Clipper could perform some of these tasks, the cost of doing so would far outweigh any derived benefits. In fact, it could be more expensive to use native code than to add a routine in C.

Adding your routines to Clipper using the preprocessor

Once you've created some new routines to enhance the functionality of Clipper, you need to add them to your Clipper program. There are two ways of doing this. You could add the calls directly to your Clipper source code, or you can define a Clipper header file and use the preprocessor to add them to your code.

The first method is acceptable if you plan to use the function only once. Of course, this brings to mind a question of why you created the function at all. Unless you created the routine to interface with some esoteric piece of hardware, it's almost certain that you need to use it more than once.

The second method adds the proper definitions to your Clipper program using the preprocessor. Because the definitions appear in a header file, the call is less error-prone. A header file either exists or it doesn't. The worst thing that could happen is that the programmer using your routine will type the wrong header filename as part of the #Include statement in the Clipper program. In addition, you can force the preprocessor to perform some formatting work for you. Figure 6-3 shows one technique for adding the function described in FIG. 6-2 to your Clipper program. Notice that this technique assumes that your routine is stand-alone. In other words, it doesn't directly enhance an existing Clipper command.

6-3 Programming example number five, header file

```
// This header file shows how you can create a new command which
// includes an external C or assembler routine.  It also shows how to
// add optional parameters like the PICTURE clause.  Notice that you
// can assign variables within a pre-processor directive as well.
// Written by: John Mueller
// Copyright 1991 John Mueller - Tab Books

#command ShowHyp <row>, <col>, <side1>, <side2>, <hyp> [, <picture>] ;
        => @ <row>, <col> get <side1> [ PICTURE <picture> ] ;
         ; @ <row> + 1, <col> get <side2> [ PICTURE <picture> ] ;
         ; read ;
         ; <hyp> := GetHyp(<side1>, <side2>) ;
         ; @ <row> + 2, <col> say <hyp> [ PICTURE <picture> ]
```

Using a header file containing the information shown in FIG. 6-3 allows you to access the function within Clipper as an independent command. It also allows you to make some modifications to the function without changing the user interface. For example, you could create a new command that adds another parameter to the function. If the user executes the function without the parameter, then it performs its original task. Executing the new command allows the same function to perform an enhanced task.

You can also modify an existing Clipper command to use your new function. Figure 6-4 shows an example of how you would accomplish this. Notice that, in this case, I've actually changed the command calling syntax, but in such a way that the user can employ the original calling syntax without error.

6-4 Programming example number six, header file

```
// This header file shows how you can modify an existing command using
// an external C or assembler routine.
// Written by: John Mueller
// Copyright 1991 John Mueller - Tab Books

#command ? HYP <row>, <col>, <side1>, <side2>, <hyp> [, <picture>] ;
        => @ <row>, <col> get <side1> [ PICTURE <picture> ] ;
         ; @ <row> + 1, <col> get <side2> [ PICTURE <picture> ] ;
         ; read ;
         ; <hyp> := GetHyp(<side1>, <side2>) ;
         ; @ <row> + 2, <col> say <hyp> [ PICTURE <picture> ]
```

The example in FIG. 6-4 shows the true extendibility of Clipper. You can enhance any aspect of the programming language without affecting backward compatibility. In fact, you could create commands that are true supersets of the original Clipper language. This, in fact, is the very reason for the existence of the Extend System—to allow you to build the tools you need without incurring a penalty.

Summary

This chapter shows you the basics of creating and using C routines with Clipper. It explains the purpose behind various construction techniques and how to use these techniques to their best advantage. It finishes by telling you how to incorporate these changes into your Clipper program. The following chapters will concentrate on building on this base of knowledge by showing you practical applications for external routines.

7
Creating new functions

This chapter will show you how to create some standard functions for your Clipper programs. In most cases they perform some direct hardware access, and concentrate on the function inherent in the 80×86 itself.

This chapter contains four main sections. The first section addresses the problem of creating date and time displays for menus. Most Clipper programmers use the Date( ) and Time( ) functions to update the display as it loops through a menu. Of course, as the program exits to a function or procedure, time (as a minimum) remains frozen. You can get around this problem by placing the Time( ) function and perhaps the Date( ) function in every procedure you write, or you can use a function that updates the display automatically. This leads to a second method of approaching the problem.

The second section examines the procedure required to create financial math functions using C or assembler. As you'll see, these functions are often more straightforward and faster than an identical function in Clipper. Of course, the main reason to use the assembler version of the function is to gain direct math coprocessor support. (Something that's impossible with C because you need to use a specific math library with Clipper.)

The third section describes some general scientific math functions. Like the financial math section, you'll find that the C and assembler functions are faster and more straightforward than their Clipper counterparts. You'll also see how you can use the math coprocessor to increase program speed even further.

The final section talks about some miscellaneous functions that you can use to enhance the appearance of your program. For example, one of the programs shows you how to exercise more control over the speaker. It explains how you can compute the values required to produce the "pure tones" created by many programs. The other examples show similarly interesting functions that can enhance your Clipper program.

Creating date and time displays for menus

Everyone wants to keep track of the time they spend engaged in specific activities. That is one of the reasons that time and date displays have become popular for PC applications. Another reason is that it reassures the program user. An active time display shows that the program is active during long computations. Some people feel that any computer operation over 5 seconds indicates that the computer is frozen. And some people feel that a time and date display dresses up an application and makes it look finished. Whatever your reason for wanting to add the time and date to your program, this part of the book will show you how.

The following sections include source code examples, sample header files, and a description of how the code works. More importantly, the examples will show you how to implement the time and date features with your Clipper programs.

Creating the date display

The date display is the easier of the two example programs. In this case, the program directly queries the appropriate peripheral chips on the computer and then converts the output it receives into a format that Clipper can use. The Clipper program retrieves the formatted date and places it on the screen. An interesting aspect of the program is that it provides the date in a format not available through Clipper. The output is in character, rather than date format. It uses the form <Day of Week>, <Day> <Full Month Name>, <Year>. While you could perform this same function using multiple Clipper functions, this new routine allows you to do it by simply calling one function.

The CharDate( ) function is an example of a routine created for ease of use rather than actual need. Figure 7-1 provides the Clipper source code used to call the CharDate( ) function. As you can see, you call it as you would any other date function. Figure 7-2 contains the CharDate( ) function assembly language code, and FIG. 7-3 provides the same code in C. Notice that the assembly language and C routines use the same general calling sequences, so the following description will apply to both languages.

As you can see, the process of retrieving the date is quite simple. It takes a few lines of code from the GetDOSDate( ) function. The function calls DOS interrupt 21h service 2Ah to read the DOS clock (as differentiated from the CMOS clock) and then places the results in variables for further processing. The processing takes a lot more code. The first task is to convert the day of the week, contained in the AL register, to a string. In assembly this is done by indexing the correct variable in the data segment. In C this is done with a switch structure.

7-1 Date programming example, Clipper source

```
// Date Programming Example
// This program is used in conjunction with either CHRDATEA.ASM or
// CHRDATEC.C to illustrate how you can obtain the date directly
// from DOS and convert it into any format desired.
// Written by: John Mueller
// Copyright 1991 John Mueller - Tab Books

// Declare program variables.

static nVarl := 0          // Place holder variable.

// Display the screen.

set scoreboard off
set color to "W+/B,RG+/R"
cls
@ 01, 00 to 24, 79 double
@ 03, 01 to 03, 78 double

// Display the date.

@ 02, 03 say CharDate()

// Display the place holder variable.

@ 05, 03 say "Enter a Number: " get nVarl picture "999.99"
read

// Exit the program.

return
```

7-2 Date programming example, assembly source

```
;*****************************************************************************
;* Character Date Programming Example                                        *
;* This program shows how to obtain the date directly from DOS.  It          *
;* then provides one example of how you could convert this information *
;* into a form usable by Clipper.  The program returns the date in the *
;* format of <Day of Week>, <Day> <Full Month Name>, <Full Year>.  You *
;* call it by typing CharDate().  This routine does not require any          *
;* input.                                                                    *
;* Written by: John Mueller                                                  *
;* Copyright 1991 John Mueller - Tab Books                                   *
;*****************************************************************************

;*****************************************************************************
;* Make any required declarations.                                           *
;*****************************************************************************
```

7-2 Continued.

```
.MODEL LARGE

INCLUDE EXTASM.INC
INCLUDE MACROS.INC

PUBLIC CharDate

;*****************************************************************
;* Declare any required variables.                               *
;*****************************************************************

.DATA

cDate  DB 40 dup (' '), 0   ; Character string used to hold date.

nYear  DW 0       ; Year in numeric form.
nMonth DB 0       ; Month in numeric form.
nDay   DB 0       ; Day in numeric form.

 ; Days of the week in character form.

cSun   DB "   Sunday, "
cMon   DB "   Monday, "
cTue   DB "  Tuesday, "
cWed   DB "Wednesday, "
cThr   DB " Thursday, "
cFri   DB "   Friday, "
cSat   DB " Saturday, "

; Months of the year in character form.

cJan   DB " January, "
cFeb   DB " February, "
cMar   DB " March, "
cApr   DB " April, "
cMay   DB " May, "
cJun   DB " June, "
cJul   DB " July, "
cAug   DB " August, "
cSep   DB " September, "
cOct   DB " October, "
cNov   DB " November, "
cDec   DB " December, "

;*****************************************************************
;* Start of the code segment and the main procedure.             *
;*****************************************************************

.CODE

CharDate       PROC    FAR
```

```
                PUSH    SI            ;Save SI.

                MOV     AX,@DATA      ;Point to our data segment.
                MOV     DS,AX
                MOV     ES,AX

                CALL    GetDOSDate ;Retrieve the date information.

                MOV     CX,11         ;Convert day of week number into a string.
                MUL     CL
                LEA     SI,cSun       ;Point to the first day of the week.
                ADD     SI,AX         ;Add enough positions to point to current day.
                LEA     DI,cDate      ;Place the string in cDate.
                REP     MOVSB

                INC     DI            ;Point to the second day position.
                MOV     AL,nDay       ;Convert the day value into a string.
                XOR     AH,AH
                CALL    HexConv

                INC     DI            ;Point one position past the end of the day
                INC     DI            ;string.
                MOV     AL,nMonth     ;Convert the month value into a string.
                XOR     AH,AH
                CALL    CheckMonth

                INC     DI            ;Point to the fourth year position.
                INC     DI
                INC     DI
                MOV     AX,nYear      ;Convert the year to a string.
                CALL    HexConv

Exit:           RetChar     cDate     ;Return the date in string form.
                POP         SI        ;Restore SI.
                RET                   ;Return to the calling procedure.

CharDate        ENDP

;**********************************************************************
;* Start of the local procedure section.                              *
;**********************************************************************

;**********************************************************************
;* This procedure checks the numeric value of the month returned by   *
;* GetDOSDate.  It places the character representation of the month in*
;* the place pointed to by ES:DI.  You place the numeric month value  *
;* in AX prior to calling the procedure.  This procedure does not     *
;* return a value.                                                    *
;**********************************************************************

CheckMonth      PROC    NEAR

                CMP     AX,1          ;Is it January?
                JNE     Month2        ;If not, check the next month.
```

7-2 Continued.

```
                LEA     SI,cJan     ;Point to the month and store it in
                MOV     CX,10       ;the position pointed to by DI.
                JMP     MonthDone

Month2:         CMP     AX,2        ;Is it February?
                JNE     Month3      ;If not, check the next month.
                LEA     SI,cFeb     ;Point to the month and store it in
                MOV     CX,11       ;the position pointed to by DI.
                JMP     MonthDone

Month3:         CMP     AX,3        ;Is it March?
                JNE     Month4      ;If not, check the next month.
                LEA     SI,cMar     ;Point to the month and store it in
                MOV     CX,8        ;the position pointed to by DI.
                JMP     MonthDone

Month4:         CMP     AX,4        ;Is it April?
                JNE     Month5      ;If not, check the next month.
                LEA     SI,cApr     ;Point to the month and store it in
                MOV     CX,8        ;the position pointed to by DI.
                JMP     MonthDone

Month5:         CMP     AX,5        ;Is it May?
                JNE     Month6      ;If not, check the next month.
                LEA     SI,cMay     ;Point to the month and store it in
                MOV     CX,6        ;the position pointed to by DI.
                JMP     MonthDone

Month6:         CMP     AX,6        ;Is it June?
                JNE     Month7      ;If not, check the next month.
                LEA     SI,cJun     ;Point to the month and store it in
                MOV     CX,7        ;the position pointed to by DI.
                JMP     MonthDone

Month7:         CMP     AX,7        ;Is it July?
                JNE     Month8      ;If not, check the next month.
                LEA     SI,cJul     ;Point to the month and store it in
                MOV     CX,7        ;the position pointed to by DI.
                JMP     MonthDone

Month8:         CMP     AX,8        ;Is it August?
                JNE     Month9      ;If not, check the next month.
                LEA     SI,cAug     ;Point to the month and store it in
                MOV     CX,9        ;the position pointed to by DI.
                JMP     MonthDone

Month9:         CMP     AX,9        ;Is it September?
                JNE     Month10     ;If not, check the next month.
                LEA     SI,cSep     ;Point to the month and store it in
                MOV     CX,12       ;the position pointed to by DI.
                JMP     MonthDone
```

```
Month10:        CMP     AX,10       ;Is it October?
                JNE     Month11     ;If not, check the next month.
                LEA     SI,cOct     ;Point to the month and store it in
                MOV     CX,10       ;the position pointed to by DI.
                JMP     MonthDone

Month11:        CMP     AX,11       ;Is it November?
                JNE     Month12     ;If not, check the next month.
                LEA     SI,cNov     ;Point to the month and store it in
                MOV     CX,11       ;the position pointed to by DI.
                JMP     MonthDone

Month12:        LEA     SI,cDec     ;Point to the month and store it in
                MOV     CX,11       ;the position pointed to by DI.

MonthDone:      REP     MOVSB       ;Move the actual data.
                RET                 ;Return to the calling procedure.

CheckMonth      ENDP

;*********************************************************************
;* Get the date and place the values obtained in specific variables.  *
;* The day of the week is left in AL.  The day is returned in nDay.   *
;* The month is returned in nMonth.  The year is returned in nYear.   *
;*********************************************************************

GetDOSDate      PROC    NEAR

                MOV     AX,2A00h    ;Obtain the date information.
                INT     21h

                MOV     nYear,CX    ;Store the values.
                MOV     nMonth,DH
                MOV     nDay,DL

                RET                 ;Return to the calling procedure.

GetDOSDate      ENDP

;*********************************************************************
;* This procedure converts a hexidecimal number to a decimal character*
;* equivalent.  AX contains the number to convert and DI the address  *
;* of the end of a storage buffer on entry.  The procedure does not   *
;* return a value.                                                    *
;*********************************************************************

HexConv         PROC    NEAR

                MOV CX,10           ;Load divisor.
DoDiv:          XOR DX,DX           ;Clear DX.
                DIV CX              ;Divide AX by 10
                ADD DX,30h          ;Change remainder to char.
                MOV [DI],DL         ;Store the number.
                DEC DI              ;Point to next number.
```

7-2 Continued.

```
                CMP AX,9        ;See if we need to divide.
                JG  DoDiv
                ADD AX,30h      ;Change quotient to char.
                MOV [DI],AL     ;Store the number.

                RET

HexConv         ENDP

END
```

7-3 Date programming example, C source

```
/* Character Date Programming Example
   This program shows how to obtain the date directly from DOS.  It
   then provides one example of how you could convert this information
   into a form usable by Clipper.  The program returns the date in the
   format of <Day of Week>, <Day> <Full Month Name>, <Full Year>.  You
   call it by typing CharDate().  This routine does not require any
   input.
   Written by: John Mueller
   Copyright 1991 John Mueller - Tab Books
*/

#include "EXTEND.H"
#include "STDIO.H"
#include "DOS.H"
#include "STRING.H"
#include "STDLIB.H"

void GetDOSDate(void);

union  REGS   inregs, outregs;

/* Declare some global variables. */

/* Year in numeric form. */
int nYear;

/* Month in numeric form. */
int nMonth;

/* Day in numeric form. */
int nDay;

/* Day of week in numeric form. */
int nDayW;

CLIPPER CharDate(void)

{
```

```
/* Character string used to hold date. */

char cDate[40];

/* Days of the week in character form. */

char cSun[] = "   Sunday, ";
char cMon[] = "   Monday, ";
char cTue[] = "  Tuesday, ";
char cWed[] = "Wednesday, ";
char cThr[] = " Thursday, ";
char cFri[] = "   Friday, ";
char cSat[] = " Saturday, ";

/* Months of the year in character form. */

char cJan[] = " January, ";
char cFeb[] = " February, ";
char cMar[] = " March, ";
char cApr[] = " April, ";
char cMay[] = " May, ";
char cJun[] = " June, ";
char cJul[] = " July, ";
char cAug[] = " August, ";
char cSep[] = " September, ";
char cOct[] = " October, ";
char cNov[] = " November, ";
char cDec[] = " December, ";

/* Declare some miscellaneous variables. */

int nRadix = 10;
char cTemp[5];

/* Beginning of main function. */

GetDOSDate();

/* Add the day of the week to cDate. */

switch(nDayW)
   {
   case 0:
      strcpy(cDate, cSun);
      break;
   case 1:
      strcpy(cDate, cMon);
      break;
   case 2:
      strcpy(cDate, cTue);
      break;
   case 3:
      strcpy(cDate, cWed);
      break;
```

7-3 Continued.

```
   case 4:
      strcpy(cDate, cThr);
      break;
   case 5:
       strcpy(cDate, cFri);
      break;
   case 6:
      strcpy(cDate, cSat);
      break;
   }

/* Convert the day from a number to a string.  Add the resulting
   string to cDate.
*/

itoa(nDay, cTemp, nRadix);
strcat(cDate, cTemp);

/* Add the full month name to cDate. */
/* Note: This was a separate function in the assembler example. */

switch(nMonth)
   {
   case 1:
      strcat(cDate, cJan);
      break;
   case 2:
      strcat(cDate, cFeb);
      break;
   case 3:
      strcat(cDate, cMar);
      break;
   case 4:
      strcat(cDate, cApr);
      break;
   case 5:
      strcat(cDate, cMay);
      break;
   case 6:
      strcat(cDate, cJun);
      break;
   case 7:
      strcat(cDate, cJul);
      break;
   case 8:
      strcat(cDate, cAug);
      break;
   case 9:
      strcat(cDate, cSep);
      break;
   case 10:
      strcat(cDate, cOct);
      break;
```

```
   case 11:
      strcat(cDate, cNov);
      break;
    case 12:
      strcat(cDate, cDec);
      break;
   }

/* Convert the year from a number to a string.  Add the resulting
   string to cDate.
*/

itoa(nYear, cTemp, nRadix);
strcat(cDate, cTemp);

/* Return the completed string to Clipper. */

_retc(cDate);

}

/* Beginning of local procedures. */

/* Get the date and place the values obtained in specific variables.
   The day of the week is left in AL.  The day is returned in nDay.
   The month is returned in nMonth.  The year is returned in nYear.
*/

void GetDOSDate(void)
{
inregs.h.ah = 0x2A;
intdos(&inregs, &outregs);
nYear = outregs.x.cx;
nMonth = outregs.h.dh;
nDay = outregs.h.dl;
nDayW = outregs.h.al;
}
```

The next task is to convert the day, found in DL, from a numeric representation to a character representation. Both C and assembler use a simple hexadecimal-to-character conversion function. The assembler example provides this routine as HexConv. C uses a built-in function, IToA( ). The conversion of the month, contained in DH, to a string follows the same procedure as the C conversion for the day of week. In this instance, both the C and the assembler examples use a case-control structure. The assembler version appears in a separate routine for the sake of clarity. Finally, you convert the year, found in the CX register, from a numeric representation to a character representation using the same procedure used for the day conversion. And finally you pass the converted date string back to Clipper using the RetC( ) function.

Because the date doesn't change very often, it's safe to use a routine that doesn't monitor the clock. This means that the routine is very efficient—it doesn't use any clock cycles by installing an interrupt-driven control. However, this method also has some drawbacks. You must rely on the program to occasionally check the date to make certain it's correct. This might not always occur, and the date displayed on the screen will be incorrect. One way to get around this problem is to create an interrupt-driven routine.

Creating the time display

Time is a natural add-on for a date display. It's just as easy to retrieve the time from DOS as it is the date. Of course, the rules for formatting a time display differ from those for creating a date. Figure 7-4 shows an enhanced

7-4 Time programming example, Clipper source

```
// Time Programming Example
// This program is used in conjunction with either CHRTIMEA.ASM or
// CHRTIMEC.C to illustrate how you can obtain the time directly
// from DOS and convert it into any format desired.  It builds on the
// previous example, CHRDATE.PRG.  Therefore, you need to add the
// CHRDATEA or CHRDATEC object file when you link the programs.
// Written by: John Mueller
// Copyright 1991 John Mueller - Tab Books

// Declare program variables.

static nVarl := 0            // Place holder variable.

// Display the screen.

set scoreboard off
set color to "W+/B,RG+/R"
cls
@ 01, 00 to 24, 79 double
@ 03, 01 to 03, 78 double

// Display the date.

@ 02, 03 say CharDate()
@ 02, 68 say CharTime()

// Display the place holder variable.

@ 05, 03 say "Enter a Number: " get nVarl picture "999.99"
read

// Exit the program.

return
```

version of the code in FIG. 7-1. Notice that it adds the time as one of the display elements. Figure 7-5 contains the assembly-language source used to create the time display. Figure 7-6 contains the C version of the same code. The important aspect to notice about these programs is that they follow much the same pattern as the date examples. The biggest differences between the two examples are the DOS function called (2Ch versus 2Ah) and the formatting technique used to produce the date output. In many other respects, the two programs are similar. Like the date display, you could use an interrupt-driven routine to automatically update the time display.

7-5 Time programming example, assembly source

```
;*************************************************************************
;* Character Time Programming Example                                    *
;* This program shows how to obtain the time directly from DOS.  It      *
;* then provides one example of how you could convert this information  *
;* into a form usable by Clipper.  The program returns the time in the  *
;* format of <Hours>:<Minutes>:<Seconds>.  You call it by typing        *
;* CharTime().  This routine does not require any input.                 *
;* Written by: John Mueller                                              *
;* Copyright 1991 John Mueller - Tab Books                               *
;*************************************************************************

;*************************************************************************
;* Make any required declarations.                                       *
;*************************************************************************

.MODEL LARGE

INCLUDE EXTASM.INC
INCLUDE MACROS.INC

PUBLIC CharTime

;*************************************************************************
;* Declare any required variables.                                       *
;*************************************************************************

.DATA

cColon      DB      ':'

cTime       DB      8 dup (' '), 0 ; Character string used to hold time.

nHour       DB 0    ; Hours in numeric form.
nMinute     DB 0    ; Minutes in numeric form.
nSecond     DB 0    ; Seconds in numeric form.

;************************************************************************
;* Start of the code segment and the main procedure.                    *
;************************************************************************
```

7-5 Continued.

```
.CODE

CharTime        PROC    FAR

                PUSH    SI          ;Save SI.

                MOV     AX,@DATA    ;Point to our data segment.
                MOV     DS,AX
                MOV     ES,AX

                CALL    GetDOSTime ;Retrieve the time information.

                LEA     DI,cTime    ;Load the starting address of time string.
                ADD     DI,7        ;Find the end of the string.

                MOV     AL,nSecond ;Convert the first number.
                XOR     AH,AH
                CALL    HexConv
                MOV     AL,cColon   ;Add a colon.
                MOV     [DI],AL
                DEC     DI          ;Point to the next position.

                MOV     AL,nMinute ;Convert the second number.
                XOR     AH,AH
                CALL    HexConv
                MOV     AL,cColon   ;Add a colon.
                MOV     [DI],AL
                DEC     DI          ;Point to the next position.

                MOV     AL,nHour    ;Convert final number.
                XOR     AH,AH
                CALL    HexConv

Exit:           RetCharcTime        ;Return the time in string form.
                POP     SI          ;Restore SI.
                RET                 ;Return to the calling procedure.

CharTime        ENDP

;*************************************************************************
;* Start of the local procedure section.                                 *
;*************************************************************************

;*************************************************************************
;* Get the time and place the values obtained in specific variables.    *
;* The Hours are returned in CH, the Minutes in CL, the Seconds in DH,*
;* and the Hundreths of a Second (not used) in DL.                       *
;*************************************************************************

GetDOSTime      PROC    NEAR
```

```
                MOV     AX,2C00h     ;Obtain the time information.
                INT     21h

                MOV     nHour,CH     ;Store the values.
                MOV     nMinute,CL
                MOV     nSecond,DH

                RET                  ;Return to the calling procedure.

GetDOSTime      ENDP

;**********************************************************************
;* This procedure converts a hexidecimal number to a decimal character*
;* equivalent.  AX contains the number to convert and DI the address  *
;* of the end of a storage buffer on entry.  The procedure does not   *
;* return a value.                                                    *
;**********************************************************************

HexConv         PROC    NEAR

                MOV     CX,10        ;Load divisor.
DoDiv:          XOR     DX,DX        ;Clear DX.
                DIV     CX           ;Divide AX by 10
                ADD     DX,30h       ;Change remainder to char.
                MOV     [DI],DL      ;Store the number.
                DEC     DI           ;Point to next number.
                CMP     AX,9         ;See if we need to divide.
                JG      DoDiv
                ADD     AX,30h       ;Change quotient to char.
                MOV     [DI],AL      ;Store the number.

                RET                  ;Return to the calling procedure.

HexConv         ENDP

END
```

7-6 Time programming example, C source

```
/* Character Time Programming Example
   This program shows how to obtain the time directly from DOS.  It
   then provides one example of how you could convert this information
   into a form usable by Clipper.  The program returns the time in the
   format of <Hours>:<Minutes>:<Seconds>.  You call it by typing
   CharTime().  This routine does not require any input.
   Written by: John Mueller
   Copyright 1991 John Mueller - Tab Books
*/

#include "EXTEND.H"
#include "STDIO.H"
#include "DOS.H"
```

7-6 Continued.

```
#include "STRING.H"
#include "STDLIB.H"

void GetDOSTime(void);

union  REGS   inregs, outregs;

/* Declare some global variables. */

/* Hours in numeric form. */
int nHour;

/* Minutes in numeric form. */
int nMinute;

/* Seconds in numeric form. */
int nSecond;

CLIPPER CharTime(void)

{

/* Character string used to hold time. */

char cTime[9];

/* Declare some miscellaneous variables. */

int nRadix = 10;
char cTemp[5];
char cColon[] = ":";

/* Beginning of main function. */

GetDOSTime();

/* Convert the hours from a number to a string.  Add the resulting
   string to CharTime.
*/

itoa(nHour, cTemp, nRadix);
strcpy(cTime, cTemp);

/* Add a colon between the hours and the minutes. */

strcat(cTime, cColon);

/* Convert the minutes from a number to a string.  Add the resulting
   string to CharTime.
*/
```

```
itoa(nMinute, cTemp, nRadix);
strcat(cTime, cTemp);

/* Add a colon between the minutes and the seconds. */

strcat(cTime, cColon);

/* Convert the seconds from a number to a string.  Add the resulting
   string to CharTime.
*/

itoa(nSecond, cTemp, nRadix);
strcat(cTime, cTemp);

/* Return the completed string to Clipper. */

_retc(cTime);

}

/* Beginning of local procedures. */

/* Get the time and place the values obtained in specific variables.
   The Hours are returned in CH, the Minutes in CL, the Seconds in DH,
   and the Hundreths of a Second (not used) in DL.
*/

void GetDOSTime(void)
{
 inregs.h.ah = 0x2C;
intdos(&inregs, &outregs);
nHour = outregs.h.ch;
nMinute = outregs.h.cl;
nSecond = outregs.h.dh;
}
```

Creating financial math functions

Financial functions are the lifeblood of any accounting program on the market. In fact, many of the available market applications use financial functions as well. For example, any cost estimation or inventory control program relies on financial functions as the basis for their predictions. In many cases, a major portion of the time that a financial program spends creating output is spent calculating the results of one or more database queries.

Because financial functions are important to the operation of so many different programs, it makes sense to ensure that they work as quickly and efficiently as possible. You could build these functions with Clipper, but C is quicker at performing the task than the same program in Clipper. The reason is simple: you can construct specific functions with less overhead than possible by using multiple generic functions. Using C is relatively simple as well. Most of the same arithmetic principles used in Clipper apply equally to the C program you create.

Due to the floating-point nature of most financial calculations, it's impractical to use assembler unless the target machine contains a math coprocessor. (In which case you cannot use C because the resulting library will conflict with Clipper.) The labor required to perform floating-point calculations with assembly language far outweigh any benefits you would see in improved program performance.

Of course, programming these functions to take advantage of a math coprocessor would make them even faster. Appendix F contains some example programs that use the math coprocessor. Unfortunately, most machines don't have access to the coprocessor. This section answers the question of how to create fast, reliable C math routines with a minimum of overhead. All the examples provided use the standard 80×86 processor found in every PC-compatible machine.

Interest calculations

There are several classifications of financial functions that you can build. The most commonly required functions are those that determine the interest and payment schedule for credit purchases. Figure 7-7 shows the Clipper program syntax for calling the C version of the functions. Figure 7-8 provides examples of both simple interest and complex interest functions written in C. As you can see, the C program uses many of the same procedures that a Clipper program would use to calculate a similar result.

Besides the obvious output of compound interest producing a higher result given similar input, FIG. 7-7 shows that calling either routine requires exactly the same syntax. In fact, you could simply substitute one for the other in any routine. The differences between the two routines is shown in the code in FIG. 7-8. As you can see, different calculations produce different procedures for each routine. The simple interest routine computes the change in principle first, then simply adds that change in a loop. The compound interest routine calculates the percentage of change and applies that percentage during each iteration of the loop. The change in the principle is calculated during the loop instead of before it.

In all other ways the two routines are the same. They begin by checking for the correct input and then place that input in local variables. Both routines store the return values into the array passed by reference from Clipper during the calculation loop. They end by passing true if they received the correct values from Clipper, or false if they didn't receive the correct values.

7-7 Simple/complex-interest example, Clipper source

```
// Interest Programming Example
// This program shows the interface between a C program used to
// calculate both simple and compound interest using the standard
// processor and the user.  It begins by polling the user for the
// numbers required to predict the future value of an investment.  The
// first routine it calls calculates the return on investment if the
// investment gains a set amount each accounting period (simple
// interest).  The second routine it calls calculates the return on
// investment if the return is compounded at a specific rate for a
// specific number of times per year (compound interest equation).  The
// program calls each C routine in turn and passes the required
// parameters.  In addition, the program passes the C routine an array
// in which to store the calculation results.  Once the C program does
// its work, it passes control back to the Clipper program after storing
// the calculated values in the array.  The Clipper program completes by
// displaying the contents of the array on screen.
// Written by: John Mueller
// Copyright 1991 John Mueller - Tab Books

local nRate      := 0,;   // Interest Rate
      nPeriodPY  := 0,;   // Compounding Periods/Year
      nPeriods   := 0,;   // Total Compounding Periods
      nPrinciple := 0,;   // Principle
      aFutureVal[256]     // Compounded Amount

static nRow, nCol, nCount // Counter Variables for Loops

// Display the background screen.

set scoreboard off
set color to "W+/B, RG+/R"
cls
@ 01, 00 to 24, 79 double
@ 02, 01 say padc(" Simple Interest Example ", 78, chr(177))
@ 03, 01 to 03, 78 double

// Get the input values from the user.

@ 05, 02 say "          Interest rate: " get nRate picture "99.999"
@ 06, 02 say "Compounding Periods/Year: " get nPeriodPY picture "99"
@ 07, 02 say "          Total Periods: " get nPeriods picture "999" range 1, 256
@ 08, 02 say "              Principle: " get nPrinciple picture "999999.99"
read

// Setup the counter variables prior to use.

nCount := 1
nCol := 2

// Display a header showing what data the co-processor will calculate.

@ 10, 01 say padc(" Future Value Results ", 78, chr(177))
```

7-7 Continued.

```
// Compute the future values on a periodic basis.

if SimpInt(nRate, nPeriodPY, nPeriods, nPrinciple, @aFutureVal)

// Display the calculated values that CompInt stored in the array.

   while nCount < nPeriods
      for nRow := 11 to 22
         @ nRow, nCol say aFutureVal[nCount] picture "$999999.99"
         nCount++
         if nCount > nPeriods
            exit
         endif
      next
   nCol := nCol + 12
   enddo
endif

// Wait for the user to finish viewing the results.

@ 23, 02 say "Press any key when ready..."
inkey(0)

// Display the background screen.

set scoreboard off
set color to "W+/B, RG+/R"
cls
@ 01, 00 to 24, 79 double
@ 02, 01 say padc(" Compound Interest Example ", 78, chr(177))
@ 03, 01 to 03, 78 double

// Get the input values from the user.

@ 05, 02 say "               Interest rate: " get nRate picture "99.999"
@ 06, 02 say "Compounding Periods/Year: " get nPeriodPY picture "99"
@ 07, 02 say "               Total Periods: " get nPeriods picture "999" range 1, 256
@ 08, 02 say "                   Principle: " get nPrinciple picture "999999.99"
read

// Setup the counter variables prior to use.

nCount := 1
nCol := 2

// Display a header showing what data the co-processor will calculate.

@ 10, 01 say padc(" Future Value Results ", 78, chr(177))

// Compute the future values on a periodic basis.
```

```
if CompInt(nRate, nPeriodPY, nPeriods, nPrinciple, @aFutureVal)

// Display the calculated values that CompInt stored in the array.

   while nCount < nPeriods
      for nRow := 11 to 22
         @ nRow, nCol say aFutureVal[nCount] picture "$999999.99"
         nCount++
         if nCount > nPeriods
            exit
         endif
      next
   nCol := nCol + 12
   enddo
endif

// Wait for the user to finish viewing the results.

@ 23, 02 say "Press any key when ready..."
inkey(0)

// Clear the display and exit the program.

set color to "W/N, N/W"
cls

return
```

7-8 Simple/complex-interest example, C source

```
/* Interest Programming Example
   This program contains two routines.  The first routine calculates
   simple interest, while the second calculates compound interest.  Both
   routines require the same five inputs: Interest Rate (in percent),
   Number of Accounting Periods/Year, Total Number of Accounting
   Periods, Amount of Principle, and an array reference in which to
   store the results.  The simple interest routine calculates the amount
   of interest in dollars that the user will see.  It then adds this
   amount to the principle for the number of interest periods.  The
   second routines calculates the interest as a percentage of the total
   amount accumulated.  For the first calculation this amount equals the
   principle.  It then multiplies the total accumulated by the interest
   rate plus one to obtain the new total.  Both programs fill the
   Clipper array during each iteration of the routine, therefore there
   is nothing to return.  The return value is used to indicate whether
   or not the routine successfully recieved the appropriate variables.
   Written by: John Mueller
   Copyright 1991 John Mueller - Tab Books */

#include "EXTEND.H"

double nRate;
```

7-8 Continued.

```
double nPeriodPY;
int nPeriods;
double nPrinciple;
double nRatePP;
double nTemp;
int nCount;
int nArray = 1;

CLIPPER SimpInt(void)
{
if (PCOUNT == 5 && ISNUM(1) && ISNUM(2) && ISNUM(3) && ISNUM(4) && ISARRAY(5))
   {

   /* Retrieve the variables from Clipper. */

   nRate = _parnd(1);
   nPeriodPY = _parnd(2);
   nPeriods = _parni(3);
   nPrinciple = _parnd(4);

   /* Make sure nArray is initialized to 1. */

   nArray = 1;

   /* Compute the interest per period.  Change the percentage figure
      obtained in Clipper to a rate by dividing by 100.  Multiply the
      result by the principle to compute the simple interest in dollars
      per period. */

   nRatePP = nRate/nPeriodPY/100*nPrinciple;

   /* Store the principle to the temporary variable. */

   nTemp = nPrinciple;

   /* Compute the principle plus interest for each period and store in
      the array passed by reference from Clipper. */

   for (nCount = 0; nCount < nPeriods; nCount++)
      {
      nTemp = nTemp + nRatePP;
      _stornd(nTemp, 5, nArray);
      nArray++;
      }

   /* Return true to show the routine recieved the proper parameters. */

   _retl(TRUE);

   }
else
   {
```

```
   /* Return false to indicate a program error. */

   _retl(FALSE);

   }
}

CLIPPER CompInt(void)
{
if (PCOUNT == 5 && ISNUM(1) && ISNUM(2) && ISNUM(3) && ISNUM(4) && ISARRAY(5))
    {

   /* Retrieve the variables from Clipper. */

   nRate = _parnd(1);
   nPeriodPY = _parnd(2);
   nPeriods = _parni(3);
   nPrinciple = _parnd(4);

   /* Make sure nArray is initialized to 1. */

   nArray = 1;

   /* Compute the interest per period.  Change the percentage figure
      obtained in Clipper to a rate by dividing by 100. */

   nRatePP = nRate/nPeriodPY/100;
   nTemp = nPrinciple;

   /* Compute the principle plus interest for each period and store in
      the array passed by reference from Clipper. */

   for (nCount = 0; nCount < nPeriods; nCount++)
      {
      nTemp = nTemp * (1 + nRatePP);
      _stornd(nTemp, 5, nArray);
      nArray++;
      }

   /* Return true to show the routine recieved the proper parameters. */

   _retl(TRUE);

   }
else
   {

   /* Return false to indicate a program error. */

   _retl(FALSE);

   }
}
```

Future value calculations

Another common financial calculation is the prediction of how much money an investor could make given a specific set of conditions. For example, if you deposit $100.00 in the bank at 5% interest for five years, compounded at one month intervals, what could you expect as a return on your investment? This type of computation is also referred to as an *annuity* in some texts. Many companies use this type of calculation to set aside enough money for capital investments and equipment repairs. Figure 7-9 presents the Clipper source code used to call the C version of the functions. Figure 7-10 provides the C source code for computing the future value of an investment given a specific set of conditions.

7-9 Annuity programming example, Clipper source

```
// Annuity Programming Example
// This program shows the interface between a C program used to
// calculate an annuity using the standard processor and the user.  It
// begins by polling the user for the numbers required to predict the
// future value of an investment.  The program then passes the variable
// to the C routine.  It includes an array in which to store the
// calculation results.  Once the C program does its work, it passes
// control back to the Clipper program after storing the calculated
// values in the array.  The Clipper program completes by displaying the
// contents of the array on screen.
// Written by: John Mueller
// Copyright 1991 John Mueller - Tab Books

local nRate      := 0,;   // Interest Rate
      nPeriodPY  := 0,;   // Compounding Periods/Year
      nPeriods   := 0,;   // Total Compounding Periods
      nPayment   := 0,;   // Payments Made Each Period
      aFutureVal[256]     // Compounded Amount

static nRow, nCol, nCount // Counter Variables for Loops

// Display the background screen.

set scoreboard off
set color to "W+/B, RG+/R"
cls
@ 01, 00 to 24, 79 double
@ 02, 01 say padc(" Annuity Example ", 78, chr(177))
@ 03, 01 to 03, 78 double

// Get the input values from the user.

@ 05, 02 say "             Interest rate: " get nRate picture "99.999"
@ 06, 02 say "Compounding Periods/Year: " get nPeriodPY picture "99"
@ 07, 02 say "             Total Periods: " get nPeriods picture "999" range 1, 256
@ 08, 02 say "     Payment Each Period: " get nPayment picture "9999.99"
read
```

```
// Setup the counter variables prior to use.

nCount := 1
  nCol := 2

// Display a header showing what data the co-processor will calculate.

@ 10, 01 say padc(" Future Value Results ", 78, chr(177))

// Compute the future values on a periodic basis.

if AnnCalc(nRate, nPeriodPY, nPeriods, nPayment, @aFutureVal)

// Display the calculated values that AnnCalc() stored in the array.

   while nCount < nPeriods
      for nRow := 11 to 22
         @ nRow, nCol say aFutureVal[nCount] picture "$999999.99"

         nCount++
         if nCount > nPeriods
            exit
         endif
      next
   nCol := nCol + 12
   enddo
endif

// Wait for the user to finish viewing the results.

@ 23, 02 say "Press any key when ready..."
inkey(0)

// Return to DOS.

return
```

7-10 Annuity programming example, C source

```
/* Annuity Programming Example
   This routine computes the future value of an annuity based on a given
   set of payments made at the end of each compounding period and a set
   interest rate.  It requires five input values: Interest Rate (in
   percent), Number of Accounting Periods/Year, Total Number of
   Accounting Periods, Amount of Payment Each Month (how much are we
   willing to add to the account at the end of every month), and an
   array reference in which to store the results.  The calculation
   assumes that the payments are made at the end of the accounting
   period and therefore no interest is earned for the first period.
   After that, the balance accumulates both compounded interest and the
   monthly payments.  As the program goes through the compuational loop,
   it fills the Clipper array.  The return value is used to indicate
```

7-10 Continued.

```
   whether or not the routine successfully recieved the appropriate
   variables.
   Written by: John Mueller
   Copyright 1991 John Mueller - Tab Books */

#include "EXTEND.H"

double nRate;
double nPeriodPY;
int nPeriods;
double nPayment;
double nRatePP;
double nTemp;
int nCount;
int nArray = 1;

CLIPPER AnnCalc(void)
{
if (PCOUNT == 5 && ISNUM(1) && ISNUM(2) && ISNUM(3) && ISNUM(4) && ISARRAY(5))
   {

   /* Retrieve the variables from Clipper. */

   nRate = _parnd(1);
   nPeriodPY = _parnd(2);
   nPeriods = _parni(3);
   nPayment = _parnd(4);

   /* Make sure nArray is initialized to 1. */

   nArray = 1;

   /* Compute the interest per period.  Change the percentage figure
      obtained in Clipper to a rate by dividing by 100. */

   nRatePP = nRate/nPeriodPY/100;

   /* Store the Payment to the temporary variable. */

   nTemp = nPayment;

   /* Compute the Balance plus the Payment plus Interest for each period
      and store in the array passed by reference from Clipper. */

   for (nCount = 0; nCount < nPeriods; nCount++)
      {
      _stornd(nTemp, 5, nArray);
      nArray++;
      nTemp = nTemp * (1 + nRatePP);
      nTemp = nTemp + nPayment;
      }
```

```
    /* Return true to show the routine recieved the proper parameters. */

    _retl(TRUE);

    }
else
    {

    /* Return false to indicate a program error. */

    _retl(FALSE);

    }
}
```

As you can see, this example looks both similar to, but also different than the interest calculations illustrated in the previous section. Notice especially that the procedure for the interest calculation follow the standard equation closely. The annuity procedure looks nothing at all like the standard equation of $S=R*(((1 + i)^n - 1) / i)$, where R is the periodic payment, i is the rate per period, n is the number of payments, and S is future value. In this case you could have used the standard equation if you wanted only the end result, the value of the annuity. To display the intermediate values, you have to use the convoluted approach to create the equation. The point of this exercise is to show that you can format the output of your external routines in any way you want.

As with the other examples presented here, this one contains the same six sections as the original example in chapter 6 (chapter 5 for assembly language). You begin by checking the five parameters for content and type. The second step is to proceed with the calculation. And finally, you output the result. The familiar error-handling routines are present as well.

Notice that all three examples require the same number and type of parameters. This makes them especially suitable for use with the preprocessor. Using the preprocessor, you could easily convert them to commands and further enhance error checking and other aspects of the function. For example, if you implemented these functions as commands, you could check for the proper type of input during compilation as well as runtime.

Determining when to use an external routine

The preceding paragraphs could lead some to believe that there is never an occasion when you should use Clipper's set of built-in primitives to compute a financial result. Nothing could be further from the truth. In many cases, it is actually more efficient to use the Clipper functions. For example, consider the instance of performing simple math on a set of numbers.

Tallying the total of a group of numbers certainly qualifies as a simple, albeit time-consuming task. The overhead involved in calling a C or assembler routine to perform the task of addition would detract from any speed benefit the program could derive. In fact, the program might actually run slower. In these instances it's better to use the built-in Clipper primitives than external routines.

When considering the advantages and disadvantages of performing financial calculations using external routines, you must take into account not only programmer effort, but the overhead incurred in calling the routine. Often, the overhead involved won't justify the use of an external routine.

Creating scientific math functions

Scientists are known for their ability to "eat" computer processing cycles when they create complex equations. Unlike financial calculations, some scientific equations are not only time-consuming, but critical as well. For example, consider an emergency-room database used to find the antidote for some type of poisoning. Unless the database operates quickly, the patient could die. Even the calculation of mundane data like the growth rate of germs could have an impact on society as a whole. Of course, not every application saves a life. Most applications perform very standard calculations and solve very ordinary problems. However, there is never a reason why your application should perform even these mundane tasks slowly.

The following sections introduce you to scientific equations and show you how to create them using external C routines. Programming these equations in assembler is possible, but time-consuming without the aid of a math coprocessor to help with the floating-point calculations. Appendix F contains some example programs that use the math coprocessor. Unfortunately, most machines don't have access to a math coprocessor. This section answers the question of how to create fast, reliable C scientific equation routines with a minimum of overhead. All the examples provided use the standard 80×86 processor found in every PC-compatible machine.

Computing event probability

Probability is used as the basis for a lot of different technologies. Most games and many theoretical applications are built on probability equations as well. For example, a business might need to know how likely a specific event is so they can invest their money wisely.

Due to the nature of some scientific fields, probability becomes an essential tool for visualizing an event or evaluating risks. The use of the probability equation, therefore, becomes a requirement rather than simply a tool. Figure 7-11 shows the Clipper source code used to call the C routine in FIG. 7-12. The purpose of the program is to compute the probability of a specific event based on the probability of a set of events.

```
// Event Probability Programming Example
// This program performs five tasks.  First, it sets up the display to
// recieve the calculated data.  Second, it polls the user for the
// number of times that each event occurs. Third, it passes the data to
// CalcProb() for analysis.  Notice that all variables are passed by
// reference so they can be reused to display the percentages.  Fourth,
// it displays the data it receives from CalcProb() on screen.  Fifth,
// it clears the display and exits to DOS.
// Written by: John Mueller
// Copyright 1991 John Mueller - Tab Books

// Declare some variables.

local nItemA := 0,;      // Number of times Item A occurred.
      nItemB := 0,;      // Number of times Item B occurred.
      nItemC := 0,;      // Number of times Item C occurred.
      nItemD := 0,;      // Number of times Item D occurred.
      nItemE := 0,;      // Number of times Item E occurred.
      nNothing := 0      // Probability that nothing happened.

// Display the background screen.

set scoreboard off
set color to "W+/B, RG+/R"
cls
@ 01, 00 to 24, 79 double
@ 02, 01 say padc(" Event Probabiliy Example ", 78, chr(177))
@ 03, 01 to 03, 78 double

// Get the input values from the user.

@ 05, 02 say "Number of times Item A occurred:" get nItemA picture "999"
@ 06, 02 say "Number of times Item B occurred:" get nItemB picture "999"
@ 07, 02 say "Number of times Item C occurred:" get nItemC picture "999"
@ 08, 02 say "Number of times Item D occurred:" get nItemD picture "999"
@ 09, 02 say "Number of times Item E occurred:" get nItemE picture "999"
read

// Calculate the weighted probability of an event occurring.

 if !(CalcProb(@nItemA, @nItemB, @nItemC, @nItemD, @nItemE, @nNothing))
   alert("The calculation failed")
   return
endif

// Display a heading for the data.

@ 11, 01 to 11, 78 double
@ 12, 01 say padc(" Probability of Event Recurring ", 78, chr(177))
@ 13, 01 to 13, 78 double

// Display the data.
```

7-11 Continued.

```
@ 15, 02 say "Item A:   " + str(nItemA, 7, 3) + "%"
@ 16, 02 say "Item B:   " + str(nItemB, 7, 3) + "%"
@ 17, 02 say "Item C:   " + str(nItemC, 7, 3) + "%"
@ 18, 02 say "Item D:   " + str(nItemD, 7, 3) + "%"
@ 19, 02 say "Item E:   " + str(nItemE, 7, 3) + "%"
@ 20, 02 say "Nothing: " + str(nNothing, 7, 3) + "%"

// Wait for the user to finish viewing the results.

@ 23, 02 say "Press any key when ready..."
inkey(0)

// Clear the display and exit to DOS.

set color to "W/N, N/W"
cls
return
```

7-12 Probability programming example, C source

```
/* Event Probability Programming Example
   This program computes the probability of any given event out of six
   events occurring.  The first five events are under the control of the
   user.  Just as in the outside world events are controlled by the
   environment, these events are controlled by our user environment.
   The sixth event is the probability of nothing happening.  We assume
   for the sake of argument that no two events may occur at the same
   time so we do not need to take any permutations into consideration.
   We also assume that the probability of any given event is equal,
   given equal input data.  The third consideration is that the actual
   probability is weighted according to the number of times the event
   actually occurs.  The program begins by calculating the average
   probability of an event occurrence and assigning that occurrence to
   Nothing.  It then finds out the total number of events and divides
   the remaining probability by that amount.  In other words, we find
   out the likelihood of any given event occurring.  Finally, we
   multiply the number of times each event occurred by the average
   probability of occurrence to obtain the actual probability for any
   given event.  The program passes these probabilities back to Clipper
   where they get displayed.
   Written by: John Mueller
   Copyright 1991 John Mueller - Tab Books */

#include "EXTEND.H"

double nItemA;
double nItemB;
double nItemC;
double nItemD;
double nItemE;
```

```
double nNothing;
double nPercent = 100;
double nTemp = 0;
double nEvents = 0;

 CLIPPER CalcProb(void)
{
if (PCOUNT == 6 && ISNUM(1) && ISNUM(2) && ISNUM(3) && ISNUM(4) && ISNUM(5))
   {

   /* Input all the values from Clipper to local variables. */

   nItemA = _parnd(1);
   nItemB = _parnd(2);
   nItemC = _parnd(3);
   nItemD = _parnd(4);
   nItemE = _parnd(5);

   /* Compute the average event probability. */

   nTemp = nPercent / 6;

   /* Store the average event probability in nNothing. */

   nNothing = nTemp;

   /* Calculate the total number of events and the probability of any
      one event occurring. */

   nTemp = nPercent - nTemp;
   nEvents = nItemA + nItemB + nItemC + nItemD + nItemE;
   nTemp = nTemp / nEvents;

   /* Calculate the weighted probability of each event. */

   nItemA = nItemA * nTemp;
   nItemB = nItemB * nTemp;
   nItemC = nItemC * nTemp;
   nItemD = nItemD * nTemp;
   nItemE = nItemE * nTemp;

   /* Store the probability values into the individual parameters. */

   _stornd(nItemA, 1);
   _stornd(nItemB, 2);
   _stornd(nItemC, 3);
   _stornd(nItemD, 4);
   _stornd(nItemE, 5);
   _stornd(nNothing, 6);

   /* Return true to show the routine recieved the proper parameters. */

   _retl(TRUE);
```

7-12 Continued.

```
    }
else
    {

    /* Return false to indicate a program error. */

    _retl(FALSE);

    }
}
```

As you can see, this routine provides an example of how to create a fully integrated function. It even provides a means of reusing all the Clipper variables, a valuable memory-saving technique. The routine essentially calculates a weighted average and uses that as the basis for the probability of an event occurring. You'll find that weighted averages and probability analyses abound in the business world, as well as both the scientific and medical community. Using this program as an example provides the fundamentals for more complex analysis techniques in the programs you create.

Determining when to use an external routine

The preceding information could lead some to believe that there's never an occasion when you should use Clipper's set of built-in primitives to compute a scientific equation. While this is certainly more true for scientific equations than the financial equations created in previous sections, Clipper can still calculate some scientific data more efficiently than calling a C or assembler routine. Again, a simple calculation, for example, determining an average value for a set of data, can be accomplished quite nicely with Clipper. The overhead involved in calling a C or assembler routine to perform this kind of task would detract from any speed benefit the program could derive. In fact, the program may actually run slower and take more programmer time to both create and maintain. In these instances it's better to use the built-in Clipper primitives than external routines.

Creating other types of useful functions

Financial and scientific calculations are just two of the areas where database management systems are in demand. It's important to measure the complexity of the equation, the investment in programmer time, and the headaches of maintaining code written in two languages, and compare these against the value of improving program execution speed. Often, speed is the only factor worth considering. Any time safety or other human factors come into play, the time invested is certainly worthwhile.

The time and date functions presented in this chapter also prove that you should not limit the external routines you create to the tried and true. You can interface Clipper to literally any device, or perform any task using external routines to enhance the programming environment. It's the creative use of external routines that makes the difference between truly exceptional program performance and the performance many users dread but expect from applications.

Summary

This chapter presents some of the functions you can create to extend the functionality of Clipper. In addition, it discusses some of the considerations you need to take into account before you can create an external routine. By using the programs and the guidelines effectively, you can create programs that are faster and more useful than you could create with Clipper alone. Often, the investment in programmer time is minimal because you can create the solution quicker in a language other than Clipper. Interface programs are the realm of assembly language, while complex equations and other types of data manipulation are the realm of C. Using the correct language to create an external routine not only makes sense, it's essential to efficient program development.

8
Using Clipper in a local-area network

Inevitably, every programmer faces the prospect of programming in a network environment. This is a natural outcome of several factors in the industry today. For example, many larger companies have found that they can satisfy at least some of their processing needs by using a local-area network (LAN) instead of a minicomputer or mainframe.

Spurring this trend are the high-powered PCs available on the market today. As these PCs become even more powerful, corporations will have even fewer reasons not to use a LAN in place of minicomputers. With this in mind, any programmer who creates database management systems for a living needs the tools to create efficient and reliable programs for networks. So it is no longer a question of if a programmer will run into a network programming situation, but when.

This chapter introduces you to some of the intricacies of programming on a network. More importantly, it discusses the theory behind networks and explains how the network environment differs from the single-user environment. There are three main topics discussed within the seven sections in this chapter.

First, you need to know what tools Clipper provides. Of course, the point here is to see what tools you have available so you don't waste time creating new ones that perform the same task. I'll show you some of the generic and esoteric uses for these commands and functions, which should provide you with ideas of how to create your routines in such a way as to make maximum use of existing Clipper commands and functions.

The second topic describes the Clipper-to-network interface. The specific focus of this section is Novell Netware. However, the same principles apply to other networks on the market as well. The term interface refers to how Clipper reacts to other users on a network as well as how it interprets the network itself. A network creates an unstable situation for your program. For example, if you store your data on a network drive, how do you know that drive will be available an hour from now? You need to know how the tools you create will react to a given set of circumstances.

Finally, the third topic discusses the theory of network programming. It provides you with insights into how the techniques you choose to employ will affect the outcome of many network situations. For example, do you check the status of the network before attempting to lock a file, or make it part of the error routine if the lock fails? In addition, I'll discuss the merits of using a particular program structure and database structure, and look at how program and database structure affect the efficiency and reliability of a network.

All three sections discuss networks with regard to the tools you have available. I assume that you're using an assembler or C compiler and that you're using Clipper 5.01, but I don't assume that you have access to one of the third-party libraries available for Netware (or any other network). Some of these libraries take so much guesswork out of handling a network that you might want to get one if you work with a network very often. If you do own one of the third-party libraries, however, this chapter will still assist you in learning about how to increase their efficiency.

Clipper commands

Chapters 1 and 2 of this book provide an overview of the commands and functions provided by Clipper. In most cases, these explanations are detailed enough to help a developer use the commands and functions effectively. However, network commands and functions are exceptionally valuable to a programmer and warrant a further discussion. This section provides a detailed description of the network commands and functions provided by Clipper (although you might not view all the functions listed as network exclusive). It includes programming examples to illustrate the real-world implementation of the descriptions provided.

CurDir([<cDriveSpec>])

Networks are more complex than most single-user situations. They use equally complex directory structures to allow everyone proper access to the data they require. Add to this the complications of drive and search mappings, and you can easily understand why a program could lose track of where it is on a network.

The CurDir( ) function allows your program to find out where it's located on a network. All you need do is call CurDir( ) without any parameters. Of course, this still isn't sufficient to tell your program what to do. Even if it does know its current location, it doesn't know where to find the files it needs. You can solve this problem by maintaining an array with the path of all the database files required by the program. Your program can now compare its current location with the location it needs to open a specific file. If they don't match, all you need do is switch to the new directory and drive.

This has another important connotation. When you experience an error with a networked program, you need all the information you can get about the status of the program before it failed. Using CurDir( ) each time you decide to change directories allows you to determine where the program failed. All you need to do is display the current path as part of the error statement. Often, you'll trace the failure to a lack of rights for the user or other noncritical error. In fact, a program might fail because the current directory simply lacked the space required to store any files you opened while there.

Some programmers place all the files used by a program in one directory. This would certainly solve the problem of having to keep track of where you are. Unfortunately, it also creates several other problems for both you and the user. First, putting all the files in one directory makes it harder to maintain proper security for sensitive files. Placing these kind of files in a separate directory reduces the risk of someone finding them by accident. Second, having too many files in one directory makes it difficult for the user to locate and thus maintain a particular file. As a result, some maintenance might get deferred, creating a potentially volatile environment for your data.

DBUnlock( )

The DBUnlock( ) function unlocks all the locks in the current work area. It's the function that the preprocessor translates the Unlock command to. The reason that you need to use this function in a network environment is obvious. If you lock a set of records or files and then fail to unlock them before you exit the program, other users on the network won't have access to them. The problem could get even worse if you log off a network without unlocking the files you were using.

Fortunately, Netware occasionally polls network users. If the user is still active, then Netware maintains the file and record locks set by the user. If the user is inactive, then Netware automatically releases the file and record locks held by the user. Other network operating systems might perform the same task. However, even if they do perform the automatic unlock, the time between logoff by the user and automatic closure by the network can easily exceed 15 minutes. This is an intolerable situation for most network applications because many users require constant and undisturbed access.

DBUnlockAll( )

The DBUnlockAll( ) function performs the same task as the DBUnlock( ) function on all work areas. Besides saving time and effort when you exit a program, the DBUnlockAll( ) function makes certain that the program releases all file and record locks. You would need to call DBUnlock( ) once for each work area, providing the potential for leaving one or more locks in place.

Directory(<cDirSpec> [, <cAttributes>])

Many programmers complain about the speed penalties of using a network. Especially for something as simple as a directory listing. However, there are a few programming tricks you can use to alleviate this situation, at least partially. If memory permits, you can perform some types of optimization with your Clipper program on a network. One technique for doing this is to cache the directory structure of the directories your program needs to work with in an array. In this fashion, you can search the directories at the speed of RAM rather than the speed of the network card. You can use the File( ) function to make absolutely certain that the file still exists before attempting to use it. This technique affords you a significant increase in speed while decreasing the possibility of program failure due to nonexistent files.

DiskSpace([<nDrive>])

One of the most common database errors on a network is running out of space to store data. It's easy to run out of space before anyone realizes the problem exists because more than one person is filling the hard drive. Using the DiskSpace( ) function before you retrieve a record to edit it can prevent this problem from occurring. This also applies to text files you create or other data you want to store.

You can also modify the Error System to recover from disk errors using this function. A program can check the error type and then recover from a disk full error by allowing the user to clear hard-disk space from another terminal. The program can then retry the failed operation. Often, this type of cooperative error recovery can make a network much easier to use and operate than the recovery techniques used by many programs on the market.

DOSError([<nNewErrorNumber>])

There are many times where the error reported for a network problem appears as a DOS error. In fact, even if Clipper provides a network error number, you can often detect more about the problem if you obtain the DOS error number as well. The DOSError( ) and NetError( ) functions are not mutually exclusive, but rather work in tandem to provide you with as much information as possible about the current error. A complete listing of the error numbers associated with both functions appears in chapter 2.

Obtaining as much information as possible before you act on a suspect error condition provides two benefits. First, you can more accurately prescribe a set of remedies for the user to perform. Many users currently object to the methods provided by programs for error handling. Some error messages are so poorly written as to obscure the true fault. The reason for this is obvious—the programmer normally needs to assume a wide range of possible error conditions. Improving the error-handling methods will improve the probability that the user will implement them.

Second, by increasing the amount of available information, your program is smarter at handling some problems automatically. This is important to you as a programmer to consider when creating your program. By allowing the program to handle some error conditions automatically, you can increase program reliability while maintaining tighter program control. For example, your code can tell you if the problem is fixed. A user-controlled situation requires that your program retrieve the correct information from the user and then verify that information through other means.

While the DOS error codes are less than complete, you can use them as a viable starting point for error routines included in your program. This will at least give you a starting point to other methods of determining the precise nature of a problem.

ErrorBlock([<bErrorHandler>])

Both DOSError( ) and NetError( ) return hardware and operating-system error information. Of course, this also includes software that creates an apparent hardware failure. Unlike these two functions, the ErrorBlock( ) works with software. It's specifically designed to work with Clipper, but it can detect other types of software errors as well. For example, failure of a mouse driver to install properly could impact the functionality of a mouse library. Left unchecked, this error could impact the Clipper program and finally the machine itself.

Error blocks help Clipper prevent this and other types of error conditions. By including external routines to enhance the native Clipper error handler, you can reduce the probability that external events will affect your Clipper program. An error block contains two components. The first element is an error object, used to pass data to the error handler. Chapter 4 contains a complete description of the Error System and how to create error objects. The second element is the error handler. In most cases, this is a function name followed by the parameters required to fully address the error. The error handler retrieves any information about the error from the error object. Therefore, one of the parameters you need to pass to your error handling routine is the error object. This means that you can't completely implement any error-handling strategy using external routines. The Extend System does not provide the means to access objects from external code. You must interface any external routines with a procedure used to interpret the error object.

When you call ErrorBlock( ), it returns the code block previously installed as the error handler. The default error handler simply retrieves the current error object and passes it to the Error System. In most cases, the error handler simply displays the procedure and line number of your program that failed and exits. This provides very little information to the user, reduces the chance that the program will recover from the error gracefully, and increases potential data damage by terminating the program abnormally. In addition, it provides little or no error handling for any external routines or libraries you include with your program.

You can redirect the error output to a user-defined function (UDF). This function could literally contain any code required to efficiently handle the error. For example, a printer error handler might attempt to reset the printer or use other means to correct a fault before alerting the user to the problem.

File(<cFileSpec>)

Sometimes it's easy to forget some of the simple error-handling techniques that Clipper provides. For example, instead of assuming that a file exists in the current directory, the program could check to make sure it exists first by using the File( ) function. This is an example of handling an error before it occurs. Using this technique allows you to preempt the problem before it actually exists. The remedy is to pop up a screen that asks the user to enter the location of the file. You can also handle the error by storing the correct directory and drive information in an array or database file. This technique is more automatic than asking the user, requires a lower level of user expertise, and reduces the risk of obtaining incorrect information. The only problem with this technique is ensuring that the directory information remains current.

FLock( )

The FLock( ) function allows you to lock the database file in the current work area before you perform some critical procedure. For example, you must lock the database before you use the Pack command. The simple rule of thumb to follow when selecting a file lock over a record lock is to determine the scope of the task and then lock accordingly. For example, an Append affects only one record in the database. That means you can use the RLock( ) function. A Delete might affect more than one record. If it does, then you need to use the FLock( ) function. Of course, you can modify your procedure to delete one record at a time. In this case, you could use the RLock( ) function.

GetEnv(<cEnvVariable>)

The GetEnv( ) function retrieves the value of a DOS environment variable. It's important to note the distinction between a DOS environment variable and any other environment variables. You create a DOS environment variable using the Set command provided with DOS and you can list any defined environment variables using the Set command without any parameters. DOS environment variables are created and maintained by DOS and they have nothing to do with either the network operating system or Clipper.

There are three ways you can use environment variables to improve network programs. First, you can use them to configure your program. In some cases you can write a generic program that reads one or more environment variables to configure itself for the user automatically.

Second, you can use environment variables to enhance error handling. For example, what do you do if one user locks a record and goes to lunch? Anyone wanting to use the information in that record cannot do so. If the record happens to contain information of importance to a lot of different workers, then your entire staff might have to stop work until the offending record is located. On the other hand, if you include the user name in a database used to store the current lock information, everyone would know in an instant who locked the record. The locked record could be located and unlocked in a matter of seconds.

The third purpose for environment variables is to identify the user. For example, what if a particular user doesn't have rights to a specific data file? You can either generate an error or check a database file containing the rights for that user. The first solution could result in an abnormal termination of your program. The second solution results in an error message telling the user they need to contact their supervisor to ask for rights to the data file.

NetErr([<lNetErrCondition>])

The default behavior for the NetErr( ) function is to return true or false based on the current network status. If you attempt to Use or Use...Exclusive a file that's currently in use by someone else on the network and Clipper stops the program because the file is locked, then NetErr( ) returns true. The other condition where NetErr( ) returns true is if you attempt to Append Blank to a locked database.

NetName( )

This function returns the name of the current workstation as a string. Unfortunately, it doesn't work with every network on the market. You'll normally need to bypass this function and use the DOS environment to identify the network user and workstation. You might even want to consider modifying this function to work with a wider variety of networks.

OS( )

Use the OS( ) function to retrieve the name of the workstation operating system as a character string. Some versions of DOS provide features that aren't supported by others. Your program can't anticipate which version of DOS will appear on every workstation on the LAN. As a result, you should always poll the workstation to determine what version of DOS it's using before you attempt to use some low-level functions within your add-on routines.

RecSize( )/LastRec( )/Header( )

There are many occasions where you will want to create a copy of a database and perform some specific task on the copy, rather than original. This is especially true of any task that could destroy data or in some way modify it. Of course, the disk you use needs to have enough space available for you to complete the task. By multiplying the record size returned by RecSize( ) by the number of records returned by LastRec( ) you can approximate the size of the database.

To determine the exact size of the database, all you need do is add the size of the header. You can retrieve this value from the Header( ) function. Once you determine the size of the database, compare it against the value returned by DiskSpace( ) to determine if the copy of the database will fit on the current disk. Unlike a single-user environment, you can't depend on the user to know how much space is available on the hard disk. That is why this particular set of functions is so important in a networking situation. Preventing an error before it occurs is always better than having the error occur and then trying to fix it.

RLock( )

The RLock( ) function allows you to lock the current record without locking the entire database. This is always preferable in a network situation. The probability of any one user requiring a specific record is much smaller than someone requiring access to the entire database. In fact, locking the entire database could put your organization on hold until the lock holder releases it. See FLock( ), previously, for the simple rule of thumb to follow when selecting a record lock or a file lock.

Clipper features

Many of the network-specific features provided by Clipper are not fully understood by the developer community. For example, most developers equate network features with the Lock( ), FLock( ), and RLock( ) functions. Unfortunately, this is where many programmers stop. There are many other features provided by Clipper that can greatly enhance the reliability of your program without drastically affecting its speed. For example, you can use the Error System to enhance the way your program handles network errors, and therefore improve the overall integrity of the system.

The following section examines those Clipper features that don't fall into the range of standard network commands or functions. I'll show you how to use code blocks and the Error System to improve error handling. This includes most nonfatal, and some near-fatal errors. You'll also see how to allow the program to fail more gracefully after a fatal network error. Finally, you'll look at some new uses for old commands, for example, how you can use the file functions to create a transaction log for your Clipper program.

Improving network error handling

One of the banes of using a network is the perceived problems of maintaining database integrity. In many cases, the problems with networked programs stem not from the inability of the database manager to perform useful work or the unreliable nature of the network, but from the lack of error handling provided with the application. The error-handling system supplied with Clipper is a good starting point, but it won't handle every situation in a single-user program, much less a networked program. As a result, you need to enhance the operation of the error handler you use with a networked program.

Chapter 4 presented some error-system enhancements in the form of Clipper's Error System. However, there are other capabilities at your disposal to make certain that errors are handled correctly. One example is the printer. What happens to your networked program when a user forgets to set the printer on-line, or if the printer experiences some other type of failure that locks it up?

In a single-workstation application, it's very likely that the printer resides in the same room as the user. If the printer fails to output any of the requested data within a specific amount of time, the user will look at the printer to find out what error occurred. On a network, the user might not be in the same room as the printer. In fact, it's very unlikely that he is. Your program needs to detect any printer errors, try an appropriate set of fixes, and then alert the user to the problem.

Figure 8-1 contains the Clipper source code required to call a typical routine for checking the status of the printer within a network. Figure 8-2 contains the assembly source for the actual printer status routine, while FIG. 8-3 contains the C version of the same code.

Of course, the problem with checking printer status is that you never know what kind of printer the local workstation is connected to. Using the CAPTURE command on Netware, you could end up with one printer in the morning and a totally different printer in the afternoon. For this reason, the provided routine uses a fairly generic test to see if the printer is available for use. Of course, what this really means is that the print server is available.

8-1 Printer-status example, Clipper source

```
// Printer Initialization and Error Trapping Example
// This program polls the user for a printer port to check.  It then
// calls a routine which resets the printer on that port (if any), and
// returns a status.  The program checks the status against known status
// information and displays a message describing the current printer
// status.  If that status is undefined, then it displays a message to
// that effect.
// Written by: John Mueller
// Copyright 1991 John Mueller - Tab Books

// Define some printer status types.

#define TimeOut   1
#define IOError   8
#define Selectd  16
#define OOPaper  32
#define PrntAck  64
#define NotBusy 128
#define ProgErr 512

// Declare some variables.

local nPrtNum := 0,;
      nStat := 0,;
      aMSelect := {"LPT1:", "LPT2:", "LPT3:"}

// Display the background screen.

set scoreboard off
set color to "W+/B, RG+/R"
cls
@ 01, 00 to 24, 79 double
@ 02, 01 say padc(" Printer Check Routine ", 78, chr(177))
@ 03, 01 to 03, 78 double

// Ask the user to select a port.

@ 04, 02 to 08, 10 double
@ 22, 03 say "Select a printer port."
nPrtNum := achoice(05, 03, 07, 09, aMSelect)

// Reset the printer, display the printer status, and wait for a
// response from the user.

@ 04, 02 clear to 23, 77
@ 04, 02 say "Resetting Printer"
nStat := PrnReset(nPrtNum)
 do case
   case nStat == TimeOut; @ 05, 02 say "Printer Timed Out"
   case nStat == IOError; @ 05, 02 say "Printer I/O Error"
   case nStat == Selectd; @ 05, 02 say "Printer Selected"
   case nStat == OOPaper; @ 05, 02 say "Printer Out of Paper"
```

```
   case nStat == PrntAck; @ 05, 02 say "Printer Acknowledged Reset"
   case nStat == NotBusy; @ 05, 02 say "Printer Not Busy"
   case nStat == ProgErr; alert("Programming Error")
   otherwise; @ 05, 02 say "Printer in Undefined State"
endcase
@ 23, 02 say "Press any key when ready..."
inkey(0)

// Clear the display and exit to DOS.

set color to "W/N, N/W"
cls
return
```

8-2 Printer-status example, assembly source

```
;************************************************************************
;* Printer Initialization and Error Trapping Example                   *
;* This program retrieves a printer port number, resets the printer    *
;* connnect to that printer port, checks its status, and returns the   *
;* status information to the calling procedure.  The reset string can  *
;* be any character combination and length.  To change the string,     *
;* modify cResetCode.  To modify the sting length, change nChar.  The  *
;* procedure uses interrupt 17h to send data to the printer port.  This*
;* ROM interrupt is trapped by most network software, therefore it     *
;* appears to the procedure as if the printer is connected to a local  *
;* port.  Since all 17h interrupts return status information, the      *
;* process of sending an initialization string and initializing the    *
;* port returns the proper printer status automatically.               *
;* Written by: John Mueller                                            *
;* Copyright 1991 John Mueller - Tab Books                             *
;************************************************************************

;************************************************************************
;* Make any required declarations.                                     *
;************************************************************************

.MODEL LARGE

INCLUDE EXTASM.INC
INCLUDE MACROS.INC

PUBLIC PrnReset

;************************************************************************
;* Declare any required variables.                                     *
;************************************************************************

.DATA

cResetCode DB      27,40   ;Esc, @ Used to Reset Printer
nChar      DW      1       ;Number of characters in reset code.
```

8-2 Continued.

```
nPrtNum     DW      0       ;Printer Selection Number, LPT1, LPT2, LPT3.
nError      DW      512     ;Error number returned for invalid parameters.

;*******************************************************************
;* Start of the code segment and the main procedure.               *
;*******************************************************************

.CODE

PrnReset    PROC    FAR

            PUSH    SI              ;Save SI.

            PCount                  ;Check the number of parameters.
            CMP     AX,0            ;If there aren't any, exit.
            JE      NoParms

            IsNum   1               ; Check the first parameter to see if
            JNE     NoParms         ; it's a character.  If not exit.

            MOV     AX,@DATA        ;Point to our data segment.
            MOV     DS,AX
            MOV     ES,AX

            GetInt  1               ;Retrieve the printer number.
            DEC     AX              ;Convert to 0 start for printer number.
            MOV     nPrtNum,AX      ;Store it for future use.

            LEA     DI,cResetCode   ;Load the reset string offset.
            MOV     CX,nChar        ;Load the number of characters to send.
            MOV     DX,nPrtNum      ;Set the printer number.
PR1:        XOR     AX,AX           ;Send a character.
            MOV     AL,[DI]
            INT     17h
            INC     DI              ;Point to the next character.
            LOOP    PR1             ;Loop until all characters sent.

            MOV     AX,0100h        ;Initialize the printer.
            MOV     DX,nPrtNum      ;Set printer number.
            INT     17h

            MOV     AL,AH           ;Move the status information to AL.
            XOR     AH,AH           ;Zero the AH register.
            PUSH    AX              ;Return the status information.
            CALL    __retni
            ADD     SP,2
            JMP     Exit            ;Exit to the calling procedure.

NoParms:    RetInt  nError          ;On error, return the error number.

Exit:       POP     SI              ;Restore SI.
```

```
          RET

PrnReset  ENDP

END
```

8-3 Printer-status example, C source

```
/* Printer Initialization and Error Trapping Example
   This program retrieves a printer port number, resets the printer
   connnect to that printer port, checks its status, and returns the
   status information to the calling procedure.  The reset string can
   be any character combination and length.  To change the string,
   modify cResetCode.  To modify the sting length, change nChar.  The
   procedure uses interrupt 17h to send data to the printer port.  This
   ROM interrupt is trapped by most network software, therefore it
   appears to the procedure as if the printer is connected to a local
   port.  Since all 17h interrupts return status information, the
   process of sending an initialization string and initializing the
   port returns the proper printer status automatically.
   Written by: John Mueller
   Copyright 1991 John Mueller - Tab Books */

#include "EXTEND.H"
#include "DOS.H"

union  REGS   regs;

/* Declare some global variables. */

int cResetCode[2] = {27, 40};
int nChar = 1;
int nPrtNum = 0;
int nError = 512;
int nCount = 0;

CLIPPER PrnReset(void)
{
if (PCOUNT == 1 && ISNUM(1))
   {

   /* Retrieve the printer number from Clipper. */

   nPrtNum = _parni(1);

   /* Adjust it for use with interrupt 17h. */

   nPrtNum--;

   /* Send the reset string to the printer. */

    regs.h.ah = 0;
```

8-3 Continued.

```
    regs.x.dx = nPrtNum;
    for(nCount = 0; nCount <= nChar; nCount++)
       {
       regs.h.al = cResetCode[nCount];
       int86(0x17, &regs, &regs);
       }

    /* Initialize the printer port. */

    regs.h.ah = 1;
    regs.x.dx = nPrtNum;
    int86(0x17, &regs, &regs);

    /* Convert the 8-bit return to a 16-bit integer. */

    regs.h.al = regs.h.ah;
    regs.h.ah = 0;

    /* Return the printer status to the calling procedure. */

    _retni(regs.x.ax);

    }
 else
    {

    /* Return the error code to indicate a program error. */

    _retni(nError);

    }
}
```

Because the print output is spooled on a network, you never find out about print errors until you physically check for the output. Because of this, Clipper provides a printer reset function, shown in FIG. 8-1, as well. You can use the reset to at least place the printer in a known condition prior to sending output to it. Novell markets a C API for Netware. If you intend to create a wide variety of network-specific programs, you might want to purchase the C API or one of the add-on libraries available on the market instead of writing your own routines.

The printer-status routine contains four sections. The first section checks the input variable for flaws. If there's more than one input variable or if that variable isn't a number, then the routine fails by sending the calling procedure an error code. The second section uses interrupt 17h to send two or more control characters to the printer. These characters usually consist of an escape sequence, which resets the printer. However, the characters don't take effect until another event takes place. You must clear the parallel port before the printer can be reset. The third section of the program initializes the printer port, clears the control characters, and resets the printer. At the same time, the interrupt polls the printer for its status. The interrupt returns this status byte in AH. The fourth part of the routine converts the 8-bit return value in AH to a 16-bit integer. It then returns the integer to the calling procedure as a printer status code.

The Clipper code used to call the printer status routine is quite simple. It displays the background screen first and then a menu for selecting a printer port. Once the user selects a printer port, the program sends the port number to the printer-status routine. When the routine returns a value, the Clipper program compares this value against some known return values to see if it can determine the printer's status.

One of the defined codes tells Clipper that the printer status routine didn't receive the proper input. The program displays an error message alerting the programmer to this situation. If the printer status routine doesn't return a known status or an error code, then the printer status is unknown. The program returns a message to this effect.

Using the file functions to improve network access

Many developers experience problems associated with bringing the network up and recovering from a power failure or other natural disaster. The file server works fine; you can use it almost immediately. However, the data files that users had open at the time of the crash might contain corrupted information. Of course, you can usually find the corrupted data by scanning the file, so you can fix it before anyone adds new data. Perhaps a worse scenario is when the record looks fine, but it contains only half of the updated information. In this case, the server crash occurred halfway through the update cycle.

The only way to find this type of error is to compare your hardcopy data with each record, or to build a transaction log. A transaction log records every change to the database before the program makes it. This way you can trace exactly what actions were pending when the file server crash occurred. Figure 8-4 shows an error-log program written with Clipper. Every major database task creates an entry in the transaction log. This program uses the example functions presented in FIG. 8-5. Notice that the example functions use the file functions provided with Clipper to maintain a transaction log. Using a transaction log can greatly increase the probability that you can recover from a fatal or near-fatal file-server crash with all your data intact.

```
// Transaction Log Example
// This program demonstrates how you would implement the transaction log
// functions found in TRANS.PRG.  It begins by recording the opening of
// the database file and index, then performing the actual task.  The
// program displays the background screen and data from the first
// record.  The loop allows the user to press the up or down arrows to
// change records, or press escape to exit the program.  Each time the
// user presses a key, the program displays the screen and records the
// record displayed.  The program closes the database and records the
// transaction before it exits to DOS.  You compile this program as you
// would any other Clipper program. You must link it with the TRANS.PRG.
// Written by: John Mueller
// Copyright 1991 John Mueller - Tab Books

// Include an required header files.

#include "INKEY.CH"

// Open the transaction log.

transopen("TEST.DOC")

// Record the opening of the database, open it, then record a successful
// open in the transaction log.

transrecord("Opening database file SAMPLE1 with index SAMPLE1.")
use SAMPLE1 index SAMPLE1
transrecord("File opened successfully.")

// Display the background screen and data.

DispScreen()
DispData()

while !(inkey(0) == K_ESC)

// Process the up and down arrow keys.  All other keys are ignored.

   do case
      case lastkey() == K_UP
         if !(bof())
            skip -1
         endif
      case lastkey() == K_DOWN
         if !(eof())
            skip
         endif
   endcase
```

```
// Display the data.

DispData()

enddo

// Close the database file.  Record that it was successfully closed,
// then close the transaction file.

cls
close all
transrecord("All files closed.")
transclose("TEST.DOC")

return

// Start of local procedures and functions.

// This procedure displays the database data.

procedure DispData

// Record that we displayed a record on screen without editing it.

transrecord("Displayed record " + ltrim(str(recno())) + ", no edit.")

// Display the data.

@ 04, 03 say "Name:        " + FIRST + " " + MIDDLE + " " + LAST
@ 06, 03 say "Address:     " + COMPANY
@ 07, 14 say ADDRESS1
@ 08, 14 say ADDRESS2
@ 09, 14 say CITY + ", " + STATE + "      " + ZIP
@ 11, 03 say "Telephone: " + TELEPHONE1
@ 12, 14 say TELEPHONE2

return

// This procedure displays the background screen.

procedure DispScreen

set scoreboard off
set color to "W+/B, RG+/R"
cls
@ 01, 00 to 24, 79 double
@ 02, 01 say padc(" Transaction Log Demonstration ", 78, chr(177))
@ 03, 01 to 03, 78 double

return
```

```
// Transaction Log Example
// This program contains three functions using the Clipper file
// functions.  Each function performs a different task related to
// creating and maintaining a transaction log.  The first function,
// TransOpen(), opens a transaction log.  If required, the function will
// create the transaction log first.  The second function,
// TransRecord(), places data in the transaction log.  Each line
// contains one entry describing what task the database was performing.
// The third function, TransClose(), closes the transaction file after
// use.  All three files contain error handling routines which detect
// most errors, programmer or otherwise.  You must compile this program
// with the Clipper /N switch.  You can link it with any program,
// although it is currently designed to work with UTRANS.PRG as an
// example.  You always place this file second in line when linking.
// Written by: John Mueller
// Copyright 1991 John Mueller - Tab Books

#define OpenErr  -1
#define LineFeed chr(10)
#define CarRetrn chr(13)
#define Blank    " "

static nHandle,;
       cOldFile := Blank,;
       lRetValue

// This function opens a transaction file.  It checks first to make
// certain that we do not have a transaction file already open.  If not,
// it tries to open the transaction file requested in cFile.

function TransOpen (cFile)

// See if we already have a transaction file open.

if (cOldFile == Blank)

   // If not, then try to open one if it exists.

   nHandle := fopen(cFile, 3)

   // If we experience an error, try creating the file.

   if nHandle == OpenErr
      nHandle := fcreate(cFile)
   endif

// Store the new filename to cOldFile for future reference.

cOldFile := cFile

// If we try to open a new file after one is already open, display an
// error message.
```

```
else

   alert("Tried to open a new transaction file;without closing;"+cOldFile)

endif

return


// This function writes the transactions to the file before we actually
// perform them.  That way we know what action was pending prior to a
// file server crash.

function TransRecord (cText)

   fwrite(nHandle, cText)
   fwrite(nHandle, LineFeed)
   fwrite(nHandle, CarRetrn)
return


// This function closes a previously opened transaction file.  It
// provides a number of safety checks, as outline below to make certain
// we do not close the wrong file.

function TransClose (cFile)

// Set the return value to true.

lRetValue := .T.

// Check to see if we're closing the correct file.

if (upper(cFile) == upper(cOldFile))

// If this is the correct file, try to close it.  If it doesn't
// close, then there is an error.  Alert the user to the problem and
// exit.  Otherwise, set the filename status to blank.

   if fclose(nHandle)
      cOldFile := Blank
   else
      alert("Error closing file;"+cFile)
      lRetValue := .F.
   endif

// If this is not the correct file, display an error message and exit.

else
   alert("You are trying to close a non-existant;transaction file;"+cFile)
   lRetValue := .F.
endif

return lRetValue
```

As you can see in FIG. 8-4, maintaining a transaction log adds only a few lines of code to your program. You could use something as simple as what's shown in FIG. 8-4, or a more complex tracking system capable of monitoring system status information and other network factors. Either choice is better than not maintaining a transaction log at all. Typing the transaction log created by the program to screen will show you why. Even with the simple provided program, you know exactly what task the database was working on and what record it was accessing during every phase of the demonstration. Of course, if you create a high-activity program, you might want to create a less verbose transaction record.

Figure 8-5 demonstrates how easy it is to create transaction-log functions. None of the functions use anything more complex than simple If...then constructs to perform their tasks. Yet, as the transaction log shows, the functions are very effective in providing you with the information you need to know after a file-server crash.

Limiting database access

Networks are fantastic work-group solutions. An entire department or even company can share information on an unprecedented level. No longer do you have to hold long and arduous meetings to share even the simplest pieces of information. Everyone can use a centralized database and retrieve the information they need with very little effort.

This sounds like a dream come true. Everyone now has access to any piece of information they require. However, this environment is not without problems. Consider the problem of maintaining company secrets. It might not be wise to let your employees know about everything going on in the company. Information of this type was closely guarded in the past with locked doors and filing cabinets. But how do you protect this information on a network that's open to everyone?

There are several solutions that work in most cases. First, you can place your files in a protected directory. Only the people who have access to that directory can read its contents. NetWare further protects the files within a library by assigning specific rights to each user within the directory. For example, one user can read the file, while another can both read and write the file.

If the information in the directory is of a very sensitive nature, you can even encrypt the file to protect it from prying eyes. Some encryption programs on the market today are nearly impossible to break. The combination of directory and file rights and a good encryption program could make your data even more secure than the filing cabinets of time past.

Unfortunately, this doesn't cover the entire range of possibilities in the average company. For example, what if you have a contact list shared by an entire department, and you want to limit access to the contents of that list to just the items people need? One employee might require total access to the database, while another might require access to only the names and addresses. The file could contain sensitive records as well. How could you keep a new client a secret from the competition?

While some stock solutions might work in some situations, they won't work in every one. You could keep new clients in a separate database that only a select group of people could access. Unfortunately, this is not only inconvenient and error-prone, but the line between those allowed access and those that don't require it is seldom clearly defined enough to implement such a solution. The situation normally contains ambiguous and less clearly defined boundaries. For example, employee A is allowed access to records 1, 3, and 5, while employee B is allowed access to records 1, 2, and 4, and employee C is allowed access to 3, 4, and 5.

Another situation is where one employee has access to a field that another employee doesn't. For example, in the contact management system mentioned earlier, one employee could have access to just names and addresses, another to names, addresses, and billing status, and a third to names, addresses, and the comments section. You could build three database files, or you could use a combination of NetWare file locks and Clipper program code to limit access. However, if the boundaries between employees are not clearly defined, you still run into problems with this stock solution.

Figure 8-6 presents the Clipper code required to implement another solution. The solution here is a combination of file commands and database fields to construct a locking mechanism. This locking mechanism is shown in the Clipper code in FIG. 8-7. As you can see, I've used the low-level file functions provided by Clipper. By constructing an access file for specially marked records, and ensuring that the access file is in a fairly unreadable format, you can allow flexible access to records based on need.

8-6 Security program example, Clipper source

```
// Program 7 - Limiting Database Access
// This program shows you how to use the functions contained in
// ACCESS.PRG.  The program begins by opening the database file and
// displaying the background screen.  It then displays the data.  The
// COMMENTS field in this database contains sensitive information, so we
// use the security program to check whether the user is supposed to
// have access to it or not.  If the CheckUser() function returns true,
// then the user is supposed to have access and we display the COMMENTS
// field.  Another function, AddUser() is called when the user presses
// Ctrl-F3.  Normally, access to this function would be limited to the
// supervisor.  We could limit access by placing another password in the
// security file and asking for it each time someone wants to add
// another user.  The program exits by closing the database file and
// returning to DOS.
// Written by: John Mueller
// Copyright 1991 John Mueller - Tab Books

// Include an required header files.
```

8-6 Continued.

```
#include "INKEY.CH"

// Create some local variables.

static cUser

// Display the background screen.

set scoreboard off
set color to "W+/B, RG+/R"
cls
@ 01, 00 to 24, 79 double
@ 02, 01 say padc(" Limited Database Access Example ", 78, chr(177))
@ 03, 01 to 03, 78 double

// Check to see if the user name is defined.  If not, exit because the
// security system will not work properly.

cUser := getenv("USERNAME")
if cUser == ""
   alert("Network Improperly Configured")
   set color to "W/N, N/W"
   cls
   return
endif

// If the user name is defined, open the database and index.  Check to
// see if the file exists.  If the user is not allowed access, then the
// filename will not appear to the File() function.  (This assumes that
// you have already verified that the directory is correct.)

if file("SAMPLE7.DBF")
   use SAMPLE7 index SAMPLE7
else
   alert("Access to Database Denied")
   set color to "W/N, N/W"
   cls
   return
endif

// Display the data.

DispData(cUser)

while !(inkey(0) == K_ESC)

// Process the up and down arrow keys.  All other keys are ignored.

   do case

      // Scroll up one record.
```

```
      case lastkey() == K_UP
         if !(bof())
            skip -1
         endif

      // Scroll down one record.

      case lastkey() == K_DOWN
         if !(eof())
            skip
         endif
         if eof()
            skip -1
         endif

      // Add new users to security file by pressing Ctrl-F3.

      case lastkey() == K_CTRL_F3
          AddUser()
   endcase

   // Display the data.

   DispData(cUser)

enddo

// Clear the display an exit to DOS.

set color to "W/N, N/W"
cls
return

// Local Procedures Begin.

// This procedure displays the data contained in the database.  If the
// person requesting the data does not have the proper access for a
// specific section of data, then the procedure does not display those
// fields.

static procedure DispData (cUser)

// Clear the display area.

@ 04, 02 clear to 23, 78

// Display the data.

@ 04, 03 say "Record: " + ltrim(str(recno()))
@ 05, 03 say "Name:      " + FIRST + " " + MIDDLE + " " + LAST
@ 07, 03 say "Address:   " + COMPANY
@ 08, 14 say ADDRESS1
@ 09, 14 say ADDRESS2
@ 10, 14 say CITY + ", " + STATE + "     " + ZIP
```

8-6 Continued.

```
@ 12, 03 say "Telephone: " + TELEPHONE1
@ 13, 14 say TELEPHONE2

// Check to see if this record requires a record access check.  If the
// RECORD_ACC field is true, then this is a sensitive field.  If the
// user is not supposed to have access to the comments field, then don't
// display them.

if (FIELD_ACC) .or. (CheckUser(cUser))
   @ 15, 03 say "Comments (Press ESC to Exit): "
   @ 16, 03 to 23, 76 double
    keyboard chr(27)
   memoedit(COMMENTS, 17, 04, 22, 75, .f.)
endif

// Return to the calling procedure.

return
```

8-7 Security program example, function source

```
// Program 7 - Limiting Database Access
// This program provides a sample of the functions required to implement
// security using the Clipper file functions.  You could perform the
// same task using either C or assembler, but in this case there is no
// speed penalty for using Clipper code.  There are four functions
// provided.  The first function, CheckUser() determines if the user
// identified by the network environment variable USERNAME is supposed
// to have access to the sensitive data contained on the current record.
// This is accomplished by comparing the user name to the names stored
// in encoded format in the security file.  If the user name matches one
// of the security file names, then function decodes the password,
// requests this information from the user, and compares.  If the
// password is correct, access is granted.  The second function,
// AddUser(), adds a new user to the security file.  All it asks the
// user is for their name, the password they wish to use, and whether
// they are supposed to have access to specific types of entries.  Of
// course, only the supervisor would normally have access to this
// function.  The third function, Encode(), takes the strings input by
// the user and encodes them into an unreadable format.  The fourth
// function, Decode(), decodes the strings encoded by the Encode()
// function.  Use the /N switch when compiling the program with Clipper.
// Written by: John Mueller
// Copyright 1991 John Mueller - Tab Books

// Include any required header files.

#include "FILEIO.CH"

// This function checks to see if the user is supposed to have access to
```

```
// the field in question.  If access is ok, then the function returns
// true.  Otherwise, it returns false.  More importantly, this function
// makes other security checks as well.  For example, it checks to make
// sure no one erased the security file.

function CheckUser (cUserName)

#define nBuffSize 42

// Declare some local variables.

local lAccess := .F.,;          // Is access allowed?
      cFileName,;               // Security file name.
      nHandle,;                 // File handle provided by file function.
      cBuffer := space(52),;    // A storage buffer for the input data.
      cUserFile := space(20),;  // User Name from File.
      cPassword := space(20),;  // User Password.
      cPassNew := space(20),;   // New User Password.
      lRecord := .T.,;          // Special Record Access?
      lField := .T.,;           // Special Field Access?
      cScreen,;                 // Saved Screen Buffer.
      cOldColor,;               // Old Screen Color
      nReadBytes                // Number of bytes read from file.

// Check for the existance of the security file.  If it does exist, then
// the file was accidently erased, purposely destroyed, or wasn't
// created in the first place.

cFileName := alias() + ".ACC"
if !(file(cFileName))
   alert("Database Security Has Been Compromised")
   lAccess := .F.
   return lAccess
endif

// Open the security file and read the first 42 bytes from the file.

nHandle := fopen(cFileName, FO_READ)
fseek(nHandle, 0, FS_SET)
nReadBytes := fread(nHandle, @cBuffer, nBuffSize)

// While there are still bytes to read in the file, look for the
// person's name to see if they are supposed to have access to the
// database field.

while !(nReadBytes == 0)

   // Store the buffer contents to various variables.

   cUserFile := substr(cBuffer, 1, 20)
   cPassword := substr(cBuffer, 21, 20)
   lRecord := substr(cBuffer, 41, 1)
   lField := substr(cBuffer, 42, 1)
```

8-7 Continued.

```
// Decode the user name.

cUserFile := decode(cUserFile)

// Check the user name against the name read from the file.  If they
// match, perform further processing.

if (rtrim(cUserFile) == rtrim(cUserName)) .and. (asc(lField) == 0)

   // Decode the password, then ask the user to enter their password.

   cPassword := decode(cPassword)
   cScreen := savescreen(00, 00, maxrow(), maxcol())
   cOldColor := setcolor("RG+/R, W+/B")
   @ 12, 20 clear to 14, 61
   @ 12, 20 to 14, 61 double
   @ 13, 21 say "Enter a password:  " get cPassNew picture "@!"
   read
   setcolor(cOldColor)
   restscreen(00, 00, maxrow(), maxcol(), cScreen)

   // If the passwords match, give the user access to the sensitive
   // information.

   if (cPassNew == cPassword)
      lAccess := .T.
   endif
exit
   endif

   // Read another name from the file if required.

   nReadBytes := fread(nHandle, @cBuffer, nBuffSize)
enddo

// Close the security file and return to the calling procedure.

fclose(nHandle)
return lAccess


// This function adds a new user to the security file.  The file uses a
// special encoding technique for the security file.  While this
// technique won't keep out an expert, it will prevent the average
// person from opening and modifying the file.  To create an even higher
// security situation, you could use special encryption techniques or
// other measures.  This function returns NIL to the calling procedure
// or function.

function AddUser

// Declare some local variables.
```

```
local lAccess,;                      // Is access allowed?
      cFileName,;                    // Security file name.
      nHandle,;                      // File handle provided by file function.
      cBuffer,;                      // A storage buffer for the input data.
      nReadBytes,;                   // Number of bytes read from file.
      cUser := space(20),;           // User Name.
      cScreen,;                      // Saved Screen Buffer.
      cPassword := space(20),;       // User Password.
      lRecord := .T.,;               // Special Record Access?
      lField := .T.,;                // Special Field Access?
      cOldColor                      // Old Screen Color

// Either open or create a filename based on the alias of the currently
// opened database file in the current work area.

cFileName := alias() + ".ACC"
if !(file(cFileName))

   // Create the file if it doesn't exist.

   nHandle := fcreate(cFileName)

else

   // Open the security file and locate the end-of-file.

   nHandle := fopen(cFileName, FO_READWRITE)
   fseek(nHandle, 0, FS_END)

endif

// Save the current display, display a dialog box asking for any
// required information, then restore the screen.

cScreen := savescreen(00, 00, maxrow(), maxcol())
cOldColor := setcolor("RG+/R, W+/B")
@ 04, 09 clear to 09, 63
@ 04, 09 to 09, 63 double
@ 05, 10 say "Enter the user's name: " get cUser picture "@!"
@ 06, 10 say "Enter a password:      " get cPassword picture "@!"
@ 07, 10 say "Allow record access?   " get lRecord
@ 08, 10 say "Allow field access?    " get lField
read
setcolor(cOldColor)
restscreen(00, 00, maxrow(), maxcol(), cScreen)

// Adjust the user name and password to a standard size and encode it.

cUser := padr(cUser, 20)
cPassword := padr(cPassword, 20)
cUser := Encode(cUser)
cPassword := Encode(cPassword)
```

8-7 Continued.

```
// Copy the new user, password, and rights to the security file.

fwrite(nHandle, cUser)
fwrite(nHandle, cPassword)
fwrite(nHandle, chr(iif(lRecord, 0, 1)))
fwrite(nHandle, chr(iif(lField, 0, 1)))

// Reset any defaults and return to the calling procedure.

fclose(nHandle)
return NIL


// This function encodes the user name and password so they are more
// difficult to read by just typing the security file.  It works by
// converting each character in the string to its ASCII number
// equivalent, subtracting 32, then converting the result back to a
// character.

function Encode(cString)

// Define some local variables.

 static nCount := 0,;              // Loop counting variable.
      cNewString                   // Encoded string.

cNewString := chr(asc(substr(cString, 1, 1)) - 32)
for nCount := 2 to 20
   cNewString := cNewString + chr(asc(substr(cString, nCount, 1)) - 32)
next

return cNewString


// This function performs the opposite task of Encode().  It decodes the
// encoded strings stored in the security file to something that Clipper
// can compare quickly.

function Decode(cString)

// Define some local variables.

static nCount := 0,;              // Loop counting variable.
      cNewString                  // Encoded string.

cNewString := chr(asc(substr(cString, 1, 1)) + 32)
for nCount := 2 to 20
   cNewString := cNewString + chr(asc(substr(cString, nCount, 1)) + 32)
next

return cNewString
```

As you can see, even though this program doesn't encode the data, it wouldn't be very hard to do. The program file shown in FIG. 8-6 calls the security program when either of two events occur. If the user presses Ctrl–F3, then the program assumes that the user wants to add a new entry to the security file. Normally, only the supervisor could use this entry. You could use a password within the security file to determine who could gain access. The second event occurs when the program sees that FIELD_ACC is true. This means that the information contained in the COMMENTS field is sensitive and therefore the user must enter a password to see it. Notice that the program automatically displays nonsensitive data. This is an extremely valuable feature to add, because you can control security at both the field and the record level.

The security functions are listed in FIG. 8-7. Notice that there are four functions, but only two are used externally. The first function, CheckUser( ), performs a security check on the user whose name appears in the environment variable USERNAME. Because this variable is automatically created as part of most NetWare systems, you can use it to detect which user wants access to sensitive data. You can also create it by adding a simple SET command, SET USERNAME = <USER NAME>, in your AUTOEXEC.BAT file. Once the function establishes that the user's name appears in the security file, it checks to see what rights the user has. If the user has the correct rights, then the function decodes the password for that user within the security file. Then if the user enters the correct password, access to the sensitive data is granted.

The AddUser( ) function adds a new user to the security file. Essentially, all it does is get the user data from the supervisor, encode it, and append it to the end of the file. Note that you have to append the data to the end of the file. Using C or assembler, you could construct a function to add the data to the beginning or even the middle of the file. However, as long as you remember to add data to the end of the file, the Clipper functions are sufficient.

The last two functions in ACCESS.PRG encode and decode the data. The functions presented in FIG. 8-7 use a fairly simple encoding technique. You could enhance it using whatever algorithm you deem necessary in order to provide an adequate level of security for both the program and the data files. Notice that you could also use these functions to encode and decode data within the database file. In fact, you could perform selective encoding and decoding based on need. Only sensitive data need suffer the speed penalty of encoding and decoding. Nonsensitive-data access speed is unaffected using this technique.

Providing network status to users

Some of the most difficult problems for a programmer to solve adequately are those related to the user interface. Often, users will determine whether or not a program works satisfactorily based on how the interface works. They expect that the program will function correctly, so solving the technical problems is usually not enough to fully satisfy anyone. Unfortunately, one area that is often not under the programmer's direct control is the one that's most annoying to the user. Even if you provide all the proper error messages and security measures, the user will want to know about the status of the network itself. If the network is operating slowly, they want to know why. The user is usually not interested in all the technical reasons why they can't get to their data; all they know is that they want to see that data right now.

Of course, there are limits to what you can do as far as detecting network errors. If one of the workstations has an interface card that's slowing the rest of the network to a crawl, there's little you can do to correct it. However, one area in which you can detect and correct problems is in finding out who has a record in the database locked. A common scenario is that the user attempts to go to the next record and they can't get to it because someone else has it open. If the network is fairly large, it might be difficult to find out who has the record locked. Often, the person viewing the record is unaware that they are impeding progress because they don't realize the file is locked. Unfortunately, the user trying to get to the record is more likely to blame the network or the application program rather than the person who has it locked.

The program shown in FIG. 8-8 contains the Clipper source code used to call and display a data file. The difference between this code and any other code that performs the same task is the use of the CheckOut( ) function presented in FIG. 8-9. CheckOut( ) places the name of the person locking the record in the CHECKOUT database. In effect, this procedure acts like a librarian. When a user needs to lock a record, they check it out from the librarian, who places their name on a checkout card, or the database record. By using this routine, you prevent the anxiety that users face when they can't get into their data. Your program can now tell them who has it locked. In the meantime, you place the blame for users' inability to see their data is where it belongs, with the user who has the record locked.

8-8 Database-status example, Clipper source

```
// Program 8 - Database Status on a Network Example
// This program demonstrates one method of keeping track of who owns the
// lock on a record.  You could use the same technique for file locks as
// well.  The program begins by displaying the background screen,
// opening the database, and displaying the data.  It then goes into a
// loop where the user can select one of four options.  They can view
// another record, edit a record, display the Edit menu, or display the
// File menu.  Viewing another record is simply a matter of skipping
// either forward or backward through the database.  Displaying either
// menu consists of saving the current display, showing the menu,
// allowing the user to make a select, restoring the display, and acting
```

```
// on the selection.  The edit data option is where the record locking
// technique comes into play.  We attempt to lock the record.  I we
// can't obtain a lock, then we call the Librarian() function to see who
// owns the lock.  We then display a message to the user allowing them
// to correct the situation, to abort the edit, or to retry the lock.
// Once we are successful creating the lock, we call the CheckOut()
// procedure to check the record out of the database.  The function then
// allows the user to edit the data.  To use this program you must link
// it with LIBRARY.PRG.  Of course, you can't see any of the effects
// unless you have a multi-tasking environment like Windows or DesqView,
// or you have a LAN handy.
// Written by: John Mueller
// Copyright 1991 John Mueller - Tab Books

// Include an required header files.

#include "INKEY.CH"

// Create some local variables.

lExit := .F.

 // Display the background screen.

set scoreboard off
set color to "W+/B, RG+/R"
cls
@ 00, 00 say padc(" Database Status Example ", 80, chr(177))
@ 01, 00 to 24, 79 double
@ 02, 02 say "File   Edit"
@ 03, 01 to 03, 78 double

// Open the database and index.  Check to see if the file exists.  If
// the user is not allowed access, then the filename will not appear to
// the File() function.  (This assumes that you have already verified
// that the directory is correct.)

if file("SAMPLE7.DBF")
   use SAMPLE7 index SAMPLE7 shared
else
   alert("Access to Database Denied")
   set color to "W/N, N/W"
   cls
   return
endif

// Display the data.

DispData()

while !(inkey(0) == K_ESC)

// Process the up and down arrow keys.  All other keys are ignored.
```

8-8 Continued.

```
   do case

      // Scroll up one record.

      case lastkey() == K_UP
         if !(bof())
            skip -1
         endif

      // Scroll down one record.

      case lastkey() == K_DOWN
         if !(eof())
            skip
         endif
         if eof()
            skip -1
         endif

      // If the user presses Alt-F, display the File menu.

      case lastkey() == K_ALT_F
         lExit := DispFile()
         if lExit

            // Clear the display an exit to DOS.

            set color to "W/N, N/W"
            cls
            return
         endif

      // If the user presses Alt-E, display the Edit menu.

      case lastkey() == K_ALT_E
         DispEdit()

      // If the user presses any character key allow them to edit the
      // data in the current record.

      case (lastkey() >= asc("0")) .and. (lastkey() <= asc("z"))
         EditData()

   endcase

   // Display the data.

   DispData()

enddo

// Clear the display an exit to DOS.
```

```
set color to "W/N, N/W"
cls
return

// Local Procedures Begin.


// This procedure displays the data contained in the database.  It
// begins by clearing any data left from the last display, then displays
// the fields one at a time.  Notice that the comments are surrounded by
// a box, making them easier to see.

static procedure DispData

 // Clear the display area.

@ 04, 02 clear to 23, 78

// Display the data.

@ 04, 03 say "Record: " + ltrim(str(recno()))
@ 05, 03 say "Name:      " + FIRST + " " + MIDDLE + " " + LAST
@ 07, 03 say "Address:   " + COMPANY
@ 08, 14 say ADDRESS1
@ 09, 14 say ADDRESS2
@ 10, 14 say CITY + ", " + STATE + "     " + ZIP
@ 12, 03 say "Telephone: " + TELEPHONE1
@ 13, 14 say TELEPHONE2
@ 15, 03 say "Comments: "
@ 16, 03 to 23, 76 double
keyboard chr(27)
memoedit(COMMENTS, 17, 04, 22, 75, .F.)

// Return to the calling procedure.

return NIL


// This function begins by displaying gets for all of the data areas.
// It waits for the user to finish editing the data and saves the
// results to the database.

static function EditData

// Declare some local variables.

static nCount := 0    // Lock attempt counter variable.

// Attempt to lock the record.

nCount := 10
while !(flock()) .and. (nCount > 0)
   nCount--
enddo
```

8-8 Continued.

```
// If we weren't successful, find out who owns the record.  Allow the
// user to select a course of action.  If we're still not successful
// locking the record, exit to the calling procedure.  Otherwise, check
// the record out of the database.

if nCount == 0
   if !(Librarian(recno()))
      return
   endif
else
   CheckOut(recno())
endif

// Allow the user to edit the data fields.

@ 05, 14 get FIRST picture "@A"
@ 05, 40 get MIDDLE picture "@A"
@ 05, 42 get LAST picture "@A"
@ 07, 14 get COMPANY
@ 08, 14 get ADDRESS1
@ 09, 14 get ADDRESS2
@ 10, 14 get CITY picture "@A"
@ 10, 51 get STATE picture "@A"
@ 10, 58 get ZIP picture "99999-9999"
@ 12, 14 get TELEPHONE1 picture "(999)999-9999"
@ 13, 14 get TELEPHONE2 picture "(999)999-9999"
read

// Allow the user to edit the memo field.

@ 15, 03 say "Comments: "
@ 16, 03 to 23, 76 double
replace COMMENTS with memoedit(COMMENTS, 17, 04, 22, 75, .T.)

// Check the record back into the database and then unlock it.

CheckIn(recno())
dbunlock()

// Return to the calling procedure.

return NIL


// This function displays the file menu at the top of the display.  It
// begins by saving the original display and color scheme and changing
// the color scheme to the one used by the menu. The next step is to
// wait for the user to make a selection.  Once the selection is made,
// the function acts on the choice.  If the user selected either About
// or Help, the function displays a dialog box. Otherwise, it returns a
// value of True in lExit to the calling procedure.  This terminates the
// program.
```

```
static function DispFile

// Define some local variables.

local aMenu := {"Quit - Esc", "Help", "About"},; // Menu array.
      cOldColor,;                          // Color string saver.
      cScreen,;                            // Screen saver.
      lExit := .F.                         // Exit the program?

// Define the user selection variable.  Notice that we use an
// unitialized static variable to preserve the value of the variable
// after each menu selection.

static nChoice

// Display the menu and obtain the user selection.

cScreen := savescreen(00, 00, maxrow(), maxcol())
cOldColor := setcolor("RG+/RB, W+/B")
@ 02, 02 say "File"
@ 03, 02 to 07, 14 double
nChoice := achoice(04, 03, 06, 13, aMenu)

// Act on the user's menu selection.

do case
   case nChoice == 1; lExit := .T.
   case nChoice == 2; alert("This Option Not Enabled;for This Demo")
   case nChoice == 3
      alert("Database Status;Copyright 1991;John Mueller-Tab Books")
endcase

// Restore the display to its original appearance.

setcolor(cOldColor)
restscreen(00, 00, maxrow(), maxcol(), cScreen)

// Return to the calling procedure.  Pass the value of lExit back.

return lExit


// This function displays the Edit menu.

static function DispEdit

// Define some local variables.

// The first variable is the Menu array.

local aMenu := {"Edit Record", "Insert Date", "Insert Time"},;
      cOldColor,;                          // Color string saver.
      cScreen                              // Screen saver.
```

8-8 Continued.

```
// Define the user selection variable.  Notice that we use an
// unitialized static variable to preserve the value of the variable
// after each menu selection.

static nChoice

// Display the menu and obtain the user selection.

cScreen := savescreen(00, 00, maxrow(), maxcol())
cOldColor := setcolor("RG+/RB, W+/B")
@ 02, 09 say "Edit"
@ 03, 09 to 07, 22 double
nChoice := achoice(04, 10, 06, 21, aMenu)

// Act on the user's menu selection.

do case
   case nChoice == 1

      // Restore the display to its original appearance.  Call the data
      // editing function.

      setcolor(cOldColor)
      restscreen(00, 00, maxrow(), maxcol(), cScreen)
      EditData()

   case nChoice == 2; alert("This Option Not Enabled;for This Demo")
   case nChoice == 3; alert("This Option Not Enabled;for This Demo")

endcase

// Restore the display to its original appearance.

setcolor(cOldColor)
restscreen(00, 00, maxrow(), maxcol(), cScreen)

// Return to the calling procedure.

return NIL
```

8-9 Database-status example, function source

```
// Program 8 - Database Status on a Network Example
// This program contains three functions.  The first function helps the
// user determine the status of a record when another user has it
// locked.  It helps the user recover from the problem by providing
// several courses of action.  The second program checks the record out
// of a library database used to determine who owns the lock on a
// record.  The third program is used to check the record back into the
// database.
```

```
// Written by: John Mueller
// Copyright 1991 John Mueller - Tab Books

// This function determines who owns a file lock and helps the user
// determine a course of action in either obtaining the lock or aborting
// the edit operation.  It returns the result of any action to the
// calling procedure.  If the locking operation is finally successful,
// then Librarian() returns true.

function Librarian(nRecord)

// Define some local variables.

local nSelect := 0,;            // User action selection.
      nLockCount := 0,;         // Number of attempts to lock the record.
      lLocked := .F.,;          // Record Locked?
      cAlias                    // Alias of current database.

// Define some choices for the user.

static aChoice := {"Correct Situation", "Abort Edit", "Retry Lock"}

// Open the record database.

cAlias := alias()
use LIBRARY index LIBRARY shared new

// Find the locked record and determine who the user is.  Allow the user
// to select a course of action based on what we find.  If we can't find
// a user, then there is most likey some type of database or network
 // error.  Advise the user to exit the program immediately.

seek nRecord
if !(found())
   alert("Database Error!;Exit immediately!;Notify your supervisor.")
   close LIBRARY
   select(cAlias)
   return lLocked
else
   nSelect := alert(USERNAME + " has the record open", aChoice)
endif

// Keep trying to lock the record until successful or the user aborts.

while !(lLocked)

   // Follow the user selected course of action.

   do case

      // Allow the user to correct the situation, then try again.

      case nSelect == 1
         @ 23, 02 say "Press any key when ready to retry lock..."
```

8-9 Continued.

```
            inkey(0)
            nLockCount := 10
            while !(flock()) .and. (nLockCount > 0)
               nLockCount--
            enddo
            if nLockCount == 0
               nSelect := alert(USERNAME + " has the record open", aChoice)
            else
               lLocked := .T.
            endif

         // Abort the edit.

         case nSelect == 2
            lLocked := .F.
            close LIBRARY
            select(cAlias)
            return

         // Retry locking the record immediately.

         case nSelect == 3
            nLockCount := 10
            while !(flock()) .and. (nCount > 0)
                nLockCount--
            enddo
            if nLockCount == 0
               nSelect := alert(USERNAME + " has the record open", aChoice)
            else
               lLocked := .T.
            endif

      endcase
   enddo

   // Close the database and exit.

   close LIBRARY
   select(cAlias)
   return lLocked

   // This function checks the desired record out of the database.

   function CheckOut(nRecord)

   // Create any required variables.

   local cUser,;           // User name as defined by the network.
         cAlias,;          // Alias of current database.
         nLockCount := 0  // Record lock count.
```

```
// Open the record database.

cAlias := alias()
use LIBRARY index LIBRARY shared new

// Find the record if available.  If not, create a new one.

seek nRecord
if !(found())
   append blank
else

   // Lock the record prior to releasing checking it out.

   nLockCount := 10
   while !(flock()) .and. (nLockCount > 0)
      nLockCount--
   enddo

endif

// Add the user name to the record.

cUser := getenv("USERNAME")
replace USERNAME with cUser
replace RECORD with nRecord

// Close the database and exit.

close LIBRARY
select(cAlias)
return NIL


// This function checks the desired record into the database.

function CheckIn(nRecord)

// Create any required variables.

local cUser,;              // User name as defined by the network.
      cAlias,;             // Alias of current database.
      cBlank := space(20) // Blank for user name.

// Open the record database.

cAlias := alias()
use LIBRARY index LIBRARY shared new

// Find the locked record.  If we can't find the specified record
// number, then there is most likey some type of database or network
// error.  Advise the user to exit the program immediately.
```

8-9 Continued.

```
seek nRecord
if !(found())
   alert("Database Error!;Exit immediately!;Notify your supervisor.")
   close LIBRARY
endif

// Lock the record prior to releasing checking it in.

nLockCount := 10
while !(flock()) .and. (nLockCount > 0)
   nLockCount--
enddo

// Blank the user name field to check the record back in.  Unlock the
// record.

replace USERNAME with cBlank
 dbunlock()

// Close the database and exit.

close LIBRARY
select(cAlias)
return NIL
```

There are several important features in the program shown in FIG. 8-8. First, it offers a menu-driven interface to the user. I'll build on this interface in later chapters. Second, it offers complete status information to users when a lock fails during editing.

There are three external functions used to perform this task. First, whenever a lock is issued, the CheckOut( ) function stores the name of the user who owns the lock in the LIBRARY database. That way, if a lock does fail, then the user requesting the lock can find out who owns it. The second function, Librarian( ), assists in finding out who owns a lock when a request fails. The third function, CheckIn( ), clears the user entry in the LIBRARY database. This checks the record in. You should clear the record rather than erasing it to reduce the time required to append and delete records in the database. Each record will contain its own entry, and searches will be a lot faster as well because the database will remain essentially in sorted order.

Figure 8-9 presents a listing of the three library functions. As you can see, CheckIn( ) and CheckOut( ) are relatively short. All you need to do with these two functions is add or subtract a name in the LIBRARY database. Notice that both CheckIn( ) and Librarian( ) include some error handling as well. If the user asks for information on a record that doesn't exist, then the CheckOut( ) function never issued one. This could indicate an error condition in either the LIBRARY or host database. The Librarian( )

function is fairly straightforward. You continue to try to appease the user's entry to the locked record until successful or if the user decides to abort the edit. The important part is that the function offers the user a range of choices.

One of the criticisms of using a technique of this sort for managing the locks on a database is that, like the host database, the LIBRARY database is subject to errors caused by network failure and other sources. This is a very real consideration. No matter what system you come up with for managing the network, there is no error-free method currently available. With that in mind, you might want to use the transaction-log method presented in the previous section to monitor the condition of the LIBRARY database as well as the host database. That way, if a failure occurs, you can reconstruct the LIBRARY database at the same time as the host database.

Interface-language considerations

Your choice of C compilers can greatly affect the performance, compatibility, and flexibility of the external routines you write for Clipper. In a single-user environment, your only concern is making sure that the compiler you choose uses libraries that are compatible with those used in Clipper. After that, it's simply a matter of following the instructions provided in the Clipper manual.

A network, however, adds a whole new layer of complexity to your programming environment. It's no longer enough to simply make certain that the compiler you choose will work with Clipper; it has to work with the network as well. For example, some compilers make assumptions about the location of the printer or other hardware. In a single-user environment, you can count on the user's printer being attached to his machine.

It's unlikely that the printer will change from day to day, so you can disregard any unfortunate choices made by the compiler vendor by programming around them. On the other hand, users on a network are not likely to have printers attached to their machines. There is always the possibility that they won't be connected to a printer at all. Even if they are connected, the chances that they'll use the same network printer every time they print are slim. They might want to use a laser printer for one report and dot-matrix for another.

For this reason you must make certain that you select a compiler that recognizes the difficulties of programming in a network environment and does not assume anything about the location or type of hardware that you'll use. This allows you the freedom of creating routines that are flexible enough to handle the diverse hardware on a network.

One problem that many programmers overlook is the cost of memory on a networked workstation. Once a user loads the network driver and shell, there is significantly less available RAM than on a single-user PC.

This, coupled with the inevitable clashes you face with network-driver interrupt conflicts, can reduce the effectiveness of your C routines. For example, if your C libraries use interrupts in a way that's incompatible with the network shell or driver, your program will behave erratically. One time the routine might work and another time it won't. All this because the network driver is either performing a task involving the interrupt or it isn't.

The memory problems become evident when you use a compiler with large or nongranular libraries. Clipper can relocate native code to disk as required to free RAM for other processes. It cannot free the RAM used by external routines. Because of this, every byte taken by your routine is one less byte available to Clipper. As the memory shortage increases, so do the accesses to the swap file on disk. Program performance suffers as a result. The program that operated fast and efficiently on a single-user machine no longer operates on the networked workstation because of a lack of available RAM.

As you can see, the choice of compiler is important. The more you work with networks, the more essential it becomes to get compilers that not only create fast and efficient code, but are compatible with a network.

Network program-structure considerations

Many programmers get frustrated writing network programs because they feel the network greatly increases the complexity of their program. Of course, this is a correct assumption for at least the first few programs you create. However, in many cases you'll face this additional complexity with every program you create. This is because many programmers fail to remember a simple word when constructing network programs—*modularity*. The more generic and flexible you can make your routines, the better.

There are two benefits that you receive when you create modular network programs. First, you need to debug the code only once. If you don't change the code for every programming effort, then it's already correct when you use it. This factor alone can save you a significant amount of time and effort. The second benefit is that you'll develop a toolbox of boilerplate code. You can put the noncreative parts of a program together in a matter of hours instead of days. This allows you the spend time on the nongeneric parts of the code. The end result is that you'll be able to create better programs in less time.

It could be argued that this same reasoning works with single-user programs as well. Anyone making this argument is correct. Creating modular, reusable code is a boon to any programmer in any environment. However, while you can get through programming projects in the single-user environment without using modular code, to do so in the multiuser environment is less than efficient.

Network database-structure considerations

A common problem with network programs is that when a file server crashes, the LAN administrator has no idea of where to begin recovering files. This problem is especially true of networked database management systems. Look in the directory of many database management systems and you'll find a few hundred files with nondescriptive names. Attempting to put this puzzle back together when it falls apart is a job that no one should have to face.

A better way of managing your database is to design the database structure from the ground floor up to be easy to understand. For example, you could place all the utility files in a directory called UTILITY. You should name each database file with a description that identifies what task that file performs. Using the same name for index files that you used for the database file is always a good idea. That way you can easily identify which files belong together. Normalizing your database so that it follows a logical pattern is another way to enhance the database design.

Network database files are inherently larger than single-user database files. There are usually more files and a more complex structure underneath as well. These factors stem from the fact that a network database services the needs of more people than a single-user database. Maximizing the potential of your database structure can reduce much of the complexity that many people experience with networked systems.

Summary

This chapter provides you with information about three areas of network programming. First, you learn about the network uses for some of the commands and functions provided by Clipper. Some of these commands are network specific, while others are general-purpose commands or functions. While chapters 1 and 2 tell you what tasks these commands perform and how to use them, this chapter introduces you to the networking purposes for which you can use these commands. Learning how to use code that's already available will often relieve you of the responsibility of creating external routines.

The second piece of information presented in this chapter deals with the practical aspects of how to prevent network disasters. I concentrate on general-purpose routines that detect errors in the network, often before they really happen. For example, by performing some simple checks on the printer before you use it, you can prevent a large number of printer-specific network errors that can occur.

Finally, I examine some of the things you can do when the inevitable happens. As with every piece of equipment, your network can experience an error that will cause it to crash. Unfortunately, you can't detect every network error by simply using Clipper-specific commands and functions. Even adding an external routine or two won't help you detect every error. Of course, the answer lies in assuming the worst-case scenario and planning in advance for it. Recovering from a file-server crash is one of the more important things that your program can do for the user. For example, I look at how you can create a transaction log using some of the file functions provided with Clipper.

9

Interfacing Clipper to other programs

Choosing a piece of software always involves making choices. One of the disadvantages to using several programs is the matter of compatibility. Whenever you need information stored in a file format that Clipper doesn't read, you have to find another means to read it. Usually this involves transferring the program to an intermediate format (ASCII, in most cases) and then bringing it into Clipper. Not only is this inconvenient, but a single error in translation can cause problems when you attempt to use the data.

Another cause for concern is getting the data back to its original format. For example, what if you wanted to import some spreadsheet data, modify it, and then place the modified information in a new spreadsheet? The process sounds easy until you consider all the intermediate steps you need to make before you end up with the completed spreadsheet file. Unfortunately, these are things you always have to consider when creating an application.

There's another way to import data from foreign files into Clipper. If you can decipher the format of the data, then you can write a C or assembler routine to read it into Clipper for you. Even if you have to pass individual pieces of information, this process is much less error-prone, faster, and more convenient than using the manual procedure discussed previously. The less often you change the format of the data, the less likely damage will occur.

This chapter will introduce you to the principles of creating import and export routines for Clipper. While this is one of the most difficult tasks you'll ever perform, it's also one of the most necessary. The emphasis on building import and export routines into your application will only increase as programs become more complex. And most users will be unable or unwilling to go through all the steps required to perform a manual transfer of the data they need from one format to another.

Spreadsheet file interface

The three major types of software applications are database managers, word processors, and spreadsheets. Of these three, spreadsheets provide some of the most interesting challenges to data conversion. Because a spreadsheet handles a wide variety of data types in its natural format, your program must handle the same variety and read a large number of data types. If you plan to create a program that performs a two-way transfer of data, then the routines you create must write data in the required formats as well.

Another interesting feature of spreadsheets is the cell structure. Clipper DBF files use a fixed-length format. Even if a field on a particular record doesn't contain data, it's represented in the file. Unlike a database manager, if a spreadsheet cell doesn't contain data, then it won't write the cell out to the file. In addition, the cells are of a variable length.

As you can see, spreadsheet files are very difficult to read because they contain variable-length cells of uncertain data types with some cells missing from the file. It would seem to be impossible to decipher a spreadsheet file with any amount of certainty. However, there are some clues as to how this process occurs. TABLE 9-1 shows some of the factors that you need to take into consideration when attempting to read a WKS format file. Because many spreadsheet files use a similar format, you can use this example as a basis for figuring out these formats as well.

Table 9-1 WKS-file opcodes

Opcode	Data bytes	Description
00h Beginning of File 2 data bytes	1028 - 1-2-3 ver 1.0/1.1 1030 - 1-2-3 ver 2.0	Shows the beginning of the data file. In addition, it describes the type of file. This is especially important when using advanced opcodes.
01h End of File 0 data bytes		Shows the end of the data file.
02h Calculation Mode 1 data byte	00h - Manual FFh - Automatic	The CalcMode opcode determine the method used to recalculate. When in manual mode the user must initiate the recalculation. This

Opcode	Data bytes	Description
		means that some datafile entries might contain old information. When in automatic mode the program recalculates the values.
03h Calculation Order 1 data byte	00h - Natural 01h - By column FFh - By row	This opcode determines the order in which the formulas contained in the spreadsheet file are recalculated.
04h Window Split 1 data byte	00h - No split 01h - Vertical FFh - Horizontal	Indicates the direction of a window split, if any.
05h Synchronize Windows 1 data byte	00h - Not synchronized FFh - Synchronized	Indicates whether or not the movement of both windows are slaved to one cursor. If not, the windows move independently.
06h File Cell Range 8 data bytes	0 - 1: Start column 2 - 3: Start row 4 - 5: End column 6 - 7: End row	When the FILE SAVE command creates the file, the range indicates the active area. When the FILE EXTRACT command creates the file, the range indicates the extract range. In both cases trailing blank rows and columns are removed. If the range does not contain any data, the starting column value equals -1. Always place this

Table 9-1 Continued.

Opcode	Data bytes	Description
		value near the Beginning of File opcode.
07h Window 1 Parameters 31 data bytes	0 - 1: Cursor column 2 - 3: Cursor row 4: Cell format byte 5: Unused (00h) 6 - 7: Column width 8 - 9: # Screen columns 10-11: # Screen rows 12-13: Leftmost column 14-15: Top row 16-17: # Title columns 18-19: # Title rows 20-21: Left title column 22-23: Top title row 24-25: Border width column 26-27: Border width row 28-29: Window width 30: Unused (00h)	The Window 1 Parameters opcode defines all the characteristics of the first display window. Using these parameters, you can rebuild the spreadsheet window, if desired. Table 9-2 describes the cell format byte shown in byte 4.
08h Window 1 Column Width 3 data bytes	0 - 1: Hex column # 2: Width	Defines the alternate column width for window number one. There is one entry for each column using an alternate column width.
09h Window 2 Parameters 31 data bytes	See the byte definitions for window number one.	The Window 2 Parameters opcode defines all the characteristics of the first display window. Using these parameters, you can rebuild the spreadsheet window, if desired. Table 9-2

Opcode	Data bytes	Description
		describes the cell format byte shown in byte 4.
0Ah Window 2 Column Width 3 data bytes	0 - 1: Hex column # 2: Width	Defines the default column width for window number two.
0Bh Range Name 24 data bytes	0 -15: NULL terminated ASCII string 16-17: Start column 18-19: Start row 20-21: End column 22-23: End row	Contains the name of the range. It also describes the area of the spreadsheet covered by the named range. Each named range is represented by its own record in the spreadsheet.
0Ch Blank Cell 5 data bytes	0: Format byte 1 - 2: Column number 3 - 4: Row number	This opcode is used to represent a blank cell within a protected or formatted area of the spreadsheet.
0Dh Integer 7 data bytes	0: Format byte 1 - 2: Column number 3 - 4: Row number 5 - 6: Integer value	The Integer opcode represents a cell containing an integer value. The cell can contain a value of ±32,767.
0Eh Number 13 data bytes	0: Format byte 1 - 2: Column number 3 - 4: Row number 5 -12: 64-bit long Real	The Number opcode describes a floating point number stored as an IEEE double precision number. This format is compatible with the long format supported by the Clipper Extend System.

Table 9-1 Continued.

Opcode	Data bytes	Description
0Fh Label > = 245 data bytes	0: Format byte 1 - 2: Column number 3 - 4: Row number 5 - 245: NULL terminated ASCII string	The Label opcode describes a cell containing a string of variable length. Because the string is NULL terminated, it is compatible with the Clipper Extend System. Byte 5 always contains | (printer command), \ (repeating characters), ` (left aligned), " (right aligned), or ^ (center aligned).
10h Formula > = 2,064 data bytes	0: Format byte 1 - 2: Column number 3 - 4: Row number 5 - 12: Numeric value 13 - 14: Formula size 15 - 2063: Formula code	This opcode designates a cell containing a formula. The numeric value might be correct, based on the current calculation mode. It evaluates to a 64-bit IEEE long real. A discussion of how a formula is evaluated is outside the scope of this book.
18h Table Range 25 data bytes	0: 0 - No table 1 - Table 1 2 - Table 2 1 - 2: Start column # 3 - 4: Start row # 5 - 6: Ending column # 7 - 8: Ending row # 9 -10: Cell 1 start column 11-12: Cell 1 start row 13-14: Cell 1 end column 15-16: Cell 1 end row 17-18: Cell 2 start column	This opcode defines a structure that contains the parameters for a data table. Tables are used for a number of purposes within 1-2-3, including various types of analyses and database operations.

Opcode	Data bytes	Description
	19-20: Cell 2 start row 21-22: Cell 2 end column 23-24: Cell 2 end row	
19h Query Range 25 data bytes	0 - 1: Input start column 2 - 3: Input start row 4 - 5: Input end column 6 - 7: Input end row 8 - 9: Output start column 10-11: Output start row 12-13: Output end column 14-15: Output end row 16-17: Criteria start column 18-19: Criteria start row 20-21: Criteria end column 22-23: Criteria end row 24: 1 - No command 2 - Find 3 - Extract 4 - Unique	The Query Range opcode provides a method of interrogating the database. You can find a value, extract a value, or locate a unique value. The query is conducted over a specific range of cells using the criteria contained in another set of cells.
1Ah Print Range 8 data bytes	0 - 1: Start column 2 - 3: Start row 4 - 5: End column 6 - 7: End row	Use this opcode to define the print range within the spreadsheet. The spreadsheet program prints only those cells falling within the specified range.
1Bh Sort Range 8 data bytes	0 - 1: Start column 2 - 3: Start row 4 - 5: End column 6 - 7: End row	This opcode defines the range of cells used during a sort. Like other opcodes of this type, the spreadsheet program acts on only those cells falling within the specified range.
1Ch Fill Range	0 - 1: Start column 2 - 3: Start row	The Fill Range opcode determines what range

Table 9-1 Continued.

Opcode	Data bytes	Description
8 data bytes	4 - 5: End column 6 - 7: End row	of cells that the spreadsheet program will fill with a specific quatity, for example, numbers based on a formula.
1Dh Primary Sort Key Range 9 data bytes	0 - 1: Start column 2 - 3: Start row 4 - 5: End column 6 - 7: End row 8: 00 - Descending order FF - Ascending order	Defines the range of cells used as the primary sort key. In addition, it determines if the sort is in ascending or descending order.
20h Distribution Range 16 data bytes	0 - 1: Values start column 2 - 3: Values start row 4 - 5: Values end column 6 - 7: Values end row 8 - 9: Bin start column 10-11: Bin start row 12-13: Bin end column 14-15: Bin end row	This opcode defines a distribution range that is used to analyze the numeric data within a group of cells.
23h Secondary Sort Key Range 9 data bytes	0 - 1: Start column 2 - 3: Start row 4 - 5: End column 6 - 7: End row 8: 00 - Descending order FF - Ascending order	Defines the range of cells used as the secondary sort key. In addition, it determines if the sort is in ascending or descending order.
24h Global Protection 1 data byte	0: 00 - Protection off 01 - Protection on	The Global Protection opcode determines whether or not all the cells in the spreadsheet are protected (i.e., read-only).
25h Footer	0 - 242: NULL terminated ASCIIZ string	Contains the footer used during

Opcode	Data bytes	Description
242 data bytes		spreadsheet printing.
26h Header 242 data bytes	0 - 242: NULL terminated ASCIIZ string	Contains the header used during spreadsheet printing.
27h Printer Setup String 39 data bytes	0 - 39: NULL terminated ASCIIZ string	Contains a set of escape sequences required to initialize the printer prior to printing.
28h Print Margins 10 data bytes	0 - 1: Left margin 2 - 3: Right margin 4 - 5: Page length 6 - 7: Top margin 8 - 9: Bottom margin	This opcode defines the margins used during printing. This refers to the output margins, not the spreadsheet margins. If the print range extends over the physical print area, then the spreadsheet prints additional pages.
29h Label Format 1 data byte	0: 27h - Left 22h - Right 5Eh - Center	Determines the alignment of text on the screen and printer output.
2Ah Print Borders (Titles) 16 data bytes	0 - 1: Row start column 2 - 3: Row start row 4 - 5: Row end column 6 - 7: Row end row 8 - 9: Column start column 10-11: Column start row 12-13: Column end column 14-15: Column end row	This opcode defines two sets of print borders. The first set is horizontal (row). The second set is verical (column). The cells defined for each group are used during display and printing as titles.
2Dh	0 - 437: Current graph	Contains the

Table 9-1 Continued.

Opcode	Data bytes	Description
Graph 437 data bytes	setting description	parameters required to create a graph of the data contained in the spreadsheet.
2Eh Named Graph 453 data bytes	0 - 453: Named graph setting description	Contains the parameters required to create a graph of the data contained in the spreadsheet. There is one entry for each named graph.
2Fh Calculation Iteration Count 1 data byte	0: Iteration count	Defines the number of iterations performed for each recalculation of the spreadsheet.
30h Unformatted 1 data byte	0: 00 - Formatted 01 - Unformatted	Determines whether output to the display and printer is formatted or unformatted.
31h Cursor Position 1 data byte	0: 01 - Cursor in window 1 02 - Cursor in window 2	Determines whether the cursor is displayed in window number one or number two.
Version 2.x specific opcodes		
4Bh Worksheet Password 4 data bytes	????	Contains a password for the decrypting the spreadsheet. Further details of the password format are unavailable.
64h Hidden Column Array 32 data bytes	Each bit refers to a different worksheet column from 1 to 256.	The Hidden Column Array opcode defines whether or not a column is hidden or displayed. If the

Opcode	Data bytes	Description
		column bit contains a 1, then the column is hidden. This array affects window number one.
65h Hidden Column Array 32 data bytes	Each bit refers to a different worksheet column from 1 to 256.	The Hidden Column Array opcode defines whether or not a column is hidden or displayed. If the column bit contains a 1, then the column is hidden. This array affects window number two.
66h Parser Range 16 data bytes	0 - 1: Input start column 2 - 3: Input start row 4 - 5: Input end column 6 - 7: Input end row 8 - 9: Output start column 10-11: Output start row 12-13: Output end column 14-15: Output end row	Defines the parser ranges for the spreadsheet. There is one record for each range defined within the worksheet.
67h Linear Regression Ranges 25 data bytes	Dependent variable range 0 - 1: Start column 2 - 3: Start row 4 - 5: End column 6 - 7: End row Independent variable range 8 - 9: Start column 10-11: Start row 12-13: End column 14-15: End row Output range 16-17: Start column 18-19: Start row 20-21: End column 22-23: End row Zero intercept	This opcode contains the parameters required to perform regression analysis on the worksheet. There is one record for each range defined.

Table 9-1 Continued.

Opcode	Data bytes	Description
	24: 0 - Not forced -1 - Forced at origin	
69h Matrix Ranges 40 data bytes	Matrix inversion source 0 - 1: Start column 2 - 3: Start row 4 - 5: End column 6 - 7: End row Matrix inversion end 8 - 9: Start column 10-11: Start row 12-13: End column 14-15: End row Matrix Multiplicand source 16-17: Start column 18-19: Start row 20-21: End column 22-23: End row Matrix Multiplier start 24-25: Start column 26-27: Start row 28-29: End column 30-31: End row Matrix product start 32-33: Start column 34-35: Start row 36-37: End column 38-39: End row	This opcode defines the parameters required to perform matrix manipulation on a range of worksheet cells. There is one record for each range.
96h Cell Pointer Index Variable number of data bytes	0 - 1: Column number 2 - 3: Low row number 4 - 5: High row number	Contains a listing of columns containing one or more active cells.

TABLE 9-1 provided a lot of information about how a spreadsheet stores data, but doesn't describe the data format. This information is presented in TABLE 9-2. As you can see, the data formatting information is contained in two bytes. The first byte describes the special format type or the number of decimal places for generic types. The second byte describes the overall type and determines if the cell is protected or not. Never confuse this with global protection, which prevents the user from modifying anything in the worksheet. This bit prevents modification of only the current cell. Notice that the generic types include most numeric combinations and the special type instruction, 7h. This allows the user to always tell the spreadsheet how many decimal places to display on screen. It doesn't affect the numeric accuracy of the stored data. The special types include text, a general format that accepts any input, and various forms of date input.

Table 9-2 Cell-format byte encoding

Bit	Description
Format types 0 through 6	
0 - 3	Number of decimal places from 0 through 15.
Format type 7 (Special)	
0 - 3	Special formatting type: 0000 - ± 0001 - General format 0010 - Day-Month-Year 0011 - Day-Month 0100 - Month-Year 0101 - Text 0110 to 1111 - Unused
Format types 0 through 7	
4 - 6	Format type: 000 - Fixed 001 - Scientific notation 010 - Currency 011 - Percent 100 - Comma 101 - Unused 110 - Unused 111 - Special format type
7	0 - Unprotected cell 1 - Protected cell

Creating the import routine

The tables in the previous section might lull you into a false sense that converting spreadsheet files is a relatively painless and fast process. After all, the contents of the worksheet are well documented and easy to understand. The code in FIG. 9-1 shows the amount of Clipper code required to display data even after you convert it and place it in an array. This code includes both the import and export code described in the next section.

9-1 WKS file import/export example, Clipper source

```
// Program 9 - WKS File Import/Export Example
// This program performs two tasks.  First it imports data from a WKS
// formatted file, then it exports data from a database to a WKS file.
// There are only two sections to the data import routine.  The first
// section polls the user for a file to convert (the example files
// contain SAMPLE1.WKS for this purpose).  The second section converts
// and displays the requested file.  Notice that this routine assumes a
// particular file format.  A more generic routine can be created using
// code that detects the format of the data and takes that into account
// as it outputs the data to the screen.  The data export routine
// consists of three sections.  First, we poll the user to see what
// output file they want to use (a suggested filename would be
// SAMPLE2.WKS).  The second section places the data information in
// arrays.  Note that we supply the data type, position that we wish it
// placed within the spreadsheet, and the actual data.  No data
// conversion is required.  The second section sends the data and
// accompanying information to the export routine.  In this case we must
// supply to other arrays.  The first array contains column numbers.
// The second array contains column widths.  The export routine uses
// this information to adjust the size of the output file columns.  The
// third section detects whether or not the conversion was successful.
// If so, it displays a success message; otherwise, an error message.
// Written by: John Mueller
// Copyright 1991 John Mueller - Tab Books

// Create some local variables.

static aType [256],;                // Data Type Array
       aRow [256],;                 // Row Position Within Worksheet
       aCol [256],;                 // Column Position Within Worksheet
       aData [256],;                // Information Stored in Cell
       cName := "            ",;    // Name of the Worksheet File
       nEntries := 0,;              // Number of Array Entries
       nCount := 0,;                // Counter Variable for Loops.
       aColNum := {0, 1, 2, 3, 4, 6, 7, 8, 9, 10, 11},;  // Column Number
       aColSiz := {25, 1, 25, 50, 50, 13, 13, 50, 35, 2} // Column Size

// Display the background screen.

set scoreboard off
set color to "W+/B, RG+/R"
```

```
cls
@ 01, 00 to 24, 79 double
@ 02, 01 say padc(" WKS File Import Example ", 78, chr(177))
@ 03, 01 to 03, 78 double

// Get the filename from the user.

@ 04, 02 say "Enter the WKS filename: " get cName picture "!!!!!!!!.WKS"
read

// Get the data from the file.

if ImpWKS(cName, @aType, @aRow, @aCol, @aData, @nEntries)

// If we successfully import the data, display a success message.

   @ 05, 02 say "Data Retrieved Successfully"

// Display the data on-screen.  (We could just as easily place it in a
// DBF file).

   for nCount := 2 to (nEntries-5) step 5
      @ row()+1, 02 say iif(valtype(aData[nCount]) = "N",;
                            CalcDate(aData[nCount]),;
                            substr(aData[nCount], 2, len(aData[nCount])))
      @ row(), 12 say substr(aData[nCount+1], 2, len(aData[nCount+1]))
      @ row(), 44 say iif(valtype(aData[nCount+2]) = "N",;
                          "$" + str(aData[nCount+2], 8, 2),;
                          substr(aData[nCount+2], 2, len(aData[nCount+2])))
      @ row(), 55 say iif(valtype(aData[nCount+3]) = "N",;
                          str(aData[nCount+3] * 100, 5, 1) + "%",;
                          substr(aData[nCount+3], 2, len(aData[nCount+3])))
      @ row(), 66 say iif(valtype(aData[nCount+4]) = "N",;
                          str(aData[nCount+4], 10, 3),;
                          substr(aData[nCount+4], 2, len(aData[nCount+4])))
   next

// If we aren't successful, display an error message and exit.

else
   @ 05, 02 say "Oops, there's an error."

   // Wait for the user to press a key.

   @ 23, 02 say "Press any key when ready..."
   inkey(0)

   // Clear the display and exit to DOS.

   set color to "W/N, N/W"
   cls
   return
endif
```

9-1 Continued.

```
// Wait for the user to press a key.

@ 23, 02 say "Press any key when ready..."
inkey(0)

// Try exporting some data.

// Display the background screen.

cls
@ 01, 00 to 24, 79 double
@ 02, 01 say padc(" WKS File Export Example ", 78, chr(177))
@ 03, 01 to 03, 78 double

// Get the filename from the user.

@ 04, 02 say "Enter the WKS filename: " get cName picture "!!!!!!!!.WKS"
read

// Open a database, places its data in the appropriate arrays, close the
// database file, and call the conversion program.

use SAMPLE1 index SAMPLE1

nEntries := 0
nCount := 0
 while !(eof())

// Add the First Name field to the array.

   nEntries++
   aData[nEntries] := FIRST
   aType[nEntries] := "Character"
   aCol[nEntries] := 0
   aRow[nEntries] := nCount

// Add the Middle Name field to the array.

   nEntries++
   aData[nEntries] := MIDDLE
   aType[nEntries] := "Character"
   aCol[nEntries] := 1
   aRow[nEntries] := nCount

// Add the Last Name field to the array.

   nEntries++
   aData[nEntries] := LAST
   aType[nEntries] := "Character"
   aCol[nEntries] := 2
   aRow[nEntries] := nCount
```

```
// Add the Address 1 field to the array.

   nEntries++
   aData[nEntries] := ADDRESS1
   aType[nEntries] := "Character"
   aCol[nEntries] := 3
   aRow[nEntries] := nCount

// Add the Address 2 field to the array.

   nEntries++
   aData[nEntries] := ADDRESS2
   aType[nEntries] := "Character"
   aCol[nEntries] := 4
   aRow[nEntries] := nCount

// Add the Zip Code field to the array.

   nEntries++
   aData[nEntries] := ZIP
   aType[nEntries] := "Character"
   aCol[nEntries] := 5
   aRow[nEntries] := nCount

// Add the Telephone 1 field to the array.

   nEntries++
   aData[nEntries] := TELEPHONE1
   aType[nEntries] := "Character"
   aCol[nEntries] := 6
   aRow[nEntries] := nCount

// Add the Telephone 2 field to the array.

   nEntries++
   aData[nEntries] := TELEPHONE2
   aType[nEntries] := "Character"
   aCol[nEntries] := 7
   aRow[nEntries] := nCount

// Add the Company field to the array.

   nEntries++
   aData[nEntries] := COMPANY
   aType[nEntries] := "Character"
   aCol[nEntries] := 8
   aRow[nEntries] := nCount

// Add the City field to the array.

   nEntries++
   aData[nEntries] := CITY
   aType[nEntries] := "Character"
   aCol[nEntries] := 9
   aRow[nEntries] := nCount
```

9-1 Continued.

```
// Add the State field to the array.

   nEntries++
   aData[nEntries] := STATE
   aType[nEntries] := "Character"
   aCol[nEntries] := 10
   aRow[nEntries] :=nCount

   nCount++
   skip
enddo

use

// Get the data from the file.

if ExpWKS(cName, @aType, @aRow, @aCol, @aData, @nEntries, aColNum, aColSiz)

// If we successfully import the data, display a success message.

   @ 05, 02 say "Data Converted Successfully"

// If we aren't successful, display an error message and exit.

else
   @ 05, 02 say "Oops, there's an error."

   // Wait for the user to press a key.

   @ 23, 02 say "Press any key when ready..."
   inkey(0)

   // Clear the display and exit to DOS.

   set color to "W/N, N/W"
   cls
   return
endif

// Wait for the user to press a key.

@ 23, 02 say "Press any key when ready..."
inkey(0)

// Clear the display and exit to DOS.

set color to "W/N, N/W"
cls
return

// Start of Local Functions

// This function takes a WKS formatted date in numeric format and
```

```
// converts it to a DBF data format.  It begins by finding the year.
// All WKS formatted dates begin at 01/01/1900.  Therefore, if we divide
// the number by 365.25 and take only the integer portion, we should
// have the number of years since 1900.  Adding 1900 to the number adds
// the century.  Finding the day since the beginning of the year
// consists of taking the modulus of the number.  If we subtract the
// correct amount for each month, then the number of months we have to
// subtract equals the correct month and the number left over is the
// current day in that month.  Once we have character versions of the
// year, month, and day, concatenate the three values into a date
// string, then convert the date string to a date.

 function CalcDate(nDate)

// Declare some local variables.

local cDay,;
      cMonth,;
      cYear,;
      nCount := 1,;
      aMonth := {31, 28, 31, 30, 31, 30, 31, 31, 30, 31, 30, 31},;
      dDate,;
      cDate

// Convert the number to a year string.

cYear := str(int(1900+nDate/365.25), 4, 0)

// Obtain the modulus of the date number to find the number of days
// since the beginning of the year.

nDate := round((nDate % 365.25), 0)

// Count the number of months since the beginning of the year.

while (nDate > aMonth[nCount])
   nDate := nDate - aMonth[nCount]
   nCount++
enddo

// Convert the month count to a string.  Take the number of days left
// over and convert it to a string for the current day of the month.

cMonth := str(nCount, 2, 0)
cDay := str(nDate, 2, 0)

// Concatenate the month, day, and year strings together to form a date
// string.  Convert the date string to a date variable.

cDate := cMonth + "/" + cDay + "/" + cYear
dDate := ctod(cDate)

// Return the date to the calling procedure.

return dDate
```

Notice that by using arrays you can make certain that the data is transferred accurately between the conversion routine written in assembly language and the Clipper program. Figure 9-2 presents the even more complex code required to actually convert the data. This code represents the most basic import and export routines that you can hope to create. You could choose to return even more information from the worksheet, but this would require a much more complex external routine.

9-2 WKS file import/export example, assembly source

```
;*************************************************************************
;* Program Number 9 - WKS Interface Example                             *
;* This program contains three routines, two of which are public.  The *
;* first routine converts data from WKS format to DBF format (or more   *
;* precisely into a format that could be placed in a DBF file).  The    *
;* second routine converts the data from DBF format to WKS format.      *
;* Notice that this routine actually create the output file with        *
;* appropriate header information so you can view it with any           *
;* spreadsheet program capable of using WKS files.  The third routine   *
;* reads a single entry from the spreadsheet file.  It is used in       *
;* conjunction with the import routine.                                 *
;* Written by: John Mueller                                             *
;* Copyright 1991 John Mueller - Tab Books                              *
;*************************************************************************

;*************************************************************************
;* Make any required declarations.                                      *
;*************************************************************************

.MODEL LARGE

INCLUDE EXTASM.INC
INCLUDE MACROS.INC
INCLUDE LOTUS.INC

PUBLIC ImpWKS, ExpWKS

;*************************************************************************
;* Declare any required variables.                                      *
;*************************************************************************

.DATA

;*************************************************************************
;* This section contains standard program variables.                    *
;*************************************************************************

nOpCode         DW      0               ;Entry Operation Code
nRecLen         DW      1               ;Length of the Data
xEData          DW      256 DUP (0)     ;Entry Data
cFName          DB      12 DUP (" "),0  ;Worksheet ASCIIZ Filename
nHandle         DW      0               ;File Handle to Worksheet
```

```
nOMode          DB      10010010b      ;Open Read/Write, Deny Others Access
cIntType        DB      "Integer",0    ;Integer type string.
cNumType        DB      "Number",0     ;Number type string.
cStrType        DB      "Character",0  ;Character type string.
nStrLen         DW      0              ;Length of a data string.

;**********************************************************************
;* This section of the data area contains a generic header for a WKS  *
;* file.  You can modify it to include the elements required for other *
;* versions of the file or to change the defaults the spreadsheet     *
;* program will see in the file you export.                           *
;**********************************************************************

WSHeader        DW      0,2,1028     ;Beginning Of File - Opcode 0
                DW      6,8          ;Range - Opcode 6
nRngSCol        DW      0            ;Range Starting Column
nRngSRow        DW      0            ;Range Starting Row
nRngECol        DW      11           ;Range Ending Column
nRngERow        DW      7            ;Range Ending Row
                DW      2Fh,1        ;Calculation Count - Opcode 2Fh
nCalCnt         DB      1            ;Number of Iterations
                DW      2,1          ;Calculation Mode - Opcode 2
nCalMode        DB      0FFh         ;Mode FF - Automatic
                DW      3,1          ;Calculation Order
nCalOrd         DB      0            ;Order 0 - Natural
                DW      4,1          ;Split - Opcode 4
nSplit          DB      0            ;0 - Window Not Split
                DW      5,1          ;Sync - Opcode 5
nSync           DB      0FFh         ;FF - Windows are Synchronized
                DW      7,1Fh        ;Window 1 Parameters
nCurCol         DW      0            ;Current Cursor Column
nCurRow         DW      0            ;Current Cursor Row
nCellFG         DB      71h          ;Global Cell Format - Unprotected General
                DB      0            ;Unused - Must be set to 0.
nColWdthG       DW      10           ;Global Column Width - 10
nNumCols        DW      5            ;5 Columns Visible on Screen
nNumRows        DW      45           ;45 Rows Visible on Screen
nLeftCol        DW      0            ;Leftmost Visible Column
nTopRow         DW      0            ;Top Visible Row
nTitCol         DW      0            ;Number of Title Columns
nTitRow         DW      0            ;Number of Title Rows
nLftTCol        DW      0            ;Leftmost Title Column
nTopTRow        DW      0            ;Top Title Row
nBWdthCol       DW      4            ;Border Width Column
nBWdthRow       DW      4            ;Border Width Row
nWinWdth        DW      72           ;Window Width
                DB      0            ;Unused - Must be set to 0.
nHLength        EQU     $-WSHeader   ;Length of Header

nNColumns       DW      0            ;Number of columns
ColChg          DW      8,3          ;Column Widths, Window 1 - Opcode 8.
nColNum         DW      0            ;Column Number to Change from Default Width.
nColSiz         DB      0            ;New Column Size.
```

9-2 Continued.

```
RestHead        DW      18h,19h             ;Table Range - Opcode 18h
                DB      0,0,17h DUP (0FFh)  ;Data
                DW      19h,19h             ;Query Range - Opcode 19h
                DB      18h DUP (0FFh), 0 ;Data
                DW      1Ah,8               ;Print Range - Opcode 1Ah
                DB      8 DUP (0FFh)        ;Data
                DW      30h,1          ;Formatted/Unformatted Toggle - Opcode 30h
                DB      0              ;Formatted
                DW      1Ch,8          ;Fill Range - Opcode 1Ch
                DB      8 DUP (0FFh)   ;Data
                DW      1Bh,8          ;Sort Range - Opcode 1Bh
                DB      8 DUP (0FFh)   ;Data
                DW      1Dh,9          ;Sort Key Range - Opcode 1Dh
                DB      8 DUP (0FFh),0 ;Data
                DW      23h,9          ;Secondary Sort Key Range - Opcode 23h
                DB      8 DUP (0FFh),0 ;Data
                DW      20h,10h        ;Distribution Range - Opcode 20h
                DB      10h DUP (0FFh) ;Data
                DW      24h,1          ;Global Protection Toggle - Opcode 24h
                DB      0              ;Protection Off
                DW      25h,0F2h       ;Footer - Opcode 25h
                DB      0F2h DUP (0)   ;No Footer Declared
                DW      26h,0F2h       ;Header - Opcode 26h
                DB      0F2h DUP (0)   ;No Header Declared
                DW      27h,28h        ;Printer Setup String - Opcode 27h
                DB      28h DUP (0)    ;No Setup String
                DW      28h,0Ah        ;Print Margins - Opcode 28h
LMarg           DW      4              ;4th space
RMarg           DW      4Ch            ;77th space
PageLen         DW      42h            ;66 lines
TopMarg         DW      2              ;2 lines
BotMarg         DW      2              ;2 lines
                DW      29h,1          ;Label Format - Opcode 29h
                DB      27h            ;Left Justified
                DW      2Ah,10h        ;Title Print Borders - Opcode 2Ah
                DB      10h DUP (0FFh) ;None Defined
                DW      2Dh,1B7h       ;Graph Data
                DB      1B7h DUP (0FFh)     ;None Defined
RHeadLen        EQU     $-RestHead

LblEntry        DW      0Fh           ;Label - Opcode 0Fh
LblLen          DW      00            ;Label Length
LblFormat       DB      7Fh           ;Special, Text
LblCol          DW      00            ;Column Number
LblRow          DW      00            ;Row Number
                DB      "'"           ;Left Justify
LblData         DB      241 DUP (0)   ;Null Terminated ASCII String

EndIt           DW      1,0           ;End of File, No Data Bytes

.CODE
```

```
;***********************************************************************
;* This procedure imports data from the specified WKS file, places any *
;* pertenant information in a set of arrays, and returns the arrays to *
;* Clipper.  The calling procedure passes the filename along with      *
;* references to four arrays.  The first array contains the data type. *
;* The second array contains the data row.  The third array contains   *
;* the data column.  The fourth array contains the actual data.        *
;***********************************************************************

ImpWKS          PROC    FAR

                PUSH    SI          ;Save SI.

                MOV     AX,@DATA    ;Point DS & ES to our data segment.
                MOV     DS,AX
                MOV     ES,AX

;**********************************************************************
;* This section of the code checks the number of parameters and their *
;* type.  It also ensures that the array was passed by reference so it*
;* can store the results of the computation.  Once the variables are  *
;* verified, it places the string passed as parameter one in cFName.  *
;**********************************************************************

                PCount              ;Check for the correct
                CMP         AX,6    ; number of parameters.
                JE          Parml   ;If so, perform next check.
                JMP         BadExit ;If not, exit.

Parml:          IsChar      1       ;Is the first parameter a string?
                JE          Parm2   ;If so, perform next check.
                JMP         BadExit ;If not, exit.

Parm2:          ParInfo     2       ;Is the second parameter an array?
                CMP         AX,Array+MPtr
                JE          Parm3   ;If so, perform next check.
                JMP         BadExit ;If not, exit.

Parm3:          ParInfo     3       ;Is the third parameter an array?
                CMP         AX,Array+MPtr
                JE          Parm4   ;If so, perform next check.
                JMP         BadExit ;If not, exit.

Parm4:          ParInfo     4       ;Is the fourth parameter an array?
                CMP         AX,Array+MPtr
                JE          Parm5   ;If so, perform next check.
                JMP         BadExit ;If not, exit.

Parm5:          ParInfo     5       ;Is the fifth parameter an array?
                CMP         AX,Array+MPtr
                JE          Parm6   ;If so, perform next check.
                JMP         BadExit ;If not, exit.

Parm6:          ParInfo     6       ;Is the sixth parameter a number?
                CMP         AX,Numeric+Mptr
```

9-2 Continued.

```
          JNE      BadExit    ;If not, exit.
          JMP      GoodParms  ;Otherwise, process the data.

BadExit:  RetFalse            ;Return false on error.
          POP      SI         ;Restore SI
          RET

GoodParms: RetTrue            ;Return true for good parameters.

          GetChar  1          ; Get the character parameter.
          PUSH     AX         ; Save the string offset.
          PUSH     DX         ; Save the Clipper DATA segment.

          GetCharLen 1        ; Retrieve the string length.
          MOV      CX,AX

          POP      DS         ; Point to the Clipper DATA segment.
          POP      SI         ; Point to the string.

          LEA      DI,cFName  ; Load the offset of SomeStr.
          REP      MOVSB      ; Move the string to our data segment.

          MOV      AX,@DATA   ; Point DS to our data segment.
          MOV      DS,AX

;**********************************************************************
;* This section of the code performs the task of opening the worksheet*
;* file.  If it isn't successful, then it returns a value of false to *
;* the calling procedure.                                             *
;**********************************************************************

          MOV      AH,3Dh     ;Open File
          MOV      AL,nOMode  ; in a specific mode.
          LEA      DX,cFName  ;Use the filename we retrieved from Clipper.
          INT      21h

          JC       BadExit    ;If we weren't successful, exit.
          MOV      nHandle,AX ;If we were, then save the file handle.

;**********************************************************************
;* This section of the code is a loop.  The loop begins when we call  *
;* ReadEntry.  When ReadEntry returns, we test the value of AX.  If AX*
;* is anything other than 0, then we were able to read information    *
;* from the WKS file.  So, we call ReadEntry again to retrieve another*
;* data value.  If AX is 0, then we've converted the entire file and  *
;* it's time to return to Clipper.                                    *
;**********************************************************************

GetData:  CALL     ReadEntry      ;Read the data.
          CMP      AX,0           ;If we reach the end of the file, exit.
          JE       EndData
          INC      nRecLen        ;Increment the entry counter.
          JMP      GetData        ;Read some more data.
```

```
;**********************************************************************
;* This section of the code stores the number of entries read from the*
;* spreadsheet, closes the file, and exits back to Clipper            *
;**********************************************************************

EndData:        StorInt     6, nRecLen      ;Store the number of entries read.

                MOV         AX,3E00h        ;Close File.
                MOV         BX,nHandle      ;Load the file handle.
                INT         21h

                POP SI                      ;Restore SI.

                RET                         ;Return to Clipper.

ImpWKS          ENDP

;**********************************************************************
;* This procedure converts a DBF file to a WKS file.                  *
;**********************************************************************

ExpWKS          PROC    FAR

                PUSH    SI              ;Save SI.

                MOV     AX,@DATA        ;Point DS & ES to our data segment.
                MOV     DS,AX
                MOV     ES,AX

;**********************************************************************
;* This section of the code checks the number of parameters and their *
;* type.  It also ensures that the array was passed by reference so it*
;* can store the results of the computation.  Once the variables are  *
;* verified, it places the string passed as parameter one in cFName.  *
;**********************************************************************

                PCount                  ;Check for the correct
                CMP         AX,8        ; number of parameters.
                JE          EParm1      ;If so, perform next check.
                JMP         EBadExit    ;If not, exit.

EParm1:         IsChar      1           ;Is the first parameter a string?
                JE          EParm2      ;If so, perform next check.
                JMP         EBadExit    ;If not, exit.

EParm2:         ParInfo     2           ;Is the second parameter an array?
                CMP         AX,Array+MPtr
                JE          EParm3      ;If so, perform next check.
                JMP         EBadExit    ;If not, exit.

EParm3:         ParInfo     3           ;Is the third parameter an array?
                CMP         AX,Array+MPtr
                JE          EParm4      ;If so, perform next check.
```

9-2 Continued.

```
EParm4:         ParInfo    4          ;Is the fourth parameter an array?
                CMP        AX,Array+MPtr
                JE         EParm5     ;If so, perform next check.
                JMP        EBadExit   ;If not, exit.

EParm5:         ParInfo    5          ;Is the fifth parameter an array?
                CMP        AX,Array+MPtr
                JE         EParm6     ;If so, perform next check.
                JMP        EBadExit   ;If not, exit.

EParm6:         ParInfo    6          ;Is the sixth parameter a number?
                CMP        AX,Numeric+Mptr
                JNE        EBadExit   ;If not, exit.
                JMP        GoodEParms ;Otherwise, process the data.

EBadExit:       RetFalse              ;Return false on error.
                POP        SI         ;Restore SI
                RET

GoodEParms:     RetTrue               ;Return true for good parameters.

                GetChar    1          ; Get the character parameter.
                PUSH       AX         ; Save the string offset.
                PUSH       DX         ; Save the Clipper DATA segment.

                GetCharLen 1          ; Retrieve the string length.
                MOV        CX,AX

                POP        DS         ; Point to the Clipper DATA segment.
                POP        SI         ; Point to the string.

                LEA        DI,cFName  ; Load the offset of SomeStr.
                REP        MOVSB      ; Move the string to our data segment.

                MOV        AX,@DATA   ;Point DS to our data segment.
                MOV        DS,AX

;*********************************************************************
;* This section of the code performs the task of opening the worksheet*
;* file.  If it isn't successful, then it returns a value of false to *
;* the calling procedure.                                             *
;*********************************************************************

                MOV        AH,3Dh     ;Open File
                MOV        AL,nOMode  ; in a specific mode.
                LEA        DX,cFName  ;Use the filename we retrieved from Clipper.
                INT        21h

                JC         CFile      ;If we weren't successful, create the file.
                MOV        nHandle,AX ;If we were, then save the file handle.
                JMP        FOpen
```

```
CFile:          MOV         AH,3Ch     ;Create a file.
                XOR         CX,CX      ;No file attributes.
                LEA         DX,cFName  ;Use the filename we retrieve from Clipper.
                INT         21h

                JC          EBadExit   ;If we still aren't successful, exit.
                MOV         nHandle,AX ;If we were, then save the file handle

;*****************************************************************************
;* This section of code places the header information into the              *
;* spreadsheet file.  This header information tells the spreadsheet         *
;* program how to configure the display.                                    *
;*****************************************************************************

FOpen:          MOV         AX,4000h        ;Write to the file
                MOV         BX,nHandle      ; pointed to by BX.
                LEA         DX,WSHeader     ;Load the address of the data.
                MOV         CX,nHLength     ;Load the length of the data.
                INT         21h             ;Write the data.

                ALength     7               ;Determine the number of non-standard columns.
                CMP         AX,0            ;See if there are any.
                JE          NoCols          ;If not, go to the next step.
                MOV         nNColumns,AX    ;Save the number of non-standard columns.

NextCol:        MOV         AX,nNColumns    ;Retrieve element X
                PUSH        AX
                MOV         AX,7            ; of the Column Number array.
                PUSH        AX
                CALL        __parni
                ADD         SP,4

                MOV         nColNum,AX      ;Save the column number.

                MOV         AX,nNColumns    ;Retrieve element X
                PUSH        AX
                MOV         AX,8            ; of the Column Size array.
                PUSH        AX
                CALL        __parni
                ADD         SP,4

                MOV         nColSiz,AL      ;Save the column size.

                MOV         AX,4000h        ;Write to the file
                MOV         BX,nHandle      ; pointed to by BX.
                LEA         DX,ColChg       ;Load the address of the data.
                MOV         CX,7            ;Load the length of the data.
                INT         21h             ;Write the data.

                DEC         nNColumns       ;Decrease the column counter by 1.
                CMP         nNColumns,0     ;See if we're finished.
                JNE         NextCol         ;If not, store some more.
```

9-2 Continued.

```
NoCols:         MOV        AX,4000h       ;Write to the file
                MOV        BX,nHandle     ; pointed to by BX.
                LEA        DX,RestHead    ;Load the address of the data.
                MOV        CX,RHeadLen    ;Load the length of the data.
                INT        21h            ;Write the data.

;*******************************************************************
;* This section of the code writes the actual data to the worksheet. *
;* In this example, we choose to ignore the data type returned by    *
;* Clipper and simply hardcode the type in.  A more generic example  *
;* would require that you add code to determine the correct data type *
;* and write this information as well.                               *
;*******************************************************************

                GetInt 6                  ;Retrieve the number of data entries.
   MOV nRecLen,AX ;Store it.

NextData:       MOV     AX,nRecLen        ;Store Current Array Index.
                PUSH    AX
                MOV     AX,5              ;Get the Data.
                PUSH    AX
                CALL    __parc
                ADD     SP,4
                PUSH    AX                ; Save the string offset.
                PUSH    DX                ; Save the Clipper DATA segment.

                MOV     AX,nRecLen        ;Store Current Array Index.
                PUSH    AX
                MOV     AX,5              ;Get the character string length.
                PUSH    AX
                CALL    __parclen
                ADD     SP,4
                MOV     CX,AX             ;Store number of bytes to move.
                ADD     AX,7              ;Add 7 to compensate for Null and position data.
                MOV     LblLen,AX         ;Save the string length.

                POP     DS                ; Point to the Clipper DATA segment.
                POP     SI                ; Point to the string.

                LEA     DI,LblData        ; Load the offset of the label data.
                REP     MOVSB             ; Move the string to our data segment.

                MOV     AX,@DATA          ;Point DS to our data segment.
                MOV     DS,AX
                MOV     BYTE PTR [DI],0      ; Null terminate the string.

                MOV     AX,nRecLen        ;Store Current Array Index.
                PUSH    AX
                MOV     AX,3              ;Get the data row.
                PUSH    AX
                CALL    __parni
```

```
        ADD     SP,4
        MOV     LblRow,AX

        MOV     AX,nRecLen      ;Store Current Array Index.
        PUSH    AX
        MOV     AX,4            ;Get the data column.
        PUSH    AX
        CALL    __parni
        ADD     SP,4
        MOV     LblCol,AX

        MOV     AX,4000h        ;Write to the file
        MOV     BX,nHandle      ; pointed to by BX.
        LEA     DX,LblEntry     ;Load the address of the data.
        MOV     CX,LblLen       ;Load the length of the data.
        ADD     CX,4            ;Offset for the data record header.
        INT     21h             ;Write the data.

        DEC     nRecLen         ;Go to the next entry.
        CMP     nRecLen,0       ;See if this was the last one.
        JNE     NextData        ;If not, go back to the beginning.

;**********************************************************************
;* This section of the code writes the end of file marker to the     *
;* worksheet.                                                         *
;**********************************************************************

        MOV     AX,4000h        ;Write to the file
        MOV     BX,nHandle      ; pointed to by BX.
        LEA     DX,EndIt        ;Load the address of the data.
        MOV     CX,4            ;Load the length of the data.
        INT     21h             ;Write the data.

;***********************************************************************
;* This section of the code closes the file and exits back to Clipper *
;***********************************************************************

        MOV     AX,3E00h        ;Close File.
        MOV     BX,nHandle      ;Load the file handle.
        INT     21h

        POP     SI              ;Restore SI.

        RET                     ;Return to Clipper.

ExpWKS  ENDP

;***********************************************************************
;* This procedure reads one entry from the WKS file.  It uses three    *
;* variables to define the entry.  The first variable, OpCode, defines *
;* the type of information that the entry contains.  Each OpCode type  *
;* for WKS files appears in LOTUS.INC.  The second entry contains the  *
;* length of the entry record.  This is the length of the data, not    *
```

9-2 Continued.

```
;* including the OpCode (always 2-bytes) or the record length (always  *
;* 2-bytes).  The third entry, Data, contains a variable length data   *
;* field.                                                             *
;*********************************************************************

ReadEntry      PROC   NEAR

DoRead:        MOV    AX,3F00h         ;Read some data from the file.
               MOV    BX,nHandle
               MOV    CX,04            ;4 bytes.
               LEA    DX,xEData        ;Load buffer location.
               INT    21h

               CMP    AX,0             ;See if we read anything.
               JNE    GoodRead         ;If successful, check the opcode.
               JMP    NoRead           ;If not, we're at the end of the file.

GoodRead:      MOV    AX,xEData        ;Move the opcode to AX.
               CMP    AX,Integer       ;Is it an integer?
               JE     StoreInt         ;If so, store it.
               CMP    AX,Number        ;Is it a floating point number?
               JE     StoreNum         ;If so, store it.
               CMP    AX,CLabel        ;Is it a string?
               JE     StoreStr         ;If so, store it.
               CMP    AX,Formula       ;Is it a formula?
               JE     StoreNum         ;If so, get the current value and store it.

               MOV    AX,3F00h         ;Otherwise, read again.
               MOV    BX,nHandle
               MOV    CX,xEData + 2    ;Load the number of data bytes.
               LEA    DX,xEData        ;Load buffer location.
               INT    21h
               JMP    DoRead           ;Check next entry.

StoreInt:      MOV    AX,3F00h         ;Read the data.
               MOV    BX,nHandle
               MOV    CX,xEData + 2    ;Load the number of data bytes.
               LEA    DX,xEData        ;Load buffer location.
               INT    21h

               MOV    AX,nRecLen       ;Select the current array element.
               PUSH   AX
               MOV    AX,5             ;Select the data array.
               PUSH   AX
               MOV    AX,xEData + 5    ;Store the data.
               PUSH   AX
               CALL   _storni          ;Send the data to Clipper.
               ADD    SP,6

               LEA CX,cIntType         ;Load the data type.
               JMP Common
```

```
StoreNum:       MOV     AX,3F00h        ;Read the data.
                MOV     BX,nHandle
                MOV     CX,xEData + 2   ;Load the number of data bytes.
                LEA     DX,xEData       ;Load buffer location.
                INT     21h

                MOV     AX,nRecLen      ;Select the current array element.
                PUSH    AX
                MOV     AX,5            ;Select the data array.
                PUSH    AX
                PUSH    WORD PTR (xEData+11)  ;Store the data.
                PUSH    WORD PTR (xEData+9)
                PUSH    WORD PTR (xEData+7)
                PUSH    WORD PTR (xEData+5)
                CALL    __stornd        ;Send the data to Clipper.
                ADD     SP,12

                LEA     CX,cNumType     ;Load the data type.
                JMP     Common

StoreStr:       MOV     AX,3F00h        ;Read the data.
                MOV     BX,nHandle
                MOV     CX,xEData + 2   ;Load the number of data bytes.
                LEA     DX,xEData       ;Load buffer location.
                INT     21h

                MOV     AX,nRecLen      ;Select the current array element.
                PUSH    AX
                MOV     AX,5            ;Select the data array.
                PUSH    AX
                MOV     DX,DS
                LEA     AX,xEData+5     ;Store the data pointer.
                PUSH    DX
                PUSH    AX
                CALL    __storc         ;Send the data to Clipper.
                ADD     SP,8

                LEA     CX,cStrType     ;Load the data type.

Common:         MOV     AX,nRecLen      ;Select the current array element.
                PUSH    AX
                MOV     AX,2            ;Select the Type array.
                PUSH    AX
                MOV     DX,DS           ;Save the Segment and offset of the
                MOV     AX,CX           ; type identifier.
                PUSH    DX
                PUSH    AX
                CALL    __storc         ;Send the type identifier to Clipper.
                ADD     SP,8

                MOV     AX,nRecLen      ;Select the current array element.
                PUSH    AX
                MOV     AX,4            ;Select the Column array.
                PUSH    AX
```

9-2 Continued.

```
                MOV     AX,xEData + 1 ;Store the column number.
                PUSH    AX
                CALL    __storni      ;Send the data to Clipper.
                ADD     SP,6

                MOV     AX,nRecLen    ;Select the current array element.
                PUSH    AX
                MOV     AX,3          ;Select the row array.
                PUSH    AX

                MOV     AX,xEData + 3 ;Store the row number.
                PUSH    AX
                CALL    __storni      ;Send the data to Clipper.
                ADD     SP,6

NoRead:         RET

ReadEntry       ENDP

END
```

As you can see, converting data between two disparate formats is no easy matter. There are several features you need to observe in the Clipper program. First, there are actually two different programs combined into one. The first program imports data from the sample worksheet, SAM PLE1.WKS. Creating a generic routine is an extremely complex process because you have to take so many different factors into account. In fact, trying to get any one client or set of clients to pay for such a routine might be difficult at best. This code shows a very specific routine for a very specific worksheet file format. In most cases you'll want to use the same type of routine in the interest of delivering a project on time and within budget.

One of the drawbacks of using assembly language to convert data is that it doesn't handle floating-point numbers very well unless you have a math coprocessor available. The routine I created for this chapter doesn't make that assumption.

There are two alternatives to using a math coprocessor. You can either create the floating-point emulation routines by hand, a very time-consuming process, or you can allow Clipper to perform the floating-point math for you, which is much slower than using assembler. In this case I've used the native Clipper floating-point support to convert the date from spreadsheet format to Clipper format. This involves a lot of floating-point division. Clipper stores the date differently than a spreadsheet does. The spreadsheet in this instance stores the date as the number of days since 01/01/1900. The function, CalcDate( ), converts the number stored by the spreadsheet into a Clipper date by performing various divisions and placing the results into strings that equate to year, month, and day. By combining the date into a string, you can convert the result into an actual Clipper date.

The assembly code shown in FIG. 9-2 contains two main and one ancillary functions. The first function imports the data. Notice that I've kept only the actual data and discarded almost everything else. A more detailed routine might use this data to enhance the quality of the information presented to Clipper. For example, you could use query ranges and other tabular information to set up similar ranges in Clipper. This would allow you to perform an analysis similar to that performed within the original worksheet.

In addition, you could convert the graph information into a format that Clipper can use. Using graphics routines you could display the data on screen using the same graph format used by the worksheet. One way this is practical is that the worksheet can perform the original analysis on a lot of small files, and then use a database manager to combine all the small files into one large database. You could then display the result using a graph that looks the same as the worksheet original.

Notice that I use a local procedure to actually read a cell. Because the cells are variable length, you can't even be sure that they will contain data. Performing the reads in this manner is more efficient than using a much longer in-line routine. In essence, you strip off the header of the worksheet file, convert the data to a form usable by Clipper, and store the result in an array. You then transfer the array to Clipper for further processing. As additional information, you can tell Clipper where the data was originally located in the worksheet and what its original format was.

The reason that you have to tell Clipper where the data was originally located is to compensate for blank cells. Remember that the worksheet doesn't store unformatted blank cells. Also, unlike DBF files, one cell in a column can contain numbers, while the very next cell could contain a string. This is an important consideration when you attempt to create a database file structure to match the worksheet.

Creating the export routine

The export routine is the most complex of all the routines presented in this chapter. A spreadsheet file, like a DBF file, requires a considerable amount of information to work properly. However, as you can see, a WKS file contains a lot more information than a DBF file. All the fields shown in the header section of the data segment must appear in the resulting WKS file or the spreadsheet program will report an error. Of course, all these parameters provide you with ample methods of enhancing the output created by your program. For the purpose of this example, all I'll do is create a generic header, tell the spreadsheet to use specific column widths, and then output the data in SAMPLE1.DBF to SAMPLE2.WKS as strings. Notice that, like the import routine, the export routine is designed to work with a specific database file format. Creating a generic export routine is easier than creating a generic import routine, but still very time-consuming.

Summary

This chapter shows you some of the basics of importing and exporting data in Clipper. While the routines provided don't address the diversity of file formats available, they do provide you with the principles involved in creating your own import and export routines. Of course, the major hurdle in creating any conversion routine is deciphering the file format of the foreign file. Without this information, any attempt to decipher a file will be futile.

10

Creating add-on libraries for Clipper

Once you start to accumulate a large number of external routines for your Clipper programs, you'll also want to find a way to manage them. It's much easier to remember that a specific function is located in a certain library than to remember where you put the object module. Even worse, recompiling all the object modules you require for every program would consume a lot of time.

Placing the object modules in a library and placing the library in your library directory wouldn't consume any time at all after you did it the first time. This is especially true of external routines. While your code generator might work fine for creating the Clipper-specific routines that you use for every program, you'll still have to go back to the DOS prompt in order to compile or assemble your external routines. Using libraries relieves you of this task.

Libraries are useful for other reasons than just saving time and energy. If you're working on a group project, they can provide one of the only methods of keeping everyone up-to-date. Checking for one library and making sure that it's up-to-date is fairly simple. You could even pass the time and date of the most current library via an e-mail system to everyone concerned. Checking for the 50 object modules that the library contains and making certain they're all current is more difficult. Someone would have to perform the time-consuming task of going through, machine by machine, to update everyone. As you can see, a library simply provides a package for your object modules and makes them easier to manage.

The following sections describe what you need in order to create and maintain libraries for your Clipper programs. They provide you with everything you need to know, including a sample procedure. This book uses the Microsoft library manager. The instructions for library managers created by other vendors might vary from the ones included here.

Understanding the library manager

Exactly what is a library manager? Many programmers know only that libraries are what you receive with your programming language, and that you need to include them on the command line to use certain functions within a program. A library manager creates the library file, adds and deletes object modules, and provides the means for listing the library contents. In most cases, this task is accomplished using a very simple set of commands. TABLE 10-1 provides a listing of these commands and describes what task they perform.

Table 10-1 Microsoft Library Manager commands and switches

Command	Description
Switches	
/? or /HELP or /H	Use any of these commmand line switches to display the LIB command options. /? displays the short help screen, while /H and /HELP display the detailed help screen.
/IGNORECASE	This command line switch tell LIB to ignore case on names. Because Clipper converts all external procedure names to uppercase, you might need to use this switch with some libraries using specific linkers. You do not need to use it with the standard Microsoft linker, RTLink, or Blinker.
/NOEXTDICTIONARY	Library files normally contain two dictionaries (indexes). The first dictionary lists the public symbols in alphabetical order and follows the public symbol name with the object module in which it appears. The second dictionary lists the object modules in alphabetical order and follows them with the public symbol names contained in that object. This option tells LIB that you do not want to build an extended dictionary. The automatic default is to build one. While adding the extended dictionary does increase the size of the library file, it decreases link time.

Command	Description
/NOIGNORECASE	This command line switch tells LIB not to ignore case on names.
/NOLOGO	Use this command line switch to inhibit the signon banner from appearing when using the LIB command. This is useful in batch operations.
/PAGESIZE:n	The library page size is the amount of memory set aside for each set library page in the file. You must specify a value between 16 and 32,768 bytes that is a power of 2. If you have a lot of small objects, then using a large value will waste space. Using a small value with large object files will increase linking time. Use a value that most closely represents the size of your object modules. To determine the correct page size, divide the average size object module that you want to include by 2.

Commands	
+name	Use the + command to add an object file to the library. If the object module does not exist in the current directory and you do not specify a path, the command will fail.
-name	This command deletes an object file from the library. It does not place a copy of the object file on disk before destroying it in the library.
-+name	Use this command to replace the specified object file contained in the library with one on disk. If the object module does not exist in the current directory and you do not specify a path, the command will fail.
*name	This command copies (extracts) an object file from the library file and places it in the current directory. The contents of the library file are unaffected.

Table 10-1 Continued.

Command	Description
-*name	Use this command to move (delete and extract) object file from a library file. This command places a copy of the object file on disk before destroying it in the library.

As you can see, the list of commands for the library manager isn't very long. Each command appears to perform a specific task related to the library as a whole. Even the combination commands appear straightforward and easy to use. And that's the point of using a library manager. It allows you to combine all the object modules that you're using into an easy-to-use package without expending a lot of energy in the process. A library manager manages your code; it doesn't let the code manage you.

While using libraries might be a nice addition to the single-programmer environment, it's absolutely essential for the work-group environment. Using libraries allows each member of the programming team to deliver his part of the code in an easy-to-use package. No longer do you need to worry if a link error message is due to not having all the parts. Another feature of using this approach is that you don't end up with a lot of out-of-date object modules, or source code sitting on individual hard disks or the network. Because every programmer delivers a single library, it's easy to check the date on the library to make certain that each member has the most up-to-date copy. Ultimately, this means that you'll have less errors caused by one programmer using an old copy of someone else's code as the baseline for his code.

Using the library manager

Creating and modifying the contents of a library is a fairly simple task. All you need to do is create your external routines, debug them, and place the object modules for any external routines in a library using the library manager. The Clipper program shown in FIG. 10-1 is typical of the programs created throughout the book. Figure 10-2 shows the assembly-language source code for the example. It differs from the other assembly examples because I've mixed a variety of public and private symbols throughout the source code.

Once you compile the code, you can use the library manager to create a library by typing LIB SOMELIB PROG11x.OBJ;. Notice that the library appears to consume more space than the object module does. This is one of the trade-offs that you need to consider when deciding to use libraries. In most cases, the extra space used by the library is worth the advantages

10-1 Using libraries example, Clipper source

```
// Program Number 11 - Library Example
// This program is used with Chapter 10 to demostrate the way to use
// libraries with your Clipper programs.  To link this program with the
// external routines contained in PROG11A.ASM, you place the external
// routines in a library, then call the linker using RTLink FI PROG11
// LIB SOMELIB.  This program also shows how to create a Gregorian to
// Julian format converter.
// Written by: John Mueller
// Copyright 1991 John Mueller - Tab Books

local dSomeDate := ctod("01/01/91"),;
      cNewDate := space(4)

// Display the background screen.

set scoreboard off
set color to "W+/B, RG+/R"
cls
@ 01, 00 to 24, 79 double
@ 02, 01 say padc(" Library Example - Date Conversion ", 78, chr(177))
@ 03, 01 to 03, 78 double

// Get a date from the user.

@ 04, 02 say "Enter a date: " get dSomeDate
read

// Convert it to Julian format.

if JDate(dSomeDate, @cNewDate)
   @ 05, 02 say "Date Conversion Successful"
   @ 06, 02 say "Julian Date Is: " + cNewDate
else
   @ 05, 02 say "Bad Input Data"
endif

// Wait for the user to press a key.

@ 23, 02 say "Press any key when ready..."
inkey(0)

// Clear the display and exit to DOS.

set color to "W/N, N/W"
cls
return
```

of convenient object-module management. Also notice that the object filename doesn't contain a dash. You can't use this character in filenames that you want to add to the library. The library manager will exit saying it can't find the object module.

```
;*************************************************************************
;* Program Number 11 - Library Example                                   *
;* This example is used in conjunction with the text in Chapter 10 to    *
;* show you how to create a library from your external routines and      *
;* Clipper object files.  It also shows you how to create a Gregorian    *
;* date format to Julian date format converter.                          *
;* Written by: John Mueller                                              *
;* Copyright 1991 John Mueller - Tab Books                               *
;*************************************************************************

;*************************************************************************
;* Make any required declarations.                                       *
;*************************************************************************

.MODEL LARGE

INCLUDE EXTASM.INC
INCLUDE MACROS.INC

PUBLIC JDate, HexConv

;*************************************************************************
;* Declare any required variables.                                       *
;*************************************************************************

.DATA

DateStr     DB 8  DUP (' ')         ; Input String Holder.
Error       DB 0                    ;Error Code for Bad Input.
cCDate      DB 5 DUP (0)            ;Converted Date Number.
nMonth      DW 0,31,59,90,120,151,181,212,243,273,304,334
cZero       DB '0'

.CODE

;*************************************************************************
;* Beginning of main procedure.  This procedure accepts the input from   *
;* Clipper and converts it to a Julian date by passing it through        *
;* several levels of conversion.                                         *
;*************************************************************************

JDate       PROC    FAR

            PUSH    SI  ;Save SI.

;*************************************************************************
;* Check the integrity of the data passed from Clipper to this           *
;* procedure.  Place the passed value in a local variable if it's the    *
;* correct type.  Remember that Clipper passes dates as strings in the   *
;* format YYYYMMDD instead of actual dates.                              *
;*************************************************************************
```

```
        PCount    ;Check the number of parameters.
        CMP    AX,0        ;If there aren't any, exit.
        JE     NoParms

        IsChar 1          ; Check the first parameter to see if
        JZ  NoParms       ; it's a character.  If not exit.

        GetDate1          ; Get the first date parameter.
        PUSH   AX         ; Save the string offset.
        PUSH   DX         ; Save the Clipper DATA segment.

        POP    DS         ; Point to the Clipper DATA segment.
        POP    SI         ; Point to the string.

        MOV    AX,@DATA   ; Point to our data segment.
        MOV    ES,AX
        LEA    DI,DateStr ; Load the offset of SomeStr.
        REP    MOVSB      ; Move the string to our data segment.

        PUSH   ES         ; Point DS to our data segment.
        POP    DS
        JMP    GoodData   ;Start the conversion.

NoParms:  RetFalse
          JMP    Exit

GoodData: RetTrue

;**********************************************************************
;* This section of the code converts the date string we recieved from  *
;* Clipper to a Julian date representation.  First, it takes the year  *
;* directly from the input string and places it in the output string.  *
;* It then converts the month to a number and finds the equivalent     *
;* number of days in a translation table.  Finally, it converts the    *
;* current day into a number and adds the number of days for the month.*
;* This results in the final output of the year plus then number of    *
;* days from 01/01.  The resulting string is in the format YDDD.       *
;**********************************************************************

      LEA    SI,DateStr            ;Load the location of the passed parameter.
      MOV    AL,BYTE PTR [SI+3]    ;Get the current year number.
      MOV    cCDate,AL             ;Store the year.

      MOV    AH,BYTE PTR [SI+4]    ;Load the month high byte.
      MOV    AL,BYTE PTR [SI+5]    ;Load the month low byte.
      CALL   MToNum                ;Convert it to a number.
      LEA    BX,nMonth             ;Point to our translation table.
      DEC    AX                    ;Offset for 0 start in translate table.
      SHL    AX,1
      MOV    DI,AX                 ;Move value to an index register.
      MOV    AX,[BX+DI]            ;Convert the month number into days.
      PUSH   AX                    ;Save the number of days.
```

10-2 Continued.

```
        MOV     AH,BYTE PTR [SI+6]     ;Load the day high byte.
        MOV     AL,BYTE PTR [SI+7]     ;Load the day low byte.
        CALL    MToNum                 ;Convert it to a number

        POP     BX                     ;Restore the number of month days.
        ADD     AX,BX                  ;Add the number of month days.

        LEA     DI,cCDate              ;Load the address of the date string.
        INC     DI                     ;Point to the end.
        INC     DI
        INC     DI
        CALL    HexConv                ;Convert the number of days since 01/01
                                       ; to a string.

        LEA     AX,cCDate              ;Load the address of the date string.
        DEC     DI                     ;Move to the first non-empty string position.
DoZero: MOV BX,DI                      ;Store the value of DI for comparison.
        CMP     AX,BX                  ;See if we need to add zeros to the string.
        JE      NoZero                 ;If not, exit.
        MOV     DL,cZero               ;Load a zero character.
        MOV     [DI],DL                ;Add a zero the current position.
        DEC     DI                     ;Point to the next position.
        JMP     DoZero

;************************************************************************
;* This section of the code stores the date in Clipper, restores any    *
;* required registers, and returns control back to the calling          *
;* procedure.                                                           *
;************************************************************************

NoZero: StorChar        2, cCDate      ;Return the converted date.

Exit:   POP             SI

        RET

JDate   ENDP

;************************************************************************
;* The whole purpose of this procedure is to convert a character to its*
;* numeric representation.                                              *
;************************************************************************

CToNum      PROC    NEAR

            SUB     AL,30h ;Convert the character to a number

            RET

CToNum      ENDP

;************************************************************************
;* This procedure recieves a two digit character-based number.  It      *
;* accepts the characters and converts them to a numeric                *
```

```
;* representation.  The low byte is passed in AL, the high byte in AH. *
;* The procedure passes the output back through AX.                     *
;***********************************************************************

MToNum      PROC    NEAR

            PUSH    AX      ;Save the current contents of AX on the stack.
            MOV     AL,AH   ;Move the high byte to AL.
            CALL    CToNum  ;Convert it to a number.
            MOV     CL,10   ;Multiply by 10.
            MUL     CL
            MOV     BX,AX   ;Save the tens value.
            POP     AX      ;Restore the ones value.
            XOR     AH,AH   ;Zero the tens value.
            CALL    CToNum  ;Convert it to a number.
            ADD     AX,BX   ;Add the tens value back in.

            RET

MToNum      ENDP

;***********************************************************************
;* This procedure converts a hexidecimal number to a decimal character*
;* equivalent.  AX contains the number to convert and DI the address   *
;* of the end of a storage buffer on entry.  The procedure does not    *
;* return a value.                                                     *
;***********************************************************************

HexConv     PROC    NEAR

            MOV     CX,10   ;Load divisor.
DoDiv:      XOR     DX,DX   ;Clear DX.
            DIV     CX      ;Divide AX by 10
            ADD     DX,30h  ;Change remainder to char.
            MOV     [DI],DL;Store the number.
            DEC     DI      ;Point to next number.
            CMP     AX,9    ;See if we need to divide.
            JG      DoDiv
            ADD     AX,30h  ;Change quotient to char.
            MOV     [DI],AL;Store the number.

            RET             ;Return to the calling procedure.

HexConv     ENDP

END
```

Now that you have a library, there are several things you can do with the library manager to make using it easier. For example, if you type LIB SOMELIB ,SOMELIB.DOC;, you'll see a new file, SOMELIB.DOC, containing a listing of the public symbols in your library. Notice that the LIB program places copies of both dictionaries in the file. In addition, observe that none of the private symbols appear in the listing. This shows another useful function for libraries. You can use them as a means for listing public symbols, while keeping private symbols hidden. Figure 10-3 contains a listing of the document created for SOMELIB.

As the listing in FIG. 10-3 shows, maintaining a listing of the library is a useful way of keeping track of the current library status. Of course, this is simply another way to manage your data. While the library manager provides a complete set of functions, the actual number of functions that you'll use from the library manager's repertoire is limited to those that add objects, list the contents of the library, and extract objects. There are times where you'll use the other functions, but these three are the most commonly used.

10-3 Library module listing

```
HEXCONV...........progl1a            JDATE.............progl1a

progl1a             Offset: 00000010H   Code and data size: 1caH
  HEXCONV             JDATE
```

Summary

This chapter provides you with an overview of what a library is. It emphasizes the importance of managing your code efficiently and explains how the library manager helps you do this. The programming example shows you how to create an object module, include it in a library, then see what your library contains at a later date without looking up the source code.

11
Using a mouse with Clipper

The graphical user interface (GUI), complete with mouse support and icons, is the rule of the day when it comes to creating user-friendly programs. One look at the success enjoyed by Windows and other GUI environments only serves to illustrate the need for this type of interface on most programs. Clipper provides many of the primitives required to create text mode GUI-like displays, but none of the required mouse interface. This chapter shows you how to create and implement these routines in three scenarios: the menu, the data-entry screen, and the print-routine display. By using these scenarios as background information, you can create a mouse interface for almost any display situation imaginable.

Using mouse services

There's no mouse support automatically provided on computers. Neither the ROM BIOS or DOS come with built-in mouse support. You must load this support as an extension to DOS through either a mouse driver in CONFIG.SYS or a command in AUTOEXEC.BAT. In fact, the mouse driver is a perfect example of an interrupt-driven, user-extendable program.

This particular driver allows you to create two types of extensions. The first type is a standard polling routine. You check the status of the mouse from time to time for movement and button presses. If there's a change in status, then you change the display appropriately. This is no different than putting a clock display in your menu loop or polling the communications port for data. The second type is event driven. You add an event driver to the mouse driver, in effect extending the DOS extension. This allows you to run your program without ever checking for mouse movement or button presses. Whenever an event occurs, the mouse driver automatically calls your routine and allows it to service the mouse.

An event-driven routine is much faster and more flexible than a standard polling routine. It has all the advantages of creating an interrupt-driven clock routine, for example. Unfortunately, it is also a bit harder to create. In many ways an event driver is even more difficult to create than a memory-resident program or an interrupt-driven program because it uses elements of both. For the purposes of this book, I'll concentrate on the first method of servicing the mouse, polling the mouse driver.

Because there are no written standards for supporting a mouse, there's a tendency to think that each mouse interface is different. However, no matter which vendor you choose, they all use approximately the same set of routines at the same interrupt to support the mouse. While you might occasionally find a difference in implementation, most mouse drivers expect and return the same parameters for a given service. The following section describes the services provided by a standard mouse driver.

Reset mouse and get status (interrupt 33H service 00H)

This service checks for the existence of a mouse. If the mouse exists, it identifies the number of mouse buttons and disables any memory-resident user handlers for mouse events. In addition, it initializes the mouse as follows:

- Places the mouse in the center of the display.
- Sets the mouse pointer display page to zero.
- Hides the mouse pointer.
- Sets the mouse pointer shape to an arrow for graphics mode and a block cursor for text mode.
- Disables the user mouse event handler.
- Enables mouse emulation of a light pen.
- Sets the horizontal mickey-to-pixel ratio at 8 to 8. Sets the vertical mickey-to-pixel ratio at 16 to 8.
- Sets the double-speed threshold to 64 mickeys per second.
- Sets the minimum and maximum horizontal and vertical pointer position limits to include the entire screen in the current display mode.

You must use this service before using any of the other mouse services. Failing to use this service might result in program failure because the mouse is not in a known state.

Register contents on entry:	
AX	0

Register contents on exit:	
AX	Status
	0000h - Mouse not available
	FFFFh - Mouse available
BX	Number of mouse buttons

Show mouse pointer (interrupt 33H service 01H)

This service displays the mouse pointer on screen. The mouse driver maintains a counter for the mouse pointer. Each time you hide the mouse, the driver decrements the counter by one. If the counter is negative, the driver increments the pointer each time you use this service. The mouse driver displays the mouse pointer when the counter contains a value of zero.

If you use services 07h or 08h (Set horizontal limits for pointer or Set vertical limits for pointer) to change the pointer limits, the mouse driver will display the mouse pointer within this defined area. If you use service 10h (Set mouse pointer exclusion area) to hide the mouse pointer, calling this service will display the mouse pointer.

Register contents on entry:	
AX	1

Hide mouse pointer (interrupt 33H service 02H)

This service removes the mouse pointer from the screen. The mouse driver continues to track the mouse position and performs any other requested mouse function. The mouse driver maintains a counter for the mouse pointer. Each time you hide the mouse, the driver decrements the counter by one. If the pointer is negative, the driver increments the counter each time you use service 01h to display the mouse. The mouse driver displays the mouse pointer when the counter contains a value of zero.

Use this service before changing any area of the screen that contains the mouse pointer. This prevents the mouse pointer from interfering with a newly displayed screen. In some cases, the mouse driver will leave a gap where the mouse pointer appeared when you move the mouse.

Register contents on entry:
AX 2

Get mouse position and button status (interrupt 33H service 03H)

This service returns the current horizontal and vertical coordinates of the mouse position along with the status of the left, right, and center mouse buttons for a three-button mouse. It returns the status of only the left and right mouse buttons for a two-button mouse. For example, if BX contains 4 on return, that means the user pressed the center mouse button.

This service always returns the mouse position in pixels. It uses the upper left corner of the display as a reference point (0, 0). The CX and DX coordinates refer to the virtual mouse screen and *not* to the text screen. To convert the virtual mouse screen coordinates to text screen coordinates, divide the coordinates by the character block size. For example, if CX returns 18, DX returns 64, and the character block size is 9 by 16, then the character position is 2, 4.

Register contents on entry:
AX 3

Register contents on exit:

BX	Mouse button status (bits true when set)
	0 - Left button down
	1 - Right button down
	2 - Center button down
	3 through 15 - Reserved (0)
CX	Horizontal (X) coordinate in pixels
DX	Vertical (Y) coordinate in pixels

Set mouse pointer position (interrupt 33H service 04H)

This service displays the mouse at a new horizontal and vertical position. The limits defined by services 07h and 08h (Set horizontal Limits for pointer and Set vertical limits for pointer) affect the mouse position. If you specify a mouse position outside the defined limits, the mouse driver automatically adjusts the requested position to the nearest limit. For example, if you set the maximum horizontal position to 85 and then use this service to place the mouse pointer at a horizontal position of 90, the mouse pointer will appear at the maximum horizontal position of 85.

Always provide the mouse position in pixels. The mouse driver uses the upper left corner of the display as a reference point (0, 0). The coordinates refer to the virtual screen mouse coordinates and *not* to the text screen coordinates. To convert the text screen coordinates to the virtual mouse screen coordinates, multiply the character position by the character block size. For example, if you want to position the mouse at row 8 column 20 and the display uses a character block size of 8 by 16, then CX contains 160 and DX contains 128.

The only time this service fails is if you fail to reset the mouse using service 00h (Reset mouse and get status) or call service 21h (Reset mouse driver). You can't see the results of this service if you haven't called service 01h (Show mouse pointer), hid the cursor using service 02h (Hide mouse pointer), or positioned the mouse pointer in an area defined by service 10h (Set mouse pointer exclusion area).

Register contents on entry:

AX	4
CX	Horizontal (X) coordinate in pixels
DX	Vertical (Y) coordinate in pixels

Get button-press information (interrupt 33H service 05H)

This service returns the status of the mouse buttons. In addition, it returns the number of presses and last position for the requested mouse button. BX determines which button this service checks. If BX is 0, then this service checks the left button. If BX is 1 or 2, this service checks the right or center buttons. The button-press value can range from 0 to 65,535. This service will not detect the overflow if you press the mouse button more than 65,535 times.

The values for the horizontal and vertical coordinates refer to the mouse pointer's position at the time the user presses a mouse button, not the current location of the mouse pointer. This service automatically resets the number of button presses for the requested button to zero. Use this service to detect user double-clicks on menu items or other areas of the display.

Register contents on entry:

AX	5
BX	Button 0 - Left button 1 - Right button 2 - Center button

Register contents on exit:

AX	Mouse button status (bits true when set)
	0 - Left button down
	1 - Right button down
	2 - Center button down
	3 through 15 - Reserved (0)
BX	Button press counter
CX	Horizontal (X) coordinate in pixels
DX	Vertical (Y) coordinate in pixels

Get button-release information (interrupt 33H service 06H)

This service returns the status of the mouse buttons. In addition, it returns the number of releases and last position for the requested mouse button. BX determines which button this service checks. If BX is 0, then this service checks the left button. If BX is 1 or 2, this service checks the right or center buttons. The button-press value can range from 0 to 65,535. This service will not detect the overflow if you press the mouse button more than 65,535 times.

The values for the horizontal and vertical coordinates refer to the mouse pointer's position at the time the user pressed a mouse button, not the current location of the mouse pointer. This service automatically resets the number of button releases for the requested button to zero. Use this service to detect user double-clicks on menu items or other areas of the display.

Register contents on entry:

AX	6
BX	Button
	0 - Left button
	1 - Right button
	2 - Center button

Register contents on exit:

AX	Mouse button status (bits true when set)
	0 - Left button down
	1 - Right button down
	2 - Center button down
	3 through 15 - Reserved (0)
BX	Button release counter
CX	Horizontal (X) coordinate in pixels
DX	Vertical (Y) coordinate in pixels

Set horizontal limits for pointer (interrupt 33H service 07H)

This service sets the minimum and maximum horizontal limits of mouse movement within the display area. If you specify a minimum limit greater than the maximum limit, this service will interchange the two values. The mouse driver automatically repositions the mouse pointer to fall within the specified horizontal limits. Use this service to provide windowing capabilities for the mouse.

Register contents on entry:

AX	7
CX	Minimum (X) coordinate in pixels
DX	Maximum (X) coordinate in pixels

Set vertical limits for pointer (interrupt 33H service 08H)

This service sets the minimum and maximum vertical limits of mouse movement within the display area. If you specify a minimum limit greater than the maximum limit, this service will interchange the two values. The mouse driver automatically repositions the mouse pointer to fall within the specified vertical limits. Use this service to provide windowing capabilities for the mouse.

Register contents on entry:

AX	8
CX	Minimum (Y) coordinate in pixels
DX	Maximum (Y) coordinate in pixels

Set graphics pointer shape (interrupt 33H service 09H)

This service defines the mouse pointer shape and hot spot in graphics mode. It does not affect the text mode pointer. To display the mouse pointer, you need to use service 01h (Show mouse pointer).

The image pointer buffer consists of two 32-byte sections for a total length of 64 bytes. The first 32-byte section contains a bit image that the mouse driver combines with the screen image using AND. The second 32-byte section contains a bit image that the mouse driver combines with the screen image using XOR.

The mouse driver uses the hot spot to determine mouse position during a button press. The mouse pointer hot spot values can range from 16 to –16. The mouse driver uses the upper left corner (0, 0) of the mouse pointer bit map as the reference point for the hot spot. You must use an even value for the horizontal hot spot offset in display modes 4 and 5.

Register contents on entry:	
AX	9
BX	Hot spot offset from left
CX	Hot spot offset from top
DX	Offset of pointer image buffer
DS	Segment of pointer image buffer

Set text pointer type (interrupt 33H service 0AH)

This service defines the mouse pointer shape and attributes in text mode. It does not affect the graphics mode cursor. You can choose two types of text cursors: software and hardware.

The software cursor does not have a shape of its own. Instead, it uses one of the 256 ASCII characters to define its shape. Just like the graphics cursor, you define both AND and XOR mask values. In addition to shape, you define the foreground and background colors, intensity, and underscoring. The mask values in CX and DX use bits 0–7 for the character value, 8–10 for the foreground color, 11 for intensity, 12–14 for the background color, and 15 for blink.

The hardware cursor appears as a block. The block width depends on the display mode you use. The block height and position on the display line depend on the value contained in the CX and DX registers. CX contains the starting scan line and DX contains the ending scan line. The maximum scan line value depends on the display mode. For example, if the current display mode uses a 9 by 16 character and you want to center a block cursor on the display, you could set CX to 1 and DX to 14. The scan line count always begins with zero for the bottom line.

Register contents on entry:	
AX	Ah
BX	Pointer type 0 - Software cursor 1 - Hardware cursor
CX	AND mask value (BX = 0), start line (BX = 1)
DX	XOR mask value (BX = 0), end line (BX = 1)

Read mouse motion counters (interrupt 33H service 0BH)

This service returns the horizontal and vertical movement of the mouse movement (measured in mickeys) since the last call. A positive value shows movement right or downwards; a negative value shows movement left or upwards. The mickey count always ranges from −32768 to 32767. This service won't detect an overflow if the mickey count exceeds these values. One mickey represents 1/200 inch mouse movement.

Register contents on entry:

AX	Bh

Register contents on exit:

CX	Horizontal (X) mickey count
DX	Vertical (Y) mickey count

Set user-defined mouse event handler (interrupt 33H service 0CH)

This service changes the address and event mask used by the mouse driver each time a mouse event occurs. The mask points to the user-defined handler for the specified mouse events. For example, if CX contains 1, then the mouse driver calls the user- defined handler every time the user moves the mouse. The mouse driver still reports events not handled by the user-defined handler. You must use service 0 to disable the user-defined handler.

When the mouse driver passes control to the user-defined handler, it makes a far call. Therefore, the user-defined handler must contain procedures using far returns. The mouse driver also fills the registers with specific information before it calls the user-defined handler. AX contains the mouse event flags. The flags appear in the same order as the event mask used to set up the user-defined handler. BX contains the button state. Bit 0 defines the left button, bit 1 defines the right button, and bit 2 defines the center button. CX contains the horizontal (X) pointer coordinate. DX contains the vertical (Y) pointer coordinate. SI contains the last raw vertical mickey count. DI contains the last raw horizontal mickey count. Finally, DS contains the mouse driver data segment.

Note: You must know how to create interrupt-driven programs before using this service. The user-defined handler uses the same techniques applied to memory-resident interrupt driven programs.

Register contents on entry:

AX	Ch
CX	Event mask (bit selected if set) 0 - Mouse movement 1 - Left button press 2 - Left button release 3 - Right button press

4 - Right button release
5 - Middle button press
6 - Middle button release
7 through 15 - Reserved (0)

DX Offset of user-defined handler
ES Segment of user-defined handler

Turn on light-pen emulation (interrupt 33H service 0DH)

This service lets the mouse emulate a light pen. You simulate pushing the pen against the screen by pressing both the left and right mouse buttons (for a three-button mouse) or both buttons (for a two-button mouse). When you release either mouse button, the pen is off the screen.

Register contents on entry:
AX Dh

Turn off light-pen emulation (interrupt 33H service 0EH)

This service disables light-pen emulation. If a program can use both a light pen and a mouse, you must disable the light-pen emulation for the program to work correctly.

Register contents on entry:
AX Eh

Set mickey-to-pixel ratio (interrupt 33H service 0FH)

This service sets the mickey-to-pixel ratio for horizontal and vertical mouse movement. The ratio determines the number of mickeys for every eight virtual-screen pixels. One mickey represents 1/200 inch of mouse travel.

The default value for the horizontal ratio is 8 mickeys to 8 virtual-screen pixels. The default value for the vertical ratio is 16 mickeys to 8 virtual-screen pixels. The mickey-to-pixel ratio can range from 1 to 32767. You can also set the mickey-to-pixels ratio using service 1Ah (Set mouse sensitivity).

Register contents on entry:

AX	Fh
CX	Horizontal mickeys (range 1 - 32,767, default 8)
DX	Vertical mickeys (range 1 - 32,767, default 16)

Set mouse pointer exclusion area (interrupt 33H service 10H)

This service defines an area where the mouse pointer won't appear on the screen. To redisplay the mouse pointer in the area defined by this service, you need to call service 00h (Reset mouse and get status) or 01h (Show cursor). You can disable the exclusion area by making a second call to this service. One use for this service is to help the user determine the availability of menu selections or usability of a screen area.

Register contents on entry:

AX	10h
CX	Upper left X coordinate
DX	Upper left Y coordinate
SI	Lower right X coordinate
DI	Lower right Y coordinate

Set double speed-threshold (interrupt 33H service 13H)

This service sets the threshold speed for doubling the movement of the mouse pointer. The threshold lets you define how fast you can move the mouse before the speed of the mouse pointer doubles. The default threshold is 64 mickeys per second.

This service makes it easier for you to move the mouse pointer long distances across the screen. You can also set the threshold speed using service 1Ah (Set mouse sensitivity).

Register contents on entry:

AX	13h
DX	Threshold speed in mickeys per second

Swap user-defined mouse event handlers (interrupt 33H service 14H)

This service changes the address and event mask used by the mouse driver each time a mouse event occurs. It returns the address of the previous event handler. The mask points to the user-defined handler for the specified mouse events. For example, if CX contains 1, then the mouse driver calls the user-defined handler every time the user moves the mouse. The mouse driver still reports events not handled by the user-defined handler. You must use service 0 to disable the user-defined handler. In essence, this service allows you to use more than one user-defined event handler, even though you can use only one at a time.

When the mouse driver passes control to the user-defined handler, it makes a far call. Therefore, the user-defined handler must contain procedures using far returns. The mouse driver also fills the registers with specific information before it calls the user-defined handler. AX contains the mouse event flags. The flags appear in the same order as the event mask used to setup the user-defined handler. BX contains the button state. Bit 0 defines the left button, bit 1 defines the right button, and bit 2 defines the center button. CX contains the horizontal (X) pointer coordinate. DX contains the vertical (Y) pointer coordinate. SI contains the last raw vertical mickey count. DI contains the last raw horizontal mickey count. Finally, DS contains the mouse driver data segment.

Register contents on entry:

AX	14h
CX	Event mask (bit selected if set)
	0 - Mouse movement
	1 - Left button press
	2 - Left button release
	3 - Right button press
	4 - Right button release
	5 - Middle button press
	6 - Middle button release
	7 through 15 - Reserved (0)
DX	Offset of user-defined handler
ES	Segment of user-defined handler

Register contents on exit:

CX	Previous event mask
DX	Offset of previous user-defined handler
ES	Segment of previous user-defined handler

Get mouse save state buffer size (interrupt 33H service 15H)

This service gets the buffer size required to store the current mouse driver state. You would use this service with service 16h (Save mouse driver state) and service 17h (Restore mouse driver state). These three services let you temporarily interrupt your program and run another program that also uses a mouse. If you temporarily exit a program and run another program that uses a mouse, the mouse might not work correctly with the second program.

Using these three services involves a two-step process. First, use service 15h (Get mouse save state buffer size) to determine if you have enough space to store the mouse driver state. Next, use service 16h (Save mouse driver state) to place the mouse driver state in the buffer. Then turn control of the mouse over to the other program. Once the second program returns control to the first program, use service 17h (Restore mouse driver state) to regain control of the mouse again.

Register contents on entry:

AX	15h

Register contents on exit:

BX	Buffer size in bytes

Save mouse driver state (interrupt 33H service 16H)

This service stores the current mouse driver state. Use this service with service 15h (Get mouse save state buffer size) and service 17h (Restore mouse driver state). Always call this service before you execute a child process using interrupt 21h service 4Bh. These three services let you temporarily interrupt your program and run another program that also uses a mouse. Just keep in mind that, if you temporarily exit a program and run another program that uses a mouse, the mouse might not work correctly with the second program.

Using these three services involves a two-step process. First, use service 15h (Get mouse save state buffer size) to determine if you have enough space to store the mouse driver state. Next, use service 16h (Save mouse driver state) to place the mouse driver state in the buffer. Then turn control of the mouse over to the other program. Once the second program returns control to the first program, use service 17h (Restore mouse driver state) to regain control of the mouse again.

Note: No documented standard exists for the format of the buffer used to store the mouse data. In fact, its format varies from vendor to vendor.

Register contents on entry:

AX	16h
DX	Buffer offset
ES	Buffer segment

Restore mouse driver state (interrupt 33H service 17H)

This service restores the current mouse driver state. Use this service with service 15h (Get mouse save state buffer size) and service 16h (Save mouse driver state). Always use this service immediately after a child process returns control of the mouse to the parent process. These three services let you temporarily interrupt your program and run another program that also uses a mouse. If you temporarily exit a program and run another program that uses a mouse, the mouse might not work correctly with the second program.

Using these three services involves a two-step process. First, use service 15h (Get mouse save state buffer size) to determine if you have enough space to store the mouse driver state. Next, use service 16h (Save mouse driver state) to place the mouse driver state in the buffer. Then turn control of the mouse over to the other program. Once the second program returns control to the first program, use service 17h (Restore mouse driver state) to regain control of the mouse again.

Note: No documented standard exists for the format of the buffer used to store the mouse data. In fact, its format varies from vendor to vendor.

Register contents on entry:

AX	17h
DX	Buffer offset
ES	Buffer segment

Set alternate mouse event handler (interrupt 33H service 18H)

This service changes the mouse event handler address for the specified event mask. It allows you to use three simultaneous event handlers. Whenever a mouse event occurs, the mouse driver calls the event handler matching the mask conditions. For example, if CX contains 1, then the mouse driver calls that user-defined handler every time the user moves the mouse. If two drivers define the same mouse event, then the driver uses the shift-key state to determine which handler to call. The mouse driver still reports events not handled by the user-defined handler. You must use service 0 to disable the user-defined handler.

Every handler defined with this service must use one of the shift-state keys (Shift, Ctrl, or Alt) defined in CX. The mouse driver uses these shift-state keys (bits 5, 6, and 7) to determine which driver to call. Make sure each driver uses a different shift-state key mask.

When the mouse driver passes control to the user-defined handler, it makes a far call. Therefore, the user-defined handler must contain procedures using far returns. The mouse driver also fills the registers with specific information before it calls the user-defined handler. AX contains the mouse event flags. The flags appear in the same order as the event mask used to setup the user-defined handler. BX contains the button state. Bit 0 defines the left button, bit 1 defines the right button, and bit 2 defines the center button. CX contains the horizontal (X) pointer coordinate. DX contains the vertical (Y) pointer coordinate. SI contains the last raw vertical mickey count. DI contains the last raw horizontal mickey count. Finally, DS contains the mouse driver data segment.

Register contents on entry:

AX	18h
CX	Event mask (bit selected if set) 0 - Mouse movement 1 - Left button press 2 - Left button release 3 - Right button press 4 - Right button release 5 - Shift key pressed during button press or release 6 - Ctrl key pressed during button press or release 7 - Alt key pressed during button press or release 8 through 15 - Reserved (0)
DX	Offset of user-defined handler
ES	Segment of user-defined handler

Register contents on exit:

AX	18h if successful, FFFFh if unsuccessful

Get address of alternate mouse event handler (interrupt 33H service 19H)

This service gets the address for the mouse event handler matching the event mask. Use this service with event handlers installed using service 18h. Because service 18h allows you to install multiple event handlers, this service allows you to find the handler you want to replace or disable.

Register contents on entry:

AX	19h
CX	Event mask (bit selected if set) 0 - Mouse movement 1 - Left button press 2 - Left button release 3 - Right button press

4 - Right button release
5 - Middle button press
6 - Middle button release
7 through 15 - Reserved (0)

Register contents on exit:

CX	0 if not successful, event mask if successful
DX	Offset of user-defined handler
ES	Segment of user-defined handler

Set mouse sensitivity (interrupt 33H service 1AH)

Mouse sensitivity defines how hard or easy the mouse pointer moves when you move the mouse. The higher the sensitivity, the faster the mouse pointer moves with little actual movement of the mouse.

The sensitivity numbers can range between 1 to 100, where 50 specifies the default mickey factor of 1. This service also lets you specify the double-speed threshold ratio. One mickey equals 1/200 inch of mouse travel.

Register contents on entry:

AX	1Ah
BX	Horizontal mickeys (range 1 - 32,767, default 8)
CX	Vertical mickeys (range 1 - 32,767, default 16)
DX	Double speed-threshold in mickeys per second

Get mouse sensitivity (interrupt 33H service 1BH)

This service gets the current number of mickeys per 8 pixels of horizontal or 16 pixels of vertical movement, plus the threshold for doubling the mouse pointer motion. One mickey equals 1/200 inch of mouse travel.

Register contents on entry:

AX	1Bh

Register contents on exit:

BX	Horizontal mickeys (range 1 - 32,767, default 8)
CX	Vertical mickeys (range 1 - 32,767, default 16)
DX	Double speed-threshold in mickeys per second

Set mouse interrupt rate (interrupt 33H service 1CH)

This service works only with the Microsoft InPort bus mouse that uses the InPort programmable chip. Calling this service will set the number of times per second the mouse driver polls the mouse for status information. For better resolution while displaying graphics, faster interrupt rates provide better resolution. However, slower interrupt rates sometimes let the program run faster. If BX contains more than one bit set, the mouse driver will select the lower interrupt rate.

NOTE: Most mouse drivers allow you to set the mouse interrupt rate. Some bus mice also support an interrupt rate feature in the hardware. Refer to your technical manual for details on changing this feature.

Register contents on entry:

AX	1Ch
BX	Interrupt rate flags (bits true when set)
	0 - No interrupts allowed
	1 - 30 interrupts per second
	2 - 50 interrupts per second
	3 - 100 interrupts per second
	4 - 200 interrupts per second
	5 through 15 - Reserved (0)

Select pointer page (interrupt 33H service 1DH)

This service selects on which display page the mouse pointer appears. Valid page numbers range from 0 to 7, depending on the display adapter used (CGA, MCGA, EGA, or VGA) and the current display mode.

Register contents on entry:

AX	1Dh
BX	Page

Get pointer page (interrupt 33H service 1EH)

This service retrieves the current mouse-pointer display-page number. Service 1Dh (Select pointer page) selects the mouse-pointer display page.

Register contents on entry:

AX	1Eh

Register contents on exit:

BX	Page

Disable mouse driver (interrupt 33H service 1FH)

This service disables the mouse and returns the address of the previous interrupt 33h handler. When you call this service, the mouse driver releases any interrupt vectors it captured (except interrupt 33h). The application program can complete the process of logically removing the mouse driver by restoring the original interrupt 33h vector. Use interrupt 21h service 25h to perform this task. Logically removing the driver does not remove the mouse driver from memory or allow other programs to allocate memory held by the mouse driver.

Register contents on entry:

AX	1Fh

Register contents on exit:

AX	001Fh if successful, FFFFh if not successful
BX	Offset of previous interrupt 33h handler
ES	Segment of previous interrupt 33h handler

Enable mouse driver (interrupt 33H service 20H)

This service enables the mouse driver and sets the interrupt 33h vector to the mouse-interrupt vector.

Register contents on entry:

AX	20h

Reset mouse driver (interrupt 33H service 21H)

This service resets the mouse driver, but doesn't perform any initialization of the mouse hardware. This allows you to reset the driver without losing any hardware-specific changes. When you use this service, the mouse driver removes the pointer from the screen, disables any user-installed interrupt handlers, and sets the default values listed below.

Default values:

Horizontal mickey-to-pixels ratio:	8
Vertical mickey-to-pixels ratio:	16
Double-speed threshold:	64 mickeys per second
Minimum horizontal cursor position:	0
Maximum horizontal cursor position:	Maximum X value - 1

Minimum vertical cursor position:	0
Maximum vertical cursor position:	Maximum Y value - 1

Register contents on entry:

AX	21h

Register contents on exit:

AX	0021h if successful, FFFFh if not successful
BX	Number of mouse buttons

Set language for mouse driver messages (interrupt 33H service 22H)

This service selects the language used for mouse-driver prompts and error messages. This interrupt works only with special international mouse-driver software.

Register contents on entry:

AX	22h
BX	Language number 0 - English 1 - French 2 - Dutch 3 - German 4 - Swedish 5 - Finnish 6 - Spanish 7 - Portuguese 8 - Italian

Get language number (interrupt 33H service 23H)

This service retrieves the current language used for mouse-driver prompts and error messages. This interrupt works only with special international mouse-driver software.

Register contents on entry:

AX	23h

Register contents on exit:

BX	Language number 0 - English 1 - French

2 - Dutch
3 - German
4 - Swedish
5 - Finnish
6 - Spanish
7 - Portuguese
8 - Italian

Get mouse information (interrupt 33H service 24H)

This service retrieves the mouse driver version, mouse type, and mouse adapter interrupt IRQ number.

Register contents on entry:

AX	24h

Register contents on exit:

BH	Major version number
BL	Minor version number
CH	Mouse type
	1 - Bus mouse
	2 - Serial mouse
	3 - InPort mouse
	4 - PS/2 mouse
	5 - HP mouse
CL	IRQ number
	0 - PS/2
	2, 3, 4, 5, or 7 - PC, PC/XT, and PC/AT

Mouse standards

There are three standards commonly used for the mouse interface. These standards include Microsoft, Logitech, and Mouse Systems. All three use the same general principles of mouse operation, but there are physical differences, like the number of buttons, and minor software differences. Often, the software differences are small or nonexistent. In fact, the major problem with software compatibility that many programmers experience is using an old mouse driver with an application expecting the features found in a new one. The following sections apply specifically to the Microsoft standard for mice, but also apply to the other two standards as well. I tested each function using both a Microsoft and Logitech mouse.

Differences between two-button and three-button mice

The main difference between most mice is the number of buttons they support. Some mice support five or six buttons. However, most mice in use today provide two or three buttons. Most software makes use of only two-button operation. However, some software allows you to assign extended functions to the extra combinations provided by a three-button mouse.

The difference in programming a three-button rather than a two-button mouse is the number of possible button-push combinations. A two-button mouse provides three combinations of button presses. The third combination involves pressing both buttons simultaneously, or *chording* the mouse buttons. Many software vendors make the right button equivalent to the Enter key, the left button equivalent to a selection key code, and the left-right button equivalent to the Escape key. Most users find that these are the three most commonly used keyboard selections. Placing these selections on the mouse enhances ease of use.

A three-button mouse allows you seven button-push combinations. This means you can add four functions to the semi-standard mouse selections. Some standard added functions include help select, file save, and menu select. Most vendors that support only two-button mice use the middle button of a three-button mouse to emulate the left-right button chord of a two-button mouse.

Using a mouse in data-entry screens

The first place that you usually see mouse support within a program is the data entry area. In fact, a lot of programs append mouse support rather than integrating it. The data-entry screen is one of the most convenient places to add this support at a basic level. It's so easy to do that many mouse vendors add an event-driven menu-creation program to their software package. The average user can add support to packages that don't currently support a mouse by simply defining a set of specific actions that they want the event-driven routine to perform.

However, as you enhance this support, the data-entry area can become one of the most complex areas to support. The reason for this range of complexity is that there's almost an endless array of features you can add to the display area, unlike a menu or other support area. To give you an idea of how far this range extends, think about some of the graphics programs you've used. Some start with a simple pick procedure. Everywhere the user points and clicks, the program moves the cursor. The next step is allowing the user to select text for editing. The program usually allows copying, cutting, and pasting as editing commands. A third level, at least for database managers, might allow the user to double-click on a blank to receive help or a pick list of choices. As you can see, the list goes on and on.

Of course, before you can implement the simplest of these procedures, you must detect and set the mouse up. The program shown in FIG. 11-1 contains a standard Clipper routine that calls an external mouse routine. Figure 11-2 contains an assembly- language routine that shows you how to detect and set up the mouse. It then illustrates some of the basic methods you can use to include mouse support within your program.

11-1 Mouse example number one, Clipper source

```
// Program Number 12 - Using a Mouse Within a Data Entry Screen Example
// This program shows you how to use the rudimentary mouse functions
// shown in PROG-12A.ASM.  There are three basic functions: determining
// if the mouse exists, obtaining information about the mouse's current
// status, and hiding the mouse.  Determining if the mouse exists
// includes displaying it if present.  The code shown below is an
// enhanced version of Program 8.  This new code adds support for the
// mouse in the display area.  If you press the left button, then the
// program allows you to edit the data.  If you press the right button,
// then the program exits to DOS.  We could have added additional
// functions, but this program is designed to show you the basics.
// Written by: John Mueller
// Copyright 1991 John Mueller - Tab Books

// Include an required header files.

#include "INKEY.CH"
#include "MOUSE.CH"

// Create some local variables.

local lExit := .F.,;            // Are we ready to exit?
      nXPosit := 0,;            // Mouse X Position.
      nYPosit := 0,;            // Mouse Y Position.
      nBPress := 0,;            // Current Mouse Key Press.
      nChoice := 0              // User Menu Selection.

public lMPresent := .F.         // Is the mouse available?

// Display the background screen.

set scoreboard off
set color to "W+/B, RG+/R"
cls
@ 00, 00 say padc(" Mouse Data Entry Screen Example ", 80, chr(177))
@ 01, 00 to 24, 79 double
@ 02, 02 say "File    Edit"
@ 03, 01 to 03, 78 double

// Check for the presence of the mouse.  If one is present, display
// the mouse cursor on screen and display the mouse present message
// at the display header.  If not, tell the user that the mouse is not
```

```
// available.

if GoMouse()
   @ 02, 40 say "Mouse Present"
   lMPresent := .T.
else
   @ 02, 40 say "Mouse Not Present"
endif

// Open the database and index.  Check to see if the file exists.  If
// the user is not allowed access, then the filename will not appear to
// the File() function.  (This assumes that you have already verified
// that the directory is correct.)

if file("SAMPLE7.DBF")
   use SAMPLE7 index SAMPLE7
else
   alert("Access to Database Denied")
   set color to "W/N, N/W"
   cls
   return
endif

// Display the data.

DispData()

while !(nChoice == K_ESC)

// Get the current mouse information if necessary.

if lMPresent
   MPosit(@nXPosit, @nYPosit, @nBPress)
   @ 02, 54 say "X: " + str(nXPosit, 2)
   @ 02, 60 say "Y: " + str(nYPosit, 2)
   @ 02, 66 say "Press: " + str(nBPress, 1)
endif

// Now that we have the mouse information, check to see if we have
// to do something with it.

do case
   case nBPress == L_BUTTON; keyboard "0"
   case nBPress == R_BUTTON; keyboard chr(K_ESC)
endcase

// See if there is a keystroke waiting to be processed.  If not,
// go back to the top and check the mouse again.  Otherwise, process
// the keystroke.

if !(nextkey() == 0)
   nChoice := inkey()
else
   loop
```

11-1 Continued.

```
endif

// Process the up and down arrow keys.  All other keys are ignored.

   do case

      // Scroll up one record.

      case lastkey() == K_UP
         if !(bof())
            skip -1
         endif

      // Scroll down one record.

      case lastkey() == K_DOWN
         if !(eof())
            skip
         endif
         if eof()
            skip -1
         endif

      // If the user presses Alt-F, display the File menu.

      case lastkey() == K_ALT_F
         lExit := DispFile()
         if lExit

            // Clear the display an exit to DOS.

            set color to "W/N, N/W"
            cls
            return
         endif

      // If the user presses Alt-E, display the Edit menu.

      case lastkey() == K_ALT_E
         DispEdit()

      // If the user presses any character key allow them to edit the
      // data in the current record.

      case (lastkey() >= asc("0")) .and. (lastkey() <= asc("z"))
         EditData()

   endcase

   // Display the data.

   DispData()
```

```
enddo

// Clear the display an exit to DOS.  Clear the mouse if required.

if lMPresent
   StopMouse()
endif
set color to "W/N, N/W"
cls
return

// Local Procedures Begin.


// This procedure displays the data contained in the database.  It
// begins by clearing any data left from the last display, then displays
// the fields one at a time.  Notice that the comments are surrounded by
// a box, making them easier to see.

static procedure DispData

// Clear the display area.

@ 04, 02 clear to 23, 78

// Display the data.

@ 04, 03 say "Record: " + ltrim(str(recno()))
@ 05, 03 say "Name:      " + FIRST + " " + MIDDLE + " " + LAST
@ 07, 03 say "Address:   " + COMPANY
@ 08, 14 say ADDRESS1
@ 09, 14 say ADDRESS2
@ 10, 14 say CITY + ", " + STATE + "     " + ZIP
@ 12, 03 say "Telephone: " + TELEPHONE1
@ 13, 14 say TELEPHONE2
@ 15, 03 say "Comments: "
@ 16, 03 to 23, 76 double
keyboard chr(27)
memoedit(COMMENTS, 17, 04, 22, 75, .F.)

// Return to the calling procedure.

return NIL


// This function begins by displaying gets for all of the data areas.
// It waits for the user to finish editing the data and saves the
// results to the database.

static function EditData

// Allow the user to edit the data fields.

@ 05, 14 get FIRST picture "@A"
```

11-1 Continued.

```
@ 05, 40 get MIDDLE picture "@A"
@ 05, 42 get LAST picture "@A"
@ 07, 14 get COMPANY
@ 08, 14 get ADDRESS1
@ 09, 14 get ADDRESS2
@ 10, 14 get CITY picture "@A"
@ 10, 51 get STATE picture "@A"
@ 10, 58 get ZIP picture "99999-9999"
@ 12, 14 get TELEPHONE1 picture "(999)999-9999"
@ 13, 14 get TELEPHONE2 picture "(999)999-9999"
read

// Allow the user to edit the memo field.

@ 15, 03 say "Comments: "
@ 16, 03 to 23, 76 double
replace COMMENTS with memoedit(COMMENTS, 17, 04, 22, 75, .T.)

// Return to the calling procedure.

return NIL


// This function displays the file menu at the top of the display.  It
// begins by saving the original display and color scheme and changing
// the color scheme to the one used by the menu.  The next step is to
// wait for the user to make a selection.  Once the selection is made,
// the function acts on the choice.  If the user selected either About
// or Help, the function displays a dialog box.  Otherwise, it returns a
// value of True in lExit to the calling procedure.  This terminates the
// program.

static function DispFile

// Define some local variables.

local aMenu := {"Quit - Esc", "Help", "About"},; // Menu array.
      cOldColor,;                              // Color string saver.
      cScreen,;                                // Screen saver.
      lExit := .F.                             // Exit the program?

// Define the user selection variable.  Notice that we use an
// unitialized static variable to preserve the value of the variable
// after each menu selection.

static nChoice

// Display the menu and obtain the user selection.

cScreen := savescreen(00, 00, maxrow(), maxcol())
cOldColor := setcolor("RG+/RB, W+/B")
@ 02, 02 say "File"
@ 03, 02 to 07, 14 double
```

```
nChoice := achoice(04, 03, 06, 13, aMenu)

// Act on the user's menu selection.

do case
   case nChoice == 1; lExit := .T.
   case nChoice == 2; alert("This Option Not Enabled;for This Demo")
   case nChoice == 3
      alert("Database Status;Copyright 1991;John Mueller-Tab Books")
endcase

// Restore the display to its original appearance.

setcolor(cOldColor)
restscreen(00, 00, maxrow(), maxcol(), cScreen)

// Return to the calling procedure.  Pass the value of lExit back.

return lExit


 // This function displays the Edit menu.

static function DispEdit

// Define some local variables.

// The first variable is the Menu array.

local aMenu := {"Edit Record", "Insert Date", "Insert Time"},;
      cOldColor,;                       // Color string saver.
      cScreen                           // Screen saver.

// Define the user selection variable.  Notice that we use an
// unitialized static variable to preserve the value of the variable
// after each menu selection.

static nChoice

// Display the menu and obtain the user selection.

cScreen := savescreen(00, 00, maxrow(), maxcol())
cOldColor := setcolor("RG+/RB, W+/B")
@ 02, 09 say "Edit"
@ 03, 09 to 07, 22 double
nChoice := achoice(04, 10, 06, 21, aMenu)

// Act on the user's menu selection.

do case
   case nChoice == 1

      // Restore the display to its original appearance.  Call the data
      // editing function.
```

11-1 Continued.

```
     setcolor(cOldColor)
     restscreen(00, 00, maxrow(), maxcol(), cScreen)
     EditData()

   case nChoice == 2; alert("This Option Not Enabled;for This Demo")
   case nChoice == 3; alert("This Option Not Enabled;for This Demo")

endcase

// Restore the display to its original appearance.

setcolor(cOldColor)
restscreen(00, 00, maxrow(), maxcol(), cScreen)

// Return to the calling procedure.

return NIL
```

11-2 Mouse example number one, assembly source

```
;*************************************************************************
;* Program Number 12 - Using a Mouse Within a Data Entry Screen          *
;* This program illustrates three of the rudimentary command required    *
;* to use a mouse with Clipper.  The first procedure, GoMouse, shows     *
;* how you determine the mouse is present, then turn it on.  This        *
;* procedure returns true if the mouse is present, or false if it        *
;* isn't.  The second procedure, StopMouse, shows how you turn the       *
;* mouse off before leaving your program.  You must always follow a      *
;* practice of hiding the mouse before you leave an application.         *
;* Failing to do so could have undesired results.  The third procedure,*
;* MPosit, returns some information about the mouse status.  These       *
;* three parameters are the minimum required information for any         *
;* program.  They include the current mouse position as X and Y          *
;* coordinates, and the current key press condition.                     *
;* Written by: John Mueller                                              *
;* Copyright 1991 John Mueller - Tab Books                               *
;*************************************************************************

;*************************************************************************
;* Make any required declarations.                                       *
;*************************************************************************

.MODEL LARGE

INCLUDE EXTASM.INC
INCLUDE MACROS.INC

PUBLIC StopMouse, GoMouse, MPosit
```

```
;*************************************************************************
;* Declare any required variables.                                       *
;*************************************************************************

.DATA

nButtons        DW      0       ;Number of Mouse Buttons.
nX              DW      0       ;Current Mouse X Position.
nY              DW      0       ;Current Mouse Y Position.
nPress          DW      0       ;Button Number Pressed.

.CODE

;*************************************************************************
;* This procedure hides the mouse pointer.                               *
;*************************************************************************

StopMouse       PROC    FAR

                PUSH    SI          ;Save SI.

                MOV     AX,0002h    ;Hide the Mouse.

                INT     33h

                RetNIL

                POP     SI          ;Restore SI.

                RET

StopMouse       ENDP
;*************************************************************************
;* This procedure initializes the mouse driver to a known state.  If    *
;* the interrupt cannot find a mouse on the current machine, it does    *
;* not return 0FFFFh in AX upon return.  If it does find a mouse, the   *
;* interrupt places the number of mouse buttons in BX.                   *
;*************************************************************************

GoMouse     PROC    FAR

            PUSH    SI              ;Save SI.

            MOV     AX,0000h        ;Initialize the mouse.
            INT     33h
            CMP     AX,0FFFFh       ;Check for pressence of mouse.
            JNE     Exit1           ;If no mouse present, exit.
            RetTrue                 ;Otherwise, report that a
            MOV     nButtons,BX     ; mouse is present and save
                                    ; the number of buttons.
            CALL    ShowMousePointer
            JMP     Exit2

Exit1:      RetFalse
```

11-2 Continued.

```
Exit2:    POP    SI              ;Restore SI.

          RET

GoMouse   ENDP

;***********************************************************************
;* This procedure obtains the current mouse position and the button    *
;* press information.  It places the mouse position in two variables,  *
;* nX and nY.  In addition, it places the current button press         *
;* information in nPress.  For example, if the user had pressed both   *
;* the right and left buttons, then nPress would contain 3.  The       *
;* procedure ends after it passes the three values back to Clipper.    *
;***********************************************************************

MPosit    PROC   FAR

          PUSH   SI            ;Save SI.

          MOV    AX,0003h      ;Get the mouse data.
          INT    33h

          MOV    AX,CX         ;Divide the X position data
          MOV    CX,3          ; by 8 to convert it to a
          SHR    AX,CL         ; character position.
          MOV    nX,AX         ;Save the current X position.

          MOV    AX,DX         ;Restore the Y position data.
          MOV    CX,3          ;Divide it by 8 to convert it
          SHR    AX,CL         ; to a character position.
          MOV    nY,AX         ;Save the current Y position.

          CMP    BX,1          ;Determine which buttons are
          JNE    BType1        ; pressed and set nPress to the
          MOV    nPress,1      ; appropriate value.
          JMP    Exit3
BType1:   CMP    BX,2
          JNE    BType2
          MOV    nPress,2
          JMP    Exit3
BType2:   CMP    BX,3
          JNE    BType3
          MOV    nPress,3
          JMP    Exit3
BType3:   CMP    BX,4
          JNE    BType4
          MOV    nPress,4
          JMP    Exit3
BType4:   CMP    BX,5
          JNE    BType5
          MOV    nPress,5
```

```
        JMP     Exit3
BType5: CMP     BX,6
        JNE     BType6
        MOV     nPress,6
        JMP     Exit3
BType6: CMP     BX,7
        JNE     BType0
        MOV     nPress,7
        JMP     Exit3
BType0: MOV     nPress,0

Exit3:  StorInt1, nX        ;Send the values we retrieved from
        StorInt2, nY        ; the mouse driver to Clipper.
        StorInt3, nPress

        POP     SI          ;Restore SI.

        RET

MPosit  ENDP

;*********************************************************************
;* This procedure displays the mouse pointer.                        *
;*********************************************************************

ShowMousePointer  PROC   NEAR

                  MOV    AX,0001h
                  INT    33h

                  RET

ShowMousePointer  ENDP

END
```

As you can see, the program develops a rudimentary set of routines for the mouse. With these routines, you can detect and display the mouse, determine the current status of the mouse, and hide the mouse from view. Before you can do anything else with the mouse you must understand these three principles. It's especially important to learn how to track the mouse. The example presented here is the most basic tracking method. There are other, more complex methods, which I'll illustrate later. In many cases, however, it's simply enough to know the real-world coordinates of the mouse, for example, in order to pick a particular entry from the display.

The current program does not support the mouse while within a get. To add support for the mouse within a get, you must change the get system in such a way that it polls the mouse during the get. In other words, when the get system isn't busy looking for characters, it should be busy looking for mouse clicks and movement. Adding this support is more complex than it might originally sound. You must poll the mouse in such a way as to not affect the inner workings of the get system.

Using a mouse in menus

Once you achieve a desired level of mouse performance within a display, you need to add support to your menus. This is often the point where people judge whether or not to append or integrate the support to the program. The difference, of course, is that you can make the mouse appear integrated with the display, but the same isn't true of a menu. You have to add in-depth treatment of mouse clicks and cursor movement when you integrate the mouse into a menu. The appended support often comes in the form of pop-up menus and other displays added to the original program. Your menu routines should provide the same feel as if the person were using cursor keys and Enter key. If the user moves the mouse up, then the menu selection should change. Clicking on a selection should initiate the same event as if the user pressed the Enter key. Even though menu support sounds difficult to master, once you understand the basic concepts it's one of the easier parts of the program to include.

Figure 11-3 shows a typical menu program in Clipper. This example builds upon the example started in FIG. 11-1 to give you the feel of a total application. Figure 11-4 shows the assembly-language code required to implement mouse support for that menu. In this instance, it adds the ability to detect the number of times the user presses the left mouse button. Notice that this program adds to the code already provided by FIGS. 11-1 and 11-2. This means that you need to link the object module for the external routine created in that program with this program.

11-3 Mouse example number two, Clipper source

```
// Program Number 13 - Using a Mouse Within a Menu Example
// This program builds on the principles started in Program Number 12.
// In this instance, we add the capability to detect single and double
// clicks to the three functions presented in PROG-12A.ASM.  To use this
// program you must link both PROG-12A.OBJ and PROG-13A.OBJ with the
// object module from this program.  Failing to do so will result in
// unresolved external calls.  The main reason to differentiate between
// single and double clicks is to allow the user to either select or
// execute a menu item.  Of course, there are other reasons to
// differentiate between them as well.  For example, you could use a
// single click to denote acceptance and a double click to denote
// rejection of a selection.  This program demonstrates a unique method
// of creating menus as well.  In Program 12 we used the AChoice()
// function to implement a menu since this is fairly straight forward.
// Unfortunately, AChoice() does not support the mouse.  To correct this
// we changed the menu routine to use a TBrowse object.  The TMenu()
// function shows you how to create a rudimentary menu using this
```

```
// technique.
// Written by: John Mueller
// Copyright 1991 John Mueller - Tab Books

// Include an required header files.

#include "INKEY.CH"
#include "MOUSE.CH"

// Create some local variables.

local lExit := .F.,;            // Are we ready to exit?
      nXPosit := 0,;            // Mouse X Position.
      nYPosit := 0,;            // Mouse Y Position.
      nBPress := 0,;            // Current Mouse Key Press.
      nChoice := 0,;            // User Menu Selection.
      lMStroke := .F.           // Last Keystroke from Mouse?

public lMPresent := .F.         // Is the mouse available?


// Display the background screen.

set scoreboard off
set color to "W+/B, RG+/R"
cls
@ 00, 00 say padc(" Mouse Controlled Menu Example ", 80, chr(177))
@ 01, 00 to 24, 79 double
@ 02, 02 say "File   Edit"
@ 03, 01 to 03, 78 double

// Check for the presence of the mouse.  If one is present, display
// the mouse cursor on screen and display the mouse present message
// at the display header.  If not, tell the user that the mouse is not
// available.

if GoMouse()
   @ 02, 40 say "Mouse Present"
   lMPresent := .T.
else
   @ 02, 40 say "Mouse Not Present"
endif

// Open the database and index.  Check to see if the file exists.  If
// the user is not allowed access, then the filename will not appear to
// the File() function.  (This assumes that you have already verified
// that the directory is correct.)

if file("SAMPLE7.DBF")
   use SAMPLE7 index SAMPLE7
else
   alert("Access to Database Denied")
   set color to "W/N, N/W"
   cls
```

11-3 Continued.

```
   return
endif

// Display the data.

DispData()

while !(nChoice == K_ESC)

// Reset the mouse stroke indicator.

lMStroke := .F.

 // Get the current mouse information if necessary.

if lMPresent
   MPosit(@nXPosit, @nYPosit, @nBPress)
   @ 02, 54 say "X: " + str(nXPosit, 2)
   @ 02, 60 say "Y: " + str(nYPosit, 2)
   @ 02, 66 say "Press: " + str(nBPress, 1)
endif

// Wait for user to release button.  Now that we have the mouse
// information, check to see if we have to do something with it.

do case
   case nBPress == R_BUTTON; keyboard chr(K_ESC)
   case nBPress == L_BUTTON
      do case
         case ((nXPosit >= 2 .and. nXPosit <= 5) .and. (nYPosit == 2))
            lMStroke := .T.
            keyboard chr(K_CTRL_F)
         case ((nXPosit >= 9 .and. nXPosit <= 12) .and. (nYPosit == 2))
            lMStroke := .T.
            keyboard chr(K_CTRL_E)
         otherwise
            keyboard "0"
      endcase
endcase

if lMPresent
   do while nBPress > 0
      MPosit(@nXPosit, @nYPosit, @nBPress)
   enddo
endif

// Zero nBPress, otherwise the program tends to act automatically.

nBPress := 0

// See if there is a keystroke waiting to be processed.  If not,
// go back to the top and check the mouse again.  Otherwise, process
// the keystroke.
```

```
if !(nextkey() == 0)
   nChoice := inkey()
else
   loop
endif

 // Process the up and down arrow keys.  All other keys are ignored.

   do case

      // Scroll up one record.

      case (lastkey() == K_UP) .and. !(lMStroke)
         if !(bof())
            skip -1
         endif

      // Scroll down one record.

      case lastkey() == K_DOWN
         if !(eof())
            skip
         endif
         if eof()
            skip -1
         endif

      // If the user presses Alt-F/Ctrl-F, display the File menu.

      case (lastkey() == K_ALT_F) .or. (lastkey() == K_CTRL_F)
         lExit := DispFile()
         if lExit

            // Clear the display an exit to DOS.  Clear the mouse if
            // required.

            if lMPresent
               StopMouse()
            endif
            set color to "W/N, N/W"
            cls
            return
         endif

      // If the user presses Alt-E/Ctrl-E, display the Edit menu.

      case (nChoice == K_ALT_E) .or. (nChoice == K_CTRL_E)
         DispEdit()

      // If the user presses any character key allow them to edit the
      // data in the current record.

      case (lastkey() >= asc("0")) .and. (lastkey() <= asc("z"))
          EditData()
```

11-3 Continued.

```
   endcase

   // Display the data.

   DispData()

enddo

// Clear the display an exit to DOS.  Clear the mouse if required.

if lMPresent
   StopMouse()
endif
set color to "W/N, N/W"
cls
return

// Local Procedures Begin.


// This procedure displays the data contained in the database.  It
// begins by clearing any data left from the last display, then displays
// the fields one at a time.  Notice that the comments are surrounded by
// a box, making them easier to see.

static procedure DispData

// Clear the display area.

@ 04, 02 clear to 23, 78

// Display the data.

@ 04, 03 say "Record: " + ltrim(str(recno()))
@ 05, 03 say "Name:       " + FIRST + " " + MIDDLE + " " + LAST
@ 07, 03 say "Address:    " + COMPANY
@ 08, 14 say ADDRESS1
@ 09, 14 say ADDRESS2
@ 10, 14 say CITY + ", " + STATE + "     " + ZIP
@ 12, 03 say "Telephone: " + TELEPHONE1
@ 13, 14 say TELEPHONE2
@ 15, 03 say "Comments: "
@ 16, 03 to 23, 76 double
keyboard chr(27)
memoedit(COMMENTS, 17, 04, 22, 75, .F.)

// Return to the calling procedure.

return NIL


// This function begins by displaying gets for all of the data areas.
```

```
// It waits for the user to finish editing the data and saves the
// results to the database.

static function EditData

// Allow the user to edit the data fields.

@ 05, 14 get FIRST picture "@A"
@ 05, 40 get MIDDLE picture "@A"
@ 05, 42 get LAST picture "@A"
@ 07, 14 get COMPANY
@ 08, 14 get ADDRESS1
@ 09, 14 get ADDRESS2
@ 10, 14 get CITY picture "@A"
@ 10, 51 get STATE picture "@A"
@ 10, 58 get ZIP picture "99999-9999"
@ 12, 14 get TELEPHONE1 picture "(999)999-9999"
@ 13, 14 get TELEPHONE2 picture "(999)999-9999"
read

// Allow the user to edit the memo field.

@ 15, 03 say "Comments: "
@ 16, 03 to 23, 76 double
replace COMMENTS with memoedit(COMMENTS, 17, 04, 22, 75, .T.)

// Return to the calling procedure.

return NIL


// This function displays the file menu at the top of the display.  It
// begins by saving the original display and color scheme and changing
// the color scheme to the one used by the menu.  The next step is to
// wait for the user to make a selection.  Once the selection is made,
// the function acts on the choice.  If the user selected either About
// or Help, the function displays a dialog box.  Otherwise, it returns
// value of True in lExit to the calling procedure.  This terminates the
// program.

static function DispFile

// Define some local variables.

local aMenu := {space(10), "Quit - Esc", "Help", "About"},; // Menu array.
      cOldColor,;                     // Color string saver.
      cScreen,;                       // Screen saver.
      lExit := .F.                    // Exit the program?

// Define the user selection variable.  Notice that we use an
// unitialized static variable to preserve the value of the variable
// after each menu selection.

static nChoice
```

11-3 Continued.

```
// Display the menu and obtain the user selection.

@ 02, 02 say "File   Edit"
cScreen := savescreen(00, 00, maxrow(), maxcol())
cOldColor := setcolor("RG+/RB, W+/B")
@ 02, 02 say "File"
@ 03, 02 to 07, 14 double
nChoice := TMenu(04, 03, 06, 13, aMenu)

// Act on the user's menu selection.

do case
   case nChoice == 1; lExit := .T.
   case nChoice == 2; alert("This Option Not Enabled;for This Demo")
   case nChoice == 3
      alert("Database Status;Copyright 1991;John Mueller-Tab Books")
endcase

// Restore the display to its original appearance.

setcolor(cOldColor)
restscreen(00, 00, maxrow(), maxcol(), cScreen)

// Return to the calling procedure.  Pass the value of lExit back.

return lExit


// This function displays the Edit menu.

static function DispEdit

 // Define some local variables.

// The first variable is the Menu array.

local aMenu := {space(11), "Edit Record", "Insert Date", "Insert Time"},;
      cOldColor,;                        // Color string saver.
      cScreen                            // Screen saver.

// Define the user selection variable.  Notice that we use an
// unitialized static variable to preserve the value of the variable
// after each menu selection.

static nChoice

// Display the menu and obtain the user selection.

@ 02, 02 say "File   Edit"
cScreen := savescreen(00, 00, maxrow(), maxcol())
cOldColor := setcolor("RG+/RB, W+/B")
@ 02, 09 say "Edit"
```

```
@ 03, 09 to 07, 22 double
nChoice := TMenu(04, 10, 06, 21, aMenu)

// Act on the user's menu selection.

do case
   case nChoice == 1

      // Restore the display to its original appearance.  Call the data
      // editing function.

      setcolor(cOldColor)
      restscreen(00, 00, maxrow(), maxcol(), cScreen)
      EditData()

   case nChoice == 2; alert("This Option Not Enabled;for This Demo")
   case nChoice == 3; alert("This Option Not Enabled;for This Demo")

endcase

// Restore the display to its original appearance.

setcolor(cOldColor)
restscreen(00, 00, maxrow(), maxcol(), cScreen)

// Return to the calling procedure.

return NIL


// This function uses a TBrowse object to display a menu.  This allows
// us to use a mouse in addition to the keyboard to manipulate the
// menus.  Single clicking the mouse highlights the object.  Double
// clicking or clicking outside the menu select the highlighted object.
// Double clicking automatically highlights the menu item under the
// mouse cursor when inside the menu box.  Notice that the function is
// designed to accept a menu placed anywhere on the screen with any
// number of menu items.  This allows us the freedom of using one
// generic routine throughout the program for menus.  Use this function
// in place of AChoice whenever a menu with mouse support is desired.

static function TMenu (nTRow, nLCol, nBRow, nRCol, aItems)

// Declare some variables

local nRowNum := 1,;             // Current row number
      nXPosit := 0,;             // Mouse X Position.
      nYPosit := 0,;             // Mouse Y Position.
      nBPress := 0,;             // Current Mouse Key Press.
      nChar := 0,;               // User input
      nI := 1                    // Array index

// Create the TBrowse object using an array.  Notice that we need to
// declare a special skipblock to make this implementation work.  Also
```

11-3 Continued.

```
// notice that we use the TBColumnNew() class function rather than
// TBColumnDB().  This is because the second class function is not
// usable with array constructs.

oBrowse := tbrowsenew (nTRow, nLCol, nBRow, nRCol)
oBrowse:skipblock := {| | nI := nI + CheckSkip(nI, len(aItems)) }
oBrowse:addcolumn(tbcolumnnew( , {|| aItems[nI]}))

// Zero the click counter so that we can monitor the number of left
// mouse clicks.

ChckClick()

// Continue this loop until the user presses ESC or ENTER.

while !(nChar == K_ESC) .and. !(nChar == K_ENTER)

   // Display the TBrowse object.

   do while !(oBrowse:stabilize())
   enddo

   // Get the current mouse information if necessary.

   if lMPresent
      set color to "W+/B, RG+/R"
      MPosit(@nXPosit, @nYPosit, @nBPress)
      @ 02, 54 say "X: " + str(nXPosit, 2)
      @ 02, 60 say "Y: " + str(nYPosit, 2)
      @ 02, 66 say "Press: " + str(nBPress, 1)
      set color to "RG+/RB, W+/B"
   endif

   // Wait for user to release button.  Now that we have the mouse
   // information, check to see if we have to do something with it.  The
   // code below appears quite complex.  In reality, we have to do a few
   // simple things a lot of times under different conditions.  First,
   // we check to see which mouse button was pressed.  If the right
   // button was pressed, then we pass an escape to the keyboard.  If
   // the left button was pressed, then we need to determine if the
   // button was single or double clicked.  If the button was single
   // clicked, then we need to determine where the mouse cursor was
   // placed.  If it appeared outside the menu, then we pass an enter
   // key to the keyboard; otherwise, we move the highlight to the
   // position directly under the mouse cursor.  A double click works
   // similar to the single click except that it always passes and enter
   // key to the keyboard.

   do case
      case nBPress == R_BUTTON; keyboard chr(K_ESC)
      case (nBPress == L_BUTTON) .and. (ChckClick() == 1)
         if (nXPosit >= nLCol) .and. (nXPosit <= nRCol)
```

```
         if (nYPosit >= nTRow) .and. (nYPosit <= nBRow)
             if oBrowse:rowPos > (nYPosit - nTRow + 1)
               while oBrowse:rowPos > (nYPosit - nTRow + 1)
                  oBrowse:up()
                  do while !(oBrowse:stabilize())
                  enddo
                  nRowNum--
               enddo
            elseif oBrowse:rowPos < (nYPosit - nTRow + 1)
               while oBrowse:rowPos < (nYPosit - nTRow + 1)
                  oBrowse:down()
                  do while !(oBrowse:stabilize())
                  enddo
                  nRowNum++
               enddo
            endif
         else
            keyboard chr(K_ENTER)
         endif
      else
         keyboard chr(K_ENTER)
      endif
   case (nBPress == L_BUTTON) .and. (ChckClick() > 1)
      if (nXPosit >= nLCol) .and. (nXPosit <= nRCol)
         if (nYPosit >= nTRow) .and. (nYPosit <= nBRow)
            if oBrowse:rowPos > (nYPosit - nTRow + 1)
               while oBrowse:rowPos > (nYPosit - nTRow + 1)
                  oBrowse:up()
                  do while !(oBrowse:stabilize())
                  enddo
                  nRowNum--
               enddo
               keyboard chr(K_ENTER)
            elseif oBrowse:rowPos < (nYPosit - nTRow + 1)
               while oBrowse:rowPos < (nYPosit - nTRow + 1)
                  oBrowse:down()
                  do while !(oBrowse:stabilize())
                  enddo
                  nRowNum++
               enddo
                  keyboard chr(K_ENTER)
               endif
            else
               keyboard chr(K_ENTER)
            endif
         else
            keyboard chr(K_ENTER)
         endif
   endcase

   if lMPresent
       do while nBPress > 0
         MPosit(@nXPosit, @nYPosit, @nBPress)
      enddo
```

11-3 Continued.

```
   endif

   // Zero nBPress, otherwise the program tends to act automatically.

   nBPress := 0

   // See if there is a keystroke waiting to be processed.  If not,
   // go back to the top and check the mouse again.  Otherwise, process
   // the keystroke.

   if !(nextkey() == 0)
      nChar := inkey()
   else
      loop
   endif

   // Interpret the InKey() value.

   do case
      case nChar == K_UP
         oBrowse:up()
         if !(oBrowse:hitTop)
            nRowNum--
         endif
      case nChar == K_DOWN
         oBrowse:down()
         if !(oBrowse:hitBottom)
            nRowNum++
         endif
   endcase

enddo

return iif(lastkey() == K_ESC, 0, nRowNum)


// We use this function to help implement a skip block for TMenu.  In
// essence, if the current cursor position is at the bottom of the menu,
// return 0.  Otherwise, return 1.

function CheckSkip(nCurRec, nItems)

if nCurRec == nItems
   return 0
else
   return 1
 endif

return 0
```

There are several unique features in the program presented in FIG. 11-3. The most unique of these features is the use of a TBrowse object to implement a menu. There are several things to consider about this part of the example. First, never limit your ideals of what you can use a command or a function for to the specification printed in a book, even this one. Even though no one told you that you could create a menu using a TBrowse object, that doesn't mean that you can't do it. The second consideration is why I used the TBrowse object in the first place.

Many of the newer features of Clipper were added to provide the flexibility you need in order to add just about any feature imaginable to your programs. You couldn't monitor the mouse using a standard menu function like AChoice( ). Because AChoice( ) does everything internally, you can't add features like mouse support. You have to use something like a TBrowse object to provide menu support within a program. Notice that the mouse code doesn't interfere with use of the keyboard. This is another important consideration. Whenever you design a new feature in your program, try to keep the old ones intact. Some people will refuse to change their habits in order to use the new features you've added, so you must allow them to use the standard methods. In this case, the standard method consists of selecting a menu item with the cursor keys and pressing Enter.

Another unique aspect of this code is a little four-line section that simply waits for the user to release the mouse button after you detect that it's been pressed. Without this section of code, the user could potentially make two selections without even knowing it. The code could react faster than the user is able to. This is an important consideration in any event- or mouse-driven program. You must add a piece of code that detects the presence of users and reacts with them instead of independently.

The code shown in FIG. 11-4 is very straightforward. All it does is make a call to the mouse driver to determine how many times the user has pressed the left mouse button since the last time it asked. Because you never know how many times the user has pressed the left button before you actually need to know this information, you must call this procedure once in order to zero the counter. I do this as part of the start-up code in the TMenu( ) function shown in FIG. 11-3. Once zeroed, you can rely on the code in FIG. 11-4 to accurately report the number of times the user pressed the left button. Of course, this code could be expanded to perform the same task with the right and middle buttons as well.

Using a mouse in print-routine screens

The print-routine screen is one of those special screens that you see implemented in a wide variety of programs. These special-purpose screens (also known as dialog boxes) are the measure of how well a programmer understands the mouse. In many cases, this is also where you will find the greatest number of problems with the mouse. Even a well-mannered routine will occasionally fail within a speciality screen. As a result, you will usually want to perform extensive testing within the speciality screen areas of your program.

Figure 11-5 shows a typical specialty screen created in Clipper code. Figure 11-6 shows the assembly language code required to implement mouse support within it. Notice that this code is more convoluted than the other examples provided in this chapter. As with the previous example, this program builds on the foundation laid by the previous two programs. You need to include the object modules for the external routines created with the other programs as part of the linking process for this program.

11-4 Mouse example number two, assembly source

```
;*************************************************************************
;* Program Number 13 - Using a Mouse Within a Menu Example               *
;* This program illustrates how to detect the number of clicks made by *
;* the user between calls to this program.  The purpose of this is to   *
;* allow you to differentiate between a single and a double click.      *
;* Many programs use a single click to select something, while they     *
;* use a double click to execute the same item.  The program consists   *
;* of a singe call to the mouse driver.  Calling the service routine    *
;* automatically resets the click counter to zero.                      *
;* Written by: John Mueller                                              *
;* Copyright 1991 John Mueller - Tab Books                               *
;*************************************************************************

;*************************************************************************
;* Make any required declarations.                                       *
;*************************************************************************

.MODEL LARGE

INCLUDE EXTASM.INC
INCLUDE MACROS.INC

PUBLIC ChckClick

;*************************************************************************
;* Declare any required variables.                                       *
;*************************************************************************

.DATA

nNumClicks     DW     0      ;Number of left button clicks.

.CODE

;*************************************************************************
;* This procedure checks the number of times that the user has pressed *
;* the left mouse button since the last time the procedure was called. *
;* This allows your programs to differentiate between single and        *
```

```
;* double clicks.                                                         *
;*************************************************************************

ChckClick       PROC    FAR

                PUSH    SI              ;Save SI.

                MOV     AX,@DATA        ;Point DS & ES to our data segment.
                MOV     DS,AX
                MOV     ES,AX

                MOV     AX,5            ;Get the mouse button release information,
                MOV     BX,0            ; for the left button.
                INT     33h

                MOV     nNumClicks,BX   ;Store the number of clicks.

                RetInt  nNumClicks      ;Return the number of clicks to Clipper.

NoSet:          POP     SI              ;Restore SI.

                RET

ChckClick       ENDP

END
```

11-5 Mouse example number three, Clipper source

```
// Program Number 14 - Using a Mouse Within Print Routine Screens
// This program concentrates on showing some of the things that you can
// use the mouse for within a dialog box.  One such example of a dialog
// box is the print routine screen presented here.  There are many ways
// to enhance mouse usage within such a display.  The two ways presented
// here consist of mouse positioning and coloring.  Since this program
// builds on the code provided by PROG-12.PRG and PROG-13.PRG, you need
// to link PROG-12A.ASM and PROG-13A.ASM with this program.  Failure to
// do so will result in unresolved external errors.
// Written by: John Mueller
// Copyright 1991 John Mueller - Tab Books

// Include an required header files.

#include "INKEY.CH"
#include "MOUSE.CH"

// Create some local variables.

local lExit := .F.,;                // Are we ready to exit?
      nXPosit := 0,;                // Mouse X Position.
      nYPosit := 0,;                // Mouse Y Position.
      nBPress := 0,;                // Current Mouse Key Press.
```

11-5 Continued.

```
      nChoice := 0,;                // User Menu Selection.
      lMStroke := .F.               // Last Keystroke from Mouse?

public lMPresent := .F.             // Is the mouse available?

// Display the background screen.

set scoreboard off
set color to "W+/B, RG+/R"
cls
@ 00, 00 say padc(" Mouse Print Routine Screen Example ", 80, chr(177))
@ 01, 00 to 24, 79 double
@ 02, 02 say "File   Edit   Print"
@ 03, 01 to 03, 78 double

// Check for the presence of the mouse.  If one is present, display
// the mouse cursor on screen.

if GoMouse()
     lMPresent := .T.
   SetMPtr(40, 12)
   SetMShape(chr(2))
endif

// Open the database and index.  Check to see if the file exists.  If
// the user is not allowed access, then the filename will not appear to
// the File() function.  (This assumes that you have already verified
// that the directory is correct.)

if file("SAMPLE7.DBF")
   use SAMPLE7 index SAMPLE7
else
   alert("Access to Database Denied")
   set color to "W/N, N/W"
   cls
   return
endif

// Display the data.

DispData()

while !(nChoice == K_ESC)

// Reset the mouse stroke indicator.

lMStroke := .F.

// Get the current mouse information if necessary.

if lMPresent
   MPosit(@nXPosit, @nYPosit, @nBPress)
```

```
endif

// Wait for user to release button.  Now that we have the mouse
// information, check to see if we have to do something with it.

do case
   case nBPress == R_BUTTON; keyboard chr(K_ESC)
   case nBPress == L_BUTTON
      do case
         case ((nXPosit >= 2 .and. nXPosit <= 5) .and. (nYPosit == 2))
            lMStroke := .T.
            keyboard chr(K_CTRL_F)
         case ((nXPosit >= 9 .and. nXPosit <= 12) .and. (nYPosit == 2))
            lMStroke := .T.
            keyboard chr(K_CTRL_E)
         case ((nXPosit >= 16 .and. nXPosit <= 21) .and. (nYPosit == 2))
            lMStroke := .T.
            keyboard chr(K_CTRL_P)
         otherwise
            keyboard "0"
      endcase
endcase

if lMPresent
   do while nBPress > 0
      MPosit(@nXPosit, @nYPosit, @nBPress)
   enddo
endif

// Zero nBPress, otherwise the program tends to act automatically.

nBPress := 0

// See if there is a keystroke waiting to be processed.  If not,
// go back to the top and check the mouse again.  Otherwise, process
// the keystroke.

if !(nextkey() == 0)
   nChoice := inkey()
else
   loop
endif

// Process the up and down arrow keys.  All other keys are ignored.

   do case

      // Scroll up one record.

      case (lastkey() == K_UP) .and. !(lMStroke)
         if !(bof())
            skip -1
         endif

      // Scroll down one record.
```

11-5 Continued.

```
      case lastkey() == K_DOWN
         if !(eof())
            skip
         endif
         if eof()
            skip -1
         endif

      // If the user presses Alt-F/Ctrl-F, display the File menu.

      case (lastkey() == K_ALT_F) .or. (lastkey() == K_CTRL_F)
         lExit := DispFile()
         if lExit

            // Clear the display an exit to DOS.  Clear the mouse if
            // required.

            if lMPresent
               StopMouse()
            endif
            set color to "W/N, N/W"
            cls
            return
         endif

      // If the user presses Alt-E/Ctrl-E, display the Edit menu.

      case (nChoice == K_ALT_E) .or. (nChoice == K_CTRL_E)
         DispEdit()

      // If the user presses Alt-P/Ctrl-P, display the Print menu.

      case (nChoice == K_ALT_P) .or. (nChoice == K_CTRL_P)
         DispPrint()

      // If the user presses any character key allow them to edit the
      // data in the current record.

      case (lastkey() >= asc("0")) .and. (lastkey() <= asc("z"))
         EditData()

   endcase

   // Display the data.

   DispData()

enddo

// Clear the display an exit to DOS.  Clear the mouse if required.
```

```
if lMPresent
   StopMouse()
 endif
set color to "W/N, N/W"
cls
return

// Local Procedures Begin.


// This procedure displays the data contained in the database.  It
// begins by clearing any data left from the last display, then displays
// the fields one at a time.  Notice that the comments are surrounded by
// a box, making them easier to see.

static procedure DispData

// Clear the display area.

@ 04, 02 clear to 23, 78

// Display the data.

@ 04, 03 say "Record: " + ltrim(str(recno()))
@ 05, 03 say "Name:       " + FIRST + " " + MIDDLE + " " + LAST
@ 07, 03 say "Address:    " + COMPANY
@ 08, 14 say ADDRESS1
@ 09, 14 say ADDRESS2
@ 10, 14 say CITY + ", " + STATE + "     " + ZIP
@ 12, 03 say "Telephone: " + TELEPHONE1
@ 13, 14 say TELEPHONE2
@ 15, 03 say "Comments: "
@ 16, 03 to 23, 76 double
keyboard chr(27)
memoedit(COMMENTS, 17, 04, 22, 75, .F.)

// Return to the calling procedure.

return NIL


// This function begins by displaying gets for all of the data areas.
// It waits for the user to finish editing the data and saves the
// results to the database.

static function EditData

// Allow the user to edit the data fields.

@ 05, 14 get FIRST picture "@A"
 @ 05, 40 get MIDDLE picture "@A"
@ 05, 42 get LAST picture "@A"
@ 07, 14 get COMPANY
@ 08, 14 get ADDRESS1
@ 09, 14 get ADDRESS2
```

11-5 Continued.

```
@ 10, 14 get CITY picture "@A"
@ 10, 51 get STATE picture "@A"
@ 10, 58 get ZIP picture "99999-9999"
@ 12, 14 get TELEPHONE1 picture "(999)999-9999"
@ 13, 14 get TELEPHONE2 picture "(999)999-9999"
read

// Allow the user to edit the memo field.

@ 15, 03 say "Comments: "
@ 16, 03 to 23, 76 double

replace COMMENTS with memoedit(COMMENTS, 17, 04, 22, 75, .T.)

// Return to the calling procedure.

return NIL


// This function displays the file menu at the top of the display.  It
// begins by saving the original display and color scheme and changing
// the color scheme to the one used by the menu.  The next step is to
// wait for the user to make a selection.  Once the selection is made,
// the function acts on the choice.  If the user selected either About
// or Help, the function displays a dialog box.  Otherwise, it returns a
// value of True in lExit to the calling procedure.  This terminates the
// program.

static function DispFile

// Define some local variables.

local aMenu := {space(10), "Quit - Esc", "Help", "About"},; // Menu array.
      cOldColor,;                     // Color string saver.
      cScreen,;                       // Screen saver.
      lExit := .F.                    // Exit the program?

// Define the user selection variable.  Notice that we use an
// unitialized static variable to preserve the value of the variable
 // after each menu selection.

static nChoice

// Display the menu and obtain the user selection.

@ 02, 02 say "File   Edit   Print"
cScreen := savescreen(00, 00, maxrow(), maxcol())
cOldColor := setcolor("RG+/RB, W+/B")
@ 02, 02 say "File"
@ 03, 02 to 07, 14 double
nChoice := TMenu(04, 03, 06, 13, aMenu)
```

```
// Act on the user's menu selection.

do case
   case nChoice == 1; lExit := .T.
   case nChoice == 2; alert("This Option Not Enabled;for This Demo")
   case nChoice == 3
      alert("Database Status;Copyright 1991;John Mueller-Tab Books")
endcase

// Restore the display to its original appearance.

setcolor(cOldColor)
restscreen(00, 00, maxrow(), maxcol(), cScreen)

// Center the mouse cursor.

if lMPresent
   SetMPtr(40, 12)
endif

// Return to the calling procedure.  Pass the value of lExit back.

return lExit


// This function displays the Edit menu.

static function DispEdit

// Define some local variables.

// The first variable is the Menu array.

local aMenu := {space(11), "Edit Record", "Insert Date", "Insert Time"},;
      cOldColor,;                    // Color string saver.
      cScreen                        // Screen saver.

 // Define the user selection variable.  Notice that we use an
// unitialized static variable to preserve the value of the variable
// after each menu selection.

static nChoice

// Display the menu and obtain the user selection.

@ 02, 02 say "File   Edit   Print"
cScreen := savescreen(00, 00, maxrow(), maxcol())
cOldColor := setcolor("RG+/RB, W+/B")
@ 02, 09 say "Edit"
@ 03, 09 to 07, 22 double
nChoice := TMenu(04, 10, 06, 21, aMenu)

// Act on the user's menu selection.
```

11-5 Continued.

```
do case
   case nChoice == 1

      // Restore the display to its original appearance.  Call the data
      // editing function.

      setcolor(cOldColor)
      restscreen(00, 00, maxrow(), maxcol(), cScreen)
      EditData()

   case nChoice == 2; alert("This Option Not Enabled;for This Demo")
   case nChoice == 3; alert("This Option Not Enabled;for This Demo")

endcase

// Restore the display to its original appearance.

setcolor(cOldColor)
restscreen(00, 00, maxrow(), maxcol(), cScreen)

// Center the mouse cursor.

if lMPresent
   SetMPtr(40, 12)
endi,

// Return to the calling procedure.

return NIL


// This function displays the Print menu.

static function DispPrint

// Define some local variables.

local cOldColor,;                 // Color string saver.
      cStdColor,;                 // 2nd color string saver.
      nXPosit := 0,;              // Mouse X Position.
      nYPosit := 0,;              // Mouse Y Position.
      nBPress := 0,;              // Current Mouse Key Press.
      nChar := 0,;                // User input
      cScreen                     // Screen saver.

// Use static variables for all the screen entries so that the program
// remembers the print parameters from one occurrence to the next.

static lSelection := .T.,;        // Print a Selection of the File?
       lOk := .T.,;               // Selections Ok?
       lDraft := .T.,;            // Draft or Final Quality?
       nRight := 10,;             // Right Print Margin
```

```
        nLeft := 75,;             // Left Print Margin
        nTop := 6,;               // Top Print Margin
        nBottom := 60,;           // Bottom Print Margin
        nLength := 66,;           // Page Length in Lines
        nCopies := 1,;            // Number of Copies
        cFilter := "                                    " // Print Filter String

// Display the menu and obtain the user selection.

@ 02, 02 say "File   Edit   Print"
cScreen := savescreen(00, 00, maxrow(), maxcol())
cOldColor := setcolor("RG+/RB, W+/B")
@ 02, 16 say "Print"
@ 05, 15 to 20, 65 double
@ 06, 16 clear to 19, 64
@ 07, 18 say "Page Length:"
@ 09, 18 say "Margins:"
@ 10, 18 say "Left:     Right:     Top:     Bottom:"
@ 12, 18 say "Copies:"
@ 14, 18 say "Quality: <Draft>  <Final>"
@ 16, 18 say "Print: <All>   <Selection>"
if lSelection
   @ 17, 18 say "Filter:"
endif
@ 19, 18 say "<Ok>   <Cancel>"

// Display any data required.

cStdColor := setcolor("RG+/R, RG+/R")
if lDraft
    @ 14, 27 say "<Draft>"
else
   @ 14, 36 say "<Final>"
endif
if lSelection
   @ 16, 33 say "<Selection>"
else
   @ 16, 25 say "<All>"
endif
if lOk
   @ 19, 18 say "<Ok>"
else
   @ 19, 25 say "<Cancel>"
endif
@ 07, 31 get nLength picture "999"
@ 10, 24 get nLeft picture "999"
@ 10, 35 get nRight picture "999"
@ 10, 44 get nTop picture "999"
@ 10, 56 get nBottom picture "999"
@ 12, 26 get nCopies picture "999"
if lSelection
   @ 17, 26 get cFilter
endif
read
```

11-5 Continued.

```
setcolor (cStdColor)

while !(nChar == K_ESC) .and. !(nChar == K_ENTER)

   // Get the current mouse information if necessary.

   if lMPresent
      MPosit(@nXPosit, @nYPosit, @nBPress)
   endif

   // Wait for user to release button.  Now that we have the mouse
   // information, check to see if we have to do something with it.

   do case
      case nBPress == R_BUTTON; keyboard chr(K_ESC)
      case nBPress == L_BUTTON; keyboard chr(K_ENTER)
   endcase

   if lMPresent
      do while nBPress > 0
         MPosit(@nXPosit, @nYPosit, @nBPress)
      enddo
   endif

   // Zero nBPress, otherwise the program tends to act automatically.

   nBPress := 0

   // See if there is a keystroke waiting to be processed.  If not,
   // go back to the top and check the mouse again.  Otherwise, process
   // the keystroke.

   if !(nextkey() == 0)
      nChar := inkey()
   else
      loop
   endif

enddo

// Restore the display to its original appearance.

setcolor(cOldColor)
restscreen(00, 00, maxrow(), maxcol(), cScreen)

// Center the mouse cursor.

if lMPresent
   SetMPtr(40, 12)
endif

// Return to the calling procedure.
```

```
return NIL


// This function uses a TBrowse object to display a menu.  This allows
// us to use a mouse in addition to the keyboard to manipulate the
// menus.  Single clicking the mouse highlights the object.  Double
// clicking or clicking outside the menu select the highlighted object.
// Double clicking automatically highlights the menu item under the
// mouse cursor when inside the menu box.  Notice that the function is
// designed to accept a menu placed anywhere on the screen with any
// number of menu items.  This allows us the freedom of using one
// generic routine throughout the program for menus.  Use this function
// in place of AChoice whenever a menu with mouse support is desired.

static function TMenu (nTRow, nLCol, nBRow, nRCol, aItems)

 // Declare some variables

local nRowNum := 1,;            // Current row number
      nXPosit := 0,;            // Mouse X Position.
      nYPosit := 0,;            // Mouse Y Position.
      nBPress := 0,;            // Current Mouse Key Press.
      nChar := 0,;              // User input
      nI := 1                   // Array index

// Create the TBrowse object using an array.  Notice that we need to
// declare a special skipblock to make this implementation work.  Also
// notice that we use the TBColumnNew() class function rather than
// TBColumnDB().  This is because the second class function is not
// usable with array constructs.

oBrowse := tbrowsenew (nTRow, nLCol, nBRow, nRCol)
oBrowse:skipblock := {| | nI := nI + CheckSkip(nI, len(aItems)) }
oBrowse:addcolumn(tbcolumnnew( , {|| aItems[nI]}))

// Zero the click counter so that we can monitor the number of left
// mouse clicks.

ChckClick()

// Continue this loop until the user presses ESC or ENTER.

while !(nChar == K_ESC) .and. !(nChar == K_ENTER)

   // Display the TBrowse object.

   do while !(oBrowse:stabilize())
   enddo

   // Get the current mouse information if necessary.

   if lMPresent
      MPosit(@nXPosit, @nYPosit, @nBPress)
   endif
```

11-5 Continued.

```
// Wait for user to release button.  Now that we have the mouse
// information, check to see if we have to do something with it.  The
// code below appears quite complex.  In reality, we have to do a few
// simple things a lot of times under different conditions.  First,
// we check to see which mouse button was pressed.  If the right
// button was pressed, then we pass an escape to the keyboard.  If
// the left button was pressed, then we need to determine if the
// button was single or double clicked.  If the button was single
// clicked, then we need to determine where the mouse cursor was
// placed.  If it appeared outside the menu, then we pass an enter
// key to the keyboard; otherwise, we move the highlight to the
// position directly under the mouse cursor.  A double click works
// similar to the single click except that it always passes and enter
// key to the keyboard.

do case
   case nBPress == R_BUTTON; keyboard chr(K_ESC)
case (nBPress == L_BUTTON) .and. (ChckClick() == 1)
   if (nXPosit >= nLCol) .and. (nXPosit <= nRCol)
      if (nYPosit >= nTRow) .and. (nYPosit <= nBRow)
         if oBrowse:rowPos > (nYPosit - nTRow + 1)
            while oBrowse:rowPos > (nYPosit - nTRow + 1)
               oBrowse:up()
               do while !(oBrowse:stabilize())
               enddo
               nRowNum--
            enddo
         elseif oBrowse:rowPos < (nYPosit - nTRow + 1)
            while oBrowse:rowPos < (nYPosit - nTRow + 1)
               oBrowse:down()
               do while !(oBrowse:stabilize())
               enddo
               nRowNum++
            enddo
         endif
      else
         keyboard chr(K_ENTER)
      endif
   else
      keyboard chr(K_ENTER)
   endif
case (nBPress == L_BUTTON) .and. (ChckClick() > 1)
   if (nXPosit >= nLCol) .and. (nXPosit <= nRCol)
      if (nYPosit >= nTRow) .and. (nYPosit <= nBRow)
         if oBrowse:rowPos > (nYPosit - nTRow + 1)
            while oBrowse:rowPos > (nYPosit - nTRow + 1)
               oBrowse:up()
                do while !(oBrowse:stabilize())
               enddo
               nRowNum--
            enddo
            keyboard chr(K_ENTER)
         elseif oBrowse:rowPos < (nYPosit - nTRow + 1)
```

```
               while oBrowse:rowPos < (nYPosit - nTRow + 1)
                  oBrowse:down()
                  do while !(oBrowse:stabilize())
                  enddo
                     nRowNum++
                  enddo
                  keyboard chr(K_ENTER)
               endif
            else
               keyboard chr(K_ENTER)
            endif
         else
            keyboard chr(K_ENTER)
         endif
   endcase

   if lMPresent
      do while nBPress > 0
         MPosit(@nXPosit, @nYPosit, @nBPress)
      enddo
   endif

   // Zero nBPress, otherwise the program tends to act automatically.

   nBPress := 0

   // See if there is a keystroke waiting to be processed.  If not,
   // go back to the top and check the mouse again.  Otherwise, process
   // the keystroke.

   if !(nextkey() == 0)
      nChar := inkey()
   else
      loop
   endif

   // Interpret the InKey() value.

   do case
      case nChar == K_UP
         oBrowse:up()
         if !(oBrowse:hitTop)
            nRowNum--
         endif
      case nChar == K_DOWN
         oBrowse:down()
         if !(oBrowse:hitBottom)
            nRowNum++
         endif
   endcase

enddo

return iif(lastkey() == K_ESC, 0, nRowNum)
```

11-5 Continued.

```
// We use this function to help implement a skip block for TMenu.  In
// essence, if the current cursor position is at the bottom of the menu,
// return 0.  Otherwise, return 1.

function CheckSkip(nCurRec, nItems)

if nCurRec == nItems
   return 0
else
   return 1
endif

return 0
```

11-6 Mouse example number three, assembly source

```
;*************************************************************************
;* Program Number 14 - Using a Mouse Within Print Routine Screens        *
;* This program allows you to perform two tasks that greatly enhance     *
;* the use of the mouse in some environments.  First, when using         *
;* dialog boxes and other GUI constructs, subtle hints to the user can *
;* greatly enhance program operation.  One of these subtle hints         *
;* consists of mouse cursor placement.  The first routine, SetMPtr()     *
;* allows you to place the cursor on a specific character position on   *
;* the display.  It requires an X and a Y position as input.  The        *
;* routine automatically converts the character positions provided       *
;* into the pixel positions required by the mouse driver.  The second    *
;* routine, SetMShape() allows you to adjust the mouse color and         *
;* shape.  In text mode you can only choose to use one of the 256        *
;* ASCII characters for characters.  Graphics mode is more flexible in *
;* this regard.  The colors in this routine are preset.  You could       *
;* just as easily pass them as variables.  Note that the colors are      *
;* not actual colors.  Instead the color values are ANDed or ORed with *
;* the current screen color to produce the mouse color.  All this        *
;* routine requires is the mouse shape you desire as input.              *
;* Written by: John Mueller                                              *
;* Copyright 1991 John Mueller - Tab Books                               *
;*************************************************************************

;*************************************************************************
;* Make any required declarations.                                       *
;*************************************************************************

 .MODEL LARGE

INCLUDE EXTASM.INC
INCLUDE MACROS.INC
```

```
PUBLIC SetMPtr, SetMShape

;*************************************************************************
;* Declare any required variables.                                       *
;*************************************************************************

.DATA

nXPosit    DW 0       ;X Position in Pixels
nYPosit    DW 0       ;Y Position in Pixels
nXSize     DB 8       ;Character Width in Pixels (Assume Standard Mode)
nYSize     DB 8       ;Character Height in Pixels (Assume Standard Mode)
cMShape    DB 0       ;Character Used for Mouse Shape
nAndMask   DB 059h    ;AND Colors Set to Magenta Background/Blue Foreground
nOrMask    DB 01Dh    ;OR Colors Set to Blue Background/Magenta Foreground

.CODE

;*************************************************************************
;* This procedure allows you to adjust the position of the mouse on     *
;* screen.  It begins by checking the position data you provide as      *
;* input to ensure accuracy.  The procedure converts this data from     *
;* character position to the pixel position required by the mouse      *
;* driver.  It then places the mouse at the position requested.  If     *
;* this position is outside the bounded limit area for the mouse, then *
;* the routine places the mouse pointer as close as possible to the     *
;* desired position without leaving the bounded area.                   *
;*************************************************************************

SetMPtr    PROC    FAR

           PUSH    SI           ;Save SI.

           MOV     AX,@DATA     ;Point DS & ES to our data segment.
           MOV     DS,AX
           MOV     ES,AX

;*************************************************************************
;* This section of the code checks the number of parameters and their *
;* type.                                                                 *
;*************************************************************************

           PCount               ;Check for the correct
           CMP     AX,2         ; number of parameters.
           JE      Parm1        ;If so, perform next check.
           JMP     BadExit      ;If not, exit.

Parm1:     IsNum   1            ;Is the first parameter a number?
           JE      Parm2        ;If so, perform next check.
           JMP     BadExit      ;If not, exit.

Parm2:     IsNum   2            ;Is the second parameter a number?
           JE      GoodParms    ;If so, retrieve the data
```

11-6 Continued.

```
BadExit:   RetFalse             ;Return false on error.
           POP     SI           ;Restore SI
           RET

GoodParms: RetTrue              ;Return true for good parameters.

;*********************************************************************
;* This section of the code retrieves the variables from Clipper and *
;* converts the character position values to pixels.  It then stores *
;* the values in local variables for later use.                      *
;*********************************************************************

           GetInt 1             ;Get the first number.
           MOV     CL,nXSize    ;Load the character width.
           MUL     CL           ;Convert character position to pixels.
           MOV     nXPosit,AX   ;Store the X position.

           GetInt 2             ;Get the second number
           MOV     CL,nYSize    ;Load the character height.
           MUL     CL           ;Convert character position to pixels.
           MOV     nYPosit,AX   ;Store the Y position.

;*********************************************************************
;* Position the mouse cursor at the desired screen coordinates.      *
;*********************************************************************

           MOV     AX,4         ;Set the mouse position to
           MOV     CX,nXPosit   ; the X position in nXPosit
           MOV     DX,nYPosit   ; and the Y position in nYPosit.
           INT     33h

           POP     SI           ;Restore SI.

           RET

SetMPtr    ENDP

;**********************************************************************
;* This procedure accepts a single character as input and uses that    *
;* character as the OR (standard) mouse pointer.  It adds one to the   *
;* character and uses the new character as the AND mouse pointer       *
;* (outside bounded limit cursor).  The routine could be adjusted to   *
;* allow you to change the AND/OR color mask as well.  Currently, it   *
;* uses colors preset for the example program.                         *
;**********************************************************************

SetMShape      PROC    FAR

               PUSH    SI          ;Save SI.

               MOV     AX,@DATA    ;Point DS & ES to our data segment.
```

```
            MOV     DS,AX
            MOV     ES,AX

;************************************************************************
;* This section of the code checks the number of parameters and their *
;* type.                                                                *
;************************************************************************

        PCount              ;Check for the correct
        CMP     AX,1        ; number of parameters.
        JE      Parm1A      ;If so, perform next check.
        JMP     BadExit2    ;If not, exit.

Parm1A:     IsChar 1            ;Is the first parameter a number?
        JE      GoodParmA   ;If so, perform next check.

BadExit2:   RetFalse            ;Return false on error.
        POP     SI          ;Restore SI
        RET

GoodParmA:  RetTrue             ;Return true for good parameters.

;************************************************************************
;* This section of the code retrieves the variables from Clipper.  It *
;* then stores the values in local variables for later use.            *
;************************************************************************

        GetChar1            ;Get the character parameter.
        PUSH    AX          ;Save the string offset.
        PUSH    DX          ;Save the Clipper DATA segment.

        POP     DS          ;Point to the Clipper DATA segment.
        POP     SI          ;Point to the string.

        MOV     CX,1        ;Assume a string length of 1.

        LEA     DI,cMShape ;Load the offset of the mouse shape.
        REP     MOVSB       ;Move the string to our data segment.

        MOV     AX,@DATA    ;Point DS to our data segment.
        MOV     DS,AX

;************************************************************************
;* This section of the code performs the task of changing the mouse   *
;* cursor shape.  It also changes the mouse pointer AND and OR masks. *
;* These masks determine what color the mouse appears on screen under *
;* various circumstances.                                               *
;************************************************************************

        MOV     AX,0Ah          ;Set the mouse shape.
        XOR     BX,BX           ;Use the software cursor.
        MOV     CL,cMShape      ;Load the AND mouse shape.
        INC     CL
        MOV     DL,cMShape      ;Load the OR mouse shape.
        MOV     CH,nAndMask     ;Load the AND color settings.
```

11-6 Continued.

```
        MOV   DH,nOrMask      ;Load the OR color settings.
        INT   33h

        POP   SI              ;Restore SI.

        RET

SetMShape  ENDP

END
```

As FIG. 11-5 shows, there are a variety of elements within a dialog box. These can consist of check boxes, radio buttons, and other forms. Often, the appearance and position of the mouse within these routines provides the best indicator to the user of what task needs to be performed. This program introduces two new routines to the other mouse routines used within the program. Figure 11-6 shows the assembly language source required to implement these routines.

The first routine simply repositions the mouse on the display. There are two reasons for using such a routine. First, if you want the user to pay special attention to something, point to it. Move the mouse cursor to the spot you want the user to look at. Second, it enhances the appearance of the display if you recenter the mouse after each routine. This is the function performed by the routines in the example program.

The second routine changes the mouse color and shape. These are very important elements of a program. For example, many programs use an hour glass shape to ask the user to wait for an action to complete before making another request. Other shapes include pointers and text cursors. While the number of shapes that you can create using ASCII character is somewhat limited, you can use a similar technique within the programs you create. For example, the smiley face is a good indicator showing that the user accomplished some task correctly. You could use a question mark cursor when the user approaches the help menu. The paragraph symbol (ASCII code 20) is useful as a text cursor. The example program uses a smiley face as a cursor since there is nothing you can do wrong within this example program.

Color is a very important aspect in creating user friendly programs. For example, you could change the mouse cursor to red if the user is approaching a function that requires some level of caution. A grey cursor could tell the user that a function is unavailable. The example program uses colors that complement the rest of the display. This is always a good choice in selecting a set of colors for you program.

Summary

This chapter provides you with insights into one method of implementing mouse support within your program. As the introduction indicated, there are other methods of implementing this support as well. However, this method is one of the easiest, most straightforward ways available. It's the best way to learn how to add mouse support to a program. While the event-driven method is more flexible and allows you to monitor the mouse without impeding the progress of your program, it does have the disadvantage of being very complex and difficult to master.

The example programs in this chapter provide three scenarios for adding mouse support. You could actually look at these three scenarios as three steps. Each step becomes progressively more difficult, but each adds to the appearance and functionality of your program as a whole. As you become proficient at each step of adding mouse support, you can add refinements to the techniques for handling user requests. You could even add separate routines for users of three-button versus two- button mice.

12 Creating a graphic interface to Clipper

Many programmers find the number of displays available today both confusing and daunting. As a result, they stick with the easiest-to-use choice among display adapters and character mode. Of course, there are better ways to display information on-screen. Windows and many other graphical user interface (GUI) environments prove this point.

Unless you want to stick with character-based displays, you need to be able to differentiate between a wide variety of display standards, and then take advantage of the features provided by each one. This chapter will illustrate two concepts you need to master in order to make full use of your display adapter. The first is how to differentiate between the different standards. You must do this as a first step or suffer the consequence of users attempting to run your VGA program on a CGA screen. The second concept is how to create many different types of display routines. Some are special versions of character-based displays, others are true graphics displays. Both display types assume that you're willing to give up compatibility with the standard Clipper display routines. This is an essential point because the internal Clipper routines cannot be modified to work with a graphics display.

Support for multiple adapter standards

The sections below discuss seven different types of display adapters. Even though more display adapter types exist, these seven kinds encompass the most common types used. The 34010 series (including BGA) accounts for a single type of adapter, even though there are many implementations of that type. Some of the display adapter descriptions have block diagrams to help you visualize the relationship between various elements of the display adapter.

Monochrome display adapter (MDA)

A monochrome display adapter differs from the Hercules graphics card discussed in the following section in memory-access and graphics-display abilities. The standard monochrome display adapter uses only 4K of video memory. Because of this memory limitation, the MDA doesn't display graphics. Figure 12-1 shows a typical MDA block diagram.

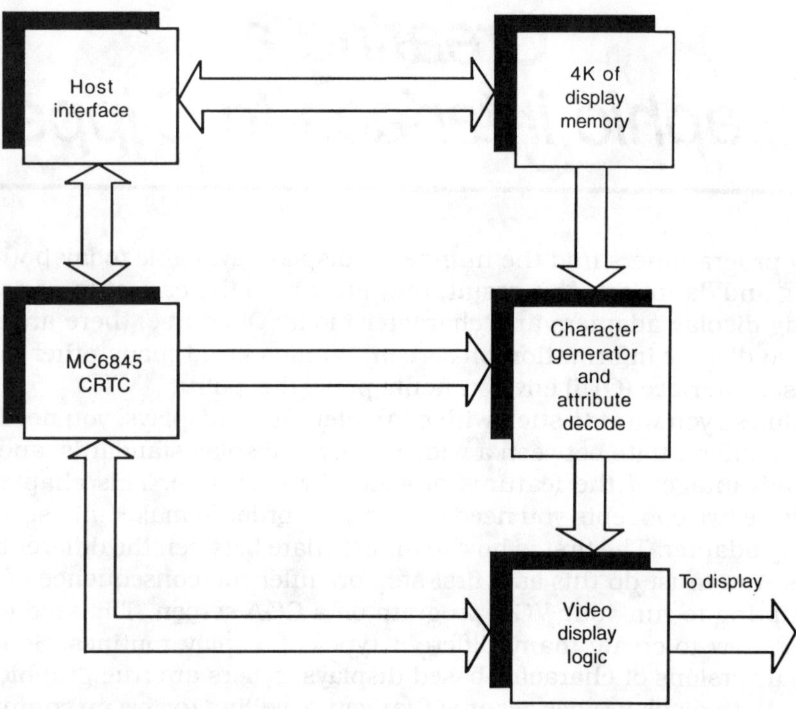

12-1 MDA block diagram

As you can see, the MDA is very simple in its design and implementation. The host simply sends ASCII characters to the display memory. The display memory of 4,096 bytes is slightly larger than what's required to hold an average display using 80 characters per line × 24 lines × 2 bytes per character, or 3,840 bytes. The 6845 cathode-ray tube controller (CRTC) provides the intelligence required to display the data. The character generator and attribute decoder reads the contents of memory and creates the required display scan lines. The video display logic performs the task of timing all the events within the display adapter. As simple as this design is, you'll find that most display adapters using a nonprocessor design contain these components for character modes of display.

Hercules graphics card (HGC)

There are actually several versions of the Hercules graphics card (HGC). Not only has Hercules improved the HGC, but clone copies of the HGC exist as well. The HGC combines the cost and resolution advantage of the MDA with the graphics capabilities of the CGA. Of course, the HGC does not provide color output. It also requires special programming to allow you to use graphics mode. There are, however, several shareware programs that allow you to simulate CGA graphics mode using the HGC.

The main difference between the HGC and the MDA is that the HGC contains the circuitry required for you to use graphics mode. The overall block diagram for the two adapters is precisely the same. Only the host interface to the CRTC and the timing circuitry differs. The HGC also contains a graphics support circuit similar to the one shown for the CGA in FIG. 12-2.

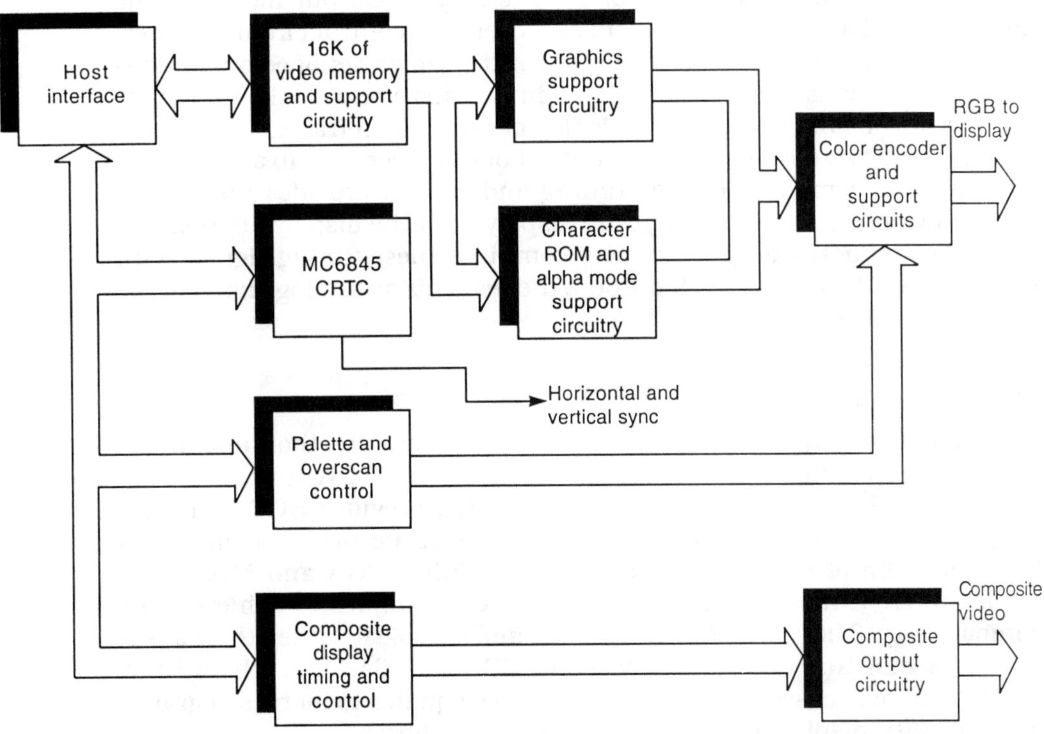

12-2 CGA block diagram

Color graphics adapter (CGA)

The color graphics adapter (CGA) adds an additional dimension to facilities offered by the MDA or HGC. It provides color output in place of the black-and-white output offered by these two devices. Because of this, instead of the 4K of RAM provided by the MDA, the CGA uses 16K. This additional memory allows the CGA to provide low-resolution graphics in four colors, and high-resolution graphics in two colors. Notice that the CGA allows you to connect to a composite monitor. Only the output to the green gun connects to the composite monitor output. Figure 12-2 shows a simplified block diagram of the structure of the CGA.

As you can see from FIG. 12-1, the CGA is an enhanced version of the MDA. While it doesn't offer the same character resolution, the CGA does offer a color display and graphics mode. It uses a few additional circuits to perform its color magic.

First, the CGA adds a graphics support circuit. This allows the adapter to display low resolution graphics in place of characters. The video-support logic circuits are replaced with the color encoder and support circuits. In addition to providing timing, these circuits output the correct signals for one of three electron guns in the display. This provides the eight base colors. The addition of an intensity-bit output increases the number of colors to 16. The palette and overscan control circuit is a new addition as well. Its main purpose is to control which set of colors the display adapter sends to the display. In addition, this circuit makes sure that the screen is blanked during nondisplay periods like retrace.

The final two circuits send the output of the green gun to a composite monitor. The composite display timing and control provides the signals required to synchronize a composite display with the display-adapter signals. The composite output circuitry combines these timing signals with the output of the green gun. It outputs the result as an analog signal to the composite video.

Enhanced graphics adapter (EGA)

The enhanced graphics adapter (EGA) is more complex than any of the display adapters discussed so far. In most cases the EGA supports HGC, CGA, and enhanced graphics modes. The EGA provides HGC and CGA support through a compatibility mode. Figure 12-3 provides a simplified block diagram of the structure of an EGA. Unlike CGA and MDA standards, different manufacturers use different techniques to achieve EGA compatibility. Therefore, FIG. 12-3 represents a typical rather than absolute block diagram. As you can see, some EGAs use 64K and others 128K of RAM. In most cases the additional memory equates to increased graphics capability, display pages, font storage, or resolution.

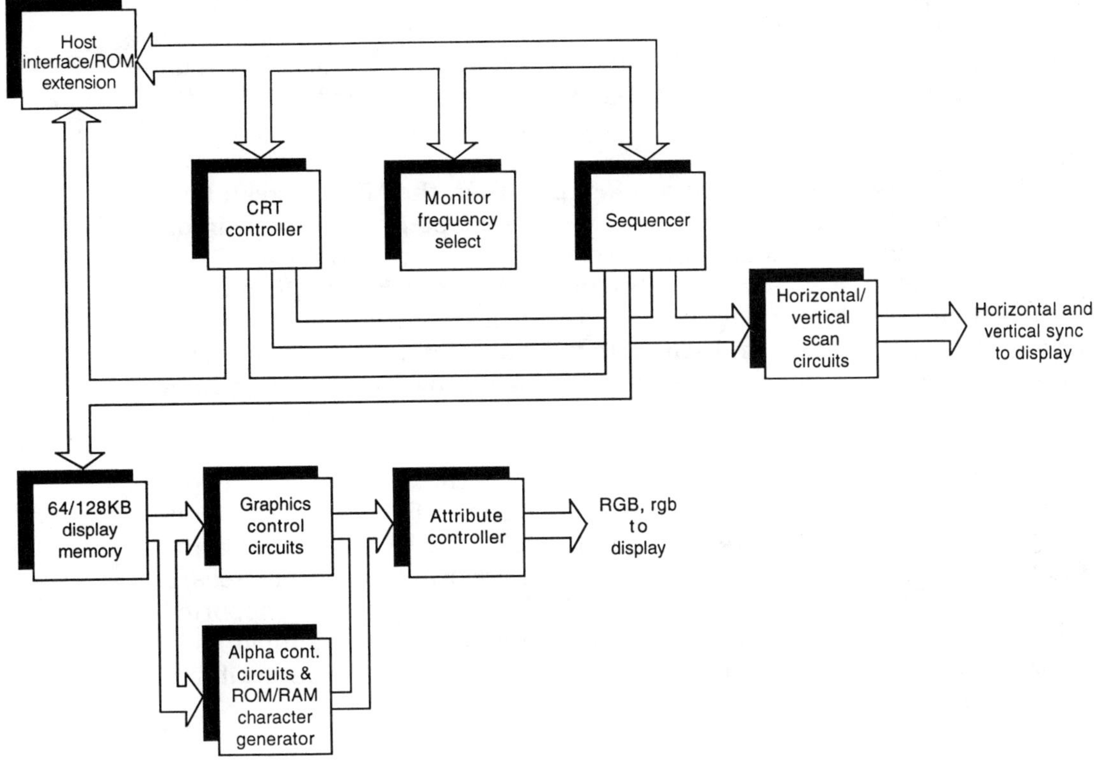

12-3 EGA block diagram

Notice that this is like the basic architecture found in the CGA. Like its predecessors, the EGA contains a host interface, CRTC, some video memory, a graphics control circuit, an alpha control circuit, and an attribute controller. Notice the enhancements to the alpha control circuits. You now have access to not only a ROM character generator, but a RAM character generator. This is one major difference between the EGA and CGA. You no longer have to accept the default character set; you can load any character set you deem necessary to perform a specific task. It is this ability that allows many programs to create GUI-like displays that use nonstandard characters. The appearance of that of graphics mode. On closer inspection, however, it becomes apparent that the display is still in character mode.

The EGA adds three more circuits to the picture. The monitor-frequency select performs the special task of allowing the EGA to emulate other display adapters. Without this circuit, the EGA would be incapable of generating the range of frequencies required to create different types of output. While the monitor-frequency select circuit is busy creating the operating frequencies required for different modes, the sequencer circuit is handling the logistics of moving data for the different modes. Each display mode uses a different set of rules in regard to data and screen handling.

The CGA uses video memory differently than the MDA. Screen handling includes every aspect of how the display adapter presents the information on screen. For example, the vertical retrace period for a CGA is different from the HGC. All this additional information is combined in the third new circuit. The horizontal/vertical scan circuits combine the output from all the other circuits and send it to the display in the form of horizontal and vertical sync signals. These sync signals allow the display adapter to tell the display which display mode to use in order to interpret the incoming data correctly.

Of course, none of this would be possible without some central control. The CRTC used in the EGA is an enhanced version of the CRTC contained in the CGA. It performs all the same tasks as the CRTC found in the CGA and MDA, but the range of tasks it must perform is greatly increased by the additional memory, support circuits, and display modes supported by the EGA. The CRTC must also support new tasks like loading fonts in RAM. All these new tasks serve to increase the complexity and flexibility of the EGA CRTC.

Virtual graphics array (VGA) and Super VGA

The virtual graphics array (VGA) is very similar to the EGA. A standard VGA provides 256K of display memory, while a Super VGA can provide 512K or more of display memory. Programs can use this extra memory for enhanced display resolutions, color combinations, and font storage. At present, there is no standard for Super VGA. The Video Electronics Standards Association (VESA) is working with vendors to produce a standard Super VGA interface. To determine the capabilities and programming interface for Super VGA modes supported by your adapter, check the vendor manual.

Figure 12-4 is a simplified block diagram of a typical VGA/Super VGA. Unlike the CGA and MDA standards, different manufacturers use different techniques to achieve VGA compatibility. Therefore, FIG. 12-4 represents a typical rather than absolute block diagram. As you can see, standard VGAs use 256K and Super VGAs use 512K or more of RAM. Some vendors might allow you to use up to 1Mb of RAM. Anything over this amount is unusual because of timing constraints that the adapter needs to observe. However, due to memory constraints, every VGA has at least 256K of RAM.

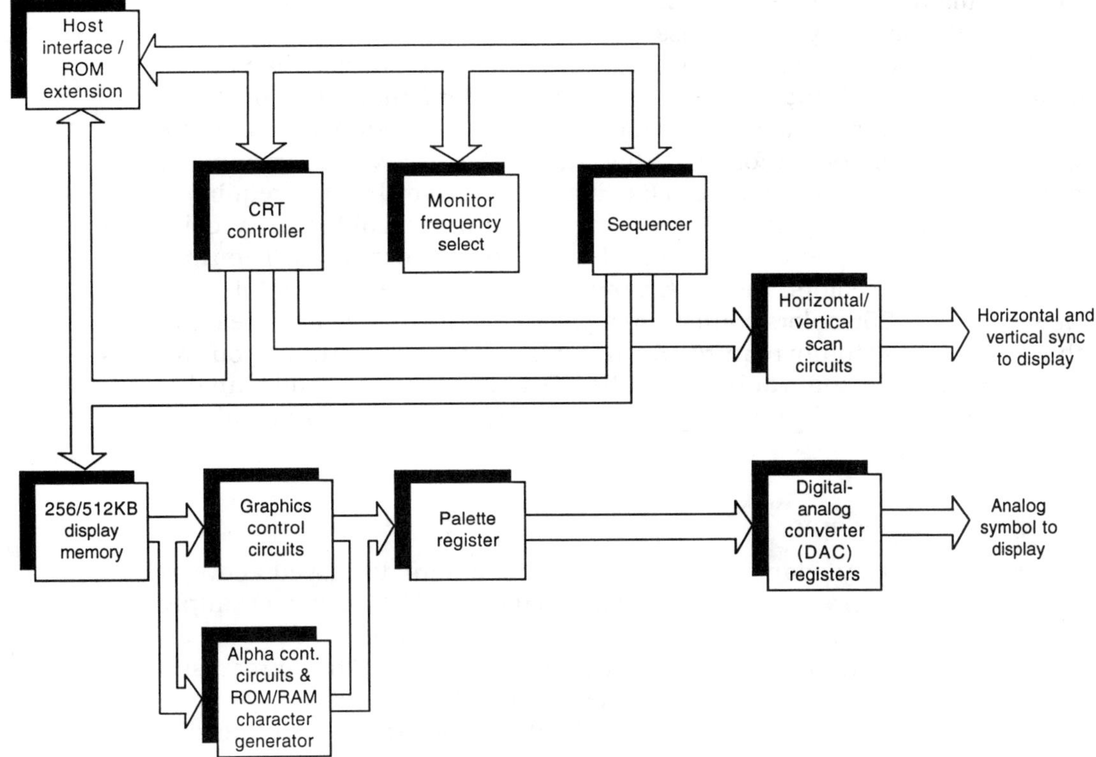

12-4 VGA block diagram

Besides some extra memory, the VGA looks essentially the same as the EGA. The only difference between the VGA and EGA is that the CRTC usually contains some extra features. These additional features usually allow the VGA to provide some extra flexibility and processing speed. In addition, the VGA provides an additional ROM, which supports the enhanced display modes. These enhanced display modes usually include several 256-color modes. The standard upper limit for Super VGA displays is 1,024 × 768 × 16 colors.

As you can see from FIG. 12-4, the VGA adds one new circuit. This circuit is called the digital-to-analog converter (DAC). The DAC converts the digital signal input provided by other display adapter circuits, and converts it to analog output. It does this by comparing the color number provided by the display circuitry to color values in a lookup table. This lookup table usually contains a standard set of colors. However, you can replace those color values with any value that the VGA is capable of displaying.

This means that the VGA is capable of color mapping, a feat that none of the other display adapters discussed so far can do.

There are a few reasons why the VGA uses analog rather than digital signals like the EGA and CGA do. The CGA provides a maximum of 16 colors. This means that the display adapter needs to output colors on three wires and intensity on a fourth. When the EGA came out, it was able to present 16 colors from a palette of 64. This means that the EGA requires 6 wires to output its signals. Three wires contain normal-intensity color information and three contain high-intensity color information. To output its standard 256 colors, the VGA would require 8 wires as a minimum. However, these 256 colors come from a palette of 262,144 colors, meaning that you would actually require 18 wires with a digital output. As you can see, this is cumbersome at best. So, the VGA uses a much simpler analog output requiring a 15-wire plug for all signals, including horizontal and vertical sync.

8514/A display adapter

The 8514/A display adapter differs from the adapters discussed above in several ways. The previous display adapters used a CRTC which is simply a controller, not a processor. The 8514/A, on the other hand, does use an on-board processor. This means that the 8514/A, like a math co-processor, can offload some of the work from the main CPU. In addition, you can directly access video memory and the display registers on the other display adapters.

Only the on-board CPU normally accesses the registers on an 8514/A. The user access consists of calls to a terminate-and-stay-resident (TSR) program called an application interface (AI). This means that you no longer have a choice; you must use AI calls when programming the 8514/A (at least if you want to make certain that an application will work properly). Another difference is that this display adapter doesn't operate by itself. It requires the addition of a VGA to access lower-resolution compatibility modes. This means that you now have a display adapter working in tandem to produce the output required from the user. Of course, this more than doubles the amount of work that the programmer must perform to create efficient, error-free displays.

As stated previously, the standard 8514/A AI consists of a TSR program. You access this program through interrupt 7Fh service 1 function 5. This means that you load AH with 01, and AL with 05. If the interrupt is successful, the CX:DX (segment:offset) pair returns a segment and offset to the program entry table, and the carry flag equals 0. This is the way that you know whether or not the machine you want to use has an 8514/A installed. If you call interrupt 7Fh with the appropriate register contents, and the carry flag returns set, then you know that the host machine doesn't contain an 8514/A. The program entry table contains 59 segment offset pairs for the calls listed in TABLE 12-1 in the order listed. Each call performs a different function in programming the 8514/A. You can look at the program entry table as an interrupt vector table for the 8514/A. Instead of calling a host processor interrupt, you're calling an 8514/A processor interrupt.

Table 12-1 8514/A application-interface AI commands

Command	Number	Function
ABLOCKCGA	53	Writes a CGA formatted alphanumeric character block.
ABLOCKMF1	52	Writes an alphanumeric character block.
ACURSOR	56	Sets the alphanumeric cursor position.
AERASE	54	Erases a character cell rectangle.
ASCROLL	55	Scrolls the character cell rectangle.
ASCUR	57	Sets the alphanumeric cursor shape.
ASFONT	58	Selects the alphanumeric character font.
AXLATE	59	Selects the alphanumeric attribute color index table.
HBAR	5	Begins a filled area.
HBBC	14	Performs Bit-BLT exclusively in display memory.
HBBCHN	13	Performs Bit-BLT to or from system memory.
HBBR	12	Defines the Bit-BLT source at an absolute address.
HBBW	10	Defines the Bit-BLT destination at an absolute address.
HCBBW	11	Defines the Bit-BLT destination at the current cursor position.
HCCHST	50	Places a text string at the current cursor position.

Table 12-1 Continued.

Command	Number	Function
HCHST	49	Places a text string at an absolute position.
HCLINE	2	Draws an absolute polyline starting at the current cursor position.
HCLOSE	16	Closes the display adapter interface.
HCMRK	9	Draws a marker symbol at the current cursor position.
HEAR	6	Ends a filled area.
HEGS	26	Clears the screen.
HESC	37	Terminate adapter processing.
HINIT	20	Initializes the task-dependent state buffer.
HINT	22	Waits for the vertical retrace signal.
HLDPAL	29	Load a palette.
HLINE	1	Draws an absolute polyline starting at an absolute cursor position.
HMRK	8	Draws a marker symbol at an absolute position.
HOPEN	15	Opens the display adapter interface.
HOCOORD	35	Gets the coordinate types.
HQCP	18	Gets the current cursor position.
HQDFPAL	19	Get default palette information.
HQDPS	38	Gets drawing process buffer size.
HQMODE	24	Gets the display adapter mode.
HQMODES	25	Sees if a display adapter mode is available.

Command	Number	Function
HRCLINE	4	Draws a relative polyline starting at the current cursor position.
HRECT	7	Draws a filled rectangle.
HRLINE	3	Draws a relative polyline starting at an absolute position.
HRLPC	33	Restores a saved line pattern position.
HRPAL	31	Restores a saved palette.
HSBCOL	45	Sets the background color.
HSBP	34	Sets the display and masking bitplane controls.
HSCMP	47	Sets the color comparison register.
HSCOL	44	Sets the foreground color.
HSCOORD	36	Sets the coordinate types.
HSCP	17	Moves the cursor to an absolute position.
HSCS	48	Selects a character set.
HSGQ	27	Sets the graphics quality/drawing styles.
HSHS	28	Clips a rectangle (scissors).
HSLPC	32	Saves the current line pattern position.
HSLT	42	Sets the current line type.
HSLW	43	Sets the current line width.
HSMARK	39	Sets the current marker shape.
HSMODE	23	Sets the display adapter mode.
HSMX	46	Sets the drawing raster operation (mix).

Table 12-1 Continued.

Command	Number	Function
HSPAL	30	Save the current palette.
HSPATT	40	Sets the current pattern shape.
HSPATTO	41	Sets the current pattern origin.
HSYNC	21	Sets the adapter to a task-dependent state.
HXLATE	51	Assigns a color index table for text.

Currently VESA is working in conjunction with various vendors to produce an 8514/A specification. Until such a specification is used by the majority of high-resolution display manufacturers, there is no certain method of programming the 8514/A registers directly. The vendor that's creating a specific display adapter is probably the best source of information regarding register programming information. In most cases, however, it's best to avoid programming the registers and use the 8514/A AI.

Business graphics array (BGA)

One of the things hindering vendors from creating even higher-resolution adapters than the Super VGA has the problem of overwhelming the main CPU. Because the CPU has to process both the video data and application data, the execution speed of a program can be greatly affected by overindulging in graphics. One solution to this problem is adding a graphics processor to the equation. If you can offload most, if not all, video processing from the host CPU, then the amount of graphics in a program becomes dependent on the speed of the graphics processor. One such processor is the TMS34010 from Texas Instruments.

The business graphics array (BGA) is one implementation of the 34010 graphics system processor (GSP). In most cases, the GSP requires discrete logic to perform its task. The addition of the 34092 BGA chip allows a simple implementation of a basic GSP design. As with all TMS340-family graphics processors, this board uses the Texas Instruments graphics architecture (an application interface) without modification. This means that the BGA should run most-TIGA compatible software, though at a lower resolution than some display adapters. Figure 12-5 shows a simplified block diagram of a typical BGA adapter.

Although the BGA produces resolutions similar to the 8514/A adapter, it has two advantages. First, you can program the 34010 like any computer. It doesn't rely on the host computer for program instructions or memory. This means that unlike a graphics coprocessor, the BGA reduces

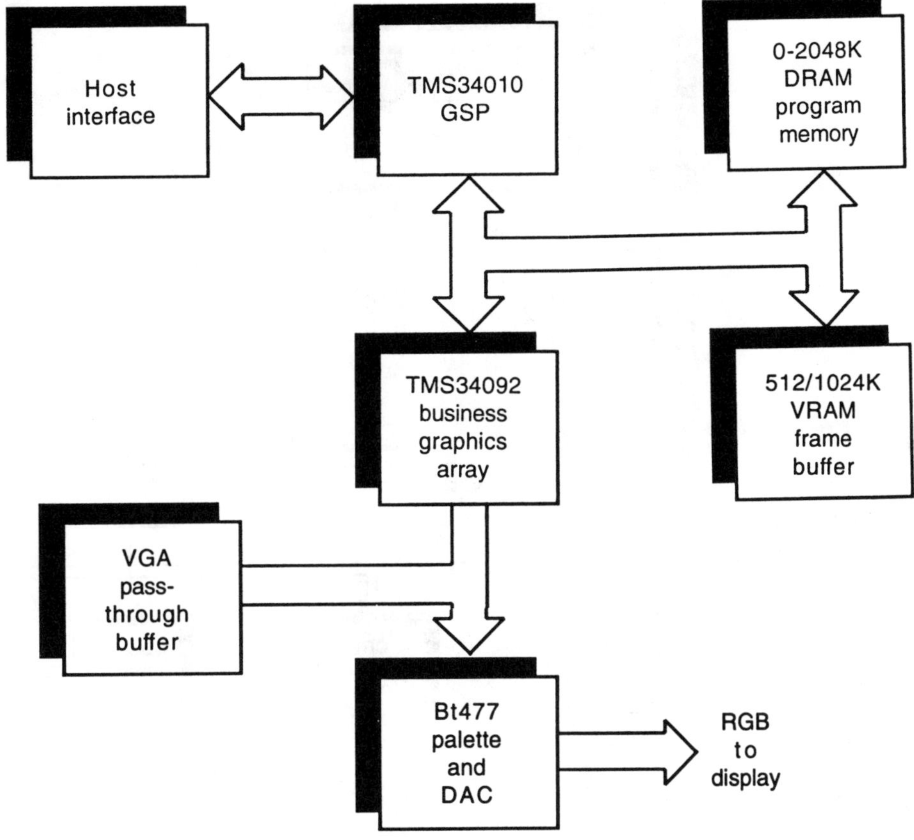

12-5 BGA block diagram

the load on the host CPU. The second advantage is speed. Because the BGA performs most of its own processing, it should update the display more quickly than coprocessor designs (depending on board design and application software).

TMS34010 graphics system processor (GSP)

GSP programming requires three pieces of information. First, you must know the memory mapping used by the interface software/ROM to provide access to the GSP. Second, you have know how to use the registers provided by the GSP to manipulate data in program and display memory. Some vendor boards don't allow direct access to either memory area. To read or write host data, you must first program the register set and then use processor commands to initiate the transfer. Third, you must know the GSP instruction set. Refer to the vendor manual for your GSP to obtain the addresses of various GSP components. Of course, you can eliminate this requirement by using the TIGA interface. Figure 12-6 shows a typical

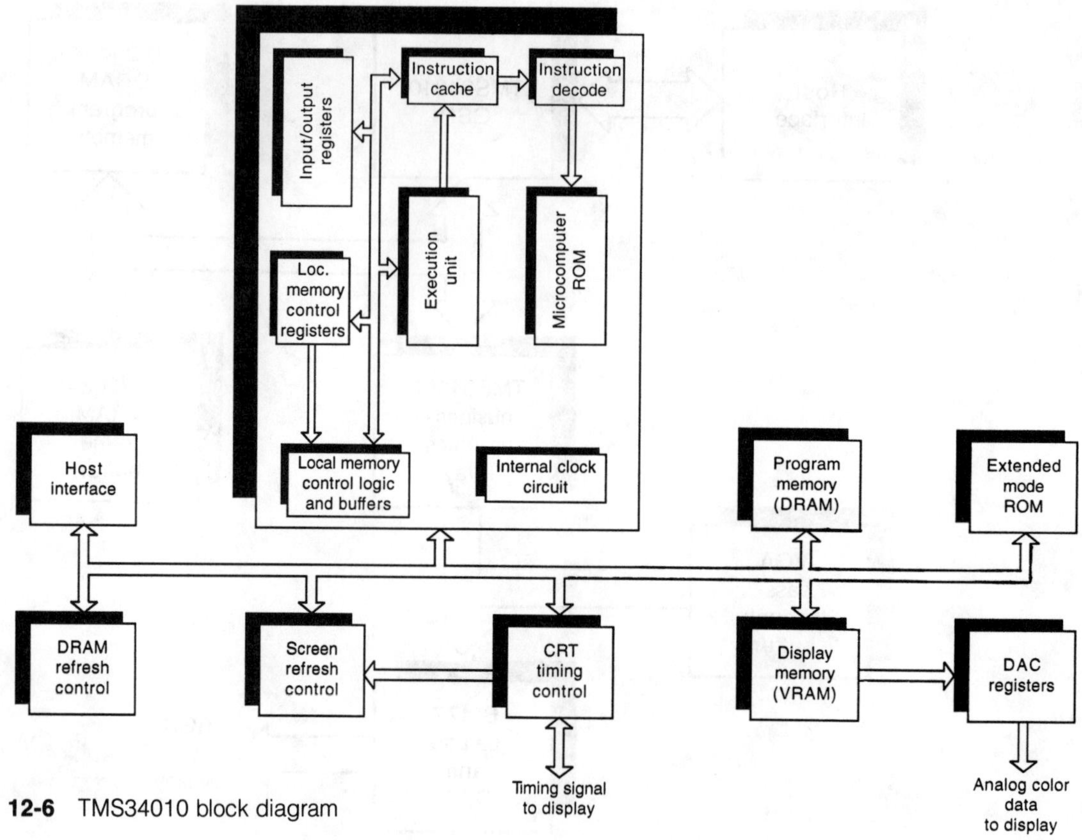

12-6 TMS34010 block diagram

TMS34010 implementation. Notice that the block diagram looks similar to other display implementations. The programmability of the GSP adds the functionality provided by this system. The block diagram shows a generalized version of a typical GSP implementation. Most manufacturers deviate from this basic design.

34010 Texas Instruments Graphics Architecture (TIGA)

The Texas Instruments Graphics Architecture (TIGA) application interface allows you to program the TMS34010 using the simplified procedures provided in multiple assembly and C libraries. TABLE 12-2 provides a summary of the TIGA instructions and their use. As with the processor instructions, this book does not provide the detailed instructions required by the novice programmer. Unlike the processor instructions, you must own a copy of the software development kit to use the TIGA interface. However, this book does provide a quick reference to the TIGA instruction set. In addition to the information provided by TABLE 12-2, you need to know the addresses used by the display adapter for the host interface. Obtain this information from the manufacturer technical manuals.

Table 12-2 TIGA instructions set

Instruction	Type	Function
Void BITBLT *(Width, Height, SRCX, SRCY, DSTX, DSTY)*	Pixel Array (Extended)	Copies data from the source bitmap to the destination bitmap. Width and height describe the size of both bitmaps. SRCX and SRCY describe the starting coordinates of the the source. DSTX and DSTY describe the starting coordinates of the destination.
Int CD_IS_ALIVE ()	Graphics System Initialization (Core)	Returns zero if the communication driver is not installed. Otherwise, returns a nonzero result.
Void CLEAR_FRAME_BUFFER *(Color)*	Clear (Core)	Clears the entire display memory by setting it to the specified color. Use the CLEAR_SCREEN function to preserve offscreen data.
Void CLEAR_PAGE *(Color)*	Clear (Core)	Clears the current drawing page by setting it to the specified color. Use the CLEAR_SCREEN function to preserve offscreen data.
Void CLEAR_SCREEN *(Color)*	Clear (Core)	Clears only the visible portion of display memory by setting it to the specified color.
Void COP2GSP *(COPID, COPADDR, GSPADDR, Length)*	Communication (Core)	Copies data from the coprocessor address space to the TMS340 address space. Transfers occur in 32-bit length words.
Short CPW *(X, Y)*	Graphics Attribute	Outputs a 4-bit outcode based on a pixel's position within a

Table 12-2 Continued.

Instruction	Type	Function
	Control (Core)	window, as shown below. *Code* — *Function* 0000 — Point lies within window. 01XX — Point lies above window. 10XX — Point lies below window. XX01 — Point lies left of window. XX10 — Point lies right of window.
Int CREATE_ALM *(RLM_Name, ALM_Name)*	Extensibility (Core)	Converts a relocatable load module to an absolute load module. Exits with a value of zero if successful.
Int CREATE_ESYM *(GM_Name)*	Extensibility (Core)	Creates an external symbol table of global symbols. The linking loader uses this table to resolve references in a relocatable load module. Exits with a value of zero if successful.
Int DELETE_FONT *(ID)*	Text (Extended)	Removes the font specified by ID (number) from the font table. Returns zero if the font was not installed. Returns nonzero value if font removed successfully.
Void DRAW_LINE *(X1, Y1, X2, Y2)*	Graphics Output (Extended)	Draws a line onscreen. X1 and Y1 contain the starting coordinate. X2 and Y2 contain the ending coordinate.
Void DRAW_OVAL *(W, H, XLeft, YTop)*	Graphics Output (Extended)	Draws an oval onscreen. W contains the width. H contains the height. XLeft and YTop

Instruction	Type	Function
		contain the coordinates of the upper left corner of the oval.
Void DRAW_OVALARC *(W, H, XLeft, YTop, Theta, Arc)*	Graphics Output (Extended)	Draws an eliptical arc onscreen. W contains the width. H contains the height. XLeft and YTop contain the coordinates of the upper left corner of the oval. Theta contains the start angle. Arc contains the number of degrees of arc.
Void DRAW_PIEARC *(W, H, XLeft, YTop, Theta, Arc)*	Graphics Output (Extended)	Draws an eliptical arc onscreen. Two lines emanate from the center of the arc to each end. W contains the width. H contains the height. XLeft and YTop contain the coordinates of the upper left corner of the oval. Theta contains the start angle. Arc contains the number of degrees of arc.
Void DRAW_POINT *(X, Y)*	Graphics Output (Extended)	Draws a single pixel onscreen. X and Y contain the coordinate of the pixel.
Void DRAW_POLYLINE *(N, Points)*	Graphics Output (Extended)	Draws a group of lines whose end points are suppied as a set of points. N indicates the number of lines to draw. Each point consists of an X and Y coordinate. To draw a closed polygon, use the same coordinates for the first and last set of points.
Void DRAW_POLYLINE *(N, Points)*	Poly Drawing (Extended)	See previous description.

Table 12-2 Continued.

Instruction	Type	Function
Void DRAW_RECT *(W, H, XLeft, YTop)*	Graphics Output (Extended)	Draws a rectangle onscreen. W contains the width. H contains the height. XLeft and YTop contain the coordinates of the upper left corner.
Unsigned Long FIELD_EXTRACT *(GPTR, FS)*	Communication (Core)	Returns the 32-bit data in the TMS340 memory space pointed to by GPTR. FS contains the field size (number of significant bits).
Void FIELD_INSERT *(GPTR, FS, Data)*	Communication (Core)	Writes data to the address in TMS340 memory pointed to by GPTR. FS contains the field size.
Void FILL_CONVEX *(N, Points)*	Graphics Output (Extended)	Draws a filled convex polygon. N indicates the number of vetices in the polygon. Each point consists of an X and Y coordinate. To draw a closed polygon, use the same coordinates for the first and last set of points.
Void FILL_CONVEX *(N, Points)*	Poly Drawing (Extended)	See previous description.
Void FILL_OVAL *(W, H, XLeft, YTop)*	Graphics Output (Extended)	Draws a filled oval onscreen. W contains the width. H contains the height. XLeft and YTop contain the coordinates of the upper left corner of the oval.
Void FILL_PIEARC *(W, H, XLeft, YTop, Theta, Arc)*	Graphics Output (Extended)	Draws a filled pie-shaped wedge onscreen. W contains the width. H contains the height. XLeft and YTop contain the coordinates of the upper left corner of the oval. Theta

Instruction	Type	Function
		contains the start angle. Arc contains the number of degrees of arc.
Void FILL_POLYGON *(N, Points)*	Graphics Output (Extended)	Draws a filled polygon. N indicates the number of vetices in the polygon. Each point consists of an X and Y coordinate. To draw a closed polygon, use the same coordinates for the first and last set of points.
Void FILL_POLYGON *(N, Points)*	Poly Drawing (Extended)	See previous description.
Void FILL_POLYGON *(N, Points)*	Workspace (Extended)	See previous description.
Void FILL_RECT *(W, H, XLeft, YTop)*	Graphics Output (Extended)	Draws a filled rectangle onscreen. W contains the width. H contains the height. XLeft and YTop contain the coordinates of the upper left corner.
Int FLUSH_ESYM ()	Extensibility (Core)	Flushes an external symbol table of external symbols. The linking loader uses this table to resolve references in a relocatable load module. Exits with a value of zero if successful.
Void FLUSH_EXTENDED ()	Extensibility (Core)	Flushes the TIGA extended functions and installed user functions. Then it removes the symbol table stored on the host.

Table 12-2 Continued.

Instruction	Type	Function
Void FRAME_OVAL *(W, H, XLeft, Ytop, DX, DY)*	Graphics Output (Extended)	Fills the area between two concentric ovals with the current foreground color. W contains the width. H contains the height. XLeft and YTop contain the coordinates of the upper left corner of the oval. DX specifies the horizontal distance between the outer and inner ovals. DY specifies the vertical distance between the two ovals.
Void FRAME_RECT *(W, H, XLeft, Ytop, DX, DY)*	Graphics Output (Extended)	Fills the area between two concentric rectangles with the current foreground color. W contains the width. H contains the height. XLeft and YTop contain the coordinates of the upper left corner. DX specifies the horizontal distance between the outer and inner rectangles. DY specifies the vertical distance between the two rectangles.
Int FUNCTION_IMPLEMENTED *(Function Code)*	Graphics System Initialization (Core)	Queries if a board supports a specific function. Some TIGA implementations do not support the following functions: COP2GSP GET_PALET GET_PALET_ENTRY GSP2COP INIT_PALET SET_PALET SET_PALET_ENTRY SET_TRANSP

Instruction	Type	Function
Void GET_COLORS *(FColor, BColor)*	Graphics Attribute Control (Core)	Obtains the foreground and background color values.
Void GET_CONFIG *(Config)*	Graphics System Initialization (Core)	Obtains the current display adapter configuration and returns it in a structure.
Int GET_CURS_STATE ()	Cursor (Core)	Returns zero if the cursor is not enabled.
Void GET_CURS_XY *(PX, PY)*	Cursor (Core)	Returns the coordinates of the cursor. Coordinates are relative to the upper left corner of the visible screen.
Void GET_ENV *(Env)*	Graphics Attribute Control (Core)	Returns the current graphics environment variable status in the structure pointed to by ENV.
Int GET_FONTINFO *(ID, PFontInfo)*	Text (Core)	Returns information about the current font in a structure pointed to by PFontInfo. ID determines which font the function polls. Zero returns system font information. -1 returns current font information.
Void GET_ISR_PRIORITIES *(NumISRs, PTR)*	Extensibility (Core)	Returns the priorities of interrupt service routines installed using the INSTALL_RLM and INSTALL_ALM functions. NumISRs contains the number of ISRs installed. PTR points to an array of short containing the priority data.

Table 12-2 Continued.

Instruction	Type	Function
Int GET_MODEINFO *(Index, ModeInfo)*	Graphics System Initialization (Core)	Returns a structure containing the board configuration supported by the current board and monitor. Index contains the mode number.
Long GET_NEAREST_COLOR *(R, G, B, I)*	Palette (Core)	Obtains the color number that most closely matches the specified parameters. R is red, G is green, B is blue, and I is intensity.
Void GET_OFFSCREEN_MEMORY *(Num_Blocks, Offscreen)*	Pointer-Based Memory Management (Core)	Returns a description of the offscreen memory areas not in use. These blocks normally consist of display memory not used for the frame buffer or alternate frame buffer. Obtain the Num_Blocks parameter using the GET_CONFIG function. Offscreen is a pointer to memory allocated for offscreen entry storage.
Void GET_PALET *(Palet Size, Palet)*	Palette (Core)	Reads an entire palette register into the palette array. You obtain the Palet Size parameter using the GET_CONFIG function.
Int GET_PALET_ENTRY *(Index, R, G, B, I)*	Palette (Core)	Reads the color values contained in a single pallete. Index specifies which pallete to read. R is red, G is green, B is blue, and I is intensity. This function returns zero if you specify an invalid index.
Long GET_PIXEL *(X, Y)*	Graphics Utility (Extended)	Returns the value of the pixel at the address specified by X and

Instruction	Type	Function
		Y. The coordinate is relative to the drawing origin.
Long GET_PMASK ()	Graphics Attribute Control (Core)	Returns the value of the plane mask (planes enabled/disabled for writing).
Int GET_PPOP ()	Graphics Attribute Control (Core)	Returns a five-bit code for the current pixel processing operation.

Code	*Function*
0	Source
1	Source AND Destination
2	Source AND NOT Destination
3	All 0s
4	Source OR NOT Destination
5	Source EQU Destination
6	NOT Destination
7	Source NOR Destination
8	Source OR Destination
9	Destination
10	Source XOR Destination
11	NOT Source AND Destination
12	All 1s
13	NOT Source OR Destination
14	Source NAND Destination
15	NOT Source
16	Source + Destination
17	ADDS (Source, Destination)
18	Destination - Source

Table 12-2 Continued.

Instruction	Type	Function
		19 SUBS (Destination, Source) 20 MAX (Source, Destination) 21 MIN (Source, Destination)
Int GET_TEXTATTR *(PControl, Count, Arg)*	Text (Extended)	Obtains the text rendering attributes. PControl is a pointer to a list of desired attributes. Current attribute values include %a (top left aligment = 0, baseline = 1) and %e (additional intercharacter spacing. Count contains the number of attributes in the control string.
Int GET_TRANSP ()	Graphics Attribute Control (Core)	Gets the state of the transparency (T) bit of the control register. Returns zero if transparency is disabled.
Unsigned Long GET_VECTOR *(TrapNum)*	Communication (Core)	Obtains the address of the trap vector specified by TrapNum.
Int GET_VIDEOMODE ()	Graphics System Initialization (Core)	Returns the current video mode emulation number.
Int GET_WINDOWING ()	Graphics Attribute Control (Core)	Gets the two-bit windowing code in the control I/O register, as shown below: *Code* *Function* 00 No windowing 01 Interrupt request on write in window 10 Interrupt request on

Instruction	Type	Function
		write outside window 11 Clip to window
Short GET_WKSP *(Addr, Pitch)*	Workspace (Core)	Returns parameters defining the current offscreen workspace. If the function returns a nonzero value, then Addr and Pitch contain the address and pitch of the workspace area.
Long GSP_CALLOC *(NMemB, Size)*	Pointer-Based Memory Management (Core)	Allocates enough TMS340 memory to contain NMemB objects of Size. Returns zero if not enough memory remains. Otherwise, returns a pointer to the memory area.
Void GSP_EXECUTE *(Entry Point)*	Graphics System Initialization (Core)	Loads and executes a nonapplication function. In other words, this function provides a portable COFF loader.
Int GSP_FREE *(PTR)*	Pointer-Based Memory Management (Core)	Deallocates the memory allocated by the GSP_MALLOC, GSP_CALLOC, or GSP_REALLOC functions. PTR points to the beginning of the memory area. Returns zero if not successful.
Long GSP_MALLOC *(Size)*	Pointer-Based Memory Management (Core)	Allocates the amount of TMS340 memory specified by Size. Returns zero if not enough memory remains. Otherwise, returns a pointer to the memory area.
Long GSP_MAXHEAP ()	Pointer-Based Memory Management (Core)	Returns the largest amount of heap available for allocation.

Table 12-2 Continued.

Instruction	Type	Function
Void GSP_MINIT *(Stack Size)*	Pointer-Based Memory Management (Core)	Deallocates all dynamically allocated memory in the TMS340 heap. Also changes the size of the stack. Providing a value of -1 allocates the default stack size.
Long GSP_REALLOC *(PTR, Size)*	Pointer-Based Memory Management (Core)	Changes the size of the previously allocated memory block pointed to by PTR. Size determines the new size of memory allocation. Returns zero if not successful.
Void GSP2COP *(COPID, GSPAddr, COPAddr, Length)*	Communication (Core)	A TMS34020 and above specific function which copies data from the TMS340 address space to the coprocessor address space.
Void GSP2GSP *(Addr1, Addr2, Length)*	Pointer-Based Memory Management (Core)	Copies data within the TMS340 address area. Addr1 contains the source address, Addr2 contains the destination address, and Length contains the length of the data.
Void GSP2HOST *(GPTR, HPTR, Length, Swizzle)*	Communication (Core)	Transfers data from TMS340 memory (GPTR) to host memory (HPTR). Length contains the length of data to transfer. If Swizzle is nonzero, the 34010 reverses the order of the bits in each byte before transfer.
Void GSP2HOSTXY *(SAddr, SPTCH, DAddr, DPTCH, SX, SY, DX, DY, XExt, YExt, PSize, Swizzle)*	Communication (Core)	Transfers a rectangular area of the TMS340 bitmap to the host. SAddr contains the source address; DAddr contains the destination address. The source area starts at SX, SY and is

Instruction	Type	Function
		transferred to DX, DY. XExt and YExt define the size of the area to transfer. PSize contains the size of the pixels transfered. SPTCH and DPTCH contain the source and destination pitch. If Swizzle is nonzero, the 34010 reverses the order of the bits in each byte before transfer.
Void HOST2GSP *(GPTR, HPTR, Length, Swizzle)*	Communication (Core)	Transfers data from host memory (HPTR) to TMS340 memory (GPTR). Length contains the length of data to transfer. If Swizzle is nonzero, the 34010 reverses the order of the bits in each byte before transfer.
Void HOST2GSPXY *(SAddr, SPTCH, DAddr, DPTCH, SX, SY, DX, DY, XExt, YExt, PSize, Swizzle)*	Communication (Core)	Transfers a rectangular area of host memory to the TMS340. SAddr contains the source address; DAddr contains the destination address. The source area starts at SX, SY and transfers to DX, DY. XExt and YExt define the area to transfer. PSize contains the size of the pixels. SPTCH and DPTCH contain source and destination pitch. If Swizzle is nonzero, the 34010 reverses the order of the bits in each byte before transfer.
Void INIT_PALET ()	Palette (Core)	Initializes the first 16 palette entries to the EGA default palette.
Void INIT_TEXT ()	Text (Core)	Removes any installed fonts from memory and selects the

Table 12-2 Continued.

Instruction	Type	Function
		standard font. Resets all text-drawing attributes.
Int INSTALL_ALM *(ALM Name)*	Extensibility (Core)	Installs the absolute load module into the TIGA graphics manager and returns a module identifier. Use the module identifier to invoke the ALM extended functions. Returns a negative number if not successful.
Short INSTALL_FONT *(PFont)*	Text (Extended)	Use this function to install a font into the font table after loading it into TMS340 memory. PFont points to the location of the font file in memory. The function returns an ID number when successful. Otherwise, it returns zero.
Int INSTALL_PRIMITIVES ()	Graphics System Initialization (Core)	Loads extended graphics primitives in memory. Returns a positive-number identifier when successful. Returns a negative-number error otherwise.
Int INSTALL_PRIMITIVES ()	Extensibility (Core)	See previous description.
Int INSTALL_RLM *(RLM Name)*	Extensibility (Core)	Installs a relocatable load module into the TIGA graphics manager and returns a module identifier. Use the module identifier to invoke the RLM extended functions. Returns a negative number if not successful.
Void INSTALL_USERERROR *(Function Name)*	Graphics System	Substitutes the default host communication error messages

Instruction	Type	Function
	Initialization (Core)	with a user-supplied error-handling routine.
Int LMO *(N)*	Graphics Utility (Core)	Calculates the position of the leftmost 1 in N. This function treats N as a 32-bit number. Returns -1 if not found. Otherwise, returns the bit position of the 1.
Unsigned Long LOADCOFF *(Filename)*	Graphics System Initialization (Core)	Provides the capability to load portable COFF code into the graphics manager. Not generally used by application programs.
Short PAGE_BUSY ()	Graphics Utility (Core)	Used with the PAGE_FLIP function. Returns a nonzero number while page flipping in progress. Otherwise, it returns zero.
Int PAGE_FLIP *(DIsplay, Drawing)*	Graphics Utility (Core)	Used with multiple frame buffers to set the display page to a particular frame buffer and the drawing page for subsequent drawing operations.
Void PATNFILL_CONVEX *(N, Points)*	Graphics Output (Extended)	Fills a covex polygon with a pattern. N defines the number of vertices in the polygon. Points is an array containing the coordinates of each vertice in the polygon. The first and last X,Y coordinate in points should be the same to make sure the polygon is closed. Uses the currently defined pattern for fill.
Void PATNFILL_CONVEX*(N, Points)*	Poly Drawing (Extended)	See previous description.

Table 12-2 Continued.

Instruction	Type	Function
Void PATNFILL_OVAL *(W, H, XLeft, YTop)*	Graphics Output (Extended)	Draws a pattern-filled oval onscreen. W contains the width. H contains the height. XLeft and YTop contain the coordinates of the upper left corner of the oval. Uses the currently defined pattern for fill.
Void PATNFILL_PIEARC *(W, H, XLeft, YTop, Theta, Arc)*	Graphics Output (Extended)	Draws a pattern-filled pie-shaped wedge onscreen. W contains the width. H contains the height. XLeft and YTop contain the coordinates of the upper left corner of the oval. Theta contains the start angle. Arc contains the number of degrees of arc. Uses the currently defined pattern for fill.
Void PATNFILL_POLYGON *(N, Points)*	Graphics Output (Extended)	Draws a pattern-filled polygon. N indicates the number of vetices in the polygon. Each point consists of an X and Y coordinate. To draw a closed polygon, use the same coordinates for the first and last set of points. Uses the currently defined pattern for fill.
Void PATNFILL_POLYGON *(N, Points)*	Poly Drawing (Extended)	See previous description.
Void PATNFILL_POLYGON *(N, Points)*	Workspace (Extended)	See previous description.
Void PATNFILL_RECT *(W, H, XLeft, YTop)*	Graphics Output (Extended)	Draws a pattern-filled rectangle onscreen. W contains the width. H contains the height. XLeft and YTop contain the coordinates of the upper left corner. Uses the currently defined pattern for fill.

Instruction	Type	Function
Void PATNFRAME_OVAL *(W, H, XLeft, Ytop, DX, DY)*	Graphics Output (Extended)	Pattern fills the area between two concentric ovals. W contains the width. H contains the height. XLeft and YTop contain the coordinates of the upper left corner of the oval. DX specifies the horizontal distance between the outer and inner ovals. DY specifies the vertical distance between the two ovals. Uses the currently defined pattern for fill.
Void PATNFRAME_RECT *(W, H, XLeft, YTop, DX, DY)*	Graphics Output (Extended)	Pattern fills the area between two concentric rectangles. W contains the width. H contains the height. XLeft and YTop contain the coordinates of the upper left corner. DX specifies the horizontal distance between the outer and inner rectangles. DY specifies the vertical distance between the two rectangles. Uses the currently defined pattern for fill.
Void PATNPEN_LINE *(X1, Y1, X2, Y2)*	Graphics Output (Extended)	Draws a patterned line onscreen. X1 and Y1 contain the starting coordinate. X2 and Y2 contain the ending coordinate. Uses the currently defined pattern for drawing. Use the SET_PENSIZE function to change pen width and height.
Void PATNPEN_OVALARC *(W, H, XLeft, YTop, Theta, Arc)*	Graphics Output (Extended)	Draws a patterned eliptical arc onscreen. W contains the width. H contains the height. XLeft and YTop contain the coordinates of the upper left corner. Theta contains the start

Table 12-2 Continued.

Instruction	Type	Function
		angle. Arc contains the degrees of arc. Uses the currently defined pattern for drawing. Use the SET_PENSIZE function to change pen width and height.
Void PATNPEN_PIEARC *(W, H, XLeft, YTop, Theta, Arc)*	Graphics Output (Extended)	Draws a patterned eliptical arc onscreen. Two lines emanate from the center of the arc to each end. W contains the width. H contains the height. XLeft and YTop contain the coordinates of the upper left corner. Theta contains the start angle. Arc contains the degrees of arc. Uses the currently defined pattern for drawing. Use the SET_PENSIZE function to change pen width and height.
Void PATNPEN_POINT *(X, Y)*	Graphics Output (Extended)	Draws rectangular set of pixels onscreen (corresponds to pen height and width). The pixel color depends on its position within the currently defined pattern. X and Y contain the coordinate of the pixel. Use the SET_PENSIZE function to change pen width and height.
Void PATNPEN_POLYLINE *(N, Points)*	Graphics Output (Extended)	Draws a group of patterned lines whose end points are suppied as a set of points. N indicates the number of lines to draw. Each point consists of an X and Y coordinate. To draw a closed polygon, use the same coordinates for the first and last set of points. Uses the currently defined pattern for drawing.

Instruction	Type	Function
		Use the SET_PENSIZE function to change pen width and height.
Void PATNPEN_POLYLINE *(N, Points)*	Poly Drawing (Extended)	See previous description.
Long PEEK_BREG *(BREG)*	Graphics Utility (Core)	Returns a 32-bit number containing the value of a B-file register. BREG contains a number from 0 to 15 corresponding to a file register number.
Void PEN_LINE *(X1, Y1, X2, Y2)*	Graphics Output (Extended)	Draws a line the width and heigth of the current pen onscreen. X1 and Y1 contain the starting coordinate. X2 and Y2 contain the ending coordinate. Use the SET_PENSIZE function to change pen width and height.
Void PEN_OVALARC *(W, H, XLeft, YTop, Theta, Arc)*	Graphics Output (Extended)	Draws an arc the width and heigth of the current pen onscreen. W contains the width. H contains the height. XLeft and YTop contain the coordinates of the upper left corner. Theta contains the start angle. Arc contains the degrees of arc. Use the SET_PENSIZE function to change pen width and height.
Void PEN_PIEARC *(W, H, XLeft, YTop, Theta, Arc)*	Graphics Output (Extended)	Draws an arc the width and heigth of the current pen onscreen. Two lines emanate from the center of the arc to each end. W contains the width. H contains the height.

Table 12-2 Continued.

Instruction	Type	Function
		XLeft and YTop contain the coordinates of the upper left corner. Theta contains the start angle. Arc contains the degrees of arc. Use the SET_PENSIZE function to change pen width and height.
Void PEN_POINT *(X, Y)*	Graphics Output (Extended)	Draws rectangular set of pixels onscreen (corresponds to pen height and width). X and Y contain the coordinate of the pixel. Use the SET_PENSIZE function to change pen width and height.
PEN_POLYLINE	Graphics Output (Extended)	Draws a group of lines the width and heigth of the current pen whose end points are suppied as a set of points. N indicates the number of lines to draw. Each point consists of an X and Y coordinate. To draw a closed polygon, use the same coordinates for the first and last set of points. Use the SET_PENSIZE function to change pen width and height.
PEN_POLYLINE	Poly Drawing (Extended)	See previous description.
Void POKE_BREG *(BREG, Value)*	Graphics Utility (Core)	Writes Value to the B-file register specified by BREG. Value is a 32-bit number.
Int RMO *(N)*	Graphics Utility (Core)	Calculates the position of the rightmost 1 in N. This function treats N as a 32-bit number. Returns -1 if not found. Otherwise, returns the bit position of the 1.

Instruction	Type	Function
Int SEED_FILL *(XSeed, YSeed, Buffer, Maxbytes)*	Graphics Output (Extended)	Fills a region of connected pixels starting a specified seed pixel. XSeed and YSeed contain the coordinates of the seed pixel. Buffer is an area of memory set aside for working storage. Maxbytes is the number of 8-bit bytes in the storage area.
Int SEED_PATNFILL *(XSeed, YSeed, Buffer, Maxbytes)*	Graphics Output (Extended)	Pattern fills a region of connected pixels starting a specified seed pixel. XSeed and YSeed contain the coordinates of the seed pixel. Buffer is an area of memory set aside for working storage. Maxbytes is the number of 8-bit bytes in the storage area. Uses the currently defined pattern for fill.
Int SELECT_FONT *(ID)*	Text (Extended)	Selects a previously installed font for use. ID is the number returned after font installation.
Void SET_BCOLOR *(Color)*	Graphics Attribute Control (Core)	Changes the background color specified in the COLOR0 B-file register to Color.
Void SET_CLIP_RECT *(W, H, XLeft, YTop)*	Graphics Attribute Control (Core)	Sets the current clipping rectangle by updating the B-file registers WSTART and WEND to match the W and H parameters. XLeft and YTop are relative to the drawing origin.
Void SET_COLORS *(FColor, BColor)*	Graphics Attribute Control (Core)	Changes the foreground color specified in the COLOR1 B-file register to FColor. Also changes the background color specified in the COLOR0 B-file register to BColor.

Table 12-2 Continued.

Instruction	Type	Function
Int SET_CONFIG *(Graphics Mode, Init Draw)*	Graphics System Initialization (Core)	The SET_CONFIG function changes the mode to match Graphics Mode. If the mode is invalid, returns 0. Otherwise, returns a nonzero result. Init Draw causes the function to reset the following parameters when set true (nonzero): Transparency is disabled (CONTROL I/O Register). Window Clipping is set (CONTROL I/O Register). Pixel Processing is set to replace (CONTROL I/O Register). PMASK I/O Register is set to 0. Foreground color is set to light grey and background color to black. Source and destination bitmaps are set to the screen. Drawing origin is set to 0, 0. Pen width and height are set to 1. Current pattern address is set to 0. All installed fonts are removed and the current selected font set to the system font. Graphics cursor placed in the center of the screen, turned off, and set to the default shape. Temporary workspace is initialized.
Void SET_CURS_SHAPE *(Shape)*	Cursor (Core)	Defines the size and shape of the cursor. Shape is a structure containing size, color, and shape bitmaps.

Instruction	Type	Function
Void SET_CURS_STATE *(Enable)*	Cursor (Core)	Displays the cursor if Enable is nonzero. Removes cursor if Enable is zero.
Void SET_CURS_XY *(X, Y)*	Cursor (Core)	Sets the pixel coordinates of the cursor hotspot. The cursor coordinates are relative to the upper left corner of the screen.
Void SET_DRAW_ORIGIN *(X, Y)*	Graphics Attribute Control (Extended)	Sets the drawing origin for future drawing operations.
Void SET_DSTBM *(Addr, Pitch, XEXT, YEXT, PSize)*	Pixel Array (Extended)	Sets the destination bitmap for future BITBLT operations. An address value of zero sets the destination to screen.
Void SET_FCOLOR *(Color)*	Graphics Attribute Control (Core)	Changes the foreground color specified in the COLOR1 B-file register to Color.
Void SET_INTERRUPT *(Level, Priority, Enable, Scan Line)*	Extensibility (Core)	Enables or disables a previously installed interrupt service routine. The Scan Line parameter is used for display interrupts only. It sets the scan line at which the interrupt becomes enabled.
Void SET_PALET *(Count, Index, Palet)*	Palette (Core)	Loads an entire palette into memory. Count contains the number of palette entries. Index contains the palette loading start point. Palet contains groups of four values (R, G, B, and I). Each group defines one palette value.
Void SET_PALET_ENTRY *(Index, R, G, B, I)*	Palette (Core)	Loads a single palette into memory. Index contains the

Table 12-2 Continued.

Instruction	Type	Function
		palette entry to replace. R, G, B, and I contain the color values for the palette entry.
Void SET_PATN *(P)*	Graphics Attribute Control (Extended)	Defines the pattern used for drawing operations. P is a pointer to a structure containing the height, width, depth, and bit pattern.
Void SET_PENSIZE *(W, H)*	Graphics Attribute Control (Extended)	Sets the width (W) and height (H) of the drawing pen.
Void SET_PMASK *(Mask)*	Graphics Attribute Control (Core)	Defines which plane-mask bits are writable. A zero in a bit position enables writing. A one in a bit position disables writing.
Void SET_PPOP *(PPOP Code)*	Graphics Attribute Control (Core)	Defines the pixel processing for future drawing operations. *Code* *Function* 0 Source 1 Source AND Destination 2 Source AND NOT Destination 3 All 0s 4 Source OR NOT Destination 5 Source EQU Destination 6 NOT Destination 7 Source NOR Destination 8 Source OR Destination 9 Destination 10 Source XOR

Instruction	Type	Function	
			Destination
		11	NOT Source AND Destination
		12	All 1s
		13	NOT Source OR Destination
		14	Source NAND Destination
		15	NOT Source
		16	Source + Destination
		17	ADDS (Source, Destination)
		18	Destination - Source
		19	SUBS (Destination, Source)
		20	MAX (Source, Destination)
		21	MIN (Source, Destination)
Void SET_SRCBM *(Addr, Pitch, XEXT, YEXT, PSize)*	Pixel Array (Extended)	Sets the source bitmap for future BITBLT operations. An address value of zero sets the source to screen.	
Int SET_TEXTATTR *(PControl, Count, Arg)*	Text (Extended)	Sets the text rendering attributes. PControl is a pointer to a list of desired attributes. Current attribute values include %a (top left aligment = 0, baseline = 1) and %e (additional intercharacter spacing). Count contains the number of attributes in the control string.	
Void SET_TIMEOUT *(Value)*	Graphics System Initialization (Core)	Sets the time in milliseconds that the host waits for a TMS340 function to complete before calling the error function.	

Table 12-2 Continued.

Instruction	Type	Function
Void SET_TRANSP *(Mode)*	Graphics Attribute Control (Core)	Changes the transparency mode (TMS34020 and above only) as shown below. (TMS34010 uses mode 2 only.) *Mode* *Function* 0 Source transparency = 0. 1 Source transparency = COLOR0 2 Result transparency = 0. 3 Result transparency = COLOR0
Unsigned SET_VECTOR *(TrapNum, NewAddr)*	Communication (Core)	Sets the specified trap number to NewAddr. Returns the address of the old interrupt.
Int SET_VIDEOMODE *(Mode, Style)*	Graphics System Initialization (Core)	The SET_VIDEOMODE function changes the current video mode and determines how to initialize the new mode. Mode can contain one of the following values: TIGA, MDA, HERCULES, CGA, EGA, VGA, AI_8514, or PREVIOUS. Style determines the initialization method. It can contain one of the following values: NO_INIT, INIT_GLOBALS, INIT, or CLR_SCREEN.
Void SET_WINDOWING *(Enable)*	Graphics Attribute Control (Core)	Sets the two-bit windowing code in the control I/O register as shown below. *Code* *Function* 00 No windowing 01 Interrupt request on write in window 10 Interrupt request on

Instruction	Type	Function
		write outside window 11 Clip to window
Void SET_WKSP *(Addr, Pitch)*	Workspace (Core)	Sets parameters defining the current offscreen workspace. Addr and Pitch contain the address and pitch of the workspace area.
Void STYLED_LINE *(X1, Y1, X2, Y2, Style, Mode)*	Graphics Output (Extended)	Uses Bresenham's algorithm to draw a styled line from X1, Y1 to X2, Y2. Style is a 32-bit value containing a repeating pattern. Mode changes the method used for drawing. *Mode* *Function* 0 Do not draw background pixels, leave gaps. Load new line-style from style argument. 1 Draw background pixels using COLOR0. Load new line-style from style argument. 2 Do not draw background pixels, leave gaps. Do not load new line-style from style argument. 3 Draw background pixels using COLOR0. Do not load new line style from style argument.
Void SWAP_BM ()	Pixel Array (Extended)	Exchanges pointers to the structures containing the source and destination bitmaps.

Table 12-2 Continued.

Instruction	Type	Function
Void SYNCHRONIZE ()	Graphics System Initialization (Core)	Synchronizes operations between two processors. Ensures the TMS340 completes an operation before the host CPU tries to manipulate the resulting data.
Int TEXT_OUT *(X, Y, PString)*	Text (Core)	Sends an ASCII string pointed to by PString to the display using the current font. X and Y specify the starting coordinates for the string.
Int TEXT_WIDTH *(PString)*	Text (Extended)	Returns the length of the specified string in pixels (using the current font for reference).
Void TRANSP_OFF ()	Graphics Attribute Control (Core)	Disables transparency for future drawing operations.
Void TRANSP_ON ()	Graphics Attribute Control (Core)	Enables transparency for future drawing operations.
Void WAIT_SCAN *(Line)*	Graphics Utility (Core)	Causes a wait state until the processor scans the specified scan line. Control returns to the calling procedure. Synchronizes drawing operations with the display.
Void ZOOM_RECT *(WS, HS, XS, YS, WD, HD, XD, YD, LineBuf)*	Pixel Array (Extended)	Expands or shrinks the specified rectangle to fit on the display. WS contains the source width. HS contains the source height. XS and YS contain the coordinates of the upper left corner of the source screen. WD contains the destination width. HD contains the destination height. XD and YD

Instruction	Type	Function
		contain the coordinates of the upper left corner of the destination screen. LineBuf is a buffer large enough to contain one line of the display.

As shown by TABLE 12-2, the TIGA instruction set falls into 14 main categories. In addition, each instruction also falls into one of two types. TIGA instruction types are core and extended. Core instructions are always available. They remain constant over the entire range of TIGA-compatible boards. You must load an extended function into the TIGA environment before using it. This allows you to substitute one instruction for another. Always consult the manufacturer documentation before using an extended function.

There are 14 TIGA instruction categories. The graphics system initialization functions allow you to determine the presence of a TIGA-compatible board and place the 340XX in a predefined state. There are different methods of performing this task. Each instruction performs the task of initialization in a different way. The cLear functions allow you to clear all or part of display memory. The graphics-attribute control functions allow you to change how the graphics processor executes various instructions. These attributes include foreground color, background color, plane mask, pixel processing, transparency, windowing, drawing origin, fill pattern, and drawing pen.

The palette function allows you to change the final color used to paint the display on screen. These functions vary in scope from manufacturer to manufacturer. The graphics-output function perform the actual drawing of objects in display memory. The poly-drawing function provide extended graphics drawing functions. The workspace functions provide a method of temporarily allocating memory to manipulate a graphics object. The pixel-array functions allow you to define pixel blocks and move them within display memory. The text functions provide the means to send text to the display. These functions depend on the availability of TIGA font files. You must install a font before using these functions.

The cursor functions change the appearance and position of the cursor on-screen. The graphics-utility functions consist of miscellaneous housekeeping instructions. The pointer-based memory management functions allow you to allocate and deallocate dynamic memory. In addition, these functions provide statistics on memory status. The communication functions determine how and when the display adapter communicates with the host. Finally, the extensibility functions allow you to add or delete functions from the TIGA environment.

As you can see, each category of TIGA instruction performs a specific task in relation to the graphics environment. Using this interface not only allows you to create portable code, but develop programs quickly and easily.

Using ROM interrupts to affect the display

This section contains descriptions for all display adapter specific ROM interrupts. The EGA and VGA BIOS extension specific information identifies which adapter uses it.

Set video mode (interrupt 10h service 0)

Use this with MDA, CGA, EGA, MCGA, and VGA. This service routine changes thc current video mode. The video mode affects both display type (graphics or text) and resolution. TABLE 12-3 contains a listing of applicable video modes. Notice that the mode doesn't always mean the same thing for each display type. In addition, the glyph-cell size (number of horizontal and vertical pixels for a character) is not applicable to the mouse. The register contents on service routine entry follow.

Register contents:

AH	0
AL	Desired video mode

Set cursor size (interrupt 10h service 1)

Use this with MDA, CGA, EGA, MCGA, and VGA. This service changes the cursor size and line position. For example, when using a CGA display, specifying a starting scan line of 0 and an ending scan line of 7 produces a block cursor. The two standard cursor types are underline and block. However, this doesn't mean that you are limited to these two sizes. TABLE 12-3 provides a character-size listing for each video mode. The character size minus one specifies the maximum cursor scan-line position.

Register contents:

AH	1
CH	Starting scan line
CL	Ending scan line

Set cursor position (interrupt 10h service 2)

Use this with MDA, CGA, EGA, MCGA, and VGA. This service changes the cursor position on screen. It therefore affects where the next text appears.

TABLE 12-3 specifies the screen dimensions for various video modes. Use these values to determine the maximum cursor row and column position for a particular video mode. TABLE 12-4 shows the correlation between video mode, display adapter type, and the number of available pages. Notice that some adapters provide more pages based on the amount of display memory available. For example, CGA in mode 2 provides only four pages, while EGA, MCGA, and VGA provide eight pages. This table is based on the standard display adapter configurations. Some Super VGA display adapters might provide more pages. Consult your vendor manual for further details.

Using this interrupt with Clipper might present some problems. For example, the interrupt won't automatically update the values returned by the Row( ) and Col( ) functions. There are other factors to consider as well. Some Clipper display functions might fail to operate correctly. In most cases you should avoid using this function and allow Clipper to position the cursor on screen.

Register contents:

AH	2
BH	Video page number
DH	Cursor row
DL	Cursor column

Table 12-3 Video-mode settings for BIOS interrupt 10 service 0

Mode	Type	Colors	Resolution	Glyph cell
*Enhanced color display **				
0h	Text	16/64	350 by 320	8 by 14
1h	Text	16/64	350 by 320	8 by 14
2h	Graphics	16/64	350 by 640	8 by 14
3h	Graphics	16/64	350 by 640	8 by 14
*Standard display **				
0h	Text	16	200 by 320	8 by 8
1h	Text	16	200 by 320	8 by 8
2h	Graphics	16	200 by 640	8 by 8
3h	Graphics	16	200 by 640	8 by 8

Table 12-3 Continued.

Mode	Type	Colors	Resolution	Glyph cell
*Enhanced color and standard displays **				
4h	Graphics	4	200 by 320	8 by 8
5h	Graphics	4	200 by 320	8 by 8
6h	Graphics	2	200 by 640	8 by 14
7h	Text	4	350 by 720	9 by 14
Dh	Graphics	16	200 by 320	8 by 8
Eh	Graphics	16	200 by 640	8 by 8
*64Kb boards **				
Fh	Graphics	4	350 by 640	8 by 14
10h	Graphics	4/64	350 by 640	8 by 14
*128Kb boards **				
Fh	Graphics	4	350 by 640	8 by 14
10h	Graphics	16/64	350 by 640	8 by 14

* Use the standard display settings for CGA and enhanced color display settings for EGA. The VGA always uses the enhanced color display and 128Kb board settings.

Table 12-4 Video display pages

Display mode	Display adapter	Pages
0	CGA, EGA, MCGA, VGA	0 - 7
1	CGA, EGA, MCGA, VGA	0 - 7
2	CGA	0 - 3
2	EGA, MCGA, VGA	0 - 7
3	CGA	0 - 3
3	EGA, MCGA, VGA	0 - 7
7	EGA, VGA	0 - 7
Dh	EGA, VGA	0 - 7
Eh	EGA, VGA	0 - 3
Fh	EGA, VGA	0 - 1
10h	EGA, VGA	0 - 1

NOTE:
Video mode/adapter combinations not listed use 1 display page.

Read cursor position and size (interrupt 10h service 3)

Use this with MDA, CGA, EGA, MCGA, and VGA. This service reads the current cursor position and size. You can use it to store the current condition of the display before manipulating it using an external routine. Failure to do so could result in unexpected output from some Clipper display functions upon return from the external routine. These values appear in the registers as stated below after interrupt execution. TABLE 12-3 shows the relationship between various display modes and the cell size of the characters used. TABLE 12-4 shows the correlation between video mode, display adapter type, and the number of available pages. The service requires that you supply the video page number as input.

Register contents on entry:

AH	3
BH	Video page number

Register contents on exit:

BH	Video page number
CH	Beginning scan line of cursor
CL	Ending scan line of cursor
DH	Cursor row
DL	Cursor column

Read light-pen position (interrupt 10h service 4)

Use this with CGA and EGA. This service returns the current light-pen position after interrupt execution. TABLE 12-3 specifies the screen dimensions for various video modes. Because the service returns the pixel position of the light pen, use these values to determine light-pen position in relation to total screen size. Only the CGA, MDA, and EGA have light-pen ports.

Register contents on entry:

AH	4

Register contents on exit (when AX equals 1):

AH	Light-pen trigger status (1 when triggered)
BX	Pixel column
CX	Pixel row
DH	Light pen row
DL	Light pen column

Select active display page (interrupt 10h service 5)

Use this with MDA, CGA, EGA, MCGA, and VGA. This service selects the active display page. A display page is a section of memory large enough to store one screen of information. For example, a screen that provides 16 different colors at a resolution of 80 characters by 25 lines requires 8,000 bytes of video memory. An EGA with 64K of video RAM could store eight such pages.

The configuration of the display adapter's registers also affects the number of display pages available. Most display adapters set an upper limit of eight pages. Each adapter allows a different number of display pages depending on the current video mode. TABLE 12-4 shows the correlation between video mode, display adapter type, and the number of available pages.

You must store the current display page before attempting to access a different display page from within Clipper. Failure to store the current display page could result in display function failure on return from the external routine. Using external interrupts doesn't update Clipper's internal counters. Therefore, changing the video state without updating the counters leaves the counters in an undetermined state.

Register contents on entry:	
AH	5
AL	Video page number

Scroll window up (interrupt 10h service 6)

Use this with MDA, CGA, EGA, MCGA, and VGA. This service scrolls the window defined by CX and DX up the number of spaces specified in AL. The service does not save any text scrolled past the top of the window. This means that scrolling the window down will not restore the current screen contents. You can use this service to move information on screen around, to clear the display (scroll the entire display up), or create special video affects. TABLE 12-3 specifies the screen dimensions for various video modes. TABLE 12-5 contains a listing of color combinations and attribute numbers.

Register contents on entry:	
AH	6
AL	Number of lines to scroll
BH	Attribute of fill character
CH	Upper left window row
CL	Upper left window column
DH	Lower right window row
DL	Lower right window column

Table 12-5 Character-attribute color values

Foreground	Background	Hex value	Dec value
Blue	Black	01h	1
Green	Black	02h	2
Cyan	Black	03h	3
Red	Black	04h	4
Magenta	Black	05h	5
Brown	Black	06h	6
White	Black	07h	7
Gray	Black	08h	8
Light blue	Black	09h	9
Light green	Black	0Ah	10
Light cyan	Black	0Bh	11
Light red	Black	0Ch	12
Light magenta	Black	0Dh	13
Yellow	Black	0Eh	14
Bright white	Black	0Fh	15
Black	Blue	10h	16
Green	Blue	12h	18
Cyan	Blue	13h	19
Red	Blue	14h	20
Magenta	Blue	15h	21
Brown	Blue	16h	22
White	Blue	17h	23
Gray	Blue	18h	24
Light blue	Blue	19h	25
Light green	Blue	1Ah	26
Light cyan	Blue	1Bh	27
Light red	Blue	1Ch	28
Light magenta	Blue	1Dh	29
Yellow	Blue	1Eh	30
Bright white	Blue	1Fh	31
Black	Green	20h	32
Blue	Green	21h	33
Cyan	Green	23h	35
Red	Green	24h	36
Magenta	Green	25h	37
Brown	Green	26h	38
White	Green	27h	39
Gray	Green	28h	40
Light blue	Green	29h	41

Table 12-5 Continued.

Foreground	Background	Hex value	Dec value
Brown	Cyan	36h	54
White	Cyan	37h	55
Gray	Cyan	38h	56
Light blue	Cyan	39h	57
Light green	Cyan	3Ah	58
Light cyan	Cyan	3Bh	59
Light red	Cyan	3Ch	60
Light magenta	Cyan	3Dh	61
Yellow	Cyan	3Eh	62
Bright white	Cyan	3Fh	63
Black	Red	40h	64
Blue	Red	41h	65
Green	Red	42h	66
Cyan	Red	43h	67
Magenta	Red	45h	69
Brown	Red	46h	70
White	Red	47h	71
Gray	Red	48h	72
Light blue	Red	49h	73
Light green	Red	4Ah	74
Light cyan	Red	4Bh	75
Light red	Red	4Ch	76
Light magenta	Red	4Dh	77
Yellow	Red	4Eh	78
Bright white	Red	4Fh	79
Black	Magenta	50h	80
Blue	Magenta	51h	81
Green	Magenta	52h	82
Light green	Green	2Ah	42
Light cyan	Green	2Bh	43
Light red	Green	2Ch	44
Light magenta	Green	2Dh	45
Yellow	Green	2Eh	46
Bright white	Green	2Fh	47
Black	Cyan	30h	48
Blue	Cyan	31h	49
Green	Cyan	32h	50
Red	Cyan	34h	52
Magenta	Cyan	35h	53

Foreground	Background	Hex value	Dec value
Cyan	Magenta	53h	83
Red	Magenta	54h	84
Brown	Magenta	56h	86
White	Magenta	57h	87
Gray	Magenta	58h	88
Light blue	Magenta	59h	89
Light green	Magenta	5Ah	90
Light cyan	Magenta	5Bh	91
Light red	Magenta	5Ch	92
Light magenta	Magenta	5Dh	93
Yellow	Magenta	5Eh	94
Bright white	Magenta	5Fh	95
Black	Brown	60h	96
Blue	Brown	61h	97
Green	Brown	62h	98
Cyan	Brown	63h	99
Red	Brown	64h	100
Magenta	Brown	65h	101
White	Brown	67h	103
Gray	Brown	68h	104
Light blue	Brown	69h	105
Light green	Brown	6Ah	106
Light cyan	Brown	6Bh	107
Light red	Brown	6Ch	108
Light magenta	Brown	6Dh	109
Yellow	Brown	6Eh	110
Bright white	Brown	6Fh	111
Black	White	70h	112
Blue	White	71h	113
Green	White	72h	114
Cyan	White	73h	115
Red	White	74h	116
Magenta	White	75h	117
Brown	White	76h	118
Gray	White	78h	120
Light blue	White	79h	121
Light green	White	7Ah	122
Light cyan	White	7Bh	123
Light red	White	7Ch	124

Table 12-5 Continued.

Foreground	Background	Hex value	Dec value
Light magenta	White	7Dh	125
Yellow	White	7Eh	126
Bright white	White	7Fh	127

NOTE:
This table lists the default combinations. Both the VGA and EGA allow other possibilities.

Scroll window down (interrupt 10h service 7)

Use this with MDA, CGA, EGA, MCGA, and VGA. This service scrolls the window defined by CX and DX down the number of spaces specified in AL. The service doesn't save any text scrolled past the bottom of the window. This means that scrolling the window up won't restore the current screen contents. You can use this service to move information on the screen around, to clear the display (scroll the entire display up), or create special video effects. TABLE 12-3 specifies the screen dimensions for various video modes. TABLE 12-5 contains a listing of color combinations and attribute numbers.

Register contents on entry:

AH	7
AL	Number of lines to scroll
BH	Attribute of fill character
CH	Upper left window row
CL	Upper left window column
DH	Lower right window row
DL	Lower right window column

Read character and attribute (interrupt 10h service 8)

Use this with MDA, CGA, EGA, MCGA, and VGA. This service returns the ASCII character number and attribute for the character at the current cursor position. Because none of the Clipper functions rely on the character or attribute information remaining constant, you can use this function to create special effects. You can also use it to detect the current screen contents. TABLE 12-4 shows the correlation between video mode, display-adapter type, and the number of available pages. TABLE 12-5 contains a listing of color combinations and attribute numbers.

Register contents on entry:	
AH	8
BH	Video page number

Register contents on exit:	
AH	Character attribute
AL	Character number

Write character and attribute (interrupt 10h service 9)

Use this with MDA, CGA, EGA, MCGA, and VGA. This service writes the specified character to the display page defined by BH using the color found in BL. Using this service is time-consuming for a large number of characters because each character must be written individually. It is, however, a very fast method of writing a few characters with inconsistent color values. TABLE 12-3 shows the correlation between video mode, display-adapter type, and the number of available pages. TABLE 12-4 contains a listing of color combinations and attribute numbers.

Register contents on entry:	
AH	9
AL	Character
BH	Video page number
BL	Character attribute/color
CX	Number of characters

Write character (interrupt 10h service Ah)

Use this with MDA, CGA, EGA, MCGA, and VGA. This service writes the number of characters specified in CX at the cursor position. The effect is not the same as writing a string to the display. AL contains the character to write. This character value doesn't change throughout the writing process. TABLE 12-4 shows the correlation between video mode, display-adapter type, and the number of available pages. Notice that this service doesn't allow you to control the display color. The service uses whatever color currently appears on the display as the color for the output character.

Register contents on entry:	
AH	Ah
AL	Character
BH	Video page number
CX	Number of characters

Set color palette (interrupt 10h service Bh)

Use this with CGA, EGA, MCGA, and VGA. This service is designed for CGA-style color manipulation. It changes the palette, background, or border color depending on the current video mode. In text mode, it selects only the border color. In 320 × 200 graphics mode, it selects the palette. The colors for palette 0 are green, red, and brown. The colors for palette 1 are cyan, magenta, and white. In all other graphics modes, this service selects the background and border color.

Register contents on entry (color select):

AH	Bh
BH	0
BL	Color

Register contents on entry (palette select):

AH	Bh
BH	1
BL	Palette

Write pixel dot (interrupt 10h service Ch)

Use this with CGA, EGA, MCGA, and VGA. This service draws a dot at the specified graphics coordinate. It assumes that the display is in graphics mode. TABLE 12-3 specifies the screen dimensions for various video modes.

Register contents on entry:

AH	Ch
AL	Pixel color value
BH	Video page number
CX	Column
DX	Row

Read pixel dot (interrupt 10h service Dh)

Use this with CGA, EGA, MCGA, and VGA. This service reads the pixel value at a specified graphics coordinate. It assumes that the display is in graphics mode. TABLE 12-3 specifies the screen dimensions for various video modes.

Register contents on entry:

AH	Dh
BH	Video page number

CX	Column
DX	Row

Register contents on exit:

AL	Pixel color value

TTY character output (interrupt 10h service Eh)

Use this with MDA, CGA, EGA, MCGA, and VGA. This service displays a character at the specified position. TABLE 12-3 specifies the screen dimensions for various video modes.

Registers contents on entry:

AH	Eh
AL	Character
BH	Video page number
BL	Foreground color (graphics modes)

Get current video state (interrupt 10h service Fh)

Use this with MDA, CGA, EGA, MCGA, and VGA. This service gets the current display mode of the video adapter. TABLE 12-3 provides the parameters for various adapter display modes. Using this service to store the current video mode allows you to present data on screen and then restore the screen before returning to Clipper. For example, you could display a graphic representation of some data and then restore the video state to return to a data entry mode. Always save the video state of the display before changing it. Failure to do so could create errors in certain Clipper display functions because most graphic routines don't automatically return the display to its previous state.

Register contents on entry:

AH	Fh

Register contents on exit:

AH	Number of screen character columns
AL	Display mode
BH	Active display page

Set individual palette register (interrupt 10h service 10h function 0)

Use this with EGA, MCGA, and VGA. This service sets the contents of a palette register to a corresponding displayable color. There are 16 palette registers numbered 0 through 15 (0–0Fh). You can safely use this service within Clipper to evoke changes to the display appearance and to produce special effects. None of the Clipper display functions rely on specific settings for the palette registers.

Register contents on entry (EGA or VGA):	
AH	10h
AL	0
BH	Color value
BL	Palette register number

Register contents on entry (MCGA):	
AH	10
AL	0
BX	0712h

Set overscan register (interrupt 10h service 10h function 1)

Use this with EGA and VGA. This service sets the contents of the overscan register to a corresponding displayable color. This changes the visible border color (normally set to black). You can use this service within Clipper without storing its previous state because none of the display functions rely on a specific overscan register state.

Register contents on entry:	
AH	10h
AL	1
BH	Color value

Set all palette registers (interrupt 10h service 10h function 2)

Use this with EGA and VGA. This service sets the contents of all the palette and overscan registers to a corresponding displayable color. Each entry is an 8-bit value. You need 16 color entries plus an overscan entry (17 total bytes) to fill the color correspondence table completely. This table must not be optimized to word boundaries as is standard in some languages. TABLE 12-4 contains a list of color numbers.

You can safely use this service within Clipper to evoke changes to the display appearance and to produce special effects. None of the Clipper display functions rely on specific settings for the palette or overscan registers. One special effect is to create gray-scale colors on an LCD display using a VGA display adapter. Other effects include the text presentation of data on screen or the use of RAM fonts to enhance display appearance.

Register contents on entry:

AH	10h
AL	2
DX	Offset to a color correspondence table
ES	Segment of a color correspondence table

Toggle intensify/blink (interrupt 10h service 10h function 3)

Use this with EGA, MCGA, and VGA. This service changes the bit used to determine whether the most significant bit of a character attribute intensifies or blinks the display. BL contains the intensify bit value. When this value equals 1, the adapter enables blinking. You can safely use this service within Clipper to evoke changes to the display appearance and to produce special effects. None of the Clipper display functions rely on specific settings for the intensify/blink register. One use for this function is to allow a greater range of color choices. Some people find it difficult to view a display that uses blinking elements. The use of enhanced color is usually less distracting.

Register contents on entry:

AH	10h
AL	3
BL	Blink/intensity bit value

Read individual palette register (interrupt 10h service 10h function 7)

Use this with VGA. This service reads the color value contained in a single palette register. There are 16 palette registers numbered 0 through 15 (0–0Fh). You can use this service to save the current state of the palette register prior to making changes in color presentation. While this isn't absolutely required for proper program execution, it is recommended so that you can quickly return the display to a known state after a specific operation.

Register contents on entry:	
AH	10h
AL	7
BL	Palette register number

Register contents on exit:	
BH	Color value

Read overscan register (interrupt 10h service 10h function 8)

Use this with VGA. This service reads the color value contained in the overscan register. The overscan register affects the screen-border color. You can use this service to save the current state of the overscan register prior to making changes in color presentation. While this isn't absolutely required for proper program execution, it is recommended so that you can quickly return the display to a known state after a specific operation.

Register contents on entry:	
AH	10h
AL	8

Register contents on exit:	
BH	Color value

Read all palette registers (interrupt 10h service 10h function 9)

Use this with VGA. This service reads the color value contained in all the palette registers and the overscan register. Use a 17-byte buffer to accept the color correspondence table. This table must not be optimized to word boundaries as is standard in some languages. TABLE 12-5 contains a list of color table values.

You can use this service to save the current state of the palette registers and the overscan register prior to making changes in color presentation. While this isn't absolutely required for proper program execution, it is recommended so that you can quickly return the display to a known state after a specific operation. Use this function whenever you intend to change all the registers. If you intend to change only a few of the registers, use the individual save routines described previously. The individual routines execute more quickly and use less memory.

Register contents on entry:	
AH	10h
AL	9
DX	Offset to a color correspondence table
ES	Segment of a color correspondence table

Register contents on exit:	
DX	Offset to a color correspondence table
ES	Segment of a color correspondence table

Set individual DAC register (interrupt 10h service 10h function 10h)

Use this with MCGA and VGA. This service programs an individual color register with a red-green-blue color combination. It provides extended control over other means of changing the color-table values. As stated in the description of the VGA display adapter, there are two different color-translation tables. The first is the palette register, which correlates a color number to an actual color. This service doesn't affect that table. The second is the digital-to-analog converter, which accepts a digital color, looks up the analog equivalent in another table, and translates it into a specific analog voltage. This service affects that table.

There are 16 or 64 colors, depending on the color-page state. Use interrupt 10h, service 10h, subfunction 1Ah to determine the number of colors. The maximum value of any color is 3Eh (64 colors) for a total of 262,144 color selections.

Register contents on entry:	
AH	10h
AL	10h
BX	Color register number
CH	Green value
CL	Blue value
DH	Red value

Set Block of DAC registers (interrupt 10h service 10h function 12h)

Use this with MCGA and VGA. This service programs a group of color registers with the red-green-blue color combinations pointed to by the ES:DX combination. It provides extended control over other means of changing the color table values. As stated in the description of the VGA display adapter, there are two different color translation tables. The first is the palette register, which correlates a color number to an actual color. This service doesn't affect that table. The second is the digital-to-analog converter, which accepts a digital color, looks up the analog equivalent in another table, and translates it into a specific analog voltage. This service affects that table.

There are 16 or 64 colors, depending on the color-page state. Use interrupt 10h, service 10h, subfunction 1Ah to determine the number of colors. As with the set all palette registers function (interrupt 10h, service 10h, function 2), you must provide enough values to fill the entire table. However, the size of the table required equals (number of color registers to program (in CX) – beginning color register number (in BX)) * 3. For example, if you wanted to program registers 30 through 60 in a 64-color table, you would need (60 – 30) * 3, or a 90-byte table. This table must not be optimized to word boundaries as is standard in some languages.

Register contents on entry:

AH	10h
AL	12h
BX	Beginning color register number
CX	Number of color registers to program
DX	Offset to a color correspondence table
ES	Segment to a color correspondence table

Select color subset (interrupt 10h service 10h function 13h)

Use this with VGA. This service selects the color-register paging mode, or an individual page of color registers. When in the paging mode, setting BH to 0 selects 4 pages of 64 registers; setting BH to 1 selects 16 pages of 16 registers. This gives you a palette of 64 (BH = 0) or 16 (BH = 1) colors. You can safely use this service within Clipper to evoke changes to the display appearance and to produce special effects. None of the Clipper display functions rely on specific settings for the color-register paging mode. Unfortunately, none of the native Clipper functions or commands will take advantage of the additional colors provided by this setting. Therefore, to make use of this setting you will also need to create your own set of display functions.

Note: You must initialize pages 4 through 15 before using them. The display adapter usually defines pages 0 through 3 when you switch page modes. Pages numbering always begins at 0.

Register contents on entry (paging mode):	
AH	10h
AL	13h
BH	Paging Mode
BL	0

Register contents on entry (color register selection):	
AH	10h
AL	13h
BH	Page
BL	1

Read individual DAC register (interrupt 10h service 10h function 15h)

Use this with MCGA and VGA. This service reads the contents of an individual color register. There are 16 or 64 total colors, depending on the color-page state. Use interrupt 10h, service 10h, subfunction 1Ah to determine the number of colors. This function returns an invalid result if you specify a register number higher than the available number of colors. You can use this service to save the current state of the DAC registers prior to making changes in color presentation. While this isn't absolutely required for proper program execution, it is recommended so that you can quickly return the display to a known state after a specific operation.

Register contents on entry:	
AH	10h
AL	15h
BX	Color register number

Register contents on exit:	
CH	Green value
CL	Blue value
DH	Red value

Read block of DAC registers (interrupt 10h service 10h function 17h)

Use this with MCGA and VGA. This service reads the contents of a group of color registers. If you intend to change only a few of the registers, use the individual save routines described previously. The individual routines execute more quickly and use less memory. The buffer used to hold the color correspondence table must allow three bytes for each register read.

There are 16 or 64 colors, depending on the color-page state. Use interrupt 10h, service 10h, subfunction 1Ah to determine the number of colors. You can use this service to save the current state of all the DAC registers prior to making changes in color presentation. While this isn't absolutely required for proper program execution, it is recommended so that you can quickly return the display to a known state after a specific operation.

As with the Read all palette registers function (interrupt 10h, service 10h, function 9), you must provide a buffer large enough to contain the entire table. However, the size of the buffer required equals (number of color registers to program (in CX) – beginning color register number (in BX)) * 3. For example, if you wanted to get the values of registers 30 through 60 in a 64-color table, you would need (60 – 30) * 3, or a 90-byte table. This table must not be optimized to word boundaries as is standard in some languages.

Register contents on entry:

AH	10h
AL	17h
BX	Beginning color register number
CX	Number of color registers to read
DX	Offset to a color correspondence table
ES	Segment to a color correspondence table

Register contents on exit:

DX	Offset to a color correspondence table
ES	Segment to a color correspondence table

Read color-page state (interrupt 10h service 10h function 1Ah)

Use this with VGA. This service returns the current color page and paging mode. The paging mode values equal 4 pages of 64 registers when BL returns 0, and 16 pages of 16 registers when BL returns 1.

Register contents on entry:

AH	10h
AL	1Ah

Register contents on exit

BH	Color page
BL	Paging mode

Sum DAC registers to gray shades (interrupt 10h service 10h function 1Bh)

Use this with MCGA and VGA. This service changes the color values in one or more color registers into their gray-scale equivalents. This is especially useful when the program you write must execute on an LCD display. In essence, this service provides you with a wider variety of color choices on a noncolor display. There are 16 or 64 colors, depending on the color-page state. Use interrupt 10h, service 10h, subfunction 1Ah to determine the number of colors.

Note: You must initialize pages 4 through 15 before using them. Summing and using an undefined page will result in a blank or otherwise unreadable display. The display adapter usually defines pages 0 through 3 when you switch page modes. Page numbering always begins at 0.

Register contents on entry:

AH	10h
AL	1Bh
BX	Beginning color register number
CX	Number of color registers to program

User alpha load (interrupt 10h service 11h function 0)

Use this with EGA, MCGA, and VGA. This service loads a user-defined font into character generator RAM. You must supply at least five pieces of information to use this function. This information includes character size, storage area on the display adapter, number of characters in the font, ASCII code of the first character, and storage area on the host. Character size is the number of bytes used by each character (usually 8, 14, or 16). Each character must use the same amount of memory.

You identify the display adapter storage area by its predefined number (block number). There are four block areas for fonts on an EGA and eight areas for a VGA. Block numbers begin at 0 and end at either 3 or 7. Use the Set block specifier function (Interrupt 10h, service 11h, function 3) to select the block if you don't use block 0 (default). Point to the host adapter storage area using a combination of ES and BP. Always save BP on the stack.

This function affects alphanumeric modes only; see interrupt 10h, service 11h, functions 20h – 24h for graphics mode functions. Execute the set block specifier function (Interrupt 10h, service 11h, function 3) immediately after this function to load the font on an MCGA display.

Note: You must use this function immediately after a mode change. Using the function at any other time produces unpredictable results.

Register contents on entry:	
AH	11h
AL	0
BH	Bytes per character
BL	Memory block
CX	Number of characters in font
DX	ASCII code of first character in font
BP	Offset of font table
ES	Segment of font table

ROM monochrome set (interrupt 10h service 11h function 1)

Use this with EGA and VGA. This service loads the default 8 × 14 ROM font table into the specified character-generator RAM block. There are four block areas for fonts on an EGA and eight areas for a VGA. Block numbers begin at 0 and end at either 3 or 7. Use the set block specifier function (interrupt 10h, service 11h, function 3) to select the block if you don't use block 0 (default).

Register contents on entry:	
AH	11h
AL	1
BL	Memory block

ROM double-dot set (interrupt 10h service 11h function 2)

Use this with EGA, MCGA, and VGA. This service loads the default 8 × 8 ROM font table into the specified character-generator RAM block. There are four block areas for fonts on an EGA and eight areas for a VGA. Block numbers begin at 0 and end at either 3 or 7. Use the Set block specifier function (interrupt 10h, service 11h, function 3) to select the block if you don't use block 0 (default).

Register contents on entry:	
AH	11h
AL	2
BL	Memory block

Set block specifier (interrupt 10h service 11h function 3)

Use this with EGA, MCGA, and VGA. This service chooses the character block selected by bit 3 of the character-attribute bytes in text-display modes. On the EGA and MCGA, bits 0 and 1 of the character-generator block select code contain the character block selected when bit 3 equals 0; bits 2 and 3 contain the character block selected when bit 3 equals 1. This provides a selection of four font-storage areas. On the VGA, bits 0, 1, and 4 of the character-generator block select code contain the character block selected when bit 3 equals 0; bits 2, 3, and 5 contain the character block selected when bit 3 equals 1. This provides a selection of eight font-storage areas.

Register contents on entry:	
AH	11h
AL	3
BL	Character generator block select code

ROM 16-row set (interrupt 10h service 11h function 4)

Use this with MCGA and VGA. This service loads the default 8 × 16 ROM font table into the specified character-generator RAM block. There are four block areas for fonts on an EGA and eight areas for a VGA. Block numbers begin at 0 and end at either 3 or 7. Use the Set block specifier function (interrupt 10h, service 11h, function 3) to select the block if you don't use block 0 (default).

Register contents on entry:	
AH	11h
AL	4
BL	Memory block

User alpha load (Pre-set block size) (interrupt 10h service 11h function 10h)

Use this with EGA, MCGA, and VGA. This service loads a user-defined font into character-generator RAM. You must supply at least five pieces of information to use this function. This information includes character size, storage area on the display adapter, number of characters in the font, ASCII code of the first character, and storage area on the host. Character size is the number of bytes used by each character (usually 8, 14, or 16). Each character must use the same amount of memory.

You identify the display adapter storage area by its predefined number (block number). There are four block areas for fonts on an EGA and eight areas for a VGA. Block numbers begin at 0 and end at either 3 or 7. Use the Set block specifier function (interrupt 10h, service 11h, function 3) to select the block if you don't use block 0 (default). Point to the host adapter storage area using a combination of ES and BP. Always save BP on the stack.

Never use this function with an MCGA display; use interrupt 10h, service 10h, function 0 instead. The MCGA reserves function 10h for future purpose and automatically defaults to function 0. This function affects alphanumeric modes only, see interrupt 10h service 11h, function 20h–24h for graphics mode functions.

Note: You must use this function immediately after a mode change. Using the function at any other time produces unpredictable results.

Register contents on entry:

AH	11h
AL	10h
BH	Bytes per character
BL	Memory block
CX	Number of characters in font
DX	ASCII code of first character in font
BP	Offset of font table
ES	Segment of font table

ROM monochrome set (interrupt 10h service 11h function 11h)

Use this with EGA and VGA. This service loads the default 8 × 14 ROM font table into the specified character-generator RAM block. Use this service only after a mode set with page 0 active. There are four block areas for fonts on an EGA and eight areas for a VGA. Block numbers begin at 0 and end at either 3 or 7. Use the Set block specifier function (interrupt 10h, service 11h, function 3) to select the block if you don't use block 0 (default).

Register contents on entry:

AH	11h
AL	11h
BL	Memory block

ROM double-dot set (interrupt 10h service 11h function 12h)

Use this with EGA, MCGA, and VGA. This service loads the default 8 × 8 ROM font table into the specified character-generator RAM block. Use this service only after a mode set with page 0 active. There are four block areas for fonts on an EGA and eight areas for a VGA. Block numbers begin at 0 and end at either 3 or 7. Use the Set block specifier function (interrupt 10h, service 11h, function 3) to select the block if you don't use block 0 (default).

Register contents on entry:	
AH	11h
AL	12h
BL	Memory block

ROM 16-row set (interrupt 10h service 11h function 14h)

Use this with MCGA and VGA. This service loads the default 8 × 16 ROM font table into the specified character-generator RAM block. Use this service only after a mode set with page 0 active. There are four block areas for fonts on an EGA and eight areas for a VGA. Block numbers begin at 0 and end at either 3 or 7. Use the Set block specifier function (interrupt 10h, service 11h, function 3) to select the block if you don't use block 0 (default).

Register contents on entry:	
AH	11h
AL	14h
BL	Memory block

User graphics characters, 8 × 8 (interrupt 10h service 11h function 20h)

Use this with EGA, MCGA, and VGA. This service sets the interrupt 1Fh pointer to the user font table. The adapter uses the values contained in the table for characters 80h through FFh, in graphics modes 4 through 6. These characters provide a compatibility-mode extended ASCII character set. Unlike the alphanumeric character set, you can load only one graphics character set at a time. A set consists of both standard and extended ASCII characters. Use this function only after a mode set. Using this function at any other time produces unpredictable results.

Register contents on entry:	
AH	11h
AL	20h
BP	Offset of font table
ES	Segment of font table

User graphics characters (interrupt 10h service 11h function 21h)

Use this with EGA, MCGA, and VGA. This service points the interrupt 43h vector to the user font table and updates the video ROM BIOS data area. The character-rows specifier shows the number of character rows per screen. A value of 1 indicates 14 rows, 2 indicates 25 rows, and 3 indicates 43 rows. When the number of rows doesn't match any of these predefined values, BL contains 0 and DL contains the number of character rows. Unlike the alphanumeric character set, you can load only one graphics character set at a time. A set consists of both standard and extended ASCII characters. Use this function only after a mode set. Using this function at any other time produces unpredictable results.

Register contents on entry:	
AH	11h
AL	21h
BL	Character rows specifier
CX	Bytes per character
DL	Character rows per screen (when BL = 0)
BP	Offset of user font table
ES	Segment of user font table

ROM 8 × 14 character-set select (interrupt 10h service 11h function 22h)

Use this with EGA, MCGA, and VGA. This service points the interrupt 43h vector to the default 8 × 14 ROM font and updates the video ROM BIOS data area. The character-rows specifier shows the number of character rows per screen. A value of 1 indicates 14 rows, 2 indicates 25 rows, and 3 indicates 43 rows. When the number of rows doesn't match any of these predefined values, BL contains 0 and DL contains the number of character rows. Unlike the alphanumeric character set, you can load only one graphics character set at a time. A set consists of both standard and extended

ASCII characters. Use this function only after a mode set. Using this function at any other time produces unpredictable results.

Register contents on entry:

AH	11h
AL	22h
BL	Character rows specifier
DL	Character rows per screen (when BL = 0)

ROM 8 × 8 character-set select (interrupt 10h service 11h function 23h)

Use this with EGA, MCGA, and VGA. This service points the interrupt 43h vector to the default 8 × 8 ROM font and updates the video ROM BIOS data area. The character-rows specifier shows the number of character rows per screen. A value of 1 indicates 14 rows, 2 indicates 25 rows, and 3 indicates 43 rows. When the number of rows doesn't match any of these predefined values, BL contains 0 and DL contains the number of character rows. Unlike the alphanumeric character set, you can load only one graphics character set at a time. A set consists of both standard and extended ASCII characters. Use this function only after a mode set. Using this function at any other time produces unpredictable results.

Register contents on entry:

AH	11h
AL	23h
BL	Character rows specifier
DL	Character rows per screen (when BL = 0)

ROM 8 × 16 character-set select (interrupt 10h service 11h function 24h)

Use this with EGA, MCGA, and VGA. This service points the interrupt 43h vector to the default 8 × 16 ROM font and updates the video ROM BIOS data area. The character-rows specifier shows the number of character rows per screen. A value of 1 indicates 14 rows, 2 indicates 25 rows, and 3 indicates 43 rows. When the number of rows doesn't match any of these predefined values, BL contains 0 and DL contains the number of character rows. Unlike the alphanumeric character set, you can load only one graphics character set at a time. A set consists of both standard and extended ASCII characters. Use this function only after a mode set. Using this function at any other time produces unpredictable results.

Register contents on entry:	
AH	11h
AL	24h
BL	Character rows specifier
DL	Character rows per screen (when BL = 0)

Return character-set information (interrupt 10h service 11h function 30h)

Use this with EGA, MCGA, and VGA. This service returns a pointer to the font character-definition table. It also returns the number of bytes per character for that font. Because this function destroys the contents of BP, always push BP on the stack. Restore BP before you perform any other operations.

Register contents on entry:	
AH	11h
AL	30h
BH	Font code 0 - Current interrupt 1Fh contents 1 - Current interrupt 43h contents 2 - 8 X 14 ROM font 3 - 8 X 8 ROM font (characters 00h - 7Fh) 4 - 8 X 8 ROM font (characters 80h - FFh) 5 - Alternate 9 X 14 ROM font 6 - 8 X 16 ROM font 7 - Alternate 9 X 16 ROM font

Register contents on exit:	
CX	Bytes per character
DL	Character rows on screen
BP	Offset of font table
ES	Segment of font table

Return memory-allocation information (interrupt 10h service 12h function 10h)

Use this with EGA and VGA. This service returns the active subsystem memory and display configuration information.

Register contents on entry:	
AH	12h
BL	10h

Register contents on exit:	
BH	Display type
	0 - Color
	1 - Monochrome
BL	Memory installed (EGA only)
	0 - 64K
	1 - 128K
	2 - 192K
	3 - 256K
CH	Feature control register bits
	0 - Output bit 0, input status bit 5
	1 - Output bit 0, input status bit 6
	2 - Output bit 1, input status bit 5
	3 - Output bit 1, input status bit 6
	4 through 7 - Not used
CL	Switch settings (one bit per switch)
	0 - Configuration switch 1
	1 - Configuration switch 2
	2 - Configuration switch 3
	3 - Configuration switch 4
	4 through 7 - Not used

Select alternate print-screen routine (interrupt 10h service 12h function 20h)

Use this with EGA and VGA. This service selects an alternate print-screen routine. Use this service when the screen length is not 25 lines. This routine won't print graphics screens.

Register contents on entry:	
AH	12h
BL	20h

Select scan lines for alpha mode (interrupt 10h service 12h function 30h)

Use this with EGA and VGA. This service selects the number of scan lines used for text modes. The selection takes effect only after a display selection interrupt (10h, function 0).

Register contents on entry:

AH	12h
AL	Scan-line code 0 - 200 lines 1 - 350 lines 2 - 400 lines
BL	30h

Register contents on exit:

AL	12h when VGA is active
AL	0 when VGA is not active

Select default palette loading (interrupt 10h service 12h function 31h)

Use this with MCGA and VGA. This service enables and disables default palette loading when a video-mode change occurs. An EGA display adapter always resets the palette after a mode change or reset. Disabling default palette loading allows a MCGA or VGA display adapter to retain special palette settings. Unsuccessful completion of this function means the display adapter is not VGA or MCGA. Failure also occurs with incompatible or failed display adapters.

Register contents on entry:

AH	12h
AL	0 to enable and 1 to disable default palette loading
BL	31h

Register contents on exit:

AL	12h for successful completion

Video enable/disable (interrupt 10h service 12h function 32h)

Use this with MCGA and VGA. This service enables and disables CPU access to the video adapter I/O ports and video refresh buffer. Use this service to protect the display-adapter memory and registers from accidental overwrite during critical drawing operations. Both areas are accessible as a default. This also prevents memory-resident programs from interfering with normal display-adapter functions. The EGA always allows access to the video adapters I/O ports and video refresh buffer. Unsuccessful completion of this function means the display adapter is not VGA or MCGA. Failure also occurs with incompatible or failed display adapters.

Register contents on entry:

AH	**12h**
AL	**0 to enable and 1 to disable access**
BL	**32h**

Register contents on exit:

AL	**12h for successful completion**

Summing to gray shades (interrupt 10h service 12h function 33h)

Use this with MCGA and VGA. This service enables and disables grayscale summing for the active display. This prevents memory-resident programs from interfering with normal display-adapter functions. When you enable summing, the display adapter uses a combination of 30% red, 59% green, and 11% blue intensity to simulate gray scales. Unsuccessful completion of this function means the display adapter is not VGA or MCGA. Failure also occurs with incompatible or failed display adapters.

Register contents on entry:

AH	**12h**
AL	**0 to enable and 1 to disable gray-scale summing**
BL	**33h**

Register contents on exit:

AL	**12h for successful completion**

Cursor emulation (interrupt 10h service 12h function 34h)

Use this with VGA. This service enables and disables cursor emulation. When enabled, cursor emulation automatically resizes the cursor to correspond to current character dimensions. When disabled, it allows you to use actual VGA lines for cursor size settings. Unsuccessful completion of this function means the display adapter is not VGA. Failure also occurs with incompatible or failed display adapters.

Register contents on entry:

AH	12h
AL	0 to enable and 1 to disable cursor emulation
BL	34h

Register contents on exit:

AL	12h for successful completion

Display switch (interrupt 10h service 12h function 35h)

Use this with MCGA and VGA. This service allows selection of one of two video adapters when port-address or memory-usage conflicts occur. Use this function to switch between an adapter installed on the motherboard and a high-resolution adapter installed in an expansion slot. To use this function correctly, you must set up a 128K video buffer. The function reroutes all calls to the expansion-slot display-adapter video RAM to this buffer. Unsuccessful completion of this function means the display adapter is not VGA or MCGA. Failure also occurs with incompatible or failed display adapters.

Register contents on entry:

AH	12h
AL	Switching function 0 - Disable initial video adapter 1 - Enable system board video adapter 2 - Disable active video adapter 3 - Enable inactive video adapter
BL	35h
DX	Offset of 128K buffer (function 0, 2, or 3)
ES	Segment of 128K buffer (function 0, 2, or 3)

Register contents on exit:

AL	12h for successful completion
DX	Offset of 128K buffer (function 0, 2, or 3)
ES	Segment of 128K buffer (function 0, 2, or 3)

Screen off/on (interrupt 10h service 12h function 36h)

Use this with VGA. This service enables and disables video refresh for the active display. This allows the host adapter to update video memory without distorting the display. Unsuccessful completion of this function means the display adapter is not VGA. Failure also occurs with incompatible or failed display adapters.

Register contents on entry:

AH	12h
AL	0 to enable and 1 to disable video refresh
BL	36h

Register contents on exit:

AL	12h for successful completion

Write string (interrupt 10h service 13h)

Use this with MDA, CGA, EGA, MCGA, and VGA. This service transfers a string to the active-display video buffer, starting at a specified position. TABLE 12-3 shows the correlation between video mode, display-adapter type, and the number of available pages. Because this function changes the contents of BP, you must save BP on the stack before using this function.

Register contents on entry:

AH 13h

AL Write mode

- 0 - Attribute in BL. String contains character codes only. Cursor position does not update after write.
- 1 - Attribute in BL. String contains character codes only. Cursor position updates after write (1 position).
- 2 - String contains alternating character codes and attribute bytes. Cursor position does not update after write.
- 3 - String contains alternating character codes and attribute bytes. Cursor position updates after write (2 positions).

BH	Video page number
BL	Attribute (write modes 0 and 1)
CX	Length of character string
DH	Starting row
DL	Starting column
BP	Offset of string
ES	Segment of string

Read display combination code(interrupt 10h service 1Ah function 0)

Use this with PS/2. This service returns a code describing the installed video-display adapter(s). TABLE 12-6 contains a list of applicable display adapters. If this function fails (does not return 1Ah in AL), then the host machine is not a PS/2 or a hardware failure occurred.

Register contents on entry:

AH	1Ah
AL	0

Register contents on exit:

AL	1Ah for successful completion
BH	Inactive display code
BL	Active display code

Table 12-6 PS/2 display-adapter codes

Code	Video subsystem type
00h	No display
01h	MDA with 5151 monitor
02h	CGA with 5153 or 5154 monitor
03h	Reserved
04h	EGA with 5153 or 5154 monitor
05h	EGA with 5151 monitor
06h	PGA with 5175 monitor
07h	VGA with analog monochrome monitor
08h	VGA with analog color monitor
09h	Reserved
0Ah	MCGA with digital color monitor
0Bh	MCGA with analog monochrome monitor
0Ch	MCGA with analog color monitor
0Dh - FEh	Reserved

Write display combination code (interrupt 10h service 1Ah function 1)

Use this with PS/2. This service writes a code describing the installed video display adapter(s) to the ROM BIOS. TABLE 12-6 contains a list of applicable display adapters. If this function fails (does not return 1Ah in AL), then the host machine is not a PS/2 or a hardware failure occurred.

Register contents on entry:

AH	1Ah
AL	1
BH	Inactive display code
BL	Active display code

Register contents on exit:

AL	1Ah for successful completion

Return functionality/state information (interrupt 10h service 1Bh)

Use this with PS/2. This service obtains information about the current display mode in a 64-byte buffer. TABLE 12-7 contains a listing of the data returned in the buffer. Bytes 0 through 3 contain a DWORD pointer to a table containing the video adapter and monitor capabilities. TABLE 12-8 contains a list of the functionality data. If this function fails (does not return 1Bh in AL), then the host machine is not a PS/2 or a hardware failure occurred.

Register contents on entry:

AH	1Bh
BX	0 (implementation type)
DI	Offset to a 64-byte buffer
ES	Segment of a 64-byte buffer

Register contents on exit:

AL	1Bh for successful completion

Table 12-7 PS/2 video-display-mode data

Byte	Contents
00h - 03h	Pointer to functionality information (Table 14-7)
04h	Current video mode
05h - 06h	Number of character columns
07h - 08h	Length of video refresh buffer
09h - 0Ah	Display upper left corner starting address
0Bh - 1Ah	Cursor position for video pages 0 - 7. First byte contains X coordinate. Second byte contains Y coordinate.
1Bh	Cursor starting line
1Ch	Cursor ending line
1Dh	Active video page number
1Eh - 1Fh	Adapter base port address
20h	Current setting of register 3B8h (monochrome) or 3D8h (color)
21h	Current setting of register 3B9h (monochrome) or 3D9h (color)
22h	Number of character rows
23h - 24h	Character height in scan lines
25h	Active display code (Table 14-5)
26h	Inactive display code (Table 14-5)
27h - 28h	Number of displayable colors
29h	Number of display pages

Byte	Contents
2Ah	Number of scan lines 00h - 200 scan lines 01h - 350 scan lines 02h - 400 scan lines 03h - 480 scan lines 04h through FFh - Reserved
2Bh	Primary character block
2Ch	Secondary character block
2Dh	Miscellaneous state information (bits) 0 - 1 when all modes on all displays active 1 - 1 if gray-scale summing active 2 - 1 if monochrome display attached 3 - 1 when default palette loading disabled 4 - 1 if cursor emulation active 5 - 1 for Intensity, 0 for Blink 6 through 7 - Reserved
2Eh - 30h	Reserved
31h	Video memory available (EGA only) 0 - 64K 1 - 128K 2 - 192K 3 - 256K
32h	Save pointer state information (bits) 0 - 1 when 512 character set active 1 - 1 when dynamic save area active 2 - 1 when alpha font override active 3 - 1 when graphics font override active 4 - 1 when palette override active 5 - 1 when DCC extension active 6 through 7 - Reserved
33h - 3Fh	Reserved

Table 12-8 PS/2 display-adapter functionality information

Byte	Bit	Meaning
00h	0	1 when video mode 0 supported
	1	1 when video mode 1 supported
	2	1 when video mode 2 supported
	3	1 when video mode 3 supported
	4	1 when video mode 4 supported
	5	1 when video mode 5 supported
	6	1 when video mode 6 supported
	7	1 when video mode 7 supported
01h	0	1 when video mode 8 supported
	1	1 when video mode 9 supported
	2	1 when video mode Ah supported
	3	1 when video mode Bh supported
	4	1 when video mode Ch supported
	5	1 when video mode Dh supported
	6	1 when video mode Eh supported
	7	1 when video mode Fh supported
02h	0	1 when video mode 10h supported
	1	1 when video mode 11h supported
	2	1 when video mode 12h supported
	3	1 when video mode 13h supported
	4 - 7	Reserved
03h - 06h		Reserved
07h	0	1 if 200 text mode scan lines available
	1	1 if 350 text mode scan lines available
	2	1 if 400 text mode scan lines available
	3	Reserved
08h		Character blocks available in text modes
09h		Maximum number of active character blocks in text modes
0Ah	0	1 when all modes on all displays active.
	1	1 if gray-scale summing active.
	2	1 if character font loading available.
	3	1 when default palette loading available.
	4	1 if cursor emulation active.

Byte	Bit	Meaning
	5	1 if EGA 64-color palette available.
	6	1 if color register loading available.
	7	1 if color register paging mode select available.
0Bh	0	1 if light pen available.
	1	1 if save/restore video state available.
	2	1 if background intensity/blinking control available.
	3	1 if get/set display combination code available.
	4 - 7	Reserved
0Ch - 0Dh		Reserved
0Eh	0	1 if display adapter supports 512 character sets.
	1	1 when dynamic save area available.
	2	1 if alpha font override available.
	3	1 if graphics font override available.
	4	1 if palette override available.
	5	1 if display combination code extension available.
	6 - 7	Reserved
0Fh		Reserved

Get video-state buffer (interrupt 10h service 1Ch function 0)

Use this with PS/2 VGA. This service obtains the memory requirements to save the current digital-to-analog (DAC) state and color registers, ROM BIOS video-driver area, or video-hardware state to RAM (as requested in the following code). If this function fails (does not return 1Ch in AL), then the host machine is not a PS/2 with a VGA or a hardware failure occurred.

Register contents on entry:

AH	1Ch
AL	0
CX	Requested states (bits)
	0 - Save video hardware state
	1 - Save video BIOS data area

	2 - Save video DAC state and color registers
	3 through 15 - Reserved
BX	Offset of buffer
ES	Segment of buffer

Register contents on exit:

AL	1Ch for successful completion
BX	Number of required 64-byte blocks

Save video state (interrupt 10h service 1Ch function 1)

Use this with PS/2 VGA. This service saves the current digital-to-analog (DAC) state and color registers, ROM BIOS video-driver area, or video-hardware state to RAM. If this function fails (does not return 1Ch in AL), then the host machine is not a PS/2 with a VGA or a hardware failure occurred.

Register Contents on Entry:

AH	1Ch
AL	1
CX	Requested states (bits)
	0 - Save video hardware state
	1 - Save video BIOS data area
	2 - Save video DAC state and color registers
	3 through 15 - Reserved
BX	Offset of buffer
ES	Segment of buffer

Register contents on exit:

AL	1Ch for successful completion

Restore video state (interrupt 10h service 1Ch function 2)

Use this with PS/2 VGA. This service restores the current digital-to-analog (DAC) state and color registers, ROM BIOS video-driver area, or video-hardware state to RAM. If this function fails (does not return 1Ch in AL), then the host machine is not a PS/2 with a VGA or a hardware failure occurred.

Register contents on entry:

AH	1Ch
AL	2
CX	Requested states (bits)

0 - Restore video hardware state
1 - Restore video BIOS data area
2 - Restore video DAC state and color registers
3 through 15 - Reserved

BX	Offset of buffer
ES	Segment of buffer

Register contents on exit:

AL	1Ch for successful completion

Using VESA interrupts

The following functions show you how to implement VESA (Video Electronics Standards Association) standards for Super VGA functions. Not all manufacturers adhere to these standards. Always check your manufacturer manual before assuming you can use these functions. Another compatibility check is using function 0 to return Super VGA information. Every Super VGA function returns the following status information in AX upon return from the interrupt. If AL equals 4Fh, the display adapter supports the specified function. Otherwise, the display adapter doesn't support the function. If AH contains 0, then the function was successful. If AH contains 1, then the function wasn't successful.

Return Super VGA information (interrupt 10h service 4Fh function 0)

This function returns information about the capabilities of the Super VGA environment supported by the manufacturer. The function returns this information in a 256-byte buffer. TABLE 12-9 contains a complete description of this buffer. If a VGA with extended capability fails to provide this information, then it doesn't adhere to the VESA standard.

Register contents on entry:

AH	4Fh
AL	0
DI	Offset of data buffer
ES	Segment of data buffer

Register contents on exit:

AX	Status

Table 12-9 **Super VGA information-block format**

Byte	Function
0 - 3 (byte)	VESA signature - Contains 'VESA'
4 - 5 (word)	VESA version number - High byte is the major revision number. Low byte is the minor revision number. VESA capabilities are upward compatible.
6 - 9 (double word)	Pointer to OEM string - Null terminated string identifying the manufacturer. The string can contain other information.
10 - 13 (byte)	Video equipment capabilities (reserved)
14 - 17 (double word)	Pointer to a list of mode numbers supported by display adapter. Each number is 16 bits long. The last number in the series is -1 (0FFFFh).
18 - 256	Reserved

Return Super VGA mode information (interrupt 10h service 4Fh function 1)

This function returns information about a specific Super VGA mode. Because some manufacturers add modes not directly supported by the Super VGA specification, you can use this function to obtain programming information for the extended mode. The function returns this information in a 256-byte buffer. TABLE 12-10 contains a complete description of this buffer. If a VGA with extended capability fails to provide this information, it doesn't adhere to the VESA standard.

Register contents on entry:

AH	4Fh
AL	1
CX	Mode number
DI	Offset of data buffer
ES	Segment of data buffer

Register contents on exit:

AX	Status

Table 12-10 Super VGA mode-information-block format

<table>
<tr><th>Byte</th><th>Function</th></tr>
<tr><td>0 - 1 (Word)</td><td>Mode attributes - Defines the characteristics of the video mode, as shown below. A value of 1 in the bit position makes the statement true. Hardware support for the mode implies that the display adapter is configured correctly and that the correct display adapter is attached. Extended mode support is provided to define the resolution, number of bit planes, and pixel format of nonVESA supported modes.

Bit Function
0 Mode supported in hardware
1 Extended mode information available
2 Output functions supported by BIOS
3 Color (true) / monochrome (false)
4 Graphics mode (true) / text mode (false)
5 - 15 Reserved</td></tr>
<tr><td>2 (Byte)</td><td>Window A attributes - Describes if the mode supports CPU windowing. It also describes how the windowing scheme is implemented, as shown below. A value of 1 in the bit position makes the statement true.

Bit Function
0 Window is supported
1 Window is readable
2 Window is writable
3 - 7 Reserve</td></tr>
<tr><td>3 (Byte)</td><td>Window B attributes - Describes if the mode supports CPU windowing. It also describes how the windowing scheme is implemented, as shown below. A value of 1 in the bit position makes the statement true.

Bit Function
0 Window is supported
1 Window is readable
2 Window is writable
3 - 7 Reserved</td></tr>
</table>

Table 12-10 Continued.

Byte	Function
4 - 5 (Word)	Window granularity - Defines the smallest window boundry size in KBytes.
6 - 7 (Word)	Window size - Defines the window size in kilobytes.
8 - 9 (Word)	Window A segment - Specifies the window segment location in the CPU address space.
10 - 11 (Word)	Window B segment - Specifies the window segment location in the CPU address space.
12 - 15 (Double Word)	Window function address - Pointer to the CPU video memory windowing function. This pointer allows you to call the windowing function directly. You can also access this function through interrupt 10h, service 4Fh, function 5.
16 - 17 (Word)	Bytes per scan line - Defines the length of a logical scan line. A logical scan line can equal or exceed the size of the physical scan line.
Extended information for nonVESA supported video modes	
18 - 19 (Word)	X-axis resolution - The width of the display. Values are in pixels for graphics mode and characters for text mode.
20 - 21 (Word)	Y-Axis resolution - The height of the display. Values are in pixels for graphics mode and characters for text mode.
22 (Byte)	X-character cell size - Width of characters in pixels.
23 (Byte)	Y-character cell size - Heigth of characters in pixels.
24 (Byte)	Number of planes - Number of memory planes available for use. This value is set to one for standard packed pixel modes.
25 (Byte)	Bits per pixel - Number of bit planes available for color display. Four bit planes provide 16 onscreen colors. Bit planes normally assume even values (except for monochrome with a single-bit plane). You can also use this field to

Byte	Function
	describe packed pixel modes. For example, a 16-color packed pixel mode would use 4 bits per pixel in one plane.
26 (Byte)	Number of banks - Defines the number of scan line banks. For example, CGA uses two banks and Hercules uses four banks. This value is set to one for modes that do not use banks (for example VGA).
27 (Byte)	Memory model - Specifies the memory model used for the mode, as shown below. *Value* *Function* 00h Text mode 01h CGA graphics 02h Hercules graphics 03h 4-plane planar 04h Packed pixel 05h Nonchain 4, 256 colors 06h-0Fh Reserved, defined by VESA 10h-FFh Reserved, defined by OEM
28 (Byte)	Bank size - The size of a scan line bank in kilobytes. For example, CGA and Hercules graphics use a bank size of 8Kb. This value is set to zero for modes that do not use banks (for example, VGA).
29 - 256	Reserved

Set Super VGA video mode (interrupt 10h service 4Fh function 2)

This function performs all the setup required to use a Super VGA mode. It initializes all registers and memory required to use the specified mode. If the mode change fails, the function leaves the environment unchanged and exits with an error code.

Register contents on entry:

AH	4Fh
AL	2

BX Video mode
Bits 0-14 - Video mode number
Bit 15 - Clear-memory flag (0 = clear memory)

Register contents on exit:
AX Status

Return current video mode (interrupt 10h service 4Fh function 3)

Returns the VESA standard or OEM-defined Super VGA mode number. Unlike the standard video-mode read function, this function doesn't return the status of the memory-clear bit. Use the Get current video state function (interrupt 10h, service Fh) to obtain this information.

Register contents on entry:
AH 4Fh
AL 3

Register contents on exit:
AX Status
BX Current video mode

Note: The services provided by function 4 are a superset of the standard VGA BIOS function 1Ch described previously. The following sections describe all three subfunctions.

Return save/restore state buffer size (interrupt 10h service 4Fh function 4 subfunction 0)

This function obtains the size buffer required to store any of four types of information. Each state occupies a separate bit of the request register (CX). You can, therefore, request the buffer size required to store any or all states. Always allocate buffer memory in blocks of 64 bytes.

Register contents on entry:
AH 4Fh
AL 4
DL 0
CX Requested states
Bit 0 - Video hardware state

Bit 1 - Video BIOS state
Bit 2 - Video DAC state
Bit 3 - Super VGA state
Bits 4 through 15 - Set to zero

Register contents on exit:

AX	Status
BX	Number of 64-byte blocks required

Save Super VGA video state (interrupt 10h service 4Fh function 4 subfunction 1)

This function stores the requested states in a buffer. Use subfunction 0 to determine the size buffer required to save the required state information.

Register contents on entry:

AH	4Fh
AL	4
DL	1
CX	Requested states
	Bit 0 - Video hardware state
	Bit 1 - Video BIOS state
	Bit 2 - Video DAC state
	Bit 3 - Super VGA state
	Bits 4 through 15 - Set to zero
BX	State buffer offset
ES	State buffer segment

Register contents on exit:

AX	Status

Restore Super VGA video state (interrupt 10h service 4Fh function 4 subfunction 2)

This function restores one or more previously saved states. When using this function, you must specify the same state information you saved. The function won't allow you to skip over unneeded data.

Register contents on entry:

AH	4Fh
AL	4

DL	2
CX	Requested states
	Bit 0 - Video hardware state
	Bit 1 - Video BIOS state
	Bit 2 - Video DAC state
	Bit 3 - Super VGA state
	Bits 4 through 15 - Set to zero
BX	State buffer offset
ES	State buffer segment

Register contents on exit:

AX	Status

Select Super VGA memory window (interrupt 10h service 4Fh function 5 subfunction 0)

This function sets the position of the specified window in memory. Before using this function, you should obtain the window data using interrupt 10h, service 4Fh, function 1 (explained previously). You can also execute this function using the far-call address obtained with function 1. The far-call method destroys the contents of AX and DX and doesn't provide any return information, but it does execute quicker than the BIOS function.

Register contents on entry:

AH	4Fh
AL	5
BH	0
BL	Window number
	0 - Window A
	1 - Window B
DX	Window position in video memory (in window granularity units)

Register contents on exit:

AX	Status

Return Super VGA memory window (interrupt 10h service 4Fh function 5 subfunction 1)

This function gets the position of the specified window in memory. Before using this function, you should obtain the window data using interrupt 10h, service 4Fh, function 1 (explained previously). You can also execute this function using the far-call address obtained using function 1. The far-call method destroys the contents of AX and DX and doesn't provide you with any return information. It does, however, execute quicker than the BIOS function.

Register contents on entry:	
AH	4Fh
AL	5
BH	1
BL	Window number 0 - Window A 1 - Window B

Register contents on exit:	
AX	Status
DX	Window position in video memory (in window granularity units)

Creating data-entry screens

Graphics displays, as stated earlier, are the wave of the future when it comes to user interfaces. Unfortunately, many programmers approach this task with the grim outlook of one condemned. There are many facilities at the programmer's disposal to reduce the labor incurred when making this transition. One such source is external libraries. Of course, there are resources even more accessible than libraries. Once you consider all the interrupts that are available to perform graphics manipulation and learn about all the different types of display adapters, it's time to create a graphics program.

Figure 12-7 contains the Clipper source code required to create the data-entry screen I've used for several other examples throughout the book. This screen is a little more basic than some of the others because the intent of the example is to concentrate on graphic-display programming basics. Figure 12-8 contains some of the assembly-language routines that you could use to fully implement a graphics display.

There are several interesting points about the Clipper code presented in FIG. 12-7. First, the code doesn't make use of the standard Clipper display routines, but it does make use of the formatting routines. This is because standard Clipper display commands and functions won't work with a graphics display. Therefore, you need to create your own display routines. There are several examples of display routines in this example. They include a routine for displaying text, another for displaying a box, and still another for creating lines. In all three cases, the new functions try to replicate the Clipper calling sequences. This means that you could use the preprocessor to convert the new routines into the old command syntax.

```
// Program 15 - Creating Graphics Mode Data Entry Screens
// This program is designed to show you some of the requirements for
// programming in graphics mode with Clipper.  The example shows several
// different routines that were examined in character mode in previous
// examples.  In addition, this program displays a little logo in the
// upper right corner of the display.  This logo could just as easily be
// an icon or other graphic form.
// Written by: John Mueller
// Copyright 1991 John Mueller - Tab Books

// Include an required header files.

#include "INKEY.CH"

// Define some local variables.

local  cLogo := chr(0)   + chr(1)   + chr(128) + chr(0)   +;
                chr(0)   + chr(3)   + chr(192) + chr(0)   +;
                chr(0)   + chr(7)   + chr(224) + chr(0)   +;
                chr(0)   + chr(15)  + chr(240) + chr(0)   +;
                chr(0)   + chr(31)  + chr(248) + chr(0)   +;
                chr(0)   + chr(63)  + chr(252) + chr(0)   +;
                chr(0)   + chr(127) + chr(254) + chr(0)   +;
                chr(0)   + chr(255) + chr(255) + chr(0)   +;
                chr(1)   + chr(255) + chr(255) + chr(128) +;
                chr(3)   + chr(255) + chr(255) + chr(192) +;
                chr(7)   + chr(255) + chr(255) + chr(224) +;
                chr(15)  + chr(255) + chr(255) + chr(240) +;
                chr(31)  + chr(255) + chr(255) + chr(248) +;
                chr(63)  + chr(255) + chr(255) + chr(252) +;
                chr(127) + chr(255) + chr(255) + chr(254) +;
                chr(255) + chr(255) + chr(255) + chr(255) +;
                chr(0)   + chr(31)  + chr(248) + chr(0)   +;
                chr(0)   + chr(31)  + chr(248) + chr(0)   +;
                chr(0)   + chr(31)  + chr(248) + chr(0)   +;
                chr(0)   + chr(31)  + chr(248) + chr(0)   +;
                chr(0)   + chr(31)  + chr(248) + chr(0)   +;
                chr(0)   + chr(0)   + chr(0)   + chr(0)   +;
                chr(0)   + chr(0)   + chr(0)   + chr(0)   +;
                chr(0)   + chr(0)   + chr(0)   + chr(0)   +;
                chr(0)   + chr(0)   + chr(0)   + chr(0)   +;
                chr(0)   + chr(0)   + chr(0)   + chr(0)   +;
                chr(0)   + chr(0)   + chr(0)   + chr(0)   +;
                chr(0)   + chr(0)   + chr(0)   + chr(0)   +;
                chr(0)   + chr(0)   + chr(0)   + chr(0)   +;
                chr(0)   + chr(0)   + chr(0)   + chr(0)

// Set up the display.  Begin by changing the graphics mode (EGA for
// this example).  Set the background color by changing the palette
// number. Display the standard text.  Notice that we can still use the
// Clipper text positioning functions.  Finally, display the company
// logo.  Notice that we use a standard string to do this.
```

```
SetGMode()
GPal(1)
WrtGMode(00, 00, padc(" Graphics Data Entry Screen ", 80, chr(177)), 31)
WrtGBoxD(01, 00, 23, 79)
WrtGMode(02, 02, "File   Edit", 31)
WrtGLineD(03, 01, 03, 78)
WrtGPixel(20, 600, 50, 632, cLogo, 10)

// Open the database and index.  Check to see if the file exists.  If
// the user is not allowed access, then the filename will not appear to
// the File() function.  (This assumes that you have already verified
// that the directory is correct.)

if file("SAMPLE7.DBF")
   use SAMPLE7 index SAMPLE7 shared
endif

// Display the data.

DispData()

while !(inkey(0) == K_ESC)

// Process the up and down arrow keys.  All other keys are ignored.

   do case

      // Scroll up one record.

      case lastkey() == K_UP
         if !(bof())
            skip -1
         endif

      // Scroll down one record.

      case lastkey() == K_DOWN
         if !(eof())
            skip
         endif
          if eof()
            skip -1
         endif

   endcase

   // Display the data.

   DispData()

enddo
// Clear the display by setting it back to text mode.  Return to DOS.

EndGMode()
```

12-7 Continued.

```
return

// Local Procedures Begin.


// This procedure displays the data contained in the database.  It
// begins by clearing any data left from the last display, then displays
// the fields one at a time.  Notice that the comments are surrounded by
// a box, making them easier to see.

static procedure DispData

// Clear the display area.

@ 04, 02 clear to 23, 78

// Display the data.

WrtGMode(04, 03, "Record: " + ltrim(str(recno())), 31)
WrtGMode(05, 03, "Name:       " + FIRST + " " + MIDDLE + " " + LAST, 31)
WrtGMode(07, 03, "Address:    " + COMPANY, 31)
WrtGMode(08, 14, ADDRESS1, 31)
WrtGMode(09, 14, ADDRESS2, 31)
WrtGMode(10, 14, CITY + ", " + STATE + "     " + ZIP, 31)
WrtGMode(12, 03, "Telephone: " + TELEPHONE1, 31)
WrtGMode(13, 14, TELEPHONE2, 31)
WrtGMode(15, 03, "Comments: ", 31)
WrtGBoxD(16, 03, 22, 76)
// memoedit(COMMENTS, 17, 04, 22, 75, .F.)

// Return to the calling procedure.

return NIL
```

12-8 Graphics-display example, assembly source

```
;*********************************************************************
;* Program 15 - Creating Graphics Mode Data Entry Screens            *
;* This program contains seven different procedures used to manipulate *
;* the display in graphics mode.  Each procedure performs a different  *
;* task related to the requirements placed on Clipper by a graphics    *
;* setup.  The SetGMode() procedure places the display in graphics     *
;* mode.  The EndGMode returns the display to the mode previous to     *
;* setting the display in graphics mode.  This could include another   *
;* graphics mode or a test mode.  WrtGMode() replaces the @...Say      *
;* command.  Clipper cannot write to a graphics display using a        *
;* standard command.  We replace the Clipper command with this         *
;* procedure.  GPal() changes the palette of the display.  This is the *
;* same as setting the background color for the display.  WrtGBoxD()   *
;* displays a double box using the specified coordinates.  WrtGLineD() *
```

```
;* displays a double line.  To display a graphic of some sort we use   *
;* the WrtGPixel() procedure.  This procedure accepts a string from    *
;* Clipper and interprets the individual bits a pixel settings.        *
;* Written by: John Mueller                                             *
;* Copyright 1991 John Mueller - Tab Books                              *
;***********************************************************************

;***********************************************************************
;* Make any required declarations.                                      *
;***********************************************************************

.MODEL LARGE

INCLUDE EXTASM.INC
INCLUDE MACROS.INC

PUBLIC SetGMode, EndGMode, WrtGMode, GPal, WrtGBoxD, WrtGLineD, WrtGPixel

;***********************************************************************
;* Declare any required variables.                                      *
;***********************************************************************

.DATA

nVMode     DB  0              ;Initial Clipper Video Mode
nDispPage  DB  0              ;Initial Clipper Display Page
nNewMode   DB  10h            ;New Video Mode (640 X 350 EGA Graphics)
nXPosit    DB  0              ;Write Character X Position.
nYPosit    DB  0              ;Write Character Y Position.
nXPosit2   DB  0              ;Second Write Character X Position.
nYPosit2   DB  0              ;Second Write Character Y Position.
nXPosit3   DW  0              ;Write Pixel X Position.
nYPosit3   DW  0              ;Write Pixel Y Position.
nXPosit4   DW  0              ;Second Write Pixel X Position.
nYPosit4   DW  0              ;Second Write Pixel Y Position.
nCharLen   DW  0              ;Length of string.
cWrtStr    DB  256 DUP (0)    ;Max String Length is 256 characters.
nStrColor  DB  0              ;String Color

.CODE

;***********************************************************************
;* This procedure set the display to a graphics mode.  The graphics    *
;* mode is stored as a mode number in nNewMode.  You could easily      *
;* enhance this procedure to accept input from Clipper, making it      *
;* more flexible.  Currently, it always changes the graphics mode to   *
;* 640 X 350 EGA with 16 colors visible.                                *
;***********************************************************************

SetGMode    PROC    FAR

            PUSH    SI              ;Save SI.

            MOV     AX,@DATA        ;Point DS & ES to our data segment.
```

12-8 Continued.

```
          MOV    DS,AX
          MOV    ES,AX

          MOV    AH,0Fh         ;Save the current video state.
          INT    10h
          MOV    nVMode,AL      ;Save the video mode number.
          MOV    nDispPage,BH   ;Save the video page number.

          XOR    AH,AH          ;Change the video mode to graphics.
          MOV    AL,nNewMode    ;Use the specified graphics mode.
          INT    10h

          POP    SI             ;Restore SI.

          RET                   ;Return to Clipper.

SetGMode  ENDP

;**********************************************************************
;* This procedure uses the defaults we saved in SetGMode() to change  *
;* the display adapter mode from graphics to text.  You could         *
;* potentially use it to restore any mode by allowing SetGMode to     *
;* return the defaults in an array and changing this procedure to     *
;* accept an array.  Currently, the procedure only restores the       *
;* previous mode.                                                     *
;**********************************************************************

EndGMode  PROC   FAR

          PUSH   SI          ;Save SI.

          MOV    AX,@DATA    ;Point DS & ES to our data segment.
          MOV    DS,AX
          MOV    ES,AX

          XOR    AH,AH       ;Change the video mode to Clipper standard.
          MOV    AL,nVMode
          INT    10h

          MOV    AH,5        ;Set the display page back to original.
          MOV    AL,nDispPage
          INT    10h

          POP    SI          ;Restore SI.

          RET                ;Return to Clipper.

EndGMode  ENDP
```

```
;***********************************************************************
;* This procedure replaces @...Say as one method of displaying text   *
;* on screen.  The standard Clipper routine will not work in graphics *
;* mode.  This one does because it uses a standard ROM interrupt to   *
;* do so.  Unfortunately, this means that you will loose some speed   *
;* in the process.  This routine also works in text mode.             *
;***********************************************************************

WrtGMode    PROC    FAR

            PUSH    SI          ;Save SI.

            MOV     AX,@DATA    ;Point DS & ES to our data segment.
            MOV     DS,AX
            MOV     ES,AX

;***********************************************************************
;* This section of the code checks the number of parameters and their *
;* type.                                                               *
;***********************************************************************

            PCount          ;Check for the correct
            CMP AX,4        ; number of parameters.
            JE  Parml       ;If so, perform next check.
            JMP BadExit     ;If not, exit.

Parml:      IsNum  1        ;Is the first parameter a number?
            JE  Parm2       ;If so, perform next check.
            JMP BadExit     ;If not, exit.

Parm2:      IsNum  2        ;Is the second parameter a number?
            JE  Parm3       ;If so, perform next check.
            JMP BadExit     ;If not, exit.

Parm3:      IsChar 3        ;Is the third parameter a character?
            JE  Parm4       ;If so, perform next check.
            JMP BadExit     ;If not, exit.

Parm4:      IsNum  4        ;Is the fourth parameter a number?
            JE  GoodParms   ;If so, retrieve the data.

BadExit:    RetFalse        ;Return false on error.
            POP SI          ;Restore SI
            RET

GoodParms: RetTrue          ;Return true for good parameters.

;***********************************************************************
;* This section of the code retrieves the various input values and    *
;* places them into variables for future use.                          *
;***********************************************************************

            GetInt      1               ;Get the first number.
            MOV         nYPosit,AL      ;Store the X position.
```

12-8 Continued.

```
        GetInt     2             ;Get the second number
        MOV        nXPosit,AL    ;Store the Y position.

        GetChar    3             ;Get the character parameter.
        PUSH       AX            ;Save the string offset.
        PUSH       DX            ;Save the Clipper DATA segment.

        GetCharLen 3             ;Retrieve the string length.
        MOV        nCharLen,AX   ;Store it for future use.
        MOV        CX,AX

        POP        DS            ;Point to the Clipper DATA segment.
        POP        SI            ;Point to the string.

        LEA        DI,cWrtStr    ;Load the offset of the display string.
        REP        MOVSB         ;Move the string to our data segment.

        MOV        AX,@DATA      ;Point DS to our data segment.
        MOV        DS,AX

        GetInt     4             ;Get the third number
        MOV        nStrColor,AL  ;Store the string color.

;*********************************************************************
;* This section of the code positions the cursor, then displays the   *
;* string starting from the specified cursor position.                *
;*********************************************************************

        MOV    AH,2          ;Position the cursor
        XOR    BX,BX         ; on display page 0
        MOV    DH,nYPosit    ; at a specific row
        MOV    DL,nXPosit    ; and a specific column.

        MOV    AH,13h        ;Display a string at the current cursor position.
        XOR    AL,AL         ;Use display mode 0.
        XOR    BH,BH         ;Use display page 0.
        MOV    BL,nStrColor  ;Use the specified color.
        MOV    CX,nCharLen   ;Load the number of characters in the string.
        MOV    DH,nYPosit    ; at a specific row
        MOV    DL,nXPosit    ; and a specific column.
        PUSH   BP            ;Save BP.
        LEA    BP,cWrtStr    ;Load the string offset.
        INT    10h           ;Display the character string.
        POP    BP            ;Restore BP.

        POP    SI            ;Restore SI.

        RET                  ;Return to Clipper.

WrtGMode    ENDP
```

```
;***********************************************************************
;* This procedure changes the background color of the display by      *
;* changing the contents of the palette register.                      *
;***********************************************************************

GPal        PROC    FAR

            PUSH    SI          ;Save SI.

            MOV     AX,@DATA    ;Point DS & ES to our data segment.
            MOV     DS,AX
            MOV     ES,AX

;***********************************************************************
;* This section of the code checks the number of parameters and their *
;* type.                                                               *
;***********************************************************************

            PCount              ;Check for the correct
            CMP     AX,1        ; number of parameters.
            JE      Parm1B      ;If so, perform next check.
            JMP     BadExitB    ;If not, exit.

Parm1B:     IsNum   1           ;Is the first parameter a number?
            JE      GoodParmB   ;If so, retrieve the data.

BadExitB:   RetFalse            ;Return false on error.
            POP     SI          ;Restore SI
            RET

GoodParmB: RetTrue              ;Return true for good parameters.

;***********************************************************************
;* This section of the code retrieves the various input values and    *
;* places them into variables for future use.                          *
;***********************************************************************

            GetInt     1    ;Get the first number.
            MOV     BL,AL   ;Store the clear color.

;***********************************************************************
;* This section of the code performs the task of clearing the         *
;* display.  It assumes that the display is 80 X 25.  You can easily  *
;* adjust it to any other size by changing the number of scroll lines *
;* in AL, and the lower right row and column positions in DH and DL.  *
;***********************************************************************

            MOV     AH,0Bh ;Clear the screen.
            XOR     BH,BH
            INT     10h

            POP     SI      ;Restore SI.

            RET             ;Return to Clipper.
```

```
GPal        ENDP

;*********************************************************************
;* This procedure draws a box using the coordinates passed by the    *
;* Clipper procedure.  This box uses the double line character set.  *
;*********************************************************************

WrtGBoxD    PROC    FAR

            PUSH    SI              ;Save SI.

            MOV     AX,@DATA        ;Point DS & ES to our data segment.
            MOV     DS,AX
            MOV     ES,AX

;*********************************************************************
;* This section of the code checks the number of parameters and their *
;* type.                                                              *
;*********************************************************************

            PCount                  ;Check for the correct
            CMP     AX,4            ; number of parameters.
            JE      Parm1C          ;If so, perform next check.
            JMP     BadExitC        ;If not, exit.

Parm1C:     IsNum   1               ;Is the first parameter a number?
            JE      Parm2C          ;If so, perform next check.
            JMP     BadExitC        ;If not, exit.

Parm2C:     IsNum   2               ;Is the second parameter a number?
            JE      Parm3C          ;If so, perform next check.
            JMP     BadExitC        ;If not, exit.

Parm3C:     IsNum   3               ;Is the third parameter a number?
            JE      Parm4C          ;If so, perform next check.
            JMP     BadExitC        ;If not, exit.

Parm4C:     IsNum   4               ;Is the fourth parameter a number?
            JE      GoodParmC       ;If so, retrieve the data.

BadExitC:   RetFalse                ;Return false on error.
            POP     SI              ;Restore SI
            RET

GoodParmC:  RetTrue                 ;Return true for good parameters.

;*********************************************************************
;* This section of the code retrieves the various input values and   *
;* places them into variables for future use.                        *
;*********************************************************************
```

```
        GetInt 1            ;Get the first number.
        MOV    nYPosit,AL   ;Store the X position.

        GetInt 2            ;Get the second number
        MOV    nXPosit,AL   ;Store the Y position.

        GetInt 3            ;Get the third number.
        MOV    nYPosit2,AL  ;Store the second X position.

        GetInt 4            ;Get the fourth number
        MOV    nXPosit2,AL  ;Store the second Y position.

;***********************************************************************
;* This section of code display the upper horizontal line.             *
;***********************************************************************

        MOV AH,2            ;Position the cursor
        XOR BX,BX           ; on display page 0
        MOV DH,nYPosit      ; at a specific row
        MOV DL,nXPosit      ; and a specific column.
        INT 10h

        XOR CH,CH           ;Zero CH
        MOV CL,nXPosit2     ;Place the ending position in CL.
        SUB CL,nXPosit      ;Subtract the beginning position to get the
        INC CX              ; number of characters to draw.
        MOV AH,0Eh          ;Display a sting of characters.
        MOV AL,205          ;Use character number 205.
        XOR BH,BH           ;Use display page zero.
        MOV BL,15           ;Use white characters.
LoopC1: INT 10h             ;Display the characters.
        Loop   LoopC1

;***********************************************************************
;* This section of code displays the lower horizontal line.            *
;***********************************************************************

       MOV AH,2            ;Position the cursor
       XOR BX,BX           ; on display page 0
       MOV DH,nYPosit2     ; at a specific row
       MOV DL,nXPosit      ; and a specific column.
       INT 10h

       XOR CH,CH           ;Zero CH
       MOV CL,nXPosit2     ;Place the ending position in CL.
       SUB CL,nXPosit      ;Subtract the beginning position to get the
       INC CX              ; number of characters to draw.
       MOV AH,0Eh          ;Display a sting of characters.
       MOV AL,205          ;Use character number 205.
       XOR BH,BH           ;Use display page zero.
       MOV BL,15           ;Use white characters.
LoopC2:INT 10h             ;Display the characters.
       Loop   LoopC2
```

12-8 Continued.

```
;*********************************************************************
;* This section of the code displays the left line.                  *
;*********************************************************************

        XOR AH,AH           ;Clear AH.
        MOV AL,nYPosit2     ;Store the ending position.
        SUB AL,nYPosit      ;Subtract the starting position.
        INC AX              ;Compensate for the last character.
        MOV SI,AX           ;Store the result in SI.

        XOR BX,BX           ;Use display page zero.
        MOV BL,15           ;Use white characters.
        MOV DH,nYPosit      ;Load the initial Y position.
        MOV DL,nXPosit      ;Load the initial X position.
        MOV CX,1            ;Display 1 character.
        MOV AL,186          ;Use character number 186.

LoopC3: MOV AH,2            ;Position the cursor.
        INT 10h

        MOV AH,0Eh          ;Display the character.
        INT 10h

        INC DH              ;Move to the next Y position.
        DEC SI              ;Decrement our character counter.
        CMP SI,0            ;Is this the last character?
        JNE LoopC3          ;If not display the next character.

;*********************************************************************
;* This section of the code displays the right line.                 *
;*********************************************************************

        XOR AH,AH           ;Clear AH.
        MOV AL,nYPosit2     ;Store the ending position.
        SUB AL,nYPosit      ;Subtract the starting position.
        INC AX              ;Compensate for the last character.
        MOV SI,AX           ;Store the result in SI.

        XOR BX,BX           ;Use display page zero.
        MOV BL,15           ;Use white characters.
        MOV DH,nYPosit      ;Load the initial Y position.
        MOV DL,nXPosit2     ;Load the initial X position.
        MOV CX,1            ;Display 1 character.
        MOV AL,186          ;Use character number 186.

LoopC4: MOV AH,2            ;Position the cursor.
        INT 10h

        MOV AH,0Eh          ;Display the character.
        INT 10h

        INC DH              ;Move to the next Y position.
        DEC SI              ;Decrement our character counter.
```

```
        CMP SI,0            ;Is this the last character?
        JNE LoopC4          ;If not display the next character.

;**********************************************************************
;* This section of the code adds the four corners to the box.         *
;**********************************************************************

     MOV DH,nYPosit      ;Load Y position for corner 1.
     MOV DL,nXPosit      ;Load X position for corner 1.
     MOV AH,2            ;Position the cursor.
     INT 10h

     MOV AL,201          ;Use character 201.
     MOV AH,0Eh          ;Display the corner.
     INT 10h

     MOV DH,nYPosit      ;Load Y position for corner 2.
     MOV DL,nXPosit2     ;Load X position for corner 2.
     MOV AH,2            ;Position the cursor.
     INT 10h

     MOV AL,187          ;Use character 187.
     MOV AH,0Eh          ;Display the corner.
     INT 10h

     MOV DH,nYPosit2     ;Load Y position for corner 3.
     MOV DL,nXPosit2     ;Load X position for corner 3.
     MOV AH,2            ;Position the cursor.
     INT 10h

     MOV AL,188          ;Use character 188.
     MOV AH,0Eh          ;Display the corner.
     INT 10h

     MOV DH,nYPosit2     ;Load Y position for corner 4.
     MOV DL,nXPosit      ;Load X position for corner 4.
     MOV AH,2            ;Position the cursor.
     INT 10h

     MOV AL,200          ;Use character 200.
     MOV AH,0Eh          ;Display the corner.
     INT 10h

     POP SI              ;Restore SI.

     RET                 ;Return to Clipper.

WrtGBoxD   ENDP


;**********************************************************************
;* This procedure draws a double line using the coordinates provided  *
;* by the calling Clipper procedure.                                  *
;**********************************************************************
```

12-8 Continued.

```
WrtGLineD      PROC   FAR

               PUSH   SI          ;Save SI.

               MOV    AX,@DATA    ;Point DS & ES to our data segment.
               MOV    DS,AX
               MOV    ES,AX

;*********************************************************************
;* This section of the code checks the number of parameters and their *
;* type.                                                              *
;*********************************************************************

            PCount              ;Check for the correct
            CMP    AX,4         ; number of parameters.
            JE     Parm1D       ;If so, perform next check.
            JMP    BadExitD     ;If not, exit.

Parm1D:     IsNum  1            ;Is the first parameter a number?
            JE     Parm2D       ;If so, perform next check.
            JMP    BadExitD     ;If not, exit.

Parm2D:     IsNum  2            ;Is the second parameter a number?
            JE     Parm3D       ;If so, perform next check.
            JMP    BadExitD     ;If not, exit.

Parm3D:     IsNum  3            ;Is the third parameter a number?
            JE     Parm4D       ;If so, perform next check.
            JMP    BadExitD     ;If not, exit.

Parm4D:     IsNum  4            ;Is the fourth parameter a number?
            JE     GoodParmD    ;If so, retrieve the data.

BadExitD:   RetFalse            ;Return false on error.
            POP SI              ;Restore SI
            RET

GoodParmD:  RetTrue             ;Return true for good parameters.

;*********************************************************************
;* This section of the code retrieves the various input values and   *
;* places them into variables for future use.                        *
;*********************************************************************

    GetInt 1            ;Get the first number.
    MOV    nYPosit,AL   ;Store the X position.

    GetInt 2            ;Get the second number
    MOV    nXPosit,AL   ;Store the Y position.

    GetInt 3            ;Get the third number.
    MOV    nYPosit2,AL    ;Store the second X position.
```

```
    GetInt 4           ;Get the fourth number
    MOV    nXPosit2,AL    ;Store the second Y position.

;*********************************************************************
;* This section of the code moves the cursor to the starting position *
;* of the line, then displays one character at a time until it      *
;* reaches the ending position.  To determine how many characters we  *
;* need to draw, we subtract the ending column from the starting     *
;* column.                                                           *
;*********************************************************************

        MOV     AH,2            ;Position the cursor
        XOR     BX,BX           ; on display page 0
        MOV     DH,nYPosit      ; at a specific row
        MOV     DL,nXPosit      ; and a specific column.
        INT     10h

        XOR     CH,CH           ;Zero CH
        MOV     CL,nXPosit2     ;Place the ending position in CL.
        SUB     CL,nXPosit      ;Subtract the beginning position to get the
        INC     CX              ; number of characters to draw.
        MOV     AH,0Eh          ;Display a sting of characters.
        MOV     AL,205          ;Use character number 205.
        XOR     BH,BH           ;Use display page zero.
        MOV     BL,15           ;Use white characters.
LoopD:  INT     10h             ;Display the characters.
        Loop    LoopD

        POP     SI              ;Restore SI.

        RET                     ;Return to Clipper.

WrtGLineD  ENDP


;*********************************************************************
;* This procedure displays a string of characters on screen as a bit- *
;* mapped image.  It accepts six parameters as input.  The first four *
;* parameters are the graphic image placement in pixels.  The first   *
;* two parameters determine the upper left corner of the screen while *
;* the second two parameters determine the lower right corner.  The   *
;* fifth parameter contains a string which the procedure interpret at *
;* a bit-map.  One bit within the string equates to one pixel on the  *
;* display.  The sixth parameter determines the color of the graphic. *
;* Since this routine interprets the graphic eight bits at a time,    *
;* your third parameter must be a multiple of eight different from    *
;* the first parameter.  For example, if the first parameter          *
;* contained 200 and the third 207, then the procedure would not work *
;* correctly.  However, a value of 208 for the second parameter would *
;* work.  The graphic image is limited to the 256 character limit for *
;* string in Clipper.                                                 *
;*********************************************************************

WrtGPixel       PROC    FAR
```

12-8 Continued.

```
              PUSH    SI          ;Save SI.

              MOV     AX,@DATA    ;Point DS & ES to our data segment.
              MOV     DS,AX
              MOV     ES,AX

;*********************************************************************
;* This section of the code checks the number of parameters and their *
;* type.                                                              *
;*********************************************************************

           PCount             ;Check for the correct
           CMP    AX,6        ; number of parameters.
           JE     Parm1E      ;If so, perform next check.
           JMP    BadExitE    ;If not, exit.

Parm1E:    IsNum  1           ;Is the first parameter a number?
           JE     Parm2E      ;If so, perform next check.
           JMP    BadExitE    ;If not, exit.

Parm2E:    IsNum  2           ;Is the second parameter a number?
           JE     Parm3E      ;If so, perform next check.
           JMP    BadExitE    ;If not, exit.

Parm3E:    IsNum  3           ;Is the first parameter a number?
           JE     Parm4E      ;If so, perform next check.
           JMP    BadExitE    ;If not, exit.

Parm4E:    IsNum  4           ;Is the second parameter a number?
           JE     Parm5E      ;If so, perform next check.
           JMP    BadExitE    ;If not, exit.

Parm5E:    IsChar 5           ;Is the third parameter a character?
           JE     Parm6E      ;If so, perform next check.
           JMP    BadExitE    ;If not, exit.

Parm6E:    IsNum  6           ;Is the fourth parameter a number?
           JE     GoodParmE   ;If so, retrieve the data.

BadExitE:  RetFalse           ;Return false on error.
           POP SI             ;Restore SI
           RET

GoodParmE: RetTrue            ;Return true for good parameters.

;*********************************************************************
;* This section of the code retrieves the various input values and   *
;* places them into variables for future use.                        *
;*********************************************************************

   GetInt     1              ;Get the first number.
   MOV        nYPosit3,AX    ;Store the X position.
```

```
GetInt      2               ;Get the second number
MOV         nXPosit3,AX     ;Store the Y position.

GetInt      3               ;Get the first number.
MOV         nYPosit4,AX     ;Store the X position.

GetInt      4               ;Get the second number
MOV         nXPosit4,AX     ;Store the Y position.

GetChar     5               ;Get the character parameter.
PUSH        AX              ;Save the string offset.
PUSH        DX              ;Save the Clipper DATA segment.

GetCharLen 5                ;Retrieve the string length.
MOV         nCharLen,AX     ;Store it for future use.
MOV         CX,AX

POP         DS              ;Point to the Clipper DATA segment.
POP         SI              ;Point to the string.

LEA         DI,cWrtStr      ;Load the offset of the display string.
REP         MOVSB           ;Move the string to our data segment.

MOV         AX,@DATA        ;Point DS to our data segment.
MOV         DS,AX

GetInt      6               ;Get the third number
MOV         nStrColor,AL    ;Store the string color.

;*********************************************************************
;* This section of the code interprets each bit of the current       *
;* character one at a time.  If the bit is not set, then it displays *
;* a pixel at that point on the display.                             *
;*********************************************************************

        MOV     AH,0Ch              ;Write a pixel dot
        MOV     AL,nStrColor        ; using the specified color
        XOR     BH,BH               ; on display page zero.
        MOV     CX,nXPosit3         ;Load the initial X position.
        MOV     DX,nYPosit3         ;Load the initial Y position.
        LEA     DI,cWrtStr          ;Load the string address.

Test1:  TEST    BYTE PTR [DI],10000000b     ;First bit a zero?
        JNE     Test2                       ;If not, perform the next check.
        INT     10h                         ;If so, display a dot.

Test2:  INC     CX                          ;Go to the next pixel
        TEST    BYTE PTR [DI],01000000b     ;Second bit a zero?
        JNE     Test3                       ;If not, perform the next check.
        INT     10h
```

12-8 Continued.

```
Test3:     INC    CX                              ;Go to the next pixel
           TEST   BYTE PTR [DI],00100000b         ;Second bit a zero?
           JNE    Test4                           ;If not, perform the next check.
           INT    10h

Test4:     INC    CX                              ;Go to the next pixel
           TEST   BYTE PTR [DI],00010000b         ;Second bit a zero?
           JNE    Test5                           ;If not, perform the next check.
           INT    10h

Test5:     INC    CX                              ;Go to the next pixel
           TEST   BYTE PTR [DI],00001000b         ;Second bit a zero?
           JNE    Test6                           ;If not, perform the next check.
           INT    10h

Test6:     INC    CX                              ;Go to the next pixel
           TEST   BYTE PTR [DI],00000100b         ;Second bit a zero?
           JNE    Test7                           ;If not, perform the next check.
           INT    10h

Test7:     INC    CX                              ;Go to the next pixel
           TEST   BYTE PTR [DI],00000010b         ;Second bit a zero?
           JNE    Test8                           ;If not, perform the next check.
           INT    10h

Test8:     INC    CX                              ;Go to the next pixel
           TEST   BYTE PTR [DI],00000001b         ;Second bit a zero?
           JNE    NextLoop                        ;If not, perform the next check.
           INT    10h

NextLoop:  INC    DI              ;Point to the next character.
           INC    CX              ;Point to the next character position.
           CMP    CX,nXPosit4     ;Check to see if this is the last position in
                                  ; this row.
           JNE Test1              ;If not, display the next character.
           MOV    CX,nXPosit3     ;If so, point to the beginning of line.
           INC    DX              ;Move to the next line.
           CMP    DX,nYPosit4     ;Is this the last line?
           JE     ExitE           ;If so, exit.
           JMP    Test1           ;Otherwise, display the next line.

   ExitE:  POP    SI              ;Restore SI.

           RET                    ;Return to Clipper.

   WrtGPixel  ENDP

   END
```

The assembly code in FIG. 12-8 at first appears very complex, but it contains a lot of repetitious code. There are seven routines required to recreate even the most basic example presented here. The first routine, SetGMode( ), places the display adapter in graphics mode. First, however, it saves the current display mode and display page number. This allows you to return to the exact mode and page number in use when the routine left Clipper.

You could use the SaveScreen( ) function to save the contents of video memory before you switch to graphics mode, and then use the RestScreen( ) function to restore the video memory when you return to text mode. In essence, Clipper would never even know that you had placed the display in graphics mode. The EndGMode( ) routine places the display adapter back into the mode that you saved prior to going into graphics mode. For the purposes of this example, I used 350- × 640- × 16-color EGA mode. You could pass a parameter to SetGMode( ) to allow use of any display mode desired.

The assembly-language source code contains a special routine for setting the background color. Unlike text mode, most ROM routines are configured to change only the foreground color of a graphics display. This means that you must change the background color separately or use some method of direct manipulation. GPal( ) is the function that changes the standard black background into blue. You can pass a value to GPal( ), which will change the background color into any color desired. Changing the background before you go into graphics mode doesn't accomplish anything, unfortunately.

As with all programs, this one writes text to the display. In most cases you won't require any fancy fonts when you do so. This example uses the default font when it calls WrtGMode( ) to send text to the display. There are several alternate fonts available in the VGA and EGA ROMs. You could select one of these as the default font using the interrupts described in previous sections. For example, there's an 8 × 8 character font that will allow you to display many more lines of text on screen.

Some of the interrupts allow you to upload your own character sets into video memory as well. This is where external programs come into play. You could create fonts using another program and then upload them for use within your Clipper routines. In essence, the WrtGMode( ) function will use whatever font you specify as the default for writing.

There are two text graphics routines included with the program. WrtGBoxD( ) and WrtGLineD( ) show you the ease with which you can include text graphics in your graphics display. While these routines look fairly complex, most of each routine's work revolves around displaying the proper character in the proper place on the display. As you can see from FIG. 12-8, most of the code is repetitious loops and counting variables. You could easily enhance these routines to draw single or combination line graphics as well. The routines illustrate that you can use text graphics whenever possible to reduce the programming load incurred by text mode.

The final routine, WrtGPixel( ), is the reason I began the graphics mode in the first place. This is an extremely rudimentary routine designed to display a logo on the screen as you work. It uses characters placed into a string and passed from Clipper as the means of describing the graphic. This technique has a lot of potential uses, but it's somewhat cumbersome and limited by the Clipper string length.

You could use the techniques shown previously in chapter 9 to import graphics from other programs or draw graphics directly on the display. Many of the common graphics programs also use well-known formats. The GIF and PCX file formats are available on many BBSs, including CompuServe. Creating your own displays from the data contained in a database is fairly easy. For example, the math coprocessor routine in appendix F uses just this technique to display the value of some trigonometric functions on screen.

Summary

This chapter provides you with the information that you need to create any type of display your program requires. It begins by describing the various types of display adapters available on the market. Understanding the differences between various display adapters will reduce the time you need to adapt your programs to work on any one type of adapter. These differences will also allow you to take advantage of various display-adapter features and help you detect the type of adapter that's resident in the host machine.

Learning the mechanical differences between various display adapter types allows you to learn about the programming differences more quickly. The second section of this chapter tells you about the ROM interrupt routines available for various types of display adapters. It also provides you with the appropriate warnings applicable to specific display-adapter types and services. Observing these warnings can enhance the displays you create and reduce the amount of time you spend debugging your program.

The third, and final section in this chapter provides you with some practical examples of how to enhance the appearance of your displays using the ROM interrupts. These examples are rudimentary in nature and designed to illustrate a concept rather than create a specific program. You can use the examples in this section as the basis for ideas for your own displays.

A

Inkey( ) return values

Value	Key	INKEY.CH define value
Cursor movement keys		
1	Home, Ctrl-A	K_HOME
2	Ctrl-right arrow, Ctrl-B	K_CTRL_RIGHT
3	Ctrl-Scroll Lock	K_CTRL_C
3	PgDn, Ctrl-C	K_PGDN
4	Right arrow, Ctrl-D	K_RIGHT
5	Up arrow, Ctrl-E	K_UP
6	End, Ctrl-F	K_END
10	Ctrl-Return	K_CTRL_RET
13	Enter, Ctrl-M	K_ENTER
13	Return, Ctrl-M	K_RETURN
18	PgUp, Ctrl-R	K_PGUP
19	Left arrow, Ctrl-S	K_LEFT
23	Ctrl-End, Ctrl-W	K_CTRL_END
24	Down arrow, Ctrl-X	K_DOWN
26	Ctrl-left arrow, Ctrl-Z	K_CTRL_LEFT
27	Esc, Ctrl-[	K_ESC
29	Ctrl-Home, Ctrl-]	K_CTRL_HOME
30	Ctrl-PgDn, Ctrl-^ ^	K_CTRL_PGDN
31	Ctrl-PgUp, Ctrl-Hyphen	K_CTRL_PGUP

Value	Key	INKEY.CH define value
Editing keys		
7	Del, Ctrl-G	K_DEL
8	Backspace, Ctrl-H	K_BS
9	Tab, Ctrl-I	K_TAB
22	Ins, Ctrl-V	K_INS
127	Ctrl-Backspace	K_CTRL_BS
271	Shift-Tab	K_SH_TAB
Function keys		
28	F1, Ctrl-\	K_F1
-1	F2	K_F2
-2	F3	K_F3
-3	F4	K_F4
-4	F5	K_F5
-5	F6	K_F6
-6	F7	K_F7
-7	F8	K_F8
-8	F9	K_F9
-9	F10	K_F10
Shift function keys		
-10	Shift-F1	K_SH_F1
-11	Shift-F2	K_SH_F2
-12	Shift-F3	K_SH_F3
-13	Shift-F4	K_SH_F4
-14	Shift-F5	K_SH_F5
-15	Shift-F6	K_SH_F6
-16	Shift-F7	K_SH_F7
-17	Shift-F8	K_SH_F8
-18	Shift-F9	K_SH_F9
-19	Shift-F10	K_SH_F10
Ctrl function keys		
-20	Ctrl-F1	K_CTRL_F1
-21	Ctrl-F2	K_CTRL_F2
-22	Ctrl-F3	K_CTRL_F3
-23	Ctrl-F4	K_CTRL_F4
-24	Ctrl-F5	K_CTRL_F5

Value	Key	INKEY.CH define value
-25	Ctrl-F6	K_CTRL_F6
-26	Ctrl-F7	K_CTRL_F7
-27	Ctrl-F8	K_CTRL_F8
-28	Ctrl-F9	K_CTRL_F9
-29	Ctrl-F10	K_CTRL_F10
Alt function keys		
-30	Alt-F1	K_ALT_F1
-31	Alt-F2	K_ALT_F2
-32	Alt-F3	K_ALT_F3
-33	Alt-F4	K_ALT_F4
-34	Alt-F5	K_ALT_F5
-35	Alt-F6	K_ALT_F6
-36	Alt-F7	K_ALT_F7
-37	Alt-F8	K_ALT_F8
-38	Alt-F9	K_ALT_F9
-39	Alt-F10	K_ALT_F10
Ctrl alpha keys		
1	Ctrl-A	K_CTRL_A
2	Ctrl-B	K_CTRL_B
3	Ctrl-C	K_CTRL_C
4	Ctrl-D	K_CTRL_D
5	Ctrl-E	K_CTRL_E
6	Ctrl-F	K_CTRL_F
7	Ctrl-G	K_CTRL_G
8	Ctrl-H	K_CTRL_H
9	Ctrl-I	K_CTRL_I
10	Ctrl-J	K_CTRL_J
11	Ctrl-K	K_CTRL_K
12	Ctrl-L	K_CTRL_L
13	Ctrl-M	K_CTRL_M
14	Ctrl-N	K_CTRL_N
15	Ctrl-O	K_CTRL_O
16	Ctrl-P	K_CTRL_P
17	Ctrl-Q	K_CTRL_Q
18	Ctrl-R	K_CTRL_R
19	Ctrl-S	K_CTRL_S
20	Ctrl-T	K_CTRL_T
21	Ctrl-U	K_CTRL_U
22	Ctrl-V	K_CTRL_V

Value	Key	INKEY.CH define value
23	Ctrl-W	K_CTRL_W
24	Ctrl-X	K_Ctrl_X
25	Ctrl-Y	K_Ctrl_Y
26	Ctrl-Z	K_CTRL_Z
Alt alpha keys		
272	Alt-Q	K_ALT_Q
273	Alt-W	K_ALT_W
274	Alt-E	K_ALT_E
275	Alt-R	K_ALT_R
276	Alt-T	K_ALT_T
277	Alt-Y	K_ALT_Y
278	Alt-U	K_ALT_U
279	Alt-I	K_ALT_I
280	Alt-O	K_ALT_O
281	Alt-P	K_ALT_P
286	Alt-A	K_ALT_A
287	Alt-S	K_ALT_S
288	Alt-D	K_ALT_D
289	Alt-F	K_ALT_F
290	Alt-G	K_ALT_G
291	Alt-H	K_ALT_H
292	Alt-J	K_ALT_J
293	Alt-K	K_ALT_K
294	Alt-L	K_ALT_L
300	Alt-Z	K_ALT_Z
301	Alt-X	K_ALT_X
302	Alt-C	K_ALT_C
303	Alt-V	K_ALT_V
304	Alt-B	K_ALT_B
305	Alt-N	K_ALT_N
306	Alt-M	K_ALT_M

B
ASCII table

Dec	Hex	Character
0	0	
1	1	☺
2	2	●
3	3	♥
4	4	♦
5	5	♣
6	6	♠
7	7	•
8	8	◘
9	9	○
10	A	◙
11	B	♂
12	C	♀
13	D	♪
14	E	♫
15	F	☼
16	10	►
17	11	◄
18	12	↕
19	13	‼
20	14	¶
21	15	§
22	16	▬
23	17	↨

Dec	Hex	Character
24	18	↑
25	19	↓
26	1A	→
27	1B	←
28	1C	∟
29	1D	↔
30	1E	▲
31	1F	▼
32	20	(space)
33	21	!
34	22	"
35	23	#
36	24	$
37	25	%
38	26	&
39	27	'
40	28	(
41	29	)
42	2A	*
43	2B	+
44	2C	,
45	2D	−
46	2E	.
47	2F	/

Dec	Hex	Character
48	30	0
49	31	1
50	32	2
51	33	3
52	34	4
53	35	5
54	36	6
55	37	7
56	38	8
57	39	9
58	3A	:
59	3B	;
60	3C	<
61	3D	=
62	3E	>
63	3F	?
64	40	@
65	41	A
66	42	B
67	43	C
68	44	D
69	45	E
70	46	F
71	47	G
72	48	H
73	49	I
74	4A	J
75	4B	K
76	4C	L
77	4D	M
78	4E	N
79	4F	O
80	50	P
81	51	Q
82	52	R
83	53	S
84	54	T
85	55	U
86	56	V
87	57	W
88	58	X
90	5A	Z
91	5B	[

Dec	Hex	Character
92	5C	\
93	5D	]
94	5E	^
95	5F	_
96	60	`
97	61	a
98	62	b
99	63	c
100	64	d
101	65	e
102	66	f
103	67	g
104	68	h
105	69	i
106	6A	j
107	6B	k
108	6C	l
109	6D	m
110	6E	n
111	6F	o
112	70	p
113	71	q
114	72	r
115	73	s
116	74	t
117	75	u
118	76	v
119	77	w
120	78	x
121	79	y
122	7A	z
123	7B	{
124	7C	|
125	7D	}
126	7E	~
127	7F	▒
128	80	Ç
129	81	ü
130	82	é
131	83	â
132	84	ä
133	85	à
134	86	å

Dec	Hex	Character
135	87	ç
136	88	ê
137	89	ë
138	8A	è
139	8B	ï
140	8C	î
141	8D	ì
142	8E	Ä
143	8F	Å
144	90	É
145	91	æ
146	92	Æ
147	93	ô
148	94	ö
149	95	ò
150	96	û
151	97	ù
152	98	ÿ
153	99	Ö
154	9A	Ü
155	9B	¢
156	9C	£
157	9D	¥
158	9E	₧
159	9F	ƒ
160	A0	á
161	A1	í
162	A2	ó
163	A3	ú
164	A4	ñ
165	A5	Ñ
166	A6	ª
167	A7	º
168	A8	¿
169	A9	⌐
170	AA	¬
171	AB	½
172	AC	¼
173	AD	¡
174	AE	«
175	AF	»
176	B0	░
177	B1	▒

Dec	Hex	Character
178	B2	▓
179	B3	│
180	B4	┤
181	B5	╡
182	B6	╢
183	B7	╖
184	B8	╕
185	B9	╣
186	BA	║
187	BB	╗
188	BC	╝
189	BD	╜
190	BE	╛
191	BF	┐
192	C0	└
193	C1	┴
194	C2	┬
195	C3	├
196	C4	─
197	C5	┼
198	C6	╞
199	C7	╟
200	C8	╚
201	C9	╔
202	CA	╩
203	CB	╦
204	CC	╠
205	CD	═
206	CE	╬
207	CF	╧
208	D0	╨
209	D1	╤
210	D2	╥
211	D3	╙
212	D4	╘
213	D5	╒
214	D6	╓
215	D7	╫
216	D8	╪
217	D9	┘
218	DA	┌
219	DB	█
220	DC	▄

Dec	Hex	Character
221	DD	▌
222	DE	▐
223	DF	▀
224	E0	α
225	E1	β
226	E2	Γ
227	E3	π
228	E4	Σ
229	E5	σ
230	E6	µ
231	E7	τ
232	E8	Φ
233	EA	Θ
234	EB	Ω
235	EC	δ
236	ED	∞
237	ED	φ
238	EE	ε

Dec	Hex	Character
239	EF	∩
240	F0	≡
241	F1	±
242	F2	≥
243	F3	≤
244	F4	⌠
245	F5	⌡
246	F6	÷
247	F7	≈
248	F8	°
249	F9	•
250	FA	·
251	FB	√
252	FC	η
253	FD	²
254	FE	■
255	FF	(blank)

Organized by type

NOTE: All ASCII codes are given in decimal notation.

Arrows

```
        24
        ↑
27 ←         → 26
        ↓
        25
```

Single horizontal and single vertical line box

```
            196 194
218 ┌     ─     ┬     ┐ 191
195 ├   197 ┼         ┤ 180
179 │   179 │         │ 179
192 └     ─     ┴     ┘ 217
            196 193
```

Single horizontal and double vertical box

```
        196 210
214 ╓   ─   ╥   ╖   183
199 ╟  215  ╫   ╢   182
186 ║  186  ║   ║   186
211 ╙   ─   ╨   ╜   189
        196 208
```

Double horizontal and single vertical box

```
        205 209
213 ╒   ═   ╤   ╕   184
198 ╞  216  ╪   ╡   181
179 │  179  │   │   179
212 ╘   ═   ╧   ╛   190
        205 207
```

Double horizontal and double vertical box

```
        205 203
201 ╔   ═   ╦   ╗   187
204 ╠  206  ╬   ╣   185
186 ║  186  ║   ║   186
200 ╚   ═   ╩   ╝   188
        205 202
```

Foreign-language characters

Ä	Å	â	ä	à	å	á	ª
142	143	131	132	133	134	160	166
Ç	ç		É	é	ê	ë	
128	135		144	130	136	137	
ï	î	ì	í	Ñ	ñ		
139	140	141	161	165	164		
Ö	ô	ö	ò	ó	º		
153	147	148	149	162	167		
Ü	ü	û	ù	ú		ÿ	Æ
154	129	150	151	163		152	146
æ	¿	¡	¢	£	¥	₧	ƒ
145	168	173	155	156	157	158	159

Mathematical symbols

½	¼	α	β	Γ	π	Σ	σ	µ
171	172	224	225	226	227	228	229	230
τ	Φ	Θ	Ω	δ	∞	φ	ϵ	∩
231	232	233	234	235	236	237	238	239
≡	±	≥	≤	⌠	⌡	÷	≈	°
240	241	242	243	244	245	246	247	248
•	·	√	η	²				
249	250	251	252	253				

C
CPU command summary

This appendix provides a brief listing of processor-specific commands. It arranges the commands in mnemonic alphabetical order. There are sections for the 8086, 8088, 80286, and 80386 processors. Each general-purpose processor builds on the commands available to its predecessor; therefore, each command appears once. Appendix F describes the math coprocessor commands. The applicable processor appears in parentheses beside the command. TABLE C-1 contains the 8086/8088 listing, TABLE C-2 contains the 80286 listing, and TABLE C-3 contains the 80386 listing. For a more complete reference with example programs, get the *Ultimate DOS Programmer's Manual*, book #3534, from Windcrest Books.

Table C-1 8088/8086 command summary

Command	Description
Arithmetic instructions	
ASCII adjust for addition (AAA)	The ASCII adjust for addition instruction changes the AL register contents from packed to unpacked decimal format. Zero the auxiliary carry flag (AF) before using this command.
ASCII adjust for division (AAD)	The ASCII adjust for division instruction changes the AX register contents from unpacked to packed decimal format.

Table C-1 Continued.

Command	Description
ASCII adjust for multiplication (AAM)	The ASCII adjust for multiplication instruction corrects the result of multiplying two unpacked decimal format numbers.
ASCII adjust for subtraction (AAS)	The ASCII adjust for subtraction instruction corrects the results of subtracting of two unpacked decimal format numbers. Zero the auxiliary carry flag (AF) before using this command.
Add with carry (ADC)	Use the add with carry instruction to add two numbers and accounts for carries generated from previous additions.
Add without carry (ADD)	This instruction adds two operands without regard for CF status.
Convert byte to word (CBW)	This instruction converts a byte value stored in AL to a word value by extending the sign-bit in AL through AH.
Compare (CMP)	This instruction compares by subtracting the value of the destination from the value of the source. It updates the AF, CF, OF, PF, SF, and ZF registers to reflect the subtraction results, but does not place the results in the destination.
Convert word to doubleword (CWD)	Use this instruction to convert a word value to a doubleword value. It extends the sign-bit in AX through DX.
Decimal adjust for addition (DAA)	The decimal adjust for addition instruction corrects the result of adding two packed decimal operands.
Decimal adjust for subtraction (DAS)	The decimal adjust for subtraction instruction corrects the result of subtracting two packed decimal operands.
Decrement (DEC)	This instruction reduces the contents of a register or memory variable by one.

Command	Description
Divide (DIV)	The divide instruction performs unsigned division. It divides the quantity in the accumulator by the divisor. When using byte values, the quotient appears in AL and the remainder appears in AH. The value divided appears in AX. When using word values, the quotient appears in AX and the remainder appears in DX. The value divided appears in the AX:DX register pair. Using doubleword values places the quotient in EAX and the remainder in EDX. The processor divides the numerator in the EAX:EDX register pair by the divisor.
Integer divide (IDIV)	The integer divide instruction performs signed division on the value contained in the accumulator. When using byte values, the quotient appears in AL and the remainder appears in AH. The value divided appears in AX. When using word values, the quotient appears in AX and the remainder appears in DX. The value divided appears in the AX:DX register pair. Using doubleword values places the quotient in EAX and the remainder in EDX. The processor divides the numerator in the EAX:EDX register pair by the divisor.
Integer multiply (IMUL)	This instruction performs signed multiplication on the value in the accumulator by the multiplicand. When using byte values, the AX register contains the double length result. Using word values returns the result in the AX:DX register pair. Doubleword values return a result in the EAX:EDX register pair.
Increment (INC)	This instruction increases the contents of a register or memory variable by one.
Multiply (MUL)	This instruction performs unsigned multiplication on the value in the accumulator by the multiplicand. When using byte values, the AX register contains the double length result. Using word values returns the result in the AX:DX register pair. Doubleword values return a result in the EAX:EDX register pair.

Table C-1 Continued.

Command	Description
Negate (NEG)	This instruction calculates the two's complement of the destination operand. This is effectively the same as subtracting the destination operand from 0.
Subtract with borrow (SBB)	This instruction subtracts the source value from the destination value and stores the result in the destination. It decrements the result by one if CF = 1. The subtract with borrow instruction affects AF, CF, OF, PF, SF, and ZF.
Subtract (SUB)	The subtract instruction subtracts the value in the source from the destination. It affects AF, CF, OF, PF, SF, and ZF.
Bit-manipulation instructions	
Logical AND on bits (AND)	Use this instruction to logically combine two values together with AND at the bit level.
Logical NOT on bits (NOT)	The NOT instruction produces the one's complement of the destination operand by inverting its bits. This instruction does not affect any flags.
Logical OR on bits (OR)	This instruction performs an inclusive OR operation of the source and destination operands. It places the results in the destination operand. A bit equals 1 in the destination operand when either or both operands contain a 1 in that bit position.
Rotate left through carry (RCL)	This instruction rotates the bits in the destination to the left the number of places specified in the count operand. The carry flag receives the value dropped from the high-order bit. The low-order bit receives the value contained in the carry flag.
Rotate right through carry (RCR)	This instruction rotates the bits in the destination to the right the number of places specified in the count operand. The carry flag receives the value dropped from the low-order bit. The high-order bit receives the value contained in the carry flag.

Command	Description
Rotate left (ROL)	This instruction rotates the bits in the destination to the left the number of places specified in the count operand. It affects both OF and CF.
Rotate right (ROR)	This instruction rotates the bits in the destination to the right the number of places specified in the count operand. It affects both OF and CF.
Arithmetic shift left (SAL)	The arithmetic shift left instruction shifts all bits in the destination operand left the number of bits specified by the source operand. It affects CF, OF, PF, SF, ZF, and AF (undefined).
Arithmetic shift right (SAR)	The arithmetic shift right instruction shifts all bits in the destination operand right the number of bits specified by the source operand. It affects CF, OF, PF, SF, ZF, and AF (undefined).
Shift left (SHL)	The shift left instruction shifts all bits in the destination operand left the number of bits specified by the source operand. It affects CF, OF, PF, SF, ZF, and AF (undefined).
Shift right (SHR)	The shift right instruction shifts all bits in the destination operand right the number of bits specified by the source operand. It affects CF, OF, PF, SF, ZF, and AF (undefined).
Test bits (TEST)	This instruction performs a logical AND of two operands then updates the flags. The flags reflect how the two operands compared. Test does nothing with the results. The flags it affects include CF, OF, PF, SF, ZF, and AF (undefined).
Logical exclusive-OR on bits (XOR)	This instruction performs an exclusive OR on two operands. It returns a value in the destination operand. XOR sets a bit in the destination operand if the corresponding bits in the comparison opperands are different. The exclusive OR instruction affects CF, OF, PF, SF, ZF, and AF (undefined).

Table C-1 Continued.

Command	Description
Control-transfer instructions	
Execute a subprogram (CALL)	The call instruction executes a subprogram. Two types of call instruction exist. The first type is a near call to subprograms ±32 kilobytes or less distant from the current instruction. For this type, the processor updates IP to the next instruction position and pushes this value on the stack. It then places the new instruction value in IP and continues execution until a return instruction appears. The second type is a far call to subprograms greater than ±32 kilobytes distant from the current instruction. The processor pushes CS and replaces it with the segment of the call instruction. Then the processor updates IP to the next instruction position and pushes this value on the stack. It then places the new instruction value in IP and continues execution until a return instruction appears.
Software interrupt (INT)	This instruction activates the following interrupt processing procedure: 1. Decrement SP by 2. Push the flags on the stack using the same format as PUSHF. 2. Clear TF and IF to prevent other single-step or maskable interrupts from occurring. 3. Decrement SP. Push CS. 4. Calculate the interrupt pointer address by multiplying the interrupt type by four and place the second word of the interrupt pointer in CS. 5. Decrement SP and push IP. Place the first word of the interrupt pointer in IP. The assembler generates a one-byte form of the instruction for interrupt 3 (known as the breakpoint interrupt). Only device drivers or operating systems normally create their own interrupt code. The only flags affected are IF and TF, which the interrupt processor sets to 1.
Interrupt on overflow (INTO)	Use this instruction to generate an interrupt 4 when the overflow flag (OF) equals 1. It operates in all respects like the interrupt instruction when executed. If OF equals 0, the processor ignores this instruction.

Command	Description
Return from interrupt (IRET)	This instruction returns control to a procedure calling an interrupt after the interrupt completes. It pops CS, IP, and all flags.
Jump if above (JA)	This instruction transfers control to the instruction pointed to by IP + Displacement when CF and ZF equal 0.
Jump if above or equal (JAE)	This instruction transfers control to the instruction pointed to by IP + Displacement when CF equals 0.
Jump if below (JB)	This instruction transfers control to the instruction pointed to by IP + Displacement when CF equals 1.
Jump if below or equal (JBE)	This instruction transfers control to the instruction pointed to by IP + Displacement when CF or ZF equal 1.
Jump on carry (JC)	This instruction transfers control to the instruction pointed to by IP + Displacement when CF equals 1.
Jump if CX equals zero (JCXZ)	This instruction transfers control to the instruction pointed to by IP + Displacement when CX equals 0.
Jump if equal (JE)	This instruction transfers control to the instruction pointed to by IP + Displacement when ZF equals 1.
Jump if greater than (JG)	This instruction transfers control to the instruction pointed to by IP + Displacement when SF equals OF or ZF equals 0.
Jump if greater than or equal (JGE)	This instruction transfers control to the instruction pointed to by IP + Displacement when SF equals OF.
Jump if less than (JL)	This instruction transfers control to the instruction pointed to by IP + Displacement when SF does not equal OF.
Jump if less than or equal (JLE)	This instruction transfers control to the instruction pointed to by IP + Displacement when SF does not equal OF or ZF equals 1.

Table C-1 Continued.

Command	Description
Jump unconditionally (JMP)	This instruction unconditionally transfers control to the instruction referenced by an operand. There are three types of unconditional jump. The first type, short, allows jumps of only ±127 bytes, but produces only 2 bytes of code. The second type, near, allows jumps of ±32 kilobytes. It produces 3 bytes of code. The third type uses both CS and IP for far jumps. It uses 5 bytes of code.
Jump if not above (JNA)	This instruction transfers control to the instruction pointed to by IP + Displacement when CF or ZF equal 1.
Jump if not above or equal (JNAE)	This instruction transfers control to the instruction pointed to by IP + Displacement when CF equals 1.
Jump if not below (JNB)	This instruction transfers control to the instruction pointed to by IP + Displacement when CF equals 0.
Jump if not below or equal (JNBE)	This instruction transfers control to the instruction pointed to by IP + Displacement when CF and ZF equal 0.
Jump on no carry (JNC)	This instruction transfers control to the instruction pointed to by IP + Displacement when CF equals 0.
Jump if not equal (JNE)	This instruction transfers control to the instruction pointed to by IP + Displacement when ZF equals 0.
Jump if not greater than (JNG)	This instruction transfers control to the instruction pointed to by IP + Displacement when SF does not equal OF or ZF equals 1.
Jump if not greater than or equal (JNGE)	This instruction transfers control to the instruction pointed to by IP + Displacement when SF does not equal OF.
Jump if not less than (JNL)	This instruction transfers control to the instruction pointed to by IP + Displacement when SF equals OF.

Command	Description
Jump if not less than or equal (JNLE)	This instruction transfers control to the instruction pointed to by IP + Displacement when SF equals OF or ZF equals 0.
Jump on no overflow (JNO)	This instruction transfers control to the instruction pointed to by IP + Displacement when OF equals 0.
Jump on no parity (JNP)	This instruction transfers control to the instruction pointed to by IP + Displacement when PF equals 0.
Jump on not sign (JNS)	This instruction transfers control to the instruction pointed to by IP + Displacement when SF equals 0.
Jump on not zero (JNZ)	This instruction transfers control to the instruction pointed to by IP + Displacement when ZF equals 0.
Jump on overflow (JO)	This instruction transfers control to the instruction pointed to by IP + Displacement when OF equals 1.
Jump on parity (JP)	This instruction transfers control to the instruction pointed to by IP + Displacement when PF equals 1.
Jump on parity even (JPE)	This instruction transfers control to the instruction pointed to by IP + Displacement when PF equals 1.
Jump on parity odd (JPO)	This instruction transfers control to the instruction pointed to by IP + Displacement when PF equals 0.
Jump on sign (JS)	This instruction transfers control to the instruction pointed to by IP + Displacement when SF equals 1.
Jump on zero (JZ)	This instruction transfers control to the instruction pointed to by IP + Displacement when ZF equals 1.
Loop (LOOP)	The loop instruction decrements CX by 1 then tests to see if CX equals 0. If CX is greater than 0, loop transfers control to the target instruction. Otherwise, it passes control to the next in-line instruction.
Loop while equal (LOOPE)	The loop instruction decrements CX by 1 then tests to see if CX equals 0. If CX is greater than 0 and ZF

Table C-1 Continued.

Command	Description
	equals 1, loop transfers control to the target instruction. Otherwise, it passes control to the next in-line instruction.
Loop while not equal (LOOPNE)	The loop instruction decrements CX by 1 then tests to see if CX equals 0. If CX is greater than 0 and ZF equals 0, loop transfers control to the target instruction. Otherwise, it passes control to the next in-line instruction.
Loop while not zero (LOOPNZ)	The loop instruction decrements CX by 1 then tests to see if CX equals 0. If CX is greater than 0 and ZF equals 0, loop transfers control to the target instruction. Otherwise, it passes control to the next in-line instruction.
Loop while zero (LOOPZ)	The loop instruction decrements CX by 1 then tests to see if CX equals 0. If CX is greater than 0 and ZF equals 1, loop transfers control to the target instruction. Otherwise, it passes control to the next in-line instruction.
Return from a subprogram (RET)	Use this instruction at the end of a subprogram to return control to the calling program. The assembler generates two types of return: far and near. The near return pops only IP from the stack. A far return pops both IP and CS from the stack.
Data-transfer instructions	
Input data from port (IN)	This instruction allows data input from a port to the AX register. Use either the DX register or a constant to specify port number less than 256. For port number greater that 255 use the DX register only. This instruction does not affect the flags.
Load the AH register with flags (LAHF)	Use this instruction during assembly language conversions from 8080/8085 processor to 8086/8088 processor format. It transfers the low order byte of the flags register to AH. The flags transfered include SF, ZF, AF, PF, and CF.

Command	Description
Load the DS register (LDS)	This instruction transfers a 32-bit pointer from the source operand (memory only) to the destination operand (offset) and the DS register (segment). The destination operand is any 16-bit general-purpose register.
Load the effective address (LEA)	The load effective address instruction transfers the offset of the source operand (rather than its value) to the destination operand. The source operand is always a memory variable. The destination is always a general purpose 16-bit register.
Load the ES register (LES)	This instruction transfers a 32-bit pointer from the source operand (memory only) to the destination operand (offset) and the ES register (segment). The destination operand is any 16-bit general purpose register.
Move (MOV)	This instruction transfers data from the source operand to a destination operand of the same length.
Output data to port (OUT)	This instruction allows data output to a port from the AX register. Use either the DX register or a constant to specify port numbers less than 256. For port numbers greater that 255 use the DX register only. This instruction does not affect the flags.
Remove data from the stack (POP)	POP removes the word pointed to by the stack pointer (SP) and places it in a memory operand or register. It then increments SP by 2.
Remove flags from the stack (POPF)	POPF removes the word pointed to by the stack pointer (SP) and places it in the flag register. It then increments SP by 2.
Place data on the stack (PUSH)	PUSH decrements SP by 2. It then adds the word contained in a register or memory operand to the location pointed to by the stack pointer (SP).
Place flags on the stack (PUSHF)	PUSHF decrements SP by 2. It then adds the flag register contents to the location pointed to by the stack pointer (SP).

Table C-1 Continued.

Command	Description
Store AH into the flag register (SAHF)	Use this instruction during assembly language conversions from 8080/8085 processor to 8086/8088 processor format. It transfers the contents of AH to low order byte of the flags register. The flags transfered include SF, ZF, AF, PF, and CF.
Exchange (XCHG)	This instruction swaps the contents of the source and destination operands. It does not affect any flags.
Translate (XLAT)	The translate instruction places the value in a table pointed to by BX in AL. The AL register initially contains an offset into the table. The translate instruction does not affect any flags.
Flag- and processor-control instructions	
Clear the carry flag (CLC)	The clear the carry flag instruction sets CF to zero.
Clear the direction flag (CLD)	The clear the direction flag instruction sets DF to zero.
Clear the interrupt flag (CLI)	The clear the interrupt flag instruction sets IF to zero.
Complement the carry flag (CMC)	This instruction toggles the value of CF.
Escape (ESC)	The escape instruction provides a means for coprocessing chips to access data using the 8086/8088/80286/80386 processing stream. It causes the processor to place the operand on the bus while internally perfoming a no operation (NOP) instruction.
Halt (HLT)	This instruction stops the processor temporarily while waiting for an interrupt. It provides a means of creating a wait state without resorting to endless software loops. The halt instruction does not affect any flags.

Command	Description
Lock the bus (LOCK)	The lock instruction prevents interference by any coprocessors during the next instruction. Always use lock with other instructions.
No operation (NOP)	This instruction tells the CPU to do nothing.
Set the carry flag (STC)	This instruction sets CF reguardless of its present condition.
Set the direction flag (STD)	This instruction sets DF reguardless of its present condition.
Set the interrupt flag (STI)	This instruction sets IF reguardless of its present condition.
Wait (WAIT)	This instuction causes the CPU to enter its wait state until it receives an external interrupt on the test line. Wait does not affect any flags.
String-manipulation instructions	
Compare strings, byte by byte (CMPSB)	This instruction changes the value of the AF, CF, OF, PF, SF, and ZF flags to show the relationship between two bytes in a string. The results of the comparison do not affect the contents of either operand. After comparing the two string bytes, the instruction updates both SI and DI to point to the next string element. DF controls the direction of comparison.
Compare strings, word by word (CMPSW)	This instruction changes the value of the AF, CF, OF, PF, SF, and ZF flags to show the relationship between two words in a string. The results of the comparison do not affect the contents of either operand. After comparing the two string words, the instruction updates both SI and DI to point to the next string element. DF controls the direction of comparison.

Table C-1 Continued.

Command	Description
Load a byte from string into AL (LODSB)	Use this instruction to transfer a byte from the string pointed to by SI to AL. The SI register automatically advances to the next string element in the direction pointed to by the direction flag.
Load a word from string into AX (LODSW)	Use this instruction to transfer a word from the string pointed to by SI to AX. The SI register automatically advances to the next string element in the direction pointed to by the direction flag.
Move string, byte by byte (MOVSB)	This instruction moves the byte pointed to by SI to the destination pointed to by DI. Using the REP instruction with this instruction, repeats the move the number of times shown in CX. After each move, the instruction advances both SI and DI to the next position in the direction indicated by DF.
Move string, word by word (MOVSW)	This instruction moves the word pointed to by SI to the destination pointed to by DI. Using the REP instruction with this instruction, repeats the move the number of times shown in CX. After each move, the instruction advances both SI and DI to the next position in the direction indicated by DF.
Repeat (REP)	Use this instruction with string manipulation instructions to repeat the instruction the number of times specified in CX.
Repeat if equal (REPE)	Use this instruction with string manipulation instructions to repeat the instruction the number of times specified in CX. It repeats only while ZF = 1 when used with the CMPSB, CMPSW, SCASB, or SCASW instructions.
Repeat if not equal (REPNE)	Use this instruction with string manipulation instructions to repeat the instruction the number of times specified in CX. It repeats only while ZF = 0 when used with the CMPSB, CMPSW, SCASB, or SCASW instructions.

Command	Description
Repeat if not zero (REPNZ)	Use this instruction with string manipulation instructions to repeat the instruction the number of times specified in CX. It repeats only while ZF = 0 when used with the CMPSB, CMPSW, SCASB, or SCASW instructions.
Repeat if zero (REPZ)	Use this instruction with string manipulation instructions to repeat the instruction the number of times specified in CX. It repeats only while ZF = 1 when used with the CMPSB, CMPSW, SCASB, or SCASW instructions.
Scan string for byte (SCASB)	Use this instruction with any of the repeat instructions to scan strings for the value contained in AL. After each scan, DI advances to point to the next string element. This instruction affects AF, CF, OF, PF, SF, and ZF.
Scan string for word (SCASW)	Use this instruction with any of the repeat instructions to scan strings for the value contained in AX. After each scan, DI advances to point to the next string element. This instruction affects AF, CF, OF, PF, SF, and ZF.
Store byte in AL at string (STOSB)	Use this instruction alone or with any repeat instruction to send the value in AL to the string pointed at by DI. DI automatically advances to the next string location after each store operation. This instruction does not affect any flags.
Store word in AX at string (STOSW)	Use this instruction alone or with any repeat instruction to send the value in AX to the string pointed at by DI. DI automatically advances to the next string location after each store operation. This instruction does not affect any flags.

Table C-2 80286 command summary

Command	Description
Bit-manipulation instructions	
Adjust RPL field of selector (ARPL)	Use this instruction to compare the two RPL bits (bits 0 and 1) of the first operand with those in the second. If the RPL bits of the first operand are less than those of the second, the instruction sets the first operand's RPL bits equal to those of the second. The adjust RPL field of selector instruction affects ZF only. It then sets ZF. Otherwise, this instruction clears ZF.
Data-transfer instructions	
Input string from port (INS)	This instruction allows string input from a port to the destination operand. Use the DX register to specify the port number and the DI register to specify destination. The instruction automatically switches between word or byte to accomadate the size of the destination operand. This instruction does not affect the flags.
Input string byte from port (INSB)	This instruction allows byte input from a port to the destination operand. Use the DX register to specify the port number and the DI register to specify destination. This instruction does not affect the flags.
Input string word from port (INSW)	This instruction allows word input from a port to the destination operand. Use the DX register to specify the port number and the DI register to specify destination. This instruction does not affect the flags.
Load access-rights byte (LAR)	This instruction overwrites the high byte of the destination with the access-rights byte and zeroes the low byte. The instruction operates only when the discriptor appears at the current privilege level and at the selector RPL. The instruction sets ZF when successful.
Load global descriptor table	Use this instruction to load the global descriptor table from the memory address operand specified. The

Command	Description
register (LGDT)	global descriptor table is six bytes long. Normally this instruction appears in protected mode operating system software only. It does not affect any registers.
Load interrupt descriptor table register (LIDT)	Use this instruction to load the interrupt descriptor table from the memory address operand specified. The interrupt descriptor table is six bytes long. Normally this instruction appears in protected mode operating system software only. It does not affect any registers.
Load local descriptor table register (LLDT)	Use this instruction to transfer the global descriptor table to the local descriptor table based on the current selector. Normally this instruction appears in protected mode operating system software only. It does not affect any registers.
Load machine status word (LMSW)	The load machine status word instruction transfers the value of the operand to the machine status word. Normally this instruction appears in operating system software only. It does not affect any registers.
Load segment limit (LSL)	This instruction loads the descriptor's limit field (if present) into the destination operand based on the selector specified in the source operand. When successful, the instruction sets ZF; otherwise, it clears ZF.
Load task register (LTR)	Use this instruction to load the task register with the value contained in the source operand. Normally this instruction appears in operating system software only. It does not affect any registers.
Output string to port (OUTS)	This instruction allows string output to a port from the source operand. Use the DX register to specify the port number and the SI register to specify source. The instruction automatically switches between word or byte to accomadate the size of the destination operand. This instruction does not affect the flags.

Table C-2 Continued.

Command	Description
Output string byte to port (OUTSB)	This instruction allows byte output to a port from the source operand. Use the DX register to specify the port number and the SI register to specify source. This instruction does not affect the flags.
Output string word to port (OUTSW)	This instruction allows byte output to a port from the source operand. Use the DX register to specify the port number and the SI register to specify source. This instruction does not affect the flags.
Pop all general registers (POPA)	POPA removes the general-purpose registers from the stack and discards the SP value. It then increments SP by 16.
Push all general registers (PUSHA)	PUSHA decrements SP by 2 for each value pushed. It then adds the register contents to the location pointed to by the stack pointer (SP). The SP value pushed equals SP before instruction execution begins.
Store global descriptor table register (SGDT)	Use this instruction to transfer the six bytes of the global descriptor table to the memeory address operand. Normally this instruction appears in protected mode operating system software only. It does not affect any registers.
Store interrupt descriptor table register (SIDT)	Use this instruction to transfer the six bytes of the interrupt descriptor table to the memeory address operand. Normally this instruction appears in protected mode operating system software only. It does not affect any registers.
Store local descriptor table register (SLDT)	Use this instruction to transfer the two bytes of the local descriptor table to the memory address operand. Normally this instruction appears in protected mode operating system software only. It does not affect any registers.
Store machine status word (SMSW)	Use this instuction to transfer the machine status word to the operand. Normally this instruction appears in operating system software only.

Command	Description
Store task register (STR)	Use this instuction to transfer the task register contents to the operand. Normally this instruction appears in operating system software only.
Flag- and processor-control instructions	
Check array index against bounds (BOUND)	This instruction compares the signed value of the first operand against the values pointed to by the second operand. The word at the second word is the lower boundry. The word after the second word is the upper boundry. This instruction generates an interrupt 5 whenever the first operand falls outside of either boundry. The bound instruction affects none of the flags.
Clear the task switched flag (CLTS)	This instruction (normally used in operating systems) clears the task switched flag of the machine register.
Make stack frame for procedure parameters (ENTER)	Use this instruction to modify the stack for entry into a high-level language. The first operand specifies the number of stack storage bytes to allocate. The second operand indicates the routine nesting level. This instruction does not modify any of the flags.
High-level procedure exit (LEAVE)	Use this instruction when leaving a high-level language procedure to reverse the effects of the ENTER instruction. It deallocates all variables, then restores SP and BP to their original state. This instruction does not affect any flags.
Verify a segment for reading (VERR)	Use this instruction to determine if the selector specified by the operand appears at the current privilege level and is readable. The instruction sets ZF for accessable selectors.
Verify a segment for writing (VERW)	Use this instruction to determine if the selector specified by the operand appears at the current privilege level and is writeable. The instruction sets ZF for accessable selectors.

Table C-3 80386 command summary

Command	Description
Arithmetic instructions	
Convert doubleword to quadword (CDQ)	Use this instruction to convert a doubleword value to a quadword value. It extends the sign-bit in EAX through EDX.
Convert word to doubleword extended (CWDE)	Use this instruction to convert a word value to a doubleword value. It extends the sign-bit in AX through EAX.
Bit-manipulation instructions	
Bit scan forward (BSF)	Use this instruction to scan the bits of the second operand (beginning at the low order bit) for any set bits. If the instruction finds a set bit, it places the bit number in the first operand and clears ZF. If it does not find any set bits, it sets ZF and does nothing to the first operand.
Bit scan reverse (BSR)	Use this instruction to scan the bits of the second operand (beginning at the high order bit) for any set bits. If the instruction finds a set bit, it places the bit number in the first operand and clears ZF. If it does not find any set bits, it sets ZF and does nothing to the first operand.
Bit test (BT)	This instruction uses the value of the second operand as a bit index to the first operand. It copies the bit at the indexed position to the carry flag.
Bit test and complement (BTC)	This instruction uses the value of the second operand as a bit index to the first operand. It copies the complement of the bit at the indexed position to the carry flag.
Bit test and reset (BTR)	This instruction uses the value of the second operand as a bit index to the first operand. It copies the bit at the indexed position to the carry flag and clears the original bit.

Command	Description
Bit test and set (BTS)	This instruction uses the value of the second operand as a bit index to the first operand. It copies the bit at the indexed position to the carry flag and sets the original bit.
Shift left, double precision (SHLD)	The shift left double precision instruction shifts all bits in the first operand left the number of bits specified by the third operand. It loses high order bits and copies low order bits from the second operand starting at the second operand's low order bit. This instruction affects CF, OF, PF, SF, ZF, and AF (undefined).
Shift right, double precision (SHRD)	The shift right double precision instruction shifts all bits in the first operand right the number of bits specified by the third operand. It loses the low order bits and copies the high order bits from the second operand start and the second operand's high order bit. This instruction affects CF, OF, PF, SF, ZF, and AF (undefined).
Control-transfer instructions	
Jump if ECX equals zero (JECXZ)	This instruction transfers control to the instruction pointed to by IP + Displacement when ECX equals 0.
Data-transfer instructions	
Input string doubleword from port (INSD)	This instruction allows doubleword input from a port to the destination operand. Use the DX register to specify the port number and the EDI register to specify destination. This instruction does not affect the flags.
Load the FS register (LFS)	This instruction transfers a 32-bit pointer from the source operand (memory only) to the destination operand (offset) and the FS register (segment). The destination operand is any 16-bit general purpose register.
Load the GS register (LGS)	This instruction transfers a 32-bit pointer from the source operand (memory only) to the destination

Table C-3 Continued.

Command	Description
	operand (offset) and the GS register (segment). The destination operand is any 16-bit general purpose register.
Load the SS register (LSS)	This instruction transfers a 32-bit pointer from the source operand (memory only) to the destination operand (offset) and the SS register (segment). The destination operand is any 16-bit general purpose register.
Move with sign extended (MOVSX)	Use this instruction to move data from a smaller to larger operand. It extends the sign-bit of the second operand to fill the first operand.
Move with zero extended (MOVZX)	Use this instruction to move data from a smaller to larger operand. It clears the bits in the first operand not filled by the second operand.
Output string doubleword to port (OUTSD)	This instruction allows doubleword output to a port from the source operand. Use the EDX register to specify the port number and the ESI register to specify source. This instruction does not affect the flags.
Pop all general doubleword registers (POPAD)	POPAD removes the extended general-purpose registers from the stack and discards the ESP value. It then increments ESP by 32.
Remove extended flags from stack (POPFD)	POPFD removes the two words pointed to by the stack pointer (ESP) and places it in the extended flag register. It then increments ESP by 4.
Push all general doubleword registers (PUSHAD)	PUSHAD decrements ESP by 4 for each value pushed. It then adds the register contents to the location pointed to by the stack pointer (ESP). The ESP value pushed equals ESP before instruction execution begins.
Place extended flags on stack (PUSHFD)	PUSHF decrements ESP by 4. It then adds the extended flag register contents to the location pointed to by the stack pointer (ESP).

Command	Description
Set byte if above (SETA)	This instruction checks the status of both CF and ZF. If both flags equal 0, then the instruction stores a 1 in the operand; otherwise, it stores a 0 in the operand.
Set byte if above or equal (SETAE)	This instruction checks the status of CF. If CF equals 0, then the instruction stores a 1 in the operand; otherwise, it stores a 0 in the operand.
Set byte if below (SETB)	This instruction checks the status of CF. If CF equals 1, then the instruction stores a 1 in the operand; otherwise, it stores a 0 in the operand.
Set byte if below or equal (SETBE)	This instruction checks the status of CF and ZF. If CF or ZF equals 1, then the instruction stores a 1 in the operand; otherwise, it stores a 0 in the operand.
Set byte on carry (SETC)	This instruction checks the status of CF. If CF equals 1, then the instruction stores a 1 in the operand; otherwise, it stores a 0 in the operand.
Set byte if equal (SETE)	This instruction checks the status of ZF. If ZF equals 1, then the instruction stores a 1 in the operand; otherwise, it stores a 0 in the operand.
Set byte if greater than (SETG)	This instruction checks the status of ZF, SF and OF. If ZF equals 0 or SF equals OF, then the instruction stores a 1 in the operand; otherwise, it stores a 0 in the operand.
Set byte if greater than or equal (SETGE)	This instruction checks the status of SF and OF. If SF equals OF, then the instruction stores a 1 in the operand; otherwise, it stores a 0 in the operand.
Set byte if less than (SETL)	This instruction checks the status of SF and OF. If SF does not equal OF, then the instruction stores a 1 in the operand; otherwise, it stores a 0 in the operand.
Set byte if less than or equal (SETLE)	This instruction checks the status of ZF, SF and OF. If SF does not equal OF or ZF equals 1, then the instruction stores a 1 in the operand; otherwise, it stores a 0 in the operand.

Table C-3 Continued.

Command	Description
Set byte if not above (SETNA)	This instruction checks the status of CF and ZF. If CF or ZF equals 1, then the instruction stores a 1 in the operand; otherwise, it stores a 0 in the operand.
Set byte if not above or equal (SETNAE)	This instruction checks the status of CF. If CF equals 1, then the instruction stores a 1 in the operand; otherwise, it stores a 0 in the operand.
Set byte if not below (SETNB)	This instruction checks the status of CF. If CF equals 0, then the instruction stores a 1 in the operand; otherwise, it stores a 0 in the operand.
Set byte if not below or equal (SETNBE)	This instruction checks the status of both CF and ZF. If both flags equal 0, then the instruction stores a 1 in the operand; otherwise, it stores a 0 in the operand.
Set byte on no carry (SETNC)	This instruction checks the status of CF. If CF equals 0, then the instruction stores a 1 in the operand; otherwise, it stores a 0 in the operand.
Set byte if not equal (SETNE)	This instruction checks the status of ZF. If ZF equals 0, then the instruction stores a 1 in the operand; otherwise, it stores a 0 in the operand.
Set byte if not greater than (SETNG)	This instruction checks the status of ZF, SF and OF. If SF does not equal OF or ZF equals 1, then the instruction stores a 1 in the operand; otherwise, it stores a 0 in the operand.
Set byte if not greater than or equal (SETNGE)	This instruction checks the status of SF and OF. If SF does not equal OF, then the instruction stores a 1 in the operand; otherwise, it stores a 0 in the operand.
Set byte if not less than (SETNL)	This instruction checks the status of SF and OF. If SF equals OF, then the instruction stores a 1 in the operand; otherwise, it stores a 0 in the operand.
Set byte if not less than or equal (SETNLE)	This instruction checks the status of ZF, SF and OF. If ZF equals 0 or SF equals OF, then the instruction stores a 1 in the operand; otherwise, it stores a 0 in the operand.

Command	Description
Set byte on no overflow (SETNO)	This instruction checks the status of OF. If OF equals 0, then the instruction stores a 1 in the operand; otherwise, it stores a 0 in the operand.
Set byte on no parity (SETNP)	This instruction checks the status of PF. If PF equals 0, then the instruction stores a 1 in the operand; otherwise, it stores a 0 in the operand.
Set byte on not sign (SETNS)	This instruction checks the status of SF. If SF equals 0, then the instruction stores a 1 in the operand; otherwise, it stores a 0 in the operand.
Set byte on not zero (SETNZ)	This instruction checks the status of ZF. If ZF equals 0, then the instruction stores a 1 in the operand; otherwise, it stores a 0 in the operand.
Set byte on overflow (SETO)	This instruction checks the status of OF. If OF equals 1, then the instruction stores a 1 in the operand; otherwise, it stores a 0 in the operand.
Set byte on parity (SETP)	This instruction checks the status of PF. If PF equals 1, then the instruction stores a 1 in the operand; otherwise, it stores a 0 in the operand.
Set byte on parity even (SETPE)	This instruction checks the status of PF. If PF equals 1, then the instruction stores a 1 in the operand; otherwise, it stores a 0 in the operand.
Set byte on parity odd (SETPO)	This instruction checks the status of PF. If PF equals 0, then the instruction stores a 1 in the operand; otherwise, it stores a 0 in the operand.
Set byte on sign (SETS)	This instruction checks the status of SF. If SF equals 1, then the instruction stores a 1 in the operand; otherwise, it stores a 0 in the operand.
Set byte on zero (SETZ)	This instruction checks the status of ZF. If ZF equals 1, then the instruction stores a 1 in the operand; otherwise, it stores a 0 in the operand.

Table C-3 Continued.

Command	Description
String-manipulation instructions	
Compare strings, doubleword by doubleword (CMPSD)	This instruction changes the value of the AF, CF, OF, PF, SF, and ZF flags to show the relationship between two doublewords in a string. The results of the comparison do not affect the contents of either operand. After comparing the two string words, the instruction updates both ESI and EDI to point to the next string element. DF controls the direction of comparison.
Load a doubleword from string into EAX (LODSD)	Use this instruction to transfer a doubleword from the string pointed to by ESI to EAX. The ESI register automatically advances to the next string element in the direction pointed to by the direction flag.
Move string, doubleword by doubleword (MOVSD)	This instruction moves the doubleword pointed to by ESI to the destination pointed to by EDI. Using the REP instruction with this instruction, repeats the move the number of times shown in ECX. After each move, the instruction advances both ESI and EDI to the next position in the direction indicated by DF.
Scan string for doubleword (SCASD)	Use this instruction with any of the repeat instructions to scan strings for the value contained in EAX. After each scan, EDI advances to point to the next string element. This instruction affects AF, CF, OF, PF, SF, and ZF.
Store doubleword in EAX at string (STOSD)	Use this instruction alone or with any repeat instruction to send to value in EAX to the string pointed at by EDI. EDI automatically advances to the next string location after each store operation. This instruction does not affect any flags.

D

Assembly-language command summary

This appendix is designed for two purposes. First, it acts as a quick reference for those familiar with macro assembler. It allows you to remind yourself of a command without referring to another manual. The second purpose is to allow you to compare the baseline assembler used for the examples in this book against those created by other vendors. Doing this will help you determine when an error in your external routine is caused by an interface error with Clipper, or if the command you chose is incompatible with the Clipper libraries.

TABLE D-1 contains the MASM command summary. It's arranged in alphabetical order and contains only MASM commands. To view the processor commands, then, you should refer to appendix C. You'll find the math coprocessor command summary in appendix F and the peripheral-chip summary in appendix G.

Table D-1 MASM 5.1 command set

Command	Description
Align types	
BYTE	The BYTE align type ensures that the segments following it always begin on a byte boundary. Using this align type reduces the space wasted padding segment boundaries. It could slow the operating speed of the 8086, 80186, 80286, and 80386 processors. This is because the processor would have to perform two memory fetches on some occasions.

Table D-1 Continued.

Command	Description
PAGE	The PAGE align type causes the segment defined to align itself on a page boundary (256 bytes per page). Using the page align type has speed benefits when using the 8086, 80286, and 80386 processors. The PAGE align type works in conjunction with the SEGMENT directive.
PARA	The PARA align type causes the segment defined to align itself on a paragraph boundary (16 bytes per paragraph). Using the paragraph align type has speed benefits when using the 8086, 80286, and 80386 processors. The PARA align type works in conjunction with the SEGMENT directive.
WORD	The WORD align type causes the segment defined to align itself on a word boundary (two bytes per word). Using the word align type has speed benefits when using the 8086, 80286, and 80386 processors. The WORD align type work in conjunction with the SEGMENT directive.
Combine types	
AT	The AT combine type is the only combine type requiring an address. When specified, the assembler references all addressing within that segment to the included address. There is no forward references allowed when using an AT combine type. All addresses must be within the referenced segment.
COMMON	The COMMON combine type creates overlapping segments. It does this by specifying the same starting address for all segments with the same name. The resulting segment length is the same as the length of the longest segment. The biggest advantage to using the COMMON combine type is in data sharing. If two segments using the COMMON combine type contain a variable with the same name, changes in one variable automatically reflect in the other.

Command	Description
MEMORY	The MEMORY combine type is the same as a PUBLIC combine type using this assembler. Other assemblers might support a different version of the MEMORY combine type.
PRIVATE	The default assembler combine type is PRIVATE. Using the PRIVATE combine type provides all segments with their own physical segment. No combining of segments takes place.
PUBLIC	This combine type causes the assembler to concatenate all segments with the same name into one continuous segment.
STACK	This combine type concatenates all segments of the same type and name into one continuous segment. The STACK combine type is the same as the PUBLIC combine type except all references are to the SS register.
Declarations	
DB, DD, DF, DQ, DT and DW	The DB, DD, DF, DQ, DT, and DW declarations tell the assembler what size data elements a variable uses. The smallest declaration is DB. It allots a byte per unit declared. The DW (declare word) declaration allots two bytes. The DD (declare double word) declaration allots four bytes. The DF (declare far word) declaration allots six bytes. The DQ (declare quad word) declaration allots eight bytes. Finally, the DT declaration allots ten bytes per unit declared.
DS	The data segment contains all of the variables used in a program. The DS declaration appears with the assume directive. It documents the label used to mark the beginning and end of the segment.
Directives	
.186	The .186 directive allows use of 80186 instructions in source code files.

Table D-1 Continued.

Command	Description
.286	The .286 directive allows use of 80286 instructions in a source code file. The assembler allows only real mode instructions when using this directive.
.286P	The .286P directive allows use of 80286 instructions in a source file. The assembler allows both real and protected mode instructions when using this directive.
.287	The .287 directive allows use of 80287 instructions in a source file.
.386	The .386 directive allows use of 80386 instructions in a source code file. The assembler allows only real mode instructions when using this directive.
.386P	The .386P directive allows use of 80386 instructions in a source code file. The assembler allows both real and protected mode instructions when using this mode. The assembler also supports multiple 8086 processor sessions.
.387	The .387 directive allows use of 80387 instructions in a source code file.
.8086	The .8086 directive allows use of 8086 instructions in a source code file. The assembler accepts none of the later processor instructions. This is the default assembler mode.
.8087	The .8087 directive allows use of 8087 instructions in a source code file. This is the default math coprocessor mode.
ALIGN	This directive allows a 8086, 80286, or 80386 processor to handle data more efficiently. The 16-bit bus of the 8086 and 80286 transfers data in a single instruction when aligned on a variable boundary. This command has no effect on the 8088 processor because it transfers data eight bits at a time. The assembler multiplies the alignment variable by a variable that is a multiple of two. The assembler

Command	Description
	aligns data on word boundaries for multiples of two and on doubleword boundaries for multiples of four. Aligning data on doubleword boundaries increases the efficiency of the 80386 processor. A 80386 processor transfers data 32 bits at a time. The penalty imposed by the align command is larger source code files. Boundary alignment of variables wastes data space in the object code generated by the assembler.
.ALPHA	The alpha directive causes the assembler to list the assembled source segments in alphanumeric order. This makes finding information in the source code much easier.
ASSUME	The assume directive tells the assembler the location of various source code segments. The directive can use actual segment values or a label to locate the segment. The word *nothing* causes the assembler to assume no value for a particular segment.
.CODE	The .code directive provides simplified segment definition. It occurs after a .model directive. The code segment ends when the assembler encounters another segment directive or the end directive.
COMM	The comm directive declares communal variables. The assembler treats communal variables as both public and external. One use for a communal variable is when several assembler routines require use of the same variable. The programmer declares the variable in an include file called by each routine. Each routine uses the variable, but it uses only one memory location.
COMMENT	The comment directive tells the assembler that text following the directive is not executable code. Assembly begins again on the next line of source code.
.CONST	The .const directive provides simplified segment definition that occurs after a .model directive. The

Table D-1 Continued.

Command	Description
	constant segment ends when the assembler encounters another segment directive or the end directive.
.CREF	The .CREF restores the listing of cross reference symbols. It usually appears after an .XCREF directive.
.DATA and .DATA?	The .data and .data? directives provide simplified segment definition. They appear after a .model directive. The data segment ends when the assembler sees another segment directive or the end directive. The .data directive defines initialized data. The .data? directive defines uninitialized data.
DOSSEG	The DOSSEG directive is similar to the .ALPHA directive. It orders the source segments according to DOS segment convention.
DWORD	The DWORD directive appears in two places. First, when an operand requires type identification. The DWORD directive specifies the operand is four bytes long. Second, during align type specification. The variables aligned to a DWORD start on doubleword address boundaries.
END, ENDIF, ENDM, ENDP and ENDS	The end, endif, endm, endp, and ends directive mark a source code termination point. Each time the assembler sees the word *end* (with or without additional letters) it ends a module, conditional statement, macro, procedure, or segment.
EQU	The EQU directive assigns a constant value to a label. The assembler uses the label to refer to a given value. The = symbol performs the same function as the EQU directive.
.ERR, .ERR1, .ERR2, .ERRB, .ERRDEF, .ERRDIF, .ERRE, .ERRIDN, .ERRNB, .ERRNDEF and .ERRNZ	The programmer can use conditional error directives to debug a program or check for assembly-time errors. When a predefined error condition occurs during assembly, the message associated with condition error directive displays on the screen.

Command	Description
EVEN	The EVEN directive works similarly to the ALIGN directive. By aligning the next byte on an even boundary, it increases the efficiency of 8086, 80286, and 80386 processors. Unlike the ALIGN directive, the EVEN directive does not allow doubleword alignment.
EXITM	The exit macro (EXITM) directive normally occurs in conditional macro blocks. It allows the program to exit from a loop or recursive call after a predefined number of iterations.
EXTRN	Use the external (EXTRN) directive when a module uses an external undefined symbol. Place it in front of the symbol name.
.FARDATA and .FARDATA?	The .FARDATA and .FARDATA? directives allow simplified segment definition. They both declare far data segments. The .FARDATA directive specifies an initialized data segment. The .FARDATA? directive specifies an uninitialized data segment.
GROUP	The GROUP directive allows several segments to have the same starting address. Use this directive when several data items contained in separate segments require access from a single register at runtime.
IF, IF1, IF2, IFB, IFDEF, IFDIF, IFE, IFIDN, IFNB and IFNDEF	All IF directives test some condition during assembly of a program. When the condition specified by the directive occurs, the assembler assembles the statements directly below the directive. An IF directive always ends with an ENDIF. The assembler uses statements located below an ELSE statement when the associated IF conditions do not occur. The IF and IFE directives test the truth value of an expression. When using the IF directive, the expression must evaluate true. The expression must test false when using the IFE directive. The IF1 and IF2 directives test the assembly pass in progress. When the assembly pass is correct for the IF value

Table D-1 Continued.

Command	Description
	given, the assembler applies the statements below the IF directive. These IF statements do not require arguments. Use the IF1 directive on the first pass and IF2 on the second pass. The IFDEF and IFNDEF directives tests symbol definition status. The only argument included with both IF statements is the name of the defined symbol. IFDEF is true for defined symbols. IFNDEF is true when the symbol is undefined. Use the IFB, IFNB, IFIDN and IFDIF directives exclusively with macros. The IFB and IFNB directives verify macro parameters. The programmer includes a single argument specifying the name, number or expression being evaluated. When the expression evaluates blank the IFB directive is true; otherwise, the IFNB directive is true. The IFIDN and IFDIF directives test two arguments. If the arguments contain the same values, IFIDN is true. IF the arguments contain different values, IFDIF is true.
INCLUDE and INCLUDELIB	The INCLUDE and INCLUDELIB directives provide a means of including data contained in other files in the program during assemble time. The INCLUDE directive uses the path and file names of a file with unassembled source code. The INCLUDELIB directive uses the path and file names of a library file containing assembled source code.
IRP and IRPC	The IRP and IRPC directives provide a means of declaring repetitive data quickly. The IRP directive accepts a variable name and a list of arguments. The IRPC directive accepts a variable and a sting. Both directives repeat the data declaration as many times as the arguments passed. Each string element passed to the IRPC directive counts as one argument.
LABEL	The LABEL directive performs two functions. In the first case, it acts as an alternative method of defining code labels. The second function is to act as a method of defining variable labels. When used as a code labeling method, the word LABEL and a distance directive (NEAR, FAR, or PROC) follow the label

Command	Description
	name. When used as a variable labeling method, the word LABEL and a type directive (BYTE, WORD, DWORD, FWORD, QWORD, or TBYTE) follow the label name.
.LALL	The .LALL directive defines how a macro expands within a source code listing. The assembler includes all information in the macro when it sees the .LALL directive included within the listing.
.LFCOND	Use this directive with both the .SFCOND and .TFCOND directives. It resumes listing of false conditional statements after a .SFCOND directive stops the listing. It selects false conditional listing before using .TFCOND directives to be sure a known beginning condition exists.
.LIST	The .LIST directive restarts the listing of program statements in the list file after an .XLIST directive. The normal program configuration lists all program statements in the list file.
LOCAL	Macros use the LOCAL directive to define variables used only within the macro. When the macro ends, it releases the memory used by the local variable.
MACRO	The MACRO directive starts all macros and requires a name prefix. The directive suffix contains all parameters passed to the macro. Commas separate the parameters.
.MODEL	There are five different memory model sizes available when using the .MODEL directive: small (64K of data and 64K of code), compact (>64K of data and 64K of code), medium (64K of data and >64K of code), large (>64K of data and >64K of code), and large (>64K of data, >64 Kb code, and >64K of arrays). The .MODEL directive provides a simplified method of defining the memory model.
.MSFLOAT	Previous to this version of macro assembler, the assembler used the Microsoft binary format for

Table D-1 Continued.

Command	Description
	assembling real numbers. This version uses a default of the IEEE format. The .MSFLOAT directive allows use of the Microsoft binary format.
NAME	Assemblers after version 5.0 ignore this directive. It was the base sourcefile name in previous versions.
NOTHING	The NOTHING directive works with the ASSUME directive. It cancels all previously assumed segment to register assignments.
ORG	The ORG directive sets the beginning offset of a segment. It sets the IP register to a specific offset during program initialization.
%OUT	This directive is a convenient means of allowing the programmer see how the assembly of a program progresses. Use it with conditional directives in the source code to tell the programmer which conditionals the assembler includes. The text included after an %OUT directive is output to the standard output device.
PAGE	The PAGE directive defines list file page printing. The two parameters controlled by the directive are page length and width. A PAGE directive without any operators creates a new page within the list file.
PROC	This directive defines the beginning of a procedure within the code. A label always prefixes the PROC directive. The NEAR or FAR type designator comes at the end of the directive. A procedure always terminates with a RET (return) statement and an ENDP directive.
PUBLIC	The PUBLIC directive defines a symbol as public so it is accessible to procedures external to the current segment.
PURGE	The PURGE directive removes macros from memory when they are no longer needed. After macro

Command	Description
	removal, the program restores any previous name redefinitions to their original condition and recovers the macro memory space.
.RADIX	The radix determines the numeric basis of all values during program assembly. The .RADIX directive selects the radix used during assembly. Any number between 2 through 16 is available. The default radix is 10.
RECORD	The assembler provides a convenient method of defining structured variables by using the RECORD directive. Define the record first, then declare variables using the record definition as shown below.
REPT	Use this directive when performing several repetitions of a sequence. The REPT directive when the LOOP directive is inappropriate. It is exceptionally useful when using the registers for other purposes.
.SALL	The .SALL directive defines macro expansion within a source code listing. The listing includes only the macro name when using the .SALL directive.
SEGMENT	Use the SEGMENT directive to define code, data, and stack segments. The SEGMENT directive also contains elements for defining the segment name (prefix), alignment type (BYTE, WORD, DWORD, PARA, and PAGE), combine type (PUBLIC, STACK, COMMON, MEMORY, and AT address), use (USE16 and USE32), and class.
.SEQ	The assembler links code segments in sequential order when the source code includes the .SEQ directive. The /A option at the command line will change the link order to alphabetical even if the source code contains a .SEQ directive.
.SFCOND	Use this directive with both the .LFCOND and .TFCOND directives. It stops the listing of false conditional statements after a .LFCOND directive starts the listing. It deselects a false conditional

Table D-1 Continued.

Command	Description
	listing before using .TFCOND directives to ensure that a known beginning condition exists.
.STACK	Use the .STACK directive with the .MODEL directive to define a simplified stack segment. The size of the argument associated with the .STACK directive is the number of bytes to allocate as stack space.
STRUC	A structure is a group of data elements evaluated as a single unit. The STRUC directive begins the definition of the data group. An ENDS directive completes the structure.
SUBTTL	The subtitle (SUBTTL) directive places the specified string under the title on all program listings. Using the SUBTTL directive without operator cancels any previously defined subtitles.
.TFCOND	Use this directive with both the .LFCOND and .SFCOND directives to toggle the listing of false conditional statements.
TITLE	The TITLE directive places a title at the top of every page of the source code listing. No title prints when the TITLE directive is absent. The assembler allows no more than one title at any time.
.XALL	The .XALL directive defines how a macro expansion occurs within a source code listing. When specified, the listing shows only code-producing lines.
.XCREF and .XLIST	The .XCREF and .XLIST directives both stop the compilation of source data to an external file. The .XCREF directive stops all cross reference data. The .XLIST directive stops listing of statements. Both control the output of unwanted assembly data.
Environment variables	
INCLUDE	The INCLUDE environment variable provides a means of assembling external files with the source code of the main file. This option is useful when using

Command	Description
	routines for more than one project. It makes the reuse of code more practical.
Equates	
@CODESIZE, @CURSEG, @DATASIZE, and @FILENAME	These equates are predefined references to specific segment or file names. The @CODESIZE and @DATASIZE equates contain the size of the current code and data segments. The value of @CODESIZE for small and compact memory models is 0. @CODESIZE equates to 1 for medium, large, and huge memory models. The value of @DATASIZE for small and compact memory models is 0, for medium and large models is 1, and for huge models 2. The @CURSEG equate contains the name of the current segment. The @FILENAME equate contains the base name of the current source file. All these equates are exceptionally useful in macros and conditional statements because the values they contain are unknown until after the program assembly.
@CODE, @DATA, @FARDATA, and @FARDATA?	The segment equates are very useful when using the segment value as an operator. Each equate contains the address of the segment name following the @ sign. The @DATA equate represents the segments defined by .DATA, .DATA?, .CONST, or .STACK type specifiers.
Operators	
&	The substitute (&) operator allows the assembler to use the actual value of a parameter. This operator is exceptionally convenient to use when several variables begin with the same name and are suffixed by a different number. A macro could differentiate between variables by using the substitute symbol and a passed parameter.
< and >	The literal text operators (< and >) change a list into a single string. This allows passing of special characters and variables to macros. It also passes variables to procedures.

Table D-1 Continued.

Command	Description
:	Use the segment-override operator to temporarily change the segment of direct and indirect memory operands. The segment definition is either a register, segment name, or group name. When using a segment or group name, assign the name to a register before using it.
!	The literal character operator suppresses the meaning of a special character. This is helpful when using special characters in displays.
%	The expression operator (&) uses the value of an expression rather than the expression itself. It evaluates the result of an expression.
;;	The macro comments operator (;;) tells the assembler that the text after the operator is not executable code.
AND, NOT, OR and XOR	The and, not, or, and xor logical operators cause the assembler to evaluate the relationship between two expressions. Conditional directives often use the results of this evaluation to determine the direction of program or assembly flow. Another use is combining a generic expression with another expression to form a result.
BYTE	The byte pointer operator works with the PTR directive. It allows indirect referencing of byte values.
DUP	Use the DUP operator with the DB, DW, DF, DQ, and DT directives. An integer prefix specifies the number of instances of a specific declaration size. The suffix contains a fill value in parentheses.
ELSE	The assembler recognizes the else operator during conditional assembles and error detections. The assembler checks to see if a given condition is true or false. If the condition is false, the assembler performs the statements following the else operator.

Command	Description
EQ, GT, GE, LT, LE and NE	The assembler uses the equals (EQ), greater than (GT), greater than or equal to (GE), less than (LT), less than or equal to (LE), and not equal to (NE) relational operators to form conditional statements. The assembler compares one expression against another using the relational operator as the evaluation criteria. The result of the evaluation determines which path an assembly pursues.
HIGH	The HIGH operator returns the high-order bytes of a constant expression. The HIGH operator is unusable with memory operands because their value changes during program execution.
LENGTH	The LENGTH operator returns the number of elements within a variable. Normally, the length operator returns a value of 1. When using nested DUP operators, the length operator returns the value of the outer DUP operator.
LOW	The LOW operator returns the low-order bytes of a constant expression. The LOW operator is unusable with memory operands because their value changes during program execution.
MASK	The MASK operator provides a means of easily manipulating records. The MASK operator outputs the defined value of the original record or record field. The NOT operator reverses the output of the MASK operator.
MOD	The modulus (MOD) operator returns the remainder of integer division. If no remainder exists, the MOD operator returns 0.
OFFSET	The OFFSET operator returns the offset of an expression. The expression is any label.
PTR	The PTR (pointer) operator specifies the type for a variable or label. The type of pointer (BYTE, WORD, DWORD, FWORD, QWORD, or TBYTE for memory

Table D-1 Continued.

Command	Description
	operands, or NEAR, FAR, or PROC for labels) precedes it. The referenced expression follows the PTR operator.
SEG	Use the SEG operator to indirectly address an expression. The expression can be any label, variable, segment name, group name, or other memory operand, but not a constant.
SHL	Do not confuse this instruction with the processor command of the same name. This operator shifts an integer constant left the number of bits specified to the left of the operator. If this value is more than 16 (32 on 80386 processors), the result is 0. The registers do not retain any bits shifted of the end of the 16-bit area.
SHORT	The SHORT operator sets the type of a specified label to short. Use the SHORT operator in JMP instructions when the jump distance is between -127 and +128 bytes.
SHR	Do not confuse this instruction with the processor command of the same name. This operator shifts an integer constant left the number of bits specified to the left of the operator. If this value is more than 16 (32 on 80386 processors), the result is 0. The registers do not retain any bits shifted of the end of the 16-bit area.
SIZE	The SIZE operator returns the number of bytes in a variable. For an array this equals the size of the number of elements times the element type. For a string and other type of variables it equals the number of positions times the variable type. Nested variables return the value of the external declaration only.
THIS	The THIS operator creates operands that contain the same offset and segment values as the current location counter. The THIS operator suffix specifies

Command	Description
	the type of the operand. The THIS operator normally appears with the EQU or = operators.
.TYPE	Do not confuse the .TYPE operator with the TYPE operator described below. The .TYPE operator determines the mode and scope of an expression. Four bit positions are output. Bit 0 is true when the expression is program related. Bit 1 is true when the expression is data related. Bit 5 is true for defined expressions. Bit 7 is true when the expression is external in scope. The .TYPE operator does not use bits 2, 3, 4, and 6. If the expression invalid, .TYPE returns a 0.
TYPE	The TYPE operator is different from the .TYPE operator described above. It returns a number that tells the expression type. There are four different values returned by the TYPE operator. If an expression is a variable, it returns the number of bytes in each element of the variable. If the expression is a string, each element is separate and TYPE returns a 1. If the expression is a structure or structure variable, it returns the number of elements in the structure. If the expression is a label, it returns 0FFFFh for NEAR labels and 0FFFEh for FAR labels.
WIDTH	Use this operator on records and record fields. It returns the number of bits contained in either the record or record field.
Symbols	
*	There are two uses for the * symbol. The first is for multiplying two numbers together. The second is for selecting a scaling factor for an index register. The 80386 mode implements the scaling factor function. In both cases the actual function is multiplication. The processor references memory in the first instance. In the second instance, the processor references its own registers. See the description of the .836 directive for more information about the 80386 mode.

Table D-1 Continued.

Command	Description
[and]	The assembler uses the [] symbols to differentiate between an address and the contents of an address. It commonly uses these symbols in memory management statements.
$	The $ symbol references and sets the location counter. The location counter is a variable maintained by the assembler to determine the current source code position. The $ symbol is especially useful when finding the location of a variable or label. The assembly will automatically insert the correct location into the assembled object file. A second use of the $ symbol is within variables. This use can cause confusion reading source code files. There is also a possibility of creating an error in the object file. Errors of this type are very hard to find.
=	The = symbol is a quick method of saying EQU (equals). The assembler uses it to make a label equal an absolute value. Acceptable absolute value types are integers, constant expressions, character string constants, or expressions that evaluate to an address. The assembler allows redefinition of the label value. The label does not consume any space in the source code.
/	The / symbol performs division during math operations. The assembler places the integer results of dividing one number by another. The operators are either numbers or variables. The result is always an integer. The processor discards the remainder. See the MOD operator description for remainder determination details.
-	The - symbol performs subtraction during math operations. The assembler places the difference between two numbers into a variable. The operand is always a variable. The assembler accepts either variables or numbers as operators.
.	The assembler uses the . symbol to differentiate between compiler directives and variable names. The

Command	Description
	assembler also allows use of the . symbol in from of variable names, if those names are not already defined. Using the . symbol in front of variable names creates confusing source code files. It also increases the risk of redefining one of the standard compiler directives, causing errors in the source code file.
+	The + symbol performs addition during math operations. The assembler places the summation of two numbers into a third variable. In all cases the third party is a variable. The assembler accepts variables and numbers as the first two operators.
?	The assembler uses the ? symbol at the end of data directives to differentiate between initialized and uninitialized data. The assembler also allows using the ? symbol as part of variable names.

Type specifiers	
BYTE	This type specifier designates the size of a variable or other memory operand. It allocates a one-byte space. Use the BYTE type specifier to declare data in different sizes. The example below shows the BYTE type specifier in use.
CODE	The linker uses the class type definitions for segment alignment purposes. The assembler links all segments with the same class type together. It links the CODE class type segments first. The linker expects all segments with executable code to have a class type of CODE. Failure to use the CODE class type might result in misalignment of the code segments. It will also make debugging the code more difficult.
FAR	The FAR type specifier defines the method used to reference a label. When using the FAR type specifier, include both the segment and offset.
FWORD	This type specifier specifies the size of a variable or other memory operand using a six-byte space. The FWORD type specifier is useful when used to declare

Table D-1 Continued.

Command	Description
	data in different sizes. The example below shows how to use the FWORD type specifier.
NEAR	A label uses a distance reference of near, far or, proc (default is near or far). When labels use the NEAR type specifier, the assembler provides only the reference offset. This reduces code size and increases execution speed.
PROC	PROC is the default type specifier for all external procedure declarations. When using the small or compact memory models, the declared distance type is near. Use a far distance declaration with medium, large, or huge memory models.
QWORD	This type specifier designates the size of a variable or other memory operand. It allocates an eight-byte space. The QWORD type specifier is useful when used to declare data in different sizes.
TBYTE	This type specifier designates the size of a variable or other memory operand. It allocates a 10-byte space. The TBYTE type specifier is useful when used to declare data in different sizes.
USE	The USE type determines the addressing mode used by a 80386 processor. The USE16 type causes the assembler to use only 16-bit addressing (the same as all other 8086 family processors with a 64K offset). The USE32 type causes the assembler to use 32-bit addresses (full 4 gigabyte offset).
WORD	This type specifier designates the size of a variable or other memory operand. It allocates a two-byte space. The WORD type specifier is useful when used to declare data in different sizes.

E
C standard command summary

This appendix is designed primarily as a quick reference for those familiar with Microsoft C, version 5.1. It allows you to remind yourself of a command without referring to another manual. It doesn't cover any commands provided by the 6.0 version of the compiler, or commands that appear in compilers created by other vendors.

Many Microsoft C version 6.0 functions are different than the ones provided with version 5.1. The difference in implementation could cause problems with the libraries provided with Clipper. This is especially true of any routines that use floating-point algorithms. To ensure that your routines will run properly with Clipper, obtain a copy of the C 5.1 libraries from Microsoft and use the /Gh switch with the C 6.0 compiler.

The second purpose of this appendix is to provide a means for comparing the baseline C used in the examples in this book against those created by other vendors. Doing this will help you determine when an error in your external routine is caused by an interface error with Clipper, or if the command you chose is incompatible with the Clipper libraries. This is exceptionally important when you experience floating-point, divide-by-zero, or other math-operation-related errors.

TABLE E-1 contains the C command summary. It's arranged in alphabetical order and contains only Microsoft C version 5.1 commands. To view the processor commands, refer to appendix C; to see the math coprocessor commands, refer to appendix F; and to see the peripheral chip commands, refer to appendix G.

Table E-1 C command summary

Command	Description
Data type declaration	
[]	Use the brackets to create an array. For example, char cSomeVar[5], creates an array of characters containing five elements.
Char (signed char)	A character with an ASCII value ranging from -128 to 127.
Double	A floating point value within the range of ±1.7E 308 (15 digits).
Float	A floating point value within the range of ±3.4E 38 (7 digits).
Int (signed, signed int)	An integer value within the range of -32,768 to 32,767.
Long (long int, signed long, signed long int)	An integer value within the range of -2,147,483,648 to 2,147,483,647
Long double	A floating point value within the range of ±1.7E 308 (19 digits).
Short (short int, signed short, signed short int)	An integer value within the range of -32,768 to 32,767.
Struct	Use the struct command to create new variable types based on one or more standard types. A structure behaves like the fields within the individual records of a database.
Union	A specialized variable which can contain different data types at different times using the same storage space.
Unsigned (unsigned int)	An integer value within the range of 0 to 65,535.

Command	Description
Unsigned char	A character with an ASCII value ranging from 0 to 255.
Unsigned long (unsigned long int)	An integer value within the range of 0 to 4,294,967,295.
Unsigned short	An integer value within the range of 0 to 65,535.
Directives	
#Define	Use the #Define directive to perform a text replacement of a variable with a value during compilation. This is the technique used by C to implement constants.
#Include	The #Include directive tells the preprocessor to add the contents of the specified file to the current file. The input code is added at the point the #Include directive appears in the target code.
#If, #Else, #Elif, #Endif	The #If directive allows conditional compilation based on the truth value of a condition. The condition is normally based on constant or expression defined during compile time. The #Endif directive defines the end of the conditional compilation block. The #Else directive defines a block of code used if the #If condition evaluates to false. The #Elif directive provides an alternate code block providing a new condition evaluates to true.
#IfDef	The #IfDef directive determines whether an expression exists at the time of compilation. If so, then the preprocessor adds the defined code block to the program.
#IfNDef	The #IfNDef directive determines whether an expression exists at the time of compilation. If not, the preprocessor adds the defined code block to the program.
#Pragma	The #Pragma directive allows you to define machine specific features.

Table E-1 Continued.

Command	Description
#UnDef	The #UnDef directive undefines a previously defined symbolic constant.
Escape sequences	
\a	Alert (bell)
\b	Backspace
\f	Form feed
\n	Newline
\r	Carriage return
\t	Horizontal tab
\v	Vertical tab
\'	Single quote
\"	Double quote
\\	Backslash
\ddd	Octal notation
\xddd	Hexadecimal notation
\0	Null
Flow control	
Break	Discontinues the current sequence of program execution and continues execution with the first statement after the current loop.
Continue	Discontinues the current sequence of program execution and continues execution with the next iteration of the current loop.

Command	Description
Do	This command executes a set of functions until the boolean expression stated as a condition of execution returns false. The do statement always tests the condition after it executes the associated functions.
For	Use this command to execute a set of functions a specific number of times. The loop continues for an amount specified from a starting point to an ending point using a specific increment.
Goto	Executes an unconditional jump to the specified label.
If	Executes the associated functions once is the specified condition is true. You may use this command with the else clause to provide an alternate execution path when the condition is false.
Switch	This command tests each of several conditions and executes the functions of any that evaluate true. If none of the conditions evaluate true, then the command will execute the default condition when supplied.
While	Performs the requested action until the boolean expression stated as a condition returns false. The while statement always tests the condition before it executes the associated functions.

Operators	
!	The logical not operator negates the logical value of a variable or expression.
!=	The not equal operator expresses the relationship between two variables or expressions. It outputs a logical value of true if the variables or expressions are not equal, or false for any other condition.
%	The modulus operator returns the remainder portion of an integer divide.

Table E-1 Continued.

Command	Description
&	The bitwise and operator performs a bit by bit comparison of two variables and outputs a result containing the result of that comparison. If bit 1 of the first variable, and bit 1 of the second variable are both 1, then the & operator outputs a 1. This symbol also acts as the address-of operator. It returns the physical location of the variable within the data segment.
&&	The logical and operator compares two values and outputs true if they both return true or false if they don't. It is usually used to combine two logical expressions.
*	Use the multiplication operator to determine the multiple of two variables or expressions. This symbol also acts as the indirection operator. You may use it to reference a variable pointed to by the value of the operand. For example, if the variable contains 1200, then you would reference the variable at memory location 1200.
+	Use the addition operator to determine the sum of two variables or expressions.
++	The increment operator increases the value of the operand by one.
,	The comma operator separates the parameters in an expression and determines their order of interpretation. C evaluates each parameter one at a time beginning from the left-most parameter and working toward the right.
-	Use the subtraction operator to determine the difference between two variables or expressions.
--	The decrement operator decreases the value of the operand by one.
/	The division operator returns the integer portion of an integer divide.

<table>
<tr><th>Command</th><th>Description</th></tr>
<tr><td><</td><td>The less than operator expresses the relationship between two variables or expressions. It outputs a logical value of true if the value of the variable on the left of the equation is less than the right, or false for any other condition.</td></tr>
<tr><td>< <</td><td>Use the shift left operator to shift the bits of the variable on the left side of the equation, the number of positions indicated by the variable on the right. For example, 3 < < 1 produces an output of 6, while 2 < < 2 produces an output of 8.</td></tr>
<tr><td>< =</td><td>The less than or equals operator expresses the relationship between two variables or expressions. It outputs a logical value of true if the value of the variable on the left of the equation is less than or equal to the right, or false for any other condition.</td></tr>
<tr><td>=</td><td>The assignment operator sets the value contained in one variable equal to the value contained in another. You can modify this outcome by prepending the +, -, *, /, %, > >, < <, &, |, or ^ symbol to the assignment operator. For example, prepending the + to the + operator results in + =, an operator that adds two values together and assigns the result to a variable.</td></tr>
<tr><td>= =</td><td>The equals operator expresses the relationship between two variables or expressions. It outputs a logical value of true if the variables or expressions are exactly equal, or false for any other condition.</td></tr>
<tr><td>></td><td>The greater than operator expresses the relationship between two variables or expressions. It outputs a logical value of true if the value of the variable on the left of the equation is greater than the right, or false for any other condition.</td></tr>
<tr><td>> =</td><td>The greater than or equals operator expresses the relationship between two variables or expressions. It outputs a logical value of true if the value of the</td></tr>
</table>

Table E-1 Continued.

Command	Description
	variable on the left of the equation is greater than or equal to the right, or false for any other condition.
>>	Use the shift right operator to shift the bits of the variable on the left side of the equation, the number of positions indicated by the variable on the right. For example, 8 >> 1 produces an output of 4, while 7 >> 2 produces an output of 1.
?:	You use the conditional operator as a shorthand version of the if else statement. For example, in the statement cSomeVar = (nVar1 == nVar2) ? "They are equal" : "They are not equal", cSomeVar will contain "They are equal" if the two values are exactly the same, or "They are not equal" if they are not.
^	The bitwise exclusive or operator performs a bit by bit comparison of two variables and outputs a result containing the result of that comparison. If bit 1 of the first variable, or bit 1 of the second variable are 1, then the ^ operator outputs a 1. However, if both variables contain the same value at the same bit position, then the output is a 0.
¦	The bitwise inclusive or operator performs a bit by bit comparison of two variables and outputs a result containing the result of that comparison. If bit 1 of the first variable, or bit 1 of the second variable are 1, then the ¦ operator outputs a 1.
¦¦	The logical or operator compares two values and outputs true if either value returns true or false if they don't. It is usually used to combine two logical expressions.
~	The complement operator reverses the bit value of a variable. Every 1 becomes a 0 and likewise, every 0 becomes a 1.
SizeOf	The SizeOf operator returns the size of the operand in bytes.

F

Accessing the math coprocessor

The math coprocessor is extremely valuable in creating fast accounting and scientific programs. If the coprocessor exists, it can greatly reduce the amount of time a program spends computing the results of various equations. Unfortunately, not every PC has a math coprocessor available. Because of this, the creators of Clipper had to make a decision.

There are three libraries provided as part of most C compilers. The first library always assumes that the math coprocessor exists. The disadvantage is obvious—that any programs created with this library will fail if the host machine doesn't contain a math coprocessor. The second library tests to see if the math coprocessor is present. If not, it emulates the coprocessor in software. The disadvantage to using this library is that the program can't make use of the most efficient means to calculate a result if the coprocessor isn't available. This means that you give up some program speed in the hope of finding a coprocessor. The third library (the one chosen by Nantucket) assumes that the math coprocessor is never present. It's extremely efficient compared to the second library when the math coprocessor is unavailable. The disadvantage to using this library is that no benefit is received when the math coprocessor is present.

While the choice to assume that the math coprocessor is not present is justified in most cases, there are instances where program speed is so important that the use of a math coprocessor is essential. This appendix examines the math coprocessor and then provide examples of its use. Notice that none of the examples are in C. You must use assembly language when programming the math coprocessor in Clipper. A C routine would request the appropriate routines from the library, creating a conflict with the library used for Clipper. The result is that a C program that attempts to use the math coprocessor will fail.

Math coprocessor command summary

This section provides a brief listing of the math coprocessor-specific commands. It arranges the commands in mnemonic alphabetical order. There is specific information for the 8087, 80287, and 80387 processors. Each math coprocessor builds upon the commands available to its predecessor in most cases; therefore, each command appears once. Each instruction also shows the applicable math coprocessor because some 8087 instructions are not present in the 80287 and 80387 processors. Appendix C describes the processor commands used with the math coprocessor. TABLE F-1 contains the 8087 listing, TABLE F-2 contains the 80287 listing, and TABLE F-3 contains the 80387 listing.

Table F-1 8087 command summary

Command	Description
Arithmetic instructions	
Absolute value (FABS) (8087/80287/80387)	Use this instruction to replace the top stack element with its absolute value. It affects the IE status bit.
Add real (FADD) (8087/80287/80387)	The add real instruction adds two numbers together and places the result in the destination operand. The instruction uses the stack as the default destination. This instruction affects the PE, UE, OE, DE, and IE status bits.
Add real and pop (FADDP) (8087/80287/80387)	This instruction adds two operands, places the result at the destination, and pops a value from the stack. The instruction uses the stack as the default destination. This instruction affects the PE, UE, OE, DE, and IE status bits.
Change sign (FCHS) (8087/80287/80387)	Use this instruction to change the sign of the top stack element. It affects the IE status bit.
Divide real (FDIV) (8087/80287/80387)	This instruction divides the destination by the source operand. It places the result in the destination. The instruction uses the stack as the default destination. The divide real instruction affects the PE, UE, OE, ZE, DE, and IE status bits.

Command	Description
Divide real and pop (FDIVP) (8087/80287/80387)	This instruction divides the destination by the source operand. It places the result in the destination and pops the stack. The instruction uses the stack as the default destination. The divide real and pop instruction affects the PE, UE, OE, ZE, DE, and IE status bits.
Divide real reversed (FDIVR) (8087/80287/80387)	This instruction divides the source by the destination operand. It places the result in the destination. The instruction uses the stack as the default destination. The divide real reversed instruction affects the PE, UE, OE, ZE, DE, and IE status bits.
Divide real reversed and pop (FDIVRP) (8087/80287/80387)	This instruction divides the source by the destination operand. It places the result in the destination and pops the stack. The instruction uses the stack as the default destination. The divide real reversed and pop instruction affects the PE, UE, OE, ZE, DE, and IE status bits.
Integer add (FIADD) (8087/80287/80387)	This instruction adds two operands as integers and stores the result at the destination. It assumes a default stack destination. The integer add instruction affects the PE, OE, DE, and IE status bits.
Integer divide (FIDIV) (8087/80287/80387)	The integer divide instruction divides the destination by the source operand as integers. It stores the result in the destination operand. The instruction uses the stack as the default destination. If affects the PE, UE, OE, ZE, DE, and IE status bits.
Integer divide reversed (FIDIVR) (8087/80287/80387)	The integer divide reversed instruction divides the source by the destination operand as integers. It stores the result in the destination operand. The instruction uses the stack as the default destination. If affects the PE, UE, OE, ZE, DE, and IE status bits.

Table F-1 Continued.

Command	Description
Integer multiply (FIMUL) (8087/80287/80387)	The integer multiply instruction multiplies the destination by the source operand as integers. It stores the result in the destination operand. The instruction uses the stack as the default destination. If affects the PE, OE, DE, and IE status bits.
Integer subtract (FISUB) (8087/80287/80387)	This instruction subtracts the source from the destination operand and places the result in the destination. The instruction assumes a stack default destination. The arithmetic instruction affects the PE, OE, DE, and IE status bits.
Integer subtract reversed (FISUBR) (8087/80287/80387)	This instruction subtracts the destination from the source operand and places the result in the destination. The instruction assumes a stack default destination. The arithmetic instruction affects the PE, OE, DE, and IE status bits.
Multiply real (FMUL) (8087/80287/80387)	This instruction multiplies the source by the destination operand. It stores the result in the destination operand. The instruction assumes a default stack destination. The multiply real instruction affects the PE, UE, OE, DE, and IE status bits.
Multiply real and pop (FMULP) (8087/80287/80387)	This instruction multiplies the source by the destination operand. It stores the result in the destination operand, then pops the stack. The instruction assumes a default stack destination. The multiply real instruction affects the PE, UE, OE, DE, and IE status bits.
Partial remainder (FPREM) (8087/80287/80387)	The partial arctangent instruction calculates the modulo of the top two stack elements. It performs this by successively subtracting the second element from the first. The calculated remainder remains in the first element. The instruction affects the C0, C1, C3, UE, DE, and IE status bits.

Command	Description
Round to an integer (FRNDINT) (8087/80287/80387)	This instruction rounds the number located on the top stack element to an integer. It affects the PE and IE status bits.
Square root (FSQRT) (8087/80287/80387)	Use this instruction to calculate the square root of the top stack element. The square root value replaces the old stack value. This instruction affects the PE, DE, and IE status bits.
Subtract real (FSUB) (8087/80287/80387)	This instruction subtracts the source from the destination operand and places the result in the destination. The instruction assumes a default destination of stack. It affects the PE, UE, OE, DE, and IE status bits.
Subtract real and pop (FSUBP) (8087/80287/80387)	This instruction subtracts the source from the destination operand and places the result in the destination. Upon instruction completion, it pops the stack. The instruction assumes a default destination of stack. It affects the PE, UE, OE, DE, and IE status bits.
Subtract real reversed (FSUBR) (8087/80287/80387)	This instruction subtracts the destination from the source operand and places the result in the destination. The instruction assumes a default destination of stack. It affects the PE, UE, OE, DE, and IE status bits.
Subtract real reversed and pop (FSUBRP) (8087/80287/80387)	This instruction subtracts the destination from the source operand and places the result in the destination. It pops the stack upon instruction completion. The instruction assumes a default destination of stack. It affects the PE, UE, OE, DE, and IE status bits.
Extract exponent and significand (FXTRACT) (8087/80287/80387)	This instruction pops the top stack element, seperates the exponent from the significand, and pushes both values on the stack. It affects only the IE status bit.

Table F-1 Continued.

Command	Description
Comparison instructions	
Compare real (FCOM) (8087/80287/80387)	This instruction compares the top stack element with the second stack element or other specified operand. It affects the C0, C1, C3, DE, and IE status bits.
Compare real and pop (FCOMP) (8087/80287/80387)	This instruction compares the top stack element with the second stack element or other specified operand. It then pops the stack. The compare real and pop instruction affects the C0, C1, C3, DE, and IE status bits.
Compare real and pop twice (FCOMPP) (8087/80287/80387)	This instruction compares the top stack element with the second stack element or other specified operand. It then pops the stack twice. The compare real and pop instruction affects the C0, C1, C3, DE, and IE status bits.
Integer compare (FICOM) (8087/80287/80387)	This instruction converts the operand to an integer (if required) and compares it to the top stack element. It then changes the condition of the status word bits to match the comparison result. The status word bits affected include C0, C2, C3, DE, and IE.
Integer compare and pop (FICOMP) (8087/80287/80387)	This instruction converts the operand to an integer (if required) and compares it to the top stack element. It then changes the condition of the status word bits to match the comparison result and pops the stack. The status word bits affected include C0, C2, C3, DE, and IE.
Test (FTST) (8087/80287/80387)	This instruction compares the top stack element with zero and sets the status bits accordingly. It affects the C0, C2, C3, DE, and IE status bits.

Command	Description
Examine (FXAM) (8087/80287/80387)	This instruction examines the top stack element and updates the status bits to reflect its condition. The examine instruction affects the C0, C1, C2, and C3 status bits.
Constant instructions	
Load value of 1.0 (FLD1) (8087/80287/80387)	This instruction pushes the constant 1.0 on the stack. It affects the IE status bit.
Load value of $\log_2 e$ (FLDL2E) (8087/80287/80387)	This instruction pushes the value of $\log_2 e$ onto the stack. It affects the IE status bit.
Load value of $\log_2 10$ (FLDL2T) (8087/80287/80387)	This instruction pushes the value of $\log_2 10$ onto the stack. It affects the IE status bit.
Load value of $\log_{10} 2$ (FLDLG2) (8087/80287/80387)	This instruction pushes the value of $\log_{10} 2$ onto the stack. It affects the IE status bit.
Load value of $\log_e 2$ (FLDLN2) (8087/80287/80387)	This instruction pushes the value of $\log_e 2$ onto the stack. It affects the IE status bit.
Load value of Pi (FLDPI) (8087/80287/80387)	This instruction pushes the value of Pi onto the stack. It affects the IE status bit.
Load value of 0.0 (FLDZ) (8087/80287/80387)	This instruction pushes 0 onto the stack. It affects the IE status bit.
Data-transfer instructions	
BCD load (FBLD) (8087/80287/80387)	Use this instruction to convert a BCD number (at the specified operand address) to a temporary real format and pushes it on the stack. This instruction affects the IE status bit.

Table F-1 Continued.

Command	Description
BCD store and pop (FBSTP) (8087/80287/80387)	This instruction pops a value from the stack, converts it to a BCD integer, and places it at the operand address. It affects the IE status bit.
Integer load (FILD) (8087/80287/80387)	This instruction converts the binary integer pointed to by the operand address to a temporary real format and pushes it on the stack. It affects only the IE status bit.
Integer store (FIST) (8087/80287/80387)	Use this instruction to round the top stack element to a binary integer and store it at the operand address. This instruction affects the PE and IE status bits.
Integer store and pop (FISTP) (8087/80287/80387)	Use this instruction to round the top stack element to a binary integer and store it at the operand address. It pops the stack after storing the integer. This instruction affects the PE and IE status bits.
Load real (FLD) (8087/80287/80387)	Use this instruction to push the source operand on the stack. It affects the DE and IE status bits.
Store real (FST) (8087/80287/80387)	The store real instruction copies the top stack element value to the position pointed to by the destination operand. This instruction affects the PE, UE, OE, and IE status bits.
Store real and pop (FSTP) (8087/80287/80387)	The store real instruction copies the top stack element value to the position pointed to by the destination operand. It pops the stack after transfering the value. This instruction affects the PE, UE, OE, and IE status bits.
Exchange registers (FXCH) (8087/80287/80387)	This instruction switches the value contained in the top stack element with the destination operand. It only affects the IE status bit.

Command	Description
Processor-control instructions	
Clear exceptions with wait (FCLEX) (8087/80287/80387)	Precede this instruction with a CPU wait prefix. It clears the B, PE, UE, OE, ZE, DE, IE, and IR status bits.
Decrement the stack pointer (FDECSTP) (8087/80287/80387)	This instruction decrements the 8087 status word stack pointer. It affects only the ST status bits.
Disable interrupts with wait (FDISI) (8087 only)	Precede this instruction with a CPU wait prefix. It sets the IEM control word bit preventing the 8087 from generating interrupts. This instruction does not affect the status word.
Enable interrupts with wait (FENI) (8087 only)	Precede this instruction with a CPU wait prefix. It clears the IEM control word bit allowing the 8087 to generate interrupts. This instruction does not affect the status word.
Free register (FFREE) (8087/80287/80387)	This instruction changes the specified stack register tag to indicate an empty element. It does not affect the status word.
Increment the stack pointer (FINCSTP) (8087/80287/80387)	This instruction increments the stack status word bits.
Initialize the processor with wait (FINIT) (8087/80287/80387)	This instruction equals a hardware reset instruction for the math coprocessor chip. Precede this instruction with a CPU wait prefix.
Load a control word (FLDCW) (8087/80287/80387)	Use this instruction to load the control word with the value pointed to by the source operand. This instruction does not affect any status bits.

Table F-1 Continued.

Command	Description
Load the environment (FLDENV) (8087/80287/80387)	The load the environment instruction restores all the environment variables from the 14-word memory location pointed to by the source operand. It affects all the status bits.
Clear exceptions (FNCLEX) (8087/80287/80387)	Use this instruction to clear the exception flags, interrupt request, and busy flags of the status word without using a CPU wait prefix. It affects the B, IR, PE, UE, OE, ZE, DE, and IE status bits.
Disable interrupts (FNDISI) (8087 only)	This instruction sets the interrupt enable mask of the control word without using a CPU wait prefix. It prevents the coprocessor from issuing interrupts. The disable interrupts instruction does not affect any status bits.
Enable interrupts (FNENI) (8087 only)	This instruction clears the interrupt enable mask of the control word without using a CPU wait prefix. It enables the coprocessor to issue interrupts. The disable interrupts instruction does not affect any status bits.
Initialize processor (FNINIT) (8087/80287/80387)	This instruction initializes the math coprocessor without issuing a CPU wait prefix. It is functionally equivalent to a hardware reset.
No operation (FNOP) (8087/80287/80387)	This instruction tells the CPU to do nothing. This instruction does not affect the status bits.
Save state (FNSAVE) (8087/80287/80387)	This instruction saves the contents of all math coprocessor registers and environment variables without issuing a CPU wait to the place pointed to by the destination operand. It requires 94 words of memory per save for an 8087 math coprocessor. The instruction then issues the equivalent of an FNINIT instruction.
Store control word (FNSTCW)	This instruction copies the control word to the place pointed to by the destination

Command	Description
(8087/80287/80387)	operand without using a CPU wait prefix. It does not affect any status bits.
Store environment (FNSTENV) (8087/80287/80387)	This instruction copies the environment variable to the place pointed to by the destination operand without using a CPU wait prefix. The store requires 14 words when using an 8087 math coprocessor. It does not affect any status bits.
Store status word (FNSTSW) (8087/80287/80387)	This instruction copies the status word to the place pointed to by the destination operand without using a CPU wait prefix. It does not affect any status bits.
Restore state (FRSTOR) (8087/80287/80387)	This instruction restores the state of all registers and environment variables from the location pointed to by the destination operand. It affects all the status bits.
Save state with wait (FSAVE) (8087/80287/80387)	This instruction saves the contents of all math coprocessor registers and environment variables to the place pointed to by the destination operand. It use the CPU wait prefix and requires 94 words of memory per save for an 8087 math coprocessor. The instruction then issues the equivalent of an FINIT instruction.
Store control word with wait (FSTCW) (8087/80287/80387)	This instruction copies the control word to the place pointed to by the destination operand using a CPU wait prefix. It does not affect any status bits.
Store environment with wait (FSTENV) (8087/80287/80387)	This instruction copies the environment variable to the place pointed to by the destination operand using a CPU wait prefix. The store requires 14 words when using an 8087 math coprocessor. It does not affect any status bits.

Table F-1 Continued.

Command	Description
Store status word with wait (FSTSW) (8087/80287/80387)	This instruction copies the status word to the place pointed to by the destination operand using a CPU wait prefix. It does not affect any status bits.
CPU wait (FWAIT) (8087/80287/80387)	The CPU wait instruction performs essentially the same function for the math coprocessor as it does for the main processor. This permits synchronization of both processors. The main processor suspends operations until the coprocessor completes its activities.
Trancendental instructions	
Value of 2^X - 1 (F2XM1) (8087/80287/80387)	This instruction calculates the value of Y = 2^X - 1. X is the top stack element. Y replaces X as the top stack element. This instruction affects the PE and UE status bits.
Partial arctangent (FPATAN) (8087/80287/80387)	This instruction computes Θ = ARCTAN (Y/X), where X is the top stack element and Y is the second stack element. It pops both stack elements and places the result on the stack. This instruction performs no input number validation. It affects the PE and UE status bits.
Partial tangent (FPTAN) (8087/80287/80387)	This instruction computes Y/X = TAN (Θ), where Θ is the top stack element. The instruction replaces the top stack element with Y, then pushes the computed X. This instruction performs no input value checking. It affects the PE and IE status bits.
Scale (FSCALE) (8087/80287/80387)	Use this instruction to calculate the value of X = X * 2^Y, where X is the value of the top stack element, and Y is the second stack element. This instruction affects the UE, OE, and IE status bits.

Command	Description
Value of Y * $\log_2$ X (FYL2X) (8087/80287/80387)	This instruction calculates the value of Z = Y * $\log_2$ X, where X is the top stack element and Y is the second stack element. The instruction pops both stack elements and pushes the new value, Z, onto the stack. This instruction does not validate the input values. It affects the PE status bit.
Value of Y * $\log_2$ (X + 1) (FYL2XP1) (8087/80287/80387)	This instruction calculates the value of Z = Y * $\log_2$ (X + 1), where X is the top stack element and Y is the second stack element. The instruction pops both stack elements and pushes the new value, Z, onto the stack. This instruction does not validate the input values. It affects the PE status bit.

Table F-2 80287 command summary

Command	Description
Processor-control instruction	
Set protected mode (FSETPM) (80287 only)	This instruction sets the 80287 to protected mode operation.

Table F-3 80387 command summary

Command	Description
Arithmetic instruction	
IEEE partial remainder (FPREM1) (80387 only)	The partial arctangent instruction calculates the modulo of the top two stack elements. It performs this by successively subtracting the second element from the first. The calculated remainder remains in the first element. The instruction affects the CO, C1, C3, UE, DE, and IE status bits.

Table F-3 Continued.

Command	Description
Comparison instruction	
Unordered compare (FUCOM) (80387 only)	This instruction converts the operand to an integer (if required) and compares it to the top stack element. It then changes the condition of the status word bits to match the comparison result. The difference between this instruction and the standard compare is that noncomparable results do not raise the invalid operation exception. The status word bits affected include C0, C2, C3, DE, and IE.
Unordered compare and pop (FUCOMP) (80387 only)	This instruction converts the operand to an integer (if required) and compares it to the top stack element. It then changes the condition of the status word bits to match the comparison result and pops the stack. The difference between this instruction and the standard compare and pop is that noncomparable results do not raise the invalid operation exception. The status word bits affected include C0, C2, C3, DE, and IE.
Unordered compare and pop twice (FUCOMPP) (80387 only)	This instruction converts the operand to an integer (if required) and compares it to the top stack element. It then changes the condition of the status word bits to match the comparison result and pops the stack twice. The difference between this instruction and the standard compare and pop twice is that noncomparable results do not raise the invalid operation exception. The status word bits affected include C0, C2, C3, DE, and IE.
Trancendental instruction	
Cosine (FCOS) (80387 only)	This instruction computes Y = COS (Θ), where Θ is the top stack element. The instruction replaces the top stack element with Y. If Θ exceeds 2^{63} then the instruction sets C2; otherwise, it clears C2. It affects the C2, PE, and IE status bits.

Command	Description
Sine (FSIN) (80387 only)	This instruction computes Y = SIN (Θ), where Θ is the top stack element. The instruction replaces the top stack element with Y. If Θ exceeds 263 then the instruction sets C2; otherwise, it clears C2. It affects the C2, PE, and IE status bits.
Sine and Cosine (FSINCOS) (80387 only)	This instruction computes Y = SIN (Θ) and X = COS (Θ), where Θ is the top stack element. The instruction replaces the top stack element with Y, then pushes X. If Θ exceeds 263 then the instruction sets C2; otherwise, it clears C2. It affects the C2, PE, and IE status bits.

The 8087, 80287, and 80387 math coprocessors do not use flags. Instead, they contain a status and control word. The status word indicates the current math coprocessor condition. The control word affects math coprocessor operation. The breakdown for both the control word and status word appears below:

Status word (bit)

0	Invalid operation exception (IE)
1	Denormalized operation exception (DE)
2	Zero divide exception (ZE)
3	Overflow exception (OE)
4	Underflow exception (UE)
5	Precision exception (PE)
7	Interrupt request (IR)
8	Condition code 0 (C0)
9	Condition code 1 (C1)
10	Condition code 2 (C2)
11 – 13	Stack top pointer (ST)
14	Condition code 3 (C3)
15	Busy signal (B)

Control word (bit)

0	Invalid operation exception mask (IM)
1	Denormalized operation exception mask (DM)
2	Zero divide exception mask (ZM)

3	Overflow exception mask (OM)
4	Underflow exception mask (UM)
5	Precision exception mask (PM)
7	Interrupt enable mask (IEM); 0 = enabled, 1 = disabled
8–9	Precision control (PC); 00 = 24 bits, 01 = (reserved), 10 = 53 bits, 11 = 64 bits
10–11	Rounding control (RC); 00 = round to nearest or even, 01 = round down, 10 = round up, 11 = truncate
12	Infinity control (IC); 0 = projective, 1 = affine
13–15	Reserved

Each math coprocessor contains eight stack elements that are 80 bits long. Bits 11 through 13 of the coprocessor status word tells you which element appears at the top of the stack. For example, if element 8 was at the top of the stack, then element 1 would appear second. Each element uses a floating-point format consisting of 64 significand bits, 15 exponent bits, and 1 sign bit. The coprocessors use these stack elements for most math operations.

Programming examples

There are two main events that you need to consider when attempting to program the math coprocessor. The first event is determining whether or not the host machine contains a math coprocessor. In most cases, you'll want to create generic math routines, so determining that it's present is enough. However, in some cases you might want to use some of the special capabilities provided by the 80387 chip to create a highly specialized program. In these instances, you'll also need to determine what type of coprocessor chip is available. Most programmers use a special procedure to check for the presence of the math coprocessor. This procedure also initializes it, so you don't need to worry about that aspect of the programming scenario.

The second event is to perform some useful work with the math coprocessor. In some cases this means a little extra work on your part because the math coprocessor is designed differently from most, if not all, the chips you might be familiar with. The math coprocessor in your PC is a *state machine*. That means that it uses a hardware stack, the register setup is completely different from the 80386, and it uses the reverse polish notation (RPN) found on many engineering calculators. You must keep this in mind as you create programs using the chip.

The following sections present three programming scenarios. The first shows you how to determine the presence and type of coprocessor installed on the host machine. The second explains how to create generic code that will work on any machine with a math coprocessor. The third provides an example of 80387 math coprocessor programming.

Determining coprocessor presence and type

One of the most important steps in using the math coprocessor is determining that the host machine has one installed. In most cases, making this determination is enough because most programs won't use the full power of the 80387 chip. The program presented in FIG. F-1 shows how to call the assembly-language program shown in FIG. F-2.

F-1 Math coprocessor detection, Clipper source

```
// Program 20 - Checking for the Math Co-Processor
// The intent of this program is to provide you with a quick routine
// for checking to see if the math co-processor is available.  The
// CheckMC() function returns true if the co-processor is present,
// and false if it isn't. The MCType() function returns a value from 0
// through 3 in most cases.  0 signifies the absence of a math
// co-processor.  1 shows that an 8087 is installed.  2 shows that an
// 80287 is installed.  3 shows that an 80387 is installed.  Any other
// return value indicates an error occurred during the determination.
// Written by: John Mueller
// Copyright 1991 John Mueller - Tab Books

local nProcType := 0

// Check for the presence of the math co-processor.

if CheckMC()
   ? "Math co-processor is present."
else
   ? "Math co-processor is not present."
endif

// Check for the type of the math co-processor.

nProcType := MCType()

do case
   case nProcType == 0
      ? "No math co-processor installed."
   case nProcType == 1
      ? "8087 math co-processor installed."
   case nProcType == 2
      ? "80287 math co-processor installed."
   case nProcType == 3
      ? "80387 math co-processor installed."
   otherwise
      ? "An error occurred with the math co-processor."
endcase

return
```

```
;*************************************************************************
;* Program 20 - Checking for the Math Co-Processor                      *
;* This program contains a routine for checking for the presence of a   *
;* math co-processor in the host machine.  One you have done that, you  *
;* can determine if you should use the math co-processor for your       *
;* programs, or the standard library routines.  The program works by    *
;* initializing the math co-processor.  If it isn't present, then       *
;* attempting to retrieve the control word will result in a null        *
;* value.  If it is present, then the control word will always return   *
;* a specific value.                                                     *
;* Written by: John Mueller                                              *
;* Copyright 1991 John Mueller - Tab Books                               *
;*************************************************************************

;*************************************************************************
;* Make any required declarations.                                       *
;*************************************************************************

.MODEL LARGE
.386p
.387

INCLUDE EXTASM.INC
INCLUDE MACROS.INC

PUBLIC CheckMC, MCType

;*************************************************************************
;* Declare any required variables.                                       *
;*************************************************************************

.DATA

CtrlWord        DW  0
CType           DW  0

;*************************************************************************
;* Start of the code segment and the main procedure.                     *
;*************************************************************************

.CODE

;*************************************************************************
;* This first procedure simply checks to see if the co-processor is     *
;* installed on the host machine.                                        *
;*************************************************************************

CheckMC     PROC    FAR

            PUSH    SI          ; Save SI.
```

```
          MOV     AX,@DATA   ;Point DS & ES to our data segment.
          MOV     DS,AX
          MOV     ES,AX

          FNINIT             ;Initialize the co-processor.
          FNSTCW CtrlWord    ;Store the control word in AX.
          MOV     AX,CtrlWord
          CMP     AH,03h     ;See if co-processor installed.
          JE      Present

NPresent: RetFalse
          JMP     Exit

Present:  RetTrue

Exit:     POP     SI         ; Restore SI.
          RET

CheckMC   ENDP

;***********************************************************************
;* This second procedure returns the specific type of co-processor    *
;* installed on the host machine.                                     *
;***********************************************************************

MCType    PROC    FAR

          PUSH    SI         ; Save SI.

          MOV     AX,@DATA   ;Point DS & ES to our data segment.
          MOV     DS,AX
          MOV     ES,AX

;***********************************************************************
;* Check for the presence of a math co-processor, then an 80287 or    *
;* 80387 math co-processor.                                           *
;***********************************************************************

    FNINIT             ;Initialize the co-processor.
    FNSTCW CtrlWord    ;Store the control word in AX.
    MOV     AX,CtrlWord
    CMP     AH,03h     ;See if co-processor installed.
    JE      Present2
    JMP     Exit2      ;If not present, exit the program.

;***********************************************************************
;* This section of the program determines the co-processor type and   *
;* returns an appropriate number.                                     *
;***********************************************************************

Present2: INC     CType              ;We know that we have an 8087 at least.

          AND     CtrlWord,0FF7Fh    ;Turn on co-processor interrupts
          FLDCW   CtrlWord           ; by loading new control word.
```

F-2 Continued.

```
            FDISI                   ;Disable interrupts (works on 8087 only)
            FSTCW  CtrlWord         ;Store the control word in AX.
            MOV    AX,CtrlWord
            TEST   AX,0080h         ;See if instruction worked.
            JE     Test2            ;If it didn't, not 8087.
            JMP    Exit2            ;If so, exit, we have an 8087.

Test2:      INC    CType            ;We know that we have an 80287 at least.

            FNINIT                  ;Re-initialize the co-processor.
            FLD1                    ;Load 1, then 0, then divide
            FLDZ                    ; to generate infinity
            FDIV
            FLD    ST               ;Generate negative inifity by pushing the current
            FCHS                    ; stack contents and changing the sign.
            FCOMPP                  ;Compare the two infinities. Equal
            FSTSW  AX               ; for 8087/80287 co-processors.
            SAHF                    ;Move AH to the flag register.
            JZ     Exit2            ;If zero, then must be 80287.
                                    ;The zero flag corresponds to condition code
                                    ; 3 on the co-processor.

            INC    CType            ;We definitely have an 80387.

Exit2:      RetInt CType            ;Return the processor type.
            POP    SI               ;Restore SI.
            RET

MCType      ENDP

END
```

You can learn several things from these two programs. The Clipper program shows that you can use one of two calls to check the math coprocessor status. CheckMC( ) simply determines if the math coprocessor is installed. Notice that the assembly code for performing this task is extremely short. This is the most efficient method of checking for the math coprocessor. The MCType( ) function returns a number that tells you what type of processor is installed. If MCType( ) returns 0, then there's no math coprocessor installed on the host machine. A value of 1 tells you that the host machine has an 8087 installed, 2 an 80287, and 3 an 80387. Notice that the assembly-language program has an exit point after checking for each type of coprocessor. Also notice that the very first check initializes the coprocessor. Using either of these two functions always prepares the math coprocessor for use.

Implementing generic math coprocessor instructions

One of the two most common applications for a math coprocessor is financial applications. Some of these applications can absorb a tremendous amount of processor time unless the math coprocessor is used. For example, consider the "what if" analysis performed by many businesses. This type of analysis is usually performed because a crisis or some other event triggers the need for a decision. The people involved at the decision-making level want the results of the analysis quickly.

One example is determining how to invest money wisely. The goal is to obtain the highest future value for the money invested now. The compound-interest equation is a simple example of such a calculation. Figure F-3 shows the Clipper code used to call CompInt( ), the compound-interest calculation function. Notice that the calling sequence provides all the required variables and returns the result in an array instead of using a standard return value. Figure F-4 shows the assembler code required to create the compound-interest calculation. Notice how the math coprocessor instructions greatly reduce the work required to perform floating-point math. Normally, you have to emulate the floating-point processor using the integer instruction provided by the CPU.

F-3 Math coprocessor financial example, Clipper source

```
// Program 21 - Math Co-Processor Financial Example
// This program shows the interface between an assembly language program
// which uses the math co-processor and the user.  It begins by polling
// the user for the numbers required to predict the future value of an
// investment if the return is compounded at a specific rate for a
// specific number of times per year (compound interest equation).  The
// program then calls the assembler routine and passes the required
// parameters.  In addition, the program passes the assembly routine an
// array in which to store the calculation results.  Once the assembly
// program does its work, it passes control back to the Clipper program
// after storing the calculated values in the array.  The Clipper
// program completes by displaying the contents of the array on screen.
// Written by: John Mueller
// Copyright 1991 John Mueller - Tab Books

local nRate       := 0,;    // Interest Rate
      nPeriodPY   := 0,;    // Compounding Periods/Year
      nPeriods    := 0,;    // Total Compounding Periods
      nPrinciple  := 0,;    // Principle
      aFutureVal[256]       // Compounded Amount

static nRow, nCol, nCount // Counter Variables for Loops

set scoreboard off
set color to "W+/B, RG+/R"
```

F-3 Continued.

```
cls
@ 01, 00 to 24, 79 double
@ 02, 01 say padc(" Math Co-Processor Financial Example ", 78, chr(177))
@ 03, 01 to 03, 78 double

// Check for the presence of the math co-processor.

if !CheckMC()
   alert("You need a math co-processor to use this program.")
endif

// Get the input values from the user.

@ 05, 02 say "              Interest rate: " get nRate picture "99.999"
@ 06, 02 say "Compounding Periods/Year: " get nPeriodPY picture "99"
@ 07, 02 say "              Total Periods: " get nPeriods picture "999" range 1, 256
@ 08, 02 say "                  Principle: " get nPrinciple picture "999999.99"
read

// Setup the counter variables prior to use.

nCount := 1
nCol := 2

// Display a header showing what data the co-processor will calculate.

@ 10, 01 say padc(" Future Value Results ", 78, chr(177))

// Compute the future values on a periodic basis.

if CompInt(nRate, nPeriodPY, nPeriods, nPrinciple, @aFutureVal)

// Display the calculated values that CompInt stored in the array.

   while nCount < nPeriods
      for nRow := 11 to 22
         @ nRow, nCol say aFutureVal[nCount] picture "$999999.99"
         nCount++
         if nCount > nPeriods
            exit
         endif
      next
   nCol := nCol + 12
   enddo
endif

// Wait for the user to finish viewing the results.

@ 23, 02 say "Press any key when ready..."
inkey(0)

// Clear the display and exit the program.
```

```
set color to "W/N, N/W"
cls

return
```

F-4 Math coprocessor financial example, assembler source

```
;*********************************************************************
;* Program 21 - Math Co-Processor Financial Example                  *
;* This program performs the task of calculating the future value of an*
;* investment and returning those results in an array to the calling  *
;* procedure.  The equation used is A = P(1+i)^n, where A is the future*
;* value, P is the principle invested, i is the rate per compounding  *
;* period, and n is the number of periods.  i is caluated by dividing *
;* the annual rate by the number of compounding periods per year.     *
;* Written by: John Mueller                                          *
;* Copyright 1991 John Mueller - Tab Books                           *
;*********************************************************************

;*********************************************************************
;* Make any required declarations.                                   *
;*********************************************************************

.MODEL LARGE

INCLUDE EXTASM.INC
INCLUDE MACROS.INC

PUBLIC CompInt

;*********************************************************************
;* Declare any required variables.                                   *
;*********************************************************************

.DATA

nPercent      DW     100

nRate         LABEL  QWORD
Rate          DW     4 DUP (0)  ;Interest Rate

nPeriodPY     LABEL  QWORD
PeriodPY      DW     4 DUP (0)  ;Number of Periods per Year

nPeriods      DW     0          ;Total Number of Periods

nPrinciple    LABEL  QWORD
Principle     DW     4 DUP (0)  ;Starting Amount

nRatePP       LABEL  QWORD
RatePP        DW     4 DUP (0)  ;Interest Rate per Period
```

F-4 Continued.

```
nPTemp         LABEL  QWORD
PTemp          DW     4 DUP (0)  ;Temporary Principle Value

;*********************************************************************
;* Start of the code segment and the main procedure.                 *
;*********************************************************************

.CODE

CompInt    PROC    FAR
           PUSH    SI          ;Save SI

           MOV     AX,@DATA    ;Point DS & ES to our data segment.
           MOV     DS,AX
           MOV     ES,AX

;*********************************************************************
;* This section of the code checks the number of parameters and their *
;* type.  It also ensures that the array was passed by reference so it*
;* can store the results of the computation.                         *
;*********************************************************************

           PCount                      ;Check for the correct
           CMP        AX,5             ; number of parameters.
           JE         Parm1            ;If so, perform next check.
           JMP        BadExit          ;If not, exit.

Parm1:     IsNum      1                ;Is the first parameter a number?
           JE         Parm2            ;If so, perform next check.
           JMP        BadExit          ;If not, exit.
Parm2:     GetDouble  1, Rate          ;Otherwise, retrieve the variable.

           IsNum      2                ;Is the second parameter a number?
           JE         Parm3            ;If so, perform next check.
           JMP        BadExit          ;If not, exit.
Parm3:     GetDouble  2, PeriodPY      ;Otherwise, retrieve the variable.

           IsNum      3                ;Is the third parameter a number?
           JE         Parm4            ;If so, perform next check.
           JMP        BadExit          ;If not, exit.
Parm4:     GetInt     3                ;Otherwise, retrieve the variable.
           MOV     nPeriods,AX

           IsNum      4                ;Is the fourth parameter a number?
           JE         Parm5            ;If so, perform next check.
           JMP        BadExit          ;If not, exit.
Parm5:     GetDouble  4, Principle     ;Otherwise, retrieve the variable.

           ParInfo5                    ;Is the fifth parameter an array?
           CMP        AX,Array+MPtr
           JNE        BadExit          ;If not, exit.
```

```
          JMP       GoodParms       ;Otherwise, process the data.

BadExit:  RetFalse                  ;Return false on error.
          POP       SI              ;Restore SI
          RET

GoodParms: RetTrue                  ;Return true for good parameters.

;*********************************************************************
;* This section of the code performs the calculation required to find *
;* the rate per period.  It then converts the percentage value passed *
;* by Clipper to an actual rate by dividing by 100.  Finally, it adds *
;* 1 to the rate so that the multiplication of the principle by the   *
;* rate results in the return of a value equal to the principle plus  *
;* interest.                                                          *
;*********************************************************************

     FLD     nRate       ;Calculate the Rate Per Period and
     FLD     nPeriodPY   ; store in nRatePP
     FDIV
     FILD    nPercent    ;Convert result from percent to rate.
     FDIV

     FLD1                ;Add 1 to the rate,
     FADD
     FST     nRatePP     ; then store it.

;*********************************************************************
;* This section of the code performs the task of calculating the      *
;* interest plus the principle for each period requrested, then       *
;* storing the result in an array.                                    *
;*********************************************************************

          FLD     nPrinciple       ;Load the principle.

          MOV     CX,[nPeriods]    ;Load the number of periods.
          INC     nPeriods         ;Point to the first period.

DoMul:    FMUL                     ;Multiply the principle by the rate.
          FST     nPTemp           ;Save the temporary value.
          FLD     nRatePP          ;Load the rate.

          MOV     AX,[nPeriods]    ;Determine the next array element to use
          SUB     AX,CX            ; for storage.
          PUSH    CX               ;Save the value of CX.
          PUSH    AX               ;Store the array index.
          MOV     AX,5             ;Store the parameter number.
          PUSH    AX
          PUSH    PTemp+6          ;Store the value of the calculation.
          PUSH    PTemp+4
          PUSH    PTemp+2
          PUSH    PTemp
          CALL    __stornd         ;Place the results in the array.
```

F-4 Continued.

```
            ADD     SP,12           ;Restore the stack.
            POP     CX              ;Restore CX.

            LOOP    DoMul           ;If required, perform the next iteration.

            POP     SI              ;Restore SI
            RET

CompInt     ENDP

END
```

The assembly-language routine performs its task in three parts. First, as always, you verify that the user passed sufficient variables of the correct type to perform the task. You also need to verify that the array was passed by reference in this case. If the user passed the correct values, then return true, otherwise return false. By testing this return value, the user can determine whether the function calculated the compound interest successfully.

The second section of the code calculates an intermediate value. You'll often find the need to calculate an intermediate value within your code. The likelihood of finding errors increases dramatically when you place the intermediate calculation code in a separate section. Finally, the assembly-language code performs the main calculation loop. Notice the relative tightness of the calculation loop. This tightness of code is what makes using the math coprocessor so necessary when program execution speed is the paramount concern.

Creating an 80387-specific program

Scientific programs often require even more processing power than accounting programs do. That is one of the reasons that some of the features of the 80387 are especially important. One of the more intriguing features is a full set of transcendental functions used for trignometric calculations. The 8087 and 80287 both lack this full set of transcendental features, along with many other conveniences provided by the 80387.

Figure F-5 contains the Clipper code required to call one of the four routines shown in FIG. 5-6. Notice that all four routines use a single trignometric calculation. In fact, you can compute both sine and cosine using one command, as illustrated in the CSDisp( ) function. Of course, the SDisp( ) function calculates the value of sine, CDisp( ) the value of cosine, and TDisp( ) the value of tangent. By using these four functions as a basis, you can calculate any trignometric function.

```
// Program 22 - Math Co-Processor Scientific Calculation Example
// This program illustrates how to create and display scientific data
// using external routines.  The Clipper portion of the program manages
// a text display and a menu for selecting a function to display.  It
// begins by displaying the background.  The program checks for the
// pressence of a math co-processor.  If one isn't found, it displays an
// error message and exit.  Otherwise, it displays the selection menu.
// The user may continue to select display options or select Quit to
// exit the program.
// To use this program correctly, you must link it with PROG-22A.ASM and
// PROG-20A.ASM.  The first file contains the scientific program
// routines.  The second file contains the math co-processor check.
// Written by: John Mueller
// Copyright 1991 John Mueller - Tab Books

// Declare any required variables.

static nSelect := 0  // User menu selection.

// Display the background screen.

DispScrn()

// Check for the presence of the math co-processor.  If one isn't
// present, display an error message and exit the program.  Note that
// the required math co-processor is an 80387 for this example.

if !(MCType() == 3)
   alert("You need a math co-processor to use this program.")
   set color to "W/N, N/W"
   cls
   return
endif

// Continue this loop until the user selects Quit.

while !(nSelect == 5)

   // Get the display selection input from the user.

   nSelect := Menu()

   // Choose between the various display options.

   do case
      case nSelect == 1
         SDisp()             // Display Sine
      case nSelect == 2
         CDisp()             // Display Cosine
      case nSelect == 3
         CSDisp()            // Display Sine/Cosine
```

F-5 Continued.

```
      case nSelect == 4
         TDisp()            // Display Tangent
   endcase

   // Display the background screen.

   DispScrn()

enddo

// Exit the program.

set color to "W/N, N/W"
cls
return

// Beginning of local functions.

// This function displays the background screen.

function DispScrn

set scoreboard off
set color to "W+/B, RG+/R"
cls
@ 01, 00 to 24, 79 double
@ 02, 01 say padc(" Scientific Programming Example ", 78, chr(177))
@ 03, 01 to 03, 78 double

return

// This function displays a menu and some explanatory text.  It asks the
// user to select from one of the display options or quit.  Once the
// user selects an option, it returns a numeric value expressing this
// selection to the calling procedure.

 function Menu()

// Create any required variables.

static nChoice := 0,;
         aMSelect := {"Sine", "Cosine", "Sine/Cosine", "Tangent", "Quit"}

// Display the menu and get the user selection.

@ 04, 02 to 10, 16 double
@ 22, 03 say "Select a display option."
nChoice := achoice(05, 03, 09, 15, aMSelect)

// Exit the function, return the user choice.

return nChoice
```

```
;*************************************************************************
;* Program 22 - Math Co-Processor Scientific Calculation Example        *
;* This program is used with PROG-22.PRG to display various             *
;* trignometric functions on screen.  There are four programs within    *
;* this file.  Each program demonstrates one of the native 80387 math   *
;* co-processor transcendental functions.  All four routines use a      *
;* similar format.  First, change the display adapter to an EGA         *
;* compatible graphics mode.  Once this task is finished, display a     *
;* title and a grid on which to display the function.  Second,          *
;* calculate the trignometric value of the angles from 0 to 360 degrees*
;* multiplied by a value of one.  Display a dot on screen showing where*
;* this value falls in reference to the scale.  Third, complete the     *
;* display by displaying a "Press any key when ready..." message and    *
;* waiting for the user to press a key.  Fourth, set the display        *
;* adapter back to standard 80 X 25 text mode.  None of the routines    *
;* require input from the calling procedure.  They all return a value   *
;* of NIL.  You must have an 80387 math co-processor installed to use   *
;* this routine.                                                        *
;* Written by: John Mueller                                             *
;* Copyright 1991 John Mueller - Tab Books                              *
;*************************************************************************

;*************************************************************************
;* Perform the program setup.                                           *
;*************************************************************************

.MODEL LARGE   ; Use a medum model size.

 INCLUDE EXTASM.INC
INCLUDE MACROS.INC

PUBLIC SDisp, CDisp, CSDisp, TDisp

.386P  ; Use the correct processor instruction set.
.387

;*************************************************************************
;* Begin the data area.  Declare all variables.                         *
;*************************************************************************
.DATA

Beep    EQU 07
LF  EQU 10
CR  EQU 13
StrEnd  EQU 36
XPosit  DW  26
YPosit  DW  0
XLen    DW  270
YLen    DW  300
XDot    DW  1
YDot    DW  1
```

F-6 Continued.

```
Two DW  2
Seventy DW  70
PtFive LABEL  QWORD
   DW  3 DUP(0),3FE0h
SineStr DB  'Value of Sine',CR,LF,StrEnd
CosineStr  DB  'Value of Cosine',CR,LF,StrEnd
CSineStr   DB  'Value of Sine/Cosine',CR,LF,StrEnd
TangStr DB  'Value of Tangent',CR,LF,StrEnd
GridStr DB  '|',CR,LF
   DB  '|',CR,LF
   DB  '|',CR,LF
   DB  '|',CR,LF
   DB  '|',CR,LF
   DB  '|',CR,LF
   DB  '|',CR,LF
   DB  '|',CR,LF
   DB  '|',CR,LF
   DB  '|',CR,LF
   DB  '|',CR,LF
   DB  '└──────────────────────────────────────────────'
   DB  '-----------------------------',CR,LF
   DB  '|',CR,LF
   DB  '|',CR,LF
   DB  '|',CR,LF
   DB  '|',CR,LF
   DB  '|',CR,LF
   DB  '|',CR,LF
   DB  '|',CR,LF
   DB  '|',CR,LF
   DB  '|',CR,LF
   DB  '|',CR,LF
   DB  '└──────────────────────────────────────────────'
   DB  '-----------------------------',CR,LF
   DB  'Press Any Key When Ready...',StrEnd


;*********************************************************************
;* Begin the code segment.                                           *
;*********************************************************************

.CODE

;*********************************************************************
;* This procedure displays a graphic representation of all the values  *
;* of sine from 0 to 360 degrees.  Since the 80387 requires radians    *
;* instead of degrees for input, the procedure uses a two step process *
;* for determining the current display position.  The display value    *
;* (fractional part of 360 degrees) is a function of the number of dots*
;* in the entire display area of 540 dots.  To find this fractional    *
;* part we divide the current X position by the total number of dots in*
;* the display, then multiply by pi.  This value provides the current  *
;* radian position within the circle.  The program then finds the value*
```

```
;* of sine for that radian value and determines the Y offset from the Y*
;* axis.                                                               *
;***********************************************************************

SDisp   PROC    FAR

        PUSH    SI          ;Save the contents of SI.

        MOV     AX,16       ;Set video adapter to graphics
        INT     10h         ; mode (640 X 350).
        MOV     AX,0200h    ;Set the cursor position.
        XOR     BX,BX
        MOV     DX,0022h
        INT     10h
        MOV     AX,0900h    ;Display the heading.
        LEA     DX,SineStr
        INT     21h
        LEA     DX,GridStr  ;Display the grid.
        INT     21h

SDispl: FILD    XDot        ;Load current X Posit.
        FILD    XLen        ;Divide by total length.
        FDIV
        FLDPI               ;Load Pi to determine the
        FMUL                ; number of radians/2.
        FSIN                ;Find the sine of angle.
        FIDIV   Two         ; values in upper half o
        FADD    PtFive      ; display. Add required
        FIMUL   YLen        ; corrections.
        FILD    YLen
        FSUBR
        FIADD   XPosit      ;Add display offset.
        FISTP   YPosit      ;Save value.

        MOV     AX,0C39h    ;Display the pixel
        XOR     BX,BX       ;Use display page 0.
        MOV     CX,XDot     ;Load the column.
        ADD     CX,5        ;Add the display offset.
        MOV     DX,YPosit   ;Load the row.
        INT     10h

        INC     XDot        ;Advance the X Posit pointer.
        CMP     XDot,541    ;See if we computed the last
        JNE     SDispl      ; display point.
        XOR     AX,AX       ;Get keyboard input.
        INT     16h
        MOV     XDot,1      ;Reset X Position pointer.
        MOV     AX,0003h    ;Reset the video mode to text.
        INT     10h

        RetNIL              ;Return NIL to calling program.

        POP     SI          ;Restore SI.
```

F-6 Continued.

```
        RET

SDisp   ENDP

;*******************************************************************
;* This procedure displays a graphic representation of all the values  *
;* of cosine from 0 to 360 degrees.  It uses the same basic procedure   *
;* as SDisp.                                                            *
;*******************************************************************

CDisp   PROC    FAR

        PUSH    SI              ;Save the contents of SI.

        MOV     AX,16           ;Set video adapter to graphics
        INT     10h             ; mode (640 X 350).
        MOV     AX,0200h        ;Set the cursor position.
        XOR     BX,BX
        MOV     DX,0021h
        INT     10h
        MOV     AX,0900h        ;Display the heading.
        LEA     DX,CosineStr
        INT     21h
        LEA     DX,GridStr      ;Display the grid.
        INT     21h

CDispl: FILD    XDot            ;Load current X Posit.
        FILD    XLen            ;Divide by total length.
        FDIV
        FLDPI                   ;Load Pi to determine the
        FMUL                    ; number of radians/2.
        FCOS                    ;Find the cosine of angle
        FIDIV   Two             ; values in upper half of
        FADD    PtFive          ; display. Add required
        FIMUL   YLen            ; corrections.
        FILD    YLen
        FSUBR
        FIADD   XPosit          ;Add display offset.
        FISTP   YPosit          ;Save value.

        MOV     AX,0C3Ah        ;Display the pixel
        XOR     BX,BX           ;Use display page 0.
        MOV     CX,XDot         ;Load the column.
        ADD     CX,5            ;Add the display offset.
        MOV     DX,YPosit       ;Load the row.
        INT     10h

        INC     XDot            ;Advance the X Posit pointer.
        CMP     XDot,541        ;See if we computed the last
        JNE     CDispl          ; display point.
        XOR     AX,AX           ;Get keyboard input.
        INT     16h
```

```
        MOV     XDot,1        ;Reset X Position pointer.
        MOV     AX,0003h      ;Reset the video mode to text.
        INT     10h

        RetNIL                ;Return NIL to calling program.

        POP     SI            ;Restore SI.

        RET

CDisp   ENDP

;*************************************************************************
;* This procedure displays a graphic representation of all the values   *
;* of sine/cosine from 0 to 360 degrees.  It uses the same basic        *
;* procedure as SDisp. Notice the procedure only performs one           *
;* transcendental function using the dual sine/cosine function.         *
;*************************************************************************

CSDisp      PROC    FAR

            PUSH    SI            ;Save the contents of SI.

            MOV     AX,16         ;Set video adapter to graphics
            INT     10h           ; mode (640 X 350).
            MOV     AX,0200h      ;Set the cursor position.
            XOR     BX,BX
            MOV     DX,001Dh
            INT     10h
            MOV     AX,0900h      ;Display the heading.
            LEA     DX,CSineStr
            INT     21h
            LEA     DX,GridStr ;Display the grid.
            INT     21h

CSDispl:    FILD    XDot          ;Load current X Posit.
            FILD    XLen          ;Divide by total length.
            FDIV
            FLDPI                 ;Load Pi to determine the
            FMUL                  ; number of radians/2.
            FSINCOS               ;Find cosine/sine of angle.
            FIDIV   Two           ; values in upper half of
            FADD    PtFive        ; display. Add required
            FIMUL   YLen          ; corrections.
            FILD    YLen
            FSUBR
            FIADD   XPosit        ;Add display offset.
            FISTP   YPosit        ;Save value.

            MOV     AX,0C3Ah      ;Display the pixel
            XOR     BX,BX         ;Use display page 0.
            MOV     CX,XDot       ;Load the column.
            ADD     CX,5          ;Add the display offset.
            MOV     DX,YPosit     ;Load the row.
            INT     10h
```

F-6 Continued.

```
        FIDIV   Two          ; values in upper half of
        FADD    PtFive       ; display. Add required
        FIMUL   YLen         ; corrections.
        FILD    YLen
        FSUBR
        FIADD   XPosit       ;Add display offset.
        FISTP   YPosit       ;Save value.

        MOV     AX,0C39h     ;Display the pixel
        XOR     BX,BX        ;Use display page 0.
        MOV     CX,XDot      ;Load the column.
        ADD     CX,5         ;Add the display offset.
        MOV     DX,YPosit    ;Load the row.
        INT     10h

        INC     XDot         ;Advance the X Posit pointer.
        CMP     XDot,541     ;See if we computed the last
        JNE     CSDispl      ; display point.
        XOR     AX,AX        ;Get keyboard input.
        INT     16h
        MOV     XDot,1       ;Reset X Position pointer.
        MOV     AX,0003h     ;Reset the video mode to text.
        INT     10h

        RetNIL               ;Return NIL to calling program.

        POP     SI           ;Restore SI.

        RET

CSDisp  ENDP

;*********************************************************************
;* This procedure displays a graphic representation of all the values *
;* of tangent from 0 to 360 degrees.  It uses the same basic procedure *
;* as SDisp.                                                          *
;*********************************************************************

TDisp   PROC    FAR

        PUSH    SI           ;Save the contents of SI.

        MOV     AX,16        ;Set video adapter to graphics
        INT     10h          ; mode (640 X 350).
        MOV     AX,0200h     ;Set the cursor position.
        XOR     BX,BX
        MOV     DX,0020h
        INT     10h
        MOV     AX,0900h     ;Display the heading.
        LEA     DX,TangStr
        INT     21h
        LEA     DX,GridStr   ;Display the grid.
        INT     21h
```

```
TDispl:FILD    XDot          ;Load current X Posit.
       FILD    XLen          ;Divide by total length.
       FDIV
       FLDPI                 ;Load Pi to determine the
       FMUL                  ; number of radians/2.
       FPTAN                 ;Find the tangent of angle
       FDIV                  ; values in upper half of
       FIDIV   Seventy       ; display. Add required
       FADD    PtFive        ; corrections.
       FIMUL   YLen
       FILD    YLen
       FSUBR
       FIADD   XPosit        ;Add display offset.
       FISTP   YPosit        ;Save value.

       MOV     AX,0C3Ch      ;Display the pixel
       XOR     BX,BX         ;Use display page 0.
       MOV     CX,XDot       ;Load the column.
       ADD     CX,5          ;Add the display offset.
       MOV     DX,YPosit     ;Load the row.
       INT     10h

       INC     XDot          ;Advance the X Posit pointer.
       CMP     XDot,541      ;See if we computed the last
       JNE     TDispl        ; display point.
       XOR     AX,AX         ;Get keyboard input.
       INT     16h
       MOV     XDot,1        ;Reset X Position pointer.
       MOV     AX,0003h      ;Reset the video mode to text.
       INT     10h

       RetNIL                ;Return NIL to calling program.

       POP     SI            ;Restore SI.

       RET

TDisp  ENDP

END
```

Figure F-6 illustrates an important concept in math-coprocessor programming. Each routine contains some code that you could relocate to a separate procedure. However, one of the reasons for using a math coprocessor is speed. Use short, compact routines to perform calculations as quickly as possible. For this reason, it's better to use in-line code to create the functions. Of course, you could have created one entry point to all four routines and allowed Clipper to pass a variable to select the proper calculation. Another concept is modularity. You want to create one modular routine to perform one task. Any other approach invites disaster when it comes time to enhance and upgrade the code.

G
Accessing the peripheral chips

Few programmers realize the wide variety of chips required to make the average PC operate. There are chips for timing, for accessing external devices like the hard and floppy disks, and for interrupting the processor to perform important work. For example, many communication programs are interrupt driven. The importance of using such chips in a program might appear minimal at first. However, once you consider being able to create a flexible interface with the outside world that acts the way you want it to, then the need for such programming becomes evident.

Consider the example of someone creating a program to directly interface with the fax board installed in their machine. There are very few fax libraries available on the market and, because most FAX boards aren't standard, it's unlikely that you'll find an exact match. The only way to create the interface, then, is to directly program the chips on the FAX board.

Peripheral chips perform a wide variety of services in a wide range of applications. The problem with using peripheral chips is discovering how to access them. In most cases, you access the chips through a combination of input/output ports and memory addresses. For example, your display adapter uses peripheral chips to modify its behavior. The data it acts upon is contained in memory located at a specific address in your machine.

Figure G-1 shows typical port relationships to the CPU. As you can see from the diagram, direct hardware manipulation using ports requires you to know three pieces of information: the port address, device reaction, and port read/write privileges. Of these three pieces of information, the port address is the most important. By knowing the port address, you can usually experiment to find the other two pieces of essential information. Writing a program and viewing the port reaction with a debugger can usually

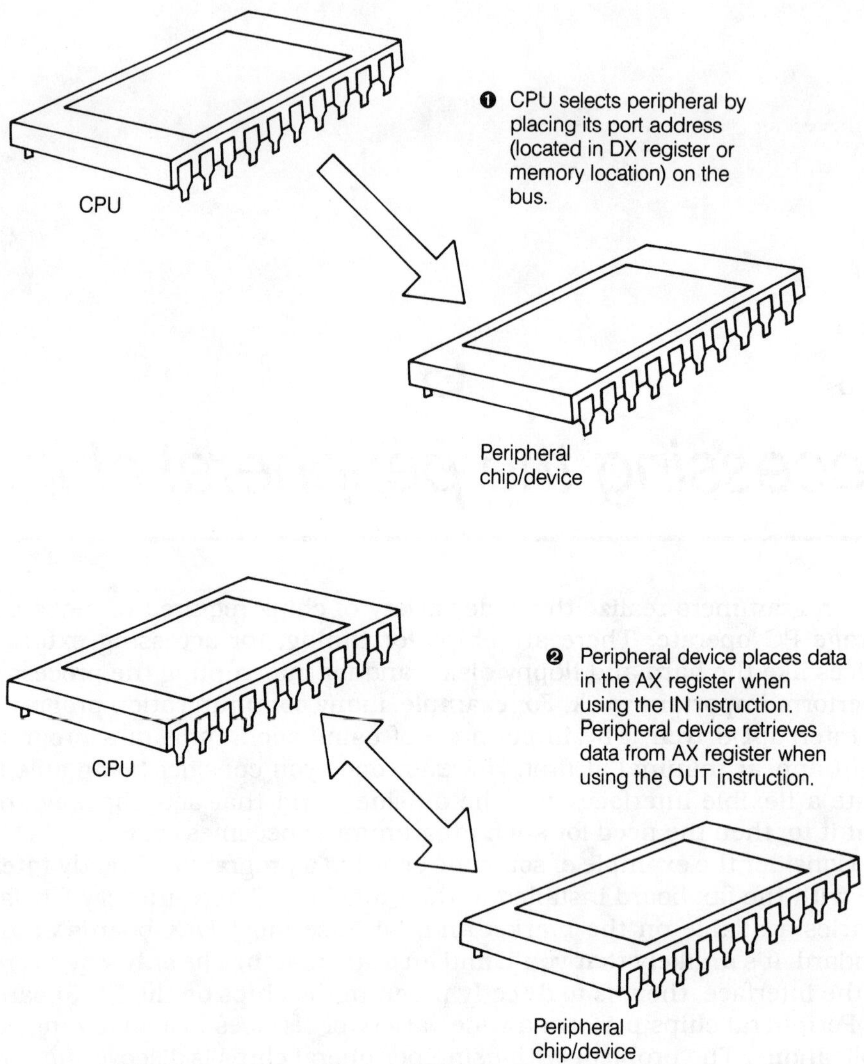

G-1 Typical CPU/port relationships.

help you determine the characteristics of the port. However, you can always achieve better results with less wasted time by knowing all three pieces from the outset.

Each port number addresses a specific device: input/output, register, or index. The CPU uses the IN instruction to retrieve information from the port. Likewise, it uses the OUT instruction to send information to the port. The DX register of the CPU or a memory location always contains the port address. The CPU uses the AL, AX, or EAX register as a buffer for port input and output. Most ROM and DOS interrupts use IN and OUT instructions to perform the tedious work of sending and receiving information to and from the port for you.

Some programs, however, need to access the ports directly in order to reduce the time required to perform an interrupt, or simply because the ROM and DOS routines don't offer the flexibility required. When using the IN and OUT instructions to control the devices at the specified address directly, you assume responsibility for knowing how it reacts. You must also know if the port allows you to read or write, or grants both privileges. The following sections describe the major processor ports and tell you how to program them. TABLE G-1 provides a listing of most processor ports and their functions.

Table G-1 Input/output port addresses

Address	Function
PC and PC/XT system board ports	
000 - 00F	8273A DMA controller
010	Manufacturer test point
020 - 021	8259A interrupt controller
040 - 043	8253 timer
060 - 063	8255A programmable peripheral interface
080 - 083	DMA page registers
0A0 - 0AF	NMI mask registers
0C8 - 0CF	Reserved
0E0 - 0EF	Reserved
PC/AT System board ports	
000 - 01F	8237A-5 DMA controller number 1
020 - 03F	8259A Interrupt controller number 1
040 - 05F	8254.2 Timer
060 - 06F	8042 Keyboard
070 - 07F	Realtime clock and NMI mask register
080 - 09F	DMA page register
0A0 - 0BF	8259A interrupt controller number 2
0C0 - 0DF	8237A-5 DMA controller number 2
0E0 - 0EF	Reserved
0F0	Clear math coprocessor busy
0F1	Reset math coprocessor
0F8 - 0FF	Math coprocessor

Table G-1 Continued.

Address	Function
PS/2 model 30 system board ports	
000 - 01F	8237A-5 DMA controller
020 - 03F	I/O support gate array, interrupt controller
040 - 05F	8253 Timer
060	I/O support gate array, keyboard input port
061 - 062	I/O support gate array, speaker and configuration control
063 - 06A	System support gate array (undocumented)
06B	System support gate array, RAM enable/remap
06C - 06F	System support gate array (undocumented)
080 - 08F	System support gate array, DMA page registers
0A0 - 0AF	I/O support gate array, NMI enable
0B0 - 0BF	Realtime clock/calendar (undocumented)
0E0 - 0EF	Realtime clock/calendar (undocumented)
PS/2 models 50, 60, and 80	
000 - 01F	8237A-5 DMA controller
020 - 021	8259A interrupt controller number 1
040	System timer
042	System timer
043	System timer
044	System timer
047	System timer
060	Keyboard auxiliary device
061	System control port B
064	Keyboard auxiliary device
070 - 071	Realtime clock and NMI mask register
074 - 076	Reserved
081 - 083	DMA page registers
087	DMA page registers
089 - 08B	DMA page registers
08F	DMA page registers
090	Central arbitration control port
091	Card selected feedback
092	System control port A
093	Reserved
094	System board setup
096 - 097	Programmable option select, channel connector select
0A0 - 0A1	8259A interrupt controller number 2
0C0 - 0DF	8237A-5 DMA controller number 2

Address	Function
0F0 - 0FF	Math coprocessor
100 - 107	Programmable option select
I/O channel ports	
1F0 - 1F8	PC/AT Hard-disk controller
200 - 20F	Game control
210 - 217	Expansion unit
21F	Voice communications adapter
220 - 24F	Reserved
278 - 27F	Parallel printer LPT3:
2C0 - 2CF	3270-PC
2E8 - 2EF	Serial port COM4:
2F0 - 2F7	Reserved
2F8 - 2FF	Serial port COM2:
300 - 31F	Prototype card
320 - 32F	Hard-disk controller (except PC/AT)
330 - 337	XT-370
360 - 36F	PC network adapter
378 - 37F	Parallel printer LPT2:
380 - 38F	Secondary bisynchronous interface
3A0 - 3AF	Primary bisynchronous interface
3B0 - 3BB	Monochrome display
3BC - 3BF	Parallel printer LPT1:
3C0 - 3CF	Enhanced graphics adapter
3D0 - 3DF	Color graphics adapter
3E0 - 3E7	Reserved
3E8 - 3EF	Serial port COM3:
3F0 - 3F7	Floppy-disk controller
3F8 - 3FF	Serial port COM1:

The 8253 and 8254 programmable timers

Both the 8253 and 8254 timers output pulses at regular intervals. The PC uses these pulses to control the sequence of events within the computer. In this way, both timers act like a clock circuit. However, they differ from a clock in two important aspects. First, a clock circuit uses a crystal to generate a specific, unchangeable frequency. The 4.77Mhz base frequency of the original PC is an example of a clock-circuit output. Changing the clock-circuit crystal provides the only way to change the circuit output. These timers accept clock input and output a changeable frequency based, in part, on that input. Second, a clock circuit does not provide a programming interface. You cannot change the clock's purpose.

A timer can perform several different functions simultaneously. The specific function depends on the status of its registers. You can use these timers within a database management system to time specific events. For example, how long do you wait for the printer to react before you generate an error message (a printer time-out)? By setting the timer and waiting for it to expire, you can avoid the problems of using timing loops within your program. Timing loops are not a reliable means of tracking time because different computers operate at different speeds. Timing circuits always track time accurately, no matter which machine you use.

Understanding timer operation

The 8253 programmable timer (used in PCs) operates at a base frequency of 1.19318Mhz. The 8254 timer (used in ATs) can operate at frequencies up to 10Mhz. For all practical purposes, both chips operate the same. They control certain system functions with three channels that can operate in one of six modes each. The listing below shows the I/O ports used for each function.

Channel 0	Port 40h
Channel 1	Port 41h
Channel 2	Port 42h
Mode control	Port 43h

Channel 0 is the system timer. This is the channel used to generate an interrupt 8h about 18 times per second. You can modify the output of this channel, but doing so will affect the speed of your entire computer. Channel 1 is used to time the periods between refreshes of system memory. You should never change the settings of this channel. Doing so could cause your computer to halt due to memory errors. Channel 2 controls the speaker normally, but you could use it for other purposes as well. It's a general-purpose channel that the computer doesn't use for any specific purpose. The mode-control port affects the appearance and method used to derive the timer output. This port is common to all three channels. Bits 6 and 7 affect which output channel you select. The mode-control functions appear in TABLE G-2.

In theory, you could change system operation by changing the output of each timer channel. However, in practice you usually change only the output of Channel 2. Some programs do derive special effects by changing the other two channels. For example, by reducing the number of memory refresh cycles per second, you could increase system performance. The computer would spend less time refreshing memory and more time servicing your program. Of course, the problem with doing this is that your system could hang or, worse yet, write corrupted data to your database.

Table G-2 8253/8254 mode-control bits

Bit	Function
0	Counter operation (1 = BCD, 0 = binary)
1 - 3	Operating mode (legal modes range from 0 through 5)
4 - 5	00b - latch present counter value 01b - Read/write only MSB 10b - Read/write only LSB 11b - Read/write LSB followed by MSB
6 - 7	Channel selection 00b - Channel 0 01b - Channel 1 10b - Channel 2

The three channels provide interrupts at given periods. To calculate the time, divide the timer base frequency (1,193,180Hz) by the channel divisor. The divisor ranges in value from 0 to 65,536. A value of zero results in a divisor of 65,536. The standard divisor for Channel 0 is 65,536, and Channel 1 is 18. Channel 2 does not use a standard divisor.

Using the timer

There are a few things you need to consider when programming the timer. First, there is only one mode-control port. You always need to make certain that the mode-control port is set to the appropriate channel before you attempt to program it. You do this by setting bits 6 and 7 of the word you output to the port to the appropriate channel. For example, to set channel 2 you would set bits 6 and 7 to 10b.

Another consideration is the method used by the channel for counting. Many programmers find that they have problems with the counter decrementing correctly (to achieve the correct interval). A BCD count uses base 10 as the counting criteria, whereas binary uses base 16. To make sure the timer decrements correctly, always set the counter operation bit, 1, to the mode you want to use for counting.

There are other factors you need to take into account as well. For example, the operating mode (output waveform type) can affect the quality of sound produced by the speaker, or your ability to detect an event. Always set the mode to the one appropriate to the task you're performing. For example, a saw-tooth waveform produces a very low-quality output from the speaker, and a sine output is very difficult to detect accurately when timing events.

Bits 4 and 5 affect the way the count is written to the channel port. You should always choose to update both the MSB and LSB of the timer channel. The other three modes are used to achieve special operating system requirements or other low-level programming needs (device drivers, for example). In most cases, these other modes are not used within application programs. The reason for this is clear. If you don't set both the LSB and MSB of the counter, then you can't be sure what they're set to. Another program could set the timer to a setting totally inappropriate to your needs.

The 8255A programmable peripheral interface (PPI)

The 8255A programmable peripheral interface controls the keyboard, speaker, and system-configuration switches. Some computers control other devices using this chip. Of all the peripheral chips, this one is the most flexible. There are five ports commonly associated with this chip. Port 60h allows you to read input from the keyboard when bit 7 of Port 61h is clear. On some PCs, setting bit 7 on Port 61h allows you to read the configuration switches using Port 60h. In all other cases, setting bit 7 returns an acknowledge to (clears) the keyboard. These are the common uses for Port 60h. Changing Port 63h bits 4, 5, and 6 allows you to use Port 60h for other purposes. As you can see, you must consider the interactions between ports carefully when programming this chip.

The listings in TABLES G-3 through G-6 provide standard 8255A port uses and bit definition. Only an AT computer normally uses port 64h, which reports the status of the 8042 controller connected to the 8255A. (This is used for reporting the status of the keyboard; the PC doesn't use a bidirectional chip, the AT does.) Most computers use ports 61h through 63h, as shown in the tables. Because each computer varies in its usage of the 8255A PPI (there is no standard configuration for this chip), consult the technical reference for your computer before using the ports. However, when all else fails, try the standard definitions to see if they'll work for your application. Another possible source of information is the manufacturer of the chip, whose name or logo you can usually obtain from the chip itself.

Port 61h status bits

The status register allows you to control the usage of the PPI. For example, by outputing a 1 in bit 0, you can tell the PPI to control the speaker through the 8253/8254 timer. This means that whatever frequency the timer channel 2 outputs is the frequency that the speaker outputs. Of course you can control the speaker directly by setting the bit to 0. Bit 1 allows you to control whether or not the speaker is on. In other words, you

Table G-3 Port 61h status bits

Bit	Function
0	Speaker control 0b = Direct 1b = Through 8253/8254 timer
1	Speaker condition 0b = Off 1b = On
2	Configuration switch selection 0b = Read spare switches port 62h (PC) 1b = Read RAM size switches port 62h (PC) AT and XT - Not used
3	Cassette motor condition/configuration switch selection 0b = Cassette motor on (PC), read configuration switch port 62h high nibble (XT) 1b - Cassette motor off (PC), read configuration switch port 62h low nibble (XT)
4	RAM parity error checking 0b = Enabled 1b = Disabled
5	Expansion port RAM parity error checking 0b = Enabled 1b = Disabled
6	Keyboard click 0b = Off 1b = On
7	0b = Keyboard enabled 1b = Read configuration switches (PC), keyboard acknowledge (XT)

can send data to the speaker, but until you turn it on you won't hear anything. Other settings include reading the switch settings on a PC and controlling the keyboard. Remember that in most cases this port does not control data flow, merely the selection of PPI function. You can read the settings of this port as well. This enables you to preserve the original settings before changing them to modify the PPI's function.

Table G-4 Port 62h status bits

Bit	Function
0 - 3	Configuration switch status (selected by port 61h bit 2 for PC and bit 3 for XT)
4	Cassette data input
5	8253/8254 timer output
6	Expansion slot RAM parity error when set
7	RAM parity error when set

Table G-5 Port 63h status bits

Bit	Function
0	Port 62h bits 0 through 3 status 0b = Output 1b = Input
1	Port 61h usage 0b = Output 1b = Input
2	Port 61h mode
3	Port 62h bits 4 through 7 status 0b = Output 1b = Input
4	Port 60h usage 0b = Output 1b = Input
5 - 6	Port 60h mode
7	Port status 0b = Active 1b = Inactive

Table G-6 Port 64h status bits

Bit position	When set	When clear
During output		
0	Ouput buffer full	Output buffer empty
1	Input buffer full	Input buffer empty
2	Return from shutdown	Normal POST
3	Last input was command	Last input was data
4	Keyboard locked	Keyboard unlocked
5	8042-6805 XMIT timeout	No timeout
6	6805-8042 XMIT timeout	No timeout
7	Parity error (6805	No parity error
During input		
0	Enable keyboard Int.	Disable keyboard int.
2	Return from shutdown	Normal POST
3	Disable keylock	Enable keylock
4	Disable keyboard	Enable keyboard
5	PC keyboard mode	AT keyboard mode
6	Translate scan codes	Does not translate

Port 62h status bits

This port allows you to monitor several of the peripheral-device inputs and outputs. One of the more useful status bits is bit 5. You can use this bit to monitor the output of the 8253/8254 timer. Instead of timing an event through timing loops or interrupts, this bit allows you to actually clock your event using channel 2 of the timer. For example, if you program channel 2 to send out a pulse every second, and you wanted to time an event for 60 seconds, then all you would need to do is poll bit 5 until you counted 60 pulses. Other interesting utilities on this port include the ability to monitor both main RAM and expansion slot RAM for errors.

Port 63h status bits

Port 63h is another control, rather than a data register. It controls the actual registers rather than PPI mode as did Port 61h. Each register is represented in the bit map of this register. You can control whether the port is configured for input or output. In some cases, you control the port mode and whether or not it's active.

Port 64h status bits

You'll never be able to use Port 64h on a PC, but you might occasionally find it present. This particular register interacts directly with the keyboard controller chip found on an AT. The AT uses a smarter controller than the PC does. This controller is two-way rather than output-only. The function of Port 64h, therefore, is to retrieve status information from the keyboard. This status information ranges from determining if the keyboard is locked to whether the last input was a command or data. You can also find out if a keyboard is being used in PC mode or AT mode. One very important piece of status information is whether or not the keyboard translates scan code. This could adversely affect the operation of your program if it's set in the wrong direction. In total, this register allow you to obtain status information about and directly control a peripheral device that is seldom under direct control by other mechanisms in your computer—the keyboard.

The 8259 programmable interrupt controller (PIC)

Every maskable hardware interrupt generated within a PC goes through a central control chip called the programmable interrupt controller. The 8259 PIC handles up to eight interrupts using a priority sequence. Every time the PIC detects a hardware interrupt, it checks to see if the CPU is servicing another interrupt. If not, the PIC passes control of the interrupt to the interrupt handler. For example, both the timer tick (channel 0 of the 8253/8254 timer) and keyboard generate hardware interrupts. When the PIC receives a timer-tick interrupt, it calls interrupt 08h to service it. Likewise, it calls interrupt 09h to service a keyboard interrupt. When the interrupt completes its service of the hardware interrupt, it clears the 8259 PIC.

The CPU follows the same basic procedure for every interrupt it processes. First it pushes all the flags. This allows the CPU to return to an exact state after processing the interrupt. Next it disables the interrupt flag. This prevents any other interrupts while the CPU processes the current interrupt. Next it pushes the code segment (CS) and instruction pointer (IP). This allows the CPU to return to a specific point in program execution. Finally, the CPU acknowledges the interrupt by signalling the 8259 PIC. The PIC places the interrupt number on the bus, and the CPU retrieves the interrupt number and multiplies it by four (the number of bytes for each interrupt in the interrupt vector table). For example, interrupt 4 uses address 0000:0016 in low memory. The CPU then passes control to the address pointed to by the interrupt vector table in low memory.

Once the CPU performs this task, it can process the interrupt. The interrupt handler must preserve the CPU registers before it services the hardware. Otherwise, the CPU will return from the interrupt in an unknown condition. After the CPU processes the interrupt, it outputs 20h to port 20h of the PIC. This allows the PIC to process other interrupts. Before the CPU returns control to the program it interrupted to service the hardware, it places the old values in CS and IP. It also pops the flags off the stack.

Each device connected to the PIC uses its own interrupt request line (IRQ). Because the AT has more devices to handle than a PC, the AT uses two cascaded 8259 PICs. The INT (output) line of the slave PIC connects to IRQ2 of the master PIC. This effectively gives the AT 15 IRQ lines. Every line is a different priority. Therefore, if two interrupts arrive at the same time, the 8259 PIC services the higher priority interrupt first, then the lower priority interrupt.

This cascading of interrupts is the source of never-ending problems on a network. Many VGA display adapters use interrupt 2 as their hardware interrupt to the CPU. Because of the cascade, however, the interrupt shows up as interrupt 9. This makes it difficult to determine which interrupt the device uses, and makes direct interrupt-driven programming of the device impossible.

The 8259 PIC uses four ports to accomplish the goal of servicing hardware interrupts. Two of the ports (22h and 23h) remain undocumented. Port 20h controls the interrupt-controller command center. The interrupt-control assembly commands control the contents of port 20h. Port 21h controls the interrupt-controller interrupt mask register. TABLE G-7 shows the use of the port at 21h.

Table G-7 8259 interrupt-controller port 21h status bits

Bit position	When set	When clear
0	System timer disabled	System timer enabled
1	Keyboard interrupt disabled	Keyboard interrupt enabled
2	Reserved	Reserved
3	COM2: interrupt disabled	COM2: interrupt enabled
4	COM1: interrupt disabled	COM1: interrupt enabled
5	Fixed-disk int. disabled	Fixed-disk int. enabled
6	Floppy-disk int. disabled	Floppy-disk int. enabled
7	Parallel port int. disabled	Parallel port int. enabled

As you can see, setting a bit in the mask register effectively disables the interrupt (in other words, there is already an interrupt pending, so you can't accept another one). Clearing the bit enables the interrupt, allowing you to accept one. This doesn't mean that the interrupt can be serviced immediately, it simply means that the interrupt is in line to be serviced. The CPU services interrupts in numeric order. So the system time and keyboard interrupt receive top priority, while the parallel port receives a much lower priority. On an AT, the math coprocessor is lower still on the interrupt service list.

Serial ports

There are four standard serial-port address ranges. Many add-in devices allow you to use more serial ports by subdividing these address ranges. The discussion below uses the values for COM1. The addresses used by the other three ports perform similar functions. Each table in this section shows the addresses for the other three ports in order. For example, the first port appearing between the parentheses is COM2.

Addresses 3F8h and 3F9h change the baud-rate setting for COM1 (beside their normal function) when a program sets bit 7 of port 3FBh. TABLE G-8 shows the baud rates resulting from various inputs to the two ports. Port 3F8h normally sends and receives data between the computer and attached device. Port 3F9h provides access to the interrupt enable/disable register. Port 3FAh provides access to the interrupt-identification register, and port 3FBh provides access to the line-control register. TABLES G-9 through G-11 show the standard uses for the ports described above.

Table G-8 Standard baud-rate divisor settings

MSB 3F9h	LSB 3F8h	Resulting baud rate
4	17h	110 bps
1	80h	300 bps
0	60h	1,200 bps
0	30h	2,400 bps
0	18h	4,800 bps
0	0Ch	9,600 bps
0	07h	19,200 bps

Table G-9
Interrupt-enable register (ports 3F9h, 2F9h, 3E9h, and 2E9h)

Bit	Function
0	Enable interrupt on data available
1	Enable interrupt on transmit holding register empty
2	Enable interrupt on receive line status change
3	Enable interrupt on modem status change
4 - 7	Not used

Table G-10 Interrupt-identification register (ports 3FAh, 2FAh, 3EAh, and 2EAh)

Bit	Function
0	Interrupt pending when clear
1 - 2	00b = Modem status change 01b = Transmitter holding register empty 10b = Received data available 11b = Receiver line status interrupt
3 - 7	Not used

Table G-11
Line-control register (ports 3FBh, 2FBh, 3EBh, and 2EBh)

Bit	Function
0 - 1	Data length 00b = 5 bits 01b = 6 bits 10b = 7 bits 11b = 8 bits
2	Number of stop bits 0b = 1 stop bit 1b = 2 Stop bits, 1.5 when bits 0 and 1 are clear
3	Parity enabled when set
4	Even parity when set
5	0 = Parity held at value in bit 4 1 = Parity operates normally
6	Transmit break condition when set
7	0 = Normal access to ports 3F8h and 3F9h 1 = Use ports 3F8h and 3F9h to specify baud rate

Understanding the baud-rate divisor settings

Many programmers think that the divisor setting of the serial port is a magic number that allows the port to function at a specific speed. There are actually two forces at work. The first is the input clock. As TABLE G-8 clearly shows, the divisor values represented in this table rely on a 1.8432Mhz input clock. If you change the clock value, then the divisor values would no longer hold true. In the past this wasn't a problem because every serial port used the same clock frequency. However, with the introduction of newer high-speed serial ports, this is no longer true. You need to know both the input clock value and the divisor value to compute the resulting baud rate.

To determine the resulting baud rate, use the equation: RESULT = (INPUT CLOCK ÷ 16) ÷ DIVISOR. For example, to obtain a baud rate of 115,200 from a serial port whose input clock is 7.3278Mhz, you would use a divisor of 4. To obtain the same result from a standard serial port, you would use a divisor of 1. As you can see, using a higher input frequency allows you to create higher baud rates. This also shows you the source of the current baud-rate limits for most devices. As the divisor becomes smaller, anomalies in the input clock become more critical. In a standard serial port, the anomalies are so critical that a poorly designed serial port cannot operate at the 115,200 baud rate used by many data-transfer programs.

Understanding the interrupt-enable register

The interrupt-enable register provides you with a wide range of choices in detecting serial-port events. These events can help you create interrupt-driven programs that operate in the background, rather than the foreground. As multitasking environment proliferate, this ability becomes more essential. Some users have noted that several communication programs don't operate well under DesqView or Windows. This is usually because the program polls the serial port rather than waiting for data to appear.

On one hand, the program is at the mercy of the multitasking environment. If the environment doesn't provide enough clock cycles to the communications program, then it can't poll the serial port often enough to retrieve the incoming data properly. On the other hand, using interrupts places communications on par with the multitasking environment. In this case, the CPU arbitrates who gets the clock cycles. If there is data waiting at the serial port to be processed, the communications program takes priority. However, data is not the only event you can track. You can also trigger your program when the transmit buffer requires filling or when the MODEM line changes status.

These different areas of interrupt allow you the freedom to create communication routines that don't rely on the benevolence of the operating environment, but rather the need of the serial port.

Using the interrupt-identification register

Once your program determines that the serial port requires servicing, you need to determine what type of service it requires. This isn't essential if you enable only one interrupt, but it is for more than one. The interrupt-identification register tells you what type of event triggered an interrupt at the serial port.

Using the line-control register

The line-control register is the one that most people are familiar with even though they don't program it directly. Every time you run the MODE command to change the setup of a serial port, you affect the contents of the line-control register. As TABLE G-11 shows, this register controls most of the physical characteristics of the port. For example, do you use even or odd parity? How many data bits does your program use? All these parameters are controlled by this register. You normally set this register once during the programming session, and then restore it at the end of the program.

Parallel ports

There are three parallel-port address ranges. The discussion of parallel-port addresses refers to LPT1. The other two parallel-port address sets perform similar functions. The tables in this section contain the appropriate addresses for the other two ports in order. For example, the first address within the parentheses is LPT2.

The first port (3BCh) outputs data to the printer. Most parallel ports are unidirectional. The parallel port on IBM PS/2 models and some other AT class machines are bidirectional, allowing both input and output. Port 3BDh accesses the printer-status register. TABLE G-12 shows the printer-status register functions. Port 3BEh accesses the printer-control register. TABLE G-13 shows the printer-control register functions. The remaining ports (3BFh, 37Bh, 37Fh, and 27Bh through 27Fh) do not serve any documented function.

Table G-12
Parallel-printer adapter-status register (ports 3BDh, 379h, and 279h)

Bit	Function
0	Time out when set
1 - 2	Not used
3	Printer error when set
4	Printer on-line when set
5	Out of paper when set
6	Acknowledged when clear
7	Printer busy when clear

Table G-13 Parallel-printer adapter-control register (ports 3BEh, 37Ah, and 27Ah)

Bit	Function
0	Output data to printer when set (strobe)
1	Enable auto linefeed when set
2	Initialize paper when set
3	Printer reads output when set
4	Enable IRQ7 for printer acknowledge
5 - 7	Not used

Using the parallel-port status register

Like many other devices connected to the computer, the devices connected to the parallel port use a specific protocol. One of these protocols is the determination of port and device status. TABLE G-12 shows the different types of parallel-port information you can determine. As you can see, most of these status bits are oriented (at least in their description) for a printer. However, any other parallel device could use them as well.

Using the parallel-port adapter-control register

As you can see, the adapter-control register is an output, rather than an input register. This port allows you to send control words to the printer or other peripheral device connected to the port. In most cases, these control words are more complex than the titles of the bits would lead you to believe. For example, to send a single character to the print head requires that you toggle bit 0, Output data to printer strobe. In fact, when in graphics mode, you must toggle this strobe once of each dot printed. In most cases it's better to allow DOS or ROM BIOS routines to handle this port. Unlike the serial port, the built-in routines for the parallel port are fairly complete.

Input/output system map

The different processors discussed in this appendix communicate with the outside world using ROM, RAM, and input/output ports. These processors have two access modes: memory and I/O port. All the processors described use 10 input/output-address lines (1,024 ports) even though they can potentially access many more. A standard 8086/8088 uses 20 memory-address lines (1Mb memory), the 80286 provides 24 memory-address lines (16Mb memory), and the 80386 uses 32 memory-address lines (4Gb memory). The memory map in TABLE G-14 shows memory allocation for basic DOS access using an 8086/8088 processor. The 80286 and 80386 processors access memory above 1Mb using operating-system-specific methods.

Table G-14 1Mb memory map (most operating systems)

Address	Function
00000 - 0003F	Hardware and software* interrupt vectors
00000 - 00003	Divide by zero
00004 - 00007	Single step
00008 - 0000B	Nonmaskable interrupt (NMI)
0000C - 0000F	Breakpoint
00010 - 00013	Overflow
00014 - 00017	BOUND exceeded, print screen* (Int 5)
00018 - 0001B	Invalid opcode, reserved* (Int 6)
0001C - 0001F	Processor extension not available, reserved* (Int 7)
00020 - 00023	Double fault, IRQ0 timer tick* (Int 8)
00024 - 00027	Segment overrun, IRQ1 keyboard* (Int 9)
00028 - 0002B	Invalid task-state segment, IRQ2 cascade from slave 8259A PIC* (Int Ah)
0002C - 0002F	Segment not present, IRQ3 serial communications COM2* (Int Bh)
00030 - 00033	Stack segment overrun, IRQ4 serial communications COM1* (Int Ch)
00034 - 00037	General protection fault, IRQ5 fixed disk - PC or parallel printer LPT2 - AT* (Int Dh)
00038 - 0003B	Page fault, IRQ6 floppy disk* (Int Eh)
0003C - 0003F	Reserved, IRQ7 parallel printer LPT1 (Int Fh)
00040 - 0007F	BIOS interrupt vectors
00040 - 00043	Numeric coprocessor error, video services* (Int 10h)
00044 - 00047	Equipment check* (Int 11h)
00044 - 0007F	Reserved
00048 - 0004B	Conventional memory size* (Int 12h)
0004C - 0004F	Disk driver* (Int 13h)
00050 - 00053	Communications driver* (Int 14h)
*00054 - 00057	Cassette driver - PC, I/O system extensions - AT* (Int 15h)
00058 - 0005B	Keyboard driver* (Int 16h)
0005C - 0005F	Printer driver* (Int 17h)
00060 - 00063	BASIC* (Int 18h)
00064 - 00067	ROM BIOS bootstrap* (Int 19h)
00068 - 0006B	Time of day* (Int 1Ah)
0006C - 0006F	Ctrl-Break* (Int 1Bh)
00070 - 00073	ROM BIOS timer tick* (Int 1Ch)
00074 - 00077	Video parameter table* (Int 1Dh)
00078 - 0007B	Floppy-disk parameters* (Int 1Eh)
0007C - 0007F	ROM BIOS font - characters 80h to FFh* (Int 1Fh)
00080 - 000FF	DOS interrupt vectors

Table G-14 Continued.

Address	Function
00080 - 00083	Terminate process* (Int 20h)
00084 - 00087	Function dispatcher* (Int 21h)
00088 - 0008B	Terminate address* (Int 22h)
0008C - 0008F	Ctrl-C handler address* (Int 23h)
00090 - 00093	Critical error handler address* (Int 24h)
00094 - 00097	Absolute disk read* (Int 25h)
00098 - 0009B	Absolute disk write* (Int 26h)
0009C - 0009F	Terminate and stay resident* (Int 27h)
00100 - 003FF	Assignable interrupt vectors
00100 - 00103	Idle interrupt* (Int 28h)
00104 - 00107	Reserved (Int 29h)
00108 - 0010B	Network redirector* (Int 2Ah)
0010C - 0011B	Reserved (Int 2Bh - 2Eh)
0011C - 0011F	Multiplex interrupt* (Int 2Fh)
00120 - 0015F	Reserved (Int 30h - 3Fh)
00400 - 004FF	ROM BIOS data area
00400 - 00416	Hardware parameters
00417 - 0043D	Keyboard buffer/status bytes
0043E - 00448	Disk status bytes
00449 - 00466	Video display data
00467 - 00470	Option ROM and timer data
00471 - 00487	Additional status bytes
00488 - 004FF	Reserved
00500 - 005FF	DOS data area
A0000 - BFFFF	Video display area
A0000 - AFFFF	EGA 64K
A0000 - BFFFF	EGA 128K
B0000 - B0FFF	Monochrome 4K
B0000 - B7FFF	EGA monochrome emulation 32K
B8000 - BBFFF	CGA 16K
B8000 - BFFFF	EGA CGA emulation 32K
C0000 - F3FFF	BIOS extensions
F4000 - FDFFF	System ROM/stand-alone BASIC
FE000 - FFFFF	ROM BIOS

* These addresses are assigned by software only. Because they aren't hardwired into the machine, they can change at any time.

Index

A

B

C

D

G

T

U

V

W

X

Y

Z